nd Engage Students

irect Observation: Competitive Intelligence
at Staples (Ch.6)

nline Focus Group Examples (Ch.7)

n-Depth Interviews Help Gannett Understand Young
Readers (Ch.7)

ow to Keep in Touch with Kids Around the Globe?
Cartoon Network Knows the Answer (Ch.7)

reative Applications of Qualitative Research Yield
Valuable Insights (Ch.7)

xamples of Test-Marketing (Ch.8)

itmus Model: Simulated Test-Marketing (Ch.8)

yundai Conducts Experimentation Exercise to Measure
Marketing Effectiveness in Rural India (Ch.8)

004 Ford F-150 Launch: Multimedia Experimentation
to Study Communication Effectiveness (Ch.8)

Measuring Brand Equity (Ch.9)

Measuring Customer Experiences (Ch.9)

allup on Sampling: How Polls Are Conducted in the
United States (Ch.11)

merican Demographics Survey: Estimation of
Maximum Sampling Error (Ch.11)

CNielsen Company: Computerized Editing of SCAN-
TRACK Data (Ch.12)

he Government's Role in Curbing Indecency in the
Media: Conservatives and Liberals Switch Their
Position (Ch.12)

ational Insurance Company Study Cross Tabulation:
Chi-Square Test Using SPSS (Ch.13)

ational Insurance Company Study: Perceived
Service Quality Differences Between Males and
Females (Ch.13)

ational Insurance Company: Computing Pearson
Correlation Among Service Quality Constructs Using
SPSS (Ch.14)

egression Applications: Illustrative Scenarios Calling
for Regression Analysis (Ch.14)

ational Insurance Company: Multiple Regression Using
SPSS (Ch.14)

ational Insurance Company: Impact of Educational
Level on Overall Perceived Quality (Ch.15)

ank Customer Perceptions Study: Factorial ANOVA
with Main and Interaction Effects (Ch.15)

ersonal Computer Study (Ch.15)

ational Insurance Study Questionnaire with Summary
of Study Findings (Ch.16)

he Roper Organization (Ch.16)

End-of-Chapter Cases are original to the text and include compelling facts and company data to illustrate the real-world use of marketing research.

D1607069

Marketing Research

Marketing Research

Second Edition

A. Parasuraman
University of Miami

Dhruv Grewal
Babson College

R. Krishnan
University of Miami

Houghton Mifflin Company **Boston** **New York**

To my beloved wife Ranga and in loving memory of her sister Sara Swany—A.P.

To my parents, wife Diana, and children Lauren and Alex—D.G.

To my parents, wife Bala, son Ram, and daughter Vidhya—R.K.

————————————

Publisher: George T. Hoffman
Development Editor: Jessica Carlisle
Project Editor: Paula Kmetz
Senior Art and Design Coordinator: Jill Haber
Senior Photo Editor: Jennifer Meyer Dare
Composition Buyer: Chuck Dutton
Senior Manufacturing Buyer: Renee Ostrowski
Marketing Manager: Mike Schenk
Marketing Specialist: Lisa E. Boden

Cover Image: Ann Cutting/Workbook Stock/Getty Image

Printed in the U.S.A.

Library of Congress Control Number: 2005936447

Instructor's exam copy:
ISBN 13: 978-0-618-66064-3
ISBN 10: 0-618-66064-X

For orders, use student text ISBNs:
ISBN 13: 978-0-618-66063-6
ISBN 10: 0-618-66063-1

123456789-DOW-10 09 08 07 06

About the Authors

A. Parasuraman

A. Parasuraman ("Parsu") is Professor and holder of the James W. McLamore Chair in Marketing (endowed by the Burger King Corporation) at the University of Miami. He obtained his bachelor of technology degree in 1970 and his master of business administration degree in 1972 from leading universities in India. His doctor of business administration degree, which he obtained in 1975, is from Indiana University, Bloomington, Indiana.

Dr. Parasuraman teaches and does research in the areas of services marketing, service-quality measurement and improvement, and the role of technology in marketing to and serving customers. In 1988 Dr. Parasuraman was selected as one of the "Ten Most Influential Figures in Quality" by the editorial board of *The Quality Review*, copublished by the American Quality Foundation and the American Society for Quality Control. He has received many distinguished teaching and research awards, including multiple Best Professor awards given by executive MBA classes and the Provost's Award for Scholarly Research at the University of Miami. In 1998 he received the American Marketing Association's Career Contributions to the Services Discipline award (an annual award bestowed on one individual who has had a sustained and far-reaching impact on the field). He received the Academy of Marketing Science's Outstanding Marketing Educator award in 2001 and was designated a Distinguished Fellow of the Academy in 2004. He has also been named to the Chartered Institute of Marketing's (U.K.) "Guru Gallery," which profiles the 50 leading marketing thinkers worldwide.

Dr. Parasuraman has published over 100 articles in journals such as *Journal of Marketing, Journal of Marketing Research, Journal of Retailing,* and *Sloan Management Review.* He served as editor of *Journal of the Academy of Marketing Science* for a three-year term (1997–2000). He is currently editor of *Journal of Service Research.* Dr. Parasuraman has coauthored three other business books written for practitioners: *Delivering Quality Service: Balancing Customer Perceptions and Expectations, Marketing Services: Competing Through Quality,* and *Techno-Ready Marketing: How and Why Your Customers Adopt Technology.* He is an active consultant and has conducted dozens of executive seminars.

Dhruv Grewal

Dhruv Grewal (Ph.D. Virginia Tech) is the Toyota Chair in Commerce and Electronic Business and Professor of Marketing at Babson College. His research and teaching interests focus on marketing research, value-based marketing, e-business, retailing, global marketing, and pricing. He was awarded the 2005 Lifetime Achievement in Behavioral Pricing Award (Fordham University) and is a Distinguished Fellow of the Academy of Marketing Science. He has served as VP, Research and Conferences on the American Marketing Association Academic Council (1999–2001) and as VP, Development for the Academy of Marketing Science (2000–2002). He co-chaired the 1993 AMS conference, the 1998 Winter AMA conference, a 1998 Marketing Science Institute conference, a 2001 AMA doctoral consortium, and he will be co-chairing the 2006 Summer AMA conference.

Dr. Grewal has won a number of awards for his teaching, including the Sherwin Williams Distinguished Teaching Award, Society for Marketing Advances (2005); the American Marketing Association Award for Innovative Excellence in

Marketing Education (2003); the Academy of Marketing Science Great Teachers in Marketing Award (1999); the Executive MBA Teaching Excellence Award (1998); School of Business Teaching Excellence Awards (1993, 1999); and Virginia Tech Certificate of Recognition for Outstanding Teaching (1989).

He has published over 70 articles in journals such as *Journal of Marketing, Journal of Consumer Research, Journal of Marketing Research, Journal of Retailing,* and *Journal of the Academy of Marketing Science.* He serves on numerous editorial review boards. He is currently co-editor of *Journal of Retailing.* His research awards include the Best Services Paper Award (2002), from the AMA Services SIG presented at the Service Frontier Conference, October 2003; the Stanley C. Hollander Best Retailing Paper, Academy of Marketing Science Conference, 2002; the M. Wayne DeLozier Best Conference Paper, Academy of Marketing Science, 2002; Best Paper Award, Pricing Track, Winter American Marketing Association Conference, 2001; and Best Paper Award, Technology Track, Summer American Marketing Association Educators' Conference, 2000. He actively works with firms as a consultant, conducts executive seminars/courses, and consults with law firms on marketing cases.

R. Krishnan

R. Krishnan (Ph.D., Virginia Tech) is Research Professor of Marketing at the School of Business Administration, University of Miami. Previously, he was Professor of Marketing and Director of Graduate Programs, Orfalea College of Business, California Polytechnic State University, San Luis Obispo. He had previously taught at the University of Miami, Virginia Tech, and the City University of New York. He has a master of industrial and production engineering degree, as well as a bachelor of mechanical engineering degree. In addition, he has worked for two years in a firm where he handled operations management responsibilities.

Dr. Krishnan's research has appeared in a number of professional and scholarly journals, including *Journal of Marketing, Sloan Management Review, California Management Review, Academy of Management Executive, Journal of Interactive Marketing, Total Quality Management, Journal of Retailing, Journal of Advertising, Journal of Advertising Research, Journal of Business Logistics, European Journal of Marketing, Industrial Marketing Management, Journal of Business Research, Journal of Consumer Psychology, Industrial Marketing Management, Journal of Marketing Management,* and *International Journal of Physical Distribution.*

Dr. Krishnan's primary interests are pricing strategies, e-commerce strategy, operations strategy and supply chain management, marketing research and quantitative analysis, marketing strategy, high-tech marketing, product and brand management, and managing change in global operations. He coedited a special issue of *Journal of Business Research:* "Marketing on the Web: E-commerce Strategies" (2001).

He has received many distinguished teaching awards, including the UM-EMBA Excellence in Teaching award, the Delta Sigma Pi Teacher Award, the College of Business Teacher Award, and Alumni Award for Best Teaching. Dr. Krishnan specializes in business strategy marketing for technology-based companies, e-commerce, new product and brand strategies, and pricing strategies and conducts marketing education programs for industries around the globe.

Brief Contents

Contents

14 Examining Associations: Correlation and Regression 437

15 Overview of Other Multivariate Techniques and Data Mining 471

Preface

Studying marketing research can and should be an interesting, enlightening, and rewarding experience. The content and format of *Marketing Research,* Second Edition, are designed to offer such an experience, especially to the typical student who approaches the subject apprehensively and reluctantly. Based on our collective teaching experience of over five decades, we believe that the best way to engage students and reinforce the importance and relevance of marketing research is to continually remind them of its applications in the real world. Therefore, as we did in the first edition, we present the various marketing research terms, tools, and concepts in an understandable, lively fashion by using numerous current examples in every chapter. In addition, we have incorporated the impact of the Internet and the latest advances in information technologies on doing and using marketing research.

This book is intended for students who are taking their first course in marketing research. The breadth and depth of topics included in the book are carefully chosen to benefit primarily those students who will be potential research users, as well as those who wish to consider marketing research as a career. To cater to this dual audience, we stress the importance of effective communication between research users and researchers, and we highlight their respective roles and responsibilities at various stages of a research project.

Features New to This Edition

This edition has a number of new features that should appeal to both students and instructors.

1. A new section on data mining has been added to the chapter on multivariate techniques (Chapter 15). Using many examples, this section discusses in an accessible fashion the capabilities and applications of, as well as recent developments in, data mining.

2. The chapter on questionnaire design (Chapter 10) has a new section discussing SurveyZ.com's Web-based survey methodology. This section helps students to gain hands-on experience in using the Web to collect data. It describes an easy-to-use approach for developing and administering online surveys.

3. Over one-third of the end-of-chapter cases are new. These focus on the role of marketing research in contemporary issues and topics, which should appeal to students. Examples include GM's launch of the Hummer (Case 1.1), developing Web-based services for government (Case 3.2), the introduction of Burger King's Enormous Omelet Sandwich (Case 7.1), and exit polls in the 2004 U.S. presidential election (Case 11.2).

4. Two new cases—"Rockbridge Associates: National Technology Readiness Survey (Part A)" (Case 12.2) and "Rockbridge Associates: National Technology Readiness Survey (Part B)" (Case 13.1)—include a large data set that is available to students. This data set is derived from a recent real-life survey of

a representative sample of 1,000 adults (18 years and over) in the United States. It contains data pertaining to consumers' technology-related attitudes and behaviors, as well as their demographics. The case questions focus on a wide range of student assignments related to data analysis—from setting up a coding scheme for the data set, to applying various techniques discussed in the data analysis chapters, to interpreting SPSS output.

5. New SPSS application questions have been added to the *Test Bank*.

6. Many new examples and Research in Use boxes have been added throughout the book to reflect the most recent developments in marketing research.

Content and Organization

The textbook contains sixteen chapters organized in five parts. Part One, consisting of three chapters, provides an overview of the nature and scope of marketing research, and the different types of marketing research. Part Two, consisting of five chapters, discusses the various types of data available to marketers, the increasing sophistication and capabilities of research-based systems to aid decision making, and the basic research approaches and designs available for conducting marketing research. Part Three, containing three chapters, focuses on the measurement instruments and sampling approaches used in data collection. Part Four highlights data analysis, with chapters on quality control and initial analysis, hypothesis testing, correlation and regression analysis, and other multivariate techniques. Part Five includes the final chapter, which highlights the importance of accurately and clearly presenting marketing research findings to decision makers.

Text Highlights

We stated earlier that this book has been designed to make the study of marketing research interesting, enlightening, and rewarding. This edition of our book preserves, and in many instances enhances, the following distinctive characteristics of the previous edition that made the subject accessible and relevant:

• Every chapter in the book has numerous carefully chosen examples that are well integrated with the textual material. Every key concept, principle, and technique is illustrated with one or more examples. Many of these examples come from international contexts, involve technology-based products and services, and focus on contemporary issues.

• The book has a readable and accessible writing style. The key ideas in each chapter are logically developed and organized to enable students to grasp them easily and quickly.

• An attractive, colorful, and engaging design presents the information in an accessible and appealing way. Charts, diagrams, and other graphic illustrations are used liberally to supplement the text discussion.

• The text provides extensive coverage of marketing research procedures that are frequently used in practice but are treated only superficially in many textbooks. For example, this book has separate chapters on geographic information systems (Chapter 5) and qualitative research (Chapter 7).

• The text offers useful frameworks and illustrations for understanding and effectively applying the more technical aspects of marketing research (for example, the probability sampling techniques covered in Chapter 11 and the hypothesis-testing procedures covered in Chapter 13).

- For those instructors who wish to familiarize students with statistical analysis software, a student version of SPSS is available for packaging with the text. In addition, in-text tutorials and screen captures provide step-by-step instructions on how to use the software to perform statistical analysis.

- The analysis chapters share a data set—the National Insurance Company data—to illustrate the use of the most appropriate techniques (including how to use SPSS to perform the analysis) based on the nature of the research question and the type of data. This common data set, obtained from a real-life survey of 285 customers of an insurance company, provides continuity across the chapters and brings to life the application of multiple analytical techniques within the same research study.

- The National Insurance Company data set, along with data sets for four other cases in the book, is included in the SPSS CD-ROM that is available with the text. The same data sets are also available on the Student Website (for Excel users and those who already have access to SPSS).

- Guidelines for using Microsoft Excel are also provided for those instructors who prefer to use this tool.

Pedagogical Features

To help highlight the most important concepts and issues in marketing research, we have incorporated a number of pedagogical features.

- Chapter-opening vignettes provide interesting and up-to-date anecdotes from the world of business, allowing immediate application of chapter concepts and setting the stage for further learning.

- Chapter Objectives identify key concepts, mapping chapter content and giving students clear direction about what they need to study most closely.

- In addition to the many in-text examples, Case in Point sections provide more in-depth examples and short case scenarios to illustrate major points.

- Research in Use boxes illustrate real-world applications of concepts or techniques covered in the chapter. Some of these have been researched firsthand and often include offbeat and unique themes.

- Key terms in each chapter are highlighted in the text and defined in the margins. The text also includes a comprehensive Glossary containing an alphabetical listing of all key terms with their definitions.

- Review and Discussion Questions, Application Exercises, and Internet or SPSS Exercises in every chapter provide a variety of tasks to help students retain the information they have learned and apply concepts in meaningful ways.

- End-of-chapter cases are original to the text. These cases include pertinent and compelling facts and company data to illustrate real-world utilization of marketing research.

Flexibility for Instructors

The content and the organization of this book are designed to offer maximum flexibility for instructors in terms of the teaching approaches they want to use and the relative emphases they wish to place on different topics. The simple writing style and liberal use of examples should minimize the amount of class time necessary to clarify concepts covered in the book. Instructors will therefore have more time to further develop key topics that they wish to emphasize and for experimental activities, such as case discussions, computer-assisted exercises, and student projects.

Each text includes a free passkey to SurveyZ.com—a website housing a professional online survey creation tool—so students will be able to conduct actual Internet surveys as part of their course work. In addition, a student version of SPSS software, containing a special tutorial program, is available for packaging with the text. For those instructors who prefer to work with Microsoft Excel, however, the text is available as a standalone product.

A Complete Package of Support Materials

Accompanying the text is a support package that focuses on generating enthusiasm in the classroom and inspiring student success. The following items are provided to help instructors plan, present, and assess more effectively:

Instructor's Resource Manual. Created by Catharine Curran-Kelly of the University of Massachusetts at Dartmouth, in association with the text authors, the *Instructor's Resource Manual* contains a variety of chapter support materials. These include chapter summaries, lists of key terms, detailed lecture notes, answers to Review and Discussion Questions, comments and guidelines for the Application Exercises and Internet or SPSS Exercises, and extensive case teaching notes. It is available on the textbook website.

Instructor Website. This password-protected site provides up-to-date research, useful Web links, and downloadable PowerPoint and *Instructor's Resource Manual* files.

Test Bank. Also developed by Catharine Curran-Kelly in association with the text authors, the *Test Bank* contains about 1,400 true/false and multiple-choice questions, several short-answer and essay questions for each chapter, and computational/problem-solving questions for the data analysis chapters.

HMTesting. This electronic version of the print *Test Bank* allows instructors to generate and change tests easily. The program includes an online testing feature that allows instructors to administer tests through their local area network or over the Web. It also has a gradebook feature that lets users set up classes, record and track grades from tests or assignments, analyze grades, and produce class and individual statistics.

Call-in Test Service. This service lets instructors select items from the *Test Bank* and call our toll-free faculty services number (800-733-1717) to order printed tests.

PowerPoint Slides. This program presents key concepts and illustrations from the text, as well as from outside the text, to enhance classroom presentations. The slides are downloadable from the Instructor Website.

Video Package. The video package provides compelling footage of real companies and situations, which helps bring the textbook concepts to life. Teaching notes and suggestions are also provided.

The following package items are available for students to enhance their knowledge and application skills:

Passkey to SurveyZ.com. A passkey for a free, six-month subscription to this website allows students to create and distribute online surveys using a professional construction tool. Downloading survey data is quick and efficient—and compatible with SPSS software.

Student Website. Content for the Student Website has been developed by the text authors and includes student tutorials, data sets relating to text exercises that can be used with either Excel or SPSS, ACE practice tests, additional marketing research information supporting text content, career search links, summaries of the latest marketing research articles with links when appropriate, and hyperlinks to research sites pertaining to technology, service, and global issues.

SPSS Software. This professional software program is available for packaging with each textbook through a special arrangement with SPSS. Step-by-step instructions, explanations, and screen shots are provided in the textbook to familiarize students with this popular statistical analysis program. In addition, a student tutorial is included with each CD-ROM. Data sets relating to exercises in the textbook are also provided.

Acknowledgments

Many individuals and organizations contributed significantly to the development of this textbook. Our sincere appreciation goes to the numerous organizations and executives who generously provided material for the cases, exercises, and illustrations in this book. Special thanks goes to Dennis Malamatinas (former CEO of Burger King), Douglass Riggan of Burger King, David Moxley of Customer Knowledge Consultants, Charles Colby and Regina D. Woodall of Rockbridge Associates, Carey Watson of Burdines, Paul Abbate of Quicktake, Christian Sager of Pankey, Michael G. Rider of Polaroid, Mark Eisner of MSR Research, Andrea Gallagher (IRI), Caroline Anawati of Taco Bell, and John Tietjen, John Watkins, Kathy Thornhill, and Jim Figura of Colgate-Palmolive. We extend our deep appreciation to Jeanne Munger for her contribution to the cases, to Catharine Curran-Kelly for her contributions to the *Instructor's Resource Manual* and *Test Bank,* and to Cornelia Perchmann for her authorship of Chapter 5, "Using Geographic Information Systems for Marketing Research." Other colleagues who provided valuable input include Ray Burke, John Hauser, Meghan McCardle, Michael Levy, David Hardesty, Anne Roggeveen and Elaine Allen. We'd also like to thank Giao Nguyen, Nancy Dlott, Morgan Wolters, Julie Rusch, and David Snavley, who helped us with research for the text, as well as our former students Betsy Russell and Kristen Presenell. In addition, our sincere appreciation goes to Dean Paul Sugrue, University of Miami; Provost Michael Fetter, Babson College; Dean Terri Swartz, California Polytechnic and State University; Professor Arun Sharma, Former Chairman, Marketing Department, University of Miami; Professor Abdul Ali, Chairman, Marketing Division, Babson College; and Professor Norm Borin, Chairman, Marketing Area, California Polytechnic and State University, for their support during this project.

We are deeply indebted to the team of professionals at Houghton Mifflin, whose excellent support and encouragement were critical in transforming our vision for the book into a finished product. In particular, our sincere thanks go to Jessica Carlisle (Development Editor), George Hoffman (Publisher), Paula Kmetz (Project Editor), and Mary Dalton-Hoffman (Permissions Editor).

We are also indebted to the following reviewers for their thoughtful and helpful comments and suggestions: David Andrus, Kansas State University; Linda Anglin,

Minnesota State University; David Ambrose, University of Nebraska, Omaha; Michael Dotson, Appalachian State University; Susan Heckler, Georgetown University; Gopal Iyer, Florida Atlantic University; John Milewicz, Jacksonville State University; Nacef Mouri, University of Central Florida; Vernon Murray, Marist College; Sabrina Neeley, Miami University; Sak Onkvisit, San Jose State University; Eric Panitz, Ferris State University; Pushkala Raman, Florida State University; Jim Roberts, Baylor University; Michael Russell, St. Bonaventure University; Daniel Rutledge, Saint Joseph's College; Charles Seifert, Siena College; David Snepenger, Montana State University; Robert Stassen, University of Arkansas; Scott Swain, Boston University; William R. Thomas; University of South Carolina; Philip Trocchia, Kansas State University; and David J. Urban, Virginia Commonwealth University.

Finally, words alone are insufficient to thank our wives and children for their generous understanding, support, and sacrifices throughout this project.

A. P.
D. G.
R. K.

Marketing Research

Introduction to Marketing Research

Part One

1 The Nature and Scope of Marketing Research

Chapter Objectives

After reading and understanding the material in this chapter, you should be able to:

- Identify the role of marketing research in strategic planning and decision making.

- Define the process of marketing research.

- Identify the three principles for generating information useful to managers.

- Explain why marketing research requires analysis and interpretation of data.

- Discuss the relationship between marketing research and decision making.

- Describe the wide variety of applications for marketing research.

- Identify various career opportunities in marketing research.

Marketing Research at Volvo[1]

Global spending on marketing research is over $16.6 billion, with the United States accounting for about 38 percent. The automotive industry is one of the biggest users of marketing research information. Volvo Cars, based in Göteborg, Sweden, is no exception. The company conducts about 400 major marketing research studies a year. Volvo employs a wide variety of methods to collect customer information. The research conducted at Volvo Cars is best seen as part of the new-product development (NPD) process.

Volvo spends a significant amount of money on sales and service satisfaction tracking to assess customers' satisfaction with their sales and service experiences at the dealerships. Although Volvo is famous for its positioning on safety, the company has recently tried to shed its traditional "boxy" design in favor of

trendier designs uncovered through marketing research. The Volvo XC90 and S40 are examples of Volvo models that were designed with help from marketing research. In designing its SUV model, Volvo recruited a group of female customers in California and sought their input in real time throughout all phases of its NPD process, to come up with a truly customer oriented design. Moreover, Volvo undertakes a variety of customer relationship management initiatives to strengthen its links with Volvo owners. Volvo managers acquire customer information through formal research studies as well as informal talks with customers and industry colleagues. ■

The aforementioned information-gathering activities are glimpses of marketing research at work. Volvo and other automakers, as well as companies in other industries, conduct a wide range of marketing research activities to help them plan and evaluate their marketing strategies. Volvo uses a methodical research approach to identify winning concepts and deliver products that satisfy a variety of stakeholders. For example, concept generation begins with market analysis for potential opportunities, as well as concept engineering and concept testing with customers and specific target groups. As the design process moves forward, customers are intimately involved in identifying key wants and needs for the new vehicle. Simultaneously, research continues to support the business case for introducing the new vehicle. Positioning, profitability and communication strategies are researched before, during, and after the launch. And dealers provide critical after-sale data regarding customer behavior, product satisfaction, and servicing issues.

The **marketing mix** is a combination of product, price, promotion, and place (the 4Ps) designed for a target market.

All marketing managers understand the importance of the **marketing mix,** or "four Ps"—product, place, price, and promotion—in developing marketing strategies. But how do managers know what specific strategies will be most effective? This is where the critical role of marketing research comes in. Research allows managers to better understand the most uncontrollable aspects of marketing: consumers and their role in the competitive environment. The most successful managers are adept at gaining insights into the needs, lifestyles, and aspirations of today's and tomorrow's customers. They use those insights to improve the quality of the product and service decisions they make. In the ambiguous and changing environments that have become the norm in many industries, identifying the real problems, considering all alternatives, and making the right decisions in a limited time frame are the most challenging managerial tasks.

Volvo is an excellent example of an organization that successfully blends marketing research with its overall business strategy. Aspects of its research demonstrate Volvo's awareness of its target market and the importance of tailoring its marketing mix to the needs of that target market. Let's take a more detailed look at the role of marketing research in strategic planning and decision making.

The Role of Marketing Research in Strategic Planning and Decision Making

A **marketing strategy** is a plan that enables an organization to make the best use of its resources to meet marketing objectives.

The **marketing plan** is a formal document that specifies the organization's resources, objectives, strategy, and implementation and control efforts in marketing a specific product.

In any organization, a multitude of decisions must be made. Our primary focus, however, will be on the role of marketing research in **marketing strategy** decisions—decisions directly related to the marketing of goods, services, or ideas to specific customers (see Exhibit 1.1). The **marketing plan** encapsulates strategic marketing decisions within a formal document that specifies organizational resources, objectives, strategy, and implementation and control efforts. The marketing plan has three major components: identifying marketing opportunities and constraints, developing and implementing marketing strategies, and evaluating the effectiveness of marketing plans.[2]

Identifying Marketing Opportunities and Constraints

Identifying marketing opportunities and constraints is a logical starting point for developing marketing strategies. In particular, firms that are considering new-product introductions or entry into new market areas with existing products will benefit from information about issues such as these:

- Who are our potential competitors, and how strong are their market positions?
- How satisfied are consumers with current offerings on the market?
- Are there any unmet consumer needs?
- How are consumers likely to perceive our offerings relative to competitors' offerings?

Marketing research can help answer these and other questions of interest to marketers.

An increasing number of firms routinely use marketing research to generate relevant information for developing effective strategies.

A case in point is T.G.I. Friday's, a leading casual-dining chain operating in 49 states and 55 countries. Every year, T.G.I. Friday's attracts more than 80 million customers. The company conducts formal interviews with customers and asks servers to be observant of what customers like and want. T.G.I. Friday's noticed that a growing number of diners were asking servers to hold the fries or to replace mashed potatoes with salads and vegetables. Moreover, the IT staff at Carlson Restaurants, T.G.I. Friday's parent company, captured data on patrons' orders that servers had entered into the restaurants' point-of-sale systems. The insights that T.G.I. Friday's derived by analyzing the point-of-sale data were consistent with conclusions from an independent report produced by ACNielsen, a leading marketing research company. The report claimed that 59 million Americans were watching their carbohydrate intake and that more than 17 percent of the nation's households had at least one person following a low-carb diet. Carlson Restaurants and Atkins Nutritionals, the company founded by the late Dr. Robert C.

Exhibit 1.1
The Role of Marketing Research in Strategic Planning and Decision Making

Atkins, jointly developed Atkins-branded low-carb lunches and dinners. According to Deborah Lipscomb, CIO of Carlson Restaurants Worldwide, "We felt the best way to communicate to our guests that we are here to help them in their lifestyle choices was to have a brand-name partnership." Close monitoring of guests' eating patterns by servers and data mining of point-of-sales data allowed T.G.I. Friday's to become aware of and capitalize on opportunities created by the low-carb trend.[3]

The craze for low-carb diets is beginning to ebb, and the companies that were slow to react to this trend missed an opportunity to cash in.[4]

Unilever, the consumer goods giant, is an example of such a company. By neglecting to conduct research on the low-carb trend, Unilever was unable to anticipate the devastating effect that the Atkins diet would have on its Slim-Fast meal-replacement business. Consequently, it was not quick enough to react to changes in the weight-management food category, almost 50 percent of which by then consisted of low-carb products. Unilever's Slim-Fast launched five low-carb products at the end of 2003, playing a catch-up game in the fast-growing low-carb category. Failure to keep up with the market cost the company dearly in 2003, while its main rival, Procter & Gamble, finished the year with double-digit growth.[5]

Pizza Hut, the well-known pizza chain, is another example of a company making effective use of marketing research to identify opportunities for improvement. Pizza Hut's marketing research initiative led to the development of new pizza. In 2003 Yum! Brands, Inc., Pizza Hut's parent company, repositioned the pizza brand to target the family and its primary decision maker, the mom. To cater to this market, Pizza Hut evaluated a record number of concepts in 2003 and introduced buffalo chicken pizza nationally after positive test market results.[6] Marketing research conducted by Pizza Hut also showed that families love variety. This insight led the chain to develop "4forAll," a new combination giving the family four topping choices in a single pizza. Pizza Hut considers 4forAll to be the most significant pizza category innovation since the introduction of stuffed crust pizza. The company expects 4forAll to become a permanent menu item and contribute significantly to profits.[7] Pizza Hut has benefited from marketing research in the international arena; based on research findings from various countries, the company customizes its pizza offerings to fit local tastes. Such indigenization has helped change Pizza Hut's image from that of an American company to that of a global company that is sensitive and responsive to local customs.[8]

As the various applications of marketing research at Pizza Hut demonstrate, strategies based on appropriate marketing research insights will benefit companies in many ways.

> The **marketing concept** is an organizational philosophy that emphasizes determining customers' needs first and then coordinating all activities to satisfy those needs.

■ **Embracing the Marketing Concept**   Conducting marketing research to understand customers and their requirements, as illustrated by the T.G.I. Friday's and Pizza Hut applications, is becoming widespread, as an increasing number of firms embrace the **marketing concept**—the philosophy of customer orientation that urges firms to uncover customer needs first and then coordinate all their activities to satisfy those needs.

By emphasizing the need to gain a good understanding of customers, the marketing concept also stresses the importance of conducting marketing research in the early stages of formulating marketing strategies. Many firms have had major new-product failures because they neglected to research market opportunities and constraints before deciding to introduce the products. A case in point is Nokia.

Nokia, a well-known mobile phone company, was trying to gain an advantage over its main rivals, Sony and Nintendo, as it entered the growing global hand-held computer game market. It launched N-Gage, a phone with high-quality gaming capabilities, without first gauging customer reactions to it. N-Gage bombed in the market, apparently because it did not match consumers' expectations for usability and functionality. This phone had to be held sideways against the face to talk, and customers mocked the product on a specially created website, www.sidetalking.com. Customers wanted a wider game selection, a larger game screen, and a user-friendly design at an affordable price. Learning from customer complaints, Nokia redesigned the N-Gage as the N-Gage QD with a longer battery life, brighter screen, and better gaming controls.[9] Paying attention to customer needs in the second round paid off for Nokia. Nearly 1 million units of N-Gage QDs were shipped around the world soon after the launch. Nevertheless, Nokia's failure to understand customers' needs before launching the original version of N-Gage allowed Sony and Nintendo sufficient time to launch their own versions of this product.

■ **Understanding the Competitive Environment**   Marketing research is vital to maintaining and improving a company's overall competitiveness. Many organizations continually collect and evaluate environmental information to identify future market opportunities and threats. A notable example is Netflix, the leading online DVD service with over 25,000 movie titles (www.netflix.com). In the first nine months of 2004, Netflix had spent almost $80 million acquiring DVDs. Over 2.5 million homes now subscribe to this online DVD rental service, paying about $20 per month for an unlimited number of DVD rentals delivered by mail.[10]

Despite its success, Netflix constantly worries about its survival. Competition in Netflix's market is intense, coming from both inside and outside the movie rental arena. Low-price DVDs and video-on-demand services from direct-broadcast satellite (DBS) and cable operators have eroded the video rental market. Netflix is also directly competing with video/DVD rental goliath Blockbuster, which dominates the market with over 48 million accounts and 8,500 stores around the globe. A growing number of people are also renting videos and DVDs from supermarkets and discount stores such as Wal-Mart, making them another force for Netflix to reckon with. Wal-Mart and Blockbuster have also introduced online services to compete with Netflix. In response to the intensifying competition, Netflix and Blockbuster dropped their prices to $18 a month from $20 to

Marketing research can help Netflix analyze competition from Wal-Mart and Amazon.com.

retain their customer base, eroding their bottom lines. Netflix has struck a deal with TiVo for online delivery of movies. And Akimbo, a privately held company, launched a video-on-demand service through Amazon.com, an online giant with a very broad reach. In short, the movie rental market is a highly volatile and dynamic one, which offers consumers a growing number of options for renting and viewing videos.

Where does marketing research fit into this scenario? Netflix needs market information to determine the actual impact of Amazon's entry into the video rental market, to update and expand its inventory of videos and DVDs, and to determine the impact of Blockbuster.com and Wal-Mart.com on its current business. Marketing research can be of great help in obtaining this information. Do Netflix customers rent from Wal-Mart, Blockbuster, grocery stores, and other online services? What segments of brick-and-mortar store customers, for example, are, or could become, Netflix customers? What could Netflix do to update its offerings consistent with changing customer preferences? What other technologies could enhance Netflix's position in the online rental market? The company needs to examine these issues on an ongoing, systematic basis to prosper in its hypercompetitive business environment.

Developing and Implementing Marketing Strategies

To benefit fully from the opportunities uncovered in the marketplace, a firm must develop an effective marketing strategy with an effective marketing mix; that is, it must make sound decisions about the nature of its product, ways to promote the product, the price charged to potential customers, and the means used to make the product available to them. Good marketing research will identify whether or not the marketing mix is effective enough to maximize the benefits to the firm (in terms of sales, profits, customer satisfaction, and value) from available opportunities. The development of many new products has been preceded by extensive marketing research to help formulate one or more elements of their marketing mixes.

Volvo generated considerable buzz by introducing at the 2004 Geneva Motor Show a car model named YCC (Your Concept Car), which was aimed at women. Extensive marketing research played a major role in the development of this car model. Volvo manufactures and sells a range of vehicle models, but until recently none was targeted specifically at the female car buyer. The YCC was an effort to appeal to females. According to CNW Marketing Research, 49 percent of new vehicles and 55 percent of used vehicles are purchased by women. By industry estimates, women can be credited with influencing up to 80 percent of new-car purchases. And 54 percent of Volvo buyers are women. Seeing an opportunity to capitalize on these facts, Volvo conducted research to determine what sort of image and features a car geared toward the female market should have. Using market surveys and insights gained from the company's 400 female workers, a team of 25 female employees was involved in designing the YCC.[11]

Evaluating the Effectiveness of Marketing Plans

Getting feedback from the marketplace and taking corrective action with elements of products or services that need fixing is often referred to as *controlling* or the *control function*. Controlling is an important component of the planning and decision-making process, and another area in which marketing research provides solutions.

To succeed in the marketplace, a firm must at least periodically monitor market conditions, usually by obtaining feedback from customers, and answer control-related questions such as: What is the market share of our product? Is its share increasing, decreasing, or staying the same? Who are its users? Are the nature of the users and the volume of their purchases consistent with our expectations (goals)? If not, why not? A firm may want to explore a number of questions like these to evaluate its market performance. Only marketing research, not marketers' intuition, can yield accurate answers to such questions.

Sprite in Ireland provides an example of marketing research in the control stage. Sprite was languishing as late as in 1999 in Ireland even though it was launched by the Coca-Cola Company in the early 1990s. 7 UP was the dominant player in the Irish lemon-lime beverage market. To revive the Sprite brand, the company invited "leading-edge teens" to talk about their attitudes and values, and evaluated their reactions to all aspects of the marketing mix, namely, product, price, distribution, and promotion. The revised marketing mix based on insights from this research was highly effective. The global promotional tag line ("Image is nothing—thirst is everything—obey your thirst") was well received by the teen participants, who were asked if they could remember the advertising message and whether it influenced their purchasing behavior. Thirty-four percent of the teens spontaneously recalled the Sprite TV ads compared to a conventional average recall of 25 percent. Fifty-eight percent recalled Sprite's outdoor advertising without prompting—20 percent above the conventional norm. Sprite sold more than double the number of bottles that had initially been budgeted. In the lemon-lime market segment, Sprite won 15 percentage share points from key competitors. The strength of demand from both consumers and retailers encouraged the Coca-Cola Company to launch larger packs, such as 2-liter bottles, more than six months ahead of the original timetable.[12]

In summary, marketing research is an essential link between marketing decision makers and the markets in which they operate. It can and should play an important role in all three stages of planning and decision making: identifying marketing opportunities and constraints, developing and implementing marketing strategies, and evaluating the effectiveness of marketing plans. Before we go further, let's look at what marketing research actually is.

Definition of Marketing Research

Students new to marketing research might define the process as

- Gathering data from your markets.
- Conducting customer surveys.
- Determining the needs of your customers.
- Evaluating customer response to advertising.
- Gathering sales and market share data of your competitors.
- Testing your product or service in the marketplace.
- Estimating the potential sales of your product or service.

Although all these definitions describe marketing research, they do not adequately reflect its full scope. They are merely examples of potential applications of marketing research rather than sound definitions.

Exhibit 1.2
The Role of Marketing Research in the Organization/Business

Marketing research is the set of techniques and principles for systematically collecting, recording, analyzing, and interpreting data to aid marketing decision makers.

According to the American Marketing Association (AMA), whose members are professionals from academic and business organizations as well as a variety of nonbusiness organizations such as government agencies, marketing research is the function that links the consumer, customer, and public to the marketer through information—information used to identify and define marketing opportunities and problems; generate, refine, and evaluate marketing actions; monitor marketing performance; and improve understanding of marketing as a process.

Marketing research specifies the information required to address these issues; designs the method for collecting information; manages and implements the data collection process; analyzes the results; and communicates the findings and their implications.[13]

Exhibit 1.2 shows graphically how marketing research informs decision makers and influences marketing decisions. As you can see, marketing research, which ultimately comes from customers and from society at large, provides the information businesses need to make organizationwide decisions. It also provides input to marketing decisions that have specific impacts on customers and on society, both of which feed information back to the organization.

A more concise definition would be as follows:

Marketing research is a set of techniques and principles for systematically collecting, recording, analyzing, and interpreting data that can aid decision makers involved in marketing goods, services, or ideas.

Note that this definition stresses both the techniques and the *principles* of marketing research. It also includes the importance of *analyzing* and *interpreting* the data collected. Marketing research also aids *decision makers;* it does not replace the decision-making function. Throughout the rest of this chapter, we will look at each of these characteristics in more detail.

Basic Marketing Research Principles

Marketing research has three principles or guidelines for generating information useful to managers:

- Attend to the timeliness and relevance of research.
- Define research objectives carefully and clearly.
- Do not conduct research to support decisions already made.

These principles are simple and perhaps even intuitive. Nevertheless, they are crucial to the proper and successful application of marketing research.

Principle 1: Attend to the Timeliness and Relevance of Research

Marketing research can lead to erroneous decisions if it is not done on a timely basis. This principle certainly applies to the auto industry. Over the past several years, U.S. auto manufacturers such as GM and Ford have been developing and selling a number of sport utility vehicles (SUVs) based on demand estimates and customer reactions obtained through their marketing research. Although the strategy of selling SUVs is quite successful, the demand for them is beginning to be adversely affected by tensions in the Middle East and the resultant rise in gasoline prices. A recent poll conducted by the market research firm Harris Interactive Inc. and the auto information service Kelley Blue Book found that one out of every six recent car buyers changed purchase plans because of higher fuel costs.[14]

Although the automakers had done extensive research prior to the release of SUVs into the market, that research fell short on an important principle of marketing research: the elapsed time between the research for and launch of new SUV models is simply too long in the rapidly changing marketplace. Although the decision to invest in product design is based on prior research, the decision to launch two to three years later is questionable. Porsche, Volkswagen, and Volvo entered the SUV market in 2004 because they had already spent considerable time and money developing a SUV based on earlier marketing research. It is worth noting that this problem of timeliness applies to other cars and products as well, especially those with a long design-to-market lead time. Thus the timeliness and relevance of the research findings are questionable.

Principle 2: Define Research Objectives Carefully and Clearly

Careful and clear definition of research objectives is a key requirement for accurate and beneficial marketing research outcomes. The experience of Microsoft is an example of what can go wrong by failing to pay careful attention to research objectives.[15] Microsoft, a global technology company, assembled a product team to develop eHome, a fully networked residential living concept. The team decided to target this concept toward the domestic home market and successfully developed the product line within the stipulated time. However, the product line never took off, because the market potential never materialized. Marketing members of the team conducted research surveys, identified profiles of potential customers for eHome, and targeted those customers. However, they failed to take into account the lack of industry standards for associated technologies required to make eHome usable. For example, Internet-enabled appliances are critical for the successful launch of eHome, but such appliances have only recently started to become available for commercial use.

Microsoft could have chosen to focus on one key area of the home first, such as the television. Subsequently, the company has focused on the release of its Windows XP Media Center product line, with its emphasis on using the Windows XP operating system to enhance the experience of watching TV, playing music, or surfing the Internet.

As the Microsoft eHome example demonstrates, the research objectives in a high-technology market should cover all aspects of emerging technology.

Principle 3: Do Not Conduct Research to Support Decisions Already Made

Conducting marketing research when potential research users have already made up their minds is not a productive use of scarce resources. Motorola's Iridium, Apple's Newton, Sony's MiniDisc, WebTV, and ITV Digital failed due to inadequate attention to this principle.[16] Apparently management in these companies was carried away by the "gee-whiz" technology and undertook research merely to see whether the results would support a decision that had already been made. Marketing research was carried out only to determine consumers' intended purchase interests and did not cover social, cultural, competitive, and economic factors surrounding these technologies. For example, the Sony MiniDisc was extremely successful in Japan but failed miserably in the United States. These studies failed to study all aspects of emerging technologies and focused only on generating support for the new products, costing the companies millions of dollars due to poor decisions. The technologies behind these products are making a comeback using a different business model.

The resources invested in conducting marketing research for SUVs (auto industry), eHomes (Microsoft), and high-technology gadgets (Motorola, Sony, WebTV, and ITV Digital) were obviously unproductive, not because of a failure to employ sophisticated research techniques, but because of inadequate attention to factors such as the timeliness of data, appropriateness of research objectives, and open-mindedness of decision makers. Such principles are as crucial to the effectiveness of marketing research as are quantitative tools and techniques.

The Importance of Analysis and Interpretation of Data

A common misconception about marketing research is that it is merely a set of tools for data collection and recording. If marketing research involved no more than the collection and recording of data, it would likely be useless for decision-making purposes. After all, companies routinely gather and record various kinds of data about their customers. However, not until the data are analyzed and the analyses interpreted will firms reap any tangible benefits from the research.

What distinguishes data from information? FedEx has vast amounts of data on customer transactions and their cost. However, these facts by themselves are not particularly helpful in determining, for instance, what should be the relationship among customer segments, marketing programs, and profitability. Rather, FedEx looks for patterns in customer data that can be correlated with customer profitability. Using its vast database, FedEx compares the costs of doing business with various customer segments and rates the segments according to profitability. For the top 20 percent of its customers, FedEx matches transaction data with demographic data to identify potential growth opportunities. Analysis and interpretation of data have helped FedEx improve the return on its marketing investments anywhere from four- to fivefold. FedEx has gone beyond merely recording and storing data to creating something much more valuable: **information** that will help managers make better decisions.

Information is data that have been analyzed and interpreted to aid in decision making.

FedEx is not the only company using this type of data analysis to differentiate customers. AT&T, Kraft, USAA, Northwestern Mutual Life Insurance Company, Capital One Financial, MCI, MBNA, and American Express are also benefiting by paying close attention to customer data analysis and interpretation. Hence, a set of data by itself cannot be viewed as useful information. Analysis and interpretation of data are essential for marketing research to be truly beneficial to decision makers.

Marketing Research Aids—But Does Not Replace—Decision Making

Marketing research by itself cannot be expected to provide sound marketing decisions. It can serve as a resource for decision makers—provided, of course, that the information it delivers is relevant, timely, and reliable. Its relevance, in turn, depends on marketers' ability to accurately diagnose the nature of the question or problem they want to solve and to ask the right questions at the right time in the data-gathering process. For instance, in the example of Microsoft eHomes, certain research-related decisions—the timing of the research studies prior to launch and the decision to forgo additional research to understand the impact of emerging technologies—contributed to the initial lackluster performance of the product.

In short, although marketing research can aid and influence decision making, its effectiveness is in turn affected by the decision makers who undertake the research. There is thus an interactive relationship between marketing research and decision making; one cannot substitute for the other.

Another reason marketing research is an aid to decision making rather than a replacement for it is that final decisions are influenced not only by research results but also by other factors both within the firm, such as resource constraints and corporate goals, and outside of it, such as competitors' activities and legal constraints, all of which must be taken into consideration. Therefore, decision makers, who should be more knowledgeable than researchers about such factors, have the ultimate responsibility for financial decisions. The experience of Kellogg Company illustrates this point.

When Research Results and Decisions Differ

Kellogg Company is the world's leading producer of ready-to-eat cereal products and other grain-based convenience foods, including toaster pastries, cereal bars, cookies, crackers, and frozen waffles. Its products are manufactured in 17 countries (on six continents) and sold in more than 180 countries worldwide, with sales of nearly $10 billion in 2004. However, Kellogg's is finding it difficult to sustain customary rates of growth and is aggressively promoting its products in foreign markets with mixed results.[17] Kellogg's has been persuading Latvians, Mexicans, and Indians to change their breakfast habits to include cereals, but has not been fully successful. According to marketing research studies, Latvians prefer a hearty plate of sausage, cold cuts, potatoes, eggs, and a few slices of thick, chewy, buttered bread. Mexicans and Indians prefer hot, spicy breakfasts. Because Kellogg's cereals' appeal is limited to a small, health-conscious group, marketing research did not forecast enthusiastic response. Nevertheless, Kellogg's chose to go ahead with its global expansion program. Latest indications are that Kellogg's is doing very well in Latin American countries, including Mexico. The Eastern European market is continuing to grow, and Latvia is going to be part of Kellogg's long-term growth. Indians, after initially showing strong interest in Kellogg's cereals, returned to their hot breakfast. High-priced Kellogg's brands and the availability of low-priced local cereal brands and cheaper breakfast alternatives are some of the reasons for its lackluster performance in India. Nevertheless, Kellogg's is willing to wait patiently for Indians to change their eating habits. This example does not imply that Kellogg's necessarily ignored the marketing research results. The research finding that consumers in different countries have different

Exhibit 1.3
Marketing Research's Relationship to Decision-Making Activity

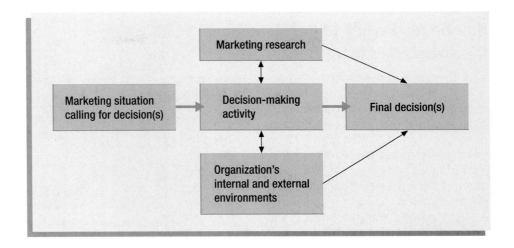

eating habits might have encouraged management to view these countries as part of a *long-term* growth strategy. In any case, the results may have been responsible for the company's decision to implement a campaign to educate the Indian market about the nutritional aspects of cereals. Only time will tell whether Kellogg's decision to continue its global expansion program was sound.

Relationship of Marketing Research to Decision Making

Exhibit 1.3 portrays the relationship of marketing research to decision-making activity. The double-headed arrows show that marketing research both influences and is influenced by decision-making activity within an organization.

Likewise, there is an interactive relationship between an organization's environment and its decision-making activity. The ultimate responsibility for decisions rests with decision makers, not with researchers, as signified by the solid arrow leading from "Decision-making activity" to "Final decision(s)." Such final decisions may be influenced by, but are not made by, those responsible for marketing research.

Marketing Research Applications

Basic research is conducted to generate knowledge.

Marketing research applications can be classified as either *basic research* or *applied research*. **Basic research** is conducted to generate or create knowledge. Examples of basic research are readily found in marketing journals such as the *Journal of Marketing Research, Journal of Consumer Research, Journal of Marketing, Journal of Retailing,* and so on. Recent articles examining the role of price promotions on value perceptions or of price and performance assessment on satisfaction are examples of basic research.[18]

Applied research is conducted to solve a problem.

Applied research is conducted to solve a problem. Marketers can use applied research to help them develop strategies for their products and services, ranging from personal computers to laundry detergents to online banking.

There are many potential applications for marketing research. In addition to being valuable in developing strategies for marketing goods and services, marketing research can aid in successfully marketing ideas.

How Do You Recruit a Nun? Marketing Research Comes to the Rescue

With most of its members more than 70 years of age, the religious order of the Sisters of St. Benedictine of Ferdinand, Indiana, faced extinction. The Benedictine order was unable to attract young recruits to continue its mission, and at last the convent's pressing need for membership forced the sisters to seek specialists with marketing research expertise. With outside help, the Sisters of St. Benedictine conducted focus groups and telephone interviews to identify their target market. Their research showed that respondents perceived a nun's life as dull and dreary. The sisters responded with humorous ads and brochures to create a more positive image of their work. The marketing campaign helped them recruit, on average, three nuns a year, a remarkable achievement compared to that of the previous decade. Thus marketing research aided St. Benedictine's efforts to successfully market the profession of Catholic

The Sisters of St. Benedictine successfully used marketing research to create a more positive image of their work.

sisterhood. Presently St. Benedictine nuns conduct annual workshops for sisters around the world, instructing them in marketing's role in reversing the declining memberships that many convents face.[a]

CASE IN POINT ▶ **Marketing Ideas** Claritas Inc. specializes in providing marketing information to companies in the media, telecommunications, financial services, and automotive industries.[19] Claritas is a key supplier of information containing the profiles and lifestyles of U.S. consumers by zip code. Jonathan Robbins, founder of Claritas, developed this information base by meticulously combining demographic data compiled by the U.S. Census Bureau with lifestyle/attitudinal data generated through various regional surveys. Each year, Claritas updates its information base by interviewing more than 150,000 households about key financial, media, and lifestyle habits. The resulting information base contains descriptive profiles of residents in each of the 36,000 five-digit zip code areas in the United States.

Recently Claritas added to its information base the Survey of Buying Power, a leading database of small-area consumer spending and retail statistics. This information base, nicknamed PRIZM (Potential Rating Index by Zip Market), has found a variety of applications in effectively marketing ideas as well as products. For example, Eddie Bauer, an upscale sportswear chain with almost 400 store locations in North America, is a Claritas client. It used the Claritas marketing and demographic data to analyze retail expenditures by area, household growth rate, and other detailed consumer information in order to determine optimal locations for new stores. Previously Eddie Bauer had been using only basic reports and Rand McNally maps, on which it marked store locations and zip code areas by hand. By utilizing the services of a firm like Claritas, the company was able to determine market expansion much more effectively and efficiently.[20] ◀

The media are also increasingly using marketing research to create news. One of the most extensive applications of marketing research for nonbusiness purposes was made by CNN during the 2004 political campaigns of incumbent president George W. Bush and Massachusetts senator John Kerry. As election day drew closer, CNN relied heavily on its daily telephone and Internet polls to gauge public opinion. CNN uses online polls daily to gauge public opinion on wide-ranging issues. CNN's QuickVote, an online poll, attracts many Internet users to its website.[21]

There are many not-for-profit, nonbusiness, or nonmarketing applications for marketing research. Organizations such as the United Way and the American Red Cross conduct marketing research to help develop strategies for effectively selling their causes to the public and for maximizing public support for their programs. The client lists of large marketing research firms in the United States include many nonbusiness organizations. For instance, the client list of Opinion Research Corporation includes the American Economic Foundation, Columbia University, the National Education Association, the National Society of Professional Engineers, the U.S. Department of Transportation, and the Veterans Administration.[22]

A novel application of marketing research is the use of customer surveys to determine the value to society of such commodities as clean air, unspoiled wilderness, and protection of endangered species.[23] Research in Use 1.1 illustrates an interesting application of marketing research for a divine cause.

In summary, marketing research is more than merely collecting and storing data and statistics. Its applications extend beyond traditional marketing situations that involve the marketing of goods and services.

Organization of and Careers in Marketing Research

In **in-house marketing research,** firms conduct research themselves.

In **external marketing research,** firms contract research to outside agencies.

Firms can acquire the information relevant for marketing decision making through **in-house marketing research** (conducting the research themselves) or **external marketing research** (contracting the research to outside agencies). Both in-house and external marketing research provide career opportunities in marketing research.

In-house marketing research is either contained within a formal marketing research department or merely assigned as a responsibility of some employees. As one would intuitively expect, large firms are more likely than small firms to have formal marketing research departments. Moreover, such departments have been found to be more prevalent in consumer product firms than in industrial product firms and service firms.[24] Thus, for those interested in careers in marketing research, such firms may offer more numerous and more varied opportunities. Positions might include project managers, product development managers, and other positions. Table 1.1 describes a variety of marketing research positions.

In a **centralized organizational structure,** one corporate department caters to all of the firm's research needs.

In a **decentralized organizational structure,** each constituency has its own marketing research arm.

A key issue facing firms with an in-house marketing research department is how to organize such a department. In particular, should it have a **centralized organizational structure,** wherein one corporate department will cater to all of the firm's research needs, or a **decentralized organizational structure,** wherein each constituency (for instance, a division or group based on product line or market segment) will have its own marketing research arm? Compare Exhibits 1.4 and 1.5. This issue is not easy to resolve, because each mode of organization

TABLE 1.1
Careers in Marketing Research

The field of marketing research provides a vast array of job opportunities including titles like the following.

- *Data Entry Clerk; Tabulation Specialist; Programmer.* These employees work for data-processing companies that compile research data and format the data to enable analysis.
- *Interviewer (Telephone or Field).* The telephone or field interviewer is employed by a data collection company specializing in interviewing consumers and professionals, recruiting respondents for focus groups or individual interviews, and central location testing.
- *Research Analyst.* The research analyst is employed by a full-service research company providing qualitative or quantitative research and is responsible for working on all stages of a project, including proposal development, survey design, questionnaire construction, data analysis, report writing, and client contact. Research analysts may also be consultants who specialize in one or more areas of expertise.
- *Marketing Research Manager.* The marketing research manager is responsible for the management of all marketing research projects within his or her area, including hiring and training of marketing research employees. Additional responsibilities include generating revenue and maintaining strong client relationships.
- *Marketing Research Director.* The marketing research director manages the entire marketing research department and provides support to account managers and sales teams. He or she develops processes and procedures for the department, establishes solid working relations and process flows with key stakeholders, participates in strategic evaluations and cost/benefit analyses of survey tools and programming packages as needed, communicates with clients and the executive team on project status, and mentors project directors.

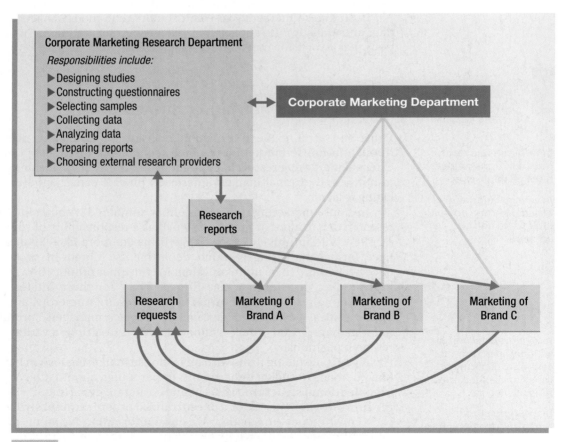

Exhibit 1.4
Illustrative Centralized Marketing Research

has distinct strengths that the other mode lacks.[25] For instance, a centralized organization will offer economies of scale. To have a corporate marketing research department with experts on questionnaire design, sample selection, and statistical techniques may be more cost efficient than to duplicate such expertise at various decentralized areas. However, a centralized research function may be less effective than a decentralized one in helping managers understand and respond to information requirements unique to each product line or market.

In a **mixed organizational structure,** a corporate research function coexists with and complements a decentralized research function.

To benefit from the strengths of both organizational modes, some firms, especially those involved in multiple lines of business, have adopted a **mixed organizational structure,** wherein a corporate research function coexists with and complements a decentralized research function (see Exhibit 1.6). Research in Use 1.2 describes the use of such a structure by Burger King Corporation. For more information on marketing research careers, see Table 1.1 and also visit this text's website at www.business.college.hmco.com.

In many businesses, marketing research activities are conducted in house by one or a few designated employees. Research in Use 1.3 describes how BISSELL Homecare, Inc., launched Steam 'n Clean largely through the efforts of one marketing research director. For people interested in more autonomy and responsibility, such businesses could be excellent career matches.

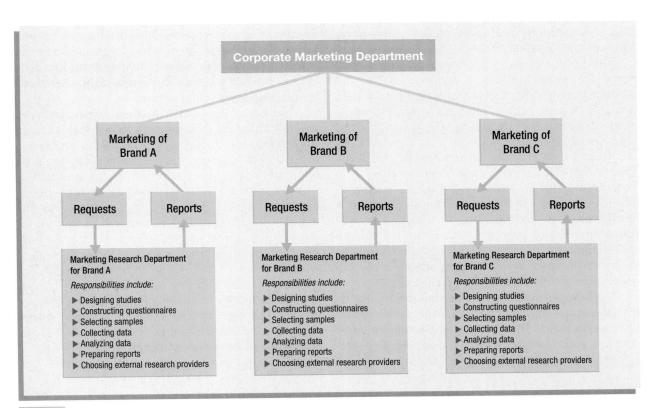

Exhibit 1.5
Illustrative Decentralized Marketing Research Function in a Multibrand Company

Marketing Research at Burger King

Burger King Corporation is a leading fast-food company in the services sector and employs well over 300,000 individuals in more than 11,000 restaurants in all 50 U.S. states and 60 countries. In fiscal year ending June 30, 2003, Burger King's worldwide sales were around $11.1 billion. Drive-through service accounts for 60 percent of Burger King's business.

Burger King's basic operations consist of product development, restaurant operation, decor, service, and advertising. Of the more than 11,000 restaurants, 92 percent are franchisee owned. Managing all the current restaurants and focusing on future growth require continuous monitoring of the environment.

Marketing research at Burger King is primarily a corporate-level (centralized) function carried out by a department known as Brand Research & Analysis. The department consists of more than 15 research professionals. The department head, a director, reports to the senior vice president of marketing, who in turn reports to the president of Burger King's North American operations. Burger King's Brand Research & Analysis Department is composed of four groups: Consumer Research, Sales Analysis, Competitive/Secondary Information, and Customer Satisfaction.

The Consumer Research Group has three managers, one research associate, and one analyst. This group works with key internal clients on a regular basis and acts as a consultant, proactively recommending needed research and suggesting actions warranted by the research findings. Typical projects conducted by this group are merchandising, restaurant design, beverage-related projects, sensory and consumer panel taste tests, pricing studies, advertising effectiveness claims, attitude and usage studies, and advertising copy testing. This group is also responsible for selecting external marketing research suppliers to carry out the studies. Actual study implementation is conducted primarily by the external marketing research suppliers under the supervision of the Consumer Research Group.

The Sales Analysis Group is responsible for analyzing sales at the unit level and classifying the units by their performance. The Competitive/Secondary Information Group analyzes published data (online and

Burger King uses both in-house and external research to understand its markets worldwide.

print media) to keep up with industry and market trends. The Customer Satisfaction Group is responsible for designing and implementing customer satisfaction programs. With the help of an external marketing research provider, this group conducts random telephone surveys to track customer satisfaction with Burger King and its competitors.

The Brand Research & Analysis Department has several control and coordination mechanisms in place to achieve the benefits of centralized marketing research. For example, the managers must get prior approval from the director of Brand Research & Analysis for particularly controversial or high-impact research projects. Moreover, the director reviews monthly status reports on all research conducted for the various internal clients. To facilitate the achievement of cross-business synergies (such as sharing knowledge and obtaining economies of scale), the managers meet monthly with the director. These regular meetings encourage informal sharing of experiences and technical approaches, facilitate collaboration on difficult research problems, and reveal opportunities for operational efficiencies.[b]

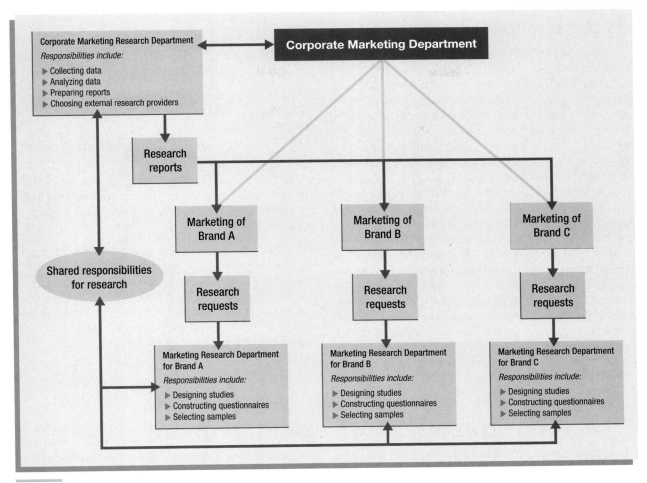

Exhibit 1.6
Illustrative Mixed-Structure Marketing Research Function in a Multibrand Company

SUMMARY

Marketing research is more than a collection of techniques for gathering data. Marketing research is essential to strategic planning and decision making. It helps a firm identify marketing opportunities and constraints, develop and implement marketing strategies, and evaluate the effectiveness of those marketing plans. It is the essential link between marketing decision makers and the markets in which they operate.

Marketing research embodies several key principles for generating information useful to managers. These principles pertain to the timeliness and relevance of research, the importance of defining objectives carefully and clearly, and the need to avoid conducting research to support decisions already made.

Marketing research also requires analysis and interpretation of data to generate relevant information. Although marketing research closely influences decision-making activity, it does not replace decision making itself.

Marketing research has a variety of applications. Marketing research can help managers develop strategies for marketing products and services—and even for marketing ideas.

Career opportunities in marketing research are numerous. Firms may acquire information through in-house marketing research or external marketing research. Each context provides many job opportunities.

RESEARCH IN USE 1.3

BISSELL's Launch of Steam 'n Clean

How useful can marketing research be? Consider the Steam Gun, a European cleaning device to be marketed by BISSELL Homecare, Inc. Erich Pagel, BISSELL's marketing research director, was instructed to figure out how to market to U.S. consumers this elongated cleaner resembling a hand-held vacuum. Despite a minuscule budget and little time, Pagel not only met his goal but also, in the process, helped improve sales for BISSELL's related products.

Pagel needed to be creative. With no resources for outside research companies, using his knowledge that women with children tended to be BISSELL's main customers, Pagel utilized a local Parent Teacher Association in Bissell's home base of Grand Rapids, Michigan. Employing ethnographics, qualitative research using observational techniques, and a donation of $1,500 to the PTA coffers, Pagel chose 20 people as his sample. Each was given a Steam Gun for two to three weeks. Their experiences with the new product were recorded in diaries, then followed up by in-home visits where Pagel himself could observe the product-consumer interactions.

Some important negative findings emerged early on:

- The American mothers expected to use chemicals and had trouble believing that hot water alone could clean as well.

- There was confusion over the many available attachments.

- The name "Steam Gun" was too similar to a weapon's in sound and name. The mothers reported that their children were "arming" themselves with the device in inappropriate play.

A more positive finding was the appeal the Steam Gun had for hard-core house cleaners. It was used to "blast away" tough, hard-to-reach grime.

Based on these research findings, BISSELL changed the product's name to Steam 'n Clean and ran infomercials. The product had an excellent response and retained its placement in 2,100 Kmarts.[c]

ACE self-test

REVIEW AND DISCUSSION QUESTIONS

1. Critically evaluate the soundness of the following definition of marketing research: "Marketing research is a set of data collection techniques that can be used by marketers to help them in their decision making."

2. What lessons about marketing research are evident in the opening vignette, "Marketing Research at Volvo"?

3. Name a *specific* purpose for which each of the following could use marketing research.
   a. A hospital
   b. A U.S. congressional representative
   c. A gas station owner
   d. The Internal Revenue Service

4. What are the three major components of marketing planning and decision making to which marketing research can contribute?

5. Provide a brief example to illustrate the importance of marketing research in determining the corrective action to take when results from the marketplace are disappointing.

6. How do in-house marketing research providers and external marketing research providers differ?

APPLICATION EXERCISES

1. Candlesticks, a producer of candles, has decided to go online. It recently purchased all the hardware and software necessary to complete this venture. It then commissioned marketing research to determine whether its customer base would find that the website adds value to the company's brick-and-mortar location. In other words, Candlesticks wanted to determine whether or not customers would use its website. The marketing research agency purchased secondary data on the value perceptions of websites. The agency relied on the secondary data (which were at least two years old) to support Candlesticks' decision and confirmed that the decision was sound.

   Using the information provided in this scenario, discuss whether Candlesticks may have violated any of the three principles of marketing research. Had you been the manager in charge of deciding whether Candlesticks should go online, what approach would you have taken in making that decision?

2. A university bookstore is considering selling university license plate covers. Describe to the store's manager the types of information he or she should collect to identify the marketing opportunities and constraints for this product.

INTERNET EXERCISES

1. Assume you are a marketing analyst working for McDonald's. You are asked to provide information that will be used to decide whether or not a new store should be opened in a particular location (pick your zip code). Use the Internet to find relevant information that would aid the chain in making this decision. (Hint: Such information might include overall population, population density, age distribution, population growth rate, income, and so on.)

2. What are some distinctions between marketing research and direct marketing? (*Hint:* Go to the ESOMAR website at www.esomar.nl and check ESOMAR's "Guidelines on Maintaining the Distinctions between Market Research and Direct Marketing"). Prepare a one-page report for your telemarketing department.

3. Go to www.monster.com and perform a search for available marketing research positions, using the following steps:

   a. Go to www.monster.com.

   b. Click on "Find Jobs."

   c. Do not type anything in "Select Location"; in "Select Job Category," click on "Advertising/Marketing/Public Relations"; in "Enter Keyword(s)," type in "Marketing Research," then click "Get Results."

   d. Pick a job that you find interesting!

   Follow these steps to find three jobs that interest you. For each job, print out the page describing it and summarize the key features that you find appealing.

CASE 1.1 LAUNCH OF THE HUMMER
(www.hummer.com)

New products can come from anywhere. All of the ARM & HAMMER products began from a simple baking ingredient, and at the other end of the simplicity spectrum there is the Hummer. The Hummer brand was developed, not as a consumer product, but from a military need. In 1979 the army required a multipurpose vehicle to suit its every need, from all-terrain pickup to ambulance. AM General developed the HMMWV, or High Mobility Multi-Purpose Wheeled Vehicle. It was not publicly known until the 1991 Gulf War, and the Hummer became recognizable only after Arnold Schwarzenegger spotted it while filming Kindergarten Cop and persuaded AM General to sell him the first civilian Humvee. This pairing quickly established the brand image for the Hummer as tough, strong, and oversized.

Sensing an attractive opportunity, AM General decided to enter the consumer market, and the civilian Hummer was in production by 1992. In 1999 AM partnered with General Motors to jointly share the marketing and distribution of the Hummer. AM produces the vehicles, and GM holds exclusive rights to the Hummer brand name. Soon after the AM-GM deal was struck, GM began work to extend the product line. After changing the Hummer's name to H1, they developed H2, a slightly smaller, sleeker version of the H1 at half the price. However, GM retained the distinctive characteristics of the original Hummer in the H2 in order to make it recognizable as a Hummer brand with the same functionality.

Marketing

Some key marketing issues had to be addressed as the H2 went into production. GM needed to understand who was going to buy an H2 and where it was going to be sold. GM thought the H2 might be different enough from its big brother the H1 to warrant a different marketing mix. It began by using marketing research to pinpoint the target market. Research results indicated that overall, 50 percent of consumers found the Hummer brand to be appealing, whereas the other 50 percent did not. Close analysis of H1 buyers indicated that they were

in a class by themselves: the cost and the uniqueness of the H1 attracted only a select group of buyers. The choice was not between buying an H1 or another SUV; rather it was between purchasing an H1 or a yacht, airplane, or second home. The H2, at half the price of the H1, appealed to a broader audience. Research further revealed that potential H2 buyers were rugged individualists and successful achievers—business people who rock climb 100-foot cliffs on the weekends, or at least those who saw themselves as the sort who would. Because this was a vastly different customer base than that of the H1, the entire marketing mix had to be adjusted for the H2.

To maximally reach the desired target market, commercials for the Hummer were aired on the CNN news network and during NFL football games, *The West Wing*, *24*, and *CSI*. The positioning strategy for the H2 was a premium vehicle that is like no other, and the tagline was "Hummer: Like Nothing Else." In other words, the H2 was positioned as a vehicle whose owners would be making a distinctive statement. GM also felt that echoing the military origins of the Hummer would appeal to this target market.

The original H1 was an expensive specialty vehicle with a small market and, therefore, few distributors. There were only 47 Hummer dealerships, and the H2 needed more distribution outlets to be able to penetrate further into the consumer market. Promoting Hummer's standards of excellence, GM dealers were chosen based on such key factors as sales, customer service, and location. In 2004 there were 170 dealerships that proudly carried the Hummer.

At a price point of just under $50,000, the success of GM's release of the H2 in 2002 left Detroit speechless. The company sold 18,861 units in the first six months and did so without any incentives. But later results indicated those days might be gone. In 2003, sales of the H2 totaled 34,529, but in the first nine months of 2004, sales dropped 20 percent. Dealers began offering leases and other financial deals to make up the slack. GM is hoping that Hummer sales will turn around during 2005–2006.

GM has also focused on continually expanding the Hummer family. The H3, a smaller, more city-compatible version, and the H1 Alpha series, a bigger and badder version of the flagship brand, hit showroom floors in 2005–2006. In addition, the H2H began its testing phase with a public face, former action star and current California governor Arnold Schwarzenegger. The H2H, with its hydrogen-fueled engine, is combating the popular environmentalist cry that SUVs are gas guzzlers. Through continuous innovation, GM hopes to keep growing the appeal of the Hummer brand and attract even more consumers to the Hummer lifestyle.

Lifestyle and Licensing

GM wants Hummer to be more than a brand and to evolve into a lifestyle. Market research had shown that Hummer buyers were unique, rugged individualists who meet life on their own terms. To allow Hummer owners to customize their vehicle, after-market parts such as roofracks, light bars, and suspension kits became available for Hummer owners. Along with the traditional hats, shirts, and other ancillary merchandise, Hummer has a tactical mountain bike that portrays everything Hummer stands for. It is a high-tech bicycle designed by the military for use by paratroopers. The premium bike folds up into a smaller, transportable load, once again echoing the military roots of the Hummer.

Another extension of the Hummer brand name is the Hummer Driving Academy. The Driving Academy is a 300-acre plot of land that tests the ability of the Hummer and its owner. Even this land is reminiscent of Hummer's origins, because it was once owned by the military to train its troops. The military serves the people, and Hummer wants this to be the purpose of its vehicles and their owners. The "Hummer Helps" program, another GM initiative, works with charity organizations and brings together the community to restore the environment.

Between Hummer merchandise, the Hummer Driving Academy, and the Hummer Helps program, GM is striving to achieve a distinctive and loyal Hummer community. This effort is reminiscent of Harley-Davidson's highly profitable lifestyle positioning of its motorcycles and other product lines. The true sign of a lifestyle product is when the owners begin to form communities around the product. Hummer owners groups are now established all across the United States and in Canada, France, Japan, and the Netherlands. Hummer owners often refer to themselves as HOGS (Hummer owners groups), but when they go to establish their domain names, they run into the other HOGs (Harley owners groups). Hummer is hoping that the newest members of the Hummer family, the H3 and the H2H, will broaden the appeal of the brand and bring new members to the HOGs.

CASE QUESTIONS

1. In what ways can marketing research help GM promote the H3 and H2H brands?
2. Could GM have done anything to capitalize better on the initial success of the Hummer brand?

This case draws on a presentation by Mike DiGiovanni (Hummer General Manager), "The Hummer Mystique" (25th Anniversary AMA Marketing Research Conference, September 20, 2004, New Orleans, LA); Mark Phelan, "GM Unveils Smaller Version of Hummer," *Knight Ridder Tribune Business News,* October 27, 2004; Danny Hakim, "Hummer Shows Signs of Losing Its Swagger," *New York Times,* May 17, 2004; www.hummer.com.

CASE 1.2 NIKE CHAINSAW AD (PART A)
(www.nike.com)

Managers at NIKE were reviewing the results of a survey that had just been tabulated by QuickTake.com (a division of Greenfield Online) as a demonstration of its research capabilities. The survey was developed to objectively assess a sample of 150 customer reactions to the controversial NIKE advertisement that appeared during NBC's coverage of the Olympic Games in Sydney, Australia. NIKE managers were concerned about what actions should be taken regarding the advertisement.

Company Background

NIKE, Inc., is the largest athletic apparel and footwear marketer in the world. Its principal business is the design, development, and worldwide marketing of high-quality footwear, apparel, equipment, and accessories. Its business is divided into four major product lines: footwear, apparel, equipment, and other brands. (Table 1 contains revenue for each product line.)

TABLE 1
NIKE, Inc., Revenue by Product Line, 2002–2004

	Fiscal Year Ended May 31, 2004		
	2004 ($million)	2003 ($million)	2002 ($million)
Footwear	6,569.9	5,983.4	5,676.6
Apparel	3,545.4	3,130.0	2,801.3
Equipment	751.0	662.9	591.2
Other	1,386.8	927.0	823.9
Total	12,253.1	10,697.0	9,893.0

Source: 10-K for NIKE, Inc., FYE May 31, 2004, available online at www.sec.gov.

TABLE 2
NIKE, Inc., Footwear, Apparel, and Equipment Revenue by Region, 2002–2004

	Fiscal Year Ended May 31, 2004		
	2004 ($million)	2003 ($million)	2002 ($million)
United States	4,793.7	4,658.4	4,669.6
EMEA	3,834.4	3,241.7	2,696.5
Asia/Pacific	1,613.4	1,349.2	1,134.9
Americas	624.8	527.0	568.1

Source: 10-K for NIKE, Inc., FYE May 31, 2004, available online at www.sec.gov.

The NIKE brand is known throughout the world, and its products are marketed in approximately 140 countries in addition to the United States. (Table 2 contains revenue by region.) NIKE products are sold through approximately 19,000 retail accounts in the United States and more than 30,000 retail accounts abroad.

NIKE itself is primarily responsible for the research, development, design, and marketing of NIKE brand products. All NIKE products are produced by independent contract manufacturers throughout the world.

The Chainsaw Ad

When NIKE chose to sponsor Suzy Favor Hamilton in its ads during the Olympics in Sydney, it was a good move. Hamilton had the fastest time in the world in her specialty, the 1,500-meter race, and she had also run in the 800-meter, the mile, the 3,000-meter, and the 5,000-meter events. In addition to international television coverage of her track events, she had gained broad exposure in print media[1] and was well known and liked by the public.

The ad was one of three in a series, all intended as humorous spots. It opened with a spooky scene of the front of a remote cabin and then cut to an interior scene featuring Hamilton. While she combed her hair, she gazed into the mirror and saw a Freddie Krueger type behind her, wearing a mask and brandishing a chainsaw. In a series of quick scene changes, the homicidal maniac pursued his target, breaking the mirror with the chainsaw, cutting through a door, and running through the woods after the frightened athlete. The only dialogue was Hamilton's bloodcurdling screams and heavy breathing. The spot ended with the exhausted pursuer falling to his knees and the Olympic runner making her way into the distant woods. The ad closed with the tag line "Why sport? You'll live longer" and the NIKE swoosh logo.

It is safe to say that the ad was designed with teenage boys in mind; they spend 60 percent of all sneakers dollars.[2] Response, however, was quite negative. NBC pulled the ad after receiving more than 2,000 complaints in only a few days, and the spot remained so controversial that it was the focus of many discussions, both favorable and unfavorable, in a variety of media. The following is a series of verbatim comments about the ad in an Internet discussion group:[3]

"Is it in poor taste? Probably. Should Mr. Knight be hung out for it? Get a grip. The ad is an attempt to make fun of the *Friday the 13th* horror flicks. The point being that if the character in the movies had had Nike shoes (and had been a world class athlete) she could have outrun the bad guy. To the folks that take offense to the ad I would say start with Hollywood and insist they stop churning out slasher movies. After you shame them into stopping, then you would be right in going after Nike for doing a parody ad."

"Pleazzzzzzzzz! Hasn't everyone seen *Friday the 13th* and the sequels and LOVED 'EM? Give me a break! This is a commercial and I thought it was creative. Nike always comes up with something better every time. Don't get too down on them."

"Our informal office poll agrees. This ad was in poor taste, a parody of a lousy movie. The basic difference is that you have to pay to see the movie and most intelligent people have a clue about what the movie is about, but the ad on TV has no such rejoinders and some of us can't click the TV remote button that fast. There is no need for ads that promote violence against women in a time when society preaches against it. I'd rather Nike used this ad money to open a safe house for women and kids, a much better usage of corporate funds and identity. Good job, NBC!"

"I thought the ad was totally uncalled for. There is nothing humorous about a maniac chasing a woman with a chainsaw. Whoever is doing the commercials for Nike better start looking for another line of work. That was awful!"

"I think Chairman Phil Knight should be asked to resign given such poor discretion in this matter. I had three small children watching NBC when that commercial came on. It is truly classic nightmare material for small children. They make such gross assumptions about the American public approving of such tasteless ads that he should be held accountable for allowing this sick ad to go on the air."

Selected Results of the Questionnaire

The questionnaire contained a total of 10 questions and was administered on the Internet to 150 individuals who had watched some of the summer Olympic Games from Sydney, Australia. A cross-sample of men and women from different income categories was included in the sample. A total of 44 percent of the respondents remembered having seen the ad, and 25 percent found the ad either offensive or inappropriate in some way. When asked what characteristic of the ad was most objectionable, 70 percent of the offended respondents indicated the use of a chainsaw to injure or kill a woman.

CASE QUESTIONS

1. Evaluate how the research results can help NIKE make strategic marketing decisions. Based on these results, should NIKE continue to run this ad?

2. What are some of the short- and long-term consequences if NIKE continues to run the ad?

CASE NOTES

1. Hamilton's website (www.suzyfavorhamilton.com/biography /index.htm) indicated that she has been featured in magazines such as *Vogue, Cosmopolitan, Rolling Stone, Runner's World, Harper's Bazaar, Men's Journal, Sports Illustrated, Sports Illustrated for Kids, Track & Field News, Women's Sports & Fitness, Running Times, Fitness,* and *Outside,* and had appeared in the 1997 Suzy Hamilton Swimsuit Calendar.

2. According to Chana R. Schoenberger, "Sneaker Attack," Forbes Magazine, October 30, 2000.

3. www.forums.ibsys.com/viewmessages.cfm?sitekey= hou&Forum=75&Topic=1037.

This case was written by Jeanne L. Munger (University of Southern Maine) in collaboration with the textbook authors, as a basis for class discussion rather than to illustrate either effective or ineffective marketing practice.

2

The Marketing Research Process

Colgate-Palmolive in Germany: CAT Shows the Way[1]

Great advertising doesn't just happen. Marketing and advertising professionals working together with marketing research partners make it happen. Marketing research professionals contribute to this process by gaining deep consumer insights through various research methods. Colgate-Palmolive (C-P) in Germany is an excellent example of how marketing research can be used to create effective advertising.

C-P in Germany has pioneered the development of competitive advertising testing, or CAT, methodology. CAT is a valuable research technique that allows the company to quantify consumers' emotional responses to advertising. Consumer responses to CAT allow C-P to determine whether its advertising actually works better than competitors'.

C-P's Palmolive body care line was languishing in Germany behind Nivea, a recognized market leader. C-P wanted to make the Palmolive brand attractive to German consumers again. Historically, German advertising had focused on functional attributes. Marianne Rose Drehmann, C-P marketing research manager, and her staff conducted numerous studies showing that, although consumers rated the advertising as informative, they found it boring. C-P's research also indicated that consumers would react more favorably if the product message were incorporated into an emotionally appealing advertising campaign.

Working with Young & Rubicam, a top-rated advertising firm, C-P developed a "natural wonder" commercial for the Palmolive brand. Originally created for the Australian market, the commercial linked Palmolive's "naturalness" (a core brand concept) to the outdoors. However, research revealed that Germans value their families and inner harmony more than an outdoor lifestyle. This key insight led to the development of a new Palmolive shower gel commercial for the German market, emphasizing family and inner harmony rather than outdoor life.

Following development, C-P initiated a series of CAT tests to measure consumer responses to its new ad and to Nivea's ad. One hundred consumers viewed the commercials and were asked to respond in two ways: by giving their first impressions in an open-ended fashion and then responding to a Viewer Response Profile (VRP). The VRP measured consumers' emotional reactions to the commercials on attributes such as relevance, personal satisfaction, involvement, uniqueness, and irritation. According to Dick Howindt, marketing manager for C-P in Germany, "We achieved outstanding results—the best test so far within our 'CAT' history! We were hoping to at the least achieve the same results as Nivea. To our surprise, the commercial won against Nivea on all important CAT dimensions." ■

The **marketing research process** is an interrelated sequence of steps that make up a marketing research project.

This example shows how Colgate-Palmolive used the marketing research process to develop a winning commercial and marketing campaign in Germany. This chapter introduces the **marketing research process,** an interrelated sequence of steps that make up a marketing research project.

Major Steps in the Marketing Research Process

Dividing the marketing research process into a series of chronological steps is convenient. In reality, however, the steps are highly interrelated; that is, each step may have an impact on the steps preceding or following it. The interrelationships will become clear as we examine each step in detail.

The major steps in the marketing research process are as follows:

1. Justify the need for marketing research.
2. Define the research objective.
3. Identify data needs.
4. Identify data sources.
5. Choose an appropriate research design and data collection method.
6. Design the research instrument or form.
7. Identify the sample.
8. Collect data, including any relevant secondary data.
9. Analyze and interpret the data.
10. Present the research findings to decision makers.

Exhibit 2.1 provides an overview of the steps in the research process. The arrows to the left emphasize the interrelationships among the steps. For instance, even at the very first step (justifying the need for marketing research), the researcher/decision maker must have some idea about what the remaining steps involve; otherwise, making a realistic assessment of whether to undertake the project may be difficult.

**Exhibit 2.1
Research Project Steps**

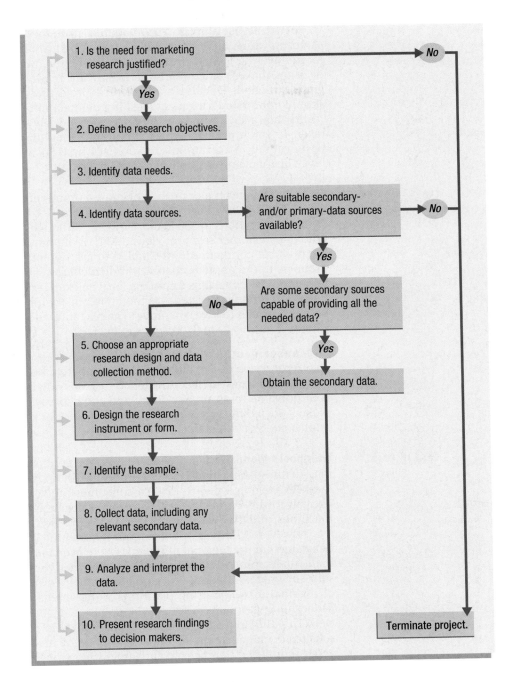

Step 1: Justify the Need for Marketing Research

A logical starting point for discussing the marketing research process is the issue of whether to conduct a proposed research project. Four considerations influence the decision: the potential usefulness of the research results; management's attitudes toward the research; the resources available for implementing the research results; and the costs of the research project versus the benefits. Although these four considerations are not necessarily independent of one another, each is important enough to be discussed separately.

■ **Potential Usefulness**   The potential usefulness of a research project is the extent to which its findings will aid in taking further action in a given situation. Alternatively, it is the extent to which the research findings are likely to reduce a decision maker's uncertainty or to provide relevant additional insights into a given situation. Obviously a proposed project with little potential usefulness should not be undertaken, at least not before appropriate revisions are made. In reality, however, companies forget this seemingly simple point. Hastily undertaken research projects typically end up generating incomplete information at best or totally irrelevant information at worst. Such information is virtually useless. The following example illustrates this point.

CASE IN POINT ▶ **KFC in Brazil**   In a major push to become a prominent player in the Brazilian market, KFC (Kentucky Fried Chicken) researched Brazilian consumers and decided to set up operations in São Paulo. However, although the research identified how a potential customer segment viewed KFC, it did not include thorough research of the possible competition. KFC failed to ask potential customers to compare its products to the popular charcoal-broiled chicken available on almost every corner in the city. Brazilians found the local chicken tastier than the Colonel's recipe. The information generated was therefore not complete enough to be useful. KFC Brazil continues to invest in order to gain a foothold in this high-potential market, where it has only a small presence today.[2] ◀

■ **Management Attitudes**   Management, or research users in general, must view a proposed research project with an open mind if the project is to be beneficial. Marketing research conducted for reasons other than aiding decision making is of no value to an organization, and the effort will be wasted unless decision makers are willing to accept the results.[3] A case in point is Whirlpool's European market analysis research.

CASE IN POINT ▶ **Whirlpool's World Washer**   When Whirlpool conducted research analyzing the market for washing machines in Europe, the findings suggested that the European market is regional due to diverse consumer preferences.[4] For instance, Swedes like galvanized washers, which withstand salty air. Britons prefer quieter washing machines, and they wash laundry more often than their European counterparts.

However, Whirlpool management ignored the research findings, apparently believing that the regional differences were overstated. Management had already made up its mind to introduce a "World Washer," a single machine that could be sold anywhere. Although this global focus helped Whirlpool reduce the number of regional manufacturing platforms worldwide, stiff competition from established European players forced the company to be more customer focused as well. The difficulties the company experienced in this globalization experience sensitized management to the importance of including in its strategic plans across-country differences in consumer preferences. This realization is reflected in the words of Dave Whitwam, Whirlpool's former chairman and CEO, who observed at that time, "We recognize that consumers are different around the world. They have different tastes, cultures, and usage patterns with our products. We want to understand better than anyone else in this industry what will satisfy a customer."[5] While Whirlpool's product-innovation teams continue to pursue economies of scale through manufacturing efficiencies, top management ensures that the teams take into account the unique needs of consumers in the diverse markets the company serves. "Think globally, but act locally" has become Whirlpool's mantra. ◀

■ **Resources Available for Implementation**   Suppose a marketing research project produces useful recommendations and management is willing to pursue those recommendations. Can we then say that this research project has been worthwhile? Not necessarily. The research will still be wasted if management lacks the resources (money, personnel, time) needed to implement the research results. Resources are especially relevant for situations in which a firm is considering marketing research to uncover market opportunities, as the following scenario illustrates.

> **SCENARIO** X-Disk Corporation is a mass producer and marketer of DVD drives. In an attempt to broaden its product assortment, it is considering a marketing research project to determine the nature and size of consumer demand for thumb drives or memory sticks. However, X-Disk currently has only limited idle-plant capacity and does not have the money to expand capacity. Moreover, it lacks the technology to produce thumb drives on a large scale. Clearly X-Disk would be wise not to spend money on marketing research on the demand for thumb drives before ensuring the availability of financial and technological resources needed to act on the research results, should those results uncover a market opportunity.

■ **Costs Versus Benefits**   The three considerations discussed so far—potential usefulness, management attitudes, and resources available for implementation—are related, although indirectly, to the costs-versus-benefits consideration. After all, each of these addresses the question of whether it is worthwhile to conduct marketing research. This section, however, focuses directly on the *monetary* costs and benefits associated with marketing research.

Research costs are much easier to quantify than research benefits. When the tasks involved in a particular research project are known, estimating the total cost of accomplishing them should be relatively easy. However, we cannot meaningfully estimate the cost of a project without knowing up front what its various stages involve. This fact emphasizes the interrelationships among the steps in the research process. From a research user's standpoint, estimating the cost of research is easiest if a research supplier will be used, because the research cost is then simply the price quoted by the supplier.

How do we quantify research benefits? There is no single standard way to put a number on them. However, because the basic purpose of any research is to aid decision makers by reducing their uncertainty, a useful starting point is to examine the nature of the uncertainty facing a decision maker. Consider the following scenarios.

> **SCENARIO A** Brenda Page, product manager for Healthy Life Corporation, is wondering whether or not to conduct marketing research to estimate the likely market share for NatSlim, a new, all-natural, diet soft drink. On the basis of production and marketing cost estimates for NatSlim, its break-even sales translate into a 10 percent share of the diet drink market. Currently 30 brands of diet drinks are on the market. Three brands have been leading sellers for a long time and enjoy a market share in excess of 20 percent each, whereas each of the other brands has a share of 5 percent or less.
>
> Page believes NatSlim is as good as any other brand on the market. However, she is uncertain about the market share NatSlim may attract if it is introduced. From her experience and understanding of the diet drink market, she estimates that NatSlim's share will range from 2 to 8 percent, with an outside chance of exceeding 8 percent. Should Page test-market NatSlim before making a decision about full-scale introduction?

Test-marketing NatSlim will provide a more precise estimate of its potential market share than Page's current estimate of 2 to 8 percent. But the monetary benefit of reducing this uncertainty will be negligible. The reason is that the break-even share required for NatSlim is 10 percent, and Page believes there is only an outside chance that its share will be greater than even 8 percent. In other words, Page can make a decision *right now* about full-scale introduction of Nat-Slim. Intuitively, unless Healthy Life Corporation is inclined to take a very heavy risk, Page may decide not to introduce NatSlim. Regardless of what Page's decision is, though, it is not likely to change because of any test-market outcome.

> **SCENARIO B** Jerry Wilson, advertising manager for Nice Smell Corporation, is uncertain about which of two television commercials, X or Y, to use for his company's brand of deodorant. Commercial X employs fear appeal: A man wears a competing brand of deodorant, only to be embarrassed later at a party where everyone avoids him, apparently because his deodorant is ineffective. Commercial Y uses romantic appeal: A man wears Nice Smell's brand of deodorant, goes to a party, and is pleased to discover that several women are attracted to him, apparently because of the effectiveness of his deodorant.

The difficulty and the risk involved in making a decision in the face of Wilson's uncertainty are much greater than in Page's case in Scenario A. Choosing the right commercial can ensure the success of Nice Smell Corporation's deodorant, whereas choosing the wrong one can ensure its failure. More important, marketing research is capable of indicating which commercial, X or Y, is more likely to be the right one. Thus the benefits of marketing research appear to be greater in Scenario B than in Scenario A.

■ **Dealing with Budget Constraints**   A major concern of researchers is that the budgets allocated to marketing research are extremely limited. Therefore, researchers must use such budgets prudently. David Gordon, past chairperson of the American Marketing Association and CEO of Angell Research Group, offers simple suggestions for conducting marketing research on a shoestring, relevant especially for small businesses:[6]

- Treat every employee as a marketing researcher. Employees should be asked to be on the lookout for how people are using the company's products or the competitors' products, what the trends are, and where people buy. Employees can provide informal reports at regular staff meetings.
- Send employees to observe customers.
- Send employees to interview trade show attendees; marketing research costs may be as low as $1,000 at a trade show, as opposed to $5,000 or more to conduct focus groups across the country.
- Use warranty cards or product registration cards to research customers, stores they shop in, and how they become aware of your brand.

Research in Use 2.1 describes how Fisher-Price makes efficient use of its marketing research dollars.

Step 2: Define the Research Objective

Questions about *what* we want to find out and *why* are crucial to the effectiveness of any research project. Indeed, our discussion of whether or not a research project is worthwhile assumed that the research purpose was well defined. We cannot meaningfully evaluate the costs and potential benefits of research unless we have

Marketing Research at Fisher-Price

Fisher-Price, Inc., is a wholly owned subsidiary of Mattel, Inc. The company's product line includes toys for preschoolers, car seats, nursery monitors, and bouncer seats. Marketing research plays an important role in helping the company launch a steady stream of new products. According to market research director Shelly Glick Gryfe, the company allocates a different percentage of its sales revenue to research every year. The budget fluctuation forces Gryfe to allocate resources based on the value of the research project. When the research budget is tight, Gryfe takes several steps to ensure that precious research dollars are spent on projects whose value can be easily justified. The following are typical steps taken by Gryfe:

1. Testing fewer products: the company tests only products that are expected to sell well; if possible, it tests more than one product at the same time.
2. Using secondary sources: the company looks at similar products, trade reaction (response of wholesalers, retailers and competitors), and price points.
3. Cutting back on strategic research.
4. Scaling back sample size.

By allocating the research budget judiciously, Fisher-Price is able to test many ideas that help the company launch a steady stream of new products.

5. Using a drawing of a product instead of a model in concept testing.

Although Gryfe always checks to ensure that the research is actionable, she admits that the effectiveness of marketing research is often compromised due to the above-mentioned reasons.[a]

clearly established the answers to *what* and *why*. Consequently, accurately defining the research problem or research objective is the key to determining whether to conduct research and, if so, what its nature should be. According to Lawrence D. Gibson, a respected researcher,

> The payoff from good marketing problem definition is enormous—nothing else we do has so much leverage on profit. When we develop our skills in problem definition, we do ourselves, our function, and our companies an extraordinary service. We begin to live up to our promise and to our potential. . . . To summarize, good marketing problem definition is a prerequisite for successful marketing research—marketing that really does solve marketing problems.[7]

The next scenario illustrates this point.

SCENARIO Pac 'n' Sac, Inc., producer of a variety of paper containers for consumer products, suffered a sales decline of 15 percent during the past year. Alarmed by this sharp decline and wondering whether or not a change in promotional strategy would help boost sales, Pac 'n' Sac's marketing manager contacted the marketing research department. The research department proposed a well-designed, comprehensive customer study to evaluate promotional strategies, including the one then being used. The marketing manager reviewed the proposed study, found it to be sound, and approved it.

Does anything appear to be wrong with the approach taken by the marketing manager and the research department in attempting to arrest Pac 'n' Sac's sales decline? Yes. The marketing manager apparently *assumed* the problem was Pac 'n' Sac's promotional strategy, and the research department went along with that assumption. However, if the assumption was incorrect, the research could be valueless. For instance, what if the cause of the sales decline were really customers' perceptions that Pac 'n' Sac's products are overpriced or have deteriorated in quality? Under these circumstances, the proposed research may be able to identify the best promotional strategy among the alternatives being considered, but employing even the best promotional strategy may do little to boost Pac 'n' Sac's sales if promotion is not the cause of the sales decline in the first place.

What if the total *industry sales* of paper containers declined by 30 percent during the past year because of stiff competition from new, nonpaper containers? In this situation, the decline in industry sales is the real problem, and Pac 'n' Sac's sales decline is merely a symptom of it. Furthermore, marketing research probably can do little to improve Pac 'n' Sac's sales, because its sales performance is actually much better than the performance of the industry as a whole, despite its 15 percent sales decline. Therefore, any marketing research expenditure will most likely be wasted.

An important lesson emerges from the Pac 'n' Sac example: at least some time and effort must be expended very early in the research process to identify the correct problem to be researched, if there is in fact a problem that marketing research can help tackle. In fact, the firm should usually conduct some exploratory research (a topic discussed at length in the next chapter) simply to define the research problem accurately before designing a project.

■ **Avoiding Mistakes in Problem Definition**   Accurate definition of a project's purpose requires (1) identifying a number of specific issues and (2) deciding which of those issues are worth examining further. Research projects focusing on ill-defined problems ultimately result in inefficient use of resources or, worse, erroneous decisions. Diageo's Captain Morgan Gold beverage provides a case in point.

CASE IN POINT ▶ **Diageo's Captain Morgan Gold**   Buoyed by its success with Smirnoff Ice vodka drinks, Diageo, the distiller, embarked on capturing more of the ready-to-drink alcoholic beverage market to revive sagging profits. The company introduced a new drink called Captain Morgan Gold, a rum-flavored malt beverage, with a $65 million marketing campaign.[8] However, Captain Morgan Gold received only lukewarm support from the drinking public despite heavy promotional spending.

Did Diageo conduct any marketing research before deciding to introduce Captain Morgan Gold? Yes, it did. In fact, the research confirmed the popularity of Captain Morgan Rum, and management was confident that Captain Morgan Gold, a ready-to-drink malt beverage, would be successful, similar to its experience with its previously released malt beverage, Smirnoff Ice.[9] What, then, went wrong? The consensus of industry analysts and experts is that the research the company commissioned did not adequately take into account consumer tastes. Quite simply, consumers did not like the taste of Captain Morgan Gold. Thus the research examined the wrong problem, in that it failed to investigate what adult consumers were looking for in a ready-to-drink malt beverage. Instead of seeking to understand the taste preferences of adult consumers, Diageo's research simply focused on the popularity of Captain Morgan Rum. The research failed to test the Captain Morgan Gold drink in the field, believing that the new product would succeed just as Smirnoff Ice had. This error, in turn, stemmed from management's apparent eagerness to respond quickly to other ready-to-drink malt beverages being introduced by competitors.

Had management been less myopic and considered the needs of the adult market rather than focusing solely on producing a similar product, the "problem" addressed by the consumer research would have encompassed more than just evaluating the popularity of its Captain Morgan Rum brand. Consequently, the money spent on the research might have yielded more relevant insights and prevented the costly introduction of Captain Morgan Gold in the first place. ◀

As the Captain Morgan Gold example shows, focusing research solely on one issue is a mistake. At least initially, the company should aim its research at *all* pertinent issues. Though this sounds like common sense, many research studies focus on the wrong problems or on problems that are too narrowly defined due to carelessness or faulty assumptions on the part of decision makers.

▪ **The Importance of Effective Communication** Effective dialogue between decision makers and researchers is critical to properly diagnosing any situation calling for marketing research. In the Pac 'n' Sac example, the marketing manager assumed that a certain type of problem existed, and the research department did not challenge that assumption. The chance that a wrong or nonexistent problem will be researched increases greatly when productive discussion between researchers and decision makers fails to take place during the problem definition stage. Effective dialogue is especially important when the purpose of a research project is to *explore opportunities* (to ask, for instance: What is the market potential for our product?) rather than to solve a specific problem. The absence of a specific problem may tempt decision makers and researchers to pay no more than lip service to defining the purpose of the research project. However, failure to establish and agree on clear-cut research objectives will decrease the effectiveness of the research and may lead to unnecessary friction between the two parties after the research has been completed.

Step 3: Identify Data Needs

What data should be collected during a research project? How easily we can answer this question depends on how clearly we have defined the purpose of the research project in the previous stage. Identifying specific data needs means scrutinizing the research purpose and listing the kinds of data required to accomplish that purpose. Consider the following scenario.

> **SCENARIO** Consolidated Bakeries, marketer of a national brand of snack food items, decides to conduct marketing research to evaluate its market position relative to competitors'. Specifically, the purpose of the research is to determine current market share and ascertain whether Consolidated's relative market position is likely to improve, stay the same, or deteriorate during the next several years. What kinds of data should Consolidated Bakeries collect through the proposed research project?

The data needed to accomplish the first part of Consolidated Bakeries' research purpose—to determine current market share—are merely its own sales figures and total industry sales figures. Data requirements for fulfilling the second, less concrete part of the research purpose—to assess Consolidated Bakeries' future market position—are not as clear-cut. A variety of data may be able to shed light on what the future looks like for Consolidated Bakeries, although none is likely to provide a complete and accurate picture. The following data are examples of the type Consolidated Bakeries should collect.

- The *brand loyalty* of consumers toward Consolidated Bakeries' products. Has Consolidated Bakeries consistently enjoyed a loyal clientele up until now? If so, its future market position will probably be as good as its current position.

- The *market shares* of Consolidated Bakeries' *competitors* and the *trends in market shares* during the past several years. Does Consolidated Bakeries have any large, strong competitors, or is its competition spread across a number of relatively weak firms? In the past, has Consolidated Bakeries' market share been increasing, holding steady, or declining? What about the shares of its competitors? Answers to these questions can provide some clues about what the future may hold for Consolidated Bakeries.

- *Consumers' perceptions* about Consolidated Bakeries' snack foods and about competing brands on dimensions such as quality, price, and availability.

Once Consolidated Bakeries has identified its data needs, the next step is to identify potential sources for the data.

Step 4: Identify Data Sources

After identifying data needs, the next logical step is to locate sources capable of providing the data. The relative ease or difficulty of locating data sources will depend on the nature of the information desired.

◼ **Secondary Data**   Usually, factual information (such as the number of units of a product sold during the past year) can be obtained through **secondary data,** data that have already been collected from other sources and are readily available from those sources. For instance, for Consolidated Bakeries, data on current and past market shares can be readily obtained from commercial research firms such as ACNielsen (offering Nielsen Retail Index[10] and ScanTrack[11] data) and Information Resources, Inc. (offering BehaviorScan[12]). Systems such as BehaviorScan can also provide data on changes in families' brand preferences over time. For example, such data can assist in accomplishing Consolidated Bakeries' research purpose by indicating the extent of brand loyalty.

When the research purpose can be accomplished through secondary data, at least some of the subsequent stages of the research process may not even be relevant. For example, suppose the sole purpose of Consolidated Bakeries' research is to determine its own and competitors' market shares. It can accomplish this by identifying appropriate secondary-data sources, obtaining data from them, analyzing the data collected, and gaining insights from this analysis. The research project will conclude at this stage. An important inference emerging from the Consolidated Bakeries example is that not every project will necessarily require all the research stages, as illustrated by the branches on the right-hand side of the flow diagram in Exhibit 2.1.

◼ **Primary Data**   Not all data may be readily available, however. For instance, consumer perceptions, listed as one of Consolidated Bakeries' data needs, can be obtained only by contacting consumers directly. Such data collected for specific research needs are called **primary data.** Collecting primary data entails a significant amount of time and effort on the researcher's part. Primary-data collection is the subject of Chapter 6.

◼ **The Importance of Time Frame**   We have thus far assumed that researchers will be able to obtain data (either secondary or primary) to fulfill all their data needs. But what if no source is available for the kinds of data needed in a particular

Secondary data are data that have already been collected by and are readily available from other sources.

Primary data are data collected for specific research needs.

project? For instance, suppose the research objective of Consolidated Bakeries is to ascertain consumer tastes and preferences for snack foods five to ten years from now. Most likely no good, trustworthy source of data will be available for this objective, because the time frame is too long. Hence, the company should abandon the research project at this stage rather than pursue it further; the results will undoubtedly not be worth it.

Step 5: Choose an Appropriate Research Design and Data Collection Method

After determining the research objectives and the nature of the data to be collected, the researchers must choose an appropriate research design, which in turn will influence what tasks they will perform in the remainder of the project. The research design may be exploratory or conclusive.

Exploratory research helps researchers gain some initial insights and may pave the way for further research. For instance, an industrial product firm wishing to generate some ideas for improving its product line can do so through informal discussions with selected customers and distributors.

Conclusive research helps researchers verify insights and select the appropriate course of action. Conclusive research can be either descriptive or experimental. For example, a department store wishing to obtain a demographic profile of its customers can use a formal, structured survey of individual customers. This data collection approach is traditionally called a *descriptive* research design. If the department store wants to examine the role that price discounts play in sales, it can systematically vary prices and examine the effects of the discounts on sales. Such an approach is called an *experimental* research design. In experimental (or causal) studies, the researcher investigates the effects of one variable on another: Does variable A modify or determine the value of variable B?

In causal studies, an independent variable is assumed to cause the observed effect on a dependent variable. The dependent variable is what the researcher is attempting to predict or explain, and the independent variable is what the researcher controls or manipulates. For example, suppose researchers are looking at the effect of sale prices on consumers' willingness to buy. Their study may investigate the impact of two levels of price discount (the independent variable)—say, a 10 percent and a 50 percent discount—on willingness to buy (the de- pendent variable). The researchers will select two similar consumer samples—one for each discount level—and ask a series of questions aimed at determining willingness to buy at each level. Any significant differences in willingness to buy between the two samples will imply that the independent variable of price discount "causes" a change in the dependent variable of willingness to buy. Such experimental studies also need to consider the timing of the independent-variable manipulation. For an independent variable to have an effect on the dependent variable, the independent one must be presented first. In the above example, subjects must be presented with a scenario explaining the price discount before they are asked questions pertaining to willingness to buy. Without this sequence, the researchers cannot make the assumption of a causal relationship.

The next chapter discusses different research designs, the circumstances under which they are appropriate, and their implications for data collection and analysis. The chosen research design serves as a blueprint for the execution of the project. This blueprint is typically cast in the form of a **research proposal,** a document that briefly describes the purpose and scope, specific objectives, sample design, data collection procedures, data analysis plan, timetable, and estimated cost for the contemplated project. The research proposal can stimulate useful

Exploratory research helps investigators gain some initial insights and may pave the way for further research.

Conclusive research helps investigators verify insights and select the appropriate course of action.

A **research proposal** is a document that briefly describes the purpose and scope, specific objectives, sample design, data collection procedures, data analysis plan, timetable, and estimated cost for the contemplated project.

| TABLE 2.1 |
| Issues a Research Proposal Should Address |

Questions that need to be answered by the client/marketing researcher team:

- Why am I conducting this research?
- How will I tell if my project has been a success?
- What method will be used?
- What questions will be asked?
- Who will be interviewed?
- How will you get contact information for potential respondents?
- When and where will data be collected?
- Which pieces will be done internally and which will be done externally?
- What statistical analysis will be performed?
- How will the results be communicated in the organization?

Source: Lori Laflin,"Planning a Successful Research Project," *Marketing News,* January 4, 1999, p. 21. © 1999 by the American Marketing Association. All rights reserved. Reprinted by permission of the American Marketing Association, Chicago, IL.

dialogue between researchers and decision makers to ensure that there is no misunderstanding between them and that the information generated will be appropriate and adequate. As a result of this dialogue, the proposal may have to be modified before a final version emerges that is acceptable to all parties.

The researcher or research department usually drafts the initial version of a research proposal. However, sometimes the department requesting the research drafts the proposal and submits it to the research department. Regardless of the origin of the initial proposal, both parties must carefully examine it, raise any concerns they have, and jointly resolve those concerns by appropriately modifying the proposal.

Table 2.1 contains key questions that the client and marketing researcher should answer while creating a research proposal. Up-front dialogue about these questions will help ensure the eventual success of the research project. An important benefit of this dialogue is that it encourages the two parties to discuss and reach agreement on various key issues before launching the project.

Step 6: Design the Research Instrument or Form

The step of developing the data collection instrument or form is relevant when a research project requires primary-data collection. Primary data are frequently collected through interviews, but in some instances they are also gathered through observation. Regardless of the method used, some instrument must be designed to record the data being collected. Although designing a data collection form may appear easy, certain aspects of the form, if not handled carefully, can seriously affect the quality and nature of the data.

A well-respected thoroughbred racing journal wanted to get personal data on its subscribers. It developed a very detailed data collection form designed to gather as much personal information as possible. The journal seemed to do things properly, first sending letters to notify subscribers to expect the questionnaire and including a dollar bill as a thank-you incentive. However, the data collection form was almost 10 pages long, with extremely detailed questions about participants' financial profiles. Such factors are likely to deter respondents from filling out a questionnaire.

Step 7: Identify the Sample

Designing a sample to collect primary data means clearly specifying who, or which units, should provide the needed data. This step may offer some general guidance for designing the sample. For instance, in a project intended to measure the public's attitudes toward government support for private schools, the source of the primary data might be specified as "individuals over 18 years of age." However, several other issues must be settled before data collection can begin: *How many* individuals over 18 years of age should be chosen for the project? *From what geographic area* should they be chosen? *How* should they be chosen?

In a **probability sample,** each element in the population has a known, non-zero chance of inclusion.

Nonprobability sampling is a subjective procedure in which the probability of selection for each population unit is unknown beforehand.

For example, the method of choosing individuals depends on whether a probability or a nonprobability sampling method is used. Very simply, in a **probability sample,** each element in the population has a known, nonzero chance of inclusion. There are various methods for building such a sample (see Chapter 11). In contrast, a **nonprobability sample** is any sample that does not fit into the definition of a probability sample. With nonprobability samples, the researcher selects subjects with a particular goal in mind, such as convenience, to choose subjects judged suitable for the study, to match the demographics of the population in question, or to select respondents based on referrals by previous respondents. Each method has pros and cons. Issues pertaining to the sampling method and sample size are discussed in detail in Chapter 11.

Step 8: Collect the Data

Once the data collection form and the sample design are ready, the next step is to collect the data. Note that, consistent with the interrelationships among the research process steps, the design of the data collection form and sample should take into account the type of collection method to be used. For example, question wording depends on whether the questionnaire is to be used in an interviewer-administered survey (such as a telephone survey) or a self-administered survey (a mail or Internet-based survey).

Interviewing customers face-to-face is one approach for collecting data.

Before data analysis can begin, the responses generated by the data collection procedures must be checked for completeness, consistency, and adherence to prespecified instructions. The process of examining the responses and taking the necessary corrective action to ensure they are of high quality is called *editing*. The edited responses also need to be put into a form that is ready for analysis. This transformation process is called *coding*.

Step 9: Analyze and Interpret the Data

As we saw in Chapter 1, analysis and interpretation are integral parts of marketing research. The types of analyses permissible in a project depend on the nature of the data, which in turn can be affected by factors such as the type of data collection method used. Chapters 12 through 15 discuss a number of methods for analyzing data and interpreting the results.

Step 10: Present Research Findings to Decision Makers

The last step in the marketing research process is to prepare a report that communicates the results of the research to decision makers. This step is critical to the process. Only through a clear and convincing report can the findings and conclusions reached by the market researcher be implemented. Given the importance of effectively communicating the research findings to decision makers, we have devoted an entire chapter (Chapter 16) to the presentation of research findings, in both oral and written form.

Interdependence of Process Steps

To summarize, any research project can be broken into a series of logical steps, starting with a determination of the worth of the project and ending with analysis and interpretation of the findings. Although we viewed the research steps as chronological for convenience, in reality few stages are independent of others.[13] Indeed, a major challenge for researchers and decision makers is to think ahead as they embark on a research project. Planning a potentially valuable research project requires a much broader perspective than focusing on only one step at a time. To give you an idea of how the various research steps fit together in a real-life setting, the next section describes marketing research projects conducted by Burger King. Of course, all marketing research projects are not as structured and formally conducted as these. However, all involve the same basic interrelated steps, as we'll see next.

New-Product Launches at Burger King

Burger King (BK) routinely conducts a Product Screen Study to determine which new concepts for menu items are most appealing to customers. Ideas are generated by the marketing department, research and development, advertising agencies, and marketing partners such as Coca-Cola.

The ideas are then tested among a national sample of consumers ages 13 to 64 who have visited a fast-food hamburger restaurant during the past four weeks. They are shown a photo of the proposed product with a short description and the selling price. They are then asked how likely they would be to make a special trip to BK to purchase the product, how unique they think the product is, and how they perceive its value for the money.

The products that achieve BK's action standards then go into testing. First, in-house sensory testing is done with employees in BK's test kitchen. Next, the product is taken to consumers across the country for further testing. Usually the product is tested in a Taste Test Study in which consumers sample it in a mall; sometimes it is served to people who qualify for the study and are willing to try it in BK restaurants. Let's look at how Burger King conducted marketing research for the BK Broiler chicken sandwich.

Marketing Research for the BK Broiler Chicken Sandwich

Step 1: Justify the Need for Marketing Research In 1998 the BK Broiler chicken sandwich was suffering from low sales. BK's customers are typically males, and the firm believed it could increase sales by appealing to women with its broiled chicken sandwich. BK needed research to identify and develop a winning positioning strategy that would appeal to women. In short, the proposed research project appeared to be worthwhile not only because the results were needed, but also because adequate resources were available to implement the research results.

■ **Step 2: Define the Research Objective**　The main objective of the research project was to find out what would be the best way to position a new broiled chicken sandwich among the target market. Potential chicken eaters' reactions to the new sandwich were of primary interest. The proposed sandwich was smaller than the current one, had fewer fat grams, and used "whole muscle" product as opposed to the existing formed-chicken patty. The sandwich was made with a corn-dusted bun, used Savory Grill sauce, and was topped with shredded vegetables. Thus the primary purpose was to obtain consumer reactions to four different ways to position the new chicken sandwich in the marketplace.

The four positionings considered for the concept/taste test were:

- Choice White Meat/Chicken Breast
- Backyard BBQ Taste
- Marinated Special Blend/Homestyle Taste
- Competitive Claim (concept only)

Consumers evaluated concept, positioning, and taste for the first three positionings. For the fourth, only the concept, Competitive Claim, was tested. The following is an actual "Choice White Meat/Chicken Breast" positioning statement used by BK in the concept test:

> Burger King introduces its new delicious flame-broiled chicken sandwich. Our specially selected choice white meat chicken breast guarantees great taste.
>
> At Burger King we always go out of our way to make our sandwiches with the highest quality ingredients, so they always taste great. That's why our new flame-broiled chicken sandwich is made from the choicest and most tender whole white meat chicken breast filet we can find. We serve it to you on a bakery fresh corn-dusted Kaiser roll and top it with our own special garden blend of crisp shredded vegetables, fresh lettuce and tomato and new mouth-watering savory sauce.
>
> Only at Burger King can you experience the great taste that you get from combining the best, high quality ingredients with flame-broiling. Try the new flame-broiled sandwich, available everyday at Burger King.[14]

■ **Steps 3 and 4: Identify Data Needs and Data Sources**　BK's data requirements fell into four classes:

1. *Purchase Intention Measures.* The purchase intention measure was to be used to assess the likelihood that respondents would buy the sandwich.
2. *Overall Product Diagnostics.* BK wanted to obtain data to understand the reasons underlying the intended purchase measures. Of interest to BK's product management were consumers' overall judgments of the product concept, measuring uniqueness or differentiation from other products, inherent interest, and value for the money.
3. *Attribute Diagnostics.* To focus further positioning and development efforts, BK needed data about specific product attributes that led people to buy chicken sandwiches.

4. *Respondent Profiling Variables.* Data on demographics were deemed important to understanding customers' fast-food eating habits.

Because most of the data were to come from potential customers' perceptions about the new chicken sandwich, some form of primary-data collection was inevitable. The company's past experience (internal secondary data on similar products) would serve as a benchmark for judging the research results.

■ **Step 5: Choose an Appropriate Research Design and Data Collection Method**   BK hired an outside research agency to design and execute the marketing research study. Because the research was intended to aid BK management in the selection of a specific course of action, the project was basically conclusive experimental research. BK and the research agency were clear about the types of information they wanted.

Choosing the Data Collection Method   The research agency decided to collect the necessary data through mall-intercept interviews. The mall-intercept approach was chosen instead of a telephone or mail survey because, to obtain meaningful data, the researcher had to prescreen the respondents to make sure they were fast-food restaurant chicken eaters. Also, those who expressed neutral or positive responses to a concept were invited to return to the mall at a later time to try the product. Given the need for such researcher-respondent interaction, other survey approaches were deemed inappropriate.

Exhibit 2.2
Purchase Intent for BK Broiler Chicken Sandwich Positionings
Source: Burger King Corporation 2001 research information used with permission from Burger King Corporation.

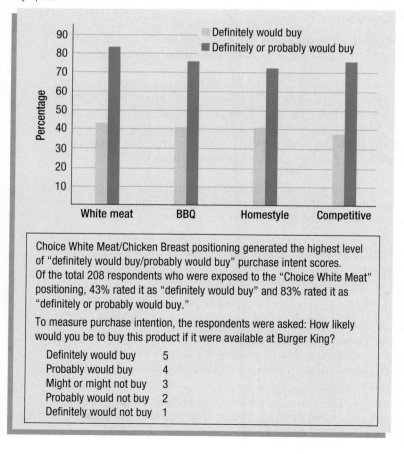

Choice White Meat/Chicken Breast positioning generated the highest level of "definitely would buy/probably would buy" purchase intent scores.
Of the total 208 respondents who were exposed to the "Choice White Meat" positioning, 43% rated it as "definitely would buy" and 83% rated it as "definitely or probably would buy."

To measure purchase intention, the respondents were asked: How likely would you be to buy this product if it were available at Burger King?

Definitely would buy	5
Probably would buy	4
Might or might not buy	3
Probably would not buy	2
Definitely would not buy	1

■ **Step 6: Design the Research Instrument or Form**   The agency developed a well-structured questionnaire to collect the necessary data about the concept and the respondents. The questionnaire consisted of the following:

• Prerecruiting screening questions
• Concept evaluation questions (only for qualified respondents)
• Taste test (only for those who gave neutral or positive responses to the concept)
• Classification questions

■ **Step 7: Identify the Sample**   The sample for this study was identified earlier as a group of people who had eaten chicken in a fast-food restaurant at least once in the past three months. The sample consisted of the following:

• Approximately 65 percent female and 35 percent male (skewed toward women to reflect the expected user base for the new broiled chicken sandwich)
• Approximately 50 percent ages 18 to 34 and 50 percent ages 35 to 54

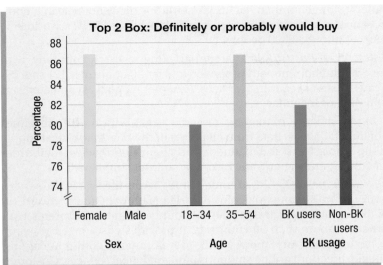

Exhibit 2.3
Purchase Intent for BK Broiler Chicken Sandwich—"Choice White Meat/Chicken Breast" Positioning—Among Key Subgroups
Source: Burger King Corporation 2001 research information used with permission from Burger King Corporation.

- Approximately 50 percent BK users and 50 percent non-BK users (within the past four weeks)

■ **Step 8: Collect the Data** A total of 835 interviews were conducted among prerecruited consumers at malls in 10 different geographic locations. Approximately 150 taste tests were conducted for the first three positionings.

■ **Step 9: Analyze and Interpret the Data** Although all four positionings generated an equally high level of "definitely would buy" purchase intent scores, the "Choice White Meat/Chicken Breast" positioning generated the highest level of *positive* interest among the non-BK users. The study found that interest in trying the product was driven by a positive predisposition toward the chicken sandwich, as well as how appetizing the product looked (in the picture). The product's healthfulness—broiled rather than fried—appeared to be a secondary driver. The "Choice White Meat/Chicken Breast" positioning generated the highest level of purchase intent (see Exhibit 2.2). In the Taste Test Study, consumers rated the product very favorably.

■ **Step 10: Present Research Findings to Decision Makers** Based on these findings, BK's Consumer Research Group recommended the "Choice White Meat/Chicken Breast" positioning. The sandwich performed well among women (the intended target market) and among non-BK users, and the 35-to-54 age group rated the sandwich very favorably (see Exhibit 2.3). However, the researchers also suggested that additional studies were needed to determine the best name and price for the sandwich.

External Providers of Marketing Research

Many organizations—those with and those without their own in-house marketing research capabilities—call on external research agencies to meet at least some of their information needs. Over 1,000 commercial marketing research firms operate in the United States. These firms vary widely in terms of both the geographic scope of their operations—ranging from local to international—and the range and nature of their services. Large commercial marketing research firms offer a full range of services, from planning through delivery of final report and recommendations. Smaller firms specialize in interviewing or other types of fieldwork, such as conducting store audit studies. A handful of large marketing research firms account for the vast majority of research services provided, with the top 25 firms controlling more than 75 percent of the dollars spent on research services. Some key firms include those listed on the next page.

- *VNU* corporation (parent company of ACNielsen) tops the list of research companies, with annual worldwide revenues of over $4 billion. VNU's worldwide operations employ about 36,000 people.[15]

- *Information Resources, Inc. (IRI)* is a large marketing research company, with revenues over $500 million, providing service in over 20 countries. IRI specializes in syndicated market scanning services. (Chapter 4 details syndicated services in a discussion of secondary data.)[16]

- *IMS Health Inc.* is a large marketing research organization with revenues around $1.4 billion. It collects data from all points of the pharmaceutical supply chain, including wholesalers, independent and chain pharmacies, mail-order firms, manufacturers, and generic and over-the-counter suppliers.[17]

- *GfK Custom Research Inc. (GfK-CRI),* founded in 1974, was the first in the service industry to win the prestigious Malcolm Baldrige National Quality Award (in 1996). GFK-CRI has offices in more than 50 countries and collaborates with research partners in more than 90 countries. It provides customized research solutions in new-product and new-service development, communications, tracking, strategic direction, online solutions, and analytical services. Customer satisfaction services provide loyalty measurement, customer satisfaction measurement, and strategic segmentation. Database solutions services integrate database and attitudinal data.[18]

Factors to Consider in Deciding to Use External Suppliers

Although numerous marketing research firms exist in the United States, a small number accounts for a large share of total marketing research industry revenues. Most of the other firms in the industry are relatively small. Organizations without in-house marketing research capabilities invariably have to hire an external provider when they want information from their marketing environment. However, even firms capable of conducting research on their own (like Burger King) can and do use external providers. Four key factors that may result in hiring external suppliers are credibility, competence, cost, and capacity (see Exhibit 2.4). Each factor is discussed next.

■ **Credibility**   *Credibility* refers to the perceived trustworthiness of the research and its findings. Even firms with full-fledged in-house marketing research departments hire outside agencies to conduct research in situations where the credibility, and hence usefulness, of the research may depend as much on *who* does the research as on *how well* it is done. For instance, suppose the board of directors of a large corporation wants to know how successful top management has been in building a favorable image for the corporation in the eyes of the public. In this situation, the board is likely to find an assessment of corporate image made by an independent research firm more credible than an assessment based on data gathered by in-house marketing research. In general, the use of external

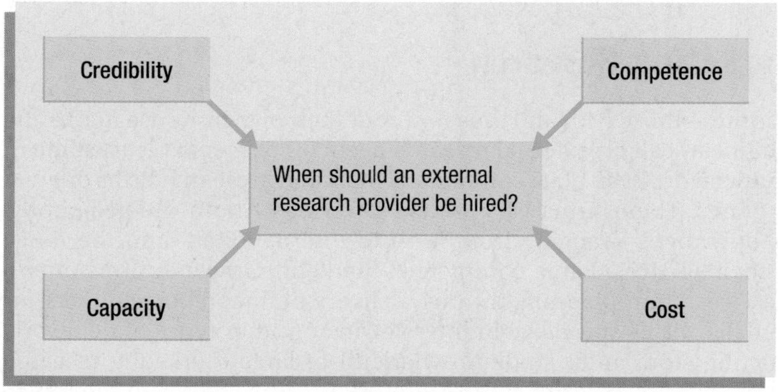

Exhibit 2.4
Factors Relevant in Deciding Whether to Use External Providers

providers is desirable when a potential conflict of interest (real or perceived) exists if a research study is conducted in-house—that is, when independence of the source of the research study is crucial to ensuring that the study's findings are credible to the intended audience.

■ **Competence**   *Competence* refers to special capabilities or facilities of an external research provider that an in-house marketing research department lacks. A firm will have to hire an appropriate external agency for projects requiring special capabilities. For instance, consider ACNielsen's national ScanTrack Service. This service, based on a nationwide sample of high-volume, scanner-equipped supermarkets, provides weekly data on product class, brand and item sales, brand share, selling prices, and so forth for numerous packaged goods. Nielsen is able to obtain such data readily because of its wide experience in store auditing and its established contacts with supermarkets. An individual packaged goods manufacturer, even one with a good in-house marketing research department, will have difficulty gaining access to the kinds of data available to Nielsen.

■ **Cost**   With certain types of research projects, using an external research provider to do part or all of the work may be less *costly* than doing the entire project in-house. For instance, many in-house marketing research departments may design research projects but hire a field service firm to perform the data collection.

■ **Capacity**   Sometimes a firm hires an external provider to conduct an important research project—one that cannot be delayed—when its in-house research department is fully tied up with ongoing research projects. In other words, external providers may be employed to expand the *capacity* of in-house marketing research temporarily to meet urgent research needs. When the timing of a research project is crucial, a firm may be forced to use the services of an external provider even if in-house marketing research personnel would be capable of handling the project if they had the time. The critical question is "How *soon* can in-house marketing research conduct the project?" rather than "Is in-house marketing research *qualified* to conduct the project?"

Criteria for Evaluating External Suppliers

When a firm decides to use external research services, it also has to decide which specific provider to hire. What criteria should a firm consider in selecting an external research provider? Several authorities have offered lists of criteria. Fortunately, the various lists agree to a great extent and lead to a handful of general guidelines. These guidelines are reflected in the four selection criteria summarized in Exhibit 2.5: prestige, past experience, personnel, and price. Each criterion is discussed next.

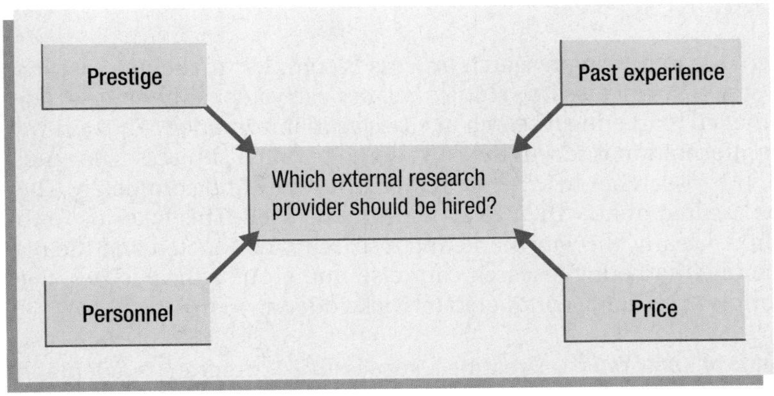

■ **Prestige**   *Prestige* refers to the reputation of a research provider and is a strong indicator of its research quality and capabilities. Like any other profession, the research industry has its

Exhibit 2.5
Criteria for Evaluating External Providers

charlatans. Hence a firm should check out the reputation of prospective research suppliers. A simple way to do this is to ask the suppliers for references or for a list of clients they serve. The reputation of a provider's clients is a useful measure of the credibility of the provider's work and the confidence its work inspires.

■ **Past Experience**   Generally, a prospective provider's ability to handle a client's project is associated with its *past research experience,* especially experience related to the research assignment. Thus, past experience is an important indicator, though not necessarily the only indicator, of a provider's competence. Another facet of past experience is the extent and nature of any past working relationship between the client firm and the provider. Rehiring the services of a provider with whom past experiences have been good may offer certain advantages, such as lower cost and better client-provider understanding.

■ **Personnel**   A key consideration in choosing an external research firm is the set of skills possessed by the provider's *personnel,* particularly those employees who will be in direct contact with client personnel. Here the term *skills* is not restricted to technical qualifications; equally important are nontechnical skills such as interpersonal skills, communication skills, the ability to understand a client's research problem, and the ability to establish rapport with client personnel.

■ **Price**   The *price* of a research firm's services is an obvious concern for any client firm. However, the cheapest buy is not necessarily the best buy. A research firm with a good reputation and high-quality research capabilities usually can, and most likely will, demand a premium price. Also, competing providers may bid different prices for the same research assignment because their perceptions of the nature and scope of the assignment may differ. In fact, a written proposal detailing what the research assignment will and will not cover should be developed and agreed to by both client and provider *before* a final research contract is signed. In other words, the price quoted by a research firm, although critical for the client firm's research budget, should not be the determining factor in provider selection. The four general considerations in choosing an external research supplier—prestige, past experience, personnel, and price—do not constitute an exhaustive set of guidelines but are good starting criteria.

Ethical Issues in Marketing Research

As we have seen, the marketing research process is complex, made up of a series of interrelated steps. Not all research studies will use each step to the same extent, but one thing that all marketing research needs is valid information. The best way to ensure such information is to win the trust of the research subjects. They must feel "safe" with the researcher in order to answer truthfully and completely. They also want to be assured of how their responses will be used. This takes us to the question of ethics. Clearly, the way marketing research is conducted and the reasons for conducting marketing research can raise numerous ethical issues. Let's look at the example of research conducted by Nickelodeon.

CASE IN POINT ▶   **Nickelodeon Wants to Know You**[19]   Creating a successful TV program is a demanding job in today's hypercompetitive entertainment industry. In 2001, for instance, only 41 percent of new shows aired on prime-time network TV in the United States were still on the air.[20]

Nickelodeon, in contrast, has created dozens of hit shows, a remarkable feat by any standard. One primary reason is its success in finding out as much as possible about what kids like to watch on TV. Research guides virtually everything that goes on the air. According to Herb Scannell, the network's president, "It's really important for Nickelodeon to look at the world from a kid's point of view. And if you want to look at the world from a kid's point of view, the most important thing is to get a kid's point of view."

How do marketing executives at Nickelodeon get a kid's point of view about what makes a TV show fun to watch?

- Nickelodeon has "adopted" a day care center, where it tests ideas for new shows or characters.
- Nickelodeon's spinoff network, Noggin, pays thousands of dollars to a school in Montclair, New Jersey, for allowing it to conduct marketing research there on a weekly basis. Children are given disposable cameras to record their activities.
- Nickelodeon's researchers conduct focus groups with school-age viewers.
- Researchers quiz the kids on all aspects of their lives, which helps Nickelodeon fine-tune its shows. For example, research showed that many young people live in nontraditional families. Thus the title character of *Hey Arnold!* lives with his grandparents, and Chucky in Rugrats doesn't have a mom. ◄

These activities are glimpses of marketing research at work. Nickelodeon uses marketing research to keep its producers informed about the needs and preferences of new generations. Angela Santomero, a researcher-turned-creator of shows like *Blue's Clues,* sums it up nicely: "I feel I'm so much smarter about my material when I know what the audience is thinking. I know why a show works or doesn't work." Nevertheless, the research conducted by Nickelodeon may raise a lot of ethical concerns.

Codes of Ethics

Marketing research ethics
ethics are principles of conduct that govern the marketing research profession.

The *Merriam-Webster Dictionary* defines *ethics* as "the principles of conduct governing an individual or a group."[21] From this definition, **marketing research ethics** may be viewed as simply the principles of conduct that govern the marketing research profession. The code of ethics drawn up by the American Marketing Association (AMA) includes these points in the area of marketing research:

- Prohibiting selling or fund raising under the guise of conducting research
- Maintaining research integrity by avoiding misrepresentation and omission of pertinent research data
- Treating outside clients and suppliers fairly[22]

Several professional marketing organizations have their own written codes of marketing research ethics. For instance, the European Society for Opinion and Marketing Research (ESOMAR®), of which the AMA is a member, and the International Chamber of Commerce (ICC) jointly developed a single International Code in 1976 and revised it in 1986 and 1994. The code lays out in detail the basic ethical and business principles that govern the practice of marketing and social research. The stakeholders of these principles typically fall into five groups:

1. External research providers (typically full-service firms) that deal directly with client organizations. These firms are traditionally known as *research suppliers.*

2. Limited-service external providers (such as data-gathering firms) that cater to research suppliers as well as to in-house marketing research departments. These firms are typically referred to as *field service firms.*

3. Research subjects or respondents who provide the data collected.

4. Clients who are the users of marketing research information.

5. The general public that may be affected by the dissemination of research results.

Each of these five groups has certain *rights,* which implies that each also has certain obligations toward the others. The ESOMAR website spells out in detail the rights and responsibilities of these stakeholders (see Exhibit 2.6).

Another organization that strives to protect the industry from abuses of research is the Council for Marketing & Opinion Research (CMOR), a federation of associations (including the AMA), research providers, and research users. One of CMOR's central goals is to encourage respondent cooperation through articulating the Respondent Bill of Rights (see Table 2.2).

Ethical Gray Areas: Code of Ethics Limitations

The rights discussed in each of these codes of ethics are self-explanatory, and any concerned researcher should be aware of them and respect them. However, looking beyond the mere definition of these rights, we can see numerous ethical gray areas in which a researcher will have to make judgment calls.

■ **An Ethical Situation? You Decide**   For instance, take an e-mailer's right to privacy. All of us will probably agree that monitoring someone else's personal e-mails is a serious violation of one's right to privacy. However, what about an e-mail service provider's scanning your e-mails using keywords for marketing campaign purposes or storing your e-mails in its servers after you have closed

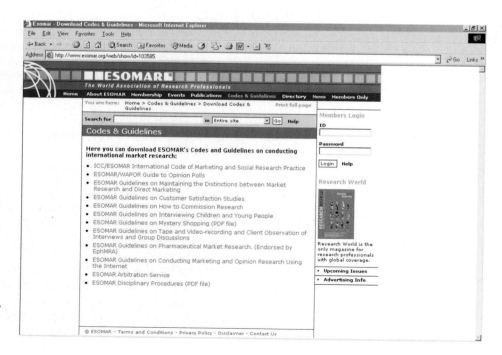

Exhibit 2.6
The ESOMAR® Website
Copyright © ESOMAR® 2005. Permission for using this material has been granted by ESOMAR® Amsterdam, Netherlands. Screen shot reprinted by permission from Microsoft Corporation.

TABLE 2.2
Council for Marketing and Opinion Research: Respondent Bill of Rights

Your participation in a legitimate research survey is very important to us, and we value the information you provide. Therefore, our relationship will be one of respect and consideration, based on the following practices:

- Your privacy and the privacy of your answers will be respected and maintained.
- Your name, address, phone number, personal information, or individual responses won't be disclosed to anyone outside the research industry without your permission.
- You will always be told the name of the person contacting you, the research company's name, and the nature of the survey.
- You will not be sold anything, or asked for money, under the guise of research.
- You will be contacted at reasonable times, but if the time is inconvenient, you may ask to be recontacted at a more convenient time.
- Your decision to participate in a study, answer specific questions, or discontinue your participation will be respected without question.
- You will be informed in advance if an interview is to be recorded and of the intended use of the recording.
- You are assured that the highest standards of professional conduct will be upheld in the collection and reporting of information you provide.

Survey research is an important part of our democratic society, allowing people to express their views on political and social issues, as well as on products and services.

Source: Reprinted by permission of the Council for Marketing and Opinion Research.

---

your e-mail account? What if the provider informs you about scanning and storing e-mails? Is this still a violation of privacy? You decide after reading the following example.

> **SCENARIO** Google launched a free e-mail service, Gmail, on April 1, 2004. Gmail is more than just a simple e-mail service. Google will scan e-mails sent through Gmail for key words and include relevant advertising messages when the e-mails are delivered. Google will also store the e-mails in its database even after users have closed their accounts. Gmail has raised a storm of protest from privacy advocates, especially in Europe, who argue that Gmail constitutes a serious violation of individual rights.[23] Earlier, European regulators had moved to adopt what are commonly known as *opt-in anti-spam rules,* which prohibit e-mail marketers from sending promotions to individuals without their prior consent.[24] About two weeks after Gmail's launch, Privacy International, a human rights advocacy group, filed complaints against Gmail simultaneously in 16 countries. Most European and U.S. regulatory agencies, however, do not see any problems with Gmail as long as Google clearly spells out the conditions for using the service at the time it signs up customers. These are in fact spelled out at Google's website (http://www.google.com/gmail/help/privacy.html). Do you think technology will further erode an individual's privacy? Does Google's ethical responsibility end with a declaration in a privacy statement? Do you think Google should be allowed to scan e-mail messages even if users consent to this arrangement?

This example illustrates real-life ethical issues with which marketers and researchers wrestle frequently. A broad ethical question for marketing researchers in today's online environment is: Where does one draw the line between a researcher's need for (or right to) information and the rights of consumers or research subjects? Such questions have no easy answers.

■ **The Difficulty of Recognizing Ethical Situations**   Empirical evidence suggests that the existence and enforcement of codes of ethics in research organizations are associated with higher levels of ethical behavior.[25] However, resolving ethical questions in specific research situations is not as simple as a written code may lead you to believe. Views about what is ethical or unethical often differ among research practitioners themselves, as well as among research agencies, their clients, and others interested in research and its findings. The practices and applications of research are too diverse and rapidly changing to yield any precise definition of ethical research, especially in a form that can be easily applied to the wide range of research problems that arise. Often, the notion of ethics also depends on the particular research project and the problem under study. In fact, some practitioners never even recognize an ethical problem when placed in a decision-making situation with an ethical component.[26] The following example illustrates this problem.

CASE IN POINT ▶ **Spyware for Marketing Data**   With the increasing popularity of the Internet as a source of information and entertainment, a growing number of marketing research companies have discovered ways of using the Internet to track consumer behavior. One such tracking method is a class of software applications called *spyware*. The main purpose of spyware is to monitor an Internet user's behavior by capturing such information as which websites the user accessed and sometimes more personal information, such as passwords and financial data. Often spyware programs are loaded onto a consumer's computer without his or her knowledge or express consent. Once there, the spyware collects consumer data behind the scenes and transmits it to a marketing firm such as Claria Corporation.

Claria, one of the leaders in online behavioral marketing, is also a leading developer of spyware programs. According to the company, "tens of millions of consumers . . . agree to receive advertising based on their actual online behavior."[27] Although the company may perceive that it is doing nothing wrong because it has obtained prior consumer consent, this scenario is an ethical gray area. User license agreements are often obtusely worded and lengthy—5,541 words long in Claria's case—and consumers rarely read the fine print.[28] In today's digital age, the key issue confronting marketing firms and researchers who employ online media to gather consumer data is recognizing and avoiding potential privacy violations. ◀

■ **Differing Interpretations of the Codes**   An additional limitation of a code of ethics is that any so-called standard in an ethical code is in reality subject to different interpretations, stemming from the values and priorities of the individuals seeking guidance from it. Research ethics are "guidelines and principles that help us uphold *our values*—to decide which goals of research are most important and to reconcile values and goals that are in conflict"[29] (emphasis added).

J. R. Sparks and S. D. Hunt conducted an interesting study that found evidence of how a person's ethical sensitivity can influence his or her perceptions about what is ethical and what is not.[30] Sparks and Hunt presented to a sample of research practitioners and students a marketing research case scenario that raised both ethical and nonethical marketing research issues. A part of the case scenario follows.

> A marketing researcher working on a project for a new client needs background information on competitive trends in the client's industry and contacts an advertising executive friend who formerly had the account of the client's chief competitor.[31]

The survey respondents were asked to briefly describe the issues that, in their opinion, this scenario raised. They were not prompted to focus on ethical, technical, or managerial issues.

Interestingly, 65 percent of the research practitioner sample did not recognize the violation of confidentiality as an ethical problem. To the remaining 35 percent, however, seeking information from someone who had acquired it "in confidence" constituted a violation of professional ethics. Apparently the majority believed it was their responsibility to make the best use of all available information. How do *you* feel about the appropriateness of the data collection method described in this scenario? As you try to answer this question, you will likely appreciate how heavily perceptions about what is ethical depend on one's own value systems and subjective judgment.

The area of ethics in marketing research is extremely important and concerns the rights of a variety of parties. Nevertheless, the resolution of real-life ethical conflicts is not always easy. Potential ethical conflicts can perhaps be minimized, but not necessarily eliminated, if all the parties in the research industry—research suppliers, field service firms, and client organizations—make a conscious effort to be aware of and respect the rights of one another as well as those of the research subjects and the general public. This section has by necessity left many questions unanswered. However, if it has sensitized you to the importance of marketing research ethics, it has accomplished its goal.

SUMMARY

This chapter introduced the various steps involved in the marketing research process used in planning and conducting marketing research projects. Certain aspects of the marketing research process deserve particular attention. First, although a research project can be viewed as a sequence of chronological steps, the steps are not necessarily independent of one another. One or more steps may have an impact on preceding or subsequent steps.

Second, some projects may not involve all the steps of the marketing research process. When all the necessary data are available through secondary sources, there is no need to develop a data collection form, design a sample, or collect primary data. At the other extreme, when no trustworthy data source (primary or secondary) capable of adequately meeting a research project's data needs is available, terminating the project is better than proceeding further.

Third, even though the marketing research process is a logical sequence of well-defined steps, it is not totally scientific. The subjective judgments of decision makers and researchers are likely to play a role in at least some of the steps, such as in the evaluation of a research project's worth. Even mathematically sophisticated approaches to making cost-versus-benefit evaluations are based on critical assumptions and require subjective inputs from decision makers. Although some degree of subjectivity in the research process is inevitable, marketing research should be conducted in a systematic fashion to be beneficial.

It is important for marketing managers to recognize that in many instances they may need to hire outside marketing research providers. Key reasons for hiring external providers include the research credibility that they bring to the table, research competence, available capacity to conduct a given project, and lower costs. Some key aspects to keep in mind in deciding which provider to hire are prestige, past experience, personnel, and price.

Marketing researchers are likely to face numerous ethical issues at every stage of the marketing research process. They have to balance the rights of a number of people. It is important that marketing research suppliers, field service firms, and clients all respect the rights of one another, the subjects, and the general public.

REVIEW AND DISCUSSION QUESTIONS

1. "In conducting a marketing research project, researchers would be unwise to spend time and effort on subsequent steps unless all previous steps have been completed." Discuss this statement.

2. State and briefly describe the criteria that are relevant in deciding whether or not to undertake a research project.

3. Explain the association between the nature of the uncertainty a decision maker faces and the potential benefit of a research project capable of reducing that uncertainty.

4. State whether you agree or disagree with this statement: "Correct identification and clear definition of the research problem are more crucial to the success of a project than sophisticated research techniques." Explain your answer.

5. Under what circumstances would a project be terminated without completing *all* of the research process steps? Give an example of your own to illustrate your answer.

6. Does every marketing research project require a formal questionnaire? Why or why not?

7. Briefly discuss why a written code of ethics is not a panacea for resolving ethical questions in marketing research.

8. List the various parties who might be involved in or affected by ethical issues in marketing research.

APPLICATION EXERCISES

1. Sears is investigating why one of its stores is experiencing declining sales in the home appliances department. Exploratory research has determined the following possible causes: (1) Wal-Mart, a large competitor of Sears, just opened a store down the street; (2) overall appliance sales for the industry have been dropping; and (3) patronage of the Sears store has decreased slightly in the past few months. Taking this information into account, answer the following questions:

   a. Describe the steps the Sears managers should go through to decide whether or not they should research the sales decline.

   b. Assuming they decide to conduct some research, what steps will they have to take to determine the project's purpose?

   c. Why is determining the project's purpose such an essential step for Sears to take in the marketing research process?

2. The population of Austin, Texas, is changing. This change is posing problems for Austin Lake Trips, a travel agency based in Austin, and is forcing the agency to take a fresh look at the market and find ways to expand its shrinking customer base. Austin Lake Trips wants to conduct some research to help create a new marketing strategy, including distribution of new promotional materials, to better reach its changing target market. The owner has come to you, a consultant, to find out what this research will entail. Explain to her the steps involved in the marketing research process. Be sure to describe how and why each step is interrelated with the other steps.

3. This chapter described how Nickelodeon conducts marketing research to develop new TV programs. In an effort to keep up with the target market, Nickelodeon, along with MTV and VH1, maintains an ongoing relationship with schools to test ideas and keep in touch with schoolchildren. For these networks, success depends on being "cool." However, some critics claim that Nickelodeon's research is too intrusive. According to Gary Ruskin, director of Commercial Alert, a watchdog group on television advertising, "It's simply wrong to use public schools for snooping into the lives of impressionable children. Schools exist to teach kids to learn to reason, not to do market research that has no educational value." Betsy Frank, head of the MTV Networks research department, counters that researchers aren't identified as working for Nickelodeon when they are in schools or day care centers. Furthermore, Nickelodeon does not sell products in schools or beam TV shows with commercials into classrooms. According to Frank, "We feel we are bringing something good to the schools and we use it to develop programs that are more in tune with what kids want."[32]

   Is Gary Ruskin right in his criticism of Nickelodeon, or do you agree with Betsy Frank's claim? What, in your opinion, is the proper thing for Nickelodeon to do in this situation? Develop a logical argument supporting your position.

4. Client, Inc., hires Research, Inc., to conduct a study to determine the extent of use of Client's brand (brand X) versus the use of competing brands. Research, Inc., conducts a study and presents the following conclusion to Client: "Of the 2,000 respondents surveyed, 1,000 refused to disclose the brand used; of the remaining 1,000 respondents, 500 used brand X, 300 used brand Y, and 200 used a variety of other brands." From this conclusion Client, Inc., develops the following ad campaign: "One out of every two consumers uses brand X, according to a study conducted by Research, Inc." What ethical issues does this example raise?

5. Papa John's became a well-known name in the United States by using its "Better Ingredients, Better Pizza" advertising slogan. In the commercial, Papa John's claimed that its pizzas beat out Pizza Hut's pizzas in a national taste test. Pizza Hut countered by arguing that the test did not compare Pizza Hut's popular pie, the pan pizza, against Papa John's.[33] Are any ethical issues involved in this example? If so, what are they?

6. A field service firm on the West Coast receives a rush order for a long-distance telephone study from a

client firm on the East Coast. Because time is short, a verbal contract is agreed to over the telephone, with the understanding that the field service firm will be reimbursed for all the study expenses as long as it completes the study on time. The field service firm completes the job on time and mails the findings to the client along with a bill for the study's costs. However, the client questions some items on the bill, such as certain long-distance telephone charges and the charge for a field supervisor's time, and refuses to pay the bill in full. Instead, the client pays only what it believes is fair. The field service firm feels cheated and is frustrated at being unable to collect from an out-of-state firm.[34] Is the client firm acting ethically? Why or why not?

7. A research supplier estimates that a study will cost $10,000, and the client agrees that this price is reasonable. But, when the study is completed, the research supplier submits a bill for $15,000, claiming that the cost increased because of changes the client wanted made during the course of the study. The client acknowledges that certain unplanned changes were made but argues that such changes should have cost no more than an additional $2,000. Who is to blame for this conflict? What, if anything, could have been done to prevent it?

8. During every presidential election, the major news media interview numerous voters about their voting intentions. On the basis of their interviews, the media rush to predict the winner, often making their predictions public to beat out competitors, even before the polls close on the West Coast. News media certainly have the right to inform the public and the right to stay ahead of the competition. But does this practice violate any of the general public's rights? Specifically, do the news media violate the rights of West Coast voters by predicting a winner before these voters can get to the polls?

 INTERNET EXERCISES

1. On the Internet, look up a source of secondary data useful for marketing research, such as a marketing research firm or a federal agency. Determine the types of data available from this source (for example, market share, general consumer behavior, specific consumer behavior for a particular product type, consumer spending). For what purposes can each type of data be useful?

2. The U.S. Census Bureau is a valuable source of marketing data. Check it out by following these steps:

   a. Go to www.factfinder.census.gov.

   b. Put in the city, county, or zip code, and then choose the state from the pull-down menu.

3. Assume you work for a bank that collects a large amount of customer data using the Internet. What are some technical and ethical issues that must be addressed when using the Internet for marketing research? (*Hint:* Go to the ESOMAR website [www.esomar.org] and search for the ESOMAR "Guideline on Conducting Marketing and Opinion Research Using the Internet.") Prepare a memo for the bank based on the guidelines.

CASE 2.1 DUNKIN' DONUTS VERSUS KRISPY KREME
(www.dunkindonuts.com)

Most people enjoy a cup of coffee and a doughnut at some time. You can stop on the way to work to pick up breakfast or sit down and relax with a hot cup. It used to be simple—all you had to do was stop at the neighborhood bakery to get that snack. Now there are more choices. The northern states of New England had Dunkin' Donuts, the chain providing their morning pick-me-up, while the South enjoyed fresh Krispy Kreme doughnuts. There were a few smaller chains around, but for years each of these doughnut giants held a proverbial monopoly in its area. Dunkin' Donuts traditionally focused more on its coffee products, while Krispy Kreme emphasized the doughnut end of the product line. But now, as each expands throughout the country, those niches are colliding. Another factor is the rising popularity of Starbucks, the gourmet coffee shop that originated in the Seattle area. With its wide variety of flavored coffees and baked goods, Starbucks is a competitor to be reckoned with.

Krispy Kreme, through popular demand and with great publicity and fanfare, went public in April 2000. Several years later, Krispy Kreme had over 400 company-owned stores and was available in 20,000 other outlets, including grocery stores and Exxon Tiger Marts. In 2004, after the hype had dwindled, Krispy Kreme began to face problems. Overexpansion and mismanagement caused it to post its first loss since its initial public offering, and the company was forced to close many stores.

Always a far larger chain than Krispy Kreme, Dunkin' Donuts franchisees own and operate over 4,400 store locations. Dunkin' Donuts' menu has expanded to offer breakfast sandwiches, iced coffee, hot coffee, muffins, bagels, and, of course, doughnuts. Although considered primarily a breakfast stop, there have been attempts to expand Dunkin' Donuts into the lunch arena. However, its best opportunity for expansion is geographic. With a goal of 15,000 stores within 10 years, Dunkin' Donuts is thinking large. The newest markets are Cleveland, Charlotte, and Tampa.

The two chains never really had to compete against each another before. But now Dunkin' Donuts, in addition to going head-to-head with Krispy Kreme, has Starbucks in its sights in terms of coffee sales. At the same time, Krispy Kreme is playing catch-up after its recent overexpansion woes. To show how much Dunkin' Donuts is willing to invest in its desire to compete with Starbucks, it introduced an $8,000 cappuccino machine. The machine's simplicity allows any employee to use it and to create and re-create the same consistent cappuccino for customers. In another competitive move, Krispy Kreme released its own versions of the popular Dunkin'

Donuts' Coolattas. In 2003 Krispy Kreme acquired a coffee line, and in 2004 it used that acquisition to roll out a new line of iced drinks, one of which tastes like its famous sugar-glazed doughnut.

CASE QUESTIONS

1. As its marketing research manager, develop a detailed marketing research proposal for Dunkin' Donuts, addressing its anticipated concerns about expansion and the competitive environment.

2. In your proposal, include the various stages of the marketing research process, starting with justification for the project and ending with what the project will deliver to management.

3. For which aspects of the research would you consider using external vendors? Why?

Rosemary Barnes, "Financial Holes Appearing in Doughnut Company Krispy Kreme," *Knight Ridder Tribune Business News,* December 11, 2004; William C. Symonds, David Kiley, and Stanley Holmes, "A Java Jolt for Dunkin' Donuts," *BusinessWeek,* December 20, 2004; Soo Yuon, "Doughnut Maker Krispy Kreme Serves up New Line of High-Calorie Cold Beverages," *Knight Ridder Tribune Business News,* July 22, 2004.

CASE 2.2   L&H MARKETING RESEARCH

It was late Saturday afternoon in mid-December. Bob Smith, a research analyst for L&H Marketing Research, was working furiously to complete the media plan portion of the Standard Grooming Products Report. Standard was considering introducing a men's hairspray and needed demographic characteristics and media habits of male hairspray users, as well as attitudinal information about such product attributes as oiliness, stickiness, masculinity, and fragrance.

The findings were to be presented Monday afternoon, and a long series of problems and delays had forced Bob to come in on Saturday to finish the report. Complicating matters, Bob felt that his boss, Barry Michaels, expected the statistical analysis to be consistent with L&H's initial recommendations to Standard. Bob, Barry, and Marjorie Glass, from Standard's advertising agency, were to meet Monday morning to finalize L&H's presentation to Standard.

Back in September, Bob had recommended surveying 250 users of men's hairspray from each of 15 metropolitan areas. Charles Chastain from Standard's marketing department had argued that conclusions about local usage in each city would not be accurate unless each city's sample size was proportional to its population. That is, the sample size for larger cities should be larger than for smaller cities. Furthermore,

Charles feared that males in metropolitan areas differed from rural males on usage or other important characteristics. Bob finally convinced Charles that sample sizes proportional to population would mean only 25 to 50 interviews in some smaller cities—too few to draw statistically valid conclusions. Furthermore, expanding the survey to include rural users would have required committing more money to the project—money Standard didn't want to spend.

In October, a Des Moines, Iowa, pretest revealed that the questionnaire's length was driving the cost per completed interview to about $18. Total expenses would be well over budget if that cost held for the 15 metro areas. If the survey costs exceeded $65,000 (counting the pilot study), precious little money would be left for the focus groups, advertising, and packaging pretesting in L&H's contract with Standard (see Table 1).

TABLE 1
Proposed Budget

Phone survey (including pilot study)	$ 58,000
Focus group study	8,000
Advertising pretesting	25,000
Package pretesting	14,000
Miscellaneous expenses	5,000
Proposed total expenses	$ 110,000

Since Standard was a new account with big potential, a long-term relationship with them would be valuable. (Business at L&H had been slow this year.) Feeling "under the gun," Bob met with Barry and Charles, who agreed to reduce the sample to 200 men in each of only 11 metropolitan areas.

In early November, a new problem arose. After surveying eight metro areas, Bob discovered that his assistant had accidentally deleted all questions on media habits from the questionnaire given to L&H's vendor for the phone interviews. When told of the missing questions problem, Barry and Charles became visibly angry at the vendor. After much discussion, they decided there was too little time to hire a new vendor and resample the eight areas. Therefore, they agreed to re-insert the media questions for the remaining three cities and just finish the survey.

Bob's task now was to make the most of the data he had. Because responses from each city came from a different region (east, west, and midwest), Bob felt confident that the three-city data were representative. Therefore, he decided to base the media plan on the large differences between his results and the national averages for adult men—making sports magazines and newspapers the primary vehicles for Standard's advertising (see Table 2).

Bob's confidence in the media plan was bolstered by a phone conversation with Marjorie Glass. Until a short time ago, her agency had handled the advertising for American Toiletries, so she had valuable information about this competitor's possible responses to Standard's new product. Marjorie liked Bob's recommendations, thought Charles would also approve, and agreed to support the media plan in Monday's meeting. Indeed, Bob thought, Marjorie had been a big help.

The Standard project had put a great deal of stress on Bob, who hated spending weekends away from his family—especially near Christmas! If the presentation went well and more business was forthcoming, Bob suspected he would be spending even more weekends here.

TABLE 2
Comparison of Media Habits: Three-City Sample of Male Hairspray Users Versus All U.S. Adult Males

		Three-City Sample	All U.S. Men
Magazines (at least one subscription of …)	News	28%	19%
	Entertainment	4	3
	Sports	39	20
	Other	9	6
Newspaper subscription (at least one daily)		35	14
Favorite radio format	Pop/rock	51	48
	Country	26	37
	EZ listening	7	6
	News/talk	5	4
	Other	11	5
Hours watching television per week	Total	17.5	23.5
	Dramas	6.3	8.4
	Comedies	7.8	7.3
	News	1.1	3.9
	Other	2.3	3.9

But if the presentation went poorly or the data collection errors became an issue, then Standard might look elsewhere for market research, thus jeopardizing Bob's future with L&H. Either way, he felt apprehensive.

CASE QUESTION

1. Are there any ethical issues involved in this case? If so, how serious are these issues?

Source: John R. Sparks and Shelby D. Hunt, "Marketing Researcher Ethical Sensitivity," *Journal of Marketing* (April 1998): 92–109. Reprinted with permission.

3 Types of Marketing Research

Chapter Objectives

After reading and understanding the material in this chapter, you should be able to:

- Distinguish between exploratory research and conclusive research, and discuss the role each plays in research projects.

- Illustrate five approaches to conducting exploratory research.

- Distinguish between the two types of conclusive research: descriptive and experimental.

- Distinguish between conducting a cross-sectional descriptive study and conducting a longitudinal descriptive study.

- Understand how to conduct experimental research.

- Determine which type of research to conduct.

Innovation Through Customer–Driven Research Revitalizes Maytag

Maytag Corporation is the United States' third largest manufacturer of washers, dryers, refrigerators, and vacuum cleaners.[1] Squeezed by the high-end (luxury) and the low-end (value-price) segments, Maytag needed innovative products to protect and strengthen its market-leader position. To help turn the company's fortunes around, Robert F. Hake, chairman and CEO of Maytag, formed a Strategic Initiatives Group.[2]

The Strategic Initiatives Group commissioned a variety of qualitative and quantitative marketing research studies covering many aspects of Maytag's business environment, including lifestyle trends, consumer perceptions of its many brands, and competition. Based on insights from preliminary studies (exploratory research) suggesting that affluent baby boomers are the primary driving force behind the high-end market for household appliances, the group decided to enter the market for small luxury kitchen appliances. Additonal marketing research of a more structured nature (descriptive research) showed that, although consumers associated the Maytag brand with performance and reliability, they associated the Jenn-Air brand with performance and style; for instance, the research subjects felt that the Jenn-Air brand is for "avid entertainers." Maytag therefore chose the Jenn-Air brand name for its line of appliances aimed at the small luxury appliance market.

To come up with Jenn-Air kitchen appliances that would appeal the most to the luxury segment, Maytag turned to Fitch:Worldwide,[3] a leading design consulting firm. Fitch researchers spent many hours studying customers in their kitchens (ethnographic and observational studies). Valuable insights from these studies helped Maytag develop over 200 product concepts for appliances such as stand mixers. Fitch and Maytag then screened these concepts and came up with 10 stand mixer prototypes. Focus groups were then used to test the prototypes (qualitative research). A stand mixer with a rounded body and a smaller head was the clear

winner, and set the course for the design and development of a full line of small Jenn-Air kitchen appliances. The final design for the Jenn-Air blender-mixer facilitated ease of use as well as pleasurable operation by incorporating three critical macro trends identified by the Cheskin/Fitch study:[4] convenience, authenticity, and mass-customization. The product had hand-blown glass bowls and pitchers that conveyed authenticity. The brand's name, *Attrezzi,* is Italian for "tools." Attrezzi's many options (color, material, and finish), intended to complement custom kitchen interiors and large appliances, reflected the mass-customization trend. This research-based and customer-driven design also led Maytag to develop the advertising tag line "Simply too beautiful to put away." ■

Chapter 2 described the general sequence of steps followed in conducting any marketing research project. However, the nature and type of marketing research vary depending on the unique characteristics of a given situation. Consider the following situations and try to identify similarities and differences among them.

Situation A. Modern Office Designs, Inc. (MOD), manufactures a broad line of office equipment and supplies. Through its sales force, it sells its products to a variety of organizations. Despite a healthy growth in industry sales, MOD's own sales and profits have declined during the past two years, much to the concern of MOD executives.

Situation B. Saver's National Bank (SNB) has grown rapidly since its inception a few years ago, apparently due to the unique set of financial services it offers. Although pleased with the bank's performance thus far, SNB's management is worried about growing competition from a variety of financial institutions. To consolidate SNB's current market position, the bank's executives want to ascertain the demographic composition of customers and their perceptions about the bank's strengths and weaknesses.

Situation C. Trent Eating Association (TEA) operates a chain of restaurants in eight communities of similar size and population. TEA currently has the image of a high-class restaurant chain serving excellent food at premium prices. Its president is wondering whether a 15 percent reduction in prices of all menu items would hurt or help sales revenues and profits.

A common feature among situations A, B, and C is the need for marketing research. Let's see what kind of research would best help clarify the situation for each marketer.

Exploratory Versus Conclusive Research

The management teams of MOD, SNB, and TEA all face uncertainties that marketing research can help reduce. However, if you examine the three situations carefully, you will also notice some differences among them. For instance, the purpose of any potential marketing research is less clear in the situation facing MOD than in those facing SNB and TEA.

Exploratory Research

The goal of the marketing research conducted in situation A should be to aid MOD's management in arresting the decline in sales and profits. However, some preliminary investigation should be done to identify the correct problem to be researched. Could MOD's poor market performance be a result of deteriorating quality in its products? Could it be due to lack of adequate motivation in MOD's sales force? Could it be due to ineffective promotion, resulting in weak customer awareness of and loyalty to MOD and its products? Could it be a result of increasing competition from online, "virtual" suppliers of office products? The MOD executives must examine such questions to pinpoint the most fruitful avenue for further research. Preliminary investigation of this nature is conventionally labeled *exploratory research*. **Exploratory research** aims to develop initial hunches or insights and to provide direction for any further needed research.

Exploratory research seeks to develop initial hunches or insights and to provide direction for any further research needed.

The primary purpose of exploratory research is to shed light on the nature of a situation and to identify any specific objectives or data needs to be addressed through additional research. Exploratory research is most useful when a decision maker wishes to better understand a situation or identify decision alternatives.

Conclusive Research

Unlike the situation facing MOD, the SNB and TEA scenarios imply a much clearer definition of research purpose and data requirements. The bank is particularly interested in obtaining a demographic profile of its customer base and uncovering customer perceptions of SNB's strengths and weaknesses. Research in this case should therefore focus on obtaining and analyzing demographic and perceptual data from a cross section of SNB's customers. Such research should, in turn, aid SNB in formulating a strategy to consolidate its market position.

TEA's president is interested in determining the impact of a price reduction on sales revenues and profits. The situation here is even more clear-cut, and a decision about whether or not to reduce prices can be made after marketing research determines the effect of a price reduction. Therefore, in both the SNB and the TEA scenarios, data requirements are clearer than in the MOD scenario, and the findings are more likely to lead to final decisions. Research of this nature is usually termed *conclusive research*. **Conclusive research** is intended to verify insights and to aid decision makers in selecting a specific course of action.

Conclusive research aims to verify insights and to aid decision makers in selecting a specific course of action.

The primary purpose of conclusive research, also known as *confirmatory research,* is to help decision makers choose the best course of action in a situation. It is especially useful when a decision maker already has in mind one or more alternatives and is specifically looking for information pertinent to evaluating them. Because data requirements are clearly specified in a situation calling for conclusive research, and because such research is intended as an aid in the final stages of the decision-making process, conclusive research is typically more formal and rigorous than exploratory research.

A Summary of the Differences

The purpose of a research project and the precision of its data requirements determine whether the research is exploratory or conclusive. Exploratory research is conducted when decision makers sense a need for marketing research but are unsure of the specific direction the research should take. Conclusive or confirmatory research is conducted when decision makers have a clearer idea about the types of information they want.

Although exploratory and conclusive research have distinct purposes, they both consist of the same research components. They differ only in terms of the degree of formalization and flexibility of the components, as Table 3.1 illustrates. Exploratory research projects are quite informal and flexible, as we'll see next.

Conducting Exploratory Research

There are several proven methods of conducting exploratory research, including surveys, focus groups, secondary-data analysis, case studies, and observations. We will discuss each approach next and offer some examples of how companies have used them to their advantage.

Key–Informant Technique

The **key-informant technique** involves interviewing knowledgeable individuals.

Conducting exploratory research by interviewing knowledgeable individuals is sometimes called the **key-informant technique.** (It is also known as an *expert-opinion survey* or a *lead-user survey.*) An effective way to do exploratory research is to seek out and talk to individuals with expertise in areas related to the situation

TABLE 3.1
Differences Between Exploratory and Conclusive Research

Research Project Components	Exploratory Research	Conclusive Research
Research purpose	General: To generate insights about a situation	Specific: To verify insights and aid in selecting a course of action
Data needs	Vague	Clear
Data sources	Ill defined	Well defined
Data collection form	Open-ended; rough	Usually structured
Sample	Relatively small; subjectively selected to maximize generalization of insights	Relatively large; objectively selected to permit generalization of findings
Data collection	Flexible; no set procedure	Rigid; well laid-out procedure
Data analysis	Informal; typically nonquantitative	Formal; typically quantitative
Inferences/recommendations	More tentative than final	More final than tentative

being investigated. For instance, in situation A described earlier, MOD executives can gain useful insights by informally discussing MOD's deteriorating market performance with a few key salespeople and customers. Discussions with knowledgeable salespeople may reveal whether lack of sales force motivation is a problem and, if so, whether or not it is serious enough to warrant further investigation.

CASE IN POINT ▶ **Keeping in Touch with Customers the Silicon Graphics Way**   Silicon Graphics, Inc. (SGI), provides a broad range of high-performance computing (supercomputing) and advanced graphics (visual computing) solutions. The firm earned $842 million for fiscal year 2004, with 65 percent of its business coming from the Americas, 25 percent from Europe, and 10 percent from the rest of the world.[5] Ed McCracken, then CEO of SGI, believes that traditional marketing research surveys are not very useful for picking up on major technological changes. SGI's best technologists call on industry experts, or "lighthouse customers," as they are normally known in the company.

Some of SGI's lighthouse customers are NASA, Industrial Light & Magic, the U.S. military, Boeing, Disney, and Merck. These customers' involvement and expertise in high-performance computing and graphics technology make them ideal for identifying next-generation products. SGI technologists spend a great deal of time interviewing lighthouse customers to learn how they are using SGI machines or how they would like to be able to use them. For example, the need for realistic images became evident as SGI interacted with experts from Industrial Light & Magic and Pacific Data Images. SGI developed high-performance machines that were used to create a cyborg made of liquid metal in *Terminator 2: Judgment Day,* the dinosaurs in *Jurassic Park,* and the sea creature in *The Abyss.* Lighthouse customers help SGI stay on the leading edge of high-performance computing. ◀

Silicon Graphics, Inc., used the key-informant technique in developing machines that helped create the *Jurassic Park* dinosaurs.

The key-informant technique is necessarily a very subjective and flexible procedure with no standard approach. In today's fast-changing technological world, very few individuals possess all of the relevant information about the market. Hence, careful attention must be given to the selection of knowledgeable people.[6] Indeed, this observation is not limited to business-to-business market settings; it is relevant in almost every context requiring exploratory research.

When properly used, the key-informant technique can be very productive in situations in which a decision maker senses the need for research but lacks well-defined research objectives.[7] Table 3.2 presents several such situations, along with examples of knowledgeable individuals capable of providing valuable insights in each case.

Focus Group Interviews

Talking to experts or knowledgeable individuals is not the only way to gain a better understanding of a situation calling for research. Another frequently used informal interviewing method is the focus

TABLE 3.2
Examples of Knowledgeable Individuals

Situation Calling for Exploratory Research	Knowledgeable Individuals with Useful Insights
The company producing brand X detergent, a leader in the detergent market, is interested in developing a new detergent to arrest sagging profits in a mature market.	Key research managers in appliance industries and key lead users from the dry-cleaning industry
A newly formed nonprofit organization to aid people with serious physical handicaps is wondering about the charitable programs it should develop and the strategies it should use to seek donations from the public.	Officers in well-established public service organizations, such as the United Way, the American Red Cross, and the Muscular Dystrophy Association
A high-technology company is interested in developing high-resolution images.	Key Hollywood animation researchers, NASA researchers, and x-ray specialists
A U.S. presidential candidate is wondering how to allocate campaign resources efficiently across various regions of the country.	State and local party officials with knowledge about public sentiment and attitudes in their areas

In a **focus group interview**, an objective discussion leader (or moderator) introduces a topic to a group of respondents and directs their discussion of that topic in a nonstructured and natural fashion.

group interview. In a **focus group interview** (sometimes called simply a *focus group*), an objective discussion leader introduces a topic to a group of respondents and directs their discussion of that topic in a nonstructured and natural fashion. Respondents (typically about 8 to 12) discuss a given topic in a fairly informal fashion. A well-trained researcher, called a *moderator*, leads the discussion. The moderator's primary tasks are to ensure that key aspects of the topic are discussed and to observe or record the participants' reactions. Focus groups are used in a variety of situations, such as for gaining insights about consumer acceptance of a new-product idea, identifying criteria that e-shoppers use in evaluating websites, observing reactions to a potential advertising theme, and determining types of questions to include in a consumer survey and how to word them. A major portion of Chapter 7 is devoted to focus group interviews.

CASE IN POINT ▶ **Focus Groups Help Charity: McDonald's Giving Meal**   When McDonald's restaurants in the San Francisco Bay Area were looking for a way to give back to the community, they developed the Giving Meal concept. A grown-up version of the company's popular kids' Happy Meal, the Giving Meal provided adults with a moderately sized meal and an opportunity to give back to the community. For each meal sold, the local McDonald's restaurants would donate 10 percent of the purchase price to the Ronald McDonald House Charities of the Bay Area.

In order to develop the concept and find out what would appeal to Bay Area consumers, the company used focus groups composed of local women and families. The focus groups had input into all aspects of this new product, from the content of the meal to the amount of money that McDonald's restaurants should donate for each Giving Meal sold.

McDonald's San Francisco management and the company's advertising agency, Hoffman/Lewis, were gratified by the rich input and the overwhelmingly positive response that they received from the focus groups. One focus group participant summed it up by saying, "The timing seems just right for McDonald's to do an uplifting idea such as this."[8] ◀

A focus group in progress, being observed by company representatives from behind a one-way mirror.

Analysis of Secondary Data

Secondary data, as we saw in the previous chapter, are data that have already been collected by someone else. Examining appropriate secondary data is a fast and inexpensive way to conduct exploratory research that can generate valuable insights. Such insights, in turn, will provide a proper focus for conclusive research. Sometimes the insights revealed by secondary-data analysis may even eliminate the need for conclusive research. Research in Use 3.1 illustrates how one company was able to make a final decision on the basis of secondary data obtained from external data sources.

CASE IN POINT ▶ **Secondary-Data Research Helps Kaplan Higher Education Target Potential Expansion Sites**   Kaplan Higher Education is a leading educational and career services company that provides postsecondary education to over 44,000 students at 47 colleges and schools located in 15 states. The company was looking to grow through competitive acquisitions as well as through expansion into more profitable markets. To obtain information about potential market areas to aid in its decision making, the company turned to market studies involving the use of secondary data. Specifically, it obtained from available secondary sources such demographic data as population by gender, median age, educational attainment, household income, own/rent ratio, and unemployment rate for different market areas. It then analyzed these data to identify the most appropriate target sites for its educational programs. By utilizing such secondary-data research, Kaplan Higher Education was able to evaluate potential sites in a fast and cost-efficient fashion.[9] ◄

The **case study method** is an in-depth examination of a unit of interest.

Case Study Method

The case study method is an in-depth examination of a unit of interest. The unit can be a customer, store, salesperson, firm, market area, website, and so on. By virtue of its insight-generating potential, the case study method is a useful form

Use of Secondary-Data Analysis in Decision Making: Low-Carb Diet Trend's Impact on Orange Juice Sales

Charles Torrey, marketing director for the refrigerator products division of Minute Maid, was seeing the sales of orange juice drop and wanted to know why. Between 1999 and 2004, overall consumption of orange juice by the U.S. population had dropped by some 10.8 percent. Households considered to be in the "heavy user" category—those consuming 12.5 gallons or more annually—experienced the most significant and noticeable decline. Since its introduction in the 1920s, orange juice had been a staple of the American diet, often offered as one of the standard breakfast beverages, along with coffee, across the country. So what was happening?

In order to determine what the cause of the decline might be, Torrey and his team started to research the issue. Utilizing surveys, Torrey found that approximately 10 percent of consumers were drinking less orange juice because of its calories, carbohydrates, and sugar content. In order to get a more complete picture, Torrey also looked at a great deal of secondary data, including nutrition journals and periodicals. What he found was that an estimated 4 percent of consumers might be avoiding the beverage because of the trend of low-carbohydrate diets.

By examining such secondary-data sources, Torrey was able to get a better understanding of consumers' eating and food-purchasing behaviors in general, and of their reduced consumption of orange juice in particular. In the process, he identified a potential consumer need that was not being met: low-carbohydrate orange juice. "When we can, we take the opportunity to do innovations to create a niche that will drive sales," said Torrey. In response to the opportunity, Minute Maid developed an orange juice line called Minute Maid Premium Light, with half the carbohydrates, sugar, and calories of regular orange juice.[a]

of exploratory research. The following example illustrates the use of case studies in a marketing context.

> **SCENARIO** Allied Associates Company (AAC) is a national chain of discount stores with more than 500 retail outlets across the country. During the past several years, the company's sales have grown rapidly, and its profitability has remained above the industry average. Top management wants to identify the key elements crucial to the company's success and to capitalize on these elements. Where and how should it start looking to accomplish these objectives?

The AAC scenario fits a research setting likely to benefit from the case study method; that is, it is a setting in which the company has a general research objective but is unsure of exactly what it is looking for. Moreover, we can view each AAC retail outlet as a separate case and gain valuable insights by thoroughly examining certain selected ones. For instance, we can study the three best-performing and the three worst-performing stores in depth on numerous dimensions. Store size and layout, product lines carried, employee morale, and trade area characteristics are but a few of the factors for which we can collect data. In a case study, only the investigator's time and imagination limit the number and types of factors to be examined.

We can gain insights about factors critical to AAC's success by looking for similarities and differences between two types of cases, namely, the best- and the worst-performing stores. For instance, if employee morale is higher in all three of the best stores than in any of the worst stores, employee morale is likely to be critical to AAC's success. In contrast, a factor such as product lines carried is likely to be less important, although not necessarily unimportant, if both types of stores carry the same product lines. Insights like these can help researchers single out key determinants of performance variations across AAC stores. Before devoting attention and resources to the critical factors identified by the case analysis, top management may want to verify the association between the factors and store performance through a focused examination of a larger number of AAC stores. Such a study would, of course, constitute conclusive research.

As the AAC example illustrates, the analysis of case data is nonquantitative and primarily involves numerous comparisons and contrasts of the data. It requires an alert investigator capable of recognizing even subtle differences across cases, as well as possible relationships among factors within a case.

▌ Observational Method

The **observational method** involves human or mechanical observation of what people actually do or what events take place during a buying or consumption situation.

The **observational method** involves human or mechanical observation of what people actually do or what events take place during a buying or consumption situation. In this method of data collection, researchers or mechanical/electronic devices witness and record information as events occur or compile evidence from past events. Observational research is useful in assessing such behavior as use of products, frequency of store visits, teens shopping with or without supervision, use of media, and time spent on specific websites. It is particularly useful in researching the behavior of young children, a group not typically amenable to many research techniques.

Mechanical, electronic, audio, and video monitors, as well as humans, can provide a variety of objective measures of behavior. Japanese managers routinely visit wholesalers and retailers to get a feel for the market. They often change their marketing strategies based on their observations.[10] Many U.S. companies increasingly rely on observational techniques to design products. Whirlpool Corporation, a U.S. appliance company based in Michigan, designed new controls for its appliances after observing users worldwide. Steelcase Inc., based in Grand Rapids, Michigan, created an entirely new office space design concept after observing interactions among clients' employees. Rubbermaid routinely sends its employees to consumers' homes to observe home storage practices. Ford Motor Company has been collecting observational data using video ethnography (which involves videotaping users interacting with products in daily life).[11]

Paul Malboeuf, manager of global advanced products research at Ford, said that the company's use of video ethnography was

> not so much to understand what people do, but to understand who they are and how they live. There is something much more real and immediate to the users of the information in seeing and interacting with the people in their own environment. Allowing the designers and engineers to experience who the target customers are and to understand how those customers may differ from you has led to a different perspective and mind-set for the people who are planning and designing our products.[12]

A major portion of Chapter 6 is devoted to observational techniques.

Exploratory research is not limited to the five methods just described—interviews with knowledgeable individuals, focus group interviews, analysis of secondary data, case studies, and observational techniques—although these are the most frequently used methods. Variations or combinations of these methods can also be employed in an exploratory research project. Research in Use 3.2 demonstrates how 3M uses various research methods to discover new product ideas.

Insights gained through exploratory research pave the way for conclusive research. In fact, many research projects involve an exploratory phase followed by a conclusive phase. The next section discusses two different kinds of conclusive research.

Discovering New Market Needs:
3M Shows the Way

Rita Shor, a senior product specialist in 3M's Medical-Surgical Markets Division, had been charged with developing a breakthrough product for the surgical drapes unit. Surgical drapes are thin plastic films applied to a patient's skin to protect from infection during surgery. Total sales of this product amounted to $100 million annually. However, the drapes market was languishing. Shor noted, "Our business unit has been going nowhere. We're number one in the surgical drapes market, but we're stagnating. We need to identify new customer needs. If we don't bring in radically new products, management may have little choice but to sell off the business."

Shor assembled a team to develop a better type of disposable surgical draping. The team researched external secondary sources and talked to experts to better understand the foundations of the markets they wanted to target and key trends in infection control. However, they soon realized that the team didn't know the needs of surgeons and hospitals in developing countries, where infectious diseases are still a major problem. They traveled in pairs to hospitals in Malaysia, Indonesia, Korea, and India to observe how doctors in less than ideal environments keep infections from spreading in the operating room (field observation).

The team found that doctors relied on antibiotics to prevent the spread of infection. This observation made them realize that the hospitals cannot afford surgical drapes and therefore require a cheaper and much more effective way to prevent infections from starting or spreading. Their eagerness to find an alternative solution led the team next to veterinarians and Hollywood makeup artists. From leading veterinary hospitals, they found that veterinarians keep infection rates low despite facing difficult conditions and cost constraints. To their surprise, the team also learned that Hollywood makeup artists use materials that do not irritate the skin and are easy to remove, an important consideration in the design of infection control materials.

The team invited several lead users (doctors, veterinarians, and Hollywood artists) to a two-and-

a-half-day workshop. The objective of the conference was to find a breakthrough, low-cost approach to infection control. The participants were divided into small groups for in-depth analysis of the problems surrounding infection control and were given the task of identifying creative ideas as well as technical constraints. The workshop generated six new-product concepts, of which the team chose three for 3M to pursue:

1. The economy line of surgical drapes, made with existing 3M technology to appeal to increasingly cost-conscious buyers.

2. The "skin doctor" line of hand-held devices, which would layer antimicrobial substances onto a patient's skin and vacuum up blood and other liquids during surgery. These products could be developed from existing 3M technology.

3. The "armor" line, which would coat catheters and tubes with antimicrobial protection. These products could also be developed from existing 3M technology and would enable 3M to compete not only in the current surface infection market but also in the blood-borne, urinary tract, and respiratory infections market.

In addition to coming up with the new concepts, the team learned from the experts that a new approach to infection control was needed. In the present environment, every patient received the same degree of protection. However, based on lead-user interviews, it became clear to the team that patients suffering from malnutrition or diabetes are particularly susceptible to infection and therefore require infection control treatment before surgery to reduce their likelihood of contracting disease during surgery. Shor's team strongly believes that the lead-user technique helped them come up with breakthrough ideas for the Medical-Surgical Markets Group that will not only revive the group's business prospects but also improve the quality of life for surgical patients around the world.[b]

Conclusive Research: Descriptive Versus Experimental

There are two basic forms of conclusive research: descriptive research and experimental research. The distinction between the two is based on the primary purpose of a conclusive research project and the nature of the inferences one can draw from it.

Descriptive Research

Descriptive research aims to describe something.

The goal of **descriptive research** is essentially, as its name implies, to describe something. Specifically, it generates data describing the composition and characteristics of relevant groups of units, such as customers, salespeople, organizations, and market areas. Data collected through descriptive research can provide valuable information about the study units along relevant characteristics and also about associations among those characteristics. The following examples illustrate the use of descriptive research in a marketing context.

CASE IN POINT ▶ **2004 World Economic Forum Survey** The World Economic Forum (www.weforum.org) is an independent international organization that brings together global leaders from all walks of life to pursue economic and social activity that will improve the state of the world. Its members include the world's 1,000 leading companies and over 200 small businesses. The forum's annual meeting of world business leaders and heads of state in Davos, Switzerland, every January helps shape the global business agenda. The forum conducts an annual global survey known as the Voice of the Leaders survey. Its Global Competitiveness Report, a popular document widely used by many business leaders and academic researchers, uses insights from the Voice of the Leaders survey. For its 2004 survey, the World Economic Forum sent its members a questionnaire about a variety of issues affecting today's business world and asked them to return the completed questionnaires by fax. A total of 132 members participated in the survey. The findings served as a backdrop for the discussions at the January annual meeting. For example, most members believed that the next generation is most likely to live in a prosperous, but unsafe, world (see Exhibit 3.1). According to the survey participants, quality of products or services, corporate brand reputation/integrity, and profitability are the three most important measures of corporate success (see Exhibit 3.2). The results also revealed that business leaders consider brand reputation/integrity to be very important to their corporate strategy (see Exhibit 3.3).[13] ◀

Experimental Research

Experimental research allows one to make causal inferences about relationships among variables.

A drawback of descriptive research is that it generally cannot provide the type of evidence necessary to make causal inferences about relationships among variables. In contrast, **experimental research** (also known as *causal research*) allows one to make such causal inferences (such as how variable X affects variable Y). To be able to say that X (for instance, shelf space assigned to a product in a supermarket or the size of a company website's "click" button for a product) has a causal influence on Y (unit sales of the product; number of times that website visitors click on the button), we must gather data under controlled conditions—that is, holding constant, or neutralizing the effect of, all variables other than X that are capable of influencing Y and systematically manipulating the levels of X to study its impact on Y. Manipulation of the presumed causal variable and control of other relevant variables are distinct features of experimental research.

Exhibit 3.1
Security and Prosperity—World Economic Forum Survey, 2004
Source: Based on 2004 Annual Meeting Survey, "A Report to World Economic Forum," January 2004, p. 7. Fleishman-Hillard Knowledge Solutions, St. Louis, MO.

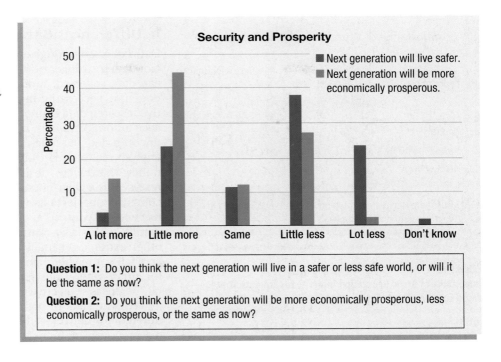

Exhibit 3.2
Measure of Corporate Success—The Top Three—World Economic Forum Survey, 2004
Source: Based on 2004 Annual Meeting Survey, "A Report to World Economic Forum," January 2004, p. 11. Fleishman-Hillard Knowledge Solutions, St. Louis, MO.

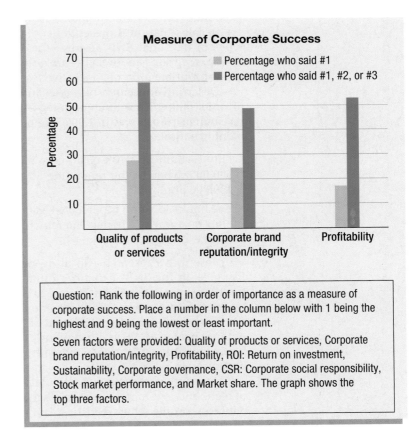

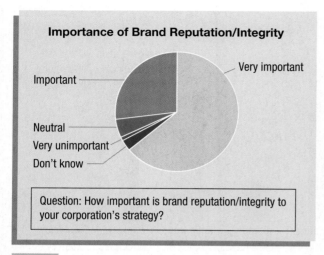

Importance of Brand Reputation/Integrity

Very important

Important

Neutral

Very unimportant

Don't know

Question: How important is brand reputation/integrity to your corporation's strategy?

Exhibit 3.3
Importance of Brand Reputation/Integrity to Corporate Strategy—World Economic Forum Survey, 2004
Source: Based on 2004 Annual Meeting Survey, "A Report to World Economic Forum," January 2004, pp. 12, 15. Fleishman-Hillard Knowledge Solutions, St. Louis, MO.

Differences Between the Two Types

Data collected through experimental research can provide much stronger evidence of cause and effect than can data collected through descriptive research. This does not necessarily mean that analysis of descriptive research data cannot suggest possible causal linkages among variables, especially when the effects of uncontrolled variables are filtered through certain analysis techniques available for that purpose. In fact, rather than view descriptive versus experimental research as a clear-cut dichotomy, we should think of conclusive projects as varying from "purely descriptive with no control" at one extreme to "purely experimental with strict control and manipulation" at the other extreme. Virtually all real-life conclusive projects fall somewhere along this continuum, although the point where "descriptive" ends and "experimental" begins is subjective and somewhat arbitrary.

For the sake of highlighting and illustrating key differences between the two types of conclusive research, we will focus for the time being on projects falling toward either end of the research continuum. In other words, in the following discussion we will use the terms *descriptive research* and *experimental research* cautiously, bearing in mind that they represent varying degrees of the same elements: control and manipulation.

Recall situation B presented earlier, about Saver's National Bank (SNB). The types of data that SNB desires—the demographic profile of its customers and their perceptions about SNB—are descriptive data. Hence, descriptive research is the appropriate form of conclusive research to use.

Descriptive research of a relevant group of units can reveal the proportion of units falling into different categories of a variable. For instance, descriptive research using a survey of 1,000 SNB customers might provide the following types of information:

- Fifty percent of SNB's customers have an annual family income of less than $30,000, whereas the remaining 50 percent have an annual family income of $30,000 or more.

- The bank's location is perceived as convenient (hence a strength) by 60 percent of its customers, whereas the remaining 40 percent perceive it as inconvenient (hence a weakness).

Descriptive research can also point out associations among variables. For instance, in the SNB scenario, simultaneous analysis of data pertaining to customer income levels and perceptions about location may reveal that, although 90 percent of customers with an income level less than $30,000 perceive SNB's location as convenient, only 30 percent of customers with an income level of $30,000 or more perceive SNB as conveniently located. In other words, customers' income levels are apparently associated with their perceptions about SNB's location, as illustrated in Table 3.3.

Descriptive research can provide profile descriptions (such as the proportion of high- and low-income customers in SNB's clientele) and point out associations between profile characteristics (such as the association between customer

TABLE 3.3
Association Between Customers' Income Level and Perceptions

	Number (%) of Customers Perceiving SNB as		
Customers' Income Level	Conveniently Located	Not Conveniently Located	Total
Less than $30,000	450 (90%)	50 (10%)	500 (100%)
$30,000 or more	150 (30%)	350 (70%)	500 (100%)

income levels and perceptions about location). But it cannot establish cause and effect between characteristics of interest. The strong association between customers' income levels and perceptions of SNB's location does not imply that the former is the cause of the latter. On the basis of descriptive data, to conclude that there is a causal linkage between higher income levels and unfavorable perceptions about location would be erroneous—and, in SNB's case, even a bit ridiculous. For instance, most of SNB's higher-income customers may reside in areas far away from SNB. If so, their perceptions about its location may have more to do with where they live than with their income level. The analysis of data on income level and perceptions did not control for the possible influence of the location of customer residences in relation to SNB's location. To make causal inferences with confidence, we must conduct experimental research, as described later in Chapter 8. General approaches used in conducting descriptive research are discussed next.

Conducting Descriptive Research

Descriptive research, or research falling closer to the descriptive end than to the experimental end of the research continuum, is by far the more frequently used form of conclusive research. On the basis of the general data collection approach used, we classify descriptive research studies into two basic types: cross-sectional studies and longitudinal studies.

Cross-sectional studies are one-time studies involving data collection at a single period in time.

Longitudinal studies are repeated-measurement studies that collect data over several periods in time.

Cross-sectional studies are one-time studies involving data collection at a single period in time. The World Economic Forum Survey presented earlier is a good example of a cross-sectional study. **Longitudinal studies** are repeated-measurement studies that collect data over several periods in time. Whereas a cross-sectional study yields a "snapshot" of a situation being researched, a longitudinal study produces a "motion picture" (or a series of snapshots) of a situation over time. In general, longitudinal studies are more informative than cross-sectional studies, just as motion pictures are more revealing than still pictures. But longitudinal studies are also more expensive. Further, the choice between the two depends on the objectives of the research.

A cross-sectional study makes use of a *cross-sectional sample,* or a group of units (consumers, stores, organizations) selected specifically and solely for the one-time data collection. The sample is disbanded after the data are collected. A longitudinal study typically employs a *panel,* or a group of units recruited to provide measurements over a period of time. At the conclusion of each measurement phase, the panel is kept intact for future use.

Thus a clear distinction exists between a cross-sectional sample and a panel. However, the distinction is blurred in practice. Sometimes cross-sectional

Interviewing the same family once every six months is an example of a longitudinal study.

samples are used in longitudinal studies, and panels (or certain segments of panels) are used in cross-sectional studies.

For example, suppose the U.S. Department of Defense wants to ascertain people's attitudes toward nuclear weapons and nuclear warfare, and to monitor changes in those attitudes over time. Specifically, suppose the Department of Defense wants to measure the public's attitudes on a quarterly basis. The appropriate research design is clearly a longitudinal study. However, researchers need not necessarily set up a panel of respondents for this purpose. Rather, they can select a separate cross-sectional sample of people for each quarterly measurement. In fact, using cross-sectional samples instead of a panel of respondents may have advantages, as we will see later. The point is that a cross-sectional study and the use of a cross-sectional sample (or a longitudinal study and the use of a panel) do not always go together.

Cross–Sectional Studies

We saw earlier that descriptive research is the more frequently used form of conclusive research. The most popular method within the domain of descriptive research is the cross-sectional study. Also, cross-sectional studies account for the majority of formal research projects involving primary-data collection.

By definition, a cross-sectional study involves data collection at only one period in time. However, we can also use cross-sectional studies to obtain data pertaining to different periods in time. In other words, the *scope* of the data collected is not necessarily limited to the time at which a cross-sectional study is conducted. The following example clarifies this point.

> **SCENARIO** Capital Online Company (COC) wants to obtain a descriptive profile of consumers who use the Internet. Specifically, COC wants to know the demographic composition and use characteristics of such consumers (for instance, shopped online, bought online, items shopped for online, frequency of purchasing online, location from which online purchases were made, likelihood of buying online in the future, disclosure of credit card and social security numbers, gift items bought online, and willingness to trade online). The company is considering a cross-sectional study involving a random sample of consumers.

Can COC obtain data other than current demographic and use characteristics through the cross-sectional study? Yes, it can. For instance, it can ask the study respondents about their past online purchases of products and services: What brands did they buy online in the past year? Was their past online usage more than, about the same as, or less than their current usage? Similarly, it can ask about *future* consumption: Do the respondents intend to continue buying products and services online? Do they plan to change their online usage during the coming year? Answers to questions like these can be valuable to COC in understanding the dynamics of online usage patterns.

The COC example implies that a cross-sectional study is capable of yielding longitudinal data of sorts, that is, data pertaining to an interval of time rather than to a single point in time. Indeed, many cross-sectional studies collect longitudinal data of this nature. However, a rather serious limitation of such data is that their accuracy depends heavily on the quality of respondents' memories of past events and intentions about future behavior. For the most part, consumers' memories are unreliable, particularly with respect to things that occurred very far in the past. Hans Zeisel makes this point clearly:

> The memory of a minor expenditure, or a fleeting observation, will disappear within days. Moreover, to rely on memory is always a treacherous undertaking, because of unconscious and even conscious forces that tend to distort it. The question, for instance, "For whom did you vote?" asked one day after election day, will always elicit too many votes for the victorious candidate.[14]

Likewise, consumer intentions may be a poor indicator of future behavior.[15] This problem becomes increasingly severe as the time frame extends further into the future. A longitudinal study is much more reliable than a cross-sectional study for monitoring changes over time, because it relies less on consumers' mental capabilities and more frequently monitors events as close to their time of occurrence as is feasible.

The sample used in a cross-sectional study is typically selected solely for one-time data collection and is disbanded after the data collection. However, several firms, especially certain commercial marketing research firms, maintain omnibus panels as a source of samples for cross-sectional studies. Firms maintaining omnibus panels have the capability to custom-design cross-sectional samples to meet specific research requirements. Such samples are composed of panel members who are returned to the panel after participating in a cross-sectional study.

CASE IN POINT ▶ **Rising Popularity of Omnibus Panels**   In recent times, omnibus panels are becoming increasingly popular as a source of consumer insights. Consolidation mania in the marketing research industry has led to the development of global omnibus panels, including many specialized niches. Global research companies are developing multicountry panels to serve their global clients. Synovate (www.synovate.com), a leading global research company, operates 11 different omnibus panels, including AsiaBUS, eNation, Global Omnibus, TeenNation, and TeleNación. Ocean Spray (www.oceanspray.com), the United States' number-one brand of canned and bottled juice drinks, has signed a multiyear agreement with Information Resources, Inc. (IRI; www.infores.com), for syndicated marketplace tracking information covering all mass core outlets, including convenience stores. IRI will also provide Ocean Spray with detailed consumer behavior insights through IRI's 75,000-member Consumer Network Household Panel. Japan's Intage Inc. (www.intage.co.jp) maintains a ladies-only panel of 10,175 participants.[16] ACNielsen (www.acnielsen.com), a unit of VNU, a global research firm, is aggressively expanding its Homescan Panel, consisting of 125,000 households, to enable client companies to better serve specific niches and to identify new ones by collecting information from specialty panels such as households with babies and households with teens. Greenfield Online's (www.greenfieldonline.com) Hispanic Panel gives access to English-dominant, bilingual, and Spanish-dominant Hispanics. Exhibit 3.4 presents descriptive profiles of Hispanics using selected characteristics based on data from the Greenfield Online Hispanic Panel. ◀

Exhibit 3.4
Greenfield Online's Hispanic
Panel—Selected Characteristics
Source: "White Paper on Online Research and
Hispanics: Clicking onto a $600 Billion Annual
Market," www.greenfieldonline.com.

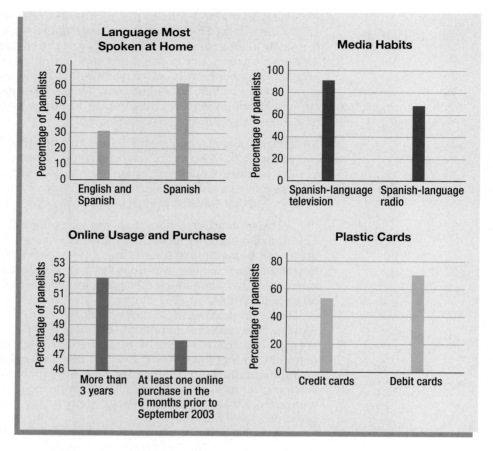

Longitudinal Studies

The primary purpose of longitudinal studies is to monitor changes over time.[17] The following examples illustrate situations calling for longitudinal studies:

- Coca-Cola is interested in keeping track of consumers' use of types and brands of beverages.

- J. D. Power and Associates wishes to monitor customers' satisfaction with national Internet service providers.

- The American Medical Association wants to ascertain whether and how people's eating and drinking habits vary from season to season.

Successive measurements in longitudinal studies can be obtained from a physically different but representative sample of units or from the same sample of units each time. Although both sample options will yield longitudinal data, the nature of the findings and the implications can differ, as the next example demonstrates.

SCENARIO   The marketer of brand X wishes to monitor X's share versus competing brands. For simplicity, let us assume that only two other brands compete with brand X: brand Y and brand Z. At the end of each suitable period (say, a month or a quarter), the marketer can survey a different cross section of product users and ascertain the brands they use. Alternatively, the marketer can form a panel of users and ask the panel members to periodically report the brands they use; in this case, the same respondents will provide data during the course of the study.

TABLE 3.4
Results of Longitudinal Brand Use Study

Use of	Period 1	Period 2
	Number of Consumers Using Each Brand at the End	
Brand X	40	42
Brand Y	30	29
Brand Z	30	29
Total	100	100

Suppose the marketer surveys a different but representative sample of 100 users for each measurement and obtains the results shown in Table 3.4. Two insights pertaining to the marketer's research objective emerge from Table 3.4. First, brand X is the leader with roughly a 40 percent share (because the sample size is 100, the number of users of a brand can be interpreted as the brand's percentage share of the market). Second, the overall percentage shares of the three brands seem to have remained stable over time.

The type of information provided by the longitudinal study would be somewhat different if the marketer had used the same sample of users for each measurement. Such a panel study, in addition to indicating overall brand shares, would have permitted the firm to monitor brands used by individual users from period to period. Tracking brand use at the individual-user level will shed light on how the brands achieved their overall shares at the end of each period. This additional information will be available only if the same sample of users is surveyed at each data collection phase.

Tables 3.5 and 3.6 demonstrate this point by providing two alternative sets of results, case 1 and case 2. In both tables, the numbers under "Row Total" represent brand shares at the end of period 1, and the numbers opposite "Column Total" represent brand shares at the end of period 2. The overall brand shares at the end of periods 1 and 2 in Tables 3.5 and 3.6 are identical to those in Table 3.4.

TABLE 3.5
Changes in Brand Shares: Case 1

Number of Consumers Using Each Brand at the End of Period 1	X	Y	Z	Row Total
	Number of Consumers Using Each Brand at the End of Period 2			
X	17	21	2	40
Y	23	5	2	30
Z	2	3	25	30
Column Total	42	29	29	100

TABLE 3.6
Changes in Brand Shares: Case 2

Number of Consumers Using Each Brand at the End of Period 1	X	Y	Z	Row Total
	Number of Consumers Using Each Brand at the End of Period 2			
X	38	1	1	40
Y	2	27	1	30
Z	2	1	27	30
Column Total	42	29	29	100

Hence, the inferences we made earlier about the overall shares of brands X, Y, and Z still hold. However, Tables 3.5 and 3.6 contain additional data about how each brand obtained its overall share. The first row of numbers in Table 3.5 reveals that, of the 40 consumers who bought brand X in period 1, 17 bought brand X again in period 2, 21 switched to brand Y, and 2 switched to brand Z. Now consider the first row of numbers in Table 3.6. These numbers reveal that, of the 40 consumers who bought brand X in period 1, 38 bought brand X again in period 2, 1 switched to brand Y, and 1 switched to brand Z. The other two rows in each table can be interpreted in similar fashion.

According to Table 3.5 (case 1), although all three brands have stable shares, only brand Z appears to enjoy brand loyalty; a majority of X and Y users switched brands during each period. In contrast, Table 3.6 (case 2) shows all three brands having stable shares and enjoying high brand loyalty. Clearly, the marketing implications emerging for brand X from case 1 are quite different from those emerging from case 2.

True-Panel Studies

A longitudinal study using the same sample of respondents will provide richer information than one using a series of different samples. Indeed, the dynamics of changes between measurements can be captured only by using the same panel of respondents. Such a panel has been labeled a *true panel* to distinguish it from omnibus panels used to generate different cross-sectional samples at various periods in time.[18]

A true-panel study, compared with a longitudinal study using different samples for the various measurements, is also capable of generating more data directly pertaining to the research purpose, for the following reasons:

1. A true panel is a captive sample of willing respondents who are likely to tolerate extended interviews or fill out lengthy questionnaires.

2. Background data such as demographic and lifestyle information need not be collected from panel respondents during each measurement. Therefore, for a given interview or questionnaire length, more data of primary research interest can be collected.[19]

Drawbacks of Consumer Panels

Consumer panels are not without drawbacks. A major difficulty in setting up a panel is identifying a representative sample of respondents who are willing to cooperate over a long period of time. Certain types of consumer groups are especially hard to recruit for panels. Examples of such groups include nonwhites, homemakers under 25, and illiterate persons. Even if a researcher initially succeeds in putting together a representative panel, some attrition of panel members will occur during a longitudinal study. As a result, the panel may no longer be representative unless the departing members are replaced with similar new members—an expensive and time-consuming task. Another potential problem with consumer panels is that the multiple-survey participation by panel members may, over a period of time, induce them to alter their natural or usual behavior. Seymour Sudman and Robert Ferber label this difficulty *panel conditioning* and illustrate it as follows:

> A homemaker who keeps a weekly purchase diary with a separate section for canned goods may feel guilty about not having made any such purchases recently and may deliberately purchase some canned goods to be able to record it in the diary. In a similar fashion, a family asked month after month

about ownership of savings accounts may decide to open a savings account, even though they originally had no such intention.[20]

Most commercial marketing research firms operating consumer panels take steps to ensure that the behavior of panel members is normal and that the reporting of such behavior is accurate. They drop families from the panel at the families' request or if the families fail to return three of their last five diaries. In addition, most companies eliminate family members after four to five years of reporting, because buying behavior may change after detailed reporting of purchases over this period of time. Obviously, precautionary procedures like these add to the expense of maintaining and operating a panel. Nevertheless, they are necessary if panel data are to be trusted.

Because of the potential limitations of true panels, researchers may be wise to restrict their use to situations in which periodic monitoring of the same respondents is essential. The unique capabilities of a true panel will not be needed when the purpose of a longitudinal study is merely to track variables at a macro, or aggregate, level. Under those circumstances, choosing several cross-sectional samples from the general population—or from a suitable omnibus panel if a special type of sample is required—may be better than using a true panel.

Conducting Experimental Research

Experimental research is intended to generate the type of evidence necessary for confidently making causal inferences about relationships among variables. This method overcomes the lack of control suffered by descriptive research projects through collecting data in an environment in which the hypothesized causal variable is manipulated and the effects of other relevant variables are controlled.

To illustrate, consider a consumer goods firm that wants to determine the impact of advertising on sales. To accomplish this objective, the firm can proceed as follows:

1. Select a group of distinct market areas that have similar demographic, socio-economic, and competitor characteristics.
2. Vary the level of advertising expenditure from market to market, keeping all other marketing variables, such as price and promotion, constant.
3. Monitor sales over a sufficient length of time.
4. Analyze the data to see whether the pattern of variation in sales across markets is consistent with the pattern of variation in advertising expenditures.

These steps constitute an experimental rather than a descriptive research approach because factors other than advertising that can influence sales are, by and large, held constant. Assuming that no major differences in external conditions (for instance, a sudden change in the unemployment rate or competitive activity in some markets but not in others) occur within the group of markets during the research period, variations in sales can be attributed to variations in advertising expenditures.

In contrast, data on advertising and sales gathered through a descriptive research project—such as a survey of a representative sample of consumer goods firms asking them to indicate their advertising expenditures and sales revenues during some past period—cannot provide as strong an indication of cause and effect. A positive correlation between advertising and sales revealed by an analysis of descriptive survey data cannot be interpreted to mean that higher advertising will lead to higher sales. There are two reasons why. First, although high advertising expenditures and high sales apparently occurred together, the latter might be due to other factors, such as the larger sizes or more favorable competitive positions of firms reporting higher sales. Second, the sample firms may have allocated a certain portion of their past sales or anticipated sales to their advertising budget, as is frequently done in practice; if so, sales levels determine advertising levels rather than vice versa.

To make causal inferences with confidence, then, we must manipulate the causal variable (in this case, advertising) and effectively control the other variables. Another condition is that the causal variable (advertising) and the effect variable (sales) must occur in the proper time sequence. To ascertain whether advertising causes sales, for instance, we must change advertising levels first, without their being influenced by anticipated sales; any changes in sales must be measured later.

To further illustrate how experimental research is conducted, consider the TEA example described in situation C earlier in the chapter. The president of TEA wants to determine the impact on sales revenues and profits when price is manipulated (price is reduced by 15 percent). An experimental research study can be set up for situation C, as outlined next.

The eight communities with TEA restaurants have similar characteristics. Hence, we can arbitrarily divide the eight restaurants into two equivalent groups: group A and group B. We drop prices by 15 percent in the group A restaurants but maintain them at current levels in the group B restaurants. After a few weeks, we compare sales revenues and profits for groups A and B. Any significant differences between the two groups will indicate a causal impact of the price reduction on sales revenues and profits. Assuming that all other factors capable of influencing sales or profits remained at similar levels in groups A and B during the research, we can unambiguously attribute any significant difference in sales revenues or profits between the two groups to the price reduction.

The design of our TEA study is a two-group experimental design using an experimental group (A) and a control group (B). Because the two groups are equivalent except for the change in the causal variable (price reduction) in group A, the control group captures all influences on the effect variable (sales or profits) other than that of the causal variable.

We can, however, use the following alternative approach if dividing the eight restaurants into equivalent experimental and control groups is not feasible. We monitor the sales revenues and profits of the eight restaurants for several weeks. We then drop prices by 15 percent in all eight restaurants but leave all other marketing variables unchanged. We then monitor sales revenues and profits of the eight restaurants again for the same number of weeks as before. Any significant differences between the before and after measurements will shed light on the causal impact of the price reduction on sales revenue and profits. This approach is known as a *one-group, before-after* experimental design.

Determining Which Type of Research to Conduct

Choosing the most appropriate type of research in a situation—exploratory or conclusive—is somewhat subjective. The choice depends not only on the nature of the situation but also on how the decision maker and researcher perceive it. Exploratory research is most appropriate in situations in which the research objectives are general and data requirements are unclear. Some form of conclusive research is appropriate in other situations. Insights gained through exploratory research typically form the foundation for more formal conclusive research. Occasionally, however, exploratory research results may strongly suggest that further research of a conclusive nature may be unnecessary or unproductive.

In situations calling for conclusive research, the choice of the type of conclusive research, descriptive or experimental, depends on whether testing causal relationships among variables is the primary research purpose. If so, some form of experimental research is appropriate; if not, descriptive research will suffice. Of course, as implied in earlier sections of this chapter, the descriptive-versus-experimental distinction exists more along a research continuum than as a clear-cut dichotomy. Therefore, we may at times be able to make tentative causal statements on the basis of data from a well-designed and -conducted descriptive research study. By the same token, we can rarely conduct a pure experimental research study. As we will see in Chapter 8, many experimental research studies suffer from varying degrees of lack of control, owing to resource, environmental, and other constraints. Exhibit 3.5 is a flow diagram that offers general guidelines for identifying the most appropriate research types to employ in a situation calling for research.

Exhibit 3.5
Flow Diagram for Selecting the Appropriate Research Type

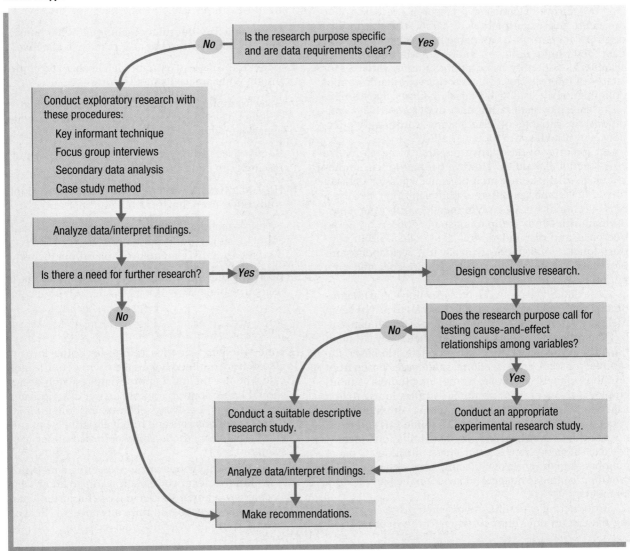

SUMMARY

We can broadly divide marketing research into exploratory research and conclusive research. Exploratory research seeks to develop initial hunches or insights and to provide direction for any further research needed, whereas conclusive research aims to verify insights and to aid decision makers in selecting a specific course of action.

Frequently used approaches for conducting exploratory research include interviewing knowledgeable individuals (the key-informant technique), focus group interviews, analysis of secondary data, the case study method, and the observation method. From the researcher's standpoint, these approaches are quite flexible. The effectiveness of exploratory research depends to a large degree on the researcher's resourcefulness and skills.

Two forms of conclusive research are descriptive re-search and experimental research. The purpose of descriptive research, as its name implies, is to generate data describing units of interest and to enable researchers to identify associations among variables or factors of interest. However, descriptive research cannot unambiguously establish causal linkages. Experimental research, by generating data under controlled conditions, is capable of establishing cause and effect between variables with more certainty.

A majority of descriptive research projects involve cross-sectional studies. However, longitudinal studies are used when the research objective calls for data on the same variables at different points in time. Because a cross-sectional study involves merely a one-time measurement, the study sample is usually chosen on an ad hoc basis and disbanded after data collection. In contrast, longitudinal studies typically use permanent samples, called *panels*, from which data are collected on a periodic basis.

The differences between cross-sectional and longitudinal studies are less clear in practice than they may seem in theory. Many cross-sectional studies of consumers collect data relating to past and future behavior, although the accuracy of such data is questionable. Moreover, the samples for some cross-sectional studies are chosen from omnibus panels. Likewise, some longitudinal studies employ a series of cross-sectional samples rather than a true panel (fixed sample) of respondents. Although a true panel is capable of generating more numerous and more revealing data, it has serious potential limitations, including lack of panel representativeness, attrition of panel members and the costs of replacing them, and panel conditioning leading to atypical behavior on the part of panel members.

Conducting experimental research involves collecting data in an environment wherein the hypothesized causal variable is manipulated and the effects of other relevant variables are controlled. A variety of approaches or designs are available for performing experimental research.

Exploratory research is useful for gaining initial insights when research objectives are general and data requirements are vague. Conclusive research is appropriate when research objectives are specific and data requirements are clear-cut.

ACE
self-test

REVIEW AND DISCUSSION QUESTIONS

1. What is the basic difference between exploratory and conclusive research?

2. Construct a scenario of your own in which exploratory research would be most appropriate. Construct another in which conclusive research would be most appropriate.

3. What is the key-informant technique? What precautions should a researcher take to make it effective?

4. When is the case study approach likely to be appropriate? What are its distinct features?

5. Give examples of your own to illustrate when to conduct descriptive research and when to conduct experimental research.

6. Briefly discuss the types of information descriptive research can and cannot provide.

7. How do the nature and purpose of a cross-sectional study differ from those of a longitudinal study?

8. "A cross-sectional study can generate data only about a single point in time." Do you agree or disagree with this statement? Explain your answer.

9. What are the advantages and the limitations of using true panels?

APPLICATION EXERCISES

1. Four different scenarios calling for some form of research are outlined below. For each scenario, indicate whether the most appropriate research design should be exploratory or conclusive; descriptive or experimental; or cross-sectional or longitudinal. Explain your answers and briefly describe what specific research methods you would use under each scenario.

   a. An industrial goods firm is expecting a recession within the next two years. It wants to know what changes, if any, it should make in its current marketing strategy to minimize any adverse effect on its performance because of a recession.

b. A firm marketing an established brand of home computer is concerned about a new brand just introduced by a competitor. It wishes to monitor how the new brand will affect the market share of its own brand and those of its competitors during the next 12 months.

c. A packaged foods firm has developed a new frozen dinner that it believes is superior to other frozen dinners already on the market. It wants to develop a unique promotional theme for the new dinner to set it apart from competing brands and appeal to a broad cross section of consumers.

d. A large bank currently has more than 20,000 loan customers. It is concerned about the increasing number of customers who are defaulting on their loans. It therefore wants to know whether customers with good payment records differ from those who have defaulted recently. Specifically, the bank wants information on each of the following characteristics: age, sex, income, occupation, marital status, and past credit record.

2. Sea Side Boats, a retail chain that sells consumer watercraft, is experiencing a sales decline in some of its retail stores. Although Sea Side is doing well overall, only two of its eight locations are performing beyond projections; the rest are lagging behind to different degrees. Sea Side is concerned about what to do with the six underperforming locations. The owner, a good friend of yours, has come to you for advice. How would you approach this problem? What type of research would you recommend and why? What specific forms of this type of research would best help Sea Side?

3. A manufacturer of beauty products has approached Jenny's Beauty Boutique to find out whether Jenny, the owner, is interested in carrying the manufacturer's line of beauty products. Jenny likes the idea of carrying beauty products in her salon. However, she wants to know more about her customers' current preferences regarding these kinds of products and has approached you for help. Jenny wants to conduct conclusive research. Do you agree? If you do, indicate to Jenny whether she should use a cross-sectional study or a longitudinal study and explain why. Then, to add to Jenny's understanding of marketing research, explain to her what the other form of conclusive research is and illustrate it with a potential application for Jenny's Beauty Boutique.

INTERNET EXERCISES

1. Go to www.greenfield.com and explore the website to find information (e.g., relevant white papers) about its Greenfield Online Panel. Answer the following questions:
   a. How does Greenfield acquire the units for its panel?
   b. How are data collected from the panel?
   c. What types of information can Greenfield supply about its panel members?
   d. What does Greenfield claim are the uses and benefits of its omnibus panel?
   e. Describe a situation in which this panel would be used.

2. Go to www.harrisinteractive.com. Go to its Harris Poll (on the right side).
   a. Read over the introductory information about Harris Polls and how they are conducted. Now go to the listing of polls by year and select the current year. Select a poll that has marketing implications. Summarize the findings.
   b. Then identify and describe the method used for data collection.
   c. Classify the type of panel involved in light of the information in Chapter 3, identifying whether it used a cross-sectional or a longitudinal design.

CASE 3.1 ALEVE
(www.aleve.com)

Over the past several years, Bayer Consumer Care, part of the HealthCare business subgroup of Bayer Corporation, undertook a series of research projects to build overall sales and market share of its Aleve brand pain reliever. Aleve had two major advantages over competing analgesics: it provided all-day relief from tough pain with just two pills, and it was available without a prescription, eliminating the need to see a doctor. A very successful advertising campaign had been built around the findings of consumer research.

Background

After winning FDA approval for the nonprescription treatment of minor pain and fever in 1994, Aleve[1] was introduced as the first new over-the-counter (OTC) analgesic in nearly a decade. Competing with aspirin, ibuprofen, and acetaminophen, Aleve was an OTC pain reliever that provided relief for a variety of conditions, such as minor arthritis pain, muscular aches, headaches, and minor aches and pains due to the common cold.

Aleve was originally the result of a joint venture between pharmaceutical manufacturer Roche Holding Ltd. and consumer packaged goods marketer Procter & Gamble (P&G). In June 1996, P&G shocked the analgesics industry by selling its 50 percent stake in the joint venture back to partner Roche Holding. After pouring $100 million into its product launch two years earlier, P&G had attained a market share of only 6 percent for Aleve, well below managers' expectations. Shortly thereafter, Bayer Consumer Care approached Roche, and over the summer the two companies reached an agreement to establish a 50-50 joint venture selling the brand. Bayer was then faced with the challenge of building the Aleve brand.

Revitalizing Aleve's Market Position[2]

Bayer confronted a real dilemma: How would it improve the market performance of a brand when a giant like P&G couldn't? Bayer brand managers realized that they needed to identify who the Aleve user actually was. They hired CLT Research Associates, a New York–based firm, to conduct 800 in-home interviews using a random sample of 18- to 75-year-old men and women who had used OTC pain relievers in the previous year. CLT determined that there was a segment, 24 percent of the sample, who were so-called pain busters. These are heavy users of OTC pain medications, who show a high degree of willingness to try multiple brands. Of the respondents in this segment, 35 percent had tried Aleve, but it was only one brand of many that they kept available. Brand managers were faced with the question of how to develop a preference for Aleve over the other choices.

This question was answered using further research. The New York–based research firm of Moskowitz Jacobs Inc. asked 249 respondents to rate a series of statements about Aleve. The men and women, ranging in age from 18 to 69, indicated that "control over pain" and/or "the freedom to do the things you want" were most important to them. A further finding was that respondents desired a reduction in the number of pills they felt they had to take to get relief from their pain. It now fell to the Aleve brand managers to develop a strategy incorporating these findings.

Aleve already claimed that two blue pills would give all-day pain relief. The strategy of comparing this to the typical OTC dosage of eight pills a day would get the attention of those in the market who were looking to cut down on their medication. A final research push using secondary data on the OTC pain reliever, integrated with a series of focus groups, determined that Aleve users suffer from arthritis and back pain to a greater degree than the average OTC analgesic user. One other useful piece of information emerged from this research. Aleve users lead very busy lives, with numerous commitments and a high degree of pride in their accomplishments.

With the help of the Moskowitz Jacobs research, the brand managers developed a personality for Aleve. Aleve would now be the brand allowing "liberation from tough pain, making a dramatic difference in the quality of life." BBDO Chicago developed an ad campaign incorporating this personality. Called "Dramatic Difference," the ads took the form of letters from grateful Aleve users, thankful that their lives had been put back in their control.

As an indication of the strategic impact of this campaign, 2000 sales of Aleve were 16 percent higher than those of 1999. Market share increased to 7 percent, its highest ever. Unaided recall of brand name increased 8 percent between 1999 and 2000, to 44 percent. Unaided recall of the "Dramatic Difference" ads themselves increased to 33 percent by 2000. It seems that, with the help of a number of marketing research providers, Bayer found the key to Aleve that P&G could not.

CASE QUESTIONS

1. Summarize the various types of research that were conducted for the Aleve brand, identifying the data collection techniques used for each.

2. Was the type of research conducted in each of the studies exploratory or conclusive? Explain why.

CASE NOTES

1. Aleve is the nonprescription strength of Anaprox, a fast-acting form of the medicine in Naprosyn, the number one selling brand in its class (antiarthritics) for many years.
2. This portion of the case draws heavily on Sara Eckel, "Road to Recovery: Bayer Consumer Care Prescribes Some Strong Medicine for an Ailing Brand," *American Demographics* (March 2001): S8.

This case was written by Jeanne L. Munger (University of Southern Maine) in collaboration with the textbook authors, as a basis for class discussion rather than to illustrate either effective or ineffective marketing practice.

CASE 3.2 GRANTS.GOV: LAUNCHING A WEB-BASED GRANT PROCESS
(www.grants.gov)

It's never easy dealing with governmental agencies. The bureaucracy can drive people either to tears or to other places. Grants.gov is doing its part to help with one bottle-necked area by consolidating the federal government's grant process into a single website for searching and applying for grants offered by 26 federal agencies and 900 individual grant programs. Over $350 billion is granted annually, and in the past, each agency had its own application process or electronic process. Moving them all to www.grants.gov required major changes in the technology infrastructures and processes. Grants.gov is touted as a success story among e-government initiatives because it represents the finest implementation of citizen-centered electronic government. For its efforts, Grants.gov was awarded the prestigious 2004 FOSE Showcase of Excellence Award. The key to its success was a continual focus on customer input and marketing research.

It was clear from the beginning of the development of Grants.gov that input from potential users, both grant applicants and grant-making agencies, was critical to designing a user-friendly and effective system. However, it was also apparent that gaining cooperation from all areas of government, including oversight groups, IT specialists, policy makers, and grant administrators, was also key to acceptance of the system. To meet these goals, Rockbridge Associates, Inc. (working as a subcontractor to IBM Business Consulting Services), employed a disciplined research process for designing an e-service.

As a first step, Rockbridge (www.rockresearch.com) conducted a series of 26 stakeholder interviews and two workshops to identify needs and expectations for the system from the perspective of key influencers. They also conducted two in-person focus groups with grant-making agency personnel (because all were in the Washington, D.C., area) and two focus groups with grant applicants (one in person in D.C. and one by telephone with grant applicants around the country) to validate the design requirements for the system. These first two phases of the research helped to create buy-in to the process, as well as to prioritize development efforts. A pilot of the system was developed upon completion of this initial research.

After development, Rockbridge conducted two navigational focus groups, one with grant applicants and one with grant-making agencies. During the focus groups, Rockbridge reviewed the pilot in detail, discussing respondents' opinions of the look and feel, navigation, and content of the Grants.gov site. The results were used to refine the system and prepare for usability testing.

After the system was launched, Rockbridge began conducting quarterly satisfaction tracking surveys with approximately 50 grant-making agency representatives and 175 grant applicants who have used the Grants.gov site in the past 60 days. The survey is conducted online and includes 15 to 20 questions. The survey covers users' overall satisfaction with the site, satisfaction with the site's features and usability, incidence of problems using the site, satisfaction with problem resolution by customer support, and how well the site meets expectations and improves the granting process. The purpose of the survey is to ensure that the system continues to meet users' needs as new features and functionality are added to the ever-evolving site. Although user-focused product development was a key driver of Grants.gov's success, Grants.gov had another challenge in encouraging initial trials of the system.

A major marketing and branding effort was undertaken to drive usage and adoption of the system. Just prior to launch, Rockbridge conducted a baseline change management survey online with 400 grant applicants and 50 grant-making agency representatives who may or may not have been familiar with Grants.gov. This survey included 25 questions and was designed to measure awareness of the Grants.gov initiative, the effects of initial communication efforts, and the market's perceptions of the grant process. This survey is conducted quarterly to guide and assess communication efforts.

The marketing research process employed by Grants.gov helped ensure its success. The research effort saved the government time and money by focusing design efforts on users' needs from the beginning of the process.

CASE QUESTIONS

1. Would you characterize the research conducted before launching the Grants.gov site as exploratory or conclusive research? What about the research conducted after the site was launched? Justify your answers. Identify the specific types of research or data collection techniques that were used in the prelaunch and postlaunch phases.

2. Were the various types of research conducted and the techniques used appropriate? If so, why? If not, why not? Would you have done anything differently? Explain your answer.

This case study was written by Regina D. Woodall, vice president, Rockbridge Associates, Inc., in collaboration with the textbook authors, as a basis for class discussion (www.rockresearch.com/case_studies/case_studies.html). The authors also appreciate the insights provided by Charles L. Colby, president, Rockbridge Associates. Reprinted by permission of Rockbridge Associates, Great Falls, VA .

Data Collection: Types and Methods

Part Two

4 Secondary Data

Chapter Objectives

After reading and understanding the material in this chapter, you should be able to:

- Compare the advantages of secondary data and primary data.

- Identify the limitations of secondary data in terms of relevance and accuracy.

- Distinguish between (1) original and secondhand sources of secondary data, and (2) internal and external sources of secondary data.

- Explain why secondary-data management is increasingly important.

- Define *marketing information system* and describe its basic components.

Quest to Acquire Information Competency—What Do Pure and Persil Detergents, Huggies Diapers, Birds Eye Fish Sticks, and Cadbury Chocolates Have in Common?

In the United Kingdom, more than 200 television channels, PCs, and the Internet vie for consumer attention. With women and men increasingly sharing grocery shopping chores, consumer goods manufacturers have a difficult time identifying the "average consumer." Although consumer goods manufacturers have knowledge about their customers, they also recognize that effective promotion requires even more in-depth knowledge.

Unilever UK, a leader in the global consumer goods industry, believed that, if Unilever learned about people's habits, attitudes, and behaviors in completely different categories, it could begin to predict how people would behave in Unilever's own categories. Unilever, in collaboration with Kimberly-Clark and Cadbury Trebor Bassett, set up a "Jigsaw Consortium" to pool customer data. The companies realized that, although their products are very different, they end up in the same grocery carts. The merged database showed that large households with children tend to consume a disproportionate amount of Unilever's Comfort Pure fabric conditioner, Persil detergent, Dove soap, Vaseline Intensive Care products, and Birds Eye fish sticks; Kimberly-Clark's Huggies; and Cadbury's chocolates. Knowing which kinds of households are most likely to buy their products helped the consortium members better target their direct-mail campaigns.

Database analysis also produced somewhat less intuitive results, such as the knowledge that empty-nesters are exceptionally heavy consumers of tea, soup, chocolate, and ice cream, and that families with children tend to stock up on diapers, detergent, and fish sticks. Using the database, the companies targeted specific groups of households with promotions tailored for each group. The direct-mail campaigns, however, were not effective. In response, Unilever decided to scale up its global relationship marketing activity and asked its global media director, Alan Rutherford, to examine Unilever's use of relationship marketing across its portfolio of FMCG (fast-moving consumer goods) brands. Under the revised strategy, the company viewed relationship marketing as another channel for promoting its products.

For instance, using the database, Birds Eye, Unilever's frozen food division, created a relationship marketing campaign aimed at families with young children. For the campaign, Unilever tapped into the Jigsaw's database of 10 million consumers. The relationship marketing program extended to 150,000 consumers drawn from the 2 million customers who had filled out questionnaires. The program included a nutritional card for mothers, a star chart to reward children for eating healthy food, an activity card showing children how to make a hideaway with a table and blanket, and a sheet of cut-out props, such as coins and a parrot.

Cadbury Trebor Bassett targeted families with an Easter direct-marketing campaign to promote its flagship Cadbury Creme Egg brand. It selected 300,000 households after profiling Jigsaw's database. The mailing included a £1 money-off coupon and a questionnaire to assist future relationship marketing.

The strong consumer database of over 10 million consumers will help Unilever and Cadbury Trebor Bassett rejuvenate their brands around faster-growing segments of the market. Some of the world's biggest marketing companies have started to investigate the opportunities that stem from building personalized databases. With ad agency Saatchi & Saatchi, P&G is developing a program called "Golden Households," which will seek to link separate brands such as Ariel and Fairy. Households are recruited to give information about how they use different P&G products to see whether they will be amenable to being cross-sold other goods. Definitive data on consumer buying behavior will allow companies to develop information competency. Information-competent companies can invest in more precisely targeted, and therefore more efficient, marketing promotions.[1] ∎

Recall that *secondary data* are data collected for some purpose other than the research situation at hand. Such data are readily available from such sources as

- Warranty cards (including date, place, and purpose of purchase) mailed or e-mailed to an appliance manufacturer by recent purchasers (for example, www.registration.whirlpoolcorp.com/registration/default.asp).

- Nielsen/NetRatings, indicating the relative popularity of various websites in a particular month (www.nielsen-netratings.com).
- Retail trade statistics in different sections of the country, estimated and released by the U.S. Census Bureau (www.census.gov).

Secondary data are usually gathered for purposes that differ from the researcher's objective. Thus a marketing researcher faces the twofold challenge of identifying which secondary data may be useful and evaluating such data in light of the requirements of the research study. This chapter explores that challenge and offers guidelines for dealing with it.

First, let's examine the pros and cons of secondary data, to highlight why a researcher must seek them out and at the same time exercise caution in using them.

Advantages of Secondary Data

There are many advantages to using secondary data. First, secondary data are readily available and therefore less costly and time consuming to obtain.

Cost and Time

A research study will invariably be less expensive and take less time to complete if it utilizes secondary rather than primary data. Consider the following small-business example that appeared in the *Los Angeles Times:*

> I am starting a pool and spa cleaning and repair service and am putting together a business plan. I am stumped by the market analysis section and cannot seem to find any information about the pool market in the San Fernando Valley. How do I find out about market size and competition? (Michael Fowler, Bell Canyon)[2]

One option available to Michael is to conduct surveys of, say, 200 households to collect the data needed to estimate the number of pools and spas in the San Fernando Valley. As you might imagine, such a primary-data collection approach will be expensive and time consuming. For instance, even if Michael spends only about $50 per interview for collecting and analyzing data—which is a conservative cost estimate—he will have to spend a total of $10,000. Given his tight financial situation, Michael would be unwise to spend that kind of money on primary-data collection, especially because useful secondary data are likely to be available at much lower cost. Furthermore, collecting primary data would consume considerably more time than using secondary data.

For instance, Michael can obtain demographic information at the U.S. Census Bureau's website (www.census.gov). He can seek information on competitors using yellowpages.com or switchboard.com. Local newspapers may also be able to offer Michael information on income levels, homes, and consumer buying habits for a nominal fee. The website www.marketingplan.com can help Michael identify other web sources. Alternatively, perhaps some other organization, such as a commercial marketing research firm, a government agency, or a trade association, has already collected data about pool and spa cleaning and repair services in various counties in California. Michael can find such data by merely clicking on the website www.poolspanews.com or by telephoning the Association of Pool & Spa Professionals (APSP)[3] or the local library.

Invariably, plunging into primary-data collection without first looking into the availability of secondary data is a mistake that squanders valuable resources:

money and time. Using secondary data to find such information as the demographic composition of a market, retail sales of a product category, changes in brand shares over time, and market potential for industrial products can be particularly cost and time efficient because a variety of rich secondary-data sources are available for these purposes.

Availability

In addition to their obvious cost and time benefits over primary data, secondary data may be more readily available. For example, the Census of Retail Trade (www.census.gov) contains data on sales of retail establishments classified according to numerous categories of outlets. This census may be the only source of accurate data available to a manufacturing firm selling its products to retailers and wishing to ascertain the size of its markets as measured by the sales of different categories of retail outlets. Given the sensitive nature of the data, the manufacturing firm may find that gathering accurate and comprehensive data on its own is difficult. However, the U.S. Census Bureau, by virtue of its legal authority, can collect and disseminate such data.

Another federal agency that has similar authority is the Securities and Exchange Commission, or SEC (www.sec.gov). A variety of publicly held business firms in the United States are required by law to file certain financial data with the SEC, which in turn makes the data public.

Although some forms of available secondary data are free (such as data contained in most government publications and in research studies published in books and journals), those made available by commercial marketing research firms are not. Secondary data sold by research firms are usually called **syndicated data.** The cost of collecting syndicated data is spread over a number of client firms; the cost to any one firm is invariably lower than the cost the firm would incur if it collected the data on its own. Consider a small firm that manufactures a line of canned vegetables and distributes its brands to supermarkets across the country through food brokers. The firm has no direct contact with the supermarkets or the customers who buy its brands. Therefore, it would be unable to learn much about who buys its brands, what its brands' shares are in various regional markets, and so on, if syndicated services, such as the National Purchase Diary Panel (www.npd.com) and the ACNielsen SCANTRACK (www.acnielsen.com) service, were not available.

> **Syndicated data** are secondary data sold by research firms.

Limitations of Secondary Data

Secondary data also have some disadvantages. These limitations involve chiefly data relevance and difficulties in ensuring accuracy.

Relevance

Available secondary data may not match the data needs of a given project on one or more of the following factors: (1) the *units* in which the data are measured; (2) the *category breakdowns* or *definitions* of variables for which the data are reported; and (3) the *time period* during which the data were measured.

Researchers can gather data on many variables of interest by using a number of alternative units of measurement. Sales of a product can be measured in dollars or in physical units; product shipments can be measured in terms of volume, weight, dollar value, or truckloads; a consumer's education level can be measured in terms of the highest degree held or the number of years of formal education completed. A particular choice of measurement units by the source of secondary data may render the data useless for certain research purposes, as the following example illustrates.

> **EXAMPLE**　Carpets Unlimited and Sentinel Corporation are two newly started firms. Carpets Unlimited manufactures a variety of carpets, and Sentinel produces a line of smoke detectors. Both firms are eager to estimate the total residential market potential for their products in different sections of the country.
>
> One way to estimate product potential in a region is to look at the average size of residential housing units in that region. However, size of residential housing can be measured in at least two ways: number of rooms and square feet of area. Residential housing size expressed in number of rooms may be adequate and appropriate for the data needs of Sentinel Corporation but not for the data needs of Carpets Unlimited. A meaningful estimate of market potential for carpeting requires size data expressed in square feet.
>
> The U.S. Census data on population and housing contain a variety of data on residential housing that may be quite useful to Sentinel Corporation in estimating market potential for smoke detectors. Data are available on total number of rooms, number of bedrooms, year in which a unit was built, and number of stories in the unit. However, these data do not yield meaningful estimates of market potential for residential carpeting.

In general, although data on a variable of interest may be readily available, the relevance of the data for a particular application depends on the measurement units used. However, we must not hastily dismiss secondary data as irrelevant just because the measurement units do not exactly match the requirements of a project. In certain situations, we can convert the reported data into the specific units of interest to us. For example, a trucking company interested in the volume of industrial chemicals transported may find secondary data reported in weight units. But such secondary data are still useful because they can be easily modified to meet the trucking company's needs by using appropriate weight-to-volume conversion factors. Similarly, total unit sales of some product—say, television sets—can be derived from total dollar sales data if a meaningful estimate of the average price per television set is available. Of course, such conversions may not always be possible. Data on total television set sales reported in dollars will be useless if we are interested in unit sales of different sizes of TVs rather than total unit sales.

> **EXAMPLE**　Digital Babysitter specializes in making digital baby-monitoring devices. The digital baby monitors facilitate the transfer of digital pictures from homes to the company's website, and parents can watch their baby from wherever they are by simply visiting the company's website. When the company decided that it wanted to grow beyond the United States, it began to look elsewhere for markets. It relied on birth rates provided by the United Nations (www.un.org) and decided to target China and India. Furthermore, it obtained information on computer penetration in urban areas and chose urban populations as its target market.
>
> Although this secondary-data analysis would have made perfect sense in a developed country, it was not meaningful in China and India, where children spend time either with their extended family or at school and are almost never alone. Due to lack of space, parents often share their room with children. Therefore, although the secondary data appeared to show a promising market for baby monitors, they were not relevant for India and China. Compounding the space problem is the fact that Internet penetration is small even in urban areas there, making India and China less attractive markets for digital baby monitors. However,

Internet usage is increasing in Asia, with nearly 7 percent of households in China having an Internet connection and a much higher percentage having access to the Internet in urban centers.[4] Internet usage in India is at a very low 0.2 percent of the population, but India's broadband policy calls for 20 million broadband subscribers and 40 million Internet subscribers by the end of 2010.[5] Internet access may not be a major stumbling block in the coming years, but cultural issues (for instance, value placed on spending time with children) will continue to be a constraint for Digital Babysitter.

Secondary data may also be irrelevant if the categories for which data are summarized are not consistent with the categories of interest to a researcher. Consider a marketer of products and services aimed primarily at senior citizens. This marketer is interested in obtaining data about the lifestyles and activities of different age groups within the category "senior citizens." Suppose a comprehensive study is available that classifies adult lifestyles and activities into five age groups: 18 to 25, 26 to 35, 36 to 45, 46 to 55, and over 55. This study is not useful to the marketer because the age variables are not consistent with the marketer's specific needs.

The mismatch between categories defined by a secondary-data source and a decision maker's desires may not always be as obvious as in this illustration. The difference may be quite subtle and, if a secondary-data user fails to recognize it, can lead to erroneous inferences. This point is forcefully made by a case study reported in *Chain Drug Review*.[6]

CASE IN POINT ▶ **Is Purell a "Liquid Soap" or an "Instant Hand Sanitizer"?** GOJO Industries launched Purell in 1995 as an "instant hand sanitizer," a product that cleans without water, and positioned it as a skin care/first aid product. However, both Nielsen and Information Resources Inc. (IRI), two leading syndicated services, categorized it as a liquid soap. Some chain drugstores, including Walgreens, placed Purell in the skin care section, some in the cough/cold section, and some in the liquid soap section following the Nielsen/IRI classification. Thus reported sales of Purell varied with its location because retailers evaluated success in terms of its performance against other items in that category. Pfizer Consumer Healthcare, a division of Pfizer Inc., has acquired Purell and positioned it as an instant hand sanitizer. This may alleviate the category mismatch problem.[7] ◀

"THE COMPUTER LINKS ME TO AN INTERNATIONAL DATABASE FOR WHO'S 'NAUGHTY AND NICE.'"

Problems with Census Data

Category mismatch is also a common problem with census data. Researchers using census data to study the nature of geographic markets must be especially cautious. Well-defined geographic areas for which census data are summarized (such as counties or states) typically do not coincide with trading areas surrounding core cities. For example, the U.S. Bureau of Economic Affairs has divided the United States into 318 economic areas whose boundaries differ from the traditional

The 2000 U.S. Census employed hundreds of field workers to collect data through personal interviews.

261 Metropolitan Statistical Areas (MSAs) and 19 Consolidated Metropolitan Statistical Areas (CMSAs).[8]

Another facet of the category problem is changes in category definition that may occur from one time period to the next. For instance, in the 1970 census Hispanics were classified as whites, whereas in the 1980 census they were assigned a separate racial category. A much more detailed breakdown of racial categories was used in the 2000 census. Before drawing inferences from secondary data obtained from multiple time periods, we must ensure that no changes occurred in the definitions of variables or their categories. Obviously, researchers interested in studying the changes in variables between 1970 and 2000 must first determine whether they can meaningfully compare the data over time.[9]

The time period during which secondary data were collected is the third factor affecting the data's relevance for a specific application. Using data that are too old can be more dangerous than using no data at all, especially in making decisions related to rapidly changing or highly volatile markets. Consider the market for Internet service providers (ISPs). Given the state of turmoil in this market, with rapidly changing competitors, prices, and applications, secondary data on the demographics of Internet users will most likely become useless shortly after collection (see Research in Use 4.1).

Data published by the U.S. Census Bureau are particularly prone to datedness. To illustrate, the Census of Population and Housing is conducted only once every 10 years. Moreover, there is a lag of about two years between collection and publication of the data. Fortunately, difficulties stemming from the recency of secondary data are somewhat mitigated by two factors: secondary-data sources usually provide periodic updates for their data, and rapid advances in computer and communications technology continue to reduce the lag between data collection and dissemination. The U.S. Census Bureau, for example, issues *Current Population Reports*, which update population data annually for major market areas. Similarly, some marketing research firms, as well as state and local agencies, periodically update census data on the basis of their own research. Certain syndicated services, such as Chase Econometrics and DRI, Inc., allow clients' computers direct access to their own computer files containing the most current demographic data.

Accuracy

In addition to ensuring the relevance of secondary data, the user must verify their accuracy. Whereas *relevance* describes the suitability of the data, *accuracy* describes their trustworthiness. Obviously the usefulness of secondary data will be diminished if they lack either of these two traits.

The key to assessing the accuracy of secondary data lies in learning as much as possible about the process of collecting them. This task may not always be easy. Indeed, in many cases a major limitation of secondary data is more the lack of information necessary to evaluate the data's accuracy than lack of accuracy per se.

Unfortunately, the proliferation of easily accessible Internet secondary data on the one hand and the scarcity of readily available information to evaluate them on the other may tempt some researchers to downplay the issue of accuracy. This temptation should be avoided; with a little effort, researchers can usually get at least some feel for the trustworthiness of secondary data.

The following set of interrelated questions plays a central role in evaluating secondary-data accuracy:

The Numbers Game: Statistics Are Only as Credible as the Sources That Produce Them

Corporate chieftains, the U.S. Congress, the FTC, and media alike are paying increasing attention to statistics concerning the problem of "spam" on the Internet. It is estimated that spam costs U.S. businesses nearly $10 billion annually in lost productivity, anti-spam technology, and technical support. These statistics produced by online research firms find their way into the press, into corporate strategy rooms, into public relations brochures, and into communications sent to investors. Congress uses the evidence to debate whether to pass anti-spam laws. Likewise, the FTC has proposed offering rewards for nabbing spammers. Many accept these spam statistics without questioning their validity, even when the projections differ significantly across competing studies (see the table in the next column). According to the table, the difference between the highest and lowest estimates of junk e-mail is as much as 41 percent for the year 2002 and 19 percent for 2004.

Many factors account for the wide variation in projections. Research firms define *spam* in many different ways. The European Union and some companies consider unsolicited bulk e-mails as spam. But the U.S. anti-spam bill says that commercial e-mail is legitimate as long as it meets certain criteria, such as letting recipients opt out of receiving future messages. The sources

Spam Projections: Which Numbers to Use?

	2002	2004
MessageLabs	19%	84%
Brightmail	39	65
Postini	60	78
FrontBridge	40	82

of data are another reason for the discrepancy. Some firms collect reports from users, a source that can be subjective. Also, anti-spam software vendors extrapolate from their clients, who may not represent a cross section of Internet users.

Conflicts of interest create credibility problems, because the estimates are provided by anti-spam software vendors, who make their money by selling their products. The tendency to release only favorable or negative results to pressure clients also creates a flawed picture of the spam market. The anti-spam market is in its infancy, and lack of historical data makes it difficult to make projections about its future, especially when the Internet market is growing exponentially. Therefore, it is important to exercise caution in interpreting these statistics before blindly jumping in with both feet.[a]

- *Who* collected the data?
- *Why* were the data collected?
- *How* were the data collected?

Now let's examine each of these questions.

■ **Who Collected the Data?** The reputation of a source of secondary data is an indicator of data accuracy. Well-known government sources, such as the U.S. Census Bureau, and many commercial marketing research firms, especially those long established in the profession, have a reputation for setting and maintaining high data quality standards. Secondary data from such sources require far less scrutiny than data offered by organizations not well established within the research profession or by sources whose credibility and competence are unknown.

■ **Why Were the Data Collected?** An examination of the explicit, or even implicit, reasons for the data collection can sometimes indicate the accuracy of the data. To illustrate, suppose a firm maintaining a Web portal site conducts, on its own, an online survey of its customers. The survey gathers data on a variety of factors, such as the demographic profiles of site visitors and the impact on visitors of banner advertisements appearing at the site. The purpose of the survey is to generate data helpful to potential advertisers in deciding whether to place banner advertisements at the website. Of course, the Web portal company also hopes the data will convince many firms to buy banner advertising space at its website.

Now think of yourself as one of the potential advertisers. Assume you have access not only to the secondary data offered by the portal site, but also to similar data offered by a marketing research firm that specializes in collecting and selling syndicated data about customers of a number of websites. Which of these two sources would you trust more? You are likely to trust the marketing research firm more, for two good reasons:

1. As an independent source with no hidden bias, the marketing research firm is more likely to provide unbiased data.

2. Because the marketing research firm specializes in website customer surveys, it is more likely to be capable of generating good-quality data. Notice that this reason also relates to the *who* question discussed earlier.

These factors do not mean you should not use the data provided by the website firm, especially because you would have to pay for the research firm's data, whereas the data provided by the website firm are free. However, they do imply that, before making any advertising decision on the basis of the website's data, you should carefully review the process involved in collecting the data, discussed next.

■ **How Were the Data Collected?**   Perhaps the most effective way to judge the accuracy of secondary data is to scrutinize the data collection process beyond the *who* and *why* aspects already discussed. What specific data collection instruments were used? How large was the sample? What types of sample units provided the data? During what specific time periods (time of day, day of week, and so on) were the data collected? Answers to questions like these are crucial in assessing data accuracy. Secondary-data suppliers with good reputations generally publish at least a brief description of their data collection procedures. Most of them will also furnish additional details if desired by potential data users.

CASE IN POINT ▶ **Gallup Poll Monthly**   The Gallup Organization, a well-known global marketing research firm, offers syndicated services, including a Web-based report entitled *Gallup Poll Monthly.* Gallup poll results are regularly published in the major print and online media, such as LexisNexis and the Roper Center, and identify numerous social trends within the general population as well as within specific demographic segments. The website www.gallup.com contains detailed descriptions of how Gallup polls are conducted, including sampling techniques, types of interviews and questions asked, and interpretation of results. ◀

Good documentation of methodology, including statements about limitations of the data, is itself an indicator of high data quality. A secondary-data source that readily offers such documentation and is willing to submit its procedures for additional examination will generally have high quality standards.

Our ability to evaluate the accuracy of secondary data also depends on whether the data are derived from the original source or from a secondhand source. The **original source** actually collects the data. A **secondhand source** uses data collected by the original source to generate its own summaries, interpretations, and the like. For example, a report issued by the Census Bureau on data gathered through the Census of Population and Housing is the original source of such data. However, a report on population characteristics issued by an independent organization that used data from the Census of Population and Housing as the basis for its report is a secondhand source of population data. The original

An **original source** is one that actually collects the data.

A **secondhand source** is one that uses data collected by the original source to generate its own summaries, interpretations, and the like.

source of secondary data is more likely than a secondhand source to spell out the procedures used in generating the data.

Moreover, a secondhand source may unintentionally or, in some cases, even deliberately restate or reinterpret the original source's data in inappropriate ways. A secondhand source may also make mistakes in transcribing the data from the original source and thus provide incorrect numbers. Hence, before using secondary data available through a secondhand source, we must, if possible, identify the original source and examine the procedures used. As a general rule, all of the relevant data should be obtained from the original source if at all feasible.

Sources and Types of Secondary Data

Internal sources are sources within the organization.

External sources are sources outside the organization.

There are literally thousands of potential sources of secondary data, too numerous to list in a book of this scope. However, from the point of view of a decision maker's organization, a useful technique is to group secondary-data sources broadly into internal sources and external sources. As the terms imply, **internal sources** are within the organization, and **external sources** are outside the organization. Secondary data are typically labeled *internal secondary data* or *external secondary data,* depending on their source.

Internal Secondary Data

A firm's historical record of sales, a public service association's list of donors, a hospital's records of services rendered to patients, and public opinion polls conducted in the past by a political candidate's campaign office are all sources of internal secondary data for those organizations. Earlier, we emphasized the usefulness of looking into the availability of secondary data before plunging into primary-data collection. Likewise, when seeking secondary data, the researcher should check out the availability of internal secondary data before turning to external sources. If available, internal secondary data may be obtained with less time, effort, and money than external secondary data. In addition, they may also be more pertinent to the situation at hand because they are from within the organization. The following example illustrates these points.

SCENARIO Burger King offered a Kids Meal program featuring 31 different *Star Wars* premiums over an extended period at nearly 8,000 locations across the United States and in 60 countries. An international TV campaign, in-store merchandising, an Internet component, print ads, and Kids Club birthday direct mailers supported the promotional campaign.[10]

Suppose the marketing manager of Burger King wants to know the effect of the company's tie-in with movies like *Star Wars.* Specifically, the manager would like to examine same-store sales trends. A marketing research firm specializing in restaurant industry research has estimates of sales for the leading fast-food restaurants. These estimates are based on a survey of a representative sample of restaurant goers in the United States and are updated semiannually.

Burger King can use internal secondary data to evaluate the effectiveness of its promotional tie-in with *Star Wars.*

> Should the manager purchase this syndicated service from the marketing research firm?
>
> The sales estimates that would be provided by the syndicated service, an external secondary-data source, would certainly offer useful insights. However, Burger King could also benefit greatly from examining same-store sales—internal secondary data that the company itself should have. The syndicated service is available on a semiannual basis only, whereas same-store sales before and after the *Star Wars* promotion would provide a clearer picture of the effect of Burger King's tie-in promotion. Furthermore, the company's sales data would be up to date all the time. In short, given the manager's specific objective, internal secondary data will be more relevant and less expensive than the syndicated data offered by the research firm.

Of course, internal secondary data may not always be suitable or adequate. For instance, if data are needed on the sales trends of competing fast-food restaurants during the same time period as the movie tie-in promotion, the manager may have to buy the syndicated data offered by the research firm. But the point of this discussion is that, once you have identified your data needs, a systematic search for data will pay off handsomely.

Exhibit 4.1 shows a flow diagram outlining the sequence of steps in a systematic data search. The logical starting point for any data search should be an examination of internal secondary-data sources. If the data available within the organization are unsuitable or inadequate, the marketer should extend the search to external secondary-data sources. Primary data should be collected only if absolutely essential.

External Sources

A variety of external sources provide secondary data. Although there is no standard way to classify them, the following groupings help to highlight key distinctions across the various sources: government sources; syndicated sources; trade associations; miscellaneous sources; and abstracts, directories, and indexes. Examples of key sources within some of these categories, along with brief descriptions of what they offer, are provided in Table 4.1. Now let's examine the main features of each category.

■ **Government Sources**   Government agencies at the federal, state, and local levels collect more data about people, firms, markets, and foreign countries than any other secondary-data source. They provide an extremely rich reservoir of data for researchers. Moreover, many of these data are freely available on the Internet (see Table 4.2). Looking into government sources of secondary data is a must if the information requirements of a project appear to relate to data in the public domain. Depending on the objective of a project, contacting an appropriate government agency or even visiting the government documents section of a library can turn up potentially valuable published data. Research in Use 4.2 provides an illustration of how one could evaluate the viability of the Brazilian market for cell phones.

Documents published by government sources are typically in the form of summary reports and tabulations based on the raw data collected. However, if additional details or different tabulations are needed, you may be able to obtain some or all of the raw data, usually for a fee. The U.S. Census Bureau, for example, sells computer CDs containing certain types of raw data collected through the variety of censuses that it conducts. One example is public-use microdata files, which contain data from the Census of Population and Housing. Public-use

Exhibit 4.1
Flow Diagram for Conducting a Data Search

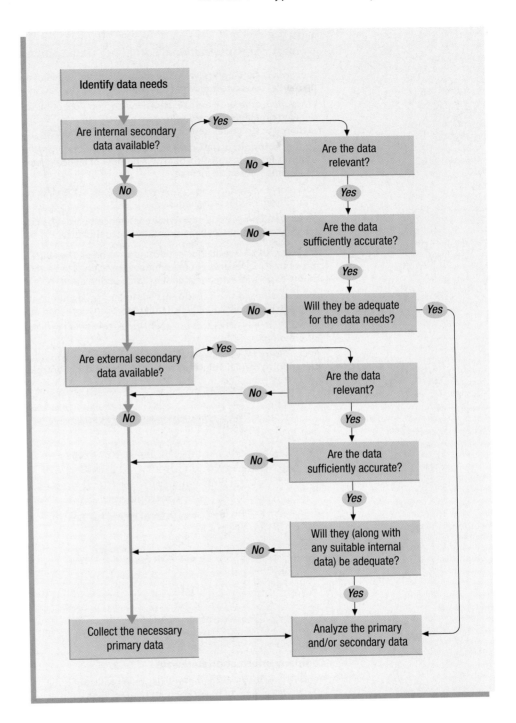

microdata files are raw-data records, stored on CDs, for a representative sample of housing units in the United States. These records provide data on the characteristics of each unit and the people living in it. However, to protect the confidentiality of respondents, the Census Bureau excludes all identifying information from the records. For the same reason, microdata records do not identify geographic areas with fewer than 100,000 people. When census data users have unique needs not

TABLE 4.1
Domestic and International Secondary-Data Sources

American Demographics (www.demographics.com). Provides access to its latest month's articles on market news and consumer research.

CIA World Factbook Country Guides (www.odci.gov/cia/publications/factbook/index.html). Has detailed profiles of countries. Provides country information on a number of facets, such as population, age structure, literacy rate, ethnic groups, language, government, and infrastructure.

Statistical Abstract of the United States (www.census.gov/prod/www/statistical-abstract-us.html). Provides statistical data on a number of facets, including population, education, health, and household income.

Consumer Expenditure Surveys (www.bls.gov/cex/). Useful for retrieving average annual expenditures from product categories.

Consumer Confidence Surveys (www.conference-board.org and www.sca.isr.umich.edu). Monthly surveys of 5,000 representative households.

Trade Statistics (www.ita.doc.gov/td/industry/otea). The Office of Trade and Economic Analysis, run by the U.S. Department of Commerce, provides a wide variety of trade data, including mport/export, investment spending, trade outlook, and more.

Economist Intelligence Unit (db.eiu.com/index.asp?layout=countries). Allows users selected access to Economist Intelligence Unit reports on more than fifty countries.

Stat-USA Internet (www.stat-usa.gov). Has useful market research reports and other consumer information.

At *Lexis-Nexis Universe* (web.lexis-nexis.com/universe) you will find articles from the past to the present on a certain industry/product in a particular country.

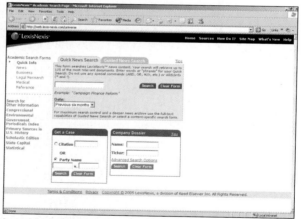

Reprinted with the permission of LexisNexis. LexisNexis and the Knowledge Burst logo are registered trademarks of Reed Elsevier Properties Inc. Used with the permission of LexisNexis. Screen shot reprinted by permission from Microsoft Corporation.

Company Information Gateways

Hoover's (www.hoovers.com). Provides brief profiles of public, private, and international companies, as well as links to major competitors, SEC filings, and news wire stories.

For information about publicly traded U.S. companies, the *Wall Street Journal* (www.wsj.com) is a great place to start. Provides *Wall Street Journal* links to several SEC filings sites, as well as various news services, stock charts, and more.

Search over forty local business weeklies for articles on local divisions and private companies at *American City Business Journals* (www.bizjournals.com).

Current Economic Conditions (www.federalreserve.gov/FOMC/BeigeBook/2004/). Also known as the *Beige Book*, a report published eight times each year by the Federal Reserve Board.

International Marketing Research Using Secondary Data: Marketing Cell Phones in Brazil

In order to market cell phones in Brazil, a country analysis needs to be conducted in order to obtain information on general consumer trends, key conditions, and key contacts. There are many online sources available for collecting this information. For example, to connect to the Country Commercial Guides, open your browser and type in the following URL: www.state.gov. Then click on the "Countries and Regions" box to find country studies.

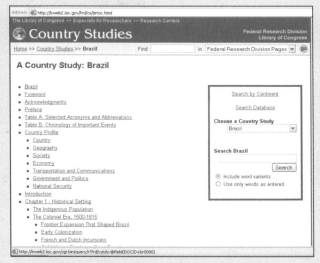

Or one can visit the Library of Congress site (lcweb2.loc.gov/frd/cs/) to obtain Country Studies. In the drop-down box on the right side of the screen, choose the country you want to study. When you click on, say, Brazil, the year of its study is indicated at the bottom of the page. This Country Study presents a comprehensive look at Brazil's commercial and social environment, including economic, political, and market analyses.

To obtain information on competing market share and industry conditions for a particular industry, GLOBUS (Global Business Opportunities) and NTDB (National Trade Data Bank) would be the best sources to use.

Screen shots reprinted by permission from Microsoft Corporation.

met by published documents, microdata files offer them the flexibility to analyze the raw data in whatever manner they desire.[11]

Many computer-based systems are available to analyze census data. One such system is known as a geographic information system (GIS). A GIS integrates maps, charts, tables, and data into a coherent structure that is related logically, quantitatively, and spatially. Typically such systems are used to organize and present information that has both geometric structure (maps, blueprints, photographs) and quantitative structure (data about population, area, density). Applications of GISs are discussed in detail in Chapter 5.

■ **Syndicated Sources**   Syndicated sources consist of marketing research firms offering syndicated services. The well-known Nielsen Retail Index is an example of a syndicated secondary-data source. Table 4.2 provides brief descriptions of several syndicated services.

Secondary data offered by marketing research firms are not free. However, because such data are syndicated, their cost is spread over a number of client organizations. Therefore, if suitable syndicated data are available, they should be more cost effective than primary data for any individual client. In contrast to secondary data from government sources, syndicated data are likely to focus directly on the needs of decision makers. Moreover, syndicated data are typically updated more frequently than government data, some as often as once a week.

Roper Reports, prepared by Roper Starch Worldwide, Inc., is one example of a syndicated service offering customization. Data are gathered from eight surveys a year through in-home personal interviews with a national sample of 2,000 adults 18 years of age or older. In addition to the standard or regularly asked questions, a tack-on custom-question service is available to Roper Reports subscribers and nonsubscribers. According to Roper Starch Worldwide, "This service offers a unique combination of frequency, speed of report delivery, quality, low cost, large sample size and extensive demographic breaks."[12]

Commercial marketing research firms are not the only sources of syndicated data. Major supermarket chains, in addition to using scanner data as internal secondary data, are making such data available as syndicated data to packaged goods producers such as Procter & Gamble, Kraft, and others.

■ **Trade Associations**   There are thousands of trade associations, each representing a group of organizations that share a common trade or line of business (for example, search www.yahoo.com for "trade associations" or "international trade associations"). Most trade associations collect background data about their members and markets, as well as other topics. Hence, they can be valuable sources of secondary data, although a researcher planning to tap such sources may face certain constraints. The data available through associations are usually quite general, and certain types of data, such as competitively sensitive data about an association's members or trade, may not be available at all. Another potential problem is that some trade associations will release data only to their members.

■ **Miscellaneous Sources**   Miscellaneous sources include those that do not fit neatly into the three previous categories. Examples are journals, magazines, research monographs, textbooks, and similar published materials. Most libraries, especially those affiliated with academic institutions, have numerous collections of such sources. Many are also available on the Internet.

A distinguishing feature of sources in this category is that the data they contain are in the form of insights, ideas, suggestions, and so forth, rather than in numerical form. Thus their primary purpose is to stimulate the thinking of researchers and decision makers, as opposed to providing them with numbers they can analyze. A miscellaneous source that is particularly useful in understanding demographic trends is *American Demographics,* a periodical available on the Web (www.americandemographics.com) and at many university libraries.

■ **Abstracts, Directories, and Indexes**   Abstracts, directories, and indexes, in contrast to the sources discussed earlier, are guides or references for identifying suitable external secondary-data sources. They are listings of available data sources, classified according to subject matter, topic area, and the like. Annotated guides are secondhand sources. A researcher would do well to locate and examine

TABLE 4.2
Syndicated Sources of Secondary Data

www.gallup.com conducts frequent surveys regarding business and the economy, social issues and policies, managing, and lifestyle.

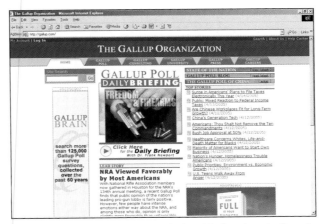

www.npd.com is dedicated principally to providing customized global reports in numerous industries.

www.acnielsen.com has a fairly extensive website to provide, for a fee, market research, information, and analysis to the consumer products and services industries.

www.arbitron.com gathers information that describes consumers' demographic, socioeconomic, and lifestyle characteristics, as well as purchase intentions, in 260 markets.

www.mediamark.com is a fee-based market data and services website.

www.smrb.com is the website for Simmons Market Research Bureau. It provides information on the products and brands that consumers are buying and, most important, the media usage of the different shopping clusters.

www.infores.com is the site for Information Resources, Inc. (IRI). IRI is a leading provider of actionable sales and marketing information, innovative software applications, and timely business solutions to the consumer packaged goods industry.

www.dialog.com is a division of The Thomson Corporation. Dialog is a leading provider of Internet-based information and technology solutions to the corporate market worldwide.

www.dnb.com offers a wide array of competitive intelligence for credit, marketing, purchasing, and receivables management in over 209 countries around the globe.

the original source, even when a summary provided by an annotated guide appears to be adequate for the purpose.

The rapid technological advances in the computer and communications fields are also revolutionizing the process of searching secondary-data guides to identify suitable data sources. Today traditional printed abstracts, directories, and indexes are being replaced by electronic files. Many search engines (www.yahoo.com, www.excite.com, www.ask.com, www.lexisnexis.com, www.altavista.com, www.lycos.com, and so on) offer online searches for locating potential sources of secondary data. To conduct a computerized search, a researcher merely specifies certain key words relating to the topic area on which data are desired. The search engine then searches the electronic files and culls all the sources containing the key words.

An obvious benefit of computerized searches is speed. What would take days or weeks to find through a traditional manual search can now be located within hours or even minutes through a computerized search. Moreover, electronic files can be updated almost as soon as a new source of data becomes available, a feature that printed guides lack. Hence, computerized searches can uncover the latest available sources.

Commercial firms specializing in computerized searches are reducing search time by providing direct communication links between their computers and clients' computers. An example is Find/SVP, a New York–based information and research firm. Find/SVP provides customized research and analysis for in-depth market and industry profiles, business and competitive intelligence, benchmarking, and exploration of new business opportunities. Client organizations receive business guidance from Find/SVP consultants via e-mail, fax, and courier. The availability of fast, efficient, and thorough computerized searches makes it all the more critical that a researcher conduct a search for secondary-data sources before embarking on any form of external-data collection, as one of Find/SVP's clients apparently discovered.

CASE IN POINT ▶ **Find/SVP Helps Clients**[13]　An industrial products and services company with a limited budget wanted to compare its plant manufacturing strategy and costs with those of competitors. The company was hoping to restructure its business following a worldwide market decline.

Find/SVP undertook a market scan of published information on competitors' plants. It consulted online databases, CD-ROMs, the Internet, Find/SVP's proprietary subject files, local newspapers, libraries, and economic development groups for hometown perspectives. The research firm also obtained press kits, product samples, and company literature from the competitors themselves. Find/SVP then obtained Environmental Protection Agency (EPA) documents, as all manufacturing industries must file reports with the EPA. EPA documents showed plant layouts, lists of equipment, operating data, and capacity. For each site, Find/SVP was able to identify eligi-bility for tax rebates, special government-financed employee recruitment and training programs, utility rate structures, taxation, and local wage rates.

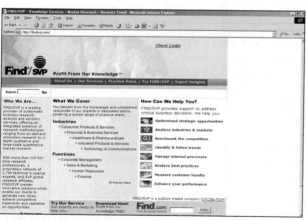

Companies like Find/SVP are a valuable source of competitive intelligence. Reprinted by permission of Find/SVP (www.find-svp.com). Screen shot reprinted by permission from Microsoft Corporation.

Find/SVP also conducted interviews (primary-data collection) with competitive plant personnel to validate and expand on the secondary data already collected. Based on Find/SVP's analysis, the industrial products and services company was able to assess cost structures of its competitors and develop benchmarks for quality, employee performance, and utility costs. Thus the company was able to immediately find virtually all the information it wanted for a few thousand dollars. ◀

This example also shows how companies can make use of marketing research to conduct competitive analysis. In the following section, we examine in more detail the role of secondary sources in competitive intelligence.

Sources of Competitive Intelligence: An Important Application of Secondary Data

Competitive intelligence means gathering data using legal and ethical means and turning them into valuable intelligence through careful analysis. It is a systematic process for creating knowledge of competition. Research in Use 4.3 illustrates how

Competitive Intelligence at Burger King

Heavy advertising, frequent price promotions, and special event promotions are the hallmark of the fast-food industry. Keeping track of all these changes in a global market is critical for developing sound marketing strategies. At Burger King Corporation, this responsibility falls on the brand information and planning analyst, who relies on a variety of sources to track major competitors.

Burger King maintains a brand research library and subscribes to analyst reports that provide a detailed view of competitors' financial and long-term plans. These syndicated reports provide sales and cost data, and describe the competition's growth plans. Magazines like *Brandweek* and *Advertising Age* provide general marketing information. The analyst routinely visits competitors' websites for general company information. The analyst also relies on trade magazines like *Nation's Restaurant News* (weekly), *Restaurant Business* (monthly), *Restaurants and Institutions* (monthly), and *Chain Leader* (monthly) for restaurant-related news.

Insights about the restaurant business can be flushed out of interviews with restaurant business leaders, published routinely in these trade journals. Of particular interest is the annual publication of a restaurant growth index published by these magazines.

Burger King's ad agency provides a monthly report on advertising activity. This report shows future advertising activity of major competitors, enabling Burger King to plan promotions more effectively. Search of the LexisNexis database often brings out useful restaurant-related news. Burger King relies heavily on NPD Group, Inc., a marketing research company, for market information on the food service industry. More details on this syndicated service are available at www.npd.com. These myriad sources provide Burger King with a wealth of knowledge about the fast-food industry, which is disseminated to relevant decision makers through a variety of methods, such as quarterly business reviews, executive summaries, e-mails, and voice mails.[b]

Burger King collects competitive intelligence. Secondary data are one important source of competitive information. They are readily available and, if used effectively, will allow companies to stay ahead of the competition.

CASE IN POINT ▶ **Novartis Keeps Tabs on Competition** Novartis, one of the world's leading pharmaceutical companies, wanted to keep track of what its competition was doing in order to stay ahead of the game. Robert Slater, executive director of the company's new-product commercialization department, noted, "There is increased competition in the market. In the past, when one developed a particular molecule, it used to take years before the competition could catch up. Now it takes only months." In order to respond to the increased competition, Novartis created a global, centralized, self-contained competitive intelligence unit within the firm, charged with keeping track of what its rivals were doing. The group usually works with short lead times, receives information requests from across the organization on such developments as new chemical compounds and therapeutic areas. The effort has paid off for Novartis, allowing it to remain one of the largest and most profitable pharmaceutical companies in the world.[14] ◀

Companies and government agencies spend enormous amounts of resources to amass large quantities of data. However, only a fraction of the data are used effectively, because in many cases the volumes are too large to manage or the data are stored in too many different systems or parts of the company to be accessed effectively.[15] To remain competitive in this information-dependent world, managers must find ways to manage data about global market environments and the impact of business decisions. In fact, managing intellectual capital may be the key to future survival. This requires a well-planned marketing information system. Before we discuss the details of a marketing information system, it is helpful to examine the evolution and process of secondary-data management.

Managing Secondary Data

The variety and richness of the available secondary data can often minimize or even eliminate the need for primary data. But merely keeping abreast of all the available data without being overwhelmed is a challenge. Capitalizing on the "information explosion" without drowning in data requires effective secondary-data management—that is, creating and operating a system for continuously monitoring various data sources and quickly retrieving needed data.

From Ad Hoc Projects to System-Oriented Projects

In Chapter 1 we saw that marketing research can provide valuable inputs at three basic stages of the marketing decision-making process: identifying marketing opportunities and constraints, developing and implementing marketing plans, and evaluating the effectiveness of marketing plans. The following are examples of questions that marketing research can help answer at each stage:

- *Identifying marketing opportunities and constraints.* What is the market potential for our product? What are the demographic and socioeconomic characteristics of the region where we wish to market our product? How many potential competitors exist in the region, and how intense is the competition among them?

- *Developing and implementing marketing plans.* In what package sizes should we offer our product? What media are most appropriate for promoting our product? Through what types of retail outlets should we sell our product?

- *Evaluating the effectiveness of marketing plans.* How effective is our current promotional strategy? To what extent are users of our product inclined to buy it again? What are the market shares of our product and the products of our leading competitors?

An **ad hoc research project** is a discrete, situation-specific project that is initiated and completed in response to a particular question or set of related questions raised by a decision maker.

Marketing research has traditionally answered such questions through ad hoc research projects. An **ad hoc research project** is a discrete, situation-specific project that is initiated and completed in response to a particular question or set of related questions raised by a decision maker. Much marketing research is still conducted in the form of discrete projects. However, during the past decade marketing research has increasingly shifted from purely project oriented to systems oriented. **Systems-oriented marketing research** makes appropriate marketing information available on a regular, integrated basis. The shift toward a systems orientation is being fueled by two related forces: (1) a growing need for marketers to constantly monitor market developments, which have been occurring more and more rapidly; and (2) an opportunity to make use of advances in information technology to gain a competitive advantage.[16]

Systems-oriented marketing research makes appropriate marketing information available on a regular, integrated basis.

Companies are using a systems approach to ensure that each research investigation integrates and builds on other investigations, so that the information they generate emerges from an overall framework. This is not to say that there will be no more ad hoc research studies. But ad hoc studies will need to provide a coherent body of knowledge about the business and its relationship to the marketplace.

In the coming years, managers will continue to decrease their reliance on ad hoc research projects to answer their market-related questions. Instead, empowered by information technologies, they will have increasing access to "frameworks of knowledge" from which they can readily extract the information they need to assist them in their decision making.

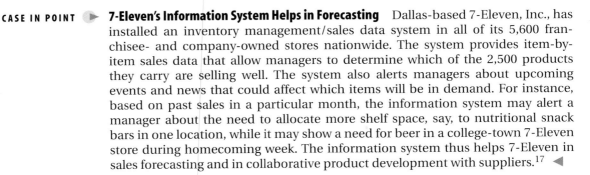

CASE IN POINT ▶ **7-Eleven's Information System Helps in Forecasting**   Dallas-based 7-Eleven, Inc., has installed an inventory management/sales data system in all of its 5,600 franchisee- and company-owned stores nationwide. The system provides item-by-item sales data that allow managers to determine which of the 2,500 products they carry are selling well. The system also alerts managers about upcoming events and news that could affect which items will be in demand. For instance, based on past sales in a particular month, the information system may alert a manager about the need to allocate more shelf space, say, to nutritional snack bars in one location, while it may show a need for beer in a college-town 7-Eleven store during homecoming week. The information system thus helps 7-Eleven in sales forecasting and in collaborative product development with suppliers.[17] ◀

The role of marketing research will expand to include assisting in the development of such information systems and serving as a constant link between decision makers and the marketplace. Therefore, marketing research will continue to be a critical component in the construction and updating of these systems.

Marketing Information Systems (MkISs)

A **marketing information system (MkIS)** is a continuing and interacting structure of people, equipment, and procedures designed to gather, sort, analyze, evaluate, and distribute pertinent, timely, and accurate information to marketing decision makers.

We have seen that a firm that obtains and utilizes marketing inputs on a regular, systematic basis can be said to have a marketing information system. A **marketing information system (MkIS)** is a continuing and interacting structure of people, equipment, and procedures designed to gather, sort, analyze, evaluate, and distribute pertinent, timely, and accurate information to marketing decision makers.[18]

Notice that the key tasks in conducting marketing research—data collection, recording, analysis, and interpretation—are implied in this definition. Thus marketing research techniques and principles are also relevant—and vital—to the proper functioning of a marketing information system. The main distinction between a marketing research project and a marketing information system is that the latter is a regular source of routine marketing reports (such as sales forecasts and market share analyses), whereas a specific marketing research project is intended to meet nonroutine information needs which cannot be adequately met by the firm's marketing information system.

The effectiveness of a marketing information system critically depends on how well the components are designed and interlinked.[19] Just as good interaction between researchers and research users is essential for the ultimate usefulness of a marketing research project, good communication between designers and potential users of a marketing information system is essential for the system's effectiveness. Moreover, designers of information systems have the delicate and difficult task of accommodating requests from multiple users and still ensuring that the system does not become too complex to be useful.

Many large companies today have sophisticated marketing information systems. Let's look at the MkIS of a leading global hotel chain headquartered in the United States. The hotel chain continuously collects a variety of data from within (for instance, occupancy rates, extent of guest satisfaction and dissatisfaction) and from outside (government and industry data on total lodging supply, demand for lodging). The collected data are analyzed to generate information that management uses to make decisions such as selecting markets for new hotels, allocating advertising spending geographically, tracking market share, and setting prices. The customer information system allows the chain to pull together information about its customers from different departments so that its representatives can anticipate and respond quickly to their needs.[20] Exhibit 4.2 outlines the hotel

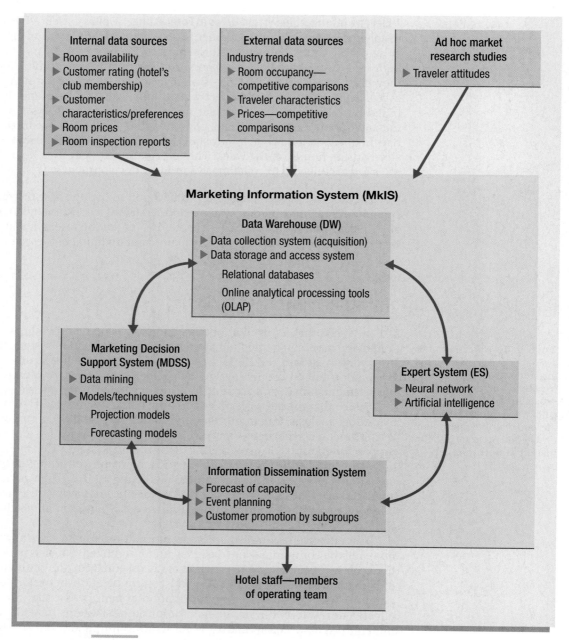

Exhibit 4.2
A Hotel Chain's Marketing Information System

chain's marketing information system. Relevant data for the chain's MkIS are obtained from within the company (internal data sources) as well as from outside (external data sources). These data are assembled, analyzed, and channeled through the chain's "information dissemination system."

The use of sophisticated marketing information systems is not limited to large firms. Smaller firms also can and do employ such systems. A case in point is Cover Concepts, a producer of book jackets with corporate advertising on the cover. Steve Shulman and Michael Yanoff, owners of Cover Concepts, covered schools' books

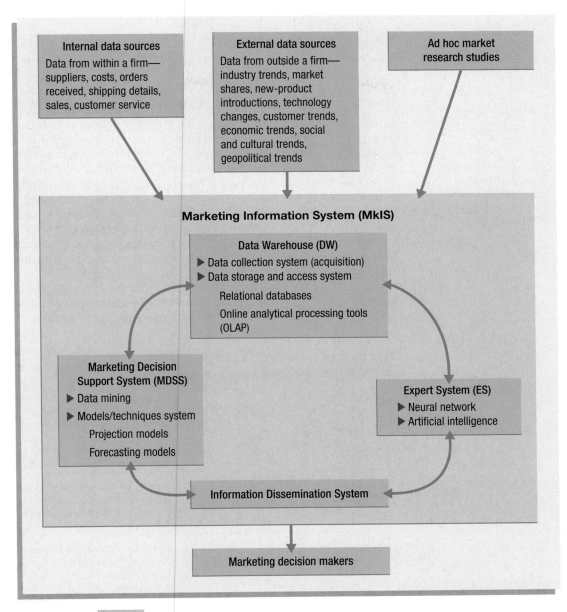

Exhibit 4.3
Structure of a Marketing Information System

with free jackets carrying advertisements and messages that appealed to kids, providing national advertisers with a cost-effective way to reach the 6- to 18-year-old market. The company's database has grown from 55 Boston-area schools in 1989 to 31,000 schools (out of a total of 85,000) and more than 21 million kids nationwide. Cover Concepts gathers the database's extensive demographic information, which it updates yearly, from the elementary, junior high, and high schools themselves, as well as from the Census Bureau, private database companies, and other sources.[21] Although the specific elements making up a firm's MkIS may be unique to that company, they will generally fall within the basic MkIS framework shown in Exhibit 4.3. Full-fledged marketing information systems contain three components.

- Information storage and retrieval system (data warehouse)
- Marketing decision support systems (data mining and modeling)
- Expert systems

Information Storage and Retrieval System: Data Warehouse

In its simplest form, a marketing information system contains an information storage and retrieval system. An important recent development accelerating the growth of marketing information storage and retrieval systems is the availability of data warehouses.[22] A **data warehouse** is a centralized database that consolidates companywide data from a variety of operational systems. Data warehouse software allows employees to ask questions and generate ad hoc reports to conduct an in-depth analysis (see Table 4.3 for more details). A well-designed data warehouse can be a valuable, multipurpose asset. For example, Staples' buyers can access their data warehouse to track sales trends, marketers can evaluate promotion expenses, store planners can exploit expansion opportunities, and senior management can track business performance store by store.[23]

Exhibit 4.4 presents an overview of a typical data warehouse operation. Data are transferred from transaction-processing systems, such as point-of-sale applications, financial information systems, and order management systems, and are

A **data warehouse** is a centralized database that consolidates companywide data from a variety of operational systems.

TABLE 4.3
Marketing Information System Components

Data warehouse	This is a centralized database that consolidates companywide data from a variety of operational systems. A data warehouse is made up of three very different functional areas: acquisition, storage, and access. Each of these must be customized to meet the needs of a business.
Acquisition	*Acquisition* involves collection of data from legacy (old) systems and outside sources. Here the data are identified, copied, formatted, and prepared for loading into the warehouse.
Storage	*Storage* is managed by relational databases (see Exhibit 4.7) like those from Sybase, Inc. (www.sybase.com) or Oracle Corp. (www.oracle.com).
Access	Different end-user PCs and workstations draw data from the warehouse with the help of query tools, neural networks, data discovery tools, queries, or reporting or analysis tools.
Data mining	This involves analysis of data to extract valuable and statistically valid information.
Online analytical processing tools (OLAP)	These help the analyst go beyond simple queries and reporting by enabling slicing and graphing of the data from any desktop.
Relational databases	These are databases stored in tables linked by various keys, such as customer code, supplier code, order code, and product code.

integrated periodically into a separate database dedicated to decision support. At the heart of each data warehouse lies a data model that contains vital statistics in the form of numeric information (Exhibit 4.5). This allows managers to easily extract and work with only the data they need.

In general, designing a simple, flexible MkIS and then expanding it as one gains experience with it is safer and faster than starting out with a complex, rigidly designed system. Many companies start with a data mart for each business process. A *data mart* is a scaled-down version of a data warehouse that contains a subset of information relevant to a particular group of users.

All MkISs contain a data warehouse. The data warehouse keeps managers in constant touch with the market by automatically channeling appropriate reports to them on a timely basis. Unlike an ad hoc research project, which gives managers a snapshot of a particular facet of a market in response to a specific request for information, a data warehouse provides managers with regular or routine sources of market information. As an illustration, at many consumer product companies, such as Colgate-Palmolive, Procter & Gamble, and Campbell Soup, regional marketing managers and field sales personnel who are constantly on the road can readily interact with the firm's marketing information support system to extract information that will help them in their interactions with customers.

Marketing Decision Support Systems: Data Mining

A **marketing decision support system (MDSS)** is a marketing information system that allows decision makers direct access to data and answers the "what if" questions raised by them.

Marketing information systems are evolving into marketing decision support systems in many firms. A marketing decision support system has greater capabilities than a marketing information system, as the following definition implies. A **marketing decision support system (MDSS)** is a marketing information system that allows decision makers direct access to information and answers the "what if" questions they raise.

Exhibit 4.4
A Typical Data Warehouse

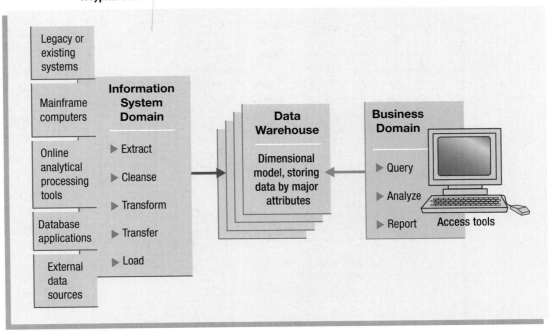

The ability of marketing decision support systems to make predictions under alternative "what if" scenarios enables managers to be proactive and to make better decisions. In contrast, managers assisted by a simple information storage and retrieval system (data warehouse) can, for the most part, react only to routine reports made available by the system. For example, Quaker Oats, marketer of such well-known brands as Gatorade and Rice-A-Roni, owes its leadership market position, at least in part, to its sophisticated marketing decision support system.[24] Its ready access provides current information in detail sufficient to assist managers in making sound decisions about allocating shelf space to different products, deciding on the product mix and sizes to offer, and setting prices. Other firms using marketing decision support systems include American Airlines (for price and route selection decisions); Frito-Lay (for price, advertising, and promotion decisions); and Sears (for evaluating potential store sites).

Competitive pressures have forced many large companies to develop MDSSs to help managers in decision making. The challenge for managers is to figure out how best to use the available data to build and sustain a competitive advantage. The two fundamental ways to explore the data warehouse are queries and data mining.

Exhibit 4.5
Database Model (Dimensional Model)

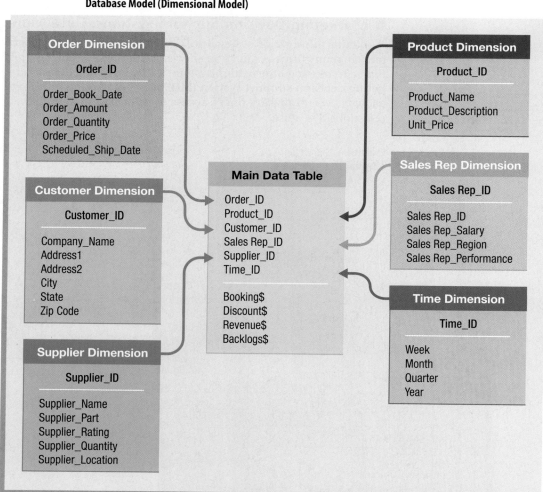

Queries enable users to search a database and obtain the desired information efficiently.

Data mining is the process of digging deeply into vast amounts of data to extract valuable and statistically valid information that cannot be obtained through queries.

Queries enable users to search a database and efficiently obtain the desired information. Users can point and click on the screen to modify data, without having to learn a specific query language. For example, a brand manager at Hershey Foods Corporation can view the entity "total sales" for the past two years and drill down (analyze to a specific level of detail) to see these sales broken down by sales territory or retail stores. The queries will help identify sales territories or retail stores with the highest total sales.

Data mining is the process of digging deeply into vast amounts of data to extract valuable and statistically valid information that cannot be obtained through queries. Increasingly, corporations worldwide are adopting data mining to make better-informed business decisions, whether the decision involves increasing customer value, analyzing customer buying profiles, identifying new markets and business trends, formulating new marketing strategies, performing cost analyses, improving management of the firm's financials, or supporting strategic decision-making. Table 4.4 presents a short list of companies that use data mining and the resultant benefits.

Some examples of data mining tools are IBM's Intelligent Miner (www.ibm.com), Angoss Software Corporation's KnowledgeSTUDIO (www.angoss.com), and Ruf Strategic Solutions' Ruf Business Targeting System (www.ruf.com). Ruf uses cluster analysis, a sophisticated statistical package, to identify subsets within a larger database that display common traits. The cluster analysis technique is described in detail at this textbook's website.

TABLE 4.4
Typical Applications of Data Mining

Companies	Benefits
Telecommunications AT&T MCI	Segmentation of prospective customers to increase new customer accounts, at the same time reducing cost per account; understanding individual customer preferences and needs, to deliver relevant long-distance products and services
Insurance Allstate BlueCross BlueShield	Improving profitability through timely valuation of insurance products; effective financial data management by balancing market, regulatory, and insurance pressures to provide superior customer/patient care
High-tech design Cadence Design Systems	Profitability analysis and product life cycle planning, leading to increased focus on nontraditional customer segments, thereby expanding the market
Retail Wal-Mart Sears Target Victoria's Secret	Demographic analysis, financial planning, and forecasting, leading to precise buying, merchandising, and marketing; improving profitability through optimal shelf space allocation; tighter end-to-end integration of internal as well as vendor systems, leading to better inventory and merchandise management; reducing returns, thereby improving margins
Banking Bank of America Capital One Chase	Consumer intelligence helps create new products and manage collections while containing delinquency rates; profitability analysis by customer segments; market penetration through personalized promotion strategies

Data mining essentially uses sophisticated statistical processing or artificial intelligence programs to automate the process of discovering useful trends and patterns from within a data warehouse. Unlike query languages that focus on associations, such as "total sales for region 1 versus region 2 for the two-year period ending 2000," data mining focuses on more significant factors. For example, a manager may want to predict the number of customers who will be lost to competitors. Using a mining technique (such as cluster analysis), the manager specifies an entity (say, "customer type") with which to analyze the database and determine all data elements that differentiate various customers (number of years doing business, repeat business, cost of doing business, and satisfaction level).[25] This will help in predicting the incremental sales that can be expected from various customer groups. Managers can then invest appropriately in various customer groups to maximize profits for the company.

Marketing Decision Support Systems: Models

The marketing response function is a mathematical model that represents the relationship between marketing input and output variables.

The ability to respond to "what if" questions posed by users requires MDSSs to have the models necessary for making the predictions. Therefore, incorporating data mining tools alone is not sufficient for upgrading a marketing information system to an effective marketing decision support system. To deliver its full potential, a marketing decision support system must also have appropriate marketing response functions built into it. A **marketing response function** is a mathematical model that represents the relationship between marketing input and output variables. Exhibit 4.6 shows an illustrative response function for how a brand's sales (an output variable) may change in response to different levels of advertising (an input variable).

■ **Marketing Response Functions**   Response functions like the one in Exhibit 4.6 must be constructed for all input variables that managers might include among the "what if" questions they pose to a marketing decision support system. Input variables other than advertising include price, expenditures on in-store promotions, amount of shelf space allocated, number of sales calls, and so on. The joint or interaction effects of several marketing inputs must also be incorporated into the system (for example, the impact on sales and profits of different advertising levels in combination with low, medium, or high prices). Moreover, an effective marketing decision support system will take into account possible variations in the response functions across different markets, owing to differences in market characteristics such as consumer demographics and levels of competition. The upshot is that building an effective marketing decision support system requires considerable groundwork to develop models capable of simulating market responses under a variety of conditions. Marketing research plays a crucial role in generating the raw material necessary to develop such models.

To illustrate, consider the advertising-sales response function. One approach to constructing such a function is to vary advertising levels systematically, collect data on advertising expenditures and sales, and analyze the data to establish the relationship between the two. An alternative approach is to analyze currently available advertising and sales data from markets in which different levels of advertising were employed in the past. Yet another approach is to ask experienced managers to draw on their market knowledge to estimate the likely sales levels at various advertising levels.[26] The estimates that managers provide can then be pooled to construct a response function. Because all these approaches involve generating

Exhibit 4.6
An Illustrative Advertising-Sales Response Function

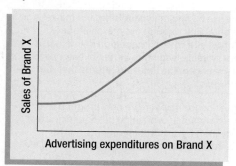

Sales of Brand X

Advertising expenditures on Brand X

and analyzing data of one form or another, marketing research is clearly an important ingredient in developing marketing decision support systems. Marketing research is also necessary to keep such systems up to date, because market characteristics and response functions can and do change over time.

MDSSs with Access to Retail Databases

Advances in research methodology and information technology are driving the use of increasingly improved marketing decision support systems in many sectors of business. Such systems are perhaps most sophisticated in the retail grocery sector. The advent of the universal product code (UPC) identification system and the availability of automated checkouts with optical scanners are facilitating easy accumulation of product, market, and sales data in the form of rich databases. These databases have greatly increased the capability of supermarket operators, as well as packaged goods manufacturers, to monitor and analyze sales trends, changes in brand shares, shifts in consumer preferences, and so on.

Retailers whose marketing decision support systems have access to the data generated by computerized optical scanners can get instant and accurate feedback about the relative sales performance of the products they carry. Such continuous feedback, when coupled with the various costs associated with carrying the products, can help retailers maximize their profits by fine-tuning their marketing mixes.

> **EXAMPLE** Numerous retail chains have installed marketing decision support systems that contain product sales data from checkouts, as well as data on virtually all factors that contribute to the cost of the products carried. (Some providers of such software include www.profitlogic.com, www.khimetrics.com, and www.demandtec.com.) These factors include shipping expenses, warehouse handling requirements, bulkiness of display, energy needs at the store, time spent on store shelves, promotional expenses, and so on. By accessing these data through the marketing decision support system, managers can perform sophisticated profitability analysis at the SKU (stock-keeping unit) or store level. Such analysis enables managers to pinpoint SKUs that are draining profits and identify corrective actions. These chain stores' profit-to-sales ratios increased sharply after a computerized decision support system was installed and put into use.

Producers of packaged goods are also benefiting from the wealth of data generated by computerized checkout scanners. They are doing so by subscribing to and linking their marketing decision support systems with one of several commercially available databases. An example is the BehaviorScan Advertising Testing conducted by Information Resources, Inc. (IRI), a pioneer in the field of scanner data research. The BehaviorScan database has grown in both size and scope since it was first established in the late 1970s. For instance, IRI has joined hands with rxremedy.com, a leading provider of syndicated, subscription-based tracking of consumer health intentions, behaviors, and outcomes, to measure the impact of television advertising on consumer health care behavior.

The heart of BehaviorScan is a central computer located at the firm's headquarters in Chicago. The computer constantly receives a variety of data from different market areas spread across the United States. These data are transmitted electronically from two sources: a panel of scanner-equipped supermarkets and a panel of households in each market area. BehaviorScan data are available at the individual household level and fall into three categories: household demographics, supermarket purchases, and television viewing.

A research firm that has developed database systems similar to BehaviorScan is ACNielsen Company, whose system is called ScanTrack. Databases such as

A **single-source database** contains, in an integrated fashion, data for individual households on household characteristics, product purchases, and exposure to marketing stimuli.

BehaviorScan and ScanTrack are known as single-source databases. A **single-source database** contains, in an integrated fashion, data on individual household characteristics, product purchases, and exposure to marketing stimuli. The last type of data includes data on exposure to a much wider range of marketing stimuli aimed at consumers by manufacturers as well as retailers. According to ACNielsen, its ScanTrack system captures a full range of data, such as those shown in Exhibit 4.7.[27] Packaged goods firms whose marketing decision support systems are linked to a database like the one in Exhibit 4.7 will have a greater ability to make sound decisions concerning a broader array of marketing mix variables. A case in point is the application of an MDSS to analyze scanner-based single-source databases and recommend a new product line. At Hershey Foods Corporation, chocolate candy sales were stagnating at $3.2 billion in 1998. Thanks to scanner data analysis by Information Resources, Inc., Hershey realized that the nonchocolate, seasonal, and assorted candy categories were growing at a rate of 32 percent and 9 percent, respectively. On the basis of this insight, Hershey has in recent years been diversifying its products.[28]

Expert Systems

The vast quantities of data available today are far outstripping the capacity of marketing decision makers to analyze them efficiently and derive the maximum possible insights from them. This data explosion, coupled with the emergence of

Exhibit 4.7
Data Captured in a Single-Source Database
Source: Paul M. Schmitt, VP and Director of Business Development, Nielsen Marketing Research, A.C. Nielsen Company, Nielsen Plaza, Northbrook, IL, 60062. Copyright © 1986, A.C. Nielsen Company. Reprinted by permission.

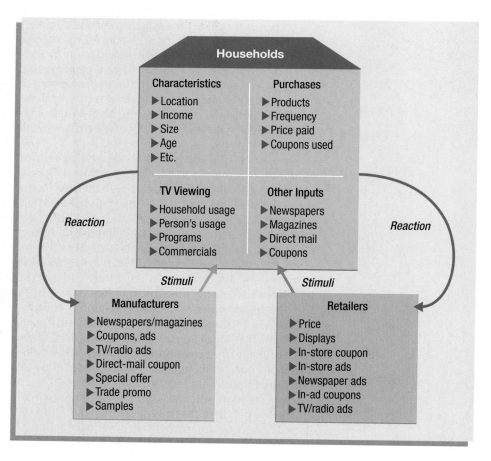

An **expert system (ES)** is a computer-based artificial intelligence system that performs tasks normally associated with human intelligence; it is programmed to reason and infer rather than to merely crunch numbers or store and retrieve information.

artificial intelligence technologies, is fueling the development of a new generation of decision support systems in the form of what is now known as an expert system. An **expert system (ES)** is a computer-based artificial intelligence system that performs tasks normally associated with human intelligence; it is programmed to reason and infer rather than merely crunch numbers or store and retrieve information. An expert system uses artificial intelligence technology that attempts to imitate the mental capabilities and reasoning processes of human experts. ESs can proactively make managers aware of market situations warranting their attention and can recommend appropriate courses of action.

CASE IN POINT ▶ **7-Eleven Maximizes Space and Selection**   An expert system employed by 7-Eleven, on sensing that the store's allocation of shelf space to different nutritional snack bar brands is suboptimal, alerts store managers and suggests how to reallocate shelf space to maximize profits from nutritional snack bar sales. 7-Eleven uses its expert system to determine the best allocation of shelf space among the various products it sells. After analyzing sales, cost, and promotional data, the system translates the results into "Plan-a-Grams," printouts that show store managers, shelf by shelf, exactly where to place their stock to maximize profits.[29] Even though marketing applications of expert systems already exist, only large firms currently employ such systems for making marketing decisions. ◀

Designing an expert system for use in the marketing field is a greater challenge than setting up a marketing decision support system. In addition to incorporating models and techniques similar to those found in a marketing decision support system, designers of a marketing expert system have to extract managers' knowledge and expertise and translate them into a set of decision rules that can be programmed into a computer. However, rudimentary applications of expert systems are emerging in several areas of marketing.

CASE IN POINT ▶ **Coca-Cola Helps Its Retail Partners**   Coca-Cola Company has created a free program to help retailers bring more customers into their stores and sell more of all the products they carry. Virtually all retailers with a scanner collect significant amounts of data on customer purchases, including universal product codes, number of items, price, time, and frequent-shopper membership purchases. Although retailers are already doing some analysis of customer data themselves, their capabilities vary. For these retailers, Coca-Cola Company offers a free service through which retailers in the program pass huge transaction files of information gathered during several months (stripped of any customer identifiers) to Coca-Cola's Atlanta headquarters. Coca-Cola's proprietary software segments shoppers by such factors as frequency of shopping, time, day, average basket size, total spending, profit generated, and category and brand choices.

The analysis is not just about soft drinks. Coca-Cola's program tries to help retailers grow the total business. One of Coca-Cola's customers, Gerland's Food Fair, allocated all of its end-of-aisle displays to snack and convenience items, to target occasional customers. However, Coca-Cola's analysis suggested that Gerland's replace the snack and convenience items with items such as pasta, soup, and tissues, sought by core customers. Gerland's implemented Coca-Cola's advice and realized a significant increase in the average basket size of its core shoppers.[30] ◀

New artificial intelligence technologies, such as neural networks, are continuing to emerge, and existing ones are being improved. At the same time, the pressure on marketing decision makers to use their ever-expanding databases more efficiently and effectively is also increasing. Therefore, expert system applications in marketing are likely to grow rapidly in the coming years.

SUMMARY

Although collected for other purposes, secondary data may be helpful in a project. In general, secondary data can be obtained more quickly and with less cost than primary data. Secondary data also can offer insights in situations in which an organization cannot collect primary data.

A potential limitation of secondary data has to do with relevance. Available secondary data may lack relevance for a given project for any of the following reasons: the units in which the data are reported may differ from the desired units of measurement; the categories in which the data are grouped may not match the requirements of the project; or the data may not be current. However, sometimes a researcher may be able to convert the measurement units, redefine the data categories, and rearrange or update the data. A researcher should explore these data modification options before dismissing available secondary data as irrelevant.

Another potential drawback of secondary data relates to accuracy, especially difficulty in verifying the trustworthiness of the data. The following interrelated questions will shed light on this issue: Who collected the data? Why were the data collected? How were the data collected? The original source of secondary data is more likely to provide the documentation necessary to answer these questions than is a secondhand source. Therefore, if at all possible, the original source should be consulted.

Secondary-data sources can be broadly divided into internal sources (those within the organization) and external sources (those outside the organization). The search for secondary data should begin with internal sources, because obtaining internal secondary data will require far less time, effort, and money than acquiring external secondary data. They may also be more pertinent to the situation being researched.

A very wide variety of external secondary-data sources exists. One useful way to classify them is as government sources; syndicated sources; trade associations; miscellaneous sources; and abstracts, directories, and indexes. Government agencies collect a huge volume of data, much of which is free and readily accessible. Data offered by syndicated sources are generally more expensive than those offered by government sources; however, they may also be more relevant to a research project. Trade associations are good sources of background data about particular trades or professions, although such data may be too general for use by a researcher or unavailable to nonmembers. Miscellaneous sources, such as journal articles, research monographs, and textbooks, are capable of providing insights, hunches, or ideas pertaining to a research project.

Abstracts, directories, and indexes serve as guides in identifying other sources of secondary data; recent technological advances have resulted in computerization of many of these sources.

One important use of secondary data involves ferreting out competitive information. Many secondary sources can provide a company with information about its competitors. Companies are increasingly relying on the Internet to obtain competitive intelligence.

Coping with the variety and abundance of secondary data available today is a major challenge. Effective management of secondary data is essential if maximum benefits are to be derived from them. Systematic procedures for identifying and scanning secondary-data sources and rapidly retrieving required data when needed are the key elements of effective secondary-data management.

A recent trend in the role of marketing research in decision making is an increasing shift from a pure project orientation to a systems orientation. This shift is being driven by a need to use marketing research inputs on a regular, integrated basis. Although the trend toward systems-oriented marketing research is still evolving, it has thus far spawned marketing information systems with increasing levels of sophistication.

The key building blocks of a marketing information system (MkIS) include an information storage and retrieval system (data warehouse), a marketing decision support system (data mining system and modeling system), and an expert system. At the simplest level, all MkISs have an information storage and retrieval system. The primary role of an information storage and retrieval system is to keep managers informed of market conditions and developments by generating regular reports and distributing them on a timely basis.

A marketing decision support system (MDSS) is an MkIS that allows managers to interact with it and raise "what if" questions. The upgrading of MkISs to MDSSs is being facilitated by data mining tools, user-friendly software packages for directly accessing and manipulating databases.

The most advanced type of marketing information system is an expert system (ES). An ES is an upgraded MDSS that makes use of artificial intelligence technology to imitate the mental and reasoning capabilities of human experts. The use of ESs in marketing is expected to expand rapidly in the near future.

REVIEW AND DISCUSSION QUESTIONS

1. "Primary data should be collected only when suitable secondary data are not available." Discuss this statement.

2. What three factors may reduce the relevance of secondary data? Give one example to illustrate each factor.

3. What is the difference between original and second-hand sources of secondary data?

4. Discuss the advantages and disadvantages of secondary data obtained from government sources and those obtained from syndicated sources.

5. What does "managing secondary data" mean? Why is it important?

6. Explain the difference between an ad hoc research project and systems-oriented marketing research.

7. What two forces are contributing to the move toward systems-oriented marketing research?

8. State three characteristics of a marketing decision support system that distinguish it from a marketing information system.

9. What is data mining? Is the availability of data mining techniques sufficient to upgrade an information storage and retrieval system to an MDSS? Why or why not?

10. What is a marketing response function? Briefly describe three approaches for developing response functions.

11. What is a single-source database? Discuss, with suitable examples, several unique benefits to a marketer who has access to a single-source database.

12. What is an expert system? Illustrate one marketing application of an ES.

APPLICATION EXERCISES

1. Assume you are the marketing manager for Revlon cosmetics (www.revlon.com) and you are considering expansion into China. Conduct a country analysis using secondary-data sources (see Tables 4.2 and 4.3 for specific sources). Specifically, provide an overview of China's economy and estimate the size of the market that may be interested in Revlon's products. To support your strategies, you need to find market share information for competing products.

2. You have just gotten an internship to work in the retail division of Pizza Hut. The restaurant chain is considering the European market. More specifically, you have been asked to focus on the market in France. Conduct a country analysis using secondary-data sources (see Tables 4.2 and 4.3 for specific sources). Specifically, provide an overview of the French marketplace and estimate the size of the market that may be interested in Pizza Hut's products.

3. Using the appropriate secondary-data sources, obtain the following information for the Metropolitan Statistical Area (MSA) in which you live or for the MSA closest to you. For each piece of information, state the sources you used and describe any calculations you made.
   a. Number of retail outlets and annual sales per outlet
   b. Number of law firms
   c. Percentage of families with children under 18 years of age
   d. The census tracts with the highest and lowest per capita incomes and their geographic locations
   e. Proportion of the total number of residential housing units less than 10 years old
   f. Proportion of residential housing units with seven or more rooms in (1) the entire MSA, (2) the census tract with the highest per capita income, and (3) the census tract with the lowest per capita income

INTERNET EXERCISES

1. Kodak (www.kodak.com) specializes in the digital imaging business. Some of its recent products include numerous digital cameras. Suppose Kodak wants to more aggressively market the product line to college students in the United States. Provide an overview of the U.S. economy and estimate the size of the college student market that may be interested in Kodak's products. To support your strategies, you need to find market potential for digital products. (*Hint:* Visit sites provided in Tables 4.2 and 4.3, such as www.census.gov for market size information.)

2. Nokia (www.nokia.com) specializes in the mobile telecommunications business. Its products include various network products and cellular phones. Suppose Nokia wants to more aggressively market the product line to consumers in Argentina. Provide an overview of Argentina's economy and estimate the size of the market that may be interested in cellular phones. (*Hint:* Visit sites provided in Tables 4.2 and 4.3, such as www.cia.gov for market information and www.stat-usa.com for information about the telecommunications market as demonstrated in Research in Use 4.2.)

Case 4.1 Time Inc.: Launching New Magazines
(www.time.com)

Quick! Name a magazine that you read! Chances are that your list included at least one of the following: *Time, Sports Illustrated, Fortune,* or *People.* These magazines, in addition to *Entertainment Weekly, InStyle, Golf Magazine,* and *Cooking Light,* are all owned by Time Inc. (www.timewarner.com). With over 130 magazines and over $5.5 billion in revenues in its portfolio, Time Inc. is well versed in actively researching and observing trends in society. These clues have aided the development of both new magazines and special issues. Time Inc. conducts research ranging from the examination of secondary data to conducting primary research.

The power of secondary data was evidenced by the sales of *People* when Selena, a multicultural pop star whose murder in 1994 shocked fans worldwide, graced the cover of a special-edition *People* (www.people.com). This issue was sold only in areas of the country where Selena's fan base primarily resided, areas with large Hispanic populations. Even with this limited distribution, that particular issue sold more than the former number-one special edition honoring the late Audrey Hepburn. These results indicated to Time Inc. that the Hispanic market was being untapped, so it developed and released a Spanish version of *People—People en Español* (www.peopleenespanol.com).

Sources of secondary data range from hard numbers derived from analyzing the sales for individual magazine issues to demographic trends taking place in the markets for those magazines. One good source for learning about trends is www.iconoculture.com. Sources like www.iconculture.com provide hard numbers about trends, such as which issues sold the most, as well as insights into shifting consumption patterns. Based at least partially on its use of secondary data, Time Inc. launched five new magazines in 2004. Some of its recent launches and specials include *Your Diet, Suede, LIFE, Real Simple,* and *Cottage Living.* These magazines are designed to exploit emerging trends discovered through secondary data.

- The diet industry targets its products at the over 180 million overweight Americans, who constitute a $40 billion market. It is no surprise that *People* magazine's covers promoting weight-related headlines invariably sell well. *Your Diet,* a special published by *People* magazine, was no exception to this trend.

- America is becoming increasingly diversified. By 2050 minorities will represent 47 percent of the U.S. population as compared to the current 25 percent. In response to this trend, Time Inc. launched *Suede,* a fashion and beauty magazine positioned for multicultural appeal.

- Consumers are making fewer trips to the supermarket—from an average of 85 in 1988 to 72 in 2003. *Life* (www.life.com) has a strong brand image from a long history of being part of Americana, and when Time Inc. relaunched the magazine as a Friday newspaper insert in Fall 2004, it started circulation with 12 million issues. The insert maintains magazine-quality pages but is distributed with newsprint.

- Social trends demonstrate that more and more consumers value good design, as evidenced by the success of Target, the well-known retailer, which concentrates on being a source of designer value. Time Inc. launched *Real Simple* (www.realsimple.com) to provide consumers with insights and solutions to designing questions.

- Recent concerns, such as terrorism in the wake of 9/11, have increased interest in the family, with the home becoming the center of our lives. Time Inc. has launched *Cottage Living* to capture the market's interest in comfort, simplicity, and style in turbulent, uncertain times.

Although headlines grab attention, there is more to creating successful magazines than just identifying changes in the target market and composing the perfect headline to titillate them. All aspects of a magazine should be designed to have an impact. Layout and design are important, in that they establish the readability and eye appeal of a magazine. Research is continually being conducted to ensure that magazines are as appealing as they can be. This is why your favorite magazines are always trying out new layouts. You may or may not like the changes, but they are designed to continually tweak the interests of the target market. Time Inc. has also determined that consumer time is increasingly valuable. The creation of bulleted points, informative visuals, and quickly read articles ensures that information is conveyed to busy consumers in a more efficient and organized manner, which research suggests is what readers want.

CASE QUESTIONS

1. What kinds of secondary data is Time Inc. using to help launch new magazines and special issues? What other kinds of secondary data, if any, are likely to be useful to Time Inc.?

2. Visit www.census.gov to identify changes in the demographic composition of the U.S. population (focus on age, gender, income, ethnicity, and education). Do the changes you identify suggest any new magazine opportunities for Time Inc.?

Ian Lewis, "Leveraging Consumer Clues for Business Impact" (25th Anniversary AMA Marketing Research Conference, New Orleans, LA, September 20, 2004); Matthew Flamm, "Relaunched Title Seeks Life Preserver," *Crain's New York Business,* December 6, 2004, 1; www.timewarner.com.

CASE 4.2 HARLEY-DAVIDSON
(www.harley-davidson.com)

With his recently minted MBA and new promotion, Christopher Dyer was excited about his first project as research director of Fast Facts, Inc. Christopher was preparing a secondary research analysis for a major global company interested in entering the U.S. premium heavyweight motorcycle industry. His goal was to better understand the market leader in the United States, Harley-Davidson, Inc., by doing some secondary research on the company. Christopher had long been a fan of Harley-Davidson motorcycles, ever since he purchased his first, a 1983 XR1000 with an overhead valve V-twin 1,000-cc engine, 11½-inch discs front and rear, and dual Dell'Orto carbs. He had absorbed a lot of Harley-Davidson history in the nearly two decades he had owned his bike and knew it to be a company with a solid reputation.

History of Harley-Davidson, Inc.

The concept of the motorcycle began in 1901 with the desire of two Milwaukee men, William Harley and Arthur Davidson, to take the work out of bicycling. Joined by Arthur's brothers Walter and William, they rolled their first products off the production line in 1903—three motorcycles. Harley-Davidson was incorporated in 1907 and enjoyed growth as people began replacing horses with motorcycles. Production increased further during World War I, as many vehicles went into military use. In 1920 Harley-Davidson became the largest manufacturer of motorcycles in the world.

After the 1929 stock market crash, sales dropped precipitously. As the U.S. economy slowly crept out of the depression, production increased. During World War II, the entire production of Harley-Davidson was dedicated to use by the Allied forces. After the war, competition heated up until 1953, when Harley-Davidson became the sole U.S. manufacturer of motorcycles.

The company went public in 1965 and by 1969 had merged with the American Machine and Foundry Company (AMF). Sales plunged again in the 1980s. In 1981, 13 senior Harley-Davidson executives purchased the company from AMF. As the company implemented design innovations in its bikes, it also developed the Harley Owners Group (H.O.G.) to encourage consumer involvement in the sport of motorcycling. As its continuous improvement initiatives began to produce fruit, the company again went public in 1986 and was approved for listing on the New York Stock Exchange in 1987.

Harley-Davidson worldwide unit shipments have steadily increased (see Exhibit 1).[1] Today, the Harley-Davidson name is revered as an American icon recognized around the world. It is the quintessential symbol of freedom, free-spiritedness, and love of the open road.

Summary

Although he was familiar with the motorcycle side of the company, Christopher needed to summarize the broader business aspects of Harley-Davidson. It was especially important to convey information pertaining to the long-term strength of the Harley-Davidson motorcycle division, because it would be a formidable competitor. Christopher identified three indicators of corporate strength that he had to find through secondary sources: growth potential, competitive strength, and sustainability of target market strategy. The fact that Fast Facts, Inc., guaranteed a 24-hour turnaround increased his motivation to obtain the information as quickly and efficiently as possible.

Exhibit 1

Worldwide Unit Shipments of Harley-Davidson Motorcycles

Numbers are in thousands and represent domestic and international shipments.

Source: Adapted from Harley-Davidson, Inc., Annual Report, 2004.

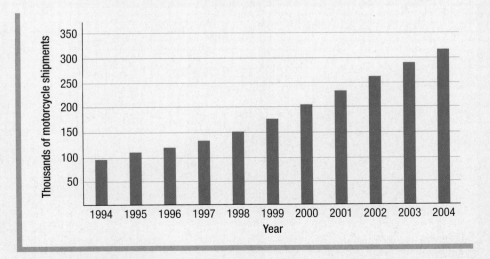

CASE QUESTIONS

1. Download Harley-Davidson's most recent annual report from its website (www.harley-davidson.com) and note its performance over the past 10 years in terms of the following: consolidated revenue, motorcycle shipments, and number of core customers as measured by Harley Owners Group (H.O.G.) memberships. How would you describe the company's *growth potential* based on this information?

2. Based on market share information contained in the annual report, what is the market share of Harley-Davidson motorcycles in the North American, European, and Asian/Pacific markets? Assess the company's *competitive strength* in each market based on this information.

3. Determine whom Harley-Davidson, Inc., considers its target customer by reviewing information from its most recent 10-K report, which can be accessed through the U.S. Securities and Exchange Commission's website (www.sec.gov). Based on U.S. Census population projections for 40-to-44- and 45-to-49-year-old males (www.census.gov), is this target market projected to grow or decline in the United States within the 2001–2020 time frame? What implications does this have for Harley-Davidson during the next two decades in terms of the sustainability of its current target market?

CASE NOTE

1. The company's history can be accessed at its website, www.harley-davidson.com.

This case was written by Jeanne L. Munger (University of Southern Maine) in collaboration with the textbook authors, as a basis for class discussion rather than to illustrate either effective or ineffective marketing practice.

Using Geographic Information Systems for Marketing Research*

What Do Starbucks, Blockbuster, and Hyundai Have in Common?

Chapter Objectives

After reading and understanding the material in this chapter, you should be able to:

■ Define geographic information system (GIS).

■ Explain how a store's trade area can be determined and how this helps in targeting customers.

■ Apply GIS to the process of choosing promising new store sites and forecasting sales at new store sites.

■ Describe how GIS and PRIZM groups are used to develop local advertising campaigns.

What do Starbucks, Blockbuster, Hyundai, and thousands of other U.S. businesses have in common? They rely on the U.S. Census to help them understand what types of people buy their products and services and how to better market to such people.[1] In effect, then, the U.S. Census is a very large marketing research project, and the 2000 census was the world's largest marketing research project ever.

The 2000 census used 400 million questionnaires that filled 500 tractor trailers, requiring 14,000 tons of paper and 15,000 gallons of ink.[2] Although the U.S. Census is conducted just once every 10 years (the next one will be in 2010), the Census Bureau also conducts periodic population surveys in off years. This effort is called the American Community Survey, and don't be surprised if someday soon you receive one of these surveys in the mail.

Why does the U.S. government invest so much money in and put such an effort into conducting the census and the American Community Survey? Government and business officials across the country and throughout the world rely on census data to gain an intimate look at the population in each neighborhood, city, county, state, and region in the United States. The census provides critical information that includes population counts and density; demographics (average age, income, education level, race); family structure (marital status, number of children); housing (homeownership and value of home, apartment rent); regional migrations; and demographic changes.[3]

Companies use these data to determine into which areas to expand, which products to offer in each area, and how to tailor their marketing and advertising campaigns appropriately to each locale. For example, Starbucks Corporation uses census data, in-store sales data, and a special type of decision support software called GIS (discussed shortly) to assess the viability of proposed new store sites. Starbucks research analysts input the addresses of suggested new store locations

*This chapter was developed by Professor Cornelia (Connie) Pechmann, Professor of Marketing at the Graduate School of Management, University of California, Irvine. She was assisted by MBA students Luke FitzSimons and Adam Chamie. Reprinted by permission.

into the GIS software, where census data are accessed and a forecasting model is used to evaluate the success of each proposed site.

Blockbuster Inc. uses census data and GIS software to ensure that each store carries the appropriate mix of movies to meet local needs. By comparing each store's movie rentals with its local market characteristics, management at Blockbuster can anticipate the demand for new movie releases and order the right number of copies to avoid being out of stock.

Hyundai identifies new markets with characteristics similar to those of its most successful car markets, then targets those promising areas with direct-mail advertising. In effect, instead of sending expensive advertisements to every household, Hyundai management identifies and mails to neighborhoods that are most likely to respond to its advertising and promotions. ■

In this chapter, you will learn how census data and other complementary data are used along with GIS decision support software to improve marketing decision making in the United States and in countries such as Canada, the United Kingdom, and Japan.

Geographic Information Systems

A **geographic information system (GIS)** is decision support computer software that stores, displays, and analyzes geographic data.

Geographic information systems are quickly becoming a standard in business and marketing research. A **geographic information system (GIS)** is decision support computer software that stores, displays, and analyzes geographic data.[4] GIS decision support software, which can be either desktop or Web based, allows users to present and interact with data on or from a map.[5] Much of the mapped data come from the U.S. Census or the American Community Survey, as discussed previously. Typically the data are purchased along with software from a GIS supplier, such as Claritas, ESRI (Environmental Systems Research Institute), or MapInfo. Many marketers also purchase data on consumers' projected product expenditures. Expenditure estimates are derived by combining census data with data from sources such as the Consumer Expenditure Survey of the U.S. Bureau of Labor Statistics. Other data are often purchased and integrated into GIS systems as well. For instance, Tele Atlas (formerly GDT) provides data on street locations and traffic, and Acxiom (www.acxiom.com) provides data on competitors' store locations and sales. Many businesses also integrate internal company data, such as store locations, store sales, and customer addresses.

GIS is an excellent analytical tool for business and marketing research. GIS software allows researchers to integrate multiple data sources, create interactive maps, and run powerful analyses. Businesses depend on GIS to learn more about existing and potential new markets, to assess the customer base and competitive situation, and to identify expansion and consolidation opportunities. They use GIS to ensure that local stores meet local needs and to forecast sales. GIS is also used to identify neighborhoods most likely to respond to local (direct-mail) advertising and to determine the most effective advertising messages for these neighborhoods. You can find out much more about GIS in several books.[6]

You have probably already used a GIS application without even knowing it. Yahoo! Maps, powered by MapQuest, provides directions to almost anywhere in the United States. By entering an address and clicking on a destination, you can create the map you need, complete with directions. Exhibit 5.1 demonstrates this GIS application. The maps in the exhibit provide directions from a person's home to the closest Domino's pizza location. From the maps, we learn that the closest Domino's is 2.7 miles away, which would not have been apparent from the addresses alone. The maps also show which direction to travel from the person's home to get to Domino's, and the shortest route to take. What else can you learn from the maps in Exhibit 5.1 that would not be clear from the addresses alone? Domino's regularly uses GIS in its pizza delivery and planning processes (see Research in Use 5.1).

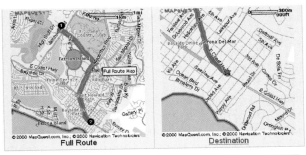

Exhibit 5.1
Using GIS to Obtain Directions to Domino's

Reproduced with permission of Yahoo! Inc. 2000 by Yahoo! Inc. YAHOO! and the YAHOO! logo are trademarks of Yahoo! Inc. Map provided by MapQuest.®

Geocoding

With GIS we are able to add information to area maps, such as customer locations, demographic information, crime reports, traffic flow data, zip code boundaries, cable network coverage, and countless other details that make a more realistic representation of that area. Maps are created by plotting data that have been geocoded. **Geocoding** is the process of assigning latitude and longitude map coordinates to a particular address.[7] For example, address geocoding matches addresses to map coordinates as shown in Exhibit 5.2. Geocoding allows users to import addresses from a spreadsheet or database file. The software matches addresses with longitude and latitude coordinates and then plots the addresses on a map. Exhibit 5.2 demonstrates this process using ESRI's popular ArcView GIS software.

> **Geocoding** (or *address geocoding*) is the process of appending latitudes and longitudes to addresses or other geographic locations to display them on a map or access related locational information.

Geocoding allows data from different sources to be integrated and examined from the perspective of a single area map. For example, within hours we can build an interactive area map that displays such detailed information as the average income of a neighborhood, which cars residents in the area tend to buy, which television shows and radio programs they tune to, and how many pizzas they eat per month on average. The benefit of GIS is that multiple data sources can be integrated for a single area and then accessed either simultaneously or selectively.[8]

Building an area map is the process of adding "thematic layers" of data to a map. Exhibit 5.3A demonstrates how layers of data are added to a map to create a fully integrated and interactive representation. These layers can be connected together because each has been geocoded, giving each point a longitude and a latitude. When a specific location is selected, data can be drawn from each layer to provide a more complete understanding of the attributes and characteristics of that location, as shown in Exhibit 5.3B.

Domino's Uses GIS

Domino's uses GIS for pizza delivery and business planning. Domino's drivers use GIS to find the shortest routes to deliver pizzas to people's homes and offices. In addition, Domino's managers use GIS to see which of its stores are most successful and why—that is, which factors are predictive of success. This analysis helps them determine where to open new Domino's stores, as we will discuss later in the chapter.

GIS helps Domino's drivers keep up with the crush of deliveries. The company is using a GIS (geographic information system), which has evolved over a couple of years, to map in advance the best delivery route to each customer's address. The company also has used GIS to select store locations based on driving distances, buying trends, and other factors; to distribute inventory efficiently; and to identify business opportunities. "The phrase 'A picture's worth a thousand words' really does apply," said Tim Monteith, senior vice president of IS at the Ann Arbor, Michigan, company [Domino's Corporation]. "It's had a huge impact on our ability to visualize and understand our market. It helps us immensely to have a common database that we can look at spatially."

Domino's GIS is powered by MapInfo's namesake desktop GIS application, which is used to analyze purchased demographic data such as household age, income, and gender. It's linked to a data warehouse fed with point-of-sale data collected from 650 Domino's-owned pizza shops and 6,100 franchisees. Using the tool, Domino's managers can, by pointing and clicking, look at detailed street maps and drill down for in-depth customer information.

Domino's Pizza uses the global positioning system (GPS) technology to track exactly where its drivers are and where their pizzas need to be delivered. Under the Domino's system, satellites will track where each driver is by using a signal transmitter in specially made trainers. Hi-tech headphones worn by the drivers will ensure that they are directed to the correct address if the signals indicate they are going astray.[a]

Micro Marketing

Marketers use GIS maps to better understand and analyze the lifestyles and product preferences of people living or working in various neighborhoods. This knowledge enables marketers to adjust their marketing mix to best reflect the preferences of their local customers. A chief goal of marketers is to design the marketing mix, or four Ps, meaning to determine the right products, prices, promotions, and places for their businesses. Tailoring the marketing mix for a local neighborhood target market is called **micro marketing**.[9] More specifically, micro marketing involves designing the right marketing mix for the local neighborhood: the right products to be sold, at the right prices, in the right places, and using the right promotions.

Micro marketing benefits both customers and businesses. Customers benefit because the locations (placements) of their local stores and the products, prices, and promotions in those stores reflect what they want and need. Businesses gain from operating efficiencies, such as increased inventory turnover, more efficient advertising, and increased goodwill from the customers they serve. This win-win relationship is based on businesses' understanding their customers better.

In sum, companies use GIS to improve their understanding of customer behavior and buying patterns. The following example demonstrates how GIS can help marketers home in on neighborhood buying patterns with a few clicks of a computer mouse. As you read the example, consider what you could do with this type of information. What are the benefits to understanding your customers and markets in this amount of detail? What might be some dangers? Which types of products might justify this type of analysis, and which might not?

Micro marketing is the process of tailoring the marketing mix for a local neighborhood.

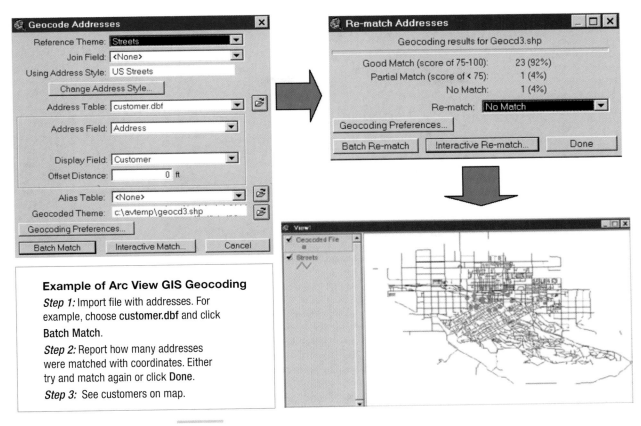

Example of Arc View GIS Geocoding

Step 1: Import file with addresses. For example, choose **customer.dbf** and click **Batch Match**.

Step 2: Report how many addresses were matched with coordinates. Either try and match again or click **Done**.

Step 3: See customers on map.

Exhibit 5.2
The Process of Geocoding Customer Address Lists So That Customers Can Be Shown on a Map

Text and Graphics reprinted from "ArcView® GIS Means Business," courtesy of ESRI. Copyright © 1997, Environmental Systems Research Institute, Inc. All rights reserved.

CASE IN POINT ▶ **Homing in on Neighborhood Buying Habits**   "[Dean Stoecker, SRC president and CEO] typed my home address into the [GIS] system and compared the buying habits of my neighbors with national averages for about 50 items including video rentals, electronic games, and alcoholic beverages. He defined an initial radius of five miles around my house. Then he tightened the radius to three miles, one mile, and one-half mile. I squirmed in my chair as the number of households in the region approached one, at which point we would be looking at my purchasing history."[10] ◀

This chapter highlights three specific GIS applications used by marketers: mapping and targeting customers, choosing new store sites, and developing local advertising campaigns. You will see how firms are adopting GIS to improve their marketing efforts and how you might use GIS in the future.

Mapping and Targeting Customers[11]

Ace Hardware Corporation (Oak Brook, Illinois) is a leading wholesale hardware cooperative, with year 2004 sales of $3.29 billion.[12] The company buys for some 5,000 retailers worldwide that compete successfully against warehouse-style superstores by offering high-quality, well-packaged products and first-rate

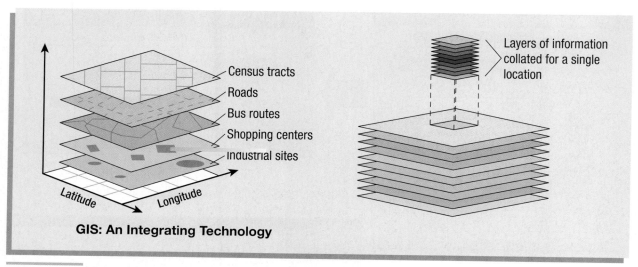

GIS: An Integrating Technology

Exhibit 5.3A, 5.3B
Displaying Layers of Information on a GIS Map

Provided courtesy of Kirsten K. Connelly, Kenneth E. Foote, and Margaret Lynch, The Geographer's Craft Project, Department of Geography, The University of Colorado at Boulder.

customer service. GIS analysis helps management target specific stores for reloca-tion, provide advertising and merchandising advice to local stores, and decide whether or not to accept new Ace retailer affiliations.

A local store in the Phoenix area, Paradise Valley Ace Hardware, conducted an in-store survey to obtain the data needed for GIS analyses. Specifically, a local con-sulting firm collected shoppers' home addresses in the Ace store over a two-week period. Two hundred addresses were sent to Ace headquarters, where the data were imported into ESRI's ArcView GIS software. The addresses were geocoded so that each customer could be plotted on an area map. Zip code boundaries were added to the map, showing that 85 percent of the store's customers came from one of three zip codes. Previously, management had defined the store's *trade area* (its service area) as consisting of 12 zip codes. Management immediately decided to restrict most advertising to the three focal zip codes to increase advertising efficiencies. Exhibit 5.4 shows the area map with the customer locations plotted as red dots.

Household income data were purchased from an outside vendor and added to the map. These data revealed that a very high-income area was located within two miles of the Paradise Valley Ace store. Despite its proximity, the store had failed to attract customers from this area. Thus management decided to create special promotions to attract these potential customers. Exhibit 5.5 shows customer locations plotted over areas that are color-coded to represent the median income of each neighbor-hood. Different colors represent differ-ent median incomes, with deep red indicating the highest median income.

Management identified products that would appeal to these high-income households—in particular, home security systems—and created a promotional mailer. Using an out-side direct-mail vendor, the company selected two zip codes with the highest

Exhibit 5.4
Zip Codes and Customer Locations Surrounding Ace Hardware Store

Text and Graphics reprinted from "ArcView® GIS Means Business," courtesy of ESRI. Copyright © 1997, Environmental Systems Research Institute, Inc. All rights reserved.

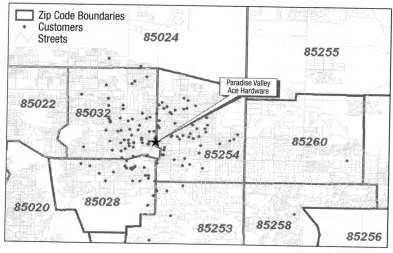

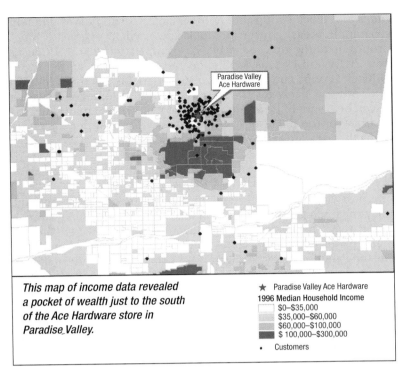

This map of income data revealed a pocket of wealth just to the south of the Ace Hardware store in Paradise Valley.

★ Paradise Valley Ace Hardware
1996 Median Household Income
□ $0–$35,000
□ $35,000–$60,000
▨ $60,000–$100,000
■ $100,000–$300,000
• Customers

Exhibit 5.5
High-Income Neighborhoods (in Red) to the South of Ace Hardware Store

Text and Graphics reprinted from "ArcView® GIS Means Business," courtesy of ESRI. Copyright © 1997, Environmental Systems Research Institute, Inc. All rights reserved.

A **Block Group** is a U.S. Census Bureau–defined geographic unit consisting of about a dozen city blocks or 340 households.

median incomes, mailed the promotional pieces, and waited for a response. On the first day of the promotion, the store recouped the entire cost of the mailing. Interest from the high-income group continued for weeks after the promotion, and management planned future targeted mailings.

Understanding the Process

In the Ace example, the objective was to better understand and market to the store's current and potential customers. The GIS analysis revealed the trade area where the store's customers came from and the median income for each neighborhood within or close to that trade area. With this knowledge, Ace was able to tailor advertising and promotional programs to specific neighborhoods, lower marketing costs, and increase sales.

Area Map

A key benefit of GIS is the ability to combine multiple data sources and create an accurate and meaningful map of the data. In this example, the first step was to create an area map around the Paradise Valley Ace hardware store. An area map generally begins with such familiar geographic boundaries as cities, counties, or zip codes. Ace used U.S. postal zip codes, as well as smaller neighborhood units called Block Groups. A **Block Group** is a U.S. Census Bureau–defined geographic unit consisting of about a dozen city blocks or 340 households.[13] If you look at the top map in Exhibit 5.6, you will note that these small neighborhoods are shown within the larger, numbered zip codes. A Block Group is far smaller than a zip code and is the smallest area for which detailed demographic information is available from the U.S. Census.

The Ace store address and the customer addresses obtained from its in-store survey were then imported from a Microsoft Excel spreadsheet and plotted on the same map (see the top map in Exhibit 5.6). ESRI's ArcView GIS software automatically assigned each address's latitude and longitude coordinates, and displayed them precisely on the map, using geocoding. Most leading GIS software applications are bundled with address geocoding capabilities, as well as geographic boundaries such as zip codes and Block Groups.

How Do Zip Codes Compare to Block Groups?

The U.S. Census Bureau releases data on small neighborhoods, or Block Groups, to provide the most detailed information it can to local governments, communities, and businesses, while preserving the confidentiality of individual household data records. However, marketers often use U.S. Postal Service zip codes, which are much larger geographic units, often the size of an entire city, to segment the population and send targeted advertisements and promotions to potential customers. How do marketers know who lives in a particular zip code? Since zip

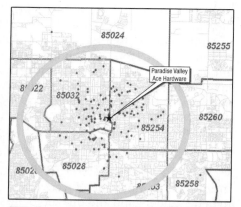

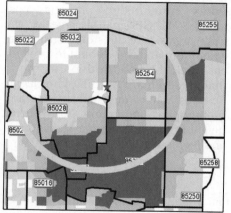

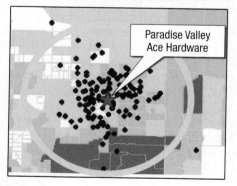

Exhibit 5.6

Multiple Views of the Trade Area Surrounding the Ace Hardware Store

Key: Top map shows the zip codes surrounding the Ace hardware store and the store's current customers (as dots). The circle represents the store's trade area.

The second map adds median household income data. Red areas represent high-income Block Groups, defined as having median household incomes of over $100,000.

The third map shows that most of the store's current customers do not come from the high-income (red) areas.

codes and Block Groups are not the same size and cover different geographic areas, conversion tools are used to aggregate Block Groups up to the zip code level. For example, the 2000 U.S. Census uses ZCTA (Zip Census Tabulation Areas) to match up zip codes to Block Groups and to provide census data for zip areas. In most GIS software packages, this conversion is automatic. However, researchers should be aware that these conversions may affect the accuracy of the data because the boundaries may not match up perfectly, and data extrapolation (estimation) may be necessary.[14]

Trade Area Identification

The next step Ace used in creating its GIS map was to show the trade area being serviced by the Paradise Valley hardware store. A **trade area** is the geographic area surrounding a store where the vast majority of its customers come from. In the maps shown in Exhibit 5.6, the Paradise Valley hardware store's trade area is indicated with yellow circles. Businesses generally find it valuable to identify their trade area. For instance, as mentioned earlier, Ace management learned that 85 percent of its customers came from just 3 zip codes, not 12, as it had believed. Because most of Ace's advertising was direct mail sent to customers by zip code, this meant that Ace could substantially reduce its advertising costs by eliminating mailings to zip codes outside its trade area.

There are many methods for defining a business's trade area. However, when a business has a customer address list, it generally plots those addresses on a map. Then it defines its trade area by drawing a circle that includes approximately 70 to 80 percent of its customers. This approach avoids using too large a trade area, which might skew the analysis. The center of the circle is the business's street address. The radius of the circle roughly indicates the drive time or travel time to the business (three or five miles). In other words, the radius indicates the distance most customers are willing to travel to the business from any direction around it.[15] (Refer again to the top map in Exhibit 5.6.)

Demographic Analysis of the Trade Area

The final step in creating the Ace trade area map was to show the median income for each Block Group in the trade area. Median income data are provided by the U.S. Census. Median income is often used as an indicator of a neighborhood's buying capacity. On the second (middle) map in Exhibit 5.6, note that each Block Group has been color-coded to show its median household income. The darkest shade of red indicates the highest-income neighborhoods (over $100,000 annually). The highest-income (red) neighborhoods were presumed to have the most money to spend in stores like Ace.

As the third map in Exhibit 5.6 shows, most people from the high-income neighborhoods were not coming to Ace for their hardware needs. Ace management responded by sending direct-mail advertisements for home security products to these households. The targeted advertising campaign was very successful, demonstrating the benefits gained by knowing one's customers and markets better.

A **trade area** is the geographic area surrounding a store where the vast majority of its customers come from.

Micro merchandising is the practice in which stores customize the products on their shelves to meet the needs of local customers.

Micro Merchandising

In this case, Ace promoted security products that it already sold in its stores to appeal to high-income buyers. Ace could also have added new products to its shelves that would appeal to high-income shoppers. When stores customize the products on their shelves to meet the needs of local customers, they are engaging in **micro merchandising.** Micro merchandising is a common practice in the retail industry and explains why different stores in the same retail chain often stock different selections. The goal is to stock products that are most likely to sell in the local neighborhood or trade area. Can you see why micro merchandising might be beneficial? Have you noticed examples of micro merchandising in stores? Would you consider micro merchandising before opening a store or while running one?

Now let's look at how GIS can help businesses choose promising new store sites.

Choosing New Store Sites

Choosing the right products and customers for a business can certainly increase profits, but choosing the right location for a business is also critical to success. How do you know where the right location is? For instance, how do casual-dining restaurant chains such as T.G.I. Friday's (TGIF), Mimi's Café, and California Pizza Kitchen find promising locations for new stores? Casual-dining restaurant chains are big business. TGIF currently operates over 500 restaurants in 47 states, with locations in over 150 MSAs (Metropolitan Statistical Areas). MSAs are urbanized areas of at least 100,000 people consisting of a core area containing a large population nucleus, together with adjacent communities that are economically and socially integrated with the core.[16]

TGIF continuously seeks growth opportunities in new MSAs. TGIF, McDonald's (see Research in Use 5.2), and many other businesses use GIS to find promising locations for new stores, a process called *new-site selection*. GIS helps firms determine which markets to enter, how many stores to put in each market, and where to locate each new store. We will discuss later how most of this process is done. In brief, firms use GIS to identify key factors leading to success in their current sites and then to find other sites where these factors are also present.

To illustrate the typical new-site selection process, we will look at a restaurant chain using the pseudonym "Connie's Café."[17] Executives from a leading marketing research firm and a casual-dining restaurant chain contributed to this case.[18] You can think of this case as "Site Selection 101."

Each year Connie's Café receives hundreds of proposals from realtors, land developers, and entrepreneurs for franchises in new locations. When a proposal for a new store site is received, management enters the location's address into GIS software so that it can be geocoded and plotted on an area map. The location's expected trade area is also shown, typically as a circle (see Exhibit 5.7). Market data for the area are added to the map. These data are purchased from outside vendors and pertain to Connie's Café's key success factors. Management uses regression analysis to measure the effects of these factors on Connie's Café sales. The results provide the basis for the sales forecasting formula the firm employs. (Regression analysis is discussed further in Chapter 14.)

Exhibit 5.7
Possible New Restaurant Locations

Key: Stars indicate possible new restaurant locations.

Red circles indicate expected trade areas for each location.

Yellow circles indicate walking distances to each location.

Graphics courtesy of Claritas, Inc., copyright 2001.

McDonald's Is Faster with GIS

Once a business knows the key factors that make a store site successful or unsuccessful, it can quickly scan large areas for potential new store sites. McDonald's uses a GIS system to overlay demographic information on maps to help decide exactly where to put new burger stands.

This is what McDonald's is doing in Japan as it aggressively plans to open 2,000 new locations in the next five years. McDonald's Japan knows the restaurants' minimum sales requirements and the factors that affect sales, and its GIS system utilizes this information to identify promising new store sites. It once took five days to review and select potential sites; now it takes less than 30 minutes with GIS. Managers at McDonald's are reviewing potential sites, forecasting sales, and opening new locations faster than you can say "cheeseburger"![b]

Managers use this approach to rank order each potential new store site. High-ranking locations are considered further; the others are rejected. The process is fast, efficient, and effective. The managers trust the screening process because it has proven successful and is based on sound statistical principles. The company has had an excellent success record using GIS to choose new store sites.

Understanding the Process

The new-site selection process requires management to define the site's likely trade area, extract relevant market data on that trade area, create a sales forecasting model, use the forecasting model to predict sales at the new site, and apply a final checklist to verify that other success factors, such as street access and appropriate zoning, are present. Next we'll discuss each step in turn.

Defining the Trade Area

The first step in the new-site selection process is to define the business's trade area or "reach." Connie's Café's trade area was drawn as a circle with a five-mile radius; that is, it extended five miles around the store in every direction. Customer data collected from its "frequent diners program" showed that 80 percent of its customers lived or worked within a five-mile radius of the Connie's Café restaurant they frequented. Management defined the trade area as a standard five-mile radius so that it could directly compare sales forecasts across potential new store sites. Note, however, that the market data from which sales forecasts are derived are based on census Block Groups. The next section discusses how Block Group data are obtained and transformed into trade area data.

Extracting Relevant Market Data

Marketing research companies as well as the U.S. Census Bureau collect market data on a regular basis, typically issuing annual reports. There are two main types of market data: population data and dollar sales potential data. *Population data* indicate how many people live or work in each geographic area and who they are in terms of their age, income, and other relevant demographic information. *Dollar sales potential* data indicate how much these people are likely to spend on various products and services, typically within a given year. Syndicated data vendors such as Claritas and R. L. Polk & Company combine these two types of market data to create a detailed description of the consumers in each U.S. Census Block

Group or neighborhood, along with their buying habits. These data are typically bundled with GIS software and sold as a package. Consumer privacy is preserved because the data do not involve individual people or households; rather, they involve neighborhoods.[19]

When a business purchases data from a vendor, the data often must be cleaned and converted to standard units. Cleaning data involves manually auditing the data for incomplete or duplicate information. Converting data to standard units means matching up the geographic areas used by the data vendors and the business. Vendors sell data on standard geographic areas such as census Block Groups. However, most businesses want to analyze the data based on trade areas. Hence, most businesses must convert the data from the outside vendors into trade area–level data before conducting their analyses. Fortunately, most GIS software can convert data from multiple Block Groups into a single number for each relevant trade area. Block Groups that are not completely within a trade area are divvied up in proportion to the amount of overlap with the trade area. Exhibit 5.8 shows how Block Groups are combined into a trade area.

Dollar Sales Potential

Management at Connie's Café had one main goal: to generate dollar sales forecasts for each proposed new store site. Management believed a significant factor that would affect sales was the trade area's dollar sales potential. Dollar sales potential for casual dining is an estimate of how much money will be spent on casual dining per year by the people who live or work in the trade area. GIS data vendors estimate dollar sales potential (also called *consumer demand* or *consumer potential*) for various products and services using a two-step process. First, U.S. Census data are used to determine how many and which types of people (for instance, students, young professionals) live or work in each Block Group in the area. Then data like those from the Consumer Expenditure Survey of the U.S. Bureau of Labor Statistics are used to determine how these people are likely to spend their money.

Management at Connie's Café purchased data from a GIS vendor on the dollar sales potential for casual dining. The data might have shown that, for instance, a typical college student spends $30 per year on casual dining. This would mean that, for each additional college student living or working in a Connie's Café trade area, the dollar sales potential for casual dining would increase by $30. The $30 is a per capita, or per person, estimate. It is based on *all* college students, including those who don't spend any money on casual dining and those who spend much more than $30 per year, so think of it as a mean, or average. Table 5.1 shows how per capita estimates are combined with population counts to calculate the dollar sales potential for casual dining within a specific trade area.

As Table 5.1 shows, the young professionals group is expected to spend $100 per capita on casual dining annually, and 10,000 of them are believed to live in the proposed new trade area. In all, then, the young professionals who live in the trade area are expected to spend $1 million per year on casual

Exhibit 5.8
Block Groups Composing a Restaurant or Retail Trade Area Are Converted into a Single Trade Area Estimate

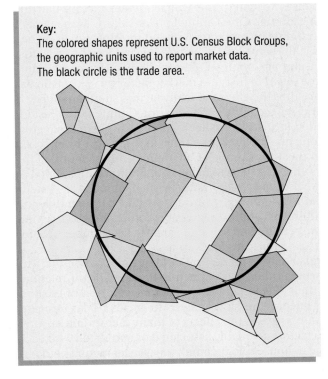

Key:
The colored shapes represent U.S. Census Block Groups, the geographic units used to report market data.
The black circle is the trade area.

TABLE 5.1
Calculating Dollar Sales Potential

Consumer Segment	Estimated per Capita Expenditures on Casual Dining (Annual)	Population in Proposed New Trade Area	Dollar Sales Potential for Casual Dining (Annual)
Young professionals	$100	10,000	$1,000,000
College students	30	10,000	300,000
Total			$1,300,000

restaurant dining ($100 x 10,000 = $1,000,000). Presumably, these young profession-als would spend at least some of this money at Connie's Café if it were to open in their neighborhood. The college student group is expected to spend only about $30 per capita on casual dining annually. Because an estimated 10,000 college students live in the trade area, they should spend approximately $300,000 ($30 × 10,000) per year. If these were the only two groups living in the trade area, the total dollar sales potential for casual dining in the area would be $1,300,000 ($1,000,000 + $300,000). If an area could be found that was more densely populated with young profession-als, it would likely be preferable to this area.

Sales Forecast Formula

Management assessed the significance of several other factors that might con-tribute to business success. Business success can be measured in many different ways. Connie's Café management used annual sales as its measure of success. Specifically, using data from a large sample of Connie's Café restaurants, manage-ment applied regression analysis to determine which market factors had the greatest systematic impact on Connie's Café's annual dollar sales.[20] Management used two kinds of regression: simple linear regression and multiple linear regres-sion. Both analyses accomplish the same goal of identifying and weighting factors that explain high versus low sales at Connie's Café restaurants. However, simple linear regression measures the effect of just one market factor on sales, whereas multiple linear regression measures the effects of many factors simultaneously.

To begin, market data and sales data from 30 existing Connie's Café restau-rants were gathered and loaded into a spreadsheet. Then a simple linear regres-sion analysis was run, using one market factor at a time, to determine its effect on sales at these 30 locations. In this way, Connie's Café management identified the number of competitors as another key success factor. Competitors are defined as direct competitors (other casual-dining restaurants) within Connie's Café's trade area. The competitor data were purchased from an outside data vendor and added to the spreadsheet. Within an instant, a regression output showed a signifi-cant relationship between competition and sales: the greater the number of com-petitors in the trade area, the lower the sales for Connie's Café.

Management repeated this analysis for several different market factors. The regression outputs showed which other market factors had significant relation-ships to sales and measured their effects. Once these factors were identified, they were plugged into a multiple linear regression analysis to create a sales forecast-ing formula. Multiple regression assesses the effects of many factors and ensures the best sales forecasts. If two factors are highly associated or correlated with each other (such as median and mean household income), the weaker factor should be dropped to avoid double counting.

In the case of Connie's Café, the number of competitors and the casual-dining dollar sales potential were plugged into the multiple regression analysis as independent (predictor) variables, and annual dollar sales at each restaurant were plugged in as the dependent (outcome) variable. The regression returned two beta coefficients that explained how much the sales at a Connie's Café restaurant would likely change for each unit change in (1) the number of competitors and (2) the casual-dining dollar sales potential. One beta coefficient might show that, as the number of competitors increases by 1, annual sales will likely decline by $400,000. The other beta coefficient might show that, for every dollar increase in casual-dining sales potential, annual sales will likely increase by a factor of 0.15. If the results turned out this way, the sales forecasting formula would look as follows:

Estimated Annual $ Sales in New Trade Area Defined as a 5-Mile Radius Around XXX Address

= Constant + (− 400,000 × Number of Casual-Dining Restaurants Already in Trade Area)

+ (0.15 × Estimated Annual Dollar Sales Potential for Casual Dining in Trade Area)

This type of formula can be used to forecast sales at each proposed new store site. The sites can then be ranked from best to worst based on forecasted sales, as shown in Exhibit 5.9.

Standard GIS software allows managers to calculate a sales forecast for any new location, provided that the relevant market data have been added and a trade area defined. Managers use GIS to screen and rank previously identified sites, as well as to search for new sites by manually moving a trade area from location to location. The ability of GIS to integrate data and run calculations makes it an effective and versatile business tool for screening new site locations and identifying sites that merit a closer look.

Final Checklist for Choosing New Store Sites

Some key success factors may be missing from the sales forecast equation because it would be too costly to collect the necessary data during the initial site-screening process. These factors might include proximity to large magnet stores, which would attract customers to a store location, street access, traffic, real estate costs, and zoning limitations. Connie's Café management uses a checklist to score a site based on such factors. Management completes this site checklist by adding data to its GIS maps, speaking with local realtors, and visiting the sites in person. A site checklist (see Table 5.2) is a quick and easy method for scoring potential locations on additional factors relevant to its success.

How do you think your city or neighborhood would score in terms of being a good location for a new casual-dining restaurant? Would there likely be high customer demand? Would a new restaurant face steep competition? Are any good locations available, such as a visible corner lot by a magnet store? Is your city promoting new-business development? Next time you drive or walk around, consider which spaces are available and score them based on your own checklist. Who knows? You may want to open your own restaurant or store someday!

TABLE 5.2
New Store Site Checklist

Site Checklist			
Proximity to magnet stores	Low	1	Score
	Moderate	3	
	High	5	___
Street access	Difficult to find	1	Score
	Within view	3	
	Corner attraction	5	___
Zoning	Many restrictions	1	Score
	Some restrictions	3	
	Restaurant ready	5	___

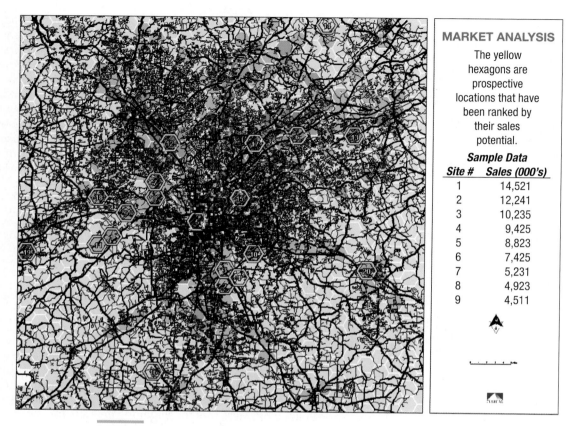

MARKET ANALYSIS

The yellow hexagons are prospective locations that have been ranked by their sales potential.

Sample Data

Site #	Sales (000's)
1	14,521
2	12,241
3	10,235
4	9,425
5	8,823
6	7,425
7	5,231
8	4,923
9	4,511

Exhibit 5.9
Ranking Potential New Site Locations Based on Forecasted Sales
Graphics courtesy of Claritas Inc., copyright 2001.

Developing Local Advertising Campaigns

Understanding your customers and choosing the best location for your business are certainly important, but without a successful advertising strategy, the business may not stay on the map. GIS can increase the effectiveness of advertising by helping businesses reach their target consumers while reducing their overall advertising expenditures. Consider how Lincoln Mercury uses GIS to maximize its advertising dollars.[21]

Lincoln Mercury, a subsidiary of Ford Motor Company, designs, manufactures, and sells many types of cars, trucks, and sport utility vehicles (SUVs). Based in Irvine, California, Mercury markets a full line of vehicles, including the Mountaineer, Cougar, Sable, Grand Marquis, and Villager.[22] Mercury uses national advertising campaigns, such as print ads in *USA Today,* to introduce new vehicles. National promotions are appropriate for announcing new products to a wide audience. However, Mercury also employs local and regional advertising campaigns that are overseen by local dealerships. This advertising targets more specific groups of consumers: those living close to the dealerships and those most interested in buying specific cars.

- 220-horsepower V-8
- Six-passenger seating
- Best-in-class trunk space
- Rear-wheel drive handling
- Remote Keyless Entry
- Electronic Automatic Temperature Control
- Digital instrumentation
- 8-way power passenger seat with power recliner and power lumbar
- 16" Teardrop aluminum wheels
- Leather seating surfaces
- AM/FM stereo/cassette Premium Sound
- Leather-wrapped steering wheel
- Electronic interior rearview mirror with compass
- HomeLink® Universal Transmitter

$2,000** Cash Back
$1,705 Package Value
$3,705 Total Package Savings

Lincoln Mercury uses GIS to locate the most appropriate target audiences for its local and regional advertisements.

GIS enables Lincoln Mercury to develop cost-effective local and regional advertising programs. GIS is used to identify past buyers of a certain vehicle and to locate similar types of consumers in the desired region. Mercury can then create direct-mail ads or newspaper inserts to reach these individuals, which can be considerably less expensive than running a local TV commercial. In Southern California, for instance, it costs approximately $3 million for Lincoln Mercury to run a TV ad campaign for three weeks.[23] Because few clients can realistically fund a multimillion-dollar local ad campaign, there is a high demand for less expensive and more targeted marketing methods, such as those based on GIS.

In June 2001, Mathews Marketing Group, a Newport, Rhode Island–based corporation, approached Mercury with a proposal for a regional newspaper insert program for the 2001/2002 Grand Marquis. This model is a five-passenger, full-size luxury vehicle with a leather interior, which retails for approximately $24,435.[24] Mathews proposed to use GIS to identify zip codes in Southern California with the greatest concentration of individuals who were most likely to buy a Grand Marquis.[25] The company would then send a glossy, magazine-quality insert to these specific households via various regional newspapers. A selected page from the insert is shown in the photo.[26]

Understanding the Process

Because we know that people differ in terms of the types of products they buy, the challenge in advertising is to direct ads toward the people who are most likely to buy a certain product and avoid those who are least likely to buy it. For example, imagine the buyers of a $6,000 compact car versus those who would purchase a $30,000 SUV. We might guess that compact car buyers would tend to have a lower income relative to high-end SUV buyers. Although our guess could be wrong, the standard descriptions of product buyers will generally hold true. These descriptions, called **buyer profiles,** explain what customers of a product are generally like on a number of different demographic variables (such as income, education, or age). Once we know the types of people who are most likely to buy a product, we can locate these people and focus our advertising efforts on them.

A **buyer profile** describes the most promising (likely) buyers of a given product or service based on a number of key demographic variables, such as income, education, and age.

Fortunately for marketers, people who are similar tend to live close to one another. The old saying "Birds of a feather flock together" is sometimes used to describe the geographic grouping of similar people. Hence, the marketer's goal is to find neighborhoods of similar people who are most interested in buying its products. Targeting entire neighborhoods can be very cost effective. Sending ads to individual homes costs a considerable amount in postage, whereas sending glossy fliers in bulk in newspapers is much less expensive. In addition, targeting neighborhoods avoids the need to collect data on individual people, which could violate privacy rights.

PRIZM Groups

The **PRIZM system,** developed by Claritas Inc., segments or divides U.S. neighborhoods into 62 different buyer types based primarily on U.S. Census Bureau demographic data.

A **PRIZM group** is one of the 62 buyer types in the PRIZM system (for example, Greenbelt Families, New Beginnings).

Claritas, a prominent GIS data vendor, has developed the PRIZM system, which helps a marketer find people who are most likely to purchase its products. Specifically, Claritas's **PRIZM system** identifies Block Groups or zip codes with the highest percentages of potential product buyers.[27] Lincoln Mercury used PRIZM to find zip codes where people were most likely to purchase the Grand Marquis automobile.

PRIZM segments, or divides, U.S. neighborhoods into 62 different "cluster groups," or buyer types, based primarily on U.S. Census Bureau demographic data. Each group has been given a unique name that briefly describes its members. The 62 **PRIZM groups** are ordered hierarchically beginning with "Blue Blood Estates" (elite, super-rich people) and ending with "Hard Scrabble" (older people in poor, isolated areas). Detailed descriptions of two PRIZM groups, "Greenbelt Families" and "New Beginnings," appear in Table 5.3. Based on these descriptions, we can conclude that New Beginnings members are probably more likely to buy compact cars than SUVs due to their smaller family size and lower-level jobs. Greenbelt Families may be more prone to buy SUVs due to their larger families and interest in sports.

To create the PRIZM system, Claritas used statistical techniques such as factor analysis to analyze the demographic characteristics of U.S. neighborhoods. *Factor analysis* is a multivariate technique (to be discussed in Chapter 15) that collapses similar variables, such as education and income, into more global explanatory variables such as social rank.[28] Using such techniques, Claritas combined the census data into six broad categories that explain most of the differences between neighborhoods and consumers.[29] These categories are Social Rank (education, income, occupation), Household Composition (family size, member ages), Mobility (length of current residence), Ethnicity (race, foreign birth), Urbanization (population density), and Housing (owner/renter, home value).[30]

Claritas has classified each U.S. neighborhood into one of the 62 PRIZM groups, based on its ratings on the six categories just described. Claritas has also researched the lifestyle characteristics of the groups, helping to further describe the consumers who constitute each group. Other firms, such as R. L. Polk, have developed similar consumer classification systems. For cost effectiveness, most systems put everyone from a neighborhood into the same group. For instance, all

TABLE 5.3
Greenbelt Families and New Beginnings PRIZM Group Descriptions
Which type of car is each group likely to buy and why?

$6,000 Compact Car or $30,000 SUV?

Greenbelt Families	New Beginnings
• This cluster is concentrated in smaller second cities and uplands. This heavily mortgaged group are young marrieds with many children. Their energies are devoted to family entertainment and outdoor sports.	• Concentrated in the boomtowns of the Southeast, the Southwest, and the Pacific Coast, this cluster is a magnet for fresh starts. Populated by well-educated youth, many are minorities. Some are divorced, whereas many others are solo parents. The majority live in multi-unit rentals and work in a variety of low-level, white-collar jobs.
• Age groups: 25–34, 35–44	• Age groups: Under 25, 25–34

of the households in a given census Block Group may be classified as New Beginnings members. Although this approach may seem simplistic, people tend to live close to others who are similar to them. To better understand this concept, consider the neighborhood where you grew up. Were you surrounded by families with similar incomes? Do you think most neighborhoods tend to be more similar than different?

Identifying Target Clusters

Now we need to identify the PRIZM groups that are most likely to buy the Grand Marquis automobile. Research firms such as MRI (Mediamark Research Inc.) and ACNielsen sell reports on each PRIZM group's propensity to purchase various products and brands, along with information about the group's media habits. However, these reports include only certain leading brands, and data for the Grand Marquis brand were not available. Further, these reports provide only national buying estimates, not regional estimates. In other words, the reports indicate how likely each PRIZM group is to buy a brand when considering the United States as a whole, not specific regions of the United States. Car-buying patterns tend to vary by region, so regional estimates are often preferred.

We can estimate each PRIZM group's regional propensity to purchase a given automobile brand through either phone surveys or vehicle registration records. Using a phone survey, we can contact members of each PRIZM group in the region and ask them if they purchased the focal automobile. Then we can calculate the percentage of each group who purchased it and use this as our estimate of the group's future propensity to purchase. However, this approach is time consuming and expensive. Also, many consumers find phone surveys annoying and intrusive.

The alternative method, used by Mathews Marketing, is to use data from vehicle registration records. Specifically, Mathews Marketing used vehicle registration records to obtain the zip code of every buyer of a Grand Marquis in Southern California during the focal time period. These data can also be purchased directly from R. L. Polk & Company, which has compiled the information from vehicle registration offices nationwide.[31] For example, if you purchased a Grand Marquis in the year 2001, Polk holds a file showing the zip code in which you registered the car. As you can see, not only is this method accurate, but it is less expensive, less time consuming, and less intrusive than conducting a survey.

Car registration data can also be used to quickly and cost effectively analyze the competition. The Grand Marquis's primary competitors include models such as the Buick LeSabre. By purchasing the zip code records of customers who purchased these competing models, we can also determine which PRIZM groups of customers buy those cars and perhaps expand our market share by targeting their zip codes as well.

A couple in the Gray Power segment, one of 62 market segments that Claritas, a GIS vendor, has identified through an elaborate analysis of demographic data provided by the U.S. Census Bureau.

TABLE 5.4
"Gray Power" PRIZM Group Description
This group is a prime target market for the Mercury Grand Marquis.

Gray Power
- This cluster represents over 2 million senior citizens who have pulled up stakes and moved to the country or the Sunbelt to retire among their peers.
- Although these neighborhoods are found nationwide, almost half are concentrated in 13 retirement areas.
- They are health and golf fanatics who maintain fat investment portfolios.
- Age groups: 55–64, 65+

Of all the PRIZM groups, the "Gray Power" group was found to have the highest propensity to purchase the Grand Marquis automobile. Table 5.4 gives the PRIZM description for Gray Power. This group is composed of older, financially secure individuals who are young at heart and physically fit. Based on the PRIZM description, we can infer that Gray Power members maintain a comfortable lifestyle in some of the United States' more pleasant climates, including Southern California. Furthermore, we can conclude that, although members of this group may not travel extensively, they would likely value the comforts of an affordable luxury car. A photo of a Gray Power couple is shown on page 133. Do they look like target customers for the Grand Marquis? Why or why not?

Converting Buyer Data to PRIZM Groups

Mathews Marketing utilizes automobile buyers' zip codes rather than addresses. The Driver's Privacy Protection Act prohibits the disclosure of personal information in motor vehicle records.[32] Although it would be easier to match a buyer with his or her proper PRIZM group using an exact street address, the buyers' zip code can still provide valuable information. Specifically, zip code data can be converted to PRIZM group data to determine which PRIZM groups are most likely to purchase the Grand Marquis. To keep things simple, we will assume that each zip code is populated by just one PRIZM group. However, in reality, adjustments are made because most zip codes are large geographic areas containing several PRIZM groups.

Table 5.5 shows hypothetical data on Grand Marquis vehicle registrations during one year for two zip codes composed of Gray Power PRIZM group members. For each zip code, if we divide the number of Grand Marquis buyers by the total adult population, we can determine the percentage of adults who purchased the Grand Marquis. For instance, in the 12345 zip code, the number of Grand Marquis buyers is 50 and the adult population is 1,000, so the percentage is 5 [(50/1,000) x 100]. The bottom row of Table 5.5 shows the percentage of Gray Power adults who purchased the Grand Marquis, averaged across the two zip codes, or 4 percent [(80/2,000) × 100]. This average percentage is our best estimate of Gray Power's propensity to buy a Grand Marquis in the future. In other words, our best guess is that 4 percent of Gray Power adults will purchase the vehicle next year. These **propensity to buy** estimates are based on the assumption that the best predictor of future behavior is past behavior.

We can use this approach to calculate the average propensity to buy for each of the 62 PRIZM groups across all the zip codes in the region. This method should give us roughly the same percentages (propensities to buy) as we would have obtained by conducting a phone survey of each PRIZM group.

Propensity to buy is the percentage likelihood that a group of consumers (for example, a PRIZM group) will purchase a certain product or service within a given time period.

TABLE 5.5
Gray Power's Propensity to Buy a Grand Marquis Automobile

PRIZM Group	Zip Code	Past Buyers of Grand Marquis	Adult Population	Propensity to Buy (Past Buyers/Adult Population) × 100
Gray Power	12345	50	1,000	5%
Gray Power	67890	30	1,000	3%
Gray Power as a whole		80	2,000	4%

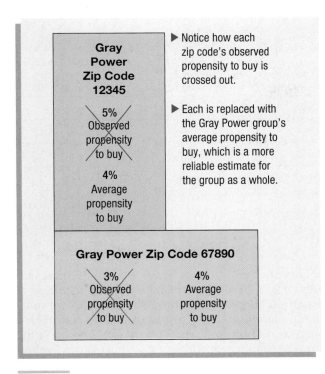

Gray Power Zip Code 12345

5% Observed propensity to buy

4% Average propensity to buy

▶ Notice how each zip code's observed propensity to buy is crossed out.

▶ Each is replaced with the Gray Power group's average propensity to buy, which is a more reliable estimate for the group as a whole.

Gray Power Zip Code 67890

3% Observed propensity to buy

4% Average propensity to buy

Exhibit 5.10
Zip Codes Where Gray Power Consumers Live Are Relabeled with the Group's Average Propensity to Buy a Grand Marquis Automobile

Handling Zip Codes with People from Different PRIZM Groups

In actuality, a zip code most likely contains people from multiple PRIZM groups. As a result, Mathews Marketing must estimate the correct PRIZM group for each Grand Marquis car buyer. This is accomplished by assigning buyers from a zip code to PRIZM groups based on each group's prevalence in that zip code. For example, suppose three buyers were from a given zip code. If that zip code were made up of one-third Gray Power and two-thirds Greenbelt Families, we would assign one buyer to Gray Power and two buyers to Greenbelt Families. Marketers that know customers' exact addresses will not need to extrapolate in this way and will be able to more accurately assign customers to appropriate PRIZM groups using those addresses.

At this point, let's briefly summarize the steps we have taken. First, we used car registration records to find the zip codes of past Grand Marquis buyers. Then we assigned the buyers in each zip code to their appropriate PRIZM groups, such as Gray Power. Next, we determined the number of Grand Marquis buyers in each PRIZM group. Finally, we divided the number of buyers in a PRIZM group by the number of adults from the region in that PRIZM group to calculate the average propensity to buy for that PRIZM group.[33]

This last step is very important because we will use the average propensity to buy from now on. In Exhibit 5.10, the two Gray Power zip codes from Table 5.5 are shown in map form. The initial propensities to buy for each zip code (3 percent and 5 percent) have been replaced with the average propensity to buy for the Gray Power group (4 percent). We make this change because the average value is a far more reliable predictor of future Gray Power behavior.

Once we know the average propensity to buy for each PRIZM group, we can identify new zip codes with high buying propensities. In Exhibit 5.11, a region has been divided into three zip codes. Above each zip code is the PRIZM group that lives there and below it is that group's average propensity to buy a Grand Marquis automobile. (Again, for simplicity, we are assuming that each zip code has just one PRIZM group living in it). As in the last exhibit, Gray Power zip code 12345 is shown to have a 4 percent average propensity to buy. The New Beginnings and Greenbelt Families zip codes are shown to have average propensities to buy of 1 and 2 percent, respectively.

Exhibit 5.11
Propensities to Buy the Grand Marquis Automobile for Three Zip Codes, Each Representing a Different PRIZM Group
Gray Power zip code 12345 is the best zip code to target. Why?

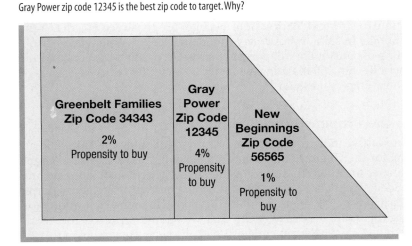

Greenbelt Families Zip Code 34343

2% Propensity to buy

Gray Power Zip Code 12345

4% Propensity to buy

New Beginnings Zip Code 56565

1% Propensity to buy

TABLE 5.6
Propensity to Buy Indices for Three Different Zip Codes

Zip Code	Zip Code's Propensity to Buy	Regional (Base) Propensity to Buy	Index Value (Zip Code Propensity/Base Propensity) × 100
12345	4%	2.33%	172
34343	2%	2.33%	86
56565	1%	2.33%	43
Regional average	N/A	2.33%	100

Creating a Propensity to Buy Index

Although it is clear that higher propensities to buy indicate more desirable zip codes for marketing purposes, it can be difficult to interpret the meaning of specific values, such as a 4 percent propensity to buy. The question we must answer is: Should we send Grand Marquis newspaper inserts to a zip code with a certain (say, 4 percent) propensity to buy, and why or why not? To clarify the meaning of the propensity to buy values, marketers often convert these values to a **propensity to buy index,** in which 100 means an average propensity to buy and thus presumably an average propensity to respond to a Grand Marquis newspaper insert. An index of 200 means twice the average propensity to buy or respond, an index of 50 means half the average, and so forth. Typically, marketers target areas with above-average propensities to buy or indices substantially above 100, such as 120 or greater. Marketing objectives and budgets also influence this decision, as you might expect.

We will now calculate a propensity to buy index using the data in Table 5.6. To create an index, we must first calculate the regional, or "base," propensity to buy. This is the average across the zip codes in the region, or 2.33 percent in the table [(4% + 2% + 1%)/3], assuming the zip codes are similar in terms of population size. Then we must divide each zip code's propensity to buy by the base (regional) propensity and multiply by 100. For instance, for zip code 12345, the index is 172 [(4/2.33) × 100]. The other index values have been calculated similarly and are shown in Table 5.6; the index ranges from 43 to 172. Zip code 12345's 172 index value demonstrates a strong (1.72 times the average) propensity to buy the Grand Marquis automobile. In sum, a propensity to buy index shows the relative likelihood that a group of consumers will purchase a certain product or service within a given time period, with 100 meaning average, 200 being two times the average, 50 being half the average, and so forth.

A **propensity to buy index** shows the likelihood that a group of consumers will purchase a certain product or service within a given time period, relative to a regional or national average. An index of 100 means average, 200 means twice the average, 50 means half the average, and so forth.

Mapping the Propensity to Buy Index

Having calculated these indices, we will now return to mapping the areas that are most promising for the Grand Marquis automobile. We will want to send Grand Marquis newspaper inserts to these promising areas. Hence, each zip code area will be color-coded. We will use blue to show the most promising areas and purple to show the least promising areas. Exhibit 5.12 shows our indexed and color-coded map. On this map, it is easy to see that we should advertise the Grand Marquis in the blue Gray Power zip code of 12345, because customers in this zip

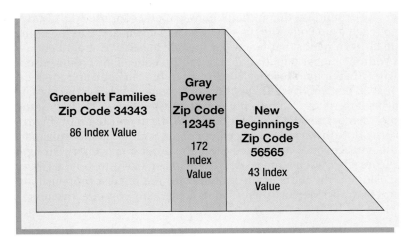

Exhibit 5.12
Propensity to Buy Indices for the Grand Marquis Automobile for Three Zip Codes, Each Representing a Different PRIZM Group
Gray Power zip code 12345 is more clearly shown to be a prime target market for the Mercury Grand Marquis automobile. How?

code appear to have a high propensity to buy the automobile. Of course, we should verify that each blue area in which we plan to advertise has reasonable access to a Lincoln Mercury dealership. This will ensure that interested buyers have a convenient place to test-drive and purchase the vehicle. For instance, we can add the Lincoln Mercury dealerships and their trade areas to the color-coded map, and mail only to blue zip codes that fall within a trade area.

Note that, because we can buy automobile registration data on our competitors' buyers, we can perform similar analyses for the Buick LeSabre and the Oldsmobile 88. We can identify zip codes with high index values for each competitor. We can pay particular attention to areas where our competitors have higher index values than the Grand Marquis. This identifies buyers who may not have purchased the Grand Marquis in the past but have a high propensity to buy a similar vehicle. This process should enable us to increase our market share by targeting a wider range of potential buyers.

Delivering the Advertisements: Direct Mail Versus Newspaper Inserts

The final step in this process is to reach our target customers with Grand Marquis advertising. The two primary ways automotive marketers deliver advertising material to specific neighborhoods are newspaper inserts and direct mail. Newspaper inserts are single or multisheet, typically full-color advertisements that are tucked inside a daily or weekly newspaper. Direct mailings are similar-style advertisements that are sent directly to your mailbox, typically in their own envelopes. Direct mail can reach 100 percent of the target market, including those who don't subscribe to newspapers. Direct mailings also tend to be more attention grabbing than newspaper inserts. The biggest disadvantage of direct mail is higher cost. Marketers must pay for the postage and envelope, on top of the actual cost of the advertisement. Newspaper inserts are far less expensive to distribute. However, newspaper inserts may be less noticeable, and marketers can reach only those consumers who actually subscribe to the newspapers. Overall, a marketer must weigh the advantages and disadvantages of direct mail versus newspaper inserts, choosing the method that is more appropriate for the product and the goal of the advertising campaign.

For the Grand Marquis, Lincoln Mercury chose to use newspaper inserts. The firm employed a colorful, three-page insert (see photo on page 131) because this stands out as a high-quality item and hopefully will be retained after the newspaper is discarded.[34] In addition, the cost savings over direct mail were considerable. The postage cost for direct mail can range from $0.30 to $1.00, whereas the three-page insert used in the Grand Marquis program cost just $0.14 to disseminate.[35]

The last step was to identify the newspapers that would most effectively reach people in the targeted zip codes. In addition to developing its own database on newspaper circulation, Mathews Marketing relies on SRDS, a research firm that specializes in providing data on media rates and coverage.[36] Using this information, Mathews Marketing is able to determine which newspapers to use to reach target zip codes. By examining the available newspapers, suppose we find two possible ways to reach a zip code: the big-city newspaper that services the entire area and the small-town paper that reaches a specific locale. We should choose the newspaper with the higher penetration into the zip code, if everything else is equal. If the big-city newspaper reaches 60 percent of the zip code and the local paper reaches just 30 percent, it would be more advantageous to use the big-city newspaper, particularly if the charge per insert is the same. For the Grand Marquis, Lincoln Mercury used a combination of 30 local and big-city (metro) newspapers to distribute the inserts to 20 percent of the Southern California market. Although the entire market was not covered, the program's primary strength was its ability to reach the customers who were most likely to buy a Grand Marquis. By focusing on the parts of the market with the highest propensity to purchase a Grand Marquis, Mercury increased its advertising cost effectiveness.

Results[37]

Lincoln Mercury distributed the Grand Marquis insert on two separate occasions in early 2001. The results for the campaign were excellent. In February 2001, the first month of the campaign, 362 Grand Marquis vehicles were sold in Southern California. That total represented the best February since 1996 for the Southern California region. In fact, the entire first quarter of 2001 saw an increase of 3 percent in Grand Marquis sales, which was very pleasing to Lincoln Mercury. As a percentage of the entire nation, California accounted for 6.4 percent of the Grand Marquis sales in February, an increase of 2.2 percent over the previous year, when a GIS newspaper insert campaign had not been used.

SUMMARY

Businesses can benefit from analyzing geographic or spatial data using GIS. It is very valuable for a business to map its geographic trade area (service area) and understand who lives or works in that area. Businesses can use this information to tailor their products, prices, and promotions to meet local customer needs. The unique capabilities of GIS to integrate multiple data sources and create intuitive maps makes this a quick and easy process.

GIS can also be used to evaluate potential new stores sites and choose the best sites based on sales forecasting models. The simplicity and speed of plotting market data and forecasting results with GIS allow businesses to make informed decisions more quickly and easily than with traditional methods.

Finally, GIS helps advertisers to target geographic areas (such as zip codes) where people have a high propensity to purchase their products or services and to avoid less promising areas. In this way, advertising can be made more cost effective. The Claritas PRIZM system and other similar systems are widely used in GIS to target the most promising customer groups and areas.[38]

ACE
self-test

REVIEW AND DISCUSSION QUESTIONS

1. What is GIS, and why do marketers use it?

2. What are some benefits to analyzing data spatially on a map rather than examining the same data in tabular form?

3. What is geocoding, and why is it important to GIS?

4. What is a Block Group? How does it differ from a zip code?

5. What is the difference between micro marketing and micro merchandising?

6. Describe two marketing applications of GIS that were discussed in this chapter.

7. Discuss how GIS is used to identify variables that can predict a store location's success or failure and why this type of analysis is useful to a business.

8. Explain how Claritas created its PRIZM system of 62 distinct buyer types and how marketers use PRIZM along with GIS.

9. What is a propensity to buy index, and how do marketers use this index?

APPLICATION EXERCISES

1. An upscale local restaurant is planning to mail promotional flyers to promote its new menu. How might it use GIS to determine which neighborhoods should receive the flyer?

2. A local sporting goods store accepts personal checks. The store owner records the customers' addresses from their checks in a database. What could the store owner do with these data using GIS?

3. Every month you must order inventory for your retail store. You have noticed that certain items are not selling very well. How can GIS help you choose better products for your store?

4. You are in charge of the national expansion of a new fast-food restaurant. You already have dozens of restaurants nationwide and are planning to open several new restaurant locations this year. You receive a proposal for a new restaurant with a specific address. How might you use GIS to forecast annual sales at the proposed new store site?

5. In a recent national advertising campaign, you targeted the group "18—Young Influentials" because you determined that this group had a high propensity to buy your company's products. In fact, their propensity to buy index was 200. Explain to your boss how you calculated the propensity to buy index and what an index of 200 means.

INTERNET EXERCISES

1. This exercise will give you some basic information on the PRIZM groups or buyer types in your hometown. You will use Claritas's "You Are Where You Live" (YAWYL) website. It will display the most common PRIZM groups in your hometown zip code. Follow these steps:

   a. Go to www.clusterbigip1.claritas.com/MyBest-Segments/Default.jsp.
   b. Click the "You Are Where You Live" button.
   c. Click the "ZIP Code Look-Up" button.
   d. Under "Enter 5-digit ZIP CODE," type in the zip code of the hometown where you grew up (or one of the hometowns where you grew up, if you moved a lot).
   e. Click "Submit."
   f. Click on each PRIZM group name and read the corresponding description.

   Based on your knowledge of the zip code, do the PRIZM groups correctly describe the population? If not, what might be some reasons for the disparity?

2. Imagine that you own a large construction company that specializes in building low-rent apartments. You would like to bid on a major government contract to construct low-rent apartments for low-income families. Your task is to locate six states with the greatest need for low-rent housing. Get data from www.factfinder.census.gov. Based on your analysis, identify the six U.S. states with the greatest apparent need for low-cost housing. (*Hint:* You may need to look at a road map or encyclopedia to identify the states by name.)

3. Imagine that you work for a company that builds sports stadiums. You attended the 2002 Winter Olympic Games in Salt Lake City and were impressed by the excitement surrounding the sport of skeleton. As in the sport of luge, skeleton athletes race on their stomach down a track, using small sleds. You believe U.S. sports enthusiasts would love to watch skeleton in person, and your supervisor has asked you to locate the best possible U.S. state in which to build a skeleton stadium. Follow these steps to complete your research:

   a. Go to www.factfinder.census.gov.
   b. Scroll down to "Data Sets."
   c. Go to the "Economic Census and Surveys" section.
   d. Click "Quick Reports" and then "Select by Industry."
   e. Under "Select a Sector," select "71: Arts, entertainment, and recreation."
   f. Under "Select a Sub-Sector," select "711: Performing arts, spectator sports, and related industries."
   g. Under "Select an Industry," select "711211: Sports teams and clubs."
   h. Click "Show Result."

   You have just generated an industry report based on U.S. Economic Census data, which is a census of U.S. businesses. Your manager has told you that the company has historically chosen new stadium locations based on shipments/sales/receipts (in dollars) divided by the population estimate. This calculation produces an estimate of dollar sales per capita (per person). Higher numbers are more promising. Using the data table shown, identify a state with high dollar sales per capita. Write a memo to your supervisor that shows your calculations, identifies a state with high dollar sales per capita, and explains why this state might be a good choice for a skeleton stadium. Also discuss other factors that you might consider in choosing a site for a skeleton stadium.

CASE 5.1 NEW-SITE SELECTION AT GOLD'S GYM
(www.goldsgym.com)

Gold's Gym is currently the largest health club chain in the world. In 1965 Gold's Gym opened its first location in Venice Beach in Southern California. It soon became known as "The Mecca of Bodybuilding," largely due to the movie *Pumping Iron* starring Arnold Schwarzenegger and Lou Ferrigno. Today, with more than 600 gyms in 46 states and 34 countries, Gold's Gym has more than 2 million members worldwide. In fact, an independent consulting firm recently identified Gold's Gym as the most recognized club name in the fitness industry.[1]

Gold's Gym's Digital Map Library

The popularity of Gold's Gym has had a sizable effect on the company, as it receives more than 500 inquiries a week requesting franchising information alone.[2] Each year, Gold's Gym Franchising Inc. considers a very large number of applications for new gym franchises. Upon receiving these applications, the franchising department must first ensure that the new gym will not infringe on a current gym's "protected territory," or primary trade area. Gold's Gym relies on a digital map library that pinpoints the precise location of each franchise in the United States and its protected territory.

New-Site Proposal

In one case, the Gold's Gym franchising manager received an application to build a gym at a specific site on Long Island, New York. The franchise team checked the digital map library and determined that the new gym's trade area would not fall within a protected territory. However, this was just the first step in evaluating the application. Next, the team determined that there were 12 established franchises on Long Island, 2 of which were located adjacent to the proposed franchise's location.

The franchise team sought to assess how the new gym might affect the two Gold's Gyms in the immediate vicinity. It was determined that the existing gyms would most probably lose customers to the new gym, because some of the customers would live closer to the new gym and switch their membership. When a new Gold's Gym steals customers away from an existing Gold's Gym, the process is called *cannibalization*. One of the franchise department's main jobs is to avoid any serious cannibalization problems. On closer inspection, the franchise group determined that, if the new gym opened, most of its members would likely come from the existing Gold's Gyms. Also, the proposed new gym was expected to attract far fewer members than the average Gold's Gym facility.

CASE QUESTIONS

1. If you were the Gold's Gym franchising manager, would you give the applicant permission to build a new Gold's Gym at the proposed site? What data would you use to support your decision?

2. How do you think the franchise group determined each gym's trade area? Could Gold's Gym customer addresses be used for this purpose and, if so, how?

3. It is often assumed that customers will join the gym closest to their home. Do you think this an appropriate assumption based on your understanding of the behavior of fitness consumers? Why or why not? How might this affect your GIS analyses?

4. Gold's Gym relies in part on the number of people ages 17 to 39 in the trade area and the average income in the area to assess health club membership. Does this approach make sense? What other data might it consider using?

CASE NOTES

1. "Best Brand in the Business," www.goldsgym.com.
2. "Gold's Gym Initial Inquiry Request for Potential Franchisees," 2002, www.goldsgym.com.

This case was based on "Franchising at Gold's Gym," previously published as Chapter 3 of Christian Harder's *ArcView GIS Means Business,* Environmental Systems Research Institute, Inc., 1997.

CASE 5.2 MAMMOGRAPHY SCREENING IN URBAN ATLANTA
(www.cancer.com)

A primary cause of cancer deaths in women is breast cancer. However, if detected early enough, breast cancer is quite survivable. As a result, one of the American Cancer Society's (ACS) key priorities is to increase mammography (breast cancer) screening. Although ACS has been successful in persuading middle-income and wealthy women to get screened, the poor and minority populations have been difficult to reach. To address this disparity, ACS turned to a marketing research firm that specializes in GIS to help it design a communication campaign to increase the number of poor and minority women seeking first-time mammography screenings in cities such as Atlanta.

Defining and Locating the Target Audience

The first step was to clearly define the target audience. Because 80 percent of breast cancer is detected in women over age 50, ACS decided to target that specific age group. Next, to reach low-income groups, ACS decided to target women with annual household incomes of less than $20,000. The city of Atlanta was chosen as the test city for the new communication campaign, in part because ACS's national office is in Atlanta.

ACS's next step was to locate the target audience within Atlanta. To achieve this end, ACS constructed a map of the Atlanta Metropolitan Statistical Area (MSA) using GIS software. The program identified geographic areas with the highest proportion of women over age 50. It also identified areas with annual household incomes below $20,000. By overlapping this information, ACS could clearly see the most promising geographic regions in which to find the target audience. In fact, the maps revealed two distinct regions where the target audience could be found: Atlanta's inner-city area and its outer ring.

Understanding the Target Audience

At this point, ACS knew where the target audience lived. The next step was to research their lifestyle characteristics. Understanding the women's lifestyles was necessary to choose appropriate media to reach them. ACS identified the customer groups that were most likely to live in the inner city and the outer ring. They discovered five main groups in the inner city and four additional groups in the outer ring. Using the descriptions of these nine groups, ACS began analyzing the target audience more fully.

ACS found that the inner-city group was largely African American and the outer ring mostly Caucasian. Members of the inner-city group were less likely to own cars than the outer-ring group, who typically had access to their own transportation. As a result, the inner-city group was more reliant on public transportation. Both groups were more likely to be single parents than the general population, and both were largely unemployed or held low-level jobs. In addition, the outer ring had a higher likelihood of being illiterate than the inner-city group. ACS then examined data on media preferences. ACS learned that both groups enjoyed radio and television programs (albeit different shows) and that a major source of entertainment for the inner-city group was going to the movies. ACS used this information to develop an advertising campaign to encourage these women to get mammograms.

The Chosen Advertising Media

Based on the inner-city group's propensity to use public transportation and attend movies, ACS selected several nontraditional forms of media to deliver its message,

including local billboards, posters at bus stops, and theater trailers. Because the outer-ring group was more likely to travel by car, ACS selected billboards. Radio was also used to reach outer-ring individuals who were illiterate. Although both groups watched TV, ACS found TV commercials to be cost prohibitive.

"A Picture Can Save Your Life"

ACS employed the slogan "A picture can save your life" to convey the importance of mammography screening. The ads stressed the importance of early detection to surviving breast cancer and provided a toll-free number for further information. During the two-month ad campaign, more than 300 low-income women called the hotline. At the same time, ACS received very few calls from women in other socioeconomic groups. As a benchmark, Atlanta compared its program with a similar ACS program in Philadelphia during the same two-month window. Philadelphia employed traditional media forms, such as hospital literature, and it received only eight calls from low-income women! ACS realized that the correct use of demographic and lifestyle data could be a major advantage in the fight against breast cancer.

CASE QUESTIONS

1. The ACS targeted low-income areas with a high proportion of women over age 50. Might it have been useful to target high-density areas with a large number of low-income women over age 50 per square mile? Why or why not?

2. Although not mentioned in this case, the outer-ring group was found to be interested in religious radio programming and religious products. How might this information be used to tailor the message or media plan to reach this group of women?

3. This case highlighted the use of geographic information systems to improve the marketing efforts of a nonprofit organization. Choose a local or national nonprofit group and discuss how it could use a similar process to understand and cost-effectively reach out to its target market. Describe the steps it should follow.

This case was based on Cynthia Currence, "Demographic and Lifestyle Data: A Practical Application to Stimulating Compliance with Mammography Guidelines Among Poor Women," previously published as Chapter 8 in *Social Marketing: Theoretical and Practical Perspectives* (Lawrence Erlbaum Associates, 1997).

Primary–Data Collection

Chapter Objectives

After reading and understanding the material in this chapter, you should be able to:

- Describe a variety of data collection methods.

- Compare the advantages and disadvantages of the questioning approach over the observation approach.

- Describe the four different formats used in questionnaires.

- Identify the appropriate questionnaire administration method for each type of primary research.

- Explain each of the five dimensions along which observation techniques can vary.

Who Are Air Travelers, and What Do They Do in the Airport? Airports Want to Know[1]

McCarran International Airport in Las Vegas surveys passengers frequently about their travel habits and shopping preferences in order to improve travelers' airport experience. Survey results showed a preference for a gym facility, and airport management promptly installed one, to the delight of travelers. Travelers are spending more time in the airport since 9/11. Airport surveys elsewhere also indicate that travelers want to engage in activities that will reduce the stress of waiting. As a result, airports are beginning to offer a variety of services, such as massages, showers, saunas, swimming pools, exercise facilities, putting greens, ice skating rinks, gambling casinos, and places to nap.

- Washington National Airport surveys passengers every two months about their travel habits and shopping preferences, and locates stores within the airport based on survey results.

- British Airports Authority (BAA), responsible for Britain's seven major airports, asks passengers to rate BAA's services on a scale of 1 to 5, from "extremely poor" to "excellent." BAA interviews more than 170,000 passengers per year about cleanliness, flight information, and baggage trolleys, as well as about aircraft access, check-in procedures, baggage claims, comfort, congestion, BAA staff, and value for money. The survey results across the various airports are tracked annually.

- Philadelphia International Airport (PHL) developed a 45,000-square-foot retail mall to overcome limited food choices and high prices. To fine-tune the retail mall plan, PHL used three focus groups consisting of 20 participants each, including business and leisure travelers as well as people who picked up and dropped off travelers. Focus groups provided information about the

specific stores they wanted and the types of food they wanted and would eat. The decision to open Philadelphia MarketPlace Food, Shops & Services paid off handsomely for the airport. According to the PHL report, 79 percent of its passengers buy food and beverages, and 62 percent buy retail, compared to other airport averages of 51 percent and 32 percent, respectively. On an interesting and surprising note, a recent survey found that, the longer the dwell time for passengers, the more satisfied they are with the airport.

- Baltimore/Washington International Airport (BWI) gathers information by taking photographs of vehicles in its parking lots. License plates revealed by these photographs give airport officials an idea of where their customers are from. BWI conducts this observational study every 18 months to pinpoint its target market. The observational study showed that the airport is servicing customers mostly from downtown Washington, southern Pennsylvania, and New Jersey. BWI shares its research with other businesses, such as banks, hotels, and airlines. ■

Primary data are collected specifically for a research project.

These examples show a variety of ways in which firms can collect data to answer specific questions. Data collected specifically for a research project are called **primary data.** When secondary data are either unavailable or inappropriate because they are irrelevant or inaccurate, the marketing researcher must collect primary data. This chapter reviews the basic methods of obtaining primary data, discusses their pros and cons, and presents guidelines for choosing among them.

Variety of Data Collection Methods

Primary data can be collected through a number of different methods, and sometimes more than one can apply to a single research problem. To illustrate, consider Gap Inc., a national chain of clothing stores, which wants to evaluate the effectiveness of a special point-of-purchase promotion for its Gap brand men's shirts. The promotion consists of a decorative display in which Gap shirts are prominently and attractively featured. The following methods illustrate the ways Gap Inc. can generate data for evaluating the effectiveness of the special display:

- *Method A.* Conduct a brief personal interview of a sample of store customers during the promotional period. Ask the customers whether or not they bought Gap men's shirts and, if so, what motivated them to make the purchase. Also ask them specific questions about their reactions to the special display.

- *Method B.* At the conclusion of the special promotion, conduct a telephone survey of residents in the store's trading area, to ascertain whether or not they visited the store during the promotional period and, if so, what their reactions and responses to the special display were.

- *Method C.* Same as method B, except that, instead of conducting a telephone survey, mail questionnaires to a sample of residents, along with stamped envelopes for returning completed questionnaires.
- *Method D.* E-mail a sample of store customers during the promotional period and request that they respond to the questionnaire posted on the company's website. Ask them whether they bought Gap men's shirts and, if so, what motivated them to make the purchase. Also ask them specific questions about their reactions to the special display.
- *Method E.* Hire someone to observe customers and record their reactions as they pass the special display. Ask the observer to record such reactions as whether or not customers stop to look at the display, how long they spend at the display, how interested in it they appear to be, and so on.
- *Method F.* Videotape the area where Gap shirts are featured, to generate a continuous record of customer reactions and behavior as they approach and pass the special display.
- *Method G.* Program the store's electronic cash registers to automatically keep track of the total number of Gap men's shirts sold during the promotional period.

Methods A, B, C, and D involve questioning customers, whereas methods E, F, and G involve observing customers or their purchases.

Questioning and observation are the two broad approaches available for collecting primary data. Numerous variations of these approaches are available, some illustrated by methods A through G. Several other forms of questioning and observation are discussed in this chapter. The key distinction between the two stems from the role that potential respondents play in the data collection process. In the questioning approach, respondents play an active role because of their interaction or communication with the researcher. Indeed, some textbooks label the questioning approach the *communication approach* to distinguish it from observation, in which respondents do not directly interact or communicate with the researcher.[2]

The use of the term *questioning approach* rather than *questionnaire approach* in the foregoing discussion is deliberate, because not all questioning or interviewing situations involve the use of formal questionnaires. Stated differently, a **questionnaire** is simply a tool that is used in many, but not all, research projects employing questioning. For instance, whereas a large-scale consumer survey invariably requires a formal questionnaire, an informal interview of a few knowledgeable persons does not, despite the fact that both fall within the questioning approach. The various questioning and observation methods are not necessarily restricted to certain types of research. Chapter 3 described three major research types—exploratory, descriptive, and experimental—of which the latter two are forms of conclusive research. Either of the two data collection methods can be used in any of these research types. To illustrate, consider methods A through G for the Gap Inc. case. Methods similar to each of these can be employed in any of the following types of research:

- *Exploratory research.* Management wants to gain some initial insights into the effectiveness of the special point-of-purchase display. Initial insights can be obtained by gathering data through questioning or observation (in a fairly informal and flexible fashion) from just one or a few stores.
- *Descriptive research.* Management wants information of a specific nature, such as what types of customers are attracted to the special display or how customers who purchase Gap shirts during the special promotion differ from those

---

A **questionnaire** is a tool used in many research projects employing questioning.

who do not. This information can be generated by simply making the data collection process more formal and specific, and by collecting data from a larger, more representative sample of stores.

- *Experimental research.* Management wants to know whether the special display has a significant impact on customer perceptions and purchases of Gap shirts. This research question can be answered by collecting data under more controlled conditions than exist in the previous (descriptive research) setting. For instance, data on customer reactions and purchases can be gathered from a sufficiently large, representative sample of stores having the special display (an experimental group) and of stores not having the special display (a control group).

Thus, although the formality or flexibility of the data collection process, the nature of the sample, and the conditions under which data are collected vary from exploratory to descriptive to experimental research, the same basic data collection methods can be used under each. The next section examines the relative advantages and limitations of questioning and observation.

Questioning Versus Observation

To put the discussion in this section into proper perspective, we must mention at the outset two points concerning questioning and observation. First, one approach is not necessarily a substitute for the other, because each has certain unique capabilities. For instance, in ascertaining young children's reactions to such stimuli as toys and educational programs, observation may be the only meaningful way to gather the required information. Research in Use 6.1 illustrates the power and benefits of observation in such circumstances.

Second, although we'll see that each approach has advantages over the other, those advantages may not hold true in every situation calling for primary-data collection. In other words, neither approach is likely to always be better than the other along each of the following dimensions.

Versatility

A major advantage of the questioning approach is its versatility in the types of data it generates. The observation approach, by definition, is limited to collecting data about visible characteristics or variables. For example, the amount of time a customer spends looking at the special display for Gap shirts can be recorded by human observers (method E) or by videotaping equipment (method F). But we cannot easily observe whether the customer is impressed, disappointed, or annoyed during the time he or she is looking at the display. In contrast, any of the questioning methods (A, B, C, or D) can tell us how the customer felt about the display. In short, observation can provide data only on overt characteristics and behavior. By contrast, direct questioning can shed light on overt variables and also provide data on respondents' feelings, motives, intentions, and other nonobservable variables. However, as we saw earlier, for certain special groups of respondents (such as young children) the questioning approach may not be viable.

Time and Cost

The questioning approach usually has an edge over observation in terms of the time and cost needed for data collection, because a researcher will have much more flexibility in the data collection process when data are collected through

How to Design a Car Interior? Johnson Controls' Automotive Systems Group Shows the Way

Johnson Controls, Inc., is the world's leading supplier of automotive and interior systems. Its sales for 2000 totaled $17.2 billion, and marketing research plays an important role in product development and selling.

Johnson Controls used imaginative observation techniques in designing new products like PlaySeat and AutoVision. Researchers observed thousands of consumers around the world in 1999 to better understand how they use their vehicle interiors, from picking up food at a drive-through restaurant to placing dry cleaning in the car. Johnson Controls gives cameras to consumers and asks them to take pictures of what they like and don't like about the interior of their cars. In addition, the company's "Kids 'n Cars" project uses videotaping to see how adults interact with children in the back and how they use control panels. Researchers also studied children in their natural environments—at home, in the car, and at day care centers—and picked up insights that would be difficult to obtain with conventional marketing research techniques.

This research led to innovations that are "child friendly," such as PlaySeat and AutoVision. PlaySeat, developed in conjunction with LEGO, comes out of the back seat armrest and is essentially a table that acts as a car playground. AutoVision turns the back seat into a mobile entertainment center for kids to watch movies or play games without disturbing the front seat occupants. According to Dana Lowell, director of product marketing, "It's not an essential product to an auto maker like seats are, but it's something that they can then use as a selling point to consumers. It's very powerful when our salespeople can show this research to customers (auto manufacturers) and then show that we've got a product that fills a need."[a]

questioning. In the Gap Inc. case, the researcher will have some latitude in data collection in each of the four questioning methods: personal interviews (method A), telephone survey (method B), mail survey (method C), or Web-based survey (method D). Therefore, he or she can schedule these methods to generate the needed data efficiently. In contrast, employing a human observer (method E) or videotaping (method F) is likely to be time consuming and expensive. The observer and videotaping equipment will not be recording anything relevant when there are no customers in the special-display area. This unproductive observation, in addition to prolonging the duration of data collection, will also add to the cost.

What about the relative data collection efficiency of method G, programming the checkout registers to keep track of Gap shirt sales during the promotional period? This method is not likely to be more time consuming and expensive than the various questionnaire methods because the total sales of Gap shirts can simply be read from the checkout registers with relatively little effort or expense. An important implication emerges here: not all observation methods may be more expensive and time consuming than questioning methods in a given situation. Alternatively, the questioning approach is usually, but not always, more efficient in terms of data collection speed and cost. In fact, recent advances in digital observation are giving marketers who effectively use such technology a distinct advantage over competitors who rely on other means of obtaining feedback from their markets. Research in Use 6.2 illustrates a case in point.

Method G, however, has one limitation that may nullify its data collection efficiency: the only type of data that method G can generate is sales of Gap shirts. Hence, it will be inadequate if Gap Inc.'s management wants richer data—such as the data capable of being generated through observation methods E and F— about customers' reactions and behavior in response to the special display.

RFID Tracking Products All the Way Home: A Cause for Concern or Information for Better Service?

Recent advances in information systems and e-commerce are bringing about the most rapid changes in retailing. For retailers, speedily identifying the most popular products in a given season and having those products in stock before consumer preferences change are extremely critical. To accomplish this, retailers have to be able to predict accurately and act fast, combining the power of electronic observation with modern communication and information technologies. Some retailers have been able to trim their long order-cycle times by using electronic techniques to obtain speedy market feedback.

Radio frequency identification (RFID) technology has been around since 1945, when it was used during World War II to distinguish British fighter planes from their German counterparts. However, only recently have retail companies been taking advantage of the technology. For example, Wal-Mart is using RFID tags to improve its efficiency by tracking products, managing inventory, and cutting down on loss and theft. By using a small RFID tag attached to a product, the company can track it all the way from its entry into each store to its placement on the shelf to the time when it eventually leaves the store through purchase by a customer.

Unlike traditional bar-code tracking systems, there is no line-of-sight requirement. All one needs to track items is a simple scanning device capable of picking up the weak radio frequencies given off by the RFID tags.

Such technology has not been without concerns, chief among them being the effect that such technology might have on individual privacy. Critics charge that RFID tags could be used to track not just products, but also people. What might be a simple way of managing inventory by one company could be used by others to find out what people are buying and where they are going. As RFID technology continues to be adopted by more and more organizations, such privacy concerns will continue to surface and beg to be resolved.

Obviously, technologies like RFID tags are increasing businesses' ability to observe consumers at the retail level and hence are becoming the cornerstone for the ability of companies like Tesco supermarkets and Wal-Mart to have the right product at the right place at the right time. How these technologies advance and what perceived value consumers themselves derive from them will likely have an impact on resolving the many privacy concerns that they raise.[b]

Data Accuracy

Data accuracy refers to the extent to which the collected data are error free and trustworthy.

Data accuracy—that is, the extent to which the collected data are error free and trustworthy—is crucial from a managerial standpoint, because it can significantly influence the soundness of decisions based on marketing research. Inaccurate data can be misleading and do more harm than good. How does the questioning approach compare with observation in terms of data accuracy? The answer depends somewhat on the characteristics of a specific research project, including its purpose and data requirements.

To illustrate, suppose Gap Inc.'s management is interested in determining the impact of the special display on sales of Gap shirts. Questioning customers about their reactions to the display and their purchases of Gap shirts may not produce accurate data. For one thing, respondents may be unable to accurately recall their reactions and purchases, especially in the case of a mail survey (method C), due to the time delay involved. For another, respondents may be unwilling to reveal their true reactions or purchases; if so, they may refuse to answer questions or, worse still, give erroneous answers.[3] The following examples illustrate how easy it is to get inaccurate data through the questioning approach.

CASE IN POINT ▶ **Companies Question the Use of Surveys for Breakthrough Products**   A growing number of companies believe that, although surveys are good for fine-tuning existing products, they are misleading for breakthrough products. Chrysler, for instance, introduced the minivan in 1984 despite a lack of support from marketing surveys, and the minivan brought Chrysler back from the brink. Facing competition from Toyota, GM, and Ford, Chrysler's designers next made the minivan more rounded and aerodynamic in appearance. Focus groups strongly supported the old 1991 model and did not endorse the new minivan. Chrysler forged ahead with the new design in the belief that what is strange today will become the accepted norm tomorrow. Chrysler was proven right again.

Compaq introduced SystemPro, a first-ever PC server designed specifically to link desktop computers into a network. In 1989 no one gave this server any chance of survival, as the industry was using PCs only for light work and the mainframe for serious work. Compaq persisted with the PC servers, and the server market finally caught on.

The marketplace abounds with many such stories. New Coke did very well in a market survey but failed miserably in the market. Arnold Schwarzenegger's *Junior* did well in screenings but performed poorly at the box office. McDonald's found strong support for diet burgers in surveys, but McDonald's McLean sales were very lean indeed.[4] ◀

Respondents' inability or unwillingness to provide accurate data is not a problem, however, if an appropriate observation method is used. For instance, management can accurately assess the sales impact of the special display by programming the cash registers to observe sales (method G) in an experimental group of stores having the special display and in a comparable control group of stores not having the display. In fact, Steelcase, Urban Outfitters, Staples, and scores of small businesses argue that the best information is often gleaned through detached observation.[5]

In summary, when the same type of data (such as sales of Gap shirts or number of customers who saw the special display for those shirts) can be obtained through either method, observation will generally yield more accurate data. Because respondents do not directly interact with researchers in the observation approach, it also minimizes data distortions stemming from respondents. Note that this doesn't mean that one should not conduct marketing research; rather, it means that the research should be done differently depending on the context.

Bear in mind, however, that the subjectivity or the carelessness of an observer may lead to inaccuracies in observational studies. For instance, in method E the observer may see a customer viewing the display for several minutes and infer that the customer is impressed by it, whereas the customer may actually be frowning at it in annoyance. Just as interviewers may bias data collected through questioning, observers may create inaccuracies in observational data.

Furthermore, as we pointed out earlier, observation cannot provide accurate data on perceptions, motives, attitudes, or people's other inner feelings. The late Stanley Marcus, founder of the upscale Neiman Marcus retail chain, admitted that his biggest mistake was a misreading of the Boston market. Based on his own experiences living there, word of mouth from luxury goods manufacturers, and observation of the way people dressed at Harvard during one of his visits, he concluded that Boston was not an attractive market. However, a demographic study conducted some time later showed that a large portion of the market went out of town to buy quality goods. Neiman Marcus opened a store in Boston, and it was a huge success. This experience taught Stanley Marcus not only to avoid relying solely on word of mouth and observation but also to use more conclusive research methods to validate the findings.[6]

Research Constraints in India

In recent years India has provided fertile resources for information technology, call center support, and accounting services. Companies seeking to increase service while decreasing costs have benefited from a highly skilled workforce capable of addressing a variety of tasks. To that end, one might conclude that marketing research from India could compare with the best research from more developed countries. After all, most Indian marketing researchers have completed an MBA-level education and have expertise in a variety of research methodologies, including advanced analysis techniques. However, many challenges, including poor infrastructure, force those researchers to "localize and innovate" in order to overcome the constraints.

First, secondary research is limited and unreliable—forcing researchers to look for primary-research opportunities to find actionable, relevant research. Face-to-face interviews have become the method of choice to compensate for unreliable mail service, varied literacy levels, and poor telephone penetration. Even in subsegments like upper-class households, where Internet and phone penetration are greater, restrictions make face-to-face interviewing the method of choice. And, unlike the situation in more developed countries, the personal interview is not as costly. Because the unemployment rate is high, freelance interviewers are available at reasonable rates.

Second, marketing research venues, such as malls or metro centers, are not widely available, and securing interview space is costly. Focus group suites do not exist. As a result, most interviews and focus groups are conducted in homes or offices. Given the costs associated with centralized interviewing, researchers are usually limited to marriage halls, educational institutions, and large residences, where they can create buying simulations or play TV ads for test studies. To some degree, this limits participation to certain groups. For example, in-home interviews are most feasible for middle-class housewives, whereas respondents for research conducted in hotel rooms with recording equipment might be upper-income males from larger towns.

Third, the constraints noted above, coupled with social conditioning, force interviewers to be skillful in their questioning. Homes tend to be small and do not lend themselves to privacy. Hosts feel compelled to be extremely nice to guests, offering gratuitous responses as dictated by social custom. Local languages lend themselves to lengthy explanations for a single thought. Constraints and customs like these call for interviewers who are sensitive to the environment and capable of conducting succinct interviews that weed out gratuitous responses.

India houses the second largest population in the world. It has over 25 states, 19 major languages (with 500 dialects), and over 50 major cultural groups. Additionally, literacy and infrastructure vary widely between rural and urban areas. This diversity, although a fertile source of a rich variety of marketing insights, also poses formidable challenges in unearthing those insights. Marketing researchers in India are up to meeting the challenge, though—they are formulating innovative solutions to reach large numbers of respondents, remove potential biases, and deliver world-class research.[c]

Respondent Convenience

By and large, observation studies will be more convenient from the respondent's standpoint and hence are superior in terms of gaining the respondent's cooperation during data collection. This conclusion follows from the fact that respondents do not actively participate in the data collection in observation studies. The few exceptions in which observation studies may be somewhat inconvenient to respondents are situations in which they have to go to a particular place at a particular time to participate in a study. (More about such studies later.)

Research in Use 6.3 discusses some of the research constraints and the trade-offs that have to be made while conducting marketing research in India.

In summary, a major limitation of the observation method is its inability to generate data about variables that are not visible. The questioning method is more versatile in this regard and therefore is more widely used in practice.[7]

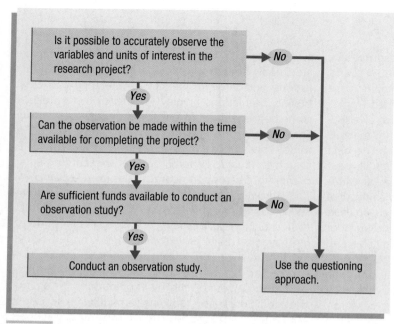

Exhibit 6.1
Choosing Between the Questioning and Observation Approaches

Another drawback of the observation method is that an observer will typically have to wait for relevant events or behavior to occur. Therefore, it is likely to involve more time and expense, although modern advances in observation methodologies (such as tracking customers on the Web) are beginning to mitigate these deficiencies. A key strength of observation studies is that they are likely to provide more accurate data because distortions arising from respondents will be much lower than in studies employing the questioning approach. Moreover, the absence of direct respondent participation in the data collection makes the observation method more convenient to respondents and minimizes the need to secure their support, a significant hurdle in most studies involving questioning of respondents. Observation appears to be the preferable method if the required data can be obtained through either of the two basic methodologies.

Exhibit 6.1 lays out a simple framework to help in choosing between them.

In some research settings, however, a combination of the two methods can be used. For instance, using method E (human observation) in the Gap Inc. case, the observer can first unobtrusively record a customer's reactions to the display. Immediately after the customer leaves the display area, the observer can conduct a personal interview interpretation of the customer's reactions. Of course, well-trained observer-interviewers, as well as adequate time and monetary resources, will be necessary for such an approach to be beneficial. Resources permitting, the observation-questioning combination may yield more valuable insights than either one used independently.[8]

Questionnaire Format

Questionnaire format is a function of the level of structure and disguise desired during data collection.

A **completely structured question** is one that is presented verbatim to every respondent and with fixed response categories.

Marketing researchers sometimes question respondents informally, with no questionnaire to guide the interviewing process. In many instances, however, they use a questionnaire, at least in the form of a checklist of items to be covered during an interview. Our discussion in this section will focus on questionnaires and their variations, although many of the concepts are relevant to questioning in general.

A questionnaire can vary in *format* as well as in terms of how it is *administered*. We will first examine format; in the next section we will examine administration. **Questionnaire format** is a function of the level of structure and disguise desired during data collection. A question presented verbatim to every respondent and with fixed response categories is a **completely structured question.** For an example, see the following question,

What are the strengths of Brand X soap in comparison with Brand Y?

(Please check as many categories as apply.)

❏ Costs less

❏ Lasts longer

❏ Smells better

❏ Produces more lather

❏ Comes in more convenient sizes

A **completely nonstructured question** is one that is not necessarily presented in exactly the same wording to every respondent and does not have fixed responses.

At the other extreme is the **completely nonstructured question,** one that is not necessarily presented in exactly the same wording to every respondent and does not have fixed responses. For example,

What are your views about Brand X soap?

_____

_____

_____

A **disguised question** is used to examine issues for which direct questions may not elicit truthful answers.

A **disguised question** is an indirect question whose true purpose is not obvious to respondents. For example,

Would people you associate with buy a cheap brand of liquid soap and dispense it from the bottle of an expensive brand to impress their guests?

❏ Yes   ❏ No

Disguised questions are used to examine issues for which direct questions may not elicit truthful answers. In the case above, if a person were asked directly if he or she would switch brands, he or she might not be inclined to answer truthfully. Using direct or nondisguised questions to investigate sensitive topics or topics that may be embarrassing to respondents will most likely yield data of questionable accuracy.

The type of research project (exploratory versus conclusive) and the extent to which respondents are willing and able to answer direct questions about the issues to be examined determine the types of questions to be used. From these two characteristics, we can identify four broad categories of questionnaire formats, as shown in Table 6.1: structured, nondisguised; nonstructured, nondisguised; structured, disguised; and nonstructured, disguised.

Structured, nondisguised questionnaires are widely used in marketing research studies, especially those with large sample sizes (conclusive research projects). Nonstructured, nondisguised questionnaires make them ideally suited for situations in which a researcher wants to give respondents a free hand in providing information. Hence, the nonstructured, nondisguised format is very popular in exploratory research projects involving personal interviews. Interviews of this nature are appropriately called _depth_ (or sometimes _in-depth_) _interviews._

TABLE 6.1
Determinants of Questionnaire Format

| | Respondent Willingness/Ability to Answer Direct Questions | |
Degree of Finality of Research	High	Low
High	Structured, nondisguised questionnaire	Structured, disguised questionnaire
Low	Nonstructured, nondisguised questionnaire	Nonstructured, disguised questionnaire

A variation of the depth interview is the focus group interview, involving the simultaneous interviewing of a group of respondents. Several examples of research projects using focus group interviews were presented in earlier chapters. Focus group interviewing is so widely used that a detailed discussion of it is presented in the next chapter.

Researchers generally use structured, disguised questionnaires to uncover people's attitudes toward sensitive issues of concern to society, such as abortion, pollution, or deregulation. A structured, disguised questionnaire consists of a number of factual items to which respondents provide structured answers, such as yes or no and true or false. A wide variety of items, ranging in degree of favorableness toward the issues being investigated, are included in the questionnaire. The items themselves can be real or fictitious.

Nonstructured, disguised questionnaires are used primarily in motivation research. *Motivation research* attempts to answer the question "Why?" and to relate behavior to underlying processes, such as people's desires, emotions, and intentions.[9] What is needed is a procedure in which a person can feel uninhibited enough to describe his or her inner feelings freely (in a nonstructured fashion) by projecting them onto a setting that is supposedly unrelated to the respondent (in other words, disguised). Such nonstructured, disguised questioning procedures are called *projective techniques*.

Questionnaire Administration Methods

A **personal interview** is one in which there is face-to-face contact between interviewers and respondents.

A **telephone survey** is one in which there is only voice contact between interviewers and respondents.

Mail surveys involve no interviewers, and the survey is sent to the respondent through the mail.

Internet- or Web-based surveys involve no interviewers, and the survey is conducted over the Web.

In the Gap Inc. example, methods A, B, C, and D describe the basic approaches to collecting data through questionnaires:

- **Personal interviews,** in which there is face-to-face contact between interviewers and respondents (method A)
- **Telephone surveys,** in which there is only voice contact between interviewers and respondents (method B)
- **Mail surveys,** in which there are no interviewers and the survey is sent to the respondent through the mail (method C)
- **Internet- or Web-based surveys,** in which there are no interviewers and the survey is conducted over the Web (method D)

Personal interviews have traditionally been conducted door to door or in the home. However, this approach has declined in popularity in the United States, due to difficulties in finding adult respondents at home during hours that are convenient for in-home interviewing and getting respondents to cooperate if they are home. In addition, setting up personal interviews takes a lot of time, another factor

Personal interviews conducted in shopping malls are a popular data collection method.

In **shopping mall intercept interviews,** respondents are intercepted in shopping malls and interviewed.

that has diminished its popularity.[10] Most personal interviews in the United States are currently conducted in shopping centers or malls. In these interviews, called **shopping mall intercept interviews,** respondents are intercepted in shopping malls and interviewed. Personal interviews are more common in the business-to-business (B2B) environment. Internet- or Web-based surveys frequently supplement other methods of collecting data. Companies desiring quick feedback are opting for Internet-based surveys to reach customers with Internet connections. Telephone surveys from central locations through WATS (Wide Area Telephone Service) are the most common method for reaching those customers who do not have an Internet connection. Mail surveys are popular for reaching a well-targeted customer base.

Not all of these methods may be equally appropriate in a given situation. Although each method has advantages and limitations, the strength of the advantages and the seriousness of the limitations depend on the specific features of the situation. Keep this point in mind throughout the following discussion of the four methods on the dimensions of versatility, time, cost, accuracy, and respondent convenience.

Versatility

A number of factors affect the versatility of questionnaire administration methods. Examples include the amount of data that can be collected, the types of questions that can be asked, and the kind of stimuli that can be presented to respondents during data collection. As you might expect, personal interviews are much more flexible and allow for the collection of a greater variety of data than telephone, mail, or Web-based surveys. Thus personal interviews are better than the other approaches for obtaining customer reactions to the appearance of a package, the taste of alternative formulations of a food product, and so on. Telephone and mail surveys are somewhat deficient in terms of presenting stimuli to respondents.

Modern technological advances are improving the versatility of Web-based surveys. For instance, researchers can present visual stimuli (including the questionnaires themselves) through respondents' PCs.[11] One of the most significant advantages of Web-based surveys is that answers to previous questions can be used to direct respondents appropriately to subsequent questions. For example, respondents clicking on the mutual funds section of a banking questionnaire can be directed to questions related to investments. Customers exhibiting an interest in credit cards can be directed to questions on credit card satisfaction. This feature of screening customers and then directing them to appropriate sections of a questionnaire increases the versatility of Web-based surveys. Audio and video capability allows a Web-based questionnaire to test reactions to new products or explain the use of service offerings.

The personal interview method is better, however, when the research requires lengthy nonstructured questionnaires, because respondent resistance to such questionnaires is likely to be especially high if administered through telephone, mail, or Web-based surveys. In a face-to-face interview, once a respondent initially agrees to cooperate, it may be psychologically difficult for him or her to terminate the interview. Face-to-face interviews—both door to door and at a central high-traffic area—constitute the most common method of data collection in developing countries. Interviewing services with facilities in shopping malls do not exist in most countries. Personal interviewing is done either in the home or through street intercepts. Some practitioners claim that Latin Americans are generally social and therefore prefer personal interviews to mail or Web-based interviews.

Telephone surveys are more flexible than mail and Web-based surveys in the sense that at least verbal contact occurs between the interviewer and respondent. This added flexibility of telephone interviews allows the interviewer to ask some open-ended questions and to probe a respondent as needed during the interview. Although mail and Web-based questionnaires can generally contain a larger number of questions than questionnaires administered over the telephone, they typically have to be quite structured to encourage respondent cooperation, which in turn reduces flexibility. In summary, with respect to overall versatility, personal interviews are perhaps the best, followed by telephone, Web-based, and mail surveys, in that order.

Time

Web-based interviewing, followed closely by telephone interviewing, is usually the best form of questionnaire administration when information is needed in a hurry. Web-based and telephone surveys avoid the time-consuming travel necessary for in-home personal interview surveys (interviewer travel time, of course, is not a drawback in surveys using shopping mall intercepts). Web-based and telephone surveys also do not suffer from the postal delays and respondent tardiness generally present in mail surveys.

The most important benefit of a Web-based survey is the timeliness of reports generated. Executives can download up-to-the-minute, real-time reports from anywhere in the world. In fiercely competitive markets, getting correct information quickly can help companies launch and establish new products faster than the competition. Connie Sanchez, Bay Networks' Web marketing manager, says of online surveys,

> Quick turnaround of results is one of on-line research's selling points. It depends on how much traffic your site generates, but we have no problem turning around 500-response surveys in a few days. Recently, for example, we were designing a new section on the web site and we wanted to find out what size screen users have, so that we can design content to take advantage of that. We were surprised to find out that 80 percent were on large screen sizes. We needed that information right away to move ahead with the design work.[12]

Researchers in the marketing research field are reporting similar experiences.[13]

The Internet is fast becoming a favorite in the marketing research world because it is cheaper, faster, and easier than surveys done in malls, by mail, or over the telephone. Online surveys can be administered in a variety of ways: open to everyone who visits the site, "opt-in," invitation only, password protected, and Internet-based panels.[14] With online surveys, supervision, data entry, and analysis are part and parcel of the survey system, thus eliminating the need for separate systems for data entry and analysis.

Although *computer-assisted telephone interviewing systems* (also known as *CATI systems*) are threatened by the advent of Web-based systems, they are popular in the United States and are increasing in use in other countries. CATI systems also reduce data collection time and the time required for data analysis. Many marketing research companies have CATI systems. Respondents in any geographic area of the United States can be interviewed through WATS interviewing stations from a centralized telephone center. The interview questionnaires appear on PCs in front of the interviewers. Responses are entered directly into these terminals. Therefore, the collected data are immediately transferred to computer memory and can be readily processed at any time. For example, a firm can conduct interviews one evening and have the responses analyzed and ready for presentation the next day.[15]

Although such facilities are common in the United States and northern Europe, they are not an option in most developing nations. Infrastructure is still in the developmental stages in most of these regions, which prevents efficient use of mail, telephone, and Web-based surveys. Hong Kong, Singapore, South Korea, and Japan have Westernlike telephone proliferation, but in China and India, the percentage of people who have a telephone is less than 10 percent, except in large cities, where it is around 40 percent. Mobile phones are becoming more popular than land lines because of infrastructure problems associated with land lines. In Japan, where telephone penetration is high, conducting a very long interview is considered a discourtesy.[16]

Personal interviews can normally generate data faster than can mail surveys, especially when adequate resources are available to hire as many interviewers as needed to collect the desired data within a specified time period. In contrast, the time needed to obtain data through mail surveys is essentially out of the hands of the researcher once the questionnaires are mailed out.

Thus, on the time dimension, the typical rank ordering of questionnaire administration methods is as follows: (1) Web-based surveys, (2) telephone surveys, (3) personal interviews (in-home less desirable than telephone, but mall intercept quite comparable), and (4) mail surveys.

Cost

Web-based surveys are not only fastest for obtaining the data, but also the least expensive, mainly because they have no interviewers, who usually account for a large share of the data collection costs in surveys using personal or telephone interviewing. Web surveys require no supervision, and data entry and analysis are automated to provide instantaneous feedback. Research companies process the data online, allowing managers to view the results in real time, 24 hours a day.

However, quickness and lower cost may sometimes compromise the usefulness of online research. For instance, many online survey companies offer quick feedback. Client companies can write their own questionnaire for a fee and get feedback within an hour from "opt-in" Internet users. These online companies recruit participants by enticing them with a sweepstakes offer or money for participation. Incentives to recruit participants and questionnaires developed by clients themselves might cast some doubt on the accuracy of the research findings.[17] Harris Interactive, a marketing research firm, offers a two-day turnaround. Its QuickQuery poll service recruits participants from an existing panel of more than 6.6 million respondents, and Harris's staff works with clients to create a professionally developed custom survey. However, the price is higher, with each question costing nearly $1,000. The bottom line is that the axiom "you get what you pay for" applies to research as well.[18] Some practitioners argue that although "call-in" online polls (whose respondents visit a website and respond to a questionnaire) offer no control of sample selection and cost little, good online research will incur significant setup costs.[19]

With long-distance costs falling rapidly, telephone interviews are also becoming cheaper. For a long time, mail surveys were cheapest for collecting data from large numbers of respondents, but they are now the slowest method for obtaining data. Research shows that fax-based short surveys are less expensive, more efficient, and significantly faster than mail surveys. Some claim that fax-based surveys are ideally suited for business-to-business markets.[20] In-home personal interviews are typically more expensive than telephone surveys because of travel expenses involved, though travel expenses are not a major concern in shopping mall intercepts. In-home personal interviews are more expensive on a per-completed-interview basis, especially if one or several callbacks are necessary before contact is made with designated respondents.

The implied ranking of the four questionnaire administration methods on the basis of cost—in-home personal interviews (most expensive), followed by telephone interviews, mail surveys, and finally Web-based surveys—is not universal. Exceptions can and do occur under certain conditions. For instance, suppose a one-page structured questionnaire is to be administered to a sample of residents within a town. The cost per completed questionnaire in this case may well be lower with telephone interviewing than with a mail survey.

Accuracy

A variety of factors, such as the format of a questionnaire, the content and wording of questions, and the mood of respondents while answering the questions, can influence data accuracy regardless of the questionnaire administration method used. However, the administration methods differ on three key determinants of data accuracy: degree of control over the sample (sampling control), degree of control over the questioning process (supervisory control), and the ability to sense and overcome any respondent difficulty in understanding or answering questions (opportunity for clarification). We will therefore focus our comparison of the questionnaire administration methods on these three dimensions.

▪ **Sampling Control**   *Sampling control* refers to the ability to collect data from a sample that adequately represents relevant segments of the population of interest. Inferences based on nonrepresentative data cannot be generalized and hence are not trustworthy. The degree to which data can be obtained from a representative sample using a particular questionnaire administration method depends on two attributes of the method: (1) the ability to identify and reach an appropriate sample of respondents and (2) the ability to secure cooperation from each respondent contacted.

Personal Interviews   The personal interview method, given its versatility, is most capable of reaching the appropriate respondents and securing cooperation. Any desired set of respondents (even those without a telephone, a mailing address, or an Internet connection) can be reached by well-trained interviewers. Moreover, refusing to participate is likely to be more difficult for a respondent when face to face with an interviewer than when contacted by telephone, mail, or e-mail. Therefore, cooperation rates are normally higher when personal interviews are used.

Telephone Surveys   Telephone surveys face several potential hurdles in attempting to reach a representative sample of households within the general population, including (1) households with unlisted telephones, (2) households without telephones, (3) answering machines, (4) caller ID, (5) cell phones, and (6) ban on computer-dialed calls in some states. Of the six, unlisted telephones, answering machines, caller ID, and cell phones are especially problematic, at least in the United States. Although most households in the United States now have telephones, a growing number of households in any given area have unlisted numbers. Moreover, households with unlisted telephones differ in significant ways from those with listed telephones.[21] Therefore, a sample of households chosen from an area's phone book will invariably be an inadequate representation of the entire area.

Telephone numbers can be chosen by using random-dialing procedures instead of a phone book, to properly represent households with unlisted telephones. Techniques such as random-digit dialing and plus-one dialing are available for this purpose. Moreover, several firms specializing in selecting up-to-date telephone samples for virtually any area of the country (such as Survey Sampling International, located in Westport, Connecticut) have highly efficient random-digit dialing procedures that eliminate inactive telephone exchanges. However, even if contact is made with respondents having unlisted telephones, a significant number of them may refuse to be interviewed.[22] Hence, respondent cooperation may not be as high as in a typical personal interview survey, although it is still likely to be better than in most mail surveys.

Computer-assisted telephone interviewing (CATI) systems can offer an additional level of sampling control that conventional telephone interviewing does not—namely, automatically ensuring that interviewers adhere to a predesignated sampling plan. For instance, suppose an area to be surveyed consists of 10 subareas, each defined by one or more telephone area codes. Further, suppose the sample of respondents from each subarea is to have the following composition: 50 males between age 20 and 65, and 50 females between age 20 and 65. In this scenario, a CATI system can be programmed to continuously keep track of the number and nature of respondents as interviews are completed, compare the profile of respondents with the desired profile, and disallow interviews with respondents who either do not fall into one of the desired demographic groups or fall into a group whose quota has already been filled. In this way, both inadvertent and deliberate interviewer errors in selecting respondents can be eliminated. This feature of CATI will be especially useful in studies involving complex sampling plans wherein the opportunity for interviewer error is likely to be high. Such screening procedures for achieving sampling control can also be programmed into Web-based surveys.

Research studies show that a significant segment of the population has answering machines and caller ID options.[23] Many people in this segment of the population routinely screen their calls, eroding their accessibility to researchers even further.

Mail Surveys   Mail surveys are generally least effective in terms of the percentage of contacts resulting in completed questionnaires. Getting back more than 50 percent of the questionnaires initially mailed is an exception. Moreover, numerous studies have shown that people who actually fill out and return questionnaires may be significantly different from nonrespondents.[24]

As you might expect, researchers have tried numerous respondent inducements to improve mail survey response rates, not all of which have been effective.[25] The more successful inducement techniques include mailing questionnaires by first-class mail, sending followup questionnaires, and enclosing incentives—monetary or nonmonetary—with the questionnaires. Using incentives has been found to be particularly effective in improving response rates, apparently because people receiving them may feel obligated to cooperate.[26]

Incentives offered to respondents, however, may increase the number of returned questionnaires without necessarily improving sample representativeness. In other words, people who respond because of an incentive may differ on critical characteristics from those who do not respond at all. Therefore, although a mail survey can reach virtually any and every potential respondent, it is generally less likely to provide a representative final sample and hence has less sampling control than personal interviews or telephone surveys.

The problem of nonrepresentative samples is not limited to mail surveys. A lack of responses from particular types of respondents, resulting in biased samples, can occur in personal, Web-based, and telephone surveys as well. But this problem is generally more extreme in mail surveys.

Web-Based Surveys The potential for nonrepresentative sample results is quite high in Web-based surveys. The most obvious benefit of using the Internet for research is the ability to reach large numbers of people. However, most websites do not attract a general audience. Therefore, conducting a survey on a website without some form of enticement is not likely to yield good results. Website surveys face two major hurdles: (1) getting respondents to go to the appropriate site containing the survey and (2) getting respondents to take the survey on the Web. Most websites do not have much traffic, and getting respondents to visit a particular website to take a survey is quite difficult. As a result, research companies now recruit respondents from leading Internet service providers, such as EarthLink, Microsoft, America Online, and Yahoo! For example, Digital Marketing Services (DMS), a Dallas-based company, recruits respondents from AOL's over 32 million members. DMS first screens visitors to AOL's Opinion Place research forum before it randomly selects users for a survey. After the survey, respondents are blocked access to AOL's Opinion Place for three months to prevent them from responding to the questionnaire again.[27]

Many consumers are nervous about Web-based surveys and are hesitant to divulge information electronically that they would freely give over the phone or to a researcher in the mall.[28] Even though Internet companies report collecting large sample sizes within hours of posting a survey on the Web, one should take adequate steps to ensure that the results can be projected to the general population. Nielsen//Net Ratings reports that nearly three out of four U.S. households with a phone line have access to the Internet, with 54 percent of Internet-connected U.S. households enjoying a high-speed connection. The incidence of high-speed connection is expected to climb to 75 percent by November 2005. Because approximately three-fourths of U.S. households have Internet access, the Internet is fast becoming a mass communication medium in the United States. Therefore, carefully executed marketing research studies can be projected to the relevant general population.[29] According to Harris Interactive, the online marketing research company mentioned earlier, Internet polls can be accurate if designed and executed properly. Research studies show that Internet penetration in most developed countries is moving rapidly to the level in the United States. Asian, Latin American, and African governments have placed a great deal of importance on developing their Internet infrastructure, and therefore we expect the Internet to become a dominant medium for collecting data not only in the United States but globally.[30]

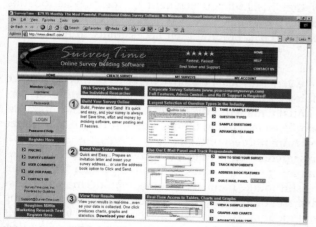

Web-based surveys facilitate fast and efficient primary-data collection, but caution must be exercised in projecting the results to the general population because of the problem of nonrepresentative samples.

Although the Internet is not suitable for conducting general surveys, it is very efficient for reaching specialized audiences, such as regular Web users, MIS managers, and online purchasers. For years, Avon Products, Inc., interviewed company representatives in 17 cities using the mall intercept interview method. In 1997 the company conducted a Web-based survey as well as a mall intercept survey of Avon representatives to estimate new-product demand. Both methods produced very similar results. However, the Internet survey was more cost effective and efficient than the mall intercept survey. Avon, to no one's surprise, has opted for Web-based surveys since 1997.[31]

Research companies are now building online panels to reduce the problem of nonrepresentativeness. Knowledge Networks, Inc., an online research company based in Menlo Park, California, uses random-digit dialing to find participants for its panel. Knowledge Networks equips all panel members with Internet hardware and connectivity at no charge so that members can respond to Web-based surveys. Knowledge Networks claims that its panel demographics closely resemble those of the U.S. population.[32] The population includes both Internet users and nonusers. However, Knowledge Networks converts nonuser households by providing them with hardware and Internet connectivity.

Some Internet research companies build panels by using an "opt-in" approach in which respondents have to sign up for online panels and communities. It is possible that those who sign up like to take surveys and that the opt-in approach leaves out non-Internet users. Therefore one must exercise caution in generalizing findings from surveys using such panels.

Supervisory control involves the ability to minimize such interviewer errors as failure to follow instructions, mistakes in recording answers, and cheating.

▪ **Supervisory Control**   The issue of **supervisory control** refers to the ability to minimize interviewer errors, such as failure to follow instructions, mistakes in recording answers, and cheating.[33] In this regard, Web-based surveys and mail surveys, because they involve no interviewers, have an edge over personal and telephone interviews. This, of course, assumes that the mail or Web-based questionnaire is well designed, with clear instructions so that respondents avoid errors when they interview themselves. Given their flexibility in detecting and in some cases correcting respondent mistakes, Web-based surveys have a distinct edge over mail surveys in terms of controlling potential errors.[34]

The personal interview method is especially prone to problems stemming from interviewer errors. Supervising the work of face-to-face interviewers is difficult, because they typically work alone in the field, although certain validity checks can be made after the data collection. Even rigorous interviewer training cannot guarantee that fieldworkers will not make mistakes.

Telephone interviews conducted from central locations are better than personal interviews in terms of supervisory control over the data collection. Most such centers have PCs and audio equipment that supervisors can use to monitor any interviewer's work as the interviewing is taking place. In this way, interviewer mistakes can be quickly spotted and corrected. Moreover, the interviewers themselves are likely to be extra careful because they know a supervisor can monitor their work at any time. In addition, as pointed out earlier, telephone interviews conducted through a CATI system can be controlled to a degree by programming the system to prevent some forms of interviewer error. Thus the system automatically offers a certain amount of "supervisory" control.

▪ **Opportunity for Clarification**   Regarding the ability to detect and overcome problems that respondents may experience in answering certain questions, mail surveys are the most problematic because there is no direct interaction with the respondent. Errors are bound to occur in mail survey data if respondents misunderstand questions or are unsure how to answer them. Web-based surveys are subject to similar errors, although technology for offering some degree of assistance to respondents experiencing problems is available and continues to improve. Personal and telephone interviews can reduce such errors by allowing respondents to seek clarification and by enabling interviewers to provide the necessary clarification. Personal interviews are perhaps the best in this regard because face-to-face contact allows interviewers to visually detect any respondent confusion or difficulty that may occur, even when respondents do not explicitly seek clarification.

In terms of overall accuracy—that is, taking into account sampling control, supervisory control, and opportunity for clarification—generalizing about which method is best and which is worst is difficult. Each has strengths and weaknesses along different dimensions pertaining to data accuracy. Therefore, which questionnaire administration method (or methods) will provide the most accurate data depends on the specific characteristics of the research setting.

Respondent Convenience

The Web-based survey and mail survey methods are the least disruptive and most flexible from a participant's perspective. Web-based surveys offer the convenience of submitting directly by simply clicking the "submit" button at the end of the questionnaire. In the case of mail questionnaires, respondents still have to mail the questionnaire after completion. Personal interviews are perhaps the worst, especially because respondents may find it difficult to say no when confronted by a persistent interviewer. Telephone surveys generally fall between the other methods with respect to respondent convenience.

Deciding Which Questionnaire Administration Method to Use

Like other decisions, the choice of questionnaire administration method depends on the research project. Table 6.2 provides a comparative summary of the four methods on the various criteria. Remember that the rankings implied by this table will not necessarily hold in every research setting. But even if they did, no method can claim to be the best on all criteria.

The purpose of our discussion concerning the relative merits and limitations of the three survey approaches is not so much to pinpoint the best approach; rather, it is to emphasize and illustrate the variety of factors to consider in selecting the most suitable approach in a research project. Situation-specific considerations are particularly crucial in collecting primary data from countries other than the United States. Table 6.3 offers a few interesting and unique research factors in other countries. These may have a significant bearing on the choice of an appropriate survey method and on the type of data that can be collected. This textbook's website contains detailed information about marketing research practices in countries around the globe.

Types of Observation Techniques

Before discussing the various questionnaire techniques, we looked at a few illustrations of observation used to collect data. This section illustrates the ways in which observation studies can vary depending on how the observations are made and exactly what is observed. The three observation methods presented in the Gap Inc. case (methods E, F, and G) serve to illustrate some of these differences.

TABLE 6.2
Comparison of Questionnaire Administration Methods

Criteria	Ranking of Methods			
	1	2	3	4
Versatility				
Number of questions	Personal	Mail	Web	Telephone
Amount/variety of information	Personal	Telephone	Web	Mail
Presentation of stimuli	Personal	Web	Telephone	Mail
Time	Web	Telephone	Personal	Mail
Cost	Web	Mail	Telephone	Personal
Accuracy				
Sampling control	Personal	Telephone	Mail	Web
Supervisory control	Web	Mail	Telephone	Personal
Opportunity for clarification	Personal	Telephone	Web	Mail
Respondent convenience	Web	Mail	Telephone	Personal

Note: The comparative rankings of the personal, telephone, mail, and Web survey techniques implied by this table are not universal; exceptions to these rankings can and do occur, depending on specific circumstances surrounding a research situation.

Recall that method E involves employing human observers, method F uses video-taping, and method G involves programming the cash registers to keep track of sales of Gap shirts. The similarities and differences across methods E, F, and G are discussed in the following subsections.

Natural Versus Contrived Observation

In **natural observation,** customer reactions and behavior are observed as they occur naturally in a real-life situation.

One feature common to methods E, F, and G is that they all involve making **natural observations;** that is, customer reactions and behavior are observed as they occur naturally in a real-life situation.

CASE IN POINT ▶ **Companies Making Observations in Natural Settings**   The following companies have used natural settings to conduct observations:

- *Wells Fargo examines the customer experience.* San Francisco–based Wells Fargo Bank had been using surveys for years to find out about customers' experiences at the bank and their level of satisfaction with the service they received. The problem with the surveys, however, was that they were expensive to administer and limited by the number of customers who could be reached. Some customers simply did not wish to take the time to be surveyed, meaning that the bank was not getting the full picture. To remedy the situation, the company installed a video surveillance system designed to analyze everything: how long customers stood in line, how much time was taken interacting with a bank teller, and even how long customers spent looking at promotional material as they waited for the next available teller. The system converts such visual information into data points that can be summarized and provided to branch managers in as little as 10 minutes. This allows the managers to identify and correct potential bottlenecks or other issues quickly, providing a better customer experience overall.[36]

TABLE 6.3
Examples of Unique Research Factors in Other Countries

Japan

- It is considered a discourtesy to conduct a very long interview over the telephone.
- The topic often determines whether it is appropriate to speak to the male or female head of the household.
- For businessmen, incentives for participating in marketing research often take the form of gifts rather than cash.
- The Japanese may not understand a letter-based performance measure, as they generally use a 100-point scale for these purposes.

Middle East

- The gender of the interviewer can have a strong impact on responses to questions.
- In Saudi Arabia, the English word *macho* does not exist, and there is no similar word or phrase to support this concept.
- In Egypt, social and cultural factors, such as a low literacy rate and low education levels, prevent the same techniques' being applied as would be used in the United States. Religious and political factors may also come into consideration.
- Israel is a multilingual society, which requires consideration in conducting surveys and interviews.
- It is difficult to gain access to upper-income groups.

South America

- An interview that takes 20 minutes in the United States could take 30 minutes in Brazil.
- As business is much more social in nature, the research method should be, too.
- In Brazil, directories are unreliable because telephone lines are bought and sold like commodities.
- In Colombia, some members of the upper class never have listed telephone numbers.
- Respondents are often very cooperative, given a low level of telemarketing and the "surprise factor" of being called from a distant location to answer a few questions.

China

- As some subcontractors are hired on a project-by-project basis, it is important to request biographies of key staff members.
- Traditional methods, such as door-to-door, central location, and focus groups, remain the backbone of marketing research in China. More advanced techniques, such as omnibus studies and panels, are making inroads. Widespread use of computers is increasing the feasibility of e-mail surveys.
- Local companies do not have a high regard for marketing research.
- Most research is conducted for multinational companies, as domestic companies consider China to be a seller's, not a buyer's, market.
- Despite being highly curious and welcoming fresh experiences, fear of crime in major urban areas has negatively influenced response rates in recent years.
- National research is impractical because long distances, low educational and literacy levels, and poor transportation are barriers.
- Observational studies are predicted to grow in popularity.
- Telephoning consumers and asking questions for research would be considered rude.
- Recent regulations have restricted the activities of research firms. Examples include approval of questionnaires, including postpilot revisions, and approval of final data.

France

- Individuals can be put off when they are called by nonnative interviewers.

(continued)

TABLE 6.3 (continued)

- Telephone interviewing is growing in popularity, with 40 percent of interviews currently being conducted via telephone.
- The French like to answer surveys because they feel their opinions will help produce better products.

India

- Due to lack of a strong research infrastructure, the available research methods are limited.
- Response rates for in-person interviews approach 60 percent for upscale markets and as high as 80 percent in other population segments.
- Due to lack of focus group facilities, hotel rooms with closed-circuit television monitoring are often used.
- Telephone and mail surveys are rarely used due to inadequate telephone penetration (1 percent of households) and low literacy rates.
- Resources such as customer databases, checkout scanners, and other automated equipment are almost nonexistent.
- Nineteen major languages and over 200 dialects make conducting a national research project extremely complex.

Germany

- Face-to-face interviewing is feasible and very popular; however, telephone interviewing is growing in popularity, as current telephone penetration is well over 80 percent.
- Business executives and government officials resist telephone interviews but are willing to be interviewed face to face.
- Mall interviewing is limited due to the lack of shopping malls. Door-to-door interviewing is becoming more difficult in major cities due to crime. Panels are becoming more popular.
- A 15-minute survey could take up to 40 minutes, as Germans like to talk more, and their language is less concise than English.
- Lower-level employees are very difficult to recruit for studies. They are often reluctant to participate without their manager's approval and are worried about accepting cash as a reward.

Mexico

- The country has some of the highest long-distance telephone rates in the world.
- Mexico's population is extremely young, and the country has a very clear social structure.
- Mexico City contains 20 percent of the country's population and generates nearly 50 percent of its GNP.
- Focus groups are often held in hotel rooms, as few high-quality facilities exist.
- Respondents view gifts as more appropriate incentives than cash.
- In-person and door-to-door studies are the best data collection techniques. Many households still lack telephones, although other telecommunications, including cellular service, are improving. When dealing with members of the upper class, interviewers often must get past servants to reach the target respondents.
- Intercept studies in shopping areas are less frequent due to the lack of facilities and the fact that there are often laws prohibiting suppliers from setting up shop in malls. They require either a relationship with a supermarket or a trailer to be set up in a high-traffic area.
- Professional standards and practices are different from those in the United States. It is not uncommon for recruiters to invite friends and family to attend a focus group.

Asia

- Vietnam and Cambodia have extremely high telephone rates. In Vietnam, it is not uncommon to have 10 families in one building sharing one telephone line.

(continued)

> **TABLE 6.3 (continued)**
>
> - In-person interviews are preferred, as they allow the researcher to show proper respect for the respondents.
> - In Thailand, only 21 percent of the population lives in urban areas, and two-thirds of that population is located in one city, Bangkok.
> - Face-to-face interviews are the most common, due to the lack of telephones and the cultural unacceptability of giving strangers information over the telephone.
> - Higher cellular, as opposed to land-line, penetration may cause low response rates in traditional telephone surveys.
> - Professionals, such as IT decision makers, have a higher response rate than in the United States because they are not yet oversurveyed.
> - A questionnaire to be administered in Singapore must have an English version as well as equivalent Malay, Hokkien, Mandarin, Tamil, and Cantonese versions.
>
> **Italy**
> - The stature of marketing research in Italy is lower than in the United States.
> - In Italy, personal relationships are vital to the commencement of business.
> - Business practices are different from those in the United States. Whereas a simple inquiry to someone's employer would be considered a small matter in the United States, in Italy it is equivalent to lodging a formal complaint.

Source: Compiled from various articles.[35]

- *Best Western learns about who makes the hotel decision.* Best Western International, Inc., asked 25 couples over the age of 55 to videotape themselves on cross-country trips so that the hotel chain could learn how they decide when and where to stop for the night. Research showed that the hotel chain does not have to increase its standard 10 percent senior citizen discount because seniors often talked the hotel clerk into giving them a better deal; it was the thrill of the deal that they wanted. These kinds of findings are hard to come by in a focus group. In fact, Best Western learned from focus groups that men decide when to stop and where to stay. However, the videotape revealed otherwise: women usually made both these decisions.[37]

- *Thriftway's use of shopping carts.* The Thriftway grocery store chain is testing the use of information technology to track the movement of shopping carts through each store. By using small sensors attached to each cart, the store is able to identify where each cart goes in the store, which direction it is facing, and how long it stays in any one location. In turn, by matching up shopping cart movements with what the customer actually purchased at the checkout lane, Thriftway is able to identify and understand customer behavior. Using such electronic observations, the company has made changes in the placement and store location of many products, creating a better shopping experience.[38]

- *The meaning of coffee.* Robert V. Kozinets developed "netnography," an online ethnographic marketing research technique, to study online communities. Kozinets's research focused on understanding the meaning of coffee consumption behavior by downloading messages from an "alt.coffee" newsgroup. The research found that analysis of newsgroups provided interesting consumption insights and was probably useful for identifying coffee trends and the views of passionate coffee drinkers (lead users).[39]

Recording consumer behavior in home settings is a form of natural observation.

- *HP develops surgical helmet.* Hewlett-Packard (HP) frequently uses observational research to design new products. HP's medical products division sent researchers to hospitals to observe surgeons during operations. The researchers noted that surgeons watched scalpel movements on a television monitor. However, other staff members often walked past the monitor while performing their duties, blocking the surgeon's view. Although the doctors did not complain, it was clear to the HP researchers that something could be done to improve the situation. Based on this insight, they developed a surgical helmet with goggles that cast images right in front of a surgeon's eyes.[40] This kind of insight clearly would have been difficult to obtain through traditional surveys or through focus groups and in-depth interviews. ◀

In **contrived observation,** observations are conducted in an environment artificially set up by the researcher.

Observations can also be made in a **contrived** setting, an environment artificially set up by the researcher. An example involving contrived observation is the BASES simulated test-marketing (STM) service offered by ACNielsen to predict how well a new product is likely to perform in the marketplace.

A key feature of the STM is a simulated, or contrived, store. The procedure used in STM research is as follows. A sample of potential customers first self-administers a background questionnaire dealing with demographics and buying habits. The respondents are then exposed to real advertising in a competitive context; for example, they may view an actual TV program containing commercials for the test product as well as for other products. Next, they are led in small groups to the store, where they are free to buy one or more of the products, or none at all. Sales of the test product and other products in the same product category are observed. These sales data, along with additional feedback obtained from the respondents after they finish their shopping trip, are used to predict the market performance of the new product.[41]

Researchers are increasingly relying on computers to conduct simulated market testing. For example, Decision Insight, a Kansas City–based marketing research firm,[42] has developed a multimedia interactive software package called SimuShop 3D to test product concepts, packaging, and design features. Hallmark Cards, with the help of Decision Insight's Virtual Insight software, created a virtual store, complete with 3-D shelves and gift-wrap samples, on the computer. Respondents were recruited using a mall intercept approach. They entered the virtual store and shopped for Christmas gift-wrapping on the computer. This virtual shopping test enabled Hallmark Cards to zero in on the designs that consumers were most likely to buy.[43] In addition to being faster, virtual market tests are significantly cheaper than the traditional in-store market tests.[44] Simulated test-marketing is becoming increasingly Web based, further reducing the time and cost of product testing.[45]

An important advantage of contrived observation over natural observation is the greater degree of control the former offers. Such control permits researchers to collect relevant data in a speedy, efficient, and less expensive fashion. A potential drawback of contrived observation is the question of whether the collected data would result in a real-life setting. This limitation may be especially serious when respondents know they are being observed, which brings up another dimension on which observation methods can differ: whether they are disguised or nondisguised.

Disguised Versus Nondisguised Observation

Disguised observation is observation of which respondents are unaware.

In **nondisguised observation,** respondents are aware they are being observed.

An observation is **disguised** when respondents are unaware they are being observed; it is **nondisguised** when respondents are aware they are being observed. One critical advantage of disguised observation is that respondents will not change their behavior as a function of the observation technique. Monitoring sales at the cash register (method G) in the Gap Inc. case is an illustration of disguised observation. Methods E and F can also be viewed as disguised observation if the researcher ensures the human observers or videotaping equipment are not visible to the store's customers.[46]

The main strength of disguised observation is that it allows for monitoring the true reactions of individuals. Data gathered through nondisguised observation, on the other hand, may be contaminated by respondent-induced errors, just as in any questionnaire method. As Michael Ray points out, "Observation measures lose their advantage over interviews if the observation becomes apparent to respondents. This can happen with simple observation if the observer appears to be unusual, carries a clipboard, etc."[47] Because disguised observation is nonintrusive, it is also more convenient from the respondent's standpoint.

One popular disguised observational technique is known as *mystery shopping*. Monitoring employee interactions with customers has become a widespread activity in many organizations, including retail chains and banks. One popular way to monitor customer service is mystery shopping. In this type of study, a mystery shopper, unknown to the retail establishment, visits the store and, using a structured script, observes and records the shopping experience.

CASE IN POINT ▶ **Companies Using Mystery Shopping**   A number of companies use mystery shopping in disguised observation:

- *Driving employee incentives at Office Depot.* Office Depot, a leading seller of office products, relies on mystery shopping in part to reward its employees.[48] Office Depot employs a mystery-shopping firm to monitor employee performance at all of its retail locations. Mystery shoppers visit each Office Depot store once a month to rate it on eight dimensions: staffing, business machine knowledge, dress code and greeting, copy and print knowledge, furniture assistance, service at registers, front-end supervisions, and cashier interaction. Every store gets a score out of a possible 100. Office Depot's corporate office receives a summary showing each store's performance. The company also surveys (using simple yes or no questions) every 50th customer about his or her satisfaction with the store. For every yes response, the store receives 5 points, with 30 being the maximum (as there are only six yes or no questions in the survey) and 0 being the minimum. Customer complaints about each store are also recorded every month. Customer complaint scores vary from 20 (for no complaints) to 0 (for one complaint or more). Office Depot then constructs a customer service index using all three pieces of information, namely, mystery-shopping score, survey score, and customer complaints. Office Depot uses this index to calculate employee bonuses.[49]

- *Driving employee incentives at Belk.* Belk Inc., a department store chain located in the U.S. Southeast, has been using a mystery-shopping program to monitor the performance of its salespeople at its stores. Belk's goal is to have every customer approached and greeted within 60 seconds of entering the store. In order to enforce the policy, the company decided to employ mystery shoppers. Some 20,000 mystery-shopper store visits are performed each year. With each visit, the mystery shopper records whether or not the goal was met and reports the results back to the corporate office. The rewards for managers who are able to enforce the policy are significant, with up to 5 percent added to their annual bonus. The store has consistently outperformed many of its department store industry competitors since the start of the program.[50] ◄

Serious ethical questions can arise, however, if disguised observation monitors aspects of respondents' behaviors that are normally private or that may not be voluntarily revealed to researchers. Moreover, data gathered through a study using disguised observation may not be as rich as those obtained from a study involving nondisguised observation. Data from a nondisguised observation are richer because observation that is not hidden from respondents is generally done with their cooperation. Consequently, respondents can be questioned before or after the observation to obtain additional data about characteristics that cannot be observed (for instance, data on demographics and buying habits collected in the STM procedure discussed earlier).

Human Versus Mechanical Observation

Human observation involves people's taking observations.

Mechanical observation involves machines' or devices' taking observations.

Data collection in observation studies can be done by human observers or by mechanical devices. Method E in the Gap Inc. example involves human observers. **Human observation** involves people's taking observations. Methods F and G use mechanical observation or, perhaps more appropriately, electronic observation. **Mechanical observation** involves machines' or devices' taking observations. With the advent of increasingly sophisticated technological gadgets, mechanical observation is rapidly replacing human observation. Of course, regardless of how observations are made, interpretation of those observations is very much a human responsibility.

A key strength of mechanical observation is that it can be used to monitor, in a more precise fashion, virtually anything a human observer is capable of monitoring. For instance, videotaping customers in the special display area for Gap shirts (method F) is likely to generate more complete and accurate observations than using human observers (method E). Moreover, method F is also likely to be less conspicuous to customers than method E, an important consideration if disguised observation is crucial.

Numerous mechanical and electronic devices are now available to observe things that human observers may find very difficult, if not impossible, to study. A comprehensive discussion of such devices is beyond the scope of this text. However, several of the most important ones are illustrated next.

■ **Brain Scan Measurement: Measuring Inner Desires**   Marketers are using functional magnetic resonance imaging (fMRI), a modification of the MRI technology used in hospitals, to study consumers' emotions and motivations. The fMRI process measures flow of blood to the brain's centers of pleasure, thought, or memory. Ford Motor Company has conducted market tests using brain scan studies in Europe. The fMRI machines are put to use to study reactions to everything from Hollywood movies to logos and packaged goods. Researchers, however, caution that desires do not always translate into actions.[51] In addition, is there any privacy issue involved here? You decide.

■ **Eye-Tracking Equipment**   Eye-tracking equipment is used to ascertain precisely which sections of an ad, product packaging, promotional display, or website attract customers' attention and how much time they spend looking at those sections.[52]

Response latency is the speed with which a respondent provides an answer.

■ **Devices to Measure Response Latency**   **Response latency** is the speed with which a respondent provides an answer. Response latency measures are being increasingly employed to determine the effectiveness of ads in influencing the strength of consumers' brand preferences.[53] The rationale underlying the use of response latency measures is that, the more quickly a respondent expresses preference for a brand, the stronger the preference is. For instance, when two customers are asked whether they prefer 7 UP or Sprite, both may say 7 UP; however, the one who responds faster, even by a fraction of a second, presumably has a lower degree of doubt in his or her mind and hence a stronger preference for 7 UP. Only electronic devices can accurately monitor and detect differences in response latency.[54]

■ **Instruments to Conduct Voice Pitch Analysis (VOPAN)**   Voice pitch analysis (VOPAN), not unlike response latency measures, is used to determine how strongly a respondent feels about an answer or how much emotional commitment is attached to it.[55] The VOPAN involves measuring the voice pitch of verbal responses during an interview. This voice pitch is then compared with the respondent's normal voice pitch used during routine conversation about such neutral topics as the weather. The extent to which the voice pitch of responses to a survey question deviates from normal voice pitch is considered a measure of the respondent's emotional commitment to the answer.[56]

■ **People Meter**   The latest development in the area of monitoring television-viewing behavior is the introduction of the people meter, an electronic device used by ACNielsen to monitor television-viewing behavior—who is watching, in addition to what shows are being watched. The people meter uses the latest electronic technology and has separate buttons for all household members as well as for visitors. The individual viewers simply press their corresponding button on the people meter when they start or stop watching TV. All the data collected by ACNielsen's people meters are automatically transmitted to its central computer.

Although the people meter has the potential to provide highly refined television audience measurements, some controversy surrounds its use. Specifically, for some TV programs, significant discrepancies in the estimates of audience size and composition have surfaced between those provided by people meters and those provided by the traditional diary method, wherein households participating in a TV panel make entries in a diary regarding who watched each program. Consequently, questions have been raised about the validity of ratings based on people meter data as well as the representativeness of households agreeing to have their television-viewing behavior monitored through people meters.[57] Efforts are being made to resolve these questions and to further refine the people meter methodology.[58]

Web-Based Observational Techniques

One of the exciting, controversial electronic observation techniques is Web-based tracking of consumers. Research in Use 6.4 illustrates the power of Web-based observation. Tracking every move the customer makes has become a reality in this Internet world. For example, DoubleClick, a U.S. online advertising

Mining Blogs: Useful Nuggets of Information in the Sea of Online Chatter

Consumers in increasing numbers are using the online medium to rave or gripe about the products they use. Companies have begun to notice this trend and are hiring researchers specializing in interpreting blogs to ferret out useful information about their products.

Volkswagen AG used Techdirt, an online marketing research service, to find out which new technologies are creating a buzz among online consumers. Techdirt compiles regular reports based on items that appear in the Techdirt blog, message boards, and mainstream news outlets.

Sony hired Intelliseek to monitor the online chatter on Sony's digital Walkman and Apple's iPod. Steve Sommers, senior manager of marketing research at Sony, likes to take the pulse of the market quickly. In his previous job at Gateway, Inc., he used Intelliseek to track consumers' thoughts on Gateway's Plasma TVs, as well as on the competition.

Blogs are especially useful for spotting negative news in a timely fashion, as illustrated by the case of Kryptonite bicycle locks. An online note on the vulnerability of Kryptonite locks was picked up by two blogs. The *New York Times*, Associated Press, and other mainstream outlets ran the story days after it appeared on the blogs. Kryptonite, a division of Ingersoll-Rand Company Ltd., was forced to act after angry customers deluged the company with questions about the lock. Monitoring and analyzing the blogs would have alerted Kryptonite to the problem much sooner, thereby limiting the damage.

According to Jonathan Carson, CEO of Internet-tracking firm BuzzMetrics, blogs are very useful for observing what customers are already saying about products and services. An airline client asked BuzzMetrics to study the check-in process. BuzzMetrics studied consumers' chatter on sites like flyertalk.com and frequentflier.com. The study showed that consumers are confused about self-service kiosks at the airport, and this insight led to the simplification of the check-in process.[d]

company, tracks consumer movements on the Internet with a tracking technology known as *cookies*. A cookie is a program that anonymously identifies an individual's computer by number. DoubleClick uses the information obtained from the cookies to select advertisements suited to individual tastes. DoubleClick is not alone in taking advantage of cookie technology.

Postel Services, a Korean company, has developed software that tracks e-mail solicitations. Whenever a recipient opens a message, Postel is alerted and in turn alerts the messenger. Such practices are becoming widespread among Internet companies. The loss of privacy is a source of concern for privacy advocates and the Federal Trade Commission, prompting many companies to post privacy policies on their website. DoubleClick acquired Abacus Direct, a direct-marketing company with a customer database of 88 million households, which contains householders' shopping habits and personal financial information. A lawsuit filed by a California woman claimed that DoubleClick, with its ability to merge two databases, could violate her privacy rights as well as those of the general public. Since then, DoubleClick has allowed individuals to "opt out" of the process of having information collected about them. Strong protests from Internet privacy advocates and a federal investigation forced DoubleClick to back off from its original plan of using name and address data to track the online activities of millions of consumers.[59] Even though the case has been settled outside the court system, the privacy controversy lingers.[60]

To overcome privacy issues, some Internet research companies have created "opt-in" Internet panels (nondisguised electronic observation) to track online consumer buying behaviors. A panel of 120,000 Internet-connected U.S. homes operated by PC Data is an example of such a panel. Information Resources, Inc.

(IRI), a leading provider of scanner-based data, has joined with PC Data, a leading provider of Internet measurement and analysis, to measure online and offline consumer buying habits. IRI maintains a 55,000-household panel to track consumer packaged goods. This strategic alliance will allow IRI to keep track of both offline (scanner-based, electronic observation) and online (Web-based, electronic observation) buying habits. Besides PC Data, other companies, such as Media Metrix, Inc., and Nielsen//NetRatings, are also in the Internet measurement market.

Tracking Web users is not without problems. Questions have been raised about the accuracy of the measurements, because there is disagreement between online merchants' own digital logs of visitors and online marketing research companies' Web traffic counts of panel members. Despite these questions, however, companies interested in ascertaining the popularity of their website relative to other sites have to rely on the numbers provided by the three companies that operate Internet panels. Moreover, these companies have demographic data for their panel members, thereby allowing them to report website traffic by demographic variables such as gender, age, income, education, and so on.[61]

Direct Versus Indirect Observation

Direct observation captures the actual behavior or phenomenon of interest.

Indirect observation examines the results or consequences of the behavior or phenomenon under study.

Suppose Mr. Smith, owner of a gift shop, wants to compare customer traffic during the last quarter of a year to traffic in the first three quarters. One option is to use human observers or mechanical/electronic monitors to count the number of people entering his store during each quarter. This procedure is called **direct observation,** because it captures the actual behavior or phenomenon of interest. Another option is to use some form of **indirect observation,** which consists of examining the results or consequences of the phenomenon. For instance, Mr. Smith could install, just inside the store entrance, a temporary patch of floor covering specially designed to wear out easily and show the extent of wear. Replacing the patch every quarter and comparing the wear on the fourth-quarter patch with the wear on patches used in previous quarters can help answer Mr. Smith's question. Research in Use 6.5 describes how Staples employs direct observational techniques to understand its competition.

Indirect observation can give only relatively crude or imprecise indications of a phenomenon. Nevertheless, it does have some attractive features. It will generally be more efficient than direct observation from the time and cost perspectives, especially if the behavior to be observed is stretched out over a long period of time and is likely to occur infrequently during that time. As we saw earlier, monitoring sales of Gap shirts at the cash register (method G), an indirect observation method, will be less time consuming and expensive than methods E and F, both of which involve direct observation. Another advantage of indirect observation is that it may be the only way to get relevant data from situations that are impractical to observe directly. An interesting example of competitive intelligence is Oracle's attempt to help the government's antitrust case against Microsoft by using a form of indirect observation. Oracle bought Microsoft's trash and hired investigators to dig into it to obtain information that government lawyers were not getting.[62]

Structured Versus Nonstructured Observation

Observation is a **structured observation** when a study's data requirements are well established and can be broken into a set of discrete, clearly defined categories.

Whether an observation is structured or nonstructured depends on the nature and type of data recorded. Observation is **structured** when a study's data requirements are well established and can be broken into a set of discrete, clearly defined categories, much like the precoded response categories in structured questions.

Direct Observation: Competitive Intelligence at Staples

Thomas Stemberg, chairman of Staples, a leading office supply chain store, likes to visit at least one of his competitors' stores and one of his own stores every week to monitor industry trends. According to Stemberg, competitive intelligence is critical to stimulating his company's growth and innovation. Stemberg also makes it a point to observe noncompeting retailers to pick up a few new pointers on retailing.

During the visit to a competitor's store, Mr. Stemberg evaluates the store on many important dimensions: visibility of the store, location accessibility, time it takes for a staff member to come with assistance, out-of-stock items, presentation of items, display of information, price ticket inaccuracies, layout of categories and accessibility, price impressions (low or high), staff response to customer questions, staff knowledge, and treatment of customers. One of the most important purposes of the visit is to identify activities that are handled better at the competitor's store and learn from them.

Stemberg, however, cautions that retailers that overly focus on one another and ignore what the customer wants may end up losing the market to a new entrant that focuses on the customer. For instance, Barnes and Noble must look not only at Borders but also at Amazon.com and other similar dot-coms to keep up with retailing trends.

Stemberg is not alone in believing that observation plays an important role in generating new ideas. Dale F. Morrison, president and CEO of Campbell Soup, shares that belief. He has put a priority on visiting retail stores to look for ideas to increase sales. This is what he has to say about observation:

> There is no substitute for getting out and about. I am an integrator of ideas, and I must get out to maximize my exposure to new ideas. Then I integrate the ideas and provide perspective and direction.[e]

Consider a restaurant manager who wants to know the number of single customers and the number of parties of two or more customers who eat at the restaurant. This setting is eminently suited for structured observation because the data requirements are clearly defined. For instance, food servers can be used as observers and asked to keep a tally of the number of single customers and the number of groups of customers they serve.

Suppose, however, that the manager wants to observe the moods and behaviors of single customers and of customer groups. Given the vagueness of the manager's objective, some form of *nonstructured observation* will be required in this situation. Observation is **nonstructured** when a study's data requirements cannot be broken into a set of discrete, clearly defined categories. For instance, the manager may use inconspicuous videotaping equipment or human observers to monitor "everything of relevance" concerning the restaurant's customers.

Although structured observation is generally easier to record and analyze than nonstructured observation, it is limited in the depth and richness of data it can provide. The pros and cons of structured observation are similar to those of structured questionnaires discussed earlier. Along the same lines, structured observation is more suitable for conclusive research projects than for exploratory research projects.

A final note on the observation method: what we have discussed so far under types of observation techniques are really five dimensions along which observation methods can vary. Numerous types of observation methods are possible through unique combinations of these dimensions. Differences among observation methods and the extent of those differences depend on how the methods vary along the five dimensions. For example, method E in the Gap Inc. case can be labeled as natural, disguised (if the observer is not conspicuous), human, direct, nonstructured observation. In contrast, method G is natural, disguised, mechanical, indirect, structured observation.

Observation is a nonstructured observation when a study's data requirements cannot be broken into a set of discrete, clearly defined categories.

SUMMARY

This chapter described a number of primary-data collection techniques that can be broadly classified into questioning and observation methods. In general, the questioning method is more versatile than the observation method, mainly because the latter can be used only to study what is visible. The questioning method is also typically, although not always, faster and cheaper. However, the observation method is less likely to suffer from respondent-induced errors and therefore is capable of generating more accurate data. The observation method is also more convenient from the respondent's perspective. In some studies, a researcher may be able to use a combination of the two methods to capitalize on the advantages of both.

The formats of questionnaires can vary along the two dimensions of structure and disguise. The more conclusive, or final, a research project, the more appropriate and advantageous structured questionnaires are. The need to use disguised questionnaires increases with anticipated respondent unwillingness or inability to answer direct questions.

On the basis of structure and disguise, questionnaires can be roughly classified into four broad categories. First are structured, nondisguised questionnaires, which are frequently used, especially in descriptive research projects. Second are nonstructured, nondisguised questionnaires, which are particularly appropriate for exploratory research projects. Third are structured, disguised questionnaires, whose typical purpose is to uncover people's attitudes about broad social issues; because of their purpose, they are not frequently used in traditional marketing research studies. Fourth are nonstructured, disguised questionnaires, which usually employ projective techniques and are used in motivation research studies to explore consumers' inner feelings and motives. Questionnaires can also be classified into four categories according to the method used to administer them: personal interviews, telephone surveys, mail surveys, and Internet- or Web-based surveys. These questionnaire administration methods differ in terms of versatility, speed, cost, accuracy, and convenience from the respondent's standpoint. That any one method will be the best on all criteria in a given situation is highly unlikely. Therefore, the researcher must carefully consider situation-specific characteristics and ascertain which criteria are most critical before selecting a questionnaire administration method. At times, the researcher may wish to improvise a hybrid questionnaire administration method possessing key strengths of all the basic methods.

A variety of techniques are available for collecting data through observation.[63] Specifically, an observation study can be (1) conducted in a natural or a contrived setting; (2) disguised or nondisguised from respondents;

(3) conducted by human observers or by mechanical/electronic means (the latter are becoming increasingly popular because of technological advances); (4) direct or indirect, depending on whether an actual occurrence or its consequence is observed; and (5) structured or nonstructured. As in the selection of a questionnaire method, the choice of an appropriate observation technique must be based on a careful examination of such factors as the nature of the research, the type of data required, and the resources available.

ACE
self-test

REVIEW AND DISCUSSION QUESTIONS

1. Can observation methods be used in exploratory research? Why or why not?

2. In what ways is the questionnaire method more versatile than the observation method?

3. What advantages do telephone surveys have over personal interviews and mail surveys?

4. What is a shopping mall intercept interview? What are its advantages over the more traditional questionnaire administration methods?

5. What is a Web-based survey? Describe a marketing research problem for which a Web-based survey would be more effective than other survey methods.

6. What are the five dimensions along which observation methods vary?

APPLICATION EXERCISES

1. The manager of a large, independent urban supermarket wants to estimate the proportion of households in the city that make a purchase in the supermarket at least once a month. What methods should the manager use to generate this estimate? Explain your answer.

2. A suburban shopping mall is planning to exhibit antiques and various types of art in its lobby area to generate more visitors. Describe a combination of the questionnaire and observation methods that can be used to ascertain the effectiveness of the antique and art exhibit.

3. Trent Eating Association (TEA) operates a chain of restaurants in eight communities of similar size and population. TEA currently has the image of a high-class restaurant chain serving excellent food at premium prices. Its president is wondering whether a 15 percent reduction in prices of all menu items would hurt or help sales revenues and profits. Assume that a marketing research study is to be conducted in this situation and that the necessary

data are to be gathered through observation. Describe an appropriate approach for collecting data in this context and indicate how you would classify that approach along each of the five observation dimensions discussed in this chapter.

 INTERNET EXERCISES

1. Visit the Gallup Organization's website (www .gallup.com) and assess how it conducts research (what survey methods it uses). Next, visit Harris Interactive's site (www.harrisinteractive.com) and ascertain its research methods. Highlight the commonalities in and differences between these two organizations in terms of their research methods.

2. Assume you are working as the marketing analyst for an Internet retailer (such as www.amazon.com, www.ebay.com, or www.bestbuy.com) and you need to assess how consumers are visiting and shopping on your firm's website. One of the leading providers of such research is Nielsen//NetRatings (www .netratings.com). After visiting the NetRatings site, outline the Internet research method you think your firm should use to observe consumer traffic. Should this study be done in-house or outsourced to a firm like Nielsen//NetRatings? In addition, what are the ethical concerns of collecting such click-through data by placing cookies on customers' computers (examine the privacy statement of DoubleClick at www.doubleclick.com).

CASE 6.1 *NATIONAL GEOGRAPHIC KIDS*
(www.nationalgeographic.com)

National Geographic is a brand that has been has been around since 1888. With a mission to "increase and diffuse geographic knowledge," the brand has been successful in expanding its reach (influence) over the years. Forty million people read National Geographic's flagship magazine, and 148 countries receive the brand's cable television channel. Even more people are touched by National Geographic through its other magazines, such as *Adventure*, *National Geographic Kids*, and *Traveler*; videos; books; and other media. In 1975, National Geographic expanded its reach to more kids by starting *World*, a nonfiction magazine for children. This kids-targeted magazine maintained close ties with the flagship magazine, but the content was redesigned to entertain the young.

World magazine enjoyed tremendous success for almost two decades after its market entry. However, after that it began to face stiff competition from explosive growth in various other media targeted toward kids—new TV shows, magazines, and various Internet sites. Recognizing the influence and buying power of children, these new outlets began to cater much more effectively to the youth market's changing tastes and preferences. *World* was missing out on these changes and needed a makeover. In an attempt to rejuvenate *World*, managers in charge of it commissioned a number of qualitative and quantitative studies focusing on children's opinions.

In conducting these studies, National Geographic had to modify its conventional research methods, which had been developed for use with adults rather than children. For instance, parental permission had to be obtained, and research instruments had to be carefully pretested to ensure their meaningfulness and clarity for children. Because children are very literal, abstract ideas do not work well for them. When using focus groups, the moderator must be aware that groupthink is more prevalent among young children than among adults. It is important to separate children by age and gender. When males and females are in the same room, males will dominate the conversation. If older and younger children are placed in the same focus group, the younger children will mimic the viewpoints of the older children.

Based on insights from the research studies, the kids' magazine's name was changed from *World* to *National Geographic Kids*. In addition, the magazine's content and appearance were modified by introducing a brighter and more intriguing font, and including more interesting pictures. The articles in the reformulated magazine are now geared to topics that kids want to read about, such as pop culture, animals, and anything fun and exciting. After the launch of the new *National Geographic Kids*, paid subscriptions rocketed to over 1 million. It is the fastest-growing kids' magazine, with a total readership of over 4 million.

To maintain the tremendous success of *National Geographic Kids*, National Geographic continues to conduct a variety of studies to track trends in and preferences of the youth market. After the release of each issue, a questionnaire with a $1 incentive and a letter from the editor in chief are sent to a random sample of 800 subscriber homes. This survey delves into readers' reactions to the cover, articles, and advertisements.

National Geographic Kids has also utilized kids' online capabilities by developing an online panel of 500 kids. Visuals are sent to the panel via regular mail to ensure the quality of the prints. The participants then log on to rate the ideas and content presented in the visuals. The results of the online survey are reviewed by editors

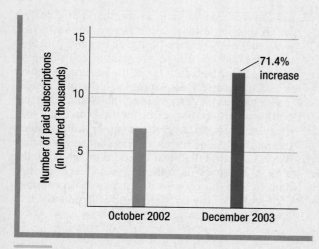

Exhibit 1
National Geographic Kids **Subscriptions**

and used as a guideline for editorial content selection. Each year the panel is renewed.

Nationwide studies are also conducted to help understand the "tween" market and its ever-changing tastes and trends. For instance, *National Geographic Kids*, in conjunction with NFO WorldGroup, conducts national surveys of 1,300 children ranging in age from 6 to 14. The goal is to gain a better understanding of their attitudes on a host of issues including learning, school, and life in general. Synthesizing and publicizing insights from these surveys helps position *National Geographic Kids* as an expert in the field and creates free positive press.

CASE QUESTIONS

1. Was the research conducted by National Geographic to regain its position in the kids' market exploratory or conclusive? Was the research approach appropriate? Why or why not?

2. What types of marketing research are being used by *National Geographic Kids* to maintain their kids-oriented focus? Are these exploratory or conclusive methods?

3. Critically evaluate the appropriateness of the research studies being conducted by *National Geographic Kids* for testing new magazine content and for tracking new trends. What changes or additional approaches, if any, would you recommend?

www.nationalgeographic.com; Lisa Wicklund, "Teaching an Old Brand New Tricks: Connecting a 116-Year-Old Brand to a 10-Year-Old" (25th Anniversary AMA Marketing Research Conference, New Orleans, LA, September 2004); National Geographic, "National Geographic Kids Survey Finds 6-to-14-Year-Olds Think Learning Is Cool," press release, June 2003.

CASE 6.2 COLGATE-PALMOLIVE MEXICO
(www.colgate-palmolive.com)

With $9 billion in annual sales, Colgate-Palmolive is a market leader in products associated with oral care, personal care, household surface care, fabric care, and pet nutrition. As a global consumer products company, Colgate-Palmolive sells its products in more than 200 countries and territories around the world. Included in its portfolio of internationally recognized brand names are Colgate, Palmolive, Mennen, Softsoap, Protex, Sorriso, Kolynos, Ajax, Axion, Soupline, Suavitel, and Fab, as well as Hill's Science Diet and Hill's Prescription Diet pet foods.

As a leading consumer products company, Colgate-Palmolive is focused on achieving consistent growth, global success, and continued company strength to benefit its consumers, employees, and shareholders. It is dedicated to serving the communities where it does business and is committed to advancing technology that can address changing consumer needs throughout the world. Its goal is to use its technology to create products that will continue to improve the quality of life for its consumers wherever they live.

Emerging Markets

As the world moves toward a global economy, businesses like Colgate-Palmolive are interested in expanding their markets. One promising front is emerging growth markets, those countries showing potential for high levels of economic growth. Although productive, these markets can exhibit substantial economic and market-related risks, and are typically viewed as long-term targets. Some of the biggest emerging markets in the 1990s were Argentina, Brazil, China, Indonesia, India, Mexico, Poland, Russia, South Africa, and Turkey.

Mexico

Mexico is an ideal target market for Colgate-Palmolive products. It has a free-market economy increasingly dominated by the private sector. Formerly state-owned enterprises have been privatized over the past two decades,[1] fostering competition in the marketplace. The economy includes both modern and outmoded industry and agriculture.

As Mexico endeavors to modernize its economy and raise the standard of living, it has seen increased employment and higher wages. These factors have fueled private consumption, further increasing economic growth. Growth in the economy, however, has not been felt equally across all socioeconomic segments of the population. An estimated 27 percent of the more than 100 million population lives below the poverty level.[2] In terms of income distribution, the top 10 percent of the population earns 36.6 percent of the income, in contrast to the lowest 10 percent, which earns 1.8 percent.[3] Furthermore, the top 20 percent of earners account for 55 percent of the income, so the majority of the discretionary income is concentrated within a small portion of the population. Much of the population struggles with low wages, underemployment, few advancement opportunities, and poverty.

Colgate-Palmolive Research[4]

Colgate-Palmolive had five separate product categories to market in Mexico: laundry care, dishwashing, house-cleaning, oral care, and hair care products. Marketing researchers set out to gain insights for crafting advertising messages and developing new products for the different socioeconomic segments of consumers. They wanted to better understand the emotions and socioeconomic factors in the lives of different consumer groups associated with use of products in each of the five categories. Their specific goals were to

1. Understand the total process involved in each of the five different product categories for the different segments.
2. Become familiar with the role of each chore in the daily lives of the consumer segments.
3. Gain a better understanding of the lifestyle of each socioeconomic segment.
4. Gain insights into each segment's predisposition to brand loyalty.
5. Better understand product substitution for each segment.

They knew that some differences existed among different socioeconomic groups, so they sought to gain insights into the broader context of use of each product category by each group.

To meet these objectives, researchers developed a unique method. They identified different socioeconomic segments, located individuals in each segment, and spent several days within each group to videotape them using each of the five product categories. Upon their return to Colgate-Palmolive headquarters, they proceeded to review the videotapes to complete descriptive reports of their findings. The researchers produced a series of five videotaped reports that summarized their findings, one for each of the different product categories. Overall, they believed they had gained tremendous insights into and understanding of the activities, attitudes, and behaviors of the different segments.

Sample Findings

The report on laundry care was representative of the types of rich qualitative information gained from the research. The research addressed each of its objectives and provided a fuller appreciation for the different lifestyles of women in the various socioeconomic groups. The following are actual excerpts from the video transcripts relating to different aspects of laundry care by different socioeconomic segments.

Comments About the Process of Doing Laundry

Urban housewife, upper-income household. Usually, the maid does the washing, at least most of the time. If she can't come to work, I have to do it myself, although I'm not used to doing laundry. I start by giving her directions, how to use the washing machine, put the soap in, sort the laundry. It doesn't make sense wasting three hours doing it by hand if there is a machine.

Urban housewife, lower-income household. I do laundry every day as my girls change clothes. I don't like clothes piling up.

Rural housewife, lower-income household. Besides washing every day, I also have other chores to do at home. Washing takes a lot of time because you have to rub the clothes hard. It's hard to combine washing with the other chores.

Rural housewife, poverty-level household. Some women wash other people's clothes and they come down here at three or four o'clock. Sometimes they spend the night here.

Comments About the Availability of Water

Urban housewife, upper-middle-income household. We don't have problems with water. Some in certain neighborhoods do, but not in ours.

Urban housewife, lower-income household. We only have water in the morning; it runs out by the evening. I do the washing by hand while there is still water. Otherwise I would have to do it the next day. Sometimes there is no water for two or three days. Usually we have water about two hours a day. We fill up barrels so we have water for other times.

Rural housewife, poverty-level household. It is easy to do laundry here in the river because I have never had water at home. I must come down here anyway. I have done the washing down here all of my life.

Comments About Treating Stains

Urban housewife, upper-income household. If I have a dress that gets a grease spot, at that point I put some talcum on it. Afterwards, I put the dress in the washing machine and the spot disappears. If the spot remains, I throw the dress away.

Urban housewife, lower-middle-income household. To take grease spots away, I use remover or Palmolive brand soap. It's an excellent brand to take away any grease, sweat spots, as well as blood, chili, and red wine stains.

Rural housewife, lower-income household. I remove stains with a bar soap. I rub it directly in the stain and leave it bleaching in the sun, which softens the spot.

Attitudes About Laundry Care

Urban housewife, upper-income household. If there are any clothes to be ironed, I leave them to the maid or to the caretaker woman. When the clothes are already dried I fold them, especially the shirts, and keep them in the closet. I have a drawer for each kind of clothing—shirts, skirts, jeans. It is a job that most of us women have to do, although maybe there are some exceptions. Unfortunately, it's a never-ending chore. It isn't well rewarded because nobody seems to notice it.

Urban housewife, upper-middle-income household. I do it because I like it. Because it makes me feel good.

Rural housewife, poverty-level household. At least I can work these days. And nobody notices it. What will I do when I get older and somebody will have to take care of me? That's what I am afraid of.

Two of the factors that influenced the behaviors of different segments were access to water and electricity. These two factors dramatically influenced activities relating to laundry care, as was evident in both the video footage and the transcripts.

CASE QUESTIONS

1. What type of research method did Colgate-Palmolive Mexico use?

2. What conclusions would you draw if you were a marketing manager for Colgate-Palmolive? Based on your conclusions, what steps would you take?

3. What additional research is needed to validate these findings?

CASE NOTES

1. According to www.cia.gov, the number of state-owned enterprises in Mexico fell from more than 1,000 in 1982 to fewer than 200 in 1999.
2. Population statistics are based on information at www.cia.gov.
3. Income distribution based on information on www.cia.gov.
4. The authors would like to thank those at Colgate-Palmolive who provided access to the research summarized in this case. Some of the content is based on a personal interview with John Tietjen and Kathy Thornhill, C-P New York, April 1999. Narratives are from the C-P video *Consumer View: Evolution of the Video Technique—Mexico.*

This case was written by Jeanne L. Munger (University of Southern Maine) in collaboration with the textbook authors, as a basis for class discussion rather than to illustrate either effective or ineffective marketing practice.

7 Qualitative Research

Focus Groups Help Gap Determine What Customers Want

Gap, one of the world's largest specialty clothing retailers, is interested in offering current fashions that customers will find attractive and fresh enough to visit Gap stores more frequently. This, according to the company, will increase its inventory turnover while maintaining high margins. Such a strategy requires Gap to find a way to stay on the cutting edge of fashion by closely monitoring consumer preferences, deliver on those preferences in a timely manner, and maintain optimum inventory levels that eliminate the need for using low-price promotions in order to clear out excess inventory.

Gap relies on focus groups to help with this challenge. Through focus groups, the company learns what customers look for in terms of fashion, preferred colors, and the most popular styles. It also uses focus groups at a more localized level to determine such preferences, allowing the company to tailor its offerings meaningfully for regional markets.

Chapter Objectives

After reading and understanding the material in this chapter, you should be able to:

■ Distinguish between qualitative and quantitative research, and explain the relationship between the two.

■ Identify the three major determinants of focus group effectiveness.

■ Explain the major advantages and disadvantages of focus groups.

■ Identify potential applications of focus groups.

■ Discuss the impact of technology on focus group research.

■ Describe other qualitative research techniques and identify situations in which you would use them.

177

Gap conducts a series of focus groups to ascertain consumers' preferences. Although it gains valuable insights from its focus groups, the company does not stop with this qualitative research. It combines the results from focus groups with more quantitative data from its point-of-sale and other information systems to develop and implement effective inventory management systems.[1] ■

Sometimes researchers need information that cannot easily be obtained through numerical data analysis. Certain types of valuable information may be obtained only through what is called *qualitative research*. As the opening vignette shows, Gap was able to gain important insights into customer needs through focus group discussions, arguably the most popular form of qualitative research.

What Is Qualitative Research?

Qualitative research is the collection, analysis, and interpretation of data that cannot be meaningfully quantified, or summarized in the form of numbers.

Qualitative research collects, analyzes, and interprets data that cannot be meaningfully quantified, or summarized in the form of numbers. For this reason, qualitative research is sometimes referred to as *soft research*. This term is unfortunate, because as subsequent sections of this chapter will show, soft research is no less valuable than so-called hard, or quantitative, research.

Any study using nonstructured questioning or observation techniques can be labeled "qualitative research." However, qualitative research typically studies relatively few respondents or units. In other words, a study of a large, representative sample would normally not be called "qualitative research" even if it used some nonstructured questions or observations.

The nonstructured and small-sample features of qualitative research techniques have an important implication. They are intended to provide initial insights, ideas, or understandings about a problem, not to recommend a final course of action. Therefore, qualitative research techniques are most appropriate in situations calling for exploratory research. Several techniques covered in previous chapters—for example, the lead-user or key-informant technique, the case study method, the focus group interview, the in-depth interview, the word association test, and nonstructured observation—are qualitative research techniques that are often used in exploratory research.

Qualitative Versus Quantitative Research

Quantitative research is the collection, analysis, and interpretation of data involving larger, more representative respondent samples and numerical calculation of results.

Quantitative research, in contrast to qualitative research, is characterized by more structure and larger, more representative respondent samples. Consequently, the logical place for quantitative research techniques (usually in the form of large-scale surveys or structured observations) is in conclusive research projects. Table 7.1 outlines several situations to juxtapose the differences between qualitative and quantitative research applications. The research settings under "Settings Best for Qualitative Research" in Table 7.1 reveal a common element of developing an initial understanding of the marketing problem and its context. A primary role of qualitative research is to generate hunches or hypotheses that can be tested through more formal research. In contrast, each of the situations under "Settings Best for Quantitative Research" calls for very specific data, capable of suggesting a final course of action. A primary role of quantitative research is to *test* hunches or hypotheses.

TABLE 7.1
Applications of Qualitative and Quantitative Research

Topic Area	Settings Best for Qualitative Research	Settings Best for Quantitative Research
Advertising	The Pennzoil-Quaker State Company, marketer of Total Shine, wants to come up with ideas for creatively communicating through a television commercial the cleaner/polisher's benefits.	Two different commercials for Total Shine have been developed; management wants to know which of the two will be more effective in favorably influencing target customers' preferences for Total Shine.
Product planning and promotion	The brand manager in charge of KitchenAid small appliances wishes to develop an understanding of how, when, where, and why consumers use kitchen appliances.	The brand manager wants to conduct a large-scale segmentation study to identify heavy users of kitchen appliances.
Personal selling	Sales of the Ford Explorer have been dropping steadily; the sales manager wants to identify possible reasons for this decline.	From discussions with several dealers, the sales manager suspects that customer satisfaction with the Ford Explorer is low and wants to confirm it by using a customer satisfaction questionnaire.
Services marketing	The administrators of Jackson Memorial Hospital in Miami want to develop a feel for the nature and extent of apprehension experienced by patients when they are in the hospital.	The administrators want to ascertain patients' ratings of specific attributes, such as patient care, food service, and medical treatment.
Politics	President George W. Bush wants to understand the concerns of U.S. citizens before formulating his specific plans for privatizing the U.S. social security system	President Bush wants to determine the degree of support for "social security privatization" among young workers.

We saw in Chapter 1 that there is much more to marketing research than numbers and statistics. This is an important point to remember, because it is tempting to believe (and some do believe) that qualitative research is somehow inferior to quantitative research and hence is not truly marketing research. However, quantification by itself does not make research any more accurate or valuable than qualitative research. One marketing researcher has this to say about the quantitative-qualitative research controversy:

> The structured questionnaire is a familiar research method that may fail to capture key information regarding the intangible characteristics of a culture. As a result, important nuances almost certainly will be overlooked. A structured questionnaire also rarely can account for contextual influences on purchase and consumption because it is based on assumptions regarding what people are conscious of or can recall about their behavior, and it presumes an understanding of the population to design, organize and frame questions. Too often, this depth of understanding is lacking. These problems, which are inherent with traditional data collection methods, are magnified when studying consumers in other cultures. Qualitative research approaches, by contrast, generally are more flexible and so more easily capture information crucial to forming effective strategy.[2]

The line between qualitative and quantitative research is not always clear. Some qualitative research yields numbers that can be statistically analyzed, and some structured questionnaires (quantitative research) contain open-ended questions requiring qualitative analysis. Both types of research have drawbacks that must be accounted for in deriving maximum value from their use. For instance, according to 16 new-product managers of US WEST (now a part of Qwest Communications),

> We move into qualitative screening, mostly one-on-one interviews where they are dealing with a prototype, or focus groups where they are dealing with a concept. . . . It's pretty well-defined that you do some quantitative analysis . . . literally taking a concept out there and saying, "Would you buy this if it were priced at X?"[3]

Both types of research play a legitimate and important role in marketing research. Qualitative is better than quantitative research if the purpose of the research is to understand a problem or develop new-product concepts.[4] Quantitative research, on the other hand, is more appropriate if the purpose of the research is to forecast sales, establish price points, or select the best potential target markets. In other words, quantitative research is necessary to address specific problems. If a company wants to estimate demand for a new-product idea or identify a potential target market, qualitative studies should always be followed by quantitative studies. The point is that, in a properly conceived study, qualitative and quantitative research techniques must *complement*, rather than *compete with*, each other. Marketing research practitioners expect an unprecedented level of integration between qualitative and quantitative research in the twenty-first century.[5] We now turn to focus group interviews, which are perhaps the most widely and frequently used form of qualitative research.

Focus Group Interviews

A **focus group** is a research technique that relies on an objective discussion leader or moderator who introduces a topic to a group of respondents and directs their discussion of that topic in a nonstructured and natural fashion.

As mentioned in Chapter 3, the *focus group interview*, often called simply "focus group," is such a popular type of qualitative research that many marketing research practitioners consider it synonymous with qualitative research. A **focus group** relies on an objective discussion leader or moderator who introduces a topic to a group of respondents and directs their discussion of that topic in a nonstructured and natural fashion. Total U.S. domestic marketing research spending in 2003 was about $6.5 billion.[6] Qualitative research accounted for 32 percent of that $6.5 billion, or roughly $2.1 billion. A significant portion of qualitative research spending goes toward focus groups.[7] Clearly, focus groups are prevalent in marketing research practice.

A useful way to get a feeling for what goes on in focus group interviews is to examine the actual procedure of a firm that conducts a large number of them. The following description provided by Burke Custom Marketing Research, a division of Burke, Inc. (www.burke.com), serves as an effective introduction to focus group interviews.

> The respondents are requested to come to the Burke studios at a specified time. There the discussion is conducted in a relaxed atmosphere, with the environment approximating that found in a home rather than an office or institution. Placing the respondents in a casual, relaxed situation is an important factor in gaining their prompt cooperation as the discussion begins. Interviewing is done during the day if only nonworking homemakers are required, or at night if working women or men are needed.

Burke discussions usually begin with the session leader explaining to the respondents the general purpose of group interviewing and the importance of their candid opinions. The discussion leader will normally have a written outline, which has been prepared to make sure all subjects relevant to the objectives of the research will be covered. This outline proceeds from the general to the specific. Very often the leader, having raised the broad general subject, will need to do very little guiding to see that all subject areas are covered. Usually these subject matters will be covered in any order brought up by respondents rather than following the written outline. This promotes normal conversation, and the discussion leader only needs to probe into details within each area and to prompt those respondents who are reluctant to voice their feelings. The discussion leader's own attitudes, of course, must never influence the discussion.[8]

This procedure is not unique to focus group interviews conducted by Burke; rather, it is a fair description of focus groups in general.

The air of informality implied in the definition does not mean that focus group interviews are easy to conduct. Quite to the contrary, focus groups as well as other qualitative research techniques must be conceived and conducted with the utmost care if they are to be useful. It is important to note that "a statistical package can do the hard work of identifying patterns in quantitative data, but identifying patterns in qualitative data requires judgment, inference, and tenacity. Making sense of one short interview seems easy enough, but a thorough and competent analysis of several lengthy interviews is harder than crunching numbers."[9] It is also important to keep in mind that "quantitative research permits objective numerical analysis, which qualitative research sacrifices for intensive analysis and fast turnaround."[10]

The potential worth of focus group interviews depends highly on factors such as group composition, moderator characteristics, and the interview atmosphere itself. Unfortunately, there is no unanimous agreement among researchers about how one should select or manipulate these factors to reap maximum benefits from focus group interviews. Therefore, remember that any general inferences about focus groups made in the following sections, although reflecting the opinions of a majority of researchers, are not absolute.

Group Composition

The effectiveness of a focus group depends very much on the number of participants and their characteristics. There is no scientific basis for determining the optimal focus group size. However, virtually all focus groups conducted by marketing research practitioners have between 6 and 12 participants.[11] Groups with fewer than 6 participants are apparently not likely to generate the momentum and group dynamics necessary for a truly beneficial focus group session. (Benefits unique to well-conducted focus groups are discussed later.) Similarly, a group with more than 12 participants may be too large to be conducive to a cohesive and natural discussion.[12]

The Importance and Implication of Homogeneity

To be effective, a focus group must be as homogeneous as possible with respect to demographic and socioeconomic characteristics. It is essential to get as much commonality in a group as possible, so that the numerous interacting demographic variables do not confuse the issues. For the group to be most productive, all the participants must be on the same wavelength.[13] However, several homogeneous focus groups representing different population segments are often necessary to get an accurate picture of the issue being investigated. The following case in point illustrates.

CASE IN POINT ▶ **Back to Realities**   Liz Claiborne Inc. (www.lizclaiborne.com) designs and markets an extensive range of women's and men's fashion apparel and accessories, including fragrances for women and men. Liz Claiborne wants to reintroduce the old fragrance brand Realities, which it discontinued in 1998. One logical starting point for Liz Claiborne is to conduct focus group interviews with target customers to get them to talk freely about their fragrance usage, satisfaction and dissatisfaction with existing brands, and recall of old brand names, including Realities. Liz Claiborne decides to conduct a focus group interview with women between the ages of 25 and 49, which is the intended target market for Realities.[14]

Clearly, whatever inferences Liz Claiborne draws from the focus group information cannot be generalized. There is no guarantee that ideas for the relaunch of Realities stemming from this group will appeal to other groups of women. This limitation is present in virtually all focus groups, because they typically rely on small, homogeneous samples. This limitation does not mean that focus groups are useless, though. The purpose of a focus group—as a matter of fact, the purpose of any qualitative research technique—is to generate preliminary insights rather than to make generalizations.

The researchers for Liz Claiborne would do well to conduct a series of focus groups, each internally homogeneous but different from the others in terms of the participants' age and employment status. Such a series of focus group interviews is likely to generate a range of new-product ideas appealing to a wide cross-section of women. Indeed, judging from what is done in practice, very seldom is just one focus group conducted for a research project. A rule of thumb is to conduct at least two focus groups aimed at a single research issue, to generate a meaningful, interpretable set of insights. Ideally, resources permitting, additional focus groups should be conducted as long as new information continues to emerge from them.[15] ◀

■ **The Danger of Drawing Definitive Conclusions**   Although conducting several focus groups may yield a rich reservoir of data, the fact remains that it is dangerous to draw any definitive conclusions from such data. This point is important to repeat, because making generalizations on the basis of focus group interviews is perhaps the most frequent misuse of the technique. One abuse is accumulating a large sample by conducting a series of focus groups and trying to quantify the data. For example, information from 100 respondents in 10 focus groups is still not representative because of the sampling and group dynamics biases. Information from

Focus groups are flexible. As shown here, participants can try products before discussing them—and generate rich insights. However, drawing definitive conclusions from those insights is dangerous.

100 randomly selected respondents interviewed individually might well be representative. The marketer should identify the type of research needed, whether qualitative or quantitative, before committing to the technique.[16]

Now let's examine the extent to which responses generated in a focus group are truthful or trustworthy. As we saw in the previous chapter, data obtained through questioning respondents can be biased due to a variety of factors, such as respondent untruthfulness and interviewer errors. Focus group interviews are no exception to this bias, especially because participants in a group interview may be tempted to provide biased responses to impress others, appear socially responsible, and so on. Moreover, a group that does not look "natural" from the participants' perspective may lead to forced or contrived responses, thereby aggravating the problem of inaccurate responses.

Intuitively, a homogeneous group in which participants can identify and feel comfortable with one another is likely to be more natural and relaxed than a heterogeneous group. Therefore, contrived responses or responses intended merely to impress others are less likely to arise in a homogeneous group. To illustrate this point, let's look at the Liz Claiborne case again. What would you expect to happen if Liz Claiborne used heterogeneous rather than homogeneous focus groups in its quest for new-product ideas? Specifically, suppose a focus group interview is to be conducted with working and nonworking women, drawn from a wide range of age groups. Because working status and age can strongly influence perceptions about the use of cosmetics, the participants in this group will most likely hold widely varying, and perhaps conflicting, opinions. Furthermore, differences in working status and age may lead to undesirable consequences; for instance, some women may become reticent, some may provide socially acceptable responses, and others may attempt to show off. The result is likely to be an unproductive focus group session, in terms of both the number of relevant insights generated and the validity of those insights. Thus homogeneous focus groups, although not capable of guaranteeing completely valid responses, are less likely to suffer from response inaccuracies than are heterogeneous groups.

■ **The Importance of Proper Screening Procedures** Proper screening procedures can ensure suitable group composition. Demographic similarity among participants in a group is desirable from the standpoint of generating useful, trustworthy data. An easy way to accomplish this similarity is to recruit respondents from organizations such as religious groups, clubs, and professional associations whose members are likely to be similar. A potential problem here, however, is whether this selection procedure will lead to any detrimental group behavior. It is generally believed that an individual should not be allowed to participate in a group containing a friend, neighbor, or relative; they will tend to talk to each other and not to the group as a whole.[17]

However, controlled studies have not demonstrated any definite problem associated with having acquaintances and friends in the same group.[18] Moreover, several well-known commercial marketing research firms apparently do recruit focus group participants from organizations like churches and schools.[19] The reality of research budgets and hard-to-recruit groups (such as doctors, business executives, and other professionals) may dictate compromise in these participant parameters. This sort of recruiting can be justified, because a well-qualified moderator can usually overcome such difficulties as participants' talking to each other rather than to the group as a whole.

A problem more serious than participants who know one another beforehand is that of so-called *professional respondents*, people who have participated in numerous focus groups before. Professional respondents are atypical consumers, and their responses during a group session can lead to serious validity problems.[20] When screening respondents for focus groups, it is a good practice to exclude those who have participated in a focus group within the previous six months. Participants should also have some experience related to the product or issue to be discussed. The reasons are obvious: respondents lacking relevant experience are not likely to make any valuable contribution to the group discussion. To the contrary, they may adversely affect the discussion by making meaningless remarks just for the sake of participating. Therefore, the screening procedure should query potential respondents about their past experience with or exposure to the focus group topic.

Exhibit 7.1 shows a screening questionnaire used by a research firm to recruit female respondents via telephone for a focus group dealing with appliance repair services. The first question is intended to ensure that potential respondents have had relevant experience. The second and third questions reflect client-imposed restrictions regarding participant characteristics. The last two questions are meant to screen out atypical and professional respondents. Only individuals who pass all five questions are recruited to participate in the focus group.

Moderator Characteristics

Of all the factors influencing the effectiveness and usefulness of a focus group, the discussion leader or moderator is perhaps the most crucial. The moderator's role is also an extremely delicate one. It requires stimulating natural discussion among all the participants while at the same time ensuring that the focus of the discussion does not stray too far from the topic. Having a relatively homogeneous group can help to a certain extent in maintaining group cohesiveness and encouraging

Exhibit 7.1
Screening Questionnaire for Recruiting Focus Group Participants
Source: Fieldwork Chicago, Inc., 5750 Old Orchard Road, Suite 500, Skokie, IL 60077 (www.fieldwork.com). Reprinted by permission.

Name:_____   Date:_____

Address: _____   Phone:_____

City and State: _____   Interview:_____

Hello, This is _____ from Fieldwork Chicago, Inc. We are planning a group discussion on the topic of appliance repair and service. Would you be interested in participating in such a session on _____ at _____?
(IF "NO" terminate and tally)

1. **Have you had an appliance (such as a television, washer, dryer, microwave oven, etc.) serviced or repaired within the last year?**
   ❑ YES...................1 CONTINUE
   ❑ NO ....2 TERMINATE AND TALLY

2. **Are you between the ages of 30 and 64?**
   ❑ YES...................1 CONTINUE
   ❑ NO ....2 TERMINATE AND TALLY

3. **Do you live in zip code 60646, 60202, 60076, or 60077?**
   ❑ YES...................1 CONTINUE
   ❑ NO ....2 TERMINATE AND TALLY

4. **Do you or any member of your family work for an advertising agency, a market research firm, or a company that makes, sells, or distributes appliances?**
   ❑ YES...................1 CONTINUE
   ❑ NO ....2 TERMINATE AND TALLY

5. **When, if ever, did you last attend a market research focus group?** _____
   (IF LESS THAN 6 MONTHS AGO—TERMINATE AND TALLY)

all individuals to participate. Nevertheless, a group in which the personalities of all participants are mutually compatible is more an exception than the rule. Focus groups usually have one or two people who strive to dominate the discussion and one or two shy individuals who are reluctant to participate. Therefore, a moderator must have good *observation, interpersonal,* and *communication* skills to recognize and overcome threats to a healthy group discussion. Table 7.2 describes several skills a good moderator should have. As the descriptions of the skill dimensions indicate, a moderator should maintain a delicate balance on each; swinging too far toward an extreme on any one of them is likely to be detrimental.

TABLE 7.2
Desirable Focus Group Moderator Skills

Kind but Firm
- Display a kind but permissive attitude toward the participants.
- Encourage them to feel at ease in the group interview environment.
- Keep the discussion germane to the problem at hand.
- Avoid tendencies of domination of the group by a single member.

Permissiveness
- Be alert to indications that the group atmosphere of cordiality is disintegrating.
- Reestablish the group purpose.
- Maintain its orientation to the subject.

Involvement
- Encourage and stimulate intensive personal involvement.
- Immerse himself or herself completely in the topic being discussed.

Incomplete Understanding
- Carefully insert noncommittal remarks, phrased in questioning tones, to encourage respondents to delve more deeply into the sources of their opinions.
- Display a genuine curiosity about the deeper sources of the participants' understanding.

Encouragement
- Should be aware of unresponsive members and try to break down their reserve and encourage their involvement.
- Ability to interpret nonverbal clues may provide a means of discovering a tactic to broaden the scope of the group's active participation.

Flexibility
- Be equipped with a topic outline of the subject matter to be covered.
- Use the outline only as a reminder of content areas omitted or covered incompletely.
- Have the ability to improvise and to alter predetermined plans amid the distractions of the group process.

Sensitivity
- Be able to identify whether or not the information is appropriate for discussion.

Sources: Thomas L. Greenbaum, "Moderator," in *Focus Group Research,* 2nd ed. (Thousand Oaks, CA: Sage, 1998), 73–87; Richard A. Krueger, "Moderating Skills," in *Focus Groups,* 2nd ed. (Thousand Oaks, CA: Sage, 1994), 100–125; Danny N. Bellenger, Kenneth L. Bernhardt, and Jac L. Goldstucker, *Qualitative Research in Marketing* (Chicago: American Marketing Association, 1976), 12–16; Naomi R. Henderson, "Insights from a Panel of Moderators," *Quirk's Marketing Research Review* (December 2000): article no. 0645; Ron Riley, "Consulting Skills as Vital as Interviewing Skills," *Marketing News,* March 1, 1999, 19.

In addition to the skills just described, moderators should have interpretive skills. Good moderators must be able to go beyond what the participants are saying by making note of such factors as tone of voice, facial expressions, and other nonverbal behaviors. Such additional information will be valuable in interpreting the content of a focus group interview. Moderators must have the skill to stimulate active participation in the discussions. Moderators must provide clients with insightful interpretations of what is said, what is not said, and what is meant.[21] Indeed, some practitioners have even suggested that a focus group is as much an observation technique as an interviewing technique.[22]

There are apparently no clear-cut guidelines regarding the physical or demographic characteristics of the moderator vis-à-vis those of the focus group participants. For instance, there is no agreement among researchers about whether the moderator should be of the same gender as the participants.[23] The ability to quickly establish rapport with the participants and make them feel at ease within the group seems to be more critical than the moderator's physical characteristics.

To summarize, not every individual, even one who may be good at one-on-one interviewing, may be an effective focus group moderator. Being able to conduct a focus group interview productively requires specific inherent personal skills as well as extensive training. Several commercial marketing research firms have ongoing, real-life training programs for their moderators. These programs conduct real-life focus groups, not for any particular client, but purely for the sake of training moderators.

Conducting Focus Groups

Focus group sessions typically last one and one-half to two hours. To use this relatively short period of time productively, the moderator must make the participants feel relaxed and comfortable with one another as quickly as possible. A skilled moderator can aid in creating an atmosphere conducive to a congenial and effective group discussion. Other means of generating a relaxed atmosphere include making the focus group room and its furnishings informal, and serving light refreshments before the session starts and throughout the session.[24]

Focus group interviews are invariably recorded, at least on audiocassettes, for subsequent replay, transcription, and analysis. They may also be recorded on videotapes, especially if conducted in a well-equipped focus group facility rather than in an improvised setting such as a hotel room. Videos improve the quality of deliverables; that is, they allow the audience (senior management, marketing and sales organization, and advertising agency) to experience the emotions of the respondents. Video captures nonverbal communication details (body language, facial expressions, and tonal variations) that usually cannot be expressed on paper. However, videotaping a focus group interview can increase costs sharply.[25]

Recording focus group interviews has another potential drawback: the recording equipment, if perceived by participants as intrusive and threatening, can make creating a relaxed atmosphere difficult. A similar limitation is associated with the presence of one-way mirrors, a feature of most focus group rooms. These mirrors enable client personnel to observe the group session without being observed themselves.[26]

One way to minimize the detrimental effects of electronic devices or other means of observing focus groups is to make the equipment as inconspicuous as possible. These measures include displaying microphones carefully to avoid distraction and running wires and cables behind dropped ceilings so they are hidden. However, such measures still may not guarantee the absence of ill effects—intrusion of the mechanical devices on the responses and outcomes of the focus groups. We do not mean that the use of recording devices and observation of focus groups by anyone other than the moderator must be avoided. In fact, a primary strength of a focus group interview is that it offers decision makers a direct report of what consumers say and how they feel about products, services, and the like. Furthermore, using videoconferencing technology, client personnel who are geographically dispersed may observe a group session in progress at a central location,[27] a valuable benefit that would be lost by a ban on the use of equipment letting outsiders observe a focus group session.

How, then, can we reconcile the need for a natural, relaxed atmosphere on the one hand with decision makers' need to get the most out of a focus group on the other? A good compromise is to use whatever devices are essential to obtain maximum benefits from a group session, but to be open with participants about them.[28] Participants should be informed about any recordings or observations that will take place during the session, and the reasons for them should be explained. Such candor, coupled with assurances from a well-trained moderator that there are no ulterior motives, can rapidly put respondents at ease. In some instances, it may be feasible and desirable to introduce guest experts to the participants and even seat them in the focus group room. The guest expert sits in the back room during the first part of the focus group. The moderator can bring in the guest expert in the second half and introduce the person as an expert on the topic of discussion. Participants may then be allowed to discuss important questions or concerns they have on the topic, letting the company prioritize the issues that are on consumers' minds.[29]

Advantages of Focus Groups

There are many specific advantages of focus groups.[30] Here is a summary of some of the general advantages they share.

Richness of Data

A well-conducted focus group interview can provide numerous important insights that a series of one-on-one depth interviews may be unable to generate.[31] Respondents are generally less likely to feel inhibited in the company of others similar to them than they are when alone with an interviewer. They are also likely to be more creative in offering insights about the topic being discussed. A comment made by one participant may trigger a stream of new ideas from the others; this reaction obviously cannot occur in a series of individual interviews.

Versatility

Focus groups can be used to gain insight into a great variety of problems. (Examples of common applications of focus groups will be described in a subsequent section.) Almost any product, service, concept, issue, or the like can be productively discussed in a focus group setting.

Focus groups are also versatile in another respect: a number of other qualitative techniques that we will cover later in this chapter (for instance, a projective question, a TAT-type picture exercise, collage-building exercises, storytelling) and stimuli (such as a product or an ad) can be used in conjunction with or during a focus group to increase the productivity of the discussion.[32] As Jonathan Hall, a marketing research consultant, puts it,

To help generate new appliance ideas, respondents were taken through the experience of entering the kitchen of their dreams, taking note of the colors, textures and smells of their kitchen, what appliances were there and what they would be doing if they owned the kitchen. After spending several minutes exploring the kitchen, the respondents were brought back to the focus group and asked to recount their thoughts. Their ideas and experience led directly to a host of innovative product functions and features.[33]

Hal Goldberg, president of an Irvine, California–based research company, takes this one step further. He hypnotizes focus group participants to tap into their subconscious reasons for product usage.[34] D'Arcy Masius Benton & Bowles (DMB&B), a New York–based communications agency, used a hypnotic focus group to have participants recollect their first glass of champagne. Most of the participants were between 30 and 55, and the task required them to go back in time (as far as 20 years) to recount their memories of that first glass of champagne. According to Maureen Craig, senior vice president of DMB&B Los Angeles, "[Hypnosis] gave us the opportunity to understand not just what people think about [a product] but how they feel . . . the emotional hot buttons that are what we call the 'the heart and soul' of advertising."[35] It is important also to recognize ethical concerns in making consumers reveal sensitive issues under such an intrusive technique as hypnosis. The basic idea behind using all these different techniques is to get consumers to act naturally, as they normally do when confronted with a new idea or a new product designed for their consumption.

Ability to Study Special Respondents

Focus groups may be the only feasible method of gathering data in situations in which conducting one-on-one interviews is unproductive or impossible, such as with children. Interviewing children on a one-on-one basis is often difficult and frustrating. A researcher using focus group interviews for research with children is likely to be more successful in generating useful information.[36] MSW Research (www.mswresearch.com) has designed PLAY*TIME PREVIEW to give children an opportunity to experience a new toy or game concept in the environment that is most comfortable and realistic for them. Although there may be major impediments to talking candidly with children, this does not mean they are uncommunicative. In fact, children communicate very well through play, which has become the linchpin of MSW's methodology for extracting information from small children in focus groups. Other groups of hard-to-interview respondents include professionals, such as doctors and lawyers, who frequently refuse to be interviewed individually. However, these professionals may be receptive to a group interview, which gives them an opportunity to be with their colleagues and compare notes with them on topics of mutual professional interest.[37]

Another company that observes children's reactions in play is Fisher-Price. Here, at the Fisher-Price PlayLab, researchers observe children's reaction to various Fisher-Price toys.

Impact on Managers

One of the pet peeves of users of marketing research is that researchers over-emphasize sophisticated techniques and statistical results. Consequently, quantitative research reports often do no more than collect dust on managers' shelves. However, qualitative research studies in general, and focus group studies in particular, stand a much better chance of being acted on. Why? Because managers have the opportunity to get actively involved in and observe a focus group study instead of merely reading a research report. Moreover, key ideas emerging from a focus group and a few crucial statements made by the participants can sometimes have a greater impact on decision makers than a report full of impressive tables and statistics. Relevant quotes from a focus group interview may be worth a thousand numbers, so to speak. Following is a case in point.

CASE IN POINT ▶ **Bayer Pharmaceuticals Corporation and GlaxoSmithKline Take On Pfizer's Viagra**
Bayer Pharmaceuticals Corporation, working in conjunction with GlaxoSmith-Kline, commissioned a series of focus groups to gain insight into how consumers viewed Viagra, Pfizer's product currently on the market for treating erectile dysfunction. Bayer was looking to introduce Levitra, a new drug that it hoped would be able to win market share away from Viagra. What the company found through the focus group feedback was that consumers were not connecting well with Viagra's intended image. Viagra was perceived as an old man's drug for sexual problems, even though Pfizer had been using younger celebrities to lure middle-aged men. For many group participants, the product's blue color was "too cool" in appearance, and they equated the color with being sick. The research revealed that middle-aged men do not want to admit their sexual problems and therefore do not consult doctors. These revelations from the focus groups conveyed a powerful message: Bayer should bring out a product that not only is at least as effective as Viagra, but also conveys a healthier, warmer image, especially to middle-aged men. Bayer should also position the product in the broadest possible terms as a remedy for a quality-of-life issue. These insights helped shape the positioning and promotional strategy for Levitra.[38]

The point here is that "colorful" and natural customer statements capable of having a significant impact on decision makers can emerge only from a focus group setting. ◀

Disadvantages of Focus Groups

Focus groups also have some disadvantages. In this section we discuss a few of the major ones.

Lack of Generalizability

To emphasize what we have already seen, focus group results cannot be viewed as conclusive. The small sample sizes and homogeneous group compositions, although crucial to conducting focus groups effectively, make any insights gained from them highly tentative. Moreover, a person who agrees to participate in a focus group interview is typically more outgoing than the average consumer. This inherent bias, coupled with the possible presence of professional respondents who routinely participate in numerous group interviews, can further erode the representativeness of a focus group.

Opportunity for Misuse

Some of the very strengths of focus groups—richness of data and impact on managers, for example—can turn into serious drawbacks when the technique is employed by careless researchers or managers. One potential misuse of focus groups occurs when managers yield to the temptation to generalize from a few key remarks made by participants, especially when similar remarks are made in several focus groups. Generalization is a serious mistake, because the primary purpose of focus groups is simply to generate insights or hypotheses, which must be verified through more formal research using representative samples.

Another potential misuse stems from the opportunity for moderators and managers to interpret focus group data arbitrarily. Although this problem can occur with the use of any qualitative research technique, it is particularly serious in focus group interviews. Because focus groups are informal, and because the data they generate are typically varied and rich, moderators and managers with preconceived notions about an issue may be able to find support for their positions by interpreting the data selectively—that is, by hearing and emphasizing only those remarks that do not dispute their opinions. If such selective perceptions occur, the focus group results will be questionable. Objective moderators and open-minded managers are essential to ensure proper use of focus groups. The former is especially critical: a moderator who is not objective can misinterpret the focus group data and also tilt the discussion in a direction consistent with his or her personal viewpoint.

Cost

A focus group interview that is professionally conducted in a research firm's facility can easily cost around $9,000. If this figure sounds high, consider the variety of expensive items essential for a well-conducted focus group. Numerous telephone calls are usually needed to recruit even a handful of qualified participants; several research firms charge around $40 to $50 just to recruit one respondent (and this cost is even higher if rare or hard-to-reach respondents are to be recruited). Normally, the firm must recruit a few extra respondents because of the possibility of no-shows at the time of the interview. In a typical consumer focus group, an incentive of around $50 is usually paid to each recruit who attends (even to those who have to be turned away if everyone recruited attends). In special focus groups involving hard-to-get respondents (such as senior business executives and doctors) the incentive per respondent is usually much higher—in the $150-to-$250 range. A qualified moderator's fee for conducting a focus group may be as much as $1,000. The addition of such costs as renting the focus group facility, transcribing and interpreting the interview, and videotaping shows why a single focus group can cost $9,000.

Some managers may perceive the total cost of even a series of focus groups as low because a typical quantitative project conducted by a research firm can carry a price tag of $30,000 to $50,000. However, this perception is mistaken, because focus groups are a prelude to, not a replacement for, quantitative research. Furthermore, on a cost-per-respondent basis, focus groups are extremely expensive. Therefore, focus groups that are conducted without a need established by management, and without thinking through what they can and cannot deliver, will be an unnecessary drain on a firm's resources. Managers who rely on focus group research, believing the technique is a quick substitute for formal research, run the risk of making bad decisions in addition to wasting valuable resources.

Focus Group Applications

Focus groups can be used in almost any situation requiring some preliminary insights (exploratory research). However, specific applications of focus groups are too numerous to discuss here. Therefore, this section simply presents three broad application categories that include the most frequent applications of the technique: understanding consumers, product planning, and advertising.

Understanding Consumers

Focus groups can be helpful in getting a feeling for consumers' perceptions of, opinions about, and behaviors concerning products or services. For example, Pillsbury, a manufacturer of cake mixes, may be interested in such questions as: What do consumers like about baking? What do they dislike? Why do they bake? How do they bake? What words/terms do they use to describe baking products and their use? Insights about these issues can be useful in a variety of situations, such as when the firm wants to identify marketing problems or opportunities worthy of further investigation, or when it is planning a formal consumer survey and wants to know what questions are worth including and how they should be worded.

Michele Holleran, managing partner of Holleran Consulting, a York, Pennsylvania, firm, describes an illustrative focus group session.

> In one memorable focus group session, the facilitator was able to uncover why poor women living in Appalachia refused to have breast screenings even when those screenings were free and offered at convenient locations. Shared one participant: "Now what am I supposed to do if I found out I did have breast cancer? I'd have to get an operation, get chemotherapy, have a long recovery and end up dead within a year anyway. I'd be worried sick the whole time and drive myself crazy, not to mention fret about the cost of medical bills. How would this affect my kids, knowing their mama is going to die? No ma'am I don't need to or want to know if I have breast cancer. I'd be better off just not knowing and letting nature take her course."

Getting behind the whats and delving into the whys of behavior helps health professionals gain insight into how to remove barriers and develop nontraditional solutions for minority populations and marketing of social programs.[39]

Product Planning

Focus groups are useful in generating ideas for new products. A case in point is the building of the Yao Ming brand by his personal group of advisers.

CASE IN POINT ▶ **Yao Ming, Inc.: Building the Yao Ming Brand**   The fast-growing Chinese market, the country's World Trade Organization (WTO) membership, and the much-awaited 2008 Beijing Olympics have transformed China's most familiar face into a major hot brand. Companies are clamoring to team up with Yao for an instant leg up in a marketplace of a billion people. The Houston Rockets' all-star center is helping businesses in America, China, and elsewhere. He is a spokesperson for PepsiCo, McDonald's, Gatorade, Walt Disney, and Reebok. His presence on the team has increased corporate sponsorship of the Houston Rockets. How did the Yao brand evolve? Focus groups played a key role in determining the market potential of Yao Ming, a Chinese NBA star.

Team Yao, consisting of his agent, a University of Chicago economics professor, a friend of Yao's, and a marketing consultant came together and

Focus groups played a major role in developing a market plan for the Yao Ming brand.

developed a five-year marketing plan. A University of Chicago Graduate School of Business new-product workshop developed a marketing plan for promoting the Yao brand. Students conducted focus groups, marketing polls, and dozens of street interviews in China. Research showed that the world of possibilities for Yao was vast. The findings suggested patience in developing the brand and wanted Yao to reflect the country's old values but represent a newer generation. Team Yao sought long-term deals with well-reputed companies in the United States, consistent with the image it wanted to project for the Yao brand.[40] ◄

Focus group interviews can also be used to suggest ideas for modifying existing products to improve their market performance.

Advertising

Perhaps the most frequent application of focus groups is in developing creative concepts and copy for advertisements. Advertising agencies face the constant challenge of updating advertisements to give them a new look and increase their impact on consumers. Ad agencies are heavy users of focus groups, as a major strength of the technique is its ability to generate new ideas. Focus groups can suggest appropriate words, slogans, copy themes, pictures, roles for TV commercial actors, and product benefits for use in advertisements, as the following example demonstrates.

CASE IN POINT ► ***Christmas with the Kranks*** In the winter of 2004, Revolution Studios released *Christmas with the Kranks*, a kind of antiholiday movie meant to poke fun at the Christmas season. The studio was hoping to take advantage of the holiday season and people's potentially negative attitudes about it to win dollars at the box office. What the company found instead was a lukewarm response from moviegoers. The studio decided to conduct focus groups to determine the culprit. What it found was that consumers reacted negatively to the film's advertising, which featured the slogan "No ho ho," and to the fact that it seemed to insult the holiday. The studio responded quickly by pulling movie posters and billboards with the "No ho ho" phrase.[41] ◄

To further demonstrate the application of focus groups and emphasize their proper use, here is another example.

CASE IN POINT ► **Marketing Jacksonville, Florida** Realizing that being the host city to Super Bowl XXXIX provided a great opportunity to market the city to potential tourists, Jacksonville, Florida, decided to put together a branding campaign. But how should the city market itself to people who might have heard the name "Jacksonville" but were aware of little else about the city? To answer this question, the city contracted a local marketing research firm to conduct focus groups and surveys to find out what people thought of Jacksonville. What the marketing research firm discovered surprised the city. According to Jim Dalton, president and CEO of the research firm, people were more aware of Jacksonville than was previously thought, "but they didn't know where we were, or anything about us."

The feedback from focus group participants helped Jacksonville tailor its branding campaign to be more effective. It realized that, first and foremost, it needed to educate the public about where it actually was. By including "Florida" in any Jacksonville advertisement, the city would be able to simultaneously educate people about its geographic location and leverage the pleasant feelings they had about the state of Florida itself. "Florida is still a desirable place," said Dalton, "and we have a lot of what Florida has to offer."[42] ◄

Impact of Technology on Focus Group Research

Technological advances have made focus group research easier and more productive. Some of the most popular applications of technology in focus groups are discussed next.

Electronic Group Interviewing (EGI)

Electronic group inter-viewing (EGI) involves using keypads or electronic devices to reduce unproductive discussion time. Each participant is provided with a keypad, which is connected to a common video display screen visible to the entire group.

Electronic group interviewing (EGI), using keypads or electronic devices to reduce unproductive discussion time, has become very popular.[43] Each participant is provided with a keypad. All keypads are connected to a common video display screen, visible to the entire group. Keypads can be used to anonymously express an opinion about an issue on a scale of 0 (no) to 10 (yes), as well as to express strength of an opinion on a scale of 0 to 100 percent. Companies can interview between 20 and 150 people at a time with EGI.

EGI using a keypad is a valuable timesaver when the moderator wants to poll the participants on some issue germane to the group discussion. Participants simply express their feelings using their keypad, and the results are instantly tabulated and displayed in the form of a histogram on the video screen. According to one practitioner who has used this technology, "EGI offers the potential benefits of greater speed, real-time feedback, better quality, more precise data and flexibility."[44] EGI provides a tangible stimulus (the video display) to guide the discussion and apparently also stimulates greater participant interest and involvement than does a traditional focus group.

CASE IN POINT ▶ **T. Rowe Price Gets Quick Feedback**   The Retirement Planning Services unit of financial services firm T. Rowe Price wanted to understand why eligible people were not enrolling in 401(k) retirement plans. To gain this understanding, the firm tested two groups of eligible people using a Perception Analyzer, an interactive dialing device that allows participants to register their reactions to an idea, product, or service by turning a dial. Clients can see immediate reactions to questions, products, ads, and so on. The immediate feedback impressed the company officials, giving them new insights. The company was able to determine that

- People had trouble linking concepts like cash, bonds, and stocks to descriptions of asset class, such as stability, income, and growth.
- Some of the basic calculations involved proved difficult for certain individuals.
- The charts and graphs included to provide details of a 401(k) plan often were not understandable to the layperson without further clarification or discussion.

"Interest might dip because we went into too much detail or talked too much about a topic," noted Carol Waddell, director of product development and technology for the company, "so we really tightened up scripts" in those areas. Based on insights from using the Perception Analyzer to understand customers' reactions, T. Rowe Price was able to change the way it communicated 401(k) information to eligible participants and nonparticipants, effectively conveying the details and the benefits of such retirement planning to both groups.[45] ◀

Videoconference Focus Groups

Advances in digital transmission and video technology are proving to be a boon to marketing researchers. Focus groups are videotaped and broadcast live for large

Videoconference focus groups allow clients at multiple sites to view focus groups from remote locations.

companies with an international base, using digital telephone lines. **Videoconference focus groups** allow clients at multiple sites to view focus groups from remote locations. Many companies, such as AT&T, have set up in-house viewing rooms so that company executives can view focus group proceedings without having to leave the office.[46] Many companies employ language translators for focus groups taking place in foreign locations, allowing executives to get an immediate impression of the proceedings. Videoconferencing greatly cuts the cost of and travel time to focus groups. Cheryl Bailey, executive vice president, managing director of planning and research, for the New York advertising firm Ammirati Puris Lintas, has this to say about videoconferencing: "We use projective techniques extensively and it's great for our creative people to be able to observe [focus group reactions to] projective techniques [via video transmission] as opposed to having someone interpret them. We find that that is usually a very rich source of ideas."

Viewers also learn in real time; they don't have to wait a week to be briefed by those who watched the groups. Bailey adds, "We used to send a team out on the road and they would phone in and brief everybody at the agency on what they had learned. And when they came back someone from the creative staff would invariably say, 'Did you ask them about this?' Or say, 'Gee, I wish I had known that because maybe we should tweak the strategy this way.'"[47]

According to industry experts, Web-based videoconferencing will replace traditional videoconferencing in the coming decade and allow consumers to participate from their home or office.[48] This development will further reduce the cost of renting a videoconference facility and may also increase respondents' willingness to participate.

Online Focus Groups

With the advent of Internet technology, businesses use e-mail, chatrooms, and message boards as new ways to connect with customers. America Online (AOL) popularized chatrooms by allowing people who are online at the same time to exchange live messages. An online focus group is a modified chatroom. Using customized software, marketing research companies have created virtual focus group facilities consisting of waiting rooms, client back rooms, and focus group rooms.[49]

Online focus groups are becoming a popular marketing research tool, promising faster turnaround, more convenience, and greater cost effectiveness in today's digital world. In addition, such groups allow companies to gain insights simultaneously from multiple locations and countries. They are ideal for hard-to-reach markets, low-incidence groups, online audiences, and geographically dispersed groups. Online focus groups can be put together in a matter of hours and much more easily than the traditional focus group. Research in Use 7.1 presents some typical online focus group examples.

In a traditional focus group, the moderator and participants discuss the topic of interest in a room while the clients watch from behind a one-way mirror. However, in an online focus group, moderator, respondents, and clients log on to a virtual focus room on the Internet from anywhere in the world and take part in the discussion from their office or home.[50] Respondents are recruited by phone and from e-mail lists, Web intercepts, banner ad intercepts, and online panels[51] and are given name identification, password, instructions, and date and time of the focus group session. The discussion guide for the moderator resembles that for a traditional focus group. The only difference is that the actual presentation of questions is in written form. The moderator signs on early and administers rescreening questions as respondents enter the virtual room to verify their identity. Participants introduce themselves and are provided instructions for entering

Online Focus Group Examples

Pennzoil-Quaker State Company used online focus groups to evaluate its new product Total Shine, a liquid cleaner/polisher that can be used for detailing all of a car except the glass. Focus group results encouraged Pennzoil-Quaker to launch the product in 1999. According to Dave Lupyan, "Internet focus groups are an effective, cost efficient tool in the development of new products as well as the evaluation and improvement of existing products. . . . We expect to refine the process continually to support and expand our already extensive product portfolio."

IPnetwork.com, an online marketplace for patents, licenses, and other forms of intellectual property, was receiving very few hits. Pressed for time and money, IPnetwork decided to conduct a pair of online focus groups to understand the reasons for the lack of traffic to the site. Online focus group results showed that the site was not easy to navigate and that there was a need for better content in its news section. IPnetwork revamped its site for easier navigation and improved the news section. The research took just a few days to finish, and the cost was very reasonable. According to Sruba De, "Traffic is up and customers are benchmarking IPnetwork.com's page more frequently and staying longer."

Janice Gjertsen, director of marketing and business development for WP Studio, a New York–based Web developer (now part of www.digitalcity.com), wanted to gauge reaction to her company's website, www.totalny.com, an information guide to the city. Gjertsen believed that people in focus groups tend to be vague about their feelings. She asked Cyber Dialogue, an online marketing research company, to conduct online focus group research. Cyber Dialogue recruited participants from its database of more than 10,000 people and provided the moderator. The focus group was held in a chatroom linked to the www.totalny.com website so that Gjertsen could watch the focus group proceedings from her office computer. She particularly liked one of Cyber Dialogue's features, the ability to interrupt the moderator at any time with e-mails, without the respondents' knowledge. Online focus groups are also cheaper, only $3,000 for a session compared to $9,000 for a traditional focus group. She received the full report in a day, considerably faster than from a traditional focus group. Online focus groups gave her plenty of ideas for attracting new members. Gjertsen is a staunch advocate of online focus groups, which is evident when she says, "People were a heck of a lot more honest on-line than they were in our traditional groups. . . . This method is so immediate, so accurate. In this world I need that."[a]

responses and asking questions. The virtual room (screen) is divided into two sections, with discussion questions appearing in one section and responses from the participants appearing in the other. The moderator follows the discussion guide to keep the focus group on target. Clients can observe the ongoing discussion and even interact with the moderator by submitting new ideas for consideration.

Online focus groups are not without limitations.[52] They operate like chatrooms, so control over the flow of the group is difficult. Emotional information (body language, facial expressions, tone of voice) cannot be obtained from an online focus group, nor can reactions to a new concept be observed in an online environment. The researcher has to settle for a written reaction to a visual concept. Projective techniques and collage-building exercises cannot be effectively done in an online focus group. Interaction among participants is limited, as participants respond at the same time. Although more than 75 percent of households in the United States have Internet access (nearly 46 percent via broadband), recruiting general audiences to participate in an online focus group takes time. However, in most countries, online focus groups are skewed toward affluent, computer-literate individuals.[53]

Companies will opt for traditional focus groups if they desire body language information and intense discussions. Those desiring speed or wishing to connect with hard-to-reach people will opt for online focus groups. Online focus groups will not completely replace their traditional in-person counterpart; industry experts believe the fascination with online focus groups will plateau in the coming years due to the inherent limitations of the medium. However, new online focus groups are continuing to emerge, and existing ones are being improved. For example, online bulletin board focus groups, in which participants are involved with the research over an extended period of time (from a few days to a month or more), allow respondents to think and respond to concepts at their own convenience and are expected to gain in popularity.[54]

Other Qualitative Research Techniques

The traditional focus group interview is the most frequently used but not the only form of qualitative research. Several nonstructured data collection techniques presented in the previous chapter (such as in-depth interviews and projective techniques) are also types of qualitative research. Next we will explore in-depth interviews (IDIs), projective techniques, and other qualitative techniques, several of which are variations of the traditional focus group interview.

In-Depth Interviews (IDIs)

Recently companies have begun requesting that researchers conduct one-on-one interviews in the consumer's natural habitat: home or office.[55] Research in Use 7.2 shows how Gannett newspapers use in-depth interviews to understand young readers.

In-depth interviews are one-on-one interviews with customers that explore issues in depth.

With **in-depth interviews,** interviewers can probe each respondent in much greater detail. Also, one respondent's viewpoints do not influence others'. In-depth interviews usually last from one-half to a full hour but can take longer depending on project requirements. Some practitioners claim that in-depth interviews deliver more quantity of information and more depth of information than a typical focus group.[56] Steve Knight, Nissan-Infiniti director of marketing, agrees. In 1994 Infiniti management wanted to introduce an upscale luxury sport utility vehicle (SUV). To nail down the specifics, Knight conducted one-on-one interviews with current Infiniti customers in New York's affluent Westchester County. According to Knight, "We've found that group dynamics are frequently steered by one or two people."[57] Researchers probed Infiniti customers about other brands considered, what existing options they would most prefer, what new options they would consider buying, and level of driving comfort desired. One-on-one interviews told Infiniti management that customers wanted an SUV with four-wheel drive that drives more like a car than like a truck. Women wanted a low step for easy boarding. In-depth interviews gave enough information for a new-car idea: an SUV that drives like a car, with a low step for boarding, priced under $40,000. Infiniti engineers created new designs based on the in-depth interviews. Two hundred nationwide users and nonusers of Infiniti were then polled about the new designs.

Research in Use 7.3 describes an atypical example of one-on-one interviews used by Cartoon Network.[58]

It is worth noting that the large sample sizes used by Cartoon Network (Research in Use 7.3) in some of its studies make its research more like a survey than like typical in-depth interview research. (Anywhere from 10 to 40 respondents, interviewed one at a time, is typically the norm in research involving in-depth interviews.) The research done by Cartoon Network combines in-depth interview techniques (nondisguised unstructured interviews, intensive probing)

In-Depth Interviews Help Gannett Understand Young Readers

Gannett, a national newspaper publishing company, was looking to understand why the circulation of its newspapers was declining among young people. Newspaper readership among 25- to 34-year-olds had been steadily declining since 2000, but it was not clear to Gannett why that was the case. Was it due to young people's being less interested in news in general, not just newspapers? Or could it be that young people's interest in news was healthy and that they were merely getting it from other sources?

To uncover the reasons, the firm conducted a series of in-depth interviews with 30 young adults from different communities. The interviews had a broad focus, asking questions not just about media habits but also about the participants' lifestyle. The participants were also asked to take pictures of the people and places most relevant to their lives.

Both the interviews and the pictures revealed that young adults had not lost interest in news; in fact, they showed that their desire for such information remained high. Rather than get their information from print newspapers, however, young adults were using many other media to obtain it—including television, e-mail, websites, and wireless mobile devices (cellular phones and PDAs). In general, the research found that young adults were finding the print media to be too static and non-engaging compared with their increasingly interactive world.

The research helped Gannett understand that, in order to respond to young people's changing tastes, the organization would need to stop being simply a newspaper publishing company and start becoming more of an on-demand, multimedia news and information provider. "Our readers and, as important, our potential readers, are changing faster than we are," says David Daugherty, Gannett's vice president of research. "We need to be quicker in adjusting to their news and information needs, and we need to be more innovative with our products, including how we deliver news and information to them."[b]

and traditional survey techniques (nondisguised structured interviews). Table 7.3 presents several factors that might influence the choice between in-depth interviews and focus groups.

Crowded One-on-One Interview

In a **crowded one-on-one interview,** up to three client personnel are present in the room and observe a depth interview as it is conducted by a professional interviewer in a conventional fashion.

A **crowded one-on-one interview** is actually a variation of the in-depth interview. In a crowded one-on-one interview, up to three client personnel are present in the room and observe a depth interview as it is conducted by a professional interviewer in a conventional fashion. After the interview is over, the client personnel can ask additional questions or seek clarification of responses already given. This type of interview is particularly effective when new concepts, designs, advertising, promotional messages, and the like are in the formulation stage, as there is still opportunity to make changes.

Projective Techniques

With **projective techniques,** a fairly ambiguous stimulus is presented to respondents who, by reacting to or describing the stimulus, indirectly reveal their inner feelings.

Although different types of **projective techniques** are available, they all share two common features: (1) a fairly ambiguous stimulus is presented to respondents, and (2) in reacting to or describing the stimulus, the respondents will indirectly reveal their own inner feelings.[59] Examples of projective techniques used in marketing research include the word association test, the sentence completion test, the thematic apperception test (commonly referred to as TAT), and the cartoon test. We will briefly examine each of these methods.

How to Keep in Touch with Kids Around the Globe?
Cartoon Network Knows the Answer

Cartoon Network is one of the most successful TV networks in the world. The network airs cartoons, and only cartoons, seven days a week. Cartoon Network reaches more than 100 million homes in over 100 countries. Marketing research plays a central role in the company's quest to become and remain a global expert on children.

To become an expert on children's preferences, Cartoon Network, with the help of the global marketing research company Taylor Nelson Sofres, conducts research with children, teens, and adults all over the world. The company starts with a brainstorming (in-depth interview) session with in-house clients, such as merchandising, programming, and sales in Asia, the United States, the European Union, and Latin America.

Brainstorming helps the network sort out research priorities. The network also conducts over 250 focus groups in more than 10 countries around the world to understand cartoon characters' popularity and viewers' perceptions of the characters.

To develop a better understanding of social influences, Cartoon Network conducts one-on-one interviews in multiple countries with hundreds of kids between 6 and 15 years old who have access to television. Face-to-face interviews examine several issues: main influences and sources of information in the kids' lives, their aspirations, ability to influence the purchase ("pester power"), computer access, and Internet usage. The results brought out commonalities and differences among global kids (see the table).[c]

Face-to-Face Interview Results

	Mexico	Argentina	Chile	Brazil	United States	Asia-Pacific
Influences and information sources	Parents/ grandparents Siblings Other adults (teachers)	Parents/ grandparents Other adults (teachers) Friends	Parents/ grandparents Siblings Other adults (teachers)	Parents/ grandparents Other adults (teachers) Friends	Grandparents Other adults (teachers) Friends	N/A
Aspirations	Get good grades Go to college Look good	Get good grades Look good Be considered cool with friends	Get good grades Go to college Look good	Get good grades Be considered cool with friends Be an individual	Get good grades Go to college Be an individual	N/A
Pester power	Clothing Shoes Toys Soda	Candy School supplies Candy	Clothing School supplies	Clothing Shoes Toys	Clothing Shoes Toys	School supplies Ice cream Movies
Computer (COM) and Internet (INT) usage	COM 59% INT 35%	COM 80% INT 26%	COM 66% INT 29%	COM 62% INT 29%	COM 97% INT 74%	COM 40% INT 20%

(continued)

Face-to-Face Interview Results (continued)

	Mexico	Argentina	Chile	Brazil	United States	Asia-Pacific
Ways kids use the Internet	Playing games Help with homework Surfing E-mail Read e-newspapers Chat	Playing games Help with homework Surfing Chat E-mail Read e-newspapers	Help with homework Playing games Surfing E-mail Chat Read e-newspapers	Help with homework Chat Playing games Read e-newspapers E-mail Surfing	Playing games E-mail Surfing Help with homework Chat Read e-newspapers	Surfing Playing games E-mail Help with homework Chat Read e-newspapers
Sample size	1,000	1,000	1,000	1,000	N/A	N/A

Source: David Kudon, "Maintaining Leadership in a Changing World: Being the Experts on the Kids' Market: The Role of Global Marketing Research" (presented at the AMA Attitude and Behavioral Research Conference, January 23–26, 2000, Phoenix, AZ). Reprinted by permission of the author.

In **word association tests,** the words are read aloud one at a time to each respondent, and the respondent is asked to say the first word that comes to mind as soon as each stimulus word is presented. These responses are then interpreted.

■ **Word Association Tests**   The stimulus in **word association tests** is a list containing a range of from just a few to more than 100 words mixed in with somewhat irrelevant or neutral words designed to preserve the disguised nature of the study. For instance, a list in a study dealing with PCs may include relevant words, such as *Internet, DVD,* and *software,* as well as neutral words, such as *cooking, exercise, furniture,* and *newspapers.* Word association tests can be especially useful in uncovering people's feelings about new products or services, brand names, and key words being considered for use in advertising copy or other promotional materials.

In a typical word association test, the words are read aloud one at a time to each respondent. The respondent is asked to say the first word that comes to mind as soon as each stimulus word is presented. Interpretation of the responses is not easy. It is based on several factors and includes analyzing the meanings of the response words, the overall nature of responses given by each respondent, the patterns of responses across respondents, the time taken to respond to each stimulus word, and the physical reactions of respondents.[60]

In **sentence completion tests,** respondents are asked to finish a set of incomplete sentences.

■ **Sentence Completion Tests**   A **sentence completion test** asks respondents to finish a set of incomplete sentences. Each incomplete sentence consists of a few words related to or neutral to the topic being researched, followed by a blank space for the response. To illustrate, a study dealing with people's inner feelings toward "Buying American" may contain the following incomplete sentences:

American automobiles . . .

Restrictions on imports . . .

Every U.S. citizen . . .

Foreign-made products . . .

Unemployment in the United States . . .

Increasing globalization . . .

TABLE 7.3
Which One to Choose: In-Depth Interview or Focus Group?

Factor	In-Depth Interview	Focus Group
Time	*Interviews.* Substantial amount of time per respondent. *Analysis.* Substantial amount of time for analyzing large volume of information.	*Interviews.* Normally take 1.5 to 3 hours for the whole group. *Analysis.* Group analysis takes a lot less time.
Group dynamics	No group interaction; probing depends on interviewer; no peer influence.	Main strength of focus groups, allowing for exchange of ideas; peer influence may affect responses.
Topic sensitivity	May be easier to deal with sensitive topics.	Respondents may be embarrassed to reveal their feelings unless brought out by some respondents.
Time for the topics	In-depth probing of each respondent is possible.	Limited time for each respondent.
Geographic constraints	Respondents can be drawn from geographically dispersed locations.	Geographic constraints exist, as respondents can be drawn only from a specific location where a focus group facility exists.
Domination of individuals	Everybody gets equal time.	Some individuals tend to dominate.
Logistics	Easier to schedule an interview.	Recruiting and running several focus groups in multiple locations is cumbersome.

Sentence completion tests are typically given to groups of respondents who are asked to finish the sentences in writing. Neither the time taken to respond to each item nor the respondents' physical reactions are monitored as they are in word association tests, so sentence completion tests are easier to administer. Moreover, they allow researchers greater flexibility in giving direction to the stimuli, so the responses obtained are more likely to be associated with the subject matter under study. In contrast, word association tests, by pressuring respondents to react quickly to single words, may lead to answers that are difficult to interpret. However, there is a price for the greater flexibility and ease of administration of sentence completion tests: respondents can think through their answers, and therefore the information obtained is limited to what each respondent is willing to divulge.

The **thematic apperception test (TAT)** is a non-structured, disguised form of questioning in which respondents are shown a series of pictures, one at a time, and asked to write a story about each.

■ **Thematic Apperception Test (TAT)**   The **thematic apperception test (TAT)** is a nonstructured, disguised form of questioning in which respondents are shown a series of pictures, one at a time, and are asked to write a story about each. The TAT was first developed by Henry A. Murray to measure personality.[61] The original TAT consisted of a set of 20 cards with pictures printed on them. In a typical administration of the TAT, the respondent is shown each picture for a short period (about 20 seconds) and asked to write a story about it in 20 minutes or so. The respondent is specifically asked to describe such things as what is happening in the picture, why it is happening, and the feelings of the characters in the picture. These stories are interpreted by specially trained analysts to ascertain the respondent's personality. The TAT can be administered individually or in groups.

Adaptations of the TAT have been employed in marketing research by using pictures specifically designed for the research topic. To illustrate, in a study of attitudes about magazine reading, "a picture was included which showed a family sitting in a living room reading. In making up stories for this picture, respondents revealed many of their views about magazines, the family and home, what the husband reads, what the wife reads, and so on."[62] Other possible applications of TAT techniques in marketing research include the evaluation of pictures being considered for use in advertisements, promotional brochures, and product packaging.

A major recent improvement on TAT is **Zaltman's Metaphor Elicitation Technique (ZMET)**.[63] ZMET tries to bring to the surface the mental models that drive consumer thinking by analyzing metaphors that consumers might use. A *metaphor* is a figure of speech that implies comparison between two unlike entities.[64] It is formed by extending everyday expressions and activities to less well known ones. It makes a qualitative leap from a reasonable comparison to a new entity sharing the characteristics of both compared entities. Thus a metaphor is a definition of one thing expressed in terms of another. Children's Hospital of Pittsburgh wanted to make sure that its new hospital was appealing to people, conveying a warm, healthy image rather than a cold, scary one. It therefore sought Zaltman's help. Patients, parents, employees, and physicians were interviewed about what images and metaphors they thought of when the hospital came to mind. Deeper probing of the emotions behind the choice of images and metaphors revealed true feelings about the facility. For example, the research revealed that patients wanted to see designs and unconventional color schemes that would help distract them from their medical conditions and relieve some of the stress associated with illness and hospitalization. Such insight might not have come out of a typical survey or focus group.[65]

A *cartoon test* (sometimes also known as a *balloon test*) is another pictorial technique like the TAT. The stimuli in cartoon tests are line drawings like the one shown in Exhibit 7.2. Such a cartoon can, for instance, be used to gain insight into customers' attitudes about PCs. The respondent in a **cartoon test (balloon test)** is asked to examine the stimulus picture and fill in the empty speech balloons with words reflecting the thoughts or verbal statements of the characters involved. Unlike the stories required in a TAT, responses to a cartoon test are limited and specific. Therefore, the responses should take less time to create and analyze.

▪ **Using Multiple Projective Techniques** The tests described so far by no means exhaust the variety of projective techniques that can be and are being used in marketing research. Often, multiple projective techniques are required to tap the underlying motivations behind a behavior.[66] For instance, charades, sentence completions, and word associations, drawing or completing pictures, and creating dialogue for balloons above characters in cartoon-style pictures are often used to understand children's behavior. Children are also frequently asked to whisper "secret votes" to the group leader or to "pretend telephone," projecting themselves into the role of parents describing a recent purchase.[67] Youngsters may be asked to "act out commercials" in a wide

Zaltman's Metaphor Elicitation Technique (ZMET) tries to bring to the surface the mental models that drive consumer thinking by analyzing metaphors that consumers might use. A metaphor is a figure of speech that implies comparison between two unlike entities.

The **cartoon test (balloon test)** is a pictorial technique like the TAT. The respondent is asked to examine the stimulus picture and fill in the empty speech balloons with words reflecting the thoughts or verbal statements of the characters involved.

Exhibit 7.2
Cartoon Test

Here is a really nice PC advertised for $999.

variety of shopping and domestic situations. From these creative play sessions, many a commercial has been restructured for more effective communication to children, prototypes for many new products have been designed based on children's uses and needs, and many products have been revitalized to enhance their appeal to children.

In short, the nonstructured, disguised, or projective method of data collection is flexible enough to be tailored to fit any research setting that calls for an examination of people's inner feelings. Projective techniques can be valuable if properly used. Unfortunately, designing valid projective tests and correctly interpreting the results of these tests is not easy. Special skills and training are required. Researchers who are fascinated by projective techniques but unqualified to use them can end up misusing them. Thus, after being widely used in the 1950s to solve marketing problems, in the 1960s projective techniques lost their popularity to focus group and survey methodologies primarily because of inappropriate use by unqualified researchers who could not deliver on their promises to decision makers. By the 1970s, there was considerable skepticism, especially among practitioners, about research employing projective techniques. However, projective techniques made a strong comeback in the 1990s, as companies were increasingly looking for deep insights into developing new products in the crowded global marketplace, and became part of focus groups and in-depth interviews.[68]

A Final Note

The list of qualitative research techniques we have covered is by no means exhaustive. A researcher's imagination is the only limit on the specific form that qualitative research takes in a given situation, as demonstrated by the variations of traditional techniques illustrated in this chapter. Research in Use 7.4 offers a couple of additional illustrations. Such flexibility and opportunity to improvise are major strengths of qualitative research. Unfortunately, these very strengths are also an invitation for ill-qualified or unscrupulous researchers to misuse and abuse qualitative research.

A high degree of subjectivity is involved in every stage of the qualitative research process, including the critical stages of sample selection, data collection, analysis, and interpretation, which has a major bearing on the validity of the results. Therefore, using qualitative research carelessly and irresponsibly can give a very misleading picture of reality, as well as waste a firm's resources.

SUMMARY

Qualitative research involves generating information that cannot be summarized in the form of numbers. It is characterized by nonstructured, flexible data collection from relatively small respondent samples. The primary purpose of qualitative research is to generate insights and ideas. Therefore, the proper place for qualitative techniques is in exploratory research projects. In contrast, quantitative techniques are more appropriate for conclusive research projects.

Qualitative research is no less important or valuable than quantitative research. The two types of research should be viewed as complementing each other; qualitative research can be a valuable, and many times necessary, prelude to quantitative research.

The most widely used qualitative research technique is the focus group interview. Three major determinants of focus group effectiveness are (1) group composition, (2) moderator characteristics, and (3) the manner in which the focus group is conducted (group atmosphere). Although there are no absolute guidelines for these factors, several rules of thumb have emerged through experience.

Focus groups typically have 6 to 12 participants. Homogeneity of group members, especially on character-

Creative Applications of Qualitative Research Yield Valuable Insights

Intel's Traveling Ethnographers

Intel's team of 10 ethnographers travels around the world to find out how to redesign existing products or come up with new ones that fit different cultures. One of the ethnographers, Genevieve Bell, visited 100 homes in Asia over three years and noticed that many Chinese were reluctant to buy PCs even if they could afford them. Bell learned that the parents were concerned that children would spend their time surfing and not paying attention to schoolwork. Intel designers used this insight to design a China Home Learning PC that can be placed in the kitchen, a popular place for a PC. The PC comes with four education applications and a physical lock and key to allow parents to control its use.

Shimano's Way: Spend Months with Customers

Shimano, Japan's leading bike parts maker is the dominant supplier of parts for higher-end bikes and is known as the "Intel of the bike business." What is the secret of its dominance? Every year, Shimano sends more than a dozen employees to work with manufacturers and retailers for several months to gauge customer trends. For instance, they spotted the craze for mountain bikes, which led to the development of the rugged derailleur for that market. Smover, a new line of computerized shifters, is being developed for today's leisure and commuting bike markets. Staying on top of customer trends has helped Shimano to dominate the high-end bike component market.[d]

istics such as gender and age, is crucial. Focus group participants must also have had some experience with or exposure to the discussion topic, and they should not be professional respondents. A generally accepted practice is to conduct at least two focus groups on a given topic.

To be effective, a focus group moderator should have good observation, interpersonal, communication, and interpretative skills. The physical or demographic characteristics of the moderator are apparently not as critical as his or her ability to establish rapport with respondents and guide the discussion in a natural yet focused fashion.

To be of maximum benefit, focus groups should be conducted in a relaxed, comfortable atmosphere. Having the appropriate physical setting and amenities can be helpful. Focus groups are invariably recorded by electronic means and are often observed unobtrusively by client personnel. An important factor here is to ensure that the means used for recording and observing do not adversely affect group atmosphere and hence the quality of the discussion.

The major advantages of focus groups include the richness of the data they can generate, their versatility (in terms of their wide application potential as well as their flexibility to be used in conjunction with other techniques), their usefulness in gathering data from otherwise hard-to-interview respondents, and their ability to make a lasting impression on managers. A limitation of focus groups is that their results are not generalizable. Moreover, the subjectivity involved in conducting and interpreting focus groups is an invitation for irresponsible

users to abuse the technique. Focus groups are also expensive, especially on a cost-per-respondent basis.

A general application of focus groups is to develop an understanding of consumers and their perceptions. Focus groups can reveal signs of potential problems, suggest reasons for existing problems, and point out possible marketing opportunities. They can also be helpful in designing formal research studies of consumers. More specific applications of focus groups occur in the area of product planning and advertising. Online focus groups are increasing in prominence and have their place in accessing hard-to-reach respondents or for situations when cost and time are of the essence. Online focus group research has many limitations and so should be used judiciously. Online focus groups will include many different forms, such as online bulletin focus groups, in the coming decade.

In-depth interviews (IDIs) are useful when the research demands intensive probing of respondents or reactions to ideas without influence from peers. IDIs facilitate a high degree of psychological depth, that is, investigation of motivations, associations, and explanations behind product/service preference. Qualitative research techniques other than the traditional focus group and in-depth interviews include some techniques that were discussed in previous chapters (case studies, mystery shoppers) as well as a variety of projective techniques. Though qualitative research can provide valuable insights, all qualitative techniques have potential limitations and must be used with caution.

ACE
self-test

REVIEW AND DISCUSSION QUESTIONS

1. Summarize the key differences between qualitative and quantitative research.

2. "Qualitative research must not be conducted in situations in which obtaining quantitative data is the ultimate objective." Discuss this statement.

3. Discuss the reasons why a focus group should consist of similar participants.

4. How many focus groups should be conducted on any given topic? Explain your answer.

5. Who are professional respondents? In what ways can they affect a focus group?

6. Briefly describe the skills that an effective focus group moderator should have.

7. "It is not advisable to record a focus group interview through electronic means." Discuss the pros and cons of this statement, indicate what your position is, and defend your position.

8. State the general advantages and disadvantages of focus groups, and describe each in a sentence or two.

9. Why are focus groups widely used in advertising?

10. State the general advantages and disadvantages of online focus groups.

11. Describe several scenarios for which online focus groups might be appropriate.

12. State and briefly describe two variations of the traditional in-depth interview.

13. Describe the distinct features of all projective techniques. Pick any one of the several projective techniques discussed in this chapter and give an example to illustrate a real-life situation in which the technique would be useful.

14. Conduct a word association test for the following names:

    a. Amazon
    b. Dell
    c. eBay
    d. Hotmail
    e. AOL

    Collect data from 10 friends. Briefly summarize the findings.

APPLICATION EXERCISES

1. For each of the following scenarios, indicate whether qualitative or quantitative research is more appropriate. Also recommend a specific technique for each and justify your answer.

    a. A manufacturer of food coloring wants to know how often and for what purposes or occasions consumers use food-coloring products.
    b. A firm marketing chewing gum has two alternative wrapper designs for the product and is wondering which one is likely to result in higher sales.
    c. A medical products company is in the final stages of perfecting a new method of contraception. It wants to gauge the reactions of men and women to the new method and their potential acceptance of the method.

2. A national charitable organization (such as the American Red Cross or United Way) wants to identify ways to sharply increase the amount of contributions from the public. Design a qualitative research study to help identify ideas to increase contributions.

INTERNET EXERCISES

1. Conduct an online chat session (available at www.yahoo.com or www.aol.com). Run the session with five to six prerecruited participants and discuss one of the following topics:

    a. Finding an internship or job
    b. Spring break
    c. What is viewed as good versus poor service at a restaurant of your choice

2. On the website for MTV (www.mtv.com) there is a link for Community. Clicking on this link brings you to a list of message boards organized by music genre or television program. The boards allow MTV viewers to discuss the most recent happenings in music and on the various MTV programs. These message boards also allow MTV to get a better understanding of their viewers' opinions about new artists as well as its programming. Choose one of these boards and discuss how MTV could use the information from the board.

CASE 7.1 BURGER KING: ENORMOUS OMELET SANDWICH
(www.bk.com)

Burger King, the worldwide fast-food restaurant, has been privately held since 2002 by the Texas Pacific Group. Before going private, Burger King boasted annual sales of over $11 billion while owned by Diageo, a British premium drink firm. Burger King currently operates more than 11,220 restaurants in 61 countries. Like many other multinational restaurants, such as McDonald's, Burger King caters to local customs in certain international outlets by offering items that are strictly regional. One example is the broiled salmon fish sandwich in Chile. In the United States, many fast-food restaurants are beginning to introduce healthier alternatives to their traditional high-fat, high-calorie menu of burgers and fries. However, Burger King seems to be skewing away from this trend. It has been using focus groups to help introduce larger, higher-calorie meals.

Burger King Corporation carried out several focus group interviews in an effort to determine unmet consumer needs. In a rather surprising result, this research pointed the company in a direction opposite to that being followed by other fast-food restaurants. Instead of expanding its low-calorie/healthy-menu options in a manner similar to McDonald's (including various Caesar, California Cobb, and bacon ranch salads), Burger King discovered an unmet need in the market, among active young men who are looking for a breakfast to fill them up. The resulting new product is the Enormous Omelet Sandwich, made with two sausage patty halves, two eggs, two slices of American cheese, and three strips of bacon served on a specialty bun. Combined, these items generate 730 calories and 47 grams of fat, excluding the hash brown rounds that come with the meal.

The Enormous Omelet Sandwich was released just four months after Hardee's, a smaller fast-food franchise, added the Monster Thickburger to its menu. Its two 1/3-pound Angus beef patties, four bacon strips, three slices of American cheese, mayonnaise, and a buttered sesame-seed bun house a whopping 107 grams of fat and 1,420 calories. The burger was modeled after Hardee's most popular menu item, the original best-selling Monster Burger. The introduction of two such seemingly undesirable offerings would appear to be an effort to buck a national trend toward combating obesity. How successful will they be in this endeavor?

CASE QUESTIONS

1. Presume that Burger King plans to use focus group interviews to determine whether the Enormous Omelet Sandwich should be sold only in specific regions. What are your recommendations for the composition of these focus groups, and in what parts of the country should they be held? What questions would you include in the screening questionnaire? Prepare an outline identifying all subjects relevant to the objective of the focus groups. Justify your recommendations.

2. What supplemental techniques would be useful in conjunction with the focus group interviews? Describe the data collection methods you recommend.

Information from www.burgerking.com; www.Mcdonalds.com; www.hardees.com; "Hardee's Unveils New Monster," www.cnnmoney.com, November 15, 2004; "A Big Breakfast at Burger King," www.cnnmoney.com, March 29, 2005; Bruce Upbin and Daniel Kruger, "Flipping Burgers," www.forbes.com, July 22, 2002.

CASE 7.2 HALLMARK
(www.hallmark.com)

Hallmark Cards is the world's leading manufacturer of social-expression and related products. The company is privately held and has annual sales of approximately $3.8 billion. Established in 1920, Hallmark has continued to grow both in size and with the times. To survive as long as Hallmark has, it has learned to navigate fads, trends, and technology. Today Hallmark is using technology to fight technology. At a time when instant communication makes trends cycle through faster and when customers have increasing control over which messages they will receive, companies must think, create, develop, and sell in ever-shorter time frames.

Hallmark has created IdEx (Idea Exchange) to capture its customers' opinions. A creative research option, IdEx provides low-cost results quickly. Hallmark invites groups of about 200 people, with some shared commonality, to exchange their thoughts and opinions in an online community setting. Such communities nurture trust and friendships, which in turn create information-rich dialogue through open-ended discussions. Some current communities are for grandparents, Latinas, children, and "Women over 45—No Kids at Home." It is important to note that there is a substantial difference between online consumer panels and online communities. Communities craft ongoing qualitative information derived from observation of discussions and probing questions, whereas panels typically meet once to answer a particular set of questions that will be used in a quantitative data set.

The accuracy of new, innovative research methods is a concern for companies. Hallmark conducted parallel testing to verify the validity of its online results and found them to be quite similar to those from more traditional methods, but faster and more cost effective. An additional benefit was that the online communities allowed Hallmark to research topics that would have been prohibitively expensive using more traditional methods. Finally, Hallmark believes that the information it gathers from IdEx is more accurate than that gathered by traditional methods, as participants feel a sense of responsibility to be honest and have a greater sense of helping and belonging.

The online communities stimulate strategic thinking and allow Hallmark to gather information on consumer needs in real time, without the delays inherent in more traditional research methods. For example, when Hallmark posed a question regarding money as a gift, 95 percent of the participants agreed that money is an acceptable gift for high school or college graduation. Based on this insight, the company increased the number of money-holder cards it designed and produced. The quick availability of results ensures that appropriate changes in wording, typography, materials, and colors

can be implemented in time for the upcoming card- or gift-giving season. IdEx allows Hallmark to gain deeper insight into emotions and trends that are usually difficult to uncover through other research methods.

CASE QUESTIONS

1. What are the advantages and disadvantages of using the IdEx data collection approach to improve the customer appeal of Hallmark's products?

2. Is this an appropriate method, considering the roles of qualitative marketing research? What other qualitative methods could supplement this research?

Information from "Idea Exchange Keeps Hallmark Connected with Consumers," Hallmark Press Room, November 2003, www.hallmark.com; Tom Brailsford, "The Hallmark Idea Exchange: Consumer Insights at Speed of Thought" (25th Anniversary AMA Marketing Research Conference, New Orleans, LA, September 21, 2004); Larry Leblanc, "The Gift of Music," *Billboard*, January 15, 2005, 41–43; Jennifer Mann, "White Hose Holiday Cards Go Out," *Knight Ridder Tribune Business News*, December 1, 2004, 1; "Research Reveals Win-Win Situation for Graduation Gift Giving," www.hallmark.com.

8 Experimentation in Marketing Research

Eddie Bauer's Electronic Windows

Eddie Bauer, the only brick-and-mortar unit of cataloguer Spiegel (www. spiegel.com), was looking for a way to draw more shoppers into its stores. It approached business students at Indiana University in Bloomington for help. The students conducted an in-store advertising experiment, using electronic window posters (images displayed on plasma screens).

To test the effectiveness of the electronic windows, Eddie Bauer selected three stores in the chain with sales and demographics similar to those of the store in the Bloomington area. The three stores served as a control group, while the Bloomington store was the experimental group. Eddie Bauer tracked how many people walked by the stores for the seven weeks immediately preceding the installation of the plasma screens in the Bloomington store.

Then the signs were installed. Eddie Bauer

Chapter Objectives

After reading and understanding the material in this chapter, you should be able to:

- Explain the difference between descriptive and experimental research.

- Identify the three conditions indicating that one variable has a causal influence on another.

- Discuss the most appropriate applications of laboratory and field experiments.

- List and explain the threats to internal and external validity of experimental results.

- Explain the difference between pre-experimental and true experimental designs.

alternated the electronic window posters to target different market sub-groups based on when they visited stores. For example, the digital images were changed to appeal to retirees in the morning and to a younger crowd in the evening. After the installation, the number of passersby who entered the control stores went up 7 percent, and in the Bloomington store, traffic increased 30 percent. Nine weeks after the experiment, sales soared 56 percent compared to sales in the weeks before the installation of digital windows. Encouraged by the results, Eddie Bauer rushed to put electronic posters in other stores.[1] ■

Decision makers in a variety of organizations frequently face questions like these:

- Will replacing commercial A with commercial B lead to a marked increase in consumer preference for our brand?
- Can we improve the profitability of our fashion clothing line by increasing its price 10 percent?
- Will an increase in the average number of sales calls per customer from six to eight per year significantly improve sales?
- Will decreasing the shelf space allocated to brand X detergent by 25 percent significantly lower its sales?
- Will it be worthwhile to mail to last year's donors an attractive (but expensive) brochure describing our organization's activities and soliciting higher contributions for this year?

Decision makers typically answer questions like these based on results of limited exploratory or descriptive research (see Chapter 3 for a discussion of these types of research) or, sometimes, based solely on their intuition. Yet, for each, an accurate answer can be ascertained only through some form of controlled research. Each question requires an investigation into the causal association between two things: the type of commercial and consumer preference in the first case, a price increase and profitability in the second, more sales calls per customer and sales in the third, reduced shelf space and sales in the fourth, and a brochure and the volume of contributions in the last case. As we saw in Chapter 3, given data pertaining to two variables, our ability to estimate the impact of one variable on the other critically depends on the conditions under which the data are gathered. The greatest assurance that a causal inference is sound will stem from experimental research. An **experiment** is a procedure in which we manipulate one (or sometimes more than one) independent (cause) variable and collect data on the dependent (effect) variable while controlling for other variables that may influence the dependent variable.

This chapter provides an overview of experiments in the field of marketing research, including the major approaches to conducting marketing experiments and the potential biases that can limit the degree of researcher control in such experiments. Later in the chapter, we cover standard experimental designs useful for marketers and discuss the advantages and disadvantages of each. To place marketing experiments in their proper perspective, we will first review the distinction between experimental and descriptive research, and the general conditions that must be met to make conclusive statements about the nature of causality between variables. The next two sections provide this review.

An **experiment** is a procedure in which one (or sometimes more than one) independent (cause) variable is systematically manipulated and data on the dependent (effect) variable are gathered, while controlling for other variables that may influence the dependent variable.

Descriptive Versus Experimental Research

In experimentation, the researcher manipulates the independent variable or variables before measuring the effect on the dependent variable. For example, the effect of price changes on sales volume of a particular product can be examined by actually varying the price of the product. In this case, the independent variable is the price change; the dependent variable is the sales volume. Thus the very basis of experimental research lies in the manipulation of independent variables. The better the researcher's control over the experimental variables, the more confident the researcher can be of the effect of the independent variable on the dependent variable.[2]

Alternatively, in descriptive research, we would simply ask consumers whether they would buy more of the product if its price were lowered. The distinction between descriptive and experimental research is a matter more of degree than of kind. Whereas descriptive survey data will merely suggest causation, data generated through experimental research will increase our degree of confidence in any suggested cause. Although, theoretically, a completely controlled experiment can indicate for certain whether something is caused by another factor, in marketing practice complete control is rarely possible. Therefore, we can seldom conclusively establish causation in practical settings.[3] This point is especially noteworthy because the term *marketing experiment* does not necessarily imply causation; evidence of association between variables based on experimental data is not proof that the association is a causal one. The discussion in the next section should further reinforce our contention that experimental research is not necessarily infallible.

Conditions for Inferring Causality

When can we confidently conclude that some variable (say, X) has a causal influence on another variable (say, Y)? The literature on experimental research suggests three rather intuitive conditions that must be satisfied for making a statement such as "If X, then Y":[4]

1. *Temporal ordering of variables.* The variable X (or a change in X) must occur before the variable Y (or a change in Y) is observed.

2. *Evidence of association.* The data on variables X and Y must suggest that the two are related in some fashion.

3. *Control of other causal factors.* Unless all potential causal factors other than X are satisfactorily controlled or accounted for, the statement "If X, then Y" may be false even when X precedes Y and evidence of association between the two exists.

All three conditions must be met before causality between X and Y can be conclusively established. The third condition is the most critical and perhaps also the most difficult to satisfy in practical research projects. We can usually infer proper temporal ordering of variables and evidence of association from observation or from questionnaire data collected through descriptive research. But some form of experimental research is invariably required to control other causal factors.

Even in experimental settings, however, we cannot always be sure that all extraneous factors have been accounted for. Sometimes experimental researchers may not even be aware of potential causal factors. Sometimes we can learn what they are and how to control them from a thorough analysis of the sales and marketing history of the product involved. In some cases, there may be no way of knowing what they are until we have done the experiments.

Fortunately, most real-life situations call for reasonable (rather than complete) assurance of control, which sound experimental studies are capable of providing. Nevertheless, we must be cautious in making causal inferences simply because the first two conditions are satisfied.

To highlight the fallacy of such inferences, consider the following example. Suppose an executive associated with the MTV cable TV channel says, "Linkin Park [a popular rock group] owes its life to MTV" and supports this belief by pointing out that Linkin Park's albums flourish in areas where cable TV carries MTV but collect dust where MTV is not seen. The implication here is that availability of the MTV channel causes a sharp increase in sales of Linkin Park albums. The former certainly preceded the latter, and there is no question that the two are strongly associated. Yet (borrowing terminology from the criminal justice system) the evidence here is mainly circumstantial and does not show beyond a reasonable doubt that MTV was responsible for the sales success of Linkin Park's albums. Other uncontrolled factors might have been responsible for what was observed. For instance, availability of the MTV channel and high sales of the albums may both have been caused independently by such unobserved factors as the socioeconomic status and interests of residents in various parts of the United States. If so, the observed association between availability of MTV and album sales is spurious. This association will vanish if we explicitly incorporate the uncontrolled factors into the analysis.

Laboratory Versus Field Experiments

Consider the following scenario, which we will use to illustrate our discussion in this and subsequent sections of the chapter. The advertising agency of Gourmet Food Products Company (GFPC) has developed two quite different television commercials (say, A and B) for the company's line of frozen pizzas. The final decision about which commercial to use in an upcoming national campaign rests with GFPC's advertising manager, Mr. Thompson. Before choosing one of the two commercials, Mr. Thompson wants to get a feeling for the potential impact of each commercial on consumer preference for GFPC's frozen pizzas. He therefore asks the ad agency to conduct an appropriate marketing experiment to assess the differential impact of one commercial over the other. The ad agency can use one of two general experimental approaches for generating the information requested by Mr. Thompson.

■ **Approach 1**   Invite a group of 100 consumers to the agency's marketing research facility. Divide the group randomly into two similar groups of 50 consumers and take each to a different television viewing room. Show each group an hour-long episode of a current television program with a normal number and variety of commercials included at appropriate time slots. Manipulate the set of commercials to be seen by the two groups such that one group will see test commercial A twice during the program and the other group will see test commercial B twice. To prevent participant knowledge of the experimental manipulation and to evoke normal reactions to the test commercials, disguise the purpose of the

A researcher in a laboratory experiment is recording a young consumer's opinions about three different flavors of a beverage.

study by telling consumers that the study's purpose is to get their reactions to the television program. After the consumers have seen the program, administer a questionnaire to obtain their reactions to the program and to the various products advertised during the program, including GFPC's frozen pizzas. Compare the mean preferences for GFPC's frozen pizzas for the two groups to assess the impacts of commercial A and commercial B.

■ **Approach 2** Select two test cities that are as similar as possible in terms of their consumer demographics and food-purchasing characteristics. Select an appropriate television program that will be shown simultaneously in both cities, but one that allows for airing different local television spots during the program. Arrange to show commercial A twice in one city and commercial B twice in the other. After the program has been aired, conduct random telephone surveys in the two cities to measure viewer reactions. Specifically, in each city, measure preference for GFPC's frozen pizzas among a sample of 50 consumers who saw the program. Compare the mean consumer preference for GFPC's frozen pizzas for the samples in the two cities to assess the impacts of commercial A and commercial B.

What similarities and differences do you see between approaches 1 and 2? Both are experimental in that they involve manipulating a causal variable (namely, the type of test commercial shown) and measuring its impact on an effect variable (namely, consumer preference for GFPC's frozen pizzas). A major difference between the two approaches, however, is the degree of control available during the manipulation and measurement process. Approach 1 clearly offers better control than approach 2 with respect to extraneous factors capable of influencing consumer preferences toward GFPC's frozen pizzas. Approach 1 is a form of laboratory experiment, whereas approach 2 is a form of field experiment. A **laboratory experiment** is a research study conducted in a contrived setting, in which the effect of all, or nearly all, influential but irrelevant independent variables is kept to a minimum. A **field experiment** is a research study conducted in a natural setting, in which the experimenter manipulates one or more independent variables under conditions controlled as carefully as the situation will permit.[5]

A **laboratory experiment** is a research study conducted in a contrived setting, in which the effect of all, or nearly all, influential but irrelevant independent variables is kept to a minimum.

A **field experiment** is a research study conducted in a natural setting, in which one or more independent variables are manipulated by the experimenter under conditions controlled as carefully as the situation will permit.

Internal validity is the extent to which observed results are due solely to the experimental manipulation.

External validity is the extent to which observed results are likely to hold beyond the experimental setting.

External and Internal Validity

The key procedural difference between the two types of experiments in terms of the research setting and the degree of control over extraneous factors has an important bearing on the validity of the experimental results. The validity of experimental results is usually evaluated on two dimensions: external validity and internal validity.[6] **Internal validity** is the extent to which observed results are due solely to the experimental manipulation; **external validity** is the extent to which observed results are likely to hold beyond the experimental setting. An ideal experiment is one whose results will have high internal as well as external validity.

The effect of in-store taste-testing of food items on their sales can be determined through a field experiment.

Unfortunately, there is usually a tradeoff between these two forms of validity. In other words, only a contrived setting typically enables an experimenter to control all extraneous factors by holding constant other causal variables, or at least estimating and filtering out the influence of such variables on the effect variable. This may cast doubt on whether the results apply to realistic settings. Thus laboratory experiments generally have an advantage over field experiments in terms of internal validity but not external validity. The opposite is true for field experiments.

Let's reexamine the two alternative experimental approaches described in the GFPC scenario in light of our discussion of laboratory versus field experiments and internal versus external validity. Suppose both approaches were used and the following results were observed:

- *Approach 1 (laboratory experiment).* In the group exposed to commercial A, 60 percent preferred GFPC's frozen pizzas over competing brands. Consumer preference for GFPC's frozen pizzas in the group exposed to commercial B was 40 percent.
- *Approach 2 (field experiment).* Consumer preference for GFPC's frozen pizzas was 25 percent among those exposed to commercial A and 30 percent among those exposed to commercial B.

The results from the two experiments are obviously at odds with each other. Can such inconsistent results occur in this scenario? They certainly can, because neither experiment can claim both high internal and high external validity.

Uncontrollable Factors

We can confidently attribute the 20-point difference in preference between the two groups in the laboratory experiment to the difference between the two test commercials because virtually everything else remained strictly controlled. The results therefore have high internal validity. There is some question, however, about whether commercial A would be so much more effective than commercial B in a real-life setting, given the artificial environment in the laboratory experiment. For instance, consumers watching television under normal circumstances may not pay as close attention to the program and the commercials in it, and as a result, consumer preferences may not differ to as great an extent as in a laboratory experiment.[7] Thus the 20-point difference in consumer preference cannot be generalized confidently.

The results of the field experiment, giving commercial B a slight edge over commercial A, may suffer from a different type of problem. Although the experimental setting itself was quite realistic, uncontrolled factors (in addition to the test commercial) may have influenced consumer preferences in different ways in the two cities. For instance, competing brands of frozen pizza may have been heavily promoted on the day of the experiment in the city in which commercial A was shown, but not in the city in which commercial B was shown. If so, the finding that commercial B is somewhat more effective than commercial A will lack internal validity and cannot be fully trusted.

Which of the two approaches should the advertising agency use? More generally, are laboratory experiments likely to be better than field experiments, or vice versa, in terms of overall usefulness of the results? There are no clear-cut answers. As we will see in the next section, a variety of situational factors play a role in the choice of an appropriate experimental approach. Nevertheless, the preceding discussion and illustrations have an important message for all researchers using marketing experiments: no matter how much control and realism you think you have incorporated into your experiment (be it a laboratory or a field experiment), unanticipated or uncontrolled conditions may influence the results. You should therefore temper your inferences accordingly when such conditions arise.

Deciding Which Type of Experiment to Use

So far we have considered only validity issues relating to laboratory versus field experiments. Other practical considerations relevant in choosing between the two types of experiments include time, cost, exposure to competition, and nature of the manipulation.

Time

As you might suspect, conducting an experiment in a real-life setting will generally be more time consuming than conducting it in a contrived setting. A field experiment will usually require additional time for such activities as identifying appropriate field locations and introducing the experimental manipulations into those locations. For instance, consider approach 2 in the GFPC scenario. Selecting two similar test cities, identifying an appropriate television program to be aired simultaneously in both cities, purchasing commercial airtime on each program, and so on, are likely to be time-consuming tasks.

Cost

As far as cost is concerned, laboratory experiments again generally have an advantage over field experiments. The larger scale on which manipulations have to be introduced and results monitored in field experiments can sharply increase their cost. For instance, in the GFPC scenario, buying commercial airtime on television programs in the two test cities is likely to make approach 2 significantly more expensive than approach 1. Given a situation requiring experimental research, a laboratory experiment can usually be conducted for a fraction of the cost of running a field experiment.

Exposure to Competition

A potential drawback of any marketing field experiment is the danger of exposing it to competitors. Exposure may invite competitors to monitor the experiment and gain valuable insights virtually free of charge. It may also prompt competitors to change the experimental environment (for example, by drastically changing their own promotional or pricing levels) and hence invalidate the experimental results. Clearly, competitive monitoring and interference in an experiment are highly undesirable from the experimenter's perspective.

Test-marketing is a form of field experiment for assessing the market's reactions to a new product and its associated marketing mix.

The threat of competitive interference is especially great in **test-marketing,** a form of field experiment for assessing the market's reactions to a new product and its associated marketing mix. Test-marketing is a formal step in the new-product planning process, prior to full-scale product introduction, for many consumer goods firms.[8] But the risk of competitive interference does not necessarily mean that laboratory experiments must be used instead of field experiments to gain insight into the potential market impact of new products. Consumer response to new products, especially to such major innovations as high-definition television (HDTV) and electric cars, simply cannot be gauged accurately in a laboratory environment. Because of consumers' lack of familiarity with new products, their reactions to conceptual descriptions or even prototypes of the product in a laboratory setting may be no better than wild guesses, which are unlikely to have external validity.[9] Furthermore, laboratory experiments cannot adequately duplicate important phenomena, such as diffusion of advertising messages through various groups of consumers and the effect of manufacturers' advertising on the inventory decisions of wholesalers and retailers, which, in turn, can influence sales.

The point of this discussion is that test-marketing, despite the risk of exposure to competition, may still be the most meaningful approach in certain situations. Research in Use 8.1 describes some real-world examples of test-marketing. A key to avoiding drawing erroneous inferences from test-market results is to take into account any unusual competitive activity when interpreting the results.

Accurate assessment and interpretation of competitive activity during a test-marketing operation may not always be easy, however. The following example illustrates this point.

CASE IN POINT ▶ **McDonald's Tests McPizza**   In an effort to strengthen its position in the adult market, McDonald's test-marketed pizza at 24 of its stores in the Evansville, Indiana, area. Successful pizza introduction would strengthen the dinner business, which McDonald's had been trying hard to improve. The introduction of pizza was designed to bring in families and adults who might not normally frequent McDonald's for dinner. When McDonald's test-marketed its McPizza, a leading competitor, Pizza Hut, reacted aggressively to McDonald's move into its territory with a buy-one-get-one-free promotion. Pizza Hut TV commercials mocked McDonald's pizza dough as "McFrozen" and claimed that McDonald's pizza was inferior to the real thing offered at Pizza Hut, using the slogan "Don't make a McStake. Come to Pizza Hut for a real pizza."

McDonald's countered with heavy advertising, emphasizing speedy service for pizza. McPizza received favorable nods in some test-markets and had partial rollout nationally. But Pizza Hut ran a buy-one-get-one-free promotion wherever McPizza was introduced, and the sales performance of McPizza did not meet management's expectations. Also, McDonald's could not make the pizza fast enough or consistent enough in quality. The results from the partial rollout discouraged McDonald's from rolling out the dough nationally.[10] ◀

As this example demonstrates, proper interpretation of test-market results requires clear knowledge not only of how competitors are reacting during the test-marketing operation, but also what they are capable of doing in the future.

■ **Nature of the Manipulation**

The type of independent variable used and the way it is to be manipulated also have a bearing on which experimental approach will be most appropriate. Laboratory experiments will be more appropriate than field experiments, especially given the time, cost, and secrecy advantages of the former, as long as the manipulations

Examples of Test-Marketing

KaBloom, a floral chain based in Massachusetts, is test-marketing selling flowers in kiosks in a variety of locations. The company sees the kiosk strategy as a possible means for expanding its geographic reach while keeping expansion costs at a minimum.

A number of electric utilities in Ohio, Virginia, and Texas are test-marketing providing Internet access through existing power lines. Using a special type of modem and low-voltage wiring in each residence, clients could be connected to the Internet without needing to use a telephone line or a cable connection. The service could be of particular interest to customers in rural areas, where the quality and quantity of high-speed Internet connections can be inconsistent.

Ford Motor Company wanted to determine the effectiveness of its advertising campaign for the new Mustang. The advertising used sophisticated computer technology to display legendary movie icon Steve McQueen interacting with both the car and a real-life actor. The company test-marketed the advertisement with a number of audiences and got the reaction it wanted: even if younger viewers were not initially aware of who Steve McQueen was, they all responded to the cool, classic image that the company was intending to convey.

Fast-food chains are test-marketing a wide variety of products spanning both ends of the nutrition spectrum. At one end of the spectrum, products are being developed to appeal to the health-conscious. After a successful test-market in Southern California, McDonald's has introduced Fruit & Walnut Salads nationwide. Some 184 Wendy's restaurants in Pittsburgh, Virginia Beach, and Portland are testing fruit bowl entrées with cantaloupe, honeydew melon, pineapple, and grapes. At the other end of the nutrition spectrum, some fast-food chains are developing high-calorie, fatty products to appeal to the 18-to-24 age group (Hardee's Monster Thickburger and Burger King's Enormous Omelet Sandwich).

Based on favorable test-marketing results, Allied Domecq, Dunkin' Donuts' British parent company, has introduced "combo" formats (combination stores) where both Dunkin' Donuts and Baskin-Robbins are offered. Nearly 53 percent of new stores are combination stores.

Kellogg's India Ltd., a wholly owned subsidiary of U.S.-based Kellogg Company, test-marketed "baked cheese snack crackers"—or Cheez-It, as it is known in the United States—in Chennai, Tamil Nadu, India. The company placed Cheez-It crackers, altered to suit the Indian palate, in select department store outlets in the state. The company has expanded nationally after its favorable test-marketing results.[a]

are likely to be meaningful in a contrived setting. For example, laboratory experiments may be quite appropriate for assessing consumer reactions to different types of package designs for a soft drink, different levels of flavoring added to an ice cream, and so on.

Field experiments are better when the manipulation is likely to be meaningless or difficult to implement in a laboratory setting. We have already seen that the potential market impact of major innovations cannot be adequately assessed through laboratory experiments because of difficulty in evoking meaningful reactions from respondents.

Although laboratory experiments may be useful in some situations, certain types of changes in the system can be investigated only by means of field experimentation. These changes are very difficult to duplicate realistically in the laboratory. Common examples are changes in website design, in salespersons' compensation, in sales force organization, in the structure of the distribution system, and in pricing policies or credit terms. The best way to study the potential impact of a change in, say, sales force strategy is to implement the change in some subset of the present territories and then compare the performance of those territories with that of the territories not receiving that treatment.

Hybrid Approaches: Simulated Test–Markets

To summarize our discussion of the pros and cons of laboratory versus field experiments, laboratory experiments are strong in terms of internal validity (ability to determine the sole impact of a causal variable), time, cost, and negligible risk of exposure to competition. Field experiments are strong in terms of external validity (generalizability of inferences) and meaningfulness of the manipulations. To capitalize on the strengths of both types of experiments and to circumvent the difficulty of making a strictly either-or decision, researchers have developed hybrid experimental approaches.[11] These hybrid approaches are essentially laboratory experiments that imitate real market conditions as much as possible and are called *simulated test-markets*. Several commercial marketing research firms have facilities especially designed for conducting experiments under conditions closely resembling actual market conditions. One such facility, called Litmus, is offered by Harris Interactive Inc., a Rochester, New York–based global research company (www.harrisinteractive.com/advantages/marketingsciences.asp). The Litmus Stimulated Test Market System provides sales volume estimates for the first one or two years following a new product or service launch. A description of the Litmus Simulated Test Market System and the way it is used is summarized in Research in Use 8.2.

Simulated test-markets are by no means completely devoid of artificiality. However, a few studies comparing results obtained from simulated and actual market experiments have shown a moderate degree of consistency between the two sets of results. Experiments conducted in simulated test-markets are likely to be more frequent in the future because they are becoming increasingly sophisticated and because they bring together the complementary strengths of laboratory and field experiments. In the GFPC scenario, for instance, testing the relative impacts of commercials A and B in a simulated market (like the one described in Research in Use 8.2) may be better than either of the two proposed approaches. The simulated test-market results will yield estimates of the immediate as well as the longer-term impacts of the commercials on sales (rather than on preference alone). Thus the information generated is likely to be richer and managerially more useful than that generated in a traditional laboratory experiment.

CASE IN POINT ▶ **Virtual Test-Markets** In recent times, the computer has come to play an important role in simulated test-marketing. Ray Burke, professor of business administration at Indiana University, has created a virtual store to determine how products catch a consumer's eye. Computer 3-D graphics create a feeling of being in a store, walking past shelves of grocery items just as in a real store. The store is interactive: consumers can pick items off the shelves to examine them more closely and can select items they would buy in real-life shopping. Virtual simulated marketing tests will enable companies to examine consumers' reactions to new products, product line extensions, prices, packaging, and merchandising. Virtual testing will allow testing of ideas in a cluttered, competitive environment. Computer-simulated test-marketing is faster to implement than traditional simulated test-marketing. It also collects more detailed information on the shopping process at a much lower cost.[12] ◀

Litmus Model: Simulated Test-Marketing (STM)

STM tests consumers with an actual product or service in an actual purchase situation to observe their actual trial, repeat, and usage behavior, and then forecasts the results in the real world. STM is not a coupon redemption study or self-reports on a five-point scale. It studies real behavior.

Simulated test-marketing puts carefully screened consumers in a special test store or service situation. The store is stocked with competitors' products as well as the new test product, based on location surveys. Customers use their own money to buy (true simulation), after being exposed to new-product ad campaigns and competitors' ad campaigns. Consumers are questioned on their attitudes before going into the store and on their reactions (1) after the ad campaign exposure, (2) after the store experience, (3) after home usage of whatever products or services they bought, and (4) at continued repurchase stages. These response data yield forecasts of trial, first and second repeat, usage rate, and other measures for use in the Litmus system. The market response testing phase also provides information on consumer diagnostics, user and nonuser demographic profiles, and the sources of new-product volume.

Because STM observes actual consumer behavior, it can use the Litmus system to develop the detailed price/marketing plan combination that will give new products optimal profits as well as sales.

The Testing Sequence

Step 1: Prerecruitment
- Appropriate sample
- Telephone
- Security screen

Step 2: Background: Habits and practices
- Security screen
- Self-administered questionnaire

- Current behavior
- Usage occasions and frequency
- Diagnostics
- Rating of ideal attributes and benefits
- Demographics

Step 3: Exposure to real advertising in a competitive context

Step 4: Simulated store purchase reflective of BDI (relative strength of a brand's sales in a particular area)/CDI (relative strength of a category in a geographic area) issues
- Shelf set and price matched to each market
- Consumers make real-money purchase

Step 5: Postpurchase inquiry
- Perceived ad message
- Reaction to price and packaging
- Anticipated purchase and usage
- Rating test with competitive brands on delivery of attributes and benefits
- Likes/dislikes

Step 6: Respondents take product home (no reference to interviewing)

Step 7: Postusage evaluation
- Telephone interview
- Reaction to product
- Degree (and reasons) for satisfaction/dissatisfaction
- Usage pattern
- Rating of brand on attributes
- Attitudinal and behavioral repeat and usage measurements[b]

Scanner Data Analysis

Availability of scanner data—data on product sales from supermarkets equipped with electronic scanners at the checkouts—is enabling marketers of packaged goods to conduct sophisticated field experiments. Several marketing research firms have established panels of scanner-equipped stores spread over areas that are representative of the major markets in the country. The data from these stores are transmitted electronically to central computers for analysis and interpretation.

Retailers and manufacturers can systematically manipulate marketing stimuli (such as price, promotion, and shelf space allocation) and ascertain their impact on product sales by analyzing scanner data from the markets participating in the experiment. Information Resources, Inc. (IRI), and ACNielsen Company offer marketers a variety of services through their information systems called BehaviorScan and ScanTrack, respectively.[13]

Web-Based Experiments

The Internet is providing an unprecedented opportunity for Web-based marketing experiments. Web-based experimentation will enable companies to test a wide range of possible marketing mix changes and statistically model consumer responses to these changes.[14] Karen Becker-Olsen conducted Web-based experiments to test the effectiveness of banner advertising and sponsored Web content. Sponsorship was defined in the study as an "investment in an activity, cause, or event—in this case, a Web community—in return for access to exploitable commercial potential." Two hundred seventy college undergraduates in an introductory marketing course were asked to view a homepage from a fictitious informational Web community. The homepage included banner advertisements and both sponsored and nonsponsored content. The study participants were then asked to fill out a questionnaire that rated each subject's response to the overall website, the content, and the banner advertisements. Three months after filling out the questionnaire, subjects were asked to participate in followup interviews to further gauge the effectiveness of the banner advertisements and sponsored content. Based on the research, Becker-Olsen concluded that, although banner advertisements were still an effective way to market products and services, there might be a better way to use the Web for marketing. The most positive results occurred when companies sponsored Web content, then followed up with banner advertising. Using such a strategy tended to increase respondents' positive feelings and attitudes about the company and its products and services.[15]

Companies can test Web designs by randomly exposing visitors to different designs and tracking their purchases over time while keeping all other marketing mix variables the same across all visitors. Although Web-based experimentation is expected to increase in the coming decade, it is important to remember that online experiments can collect information only from consumers who use the Internet. This leaves out a significant portion of the U.S. population and many more in other countries. Nevertheless, Web-based panels are becoming increasingly popular, and initial indications are that the results from such panels show a degree of representativeness.[16]

Threats to Internal and External Validity

We have so far seen specific illustrations of biases (in the context of the GFPC scenario and in the banner ad testing experiment) that can lower the validity of experimental results. In the next two sections, we will examine certain standard threats to the internal and external validity of experiments in general. As you examine those threats, keep in mind that not all of them may be present in every experiment. The type of experiment (laboratory or field) and the type of units from which data are gathered (whether consumers or stores) will have a bearing on which threats are likely to be serious.

Internal Validity

Internal validity, as was discussed earlier, refers to the extent to which we can be confident that the manipulated independent variable is solely responsible for observed changes in the dependent variable. Therefore, the presence of any condition or occurrence (other than the independent variable manipulation) that can offer a competing explanation for the experimental results is a threat to internal validity. We will discuss the following effects that can lower the internal validity of experiments: history, maturation, pretesting, instrument variation, selection, and mortality.[17]

History effects are specific external events or occurrences during an experiment that are likely to affect the dependent variable.

■ **History Effect** **History effects** are specific external events or occurrences during an experiment that are likely to affect the dependent variable. The history effect is not a frequent problem in laboratory experiments. Because of the controlled environments in which such experiments are conducted, the researcher is in a good position to prevent, or at least monitor and account for, any extraneous event or occurrence other than the planned manipulation. The history effect is potentially a more serious problem in field experiments. Unusual shifts in competitors' marketing mix variables when a field experiment is in progress are the most likely form of the history effect.

SCENARIO Suppose Dole wishes to study the impact of a special store display on sales of its branded canned fruits. It selects a representative group of stores in a test area and monitors sales of Dole canned fruits in these stores for a one-month period. The company then introduces the special display and monitors sales for another month. The difference between the first and the second month's sales of Dole canned fruits in the test stores should reveal the impact of the special display. But what happens if the price of or promotional strategy for Del Monte canned fruits changes significantly during the two-month experimental period or if Del Monte experiences distribution problems during that period and stocks out in several of the test stores? Occurrences like these are history effects and may be responsible, at least in part, for any difference between sales of Dole canned fruits with and without the special display. Consequently, the experimental findings cannot be taken at face value.

The **maturation effect** is the effect on the dependent variable of physiological or physical changes that occur with the passage of time.

■ **Maturation Effect** The effect of physiological or physical changes that occur with the passage of time in the dependent variable being measured constitutes a **maturation effect.** Unlike the history effect, which stems from the external experimental environment, the maturation effect stems from the experimental units.

SCENARIO Consider a laboratory experiment to ascertain the impact of a new Honda commercial on consumer opinions about Honda cars. A representative group of consumers is brought to a laboratory setting, and their current opinions about Honda cars are measured through an appropriate questionnaire. They watch an hour-long television program in which the test commercial is inserted. Next, the researchers measure the consumers' opinions about Honda cars once again. Could any physiological changes have occurred in the respondents during this experiment? Yes, because some of them might have started feeling hungry toward the end of the experiment, others might have become tired, and so on. If such changes prompted the respondents to "just get the whole thing over with," their opinions as measured through the second questionnaire would be inaccurate due to the maturation effect.

The **pretesting effect** occurs when responses given during a later measurement are influenced by those given during a previous measurement.

■ Pretesting Effect

The **pretesting effect** occurs when consumer responses during a later measurement are influenced by those they gave during a previous measurement, regardless of what happened between the measurements. The difference between the pretest and posttest measures of the dependent variable will then inaccurately reflect the impact of the experimental manipulation, thereby lowering internal validity. The pretesting effect stems from the tendency (for whatever underlying reasons) to remain consistent or to change between pretest and posttest measurements. Because this tendency is a purely human phenomenon, the pretesting effect is rarely a threat to the internal validity of experiments in which measurements are obtained from stores.

Recall the laboratory experiment to measure the impact of a new Honda television commercial. Suppose we now measure consumers' opinions before and after exposure to the commercial through a series of 10-point rating scales relating to various attributes of Honda cars (rating scales and their development are discussed in Chapter 9). While responding to the second measurement, the respondents may remember how they rated Honda on each scale during the first measurement. Furthermore, some of these respondents may provide the same ratings they gave in the previous measurement, perhaps through a desire to appear consistent. If so, the difference between the two measurements will reveal nothing about the true impact the Honda commercial may have had on these respondents. Alternatively, some respondents may provide a different set of ratings during the second measurement, not because their opinions about Honda cars have changed, but because they do not want to give the same set of ratings twice. In either case, the result is a lowering of internal validity: the difference, or lack of difference, between pretest and posttest opinions about Honda cars cannot be attributed solely to the Honda commercial.

The **instrument variation effect** is a bias that relates to differences between pretest and posttest measurements owing to changes in the instruments (questionnaires) or procedures used to measure the dependent variable.

■ Instrument Variation Effect

The **instrument variation effect** is a bias relating to differences between pretest and posttest measurements owing to changes in the instruments (questionnaires) or procedures used to measure the dependent variable. It is a potential internal validity threat only in experiments involving more than one measurement of the same dependent variable. However, it is unlikely to be a problem when the units from which measurements are obtained are stores. In other words, dependent variables on which data are obtained from stores, such as sales, inventory turnover, and brand share, are typically straightforward, with little room for variation in their measurement. Of course, if the definitions of these variables or the ways in which they are measured do change during the experiment, the instrument variation effect will be a problem. But to the extent that the researcher can prevent such changes in measuring at the store level, the threat of the instrument variation effect is unlikely to be serious.

The instrument variation effect is a much more serious threat to the internal validity of experiments involving respondents. Dependent variables in such experiments are invariably nebulous constructs like attitudes, opinions, preferences, or purchase intentions. In discussing the banner ad testing experiment, we raised serious doubts about the validity of ad effectiveness measurement. All the questions centered on measurement and are therefore susceptible to instrument variation effects. Measuring such variables typically requires a questionnaire and calls for some form of interaction between respondents and an interviewer. Any changes in the questionnaire or the interviewer between pre- and postmeasurements can, in and of itself, produce a difference in the results obtained.[18]

The **selection effect** occurs when multiple groups participating in an experiment differ on characteristics that have a bearing on the dependent variable.

■ **Selection Effect**   The **selection effect** is a potential problem in experiments with more than one group of units. This bias is present when multiple groups participating in an experiment differ on characteristics that have a bearing on the dependent variable. For instance, both the laboratory and field experiment approaches proposed in the GFPC scenario to test the relative effectiveness of commercials A and B involved two groups of respondents. Suppose the group exposed to commercial A was dominated by heavy users of frozen dinners, whereas the group exposed to commercial B was dominated by consumers who typically ate only home-cooked meals. Also suppose that 40 percent of those who saw commercial A indicated a preference for GFPC's frozen pizzas, whereas only 5 percent of those who saw commercial B did so. These results cannot necessarily be interpreted as showing commercial A to be more effective than commercial B. All or part of the observed difference in preferences may be due to the critical difference between the general food preferences of the two groups rather than to the experimental manipulation (the difference between the two commercials). The internal validity of the experiment under these circumstances is likely to be quite low because of the presence of the selection effect.

The **mortality effect** occurs when certain participating units drop out of an experiment, and as a result, the set of units completing the experiment differs significantly from the original set of units.

■ **Mortality Effect**   The **mortality effect** occurs when certain participating units drop out of an experiment, and as a result, the set of units completing the experiment differs significantly from the original set of units. To illustrate the mortality effect, consider an in-home product-testing experiment for evaluating the effectiveness of a new and improved bathtub and tile cleaner. An initial sample of 100 users of the current version of the product is chosen for this experiment. In a pretest interview, researchers ask these participants to state their overall opinion of the old version of the bathtub and tile cleaner on a scale of 1 to 10 (the higher the number, the more favorable the opinion). Assume that the mean rating across all 100 participants turns out to be 6. The participants receive samples of the new and improved version, and use it over a two-month period. At the end of this period, suppose only 70 participants take part in a posttest interview to measure reactions to the new version; the rest simply refuse to be interviewed. Assume that the mean rating across the 70 participants is 8 on the same 10-point scale. The key question now is whether the 2-point improvement in the mean opinion rating can be attributed to the new and improved version of the product or is due to the difference between the pre- and posttest groups.

The answer to this question critically depends on the composition of the dropout group compared to the original set of participants. For instance, if the 30 who dropped out were people with negative reactions to the product, the post-measured mean rating of 8 could be inflated. In other words, the difference in mean opinion ratings is not a true reflection of the effectiveness of the new and improved version, because the composition of participants changed critically between measurements. Thus the mortality effect is present. Of course, if the 30 people who dropped out were random dropouts—that is, if the characteristics of those dropping out had no systematic connection to the dependent variable—the pre- and postinterview groups would differ in size but not in composition. Hence, there would be little or no mortality effect. The mortality effect is a problem only when such a loss results in a group that differs critically from the original group. Therefore, an experimenter should collect data on critical participant characteristics (demographics, extent, and frequency of product use) during both pre- and postinterviews. In the event of loss of participants during an experiment, such data can be valuable in ascertaining whether and in what ways group composition has changed. This information will lower the risk of making erroneous inferences.

Consumers' reactions to products being evaluated in a laboratory experiment such as the one shown here may differ from their reactions in a natural setting because of potential reactive bias.

External Validity

External validity of experimental results relates to their generalizability. The various internal validity threats we have discussed also indirectly affect external validity, because it would be meaningless to generalize experimental findings that are not even internally valid. In other words, internal validity can be viewed as a necessary but not a sufficient condition for external validity. Our discussion in this section will focus on conditions that must be met beyond those needed for internal validity to conclude that experimental findings have external validity. We will examine biases that stand in the way of generalizing experimental results even when they have high internal validity. Specifically, we will discuss the following three biases: reactive bias, pretest-manipulation interaction bias, and nonrepresentative-sample bias.[19]

■ **Reactive Bias** **Reactive bias** is the problem of participants' exhibiting abnormal or unusual behavior simply because they are participating in an experiment. This bias is limited to experiments with consumers and is likely to occur only when they know they are participating in an experiment. Reactive bias can be quite severe in laboratory experiments, because the artificial environment and the attention paid to participants by the experimenter are especially conducive to this type of bias. As Fred N. Kerlinger and Howard B. Lee observe, "Almost any change, any extra attention, any experimental manipulation, or even the absence of manipulation but the knowledge that a study is being done, is enough to cause subjects to change. In short, if we pay attention to people, they respond."[20]

In **reactive bias**, participants exhibit abnormal or unusual behavior simply because they are participating in an experiment.

Although reactive bias is more likely to occur in laboratory experiments, field experiments with consumers are by no means immune to it. In Chapter 3 we discussed consumer panels, permanent samples of respondents who are repeatedly measured over time. Many field experiments use data obtained from consumer panels. For example, we can estimate the impact of a campaign using a 50-cents-off coupon for a brand of detergent by comparing purchases of the detergent made by panel members before and after the campaign. Reactive bias is a potential problem with this approach because, if panel members know their purchases are being monitored, they may behave differently than normal consumers.

Pretest-manipulation interaction bias is a special form of reactive bias that is unique to experiments relying on premeasurement of consumers before they are exposed to the experimental manipulation; it arises when the premeasurement increases or decreases respondents' sensitivity to the experimental manipulation.

■ **Pretest–Manipulation Interaction Bias** **Pretest-manipulation interaction bias** is simply a special form of reactive bias that is unique to experiments relying on premeasurement of consumers before they are exposed to the experimental manipulation. Whereas reactive bias stems from the influence of the experiment as a whole, pretest-manipulation interaction bias stems from the influence of the premeasurement. Specifically, pretest-manipulation interaction bias will arise when the premeasurement increases or decreases respondents' sensitivity to the experimental manipulation.

■ Nonrepresentative–Sample Bias

Nonrepresentative-sample bias occurs when the units participating in an experiment are not representative of the larger body of units to which the experimental results are to be generalized. This bias stems from improper or inadequate recruiting of units and is a sampling problem. When the composition of units participating in an experiment critically differs from that of the total collection of units, the experimental results will lack external validity, no matter how internally valid they are.

Nonrepresentative-sample bias is a major issue in Web-based experiments. Because Web-based experiments tend to attract only those participants with computers and Internet access, those selected may be quite different from the general population. Although the severity of this problem may decrease in time, as more and more people start using the Internet and respondents are recruited from research firms' Internet panels, we still have a long way to go before we can generalize the findings. Also, Internet studies (like the banner ad experiment described earlier) choose respondents only from those who visit websites, another source of nonrepresentative-sample bias because only those who have a special interest visit a particular site. Recently, however, companies conducting online experiments or surveys have begun recruiting respondents from general-purpose websites like those maintained by AOL, thereby minimizing the impact of the nonrepresentative-sample bias. This bias cannot be completely eliminated, however, because online surveys still appeal only to those who have Internet access.

Nonrepresentative-sample bias can be a potential threat to external validity in all types of experiments, laboratory as well as field, and those involving consumers or stores. It is particularly likely to be present in laboratory experiments and experiments involving consumer panels. There is always the risk that participants willing to expend the effort to take part in a laboratory experiment, or to respond to the repeated measurements to which panel members are subjected, may differ in significant ways from the population at large.[21]

■ Determining the Seriousness of Threats to Validity

The preceding two sections covered a number of problems that can lower the internal or external validity of experimental results. These problems, although not exhaustive, are the ones that underlie the practical constraints we most frequently encounter in conducting experimental research in marketing.[22] An additional complication is that there are often tradeoffs between these problems; that is, minimizing one problem may aggravate another. For example, an attempt to reduce the pretesting effect by using different questionnaires (questionnaires with the same content but different formats) for the pre- and postmeasurements is likely to lead to the instrument variation effect. An attempt to circumvent the mortality effect by analyzing data from only those units completing all phases of an experiment may result in nonrepresentative-sample bias. The point is that an experimenter, in striving to avoid specific threats to validity, should not lose sight of the possible increased risk of other threats. If the number and variety of potential problems give you the hopeless feeling that experimental research in marketing is useless, do not despair. First, not all problems are likely to be severe in every marketing experiment. As discussed earlier, the seriousness of problems depends on the nature of the experiment (laboratory or field) and the nature of the participating units (consumers or stores). Table 8.1 summarizes the circumstances in which each validity threat is likely to be serious.

Second, although a researcher may not be able to eliminate certain threats in a situation, he or she may still be able to account for them by filtering out their influences from the experimental results.

TABLE 8.1
Circumstances Under Which Various Validity Threats May Be Serious

	Threat May Be Serious For	
Type of Threat	Experiment	Participants
History effect	Field experiment	Consumers or stores
Maturation effect	Laboratory or field experiment	Consumers or stores
Pretesting effect	Laboratory or field experiment	Consumers
Instrument variation effect	Laboratory or field experiment	Consumers
Selection effect	Laboratory or field experiment	Consumers or stores
Mortality effect	Field experiment	Consumers or stores
Reactive bias	Laboratory experiment	Consumers
Pretest-manipulation interaction bias	Laboratory or field experiment	Consumers
Nonrepresentative-sample bias	Laboratory or field experiment	Consumers or stores

Third, recall from our discussion at the beginning of the chapter that to conclusively establish causality between variables is virtually impossible. Therefore, the realistic role of experimentation in marketing is not so much to prove causality as to increase our confidence in making causal inferences. Viewed from this perspective, carefully conducted experimental research, even if less than perfect, can provide more meaningful and accurate causal insights than descriptive research can.

Experimental Design

Now we will discuss several standard experimental designs that frequently serve as the basis for causal inferences in marketing. Before we examine these designs, a few points concerning them are in order. First, most of the standard designs can be employed in laboratory or field settings and can rely on consumers or stores as the observational units. Therefore, although each design has certain inherent weaknesses, how serious those weaknesses are likely to be may depend on the particular context in which the design is employed. (Recall that the seriousness of several of the validity threats depends on these features; see Table 8.1.) Second, the experimental designs we will look at are not the only ones available.[23] Third, depending on the unique feature of a given situation and the experimenter's ingenuity, the experimenter may be able to create an ad hoc design to fit the situation by modifying one of the standard designs or borrowing ideas from several of them. In other words, a standard design does not necessarily mean the design should be used without modification. Research in Use 8.3 describes one such experiment, conducted by Hyundai Motor Company to measure marketing effectiveness in rural India.

The designs we will examine in this chapter are classified into two groups: pre-experimental designs and true experimental designs. We will use the following symbolic notation to depict these designs and to aid in easy comparisons

Hyundai Conducts Experimentation Exercise to Measure Marketing Effectiveness in Rural India

Hyundai Motor Company has been employing a novel strategy to both test and increase its brand awareness in rural India. Establishing relationships with key village leaders, company sales representatives give the leaders exclusive test drives of Hyundai vehicles. The next day, the sales representatives return to the village with a van equipped with a video screen, which they use to display Hyundai advertisements to the gathered villagers and leaders. In some cases, the village leader who has been given the exclusive test drive takes the opportunity to announce to those gathered that he has decided to buy the vehicle.

Such experiments allow Hyundai to determine how best to market its vehicles to those in rural areas. The company has identified the best way to increase its brand awareness and its vehicle sales by targeting influential community members, who effectively operate as opinion leaders from whom others seek input and advice before making major decisions—from marriage to large purchases. These field experiments are not conventional research experiments intended to understand relationships between variables. Instead, they are intended to help companies gauge the effectiveness of novel marketing techniques in rural markets.[c]

across designs (this notational scheme is very similar to the schemes followed in several standard books):

O Any formal observation or measurement of the dependent (or effect) variable that is made as part of the experimental study (we will use symbols O_1, O_2, and so on, when two or more measurements are involved during the experiment)

Note: In many experiments, we must also make formal measurements of the independent (causal) variables to make sure the experimental manipulations worked as planned. Such measurements, called **manipulation checks,** will not be explicitly shown in the designs we will look at, to keep the designs simple.[24]

Manipulation checks consist of formal measurements of the independent (or causal) variables to make sure the experimental manipulations worked as planned.

X Exposure of units participating in the study to the experimental manipulation or treatment (we will use symbols X_1, X_2, and so on, when two or more experimental treatments are involved)

Note: The ordering of Os and Xs from left to right will represent the time sequence in which they occur.

The **experimental group** consists of units that get exposed to the experimental treatment.

EG An **experimental group** of units that get exposed to the experimental treatment (we will use symbols EG_1, EG_2, and so on, when the experiment has more than one experimental group)

CG A **control group** of units participating in the experiment but not exposed to the experimental treatment (we will use symbols CG_1, CG_2, and so on, when there are multiple control groups)

The **control group** consists of units participating in the experiment but not exposed to the experimental treatment.

(R) A symbol used to indicate that units participating in the study have been randomly assigned to the groups (more on random assignment later)

Pre–Experimental Designs

Pre-experimental designs exert little or no control over the influence of extraneous factors.

Pre-experimental designs exert little or no control over the influence of extraneous factors. These studies are not much better than descriptive studies when it comes to making causal inferences. Although pre-experimental studies can certainly lead to hypotheses about causal relationships, we cannot have much confidence in the existence of such relationships without additional research. The label "pre-experimental" emphasizes the fact that these studies are more exploratory than conclusive as far as causal inferences are concerned.

Why should we even bother to discuss pre-experimental designs when they are not really experiments? There are two good reasons for doing so. First, studies employing pre-experimental designs often form the basis for causal inferences in the real world, and we need to be aware of their pitfalls to avoid interpreting their findings at face value. Second, comparisons with pre-experimental designs can help highlight the merits of true experimental designs.

∎ One–Group, After–Only Design   Consider the following two situations:

Situation A. A company introduces a new brand of margarine in four test-market areas and employs a unique and revolutionary promotional campaign for it. The brand captures at least a 10 percent share in each market within two months after introduction. The company's management concludes that the revolutionary promotional campaign played a major role in the market share achieved by the brand.

Situation B. The president of the United States makes a television speech soliciting public support for legislation favoring prayer in public schools. A telephone survey of those who viewed the presidential speech indicates that 70 percent favor such legislation. The president's speech is therefore considered to have had a significant impact on the U.S. public.

Each of these situations implies a causal inference. However, although the inferences seem to be intuitively sound, they cannot be entirely trusted. To see why, let's first depict the experimental design underlying the two situations in terms of the symbols defined earlier. Both situations involve the following *one-group, after-only design:*

$$EG \quad X \quad O$$

One group of units (*EG*)—the four test markets in situation A and the television audience for the president's speech in situation B—was exposed to a manipulation (*X*)—the new brand's promotional campaign in situation A and the presidential speech in situation B. Then a single measurement (*O*) was made—the brand's market share in situation A and support for school prayer legislation in situation B. A readily apparent problem with this design is the lack of control of extraneous influences. Stated differently, factors other than *X* may well be partly or fully responsible for the observed results (*O*). Another obvious limitation is the absence of any objective standard against which the results can be compared in ascertaining whether and to what extent *X* influenced *O*.

In situation A, the inference that the promotional campaign was responsible for the brand's market share was quite subjective; it was based on an assumption that the brand's market share would have been significantly less than 10 percent without the promotional campaign. Similarly, in situation B the inferred effectiveness of the president's speech stemmed from a subjective notion that the percentage of respondents favoring the legislation would have been substantially less than 70 percent had the president's speech not been aired. The potential fallacy of such causal inferences based on data from one-group, after-only designs is clear because it is difficult, if not impossible, to interpret any consumer research number in a vacuum. Knowing, for example, that 70 percent of a sample of viewers rated prayer legislation favorably after the president's speech doesn't mean much to anyone without knowing how many held a similarly supportive view before the speech.

■ **One–Group, Before–After Design**   The *one-group, before-after design* is an improvement over the previous design because it includes a premeasurement. The symbolic representation of this design is as follows:

$$EG \quad O_1 \quad X \quad O_2$$

The premeasurement serves as a benchmark against which the postmeasurement is compared to determine the impact of the experimental manipulation. Several experiments described earlier in the chapter to illustrate validity threats—the laboratory experiment to assess the impact of a new Honda commercial on consumers' opinions about Honda cars; the field experiment to study the impact on the brand's sales of a special store display for Dole canned fruits—used this design. Each of these experiments had serious internal validity, and possibly some external validity, problems, as was demonstrated by our discussion in the earlier section. Potential validity threats that can become serious in studies employing the one-group, before-after design are summarized next.

- In laboratory experiments, which invariably involve measurement of consumers, like the one for assessing the impact of the new Honda commercial: maturation effect, pretesting effect, instrument variation effect, reactive bias, and pretest-manipulation interaction bias
- In field experiments involving measurements of stores, like the one for studying the effect of the special store display for Dole canned fruits: history effect and mortality effect
- In field experiments involving measurement of consumers, like the in-home test of the new and improved bathtub and tile cleaner: history effect, pretesting effect, instrument variation effect, mortality effect, reactive bias, and pretest-manipulation interaction bias

Each of these experiments can also suffer from nonrepresentative-sample bias if the units chosen for the experimental study do not adequately represent the total body of units. Of course, nonrepresentative-sample bias stems from inadequate sampling and can occur in any experimental design.

In short, although the one-group, before-after design is slightly better than the one-group, after-only design, its potential validity problems make it no more than a pre-experimental design.

Field experiments can help managers evaluate the effectiveness of alternative store displays.

■ **Two–Group, Ex Post Facto Design** The *two-group, ex post facto design* has two groups of units: one exposed and the other unexposed to the experimental manipulation. There is no premeasurement, and both groups are measured after the manipulation has been introduced. The symbolic representation of this design is as follows:

$$EG \quad X \quad O_1$$
$$CG \qquad O_2$$

Recall situation B, the study to evaluate the effectiveness of the president's speech on school prayer. A major weakness of this study was the absence of a benchmark against which to compare the finding that 70 percent of those who viewed the television speech favored the school prayer legislation. Suppose the telephone survey conducted in this study covered a random sample of the public, including those who did *not* view the speech, instead of being limited to those who viewed it. In other words, let's assume the survey sought the opinions of those who said they viewed the speech as well as those who said they did not. Also, suppose 20 percent of the latter group of respondents (nonviewers) favored the school prayer legislation, in contrast to the 70 percent of the viewers who favored it.

Do these results imply that the president's speech was effective in swaying public opinion in favor of the school prayer legislation? It is tempting to think so, because the experimental group of respondents seems to be much more favorable toward the legislation than the control group. Yielding to such a temptation can be a serious mistake, however. Although opinions from an exposed and an unexposed group were sought and compared, the critical factor is that the groups were self-selected. In other words, determination of who belonged to the experimental group and who belonged to the control group was made solely on the basis of what the respondents said in the survey following the speech. The researcher had no control over the composition of the two groups and hence no way to ensure they had similar feelings about school prayer before the president's speech. For instance, respondents who watched the speech may have shared the president's viewpoints to begin with, including those relating to school prayer. By the same token, the majority of people who did not watch the speech may have been individuals whose opinions were at odds with those of the president. Such a sharp discrepancy between the groups with respect to their prior opinions about school prayer is bound to result in serious selection effect, a major internal validity threat.

The very term *ex post facto* (meaning "after the fact") in the label for this design underlines its inherent weakness: that the compositions of *EG* and *CG* are determined *after* the manipulation has been introduced, with no way to ensure prior similarity between the groups. An additional problem associated with self-selection when consumers are involved is that some, either intentionally or unintentionally, might state that they were exposed to the manipulation when they really were not, or vice versa. Hence, there is no guarantee that all units in *EG* were exposed to *X* and that all units in *CG* were not exposed to *X*.

Why the ex post facto design is a pre-experimental design should be clear by now. The results of a study using this design are no better than cross-tabulations or correlation of data obtained through descriptive research studies. Because the researcher has no control over group composition or overexposure or non-exposure to the manipulation, any causal inference is based solely on the post-measurement survey. Specifically, the survey data on the dependent variable are cross-tabulated according to units that happened to be exposed to the manipulation and those that happened not to be. To make causal inferences merely from evidence of associations is risky. Yet it is not uncommon to find causal inferences being made on the basis of studies using a two-group, ex post facto design. A case in point is the example discussed earlier concerning the impact of MTV on sales of Linkin Park albums in the United States. Researchers and managers must be wary of such causal inferences.

True Experimental Designs

True experimental designs have built-in safeguards for controlling all threats to internal and external validity.

In sharp contrast to pre-experimental designs, **true experimental designs** have built-in safeguards for controlling all threats to internal and external validity. As we will see, the effectiveness with which various threats are neutralized by true experimental designs may still depend to some extent on the context in which they are applied. Nevertheless, these designs are generally far superior to pre-experimental designs in terms of making causal inferences with confidence.

True experimental designs have two key features that enable them to exercise tight control over extraneous influences: the presence of one or more control groups and, more important, the random assignment of units to various experimental and control groups. **Random assignment** distributes the sample units chosen for a study to various groups on a strictly objective basis, so that the group compositions can be equivalent before starting the experiment. As Louise Kidder observes,

> Random assignment controls for the influence of all the extraneous subject [sample unit] variables that you do not want to study but also do not want to hold constant because holding them constant limits the generalizability of your study. It is the defining feature of a true experiment.[25]

Because random assignment is a critical characteristic of true experiments, we should examine how it differs from an alternative, often-used approach for ensuring group equivalence called *matching*. **Matching** forms groups in such a way that the composition of units is similar across groups with respect to one or more specific characteristics.[26] To illustrate, suppose a sample of respondents is to be divided into two groups in a laboratory experiment for testing the relative effectiveness of two different commercials for a new car. Assuming that respondents' income levels, for instance, might have a bearing on how they react to the commercials, forming two matched groups ensures that the two groups have similar income distributions. Any differences in reactions to the two commercials that can be attributed to income levels will then cancel out between the two groups.

A potential limitation of matching, however, is that the groups can differ on key characteristics on which they are not explicitly matched. For example, the two groups with matched income distributions may differ significantly on characteristics such as their interests and driving habits, which in turn may result in differential impact of the commercials, thereby lowering internal validity. Another practical limitation of matching is that data on the matching characteristics must be readily available in order to form the groups. Matching obviously will not be possible when such data are not available.

Random assignment, in contrast to matching, equalizes groups on all relevant characteristics, with no special emphasis on any one characteristic. Furthermore, random assignment does not require any data on characteristics of the initial sample of units. Between matching and random assignment, the latter is therefore the generally recommended approach for forming equivalent groups.

Strict random assignment may not always be desirable. Specifically, forming matched sets of units first and then randomly assigning units within each set to the various groups may be a better strategy when the number of units available for an experimental study is small. For instance, consider a field experiment to test the effectiveness of point-of-purchase material for a brand of cookies. Let's say that eight supermarkets in a test area have agreed to participate in the experiment. Four of the eight stores are to be in an experimental group in which the point-of-purchase material will be displayed, and the rest are to form a control group.

Assigning four stores each to the experimental and control groups on a completely random basis may be risky in this case. For instance, what if the four stores in one group turn out be the largest of the eight? Or what if all four stores happen to be located in neighborhoods that are wealthier than those in which the other stores are located? The obvious danger here is that the skewed group compositions will lead to the selection effect. Therefore, a better procedure is to first form pairs of stores subjectively so that the stores within each paired set are similar on critical characteristics, such as size and location. This pairing results in four pairs of stores. One store from each pair is now randomly selected and assigned to one group (experimental or control), and the remaining store is assigned to the other group.

■ **Two–Group, Before–After Design**   One type of true experimental design is the *two-group, before-after design*. Its symbolic representation is as follows:

$$EG(R) \quad O_1 \quad X \quad O_2$$
$$CG(R) \quad O_3 \quad\quad O_4$$

We will first examine the general features of this design and then discuss specific applications. Because the study units in this design are randomly assigned to *EG* and *CG*, the two groups can be considered equivalent. In other words, they will be influenced by the same extraneous factors and are likely to go through similar experiences, except for the exposure to the experimental manipulation (X), which will occur in *EG* but not in *CG*. Therefore, the difference between the pre- and postmeasurements of *CG* (that is, $O_4 - O_3$) should give a good indication of all extraneous influences experienced by *EG*. The difference between the pre- and postmeasurements of *EG* (that is, $O_2 - O_1$) reflects the impact of X as well as any extraneous influences. Hence, the true impact of X is given by

$$(O_2 - O_1) - (O_4 - O_3)$$

This expression completely accounts for and neutralizes all validity threats except for the mortality effect, reactive bias, pretest-manipulation interaction bias, and nonrepresentative-sample bias.

We will now look at three illustrative applications of the two-group, before-after design.

Experiment 1. A field experiment is conducted to study the impact of a price reduction on the sales of a brand of paper towels. A sample of 50 supermarkets in a designated region is divided into *EG* and *CG*, each containing 25 stores, through random assignment. Unit sales of the paper towel brand are monitored for a four-week period in *EG* and *CG*, and constitute the O_1 and O_3 measurements. Then the price of the brand is reduced 10 percent (that is, X is introduced) in *EG* but is left unchanged in *CG* for a four-week period. Unit sales are once again monitored during this period to yield the O_2 and O_4 measurements.

Experiment 2. A field experiment is conducted to measure the impact of a two-page brochure describing the harmful effects of sugar on consumption of sugar-free soft drinks. A sample of 200 households is chosen from an area. Half the sample is randomly assigned to *EG* and the other half to *CG*. A questionnaire about general food consumption behavior is completed by all households. Part of this questionnaire deals with current consumption levels of sugar-free soft drinks in the various households and provides the O_1 and O_3 measurements. A booklet on general nutrition and good eating habits is left behind in all households, with one key difference: the booklets given to households in *EG* contain the two-page brochure on the ill effects of sugar, but those given to households in *CG* do not. The heads of households in both groups are requested to read the booklets at their leisure. After an interval of three months, the households are recontacted and requested to fill out the same questionnaire once again. The O_2 and O_4 measurements are obtained through this questionnaire.

Experiment 3. A laboratory experiment is conducted to determine the impact of a personal computer commercial (demonstrating how easy it is to use the product) on consumer perceptions about its ease of use. One hundred consumers are recruited for this experiment and randomly divided into two groups (*EG* and *CG*). Both groups are administered a questionnaire dealing with a variety of home appliances. Through this questionnaire, current perceptions about the personal computer are measured (O_1 and O_3). The *EG* and the *CG* are then shown, in different viewing rooms, the same hour-long television program that includes commercials for a variety of products. The test commercial (*X*) is inserted in the version of the program seen by *EG* but not by *CG*. Then the relevant O_2 and O_4 measurements are obtained through the same questionnaire.

The type of validity threats present and their degree of seriousness vary somewhat across experiments 1, 2, and 3, even though all three employ the same design. Table 8.2 lists the validity threats and, for each experiment, indicates which threats are controlled by the design and which are not.

■ **Modified Designs** The standard experimental designs we have examined are not the only ones available for studying causal associations between variables. We can modify standard designs to fit a given situation by incorporating specific features and controls germane to the situation. Marketing researchers frequently employ modified designs like the one used in the controlled market testing by Marketing Evolution. Research in Use 8.4 illustrates how Marketing Evolution used an experiment to study the effectiveness of multimedia communication of the 2004 Ford F-150 launch.

TABLE 8.2
Validity Threats in Experiments 1, 2, and 3

Type of Threat	Experiment 1	Experiment 2	Experiment 3
History effect	May occur but is controlled	May occur but is controlled	Unlikely to occur controlled
Maturation effect	May occur but is controlled	May occur but is controlled	May occur but is controlled
Pretesting effect	Unlikely to occur	May occur but is controlled	May occur but is controlled
Instrument variation effect	Unlikely to occur	May occur but is controlled	May occur but is controlled
Selection effect	Unlikely to occur	Unlikely to occur	May occur but is controlled
Mortality effect	May occur; whether it does depends on the nature of the units dropping out	May occur; whether it does depends on the nature of the units dropping out	Unlikely to occur
Reactive bias	Unlikely to occur	May occur; if so, the *EG* and *CG* equivalence should still preserve internal validity, although external validity may be lowered	May occur; if so, the *EG* and *CG* equivalence should still preserve internal validity, although external validity may be lowered
Pretest-manipulation interaction effect	Unlikely to occur	May occur; if so, it is not controlled	May occur; if so, it is not controlled

Note: Nonrepresentative-sample bias is not listed because it stems from inadequacies in initial sample selection and is not unique to any particular experimental design.

2004 Ford F-150 Launch: Multimedia Experimentation to Study Communication Effectiveness

Companies are employing the so-called surround-sound strategy, recognizing that consumers are influenced by multiple marketing cues from TV, the Internet, cell phones, radio, magazines, and so on. Trying to assess the effectiveness of multimedia advertising is a difficult task. It became an important priority for Ford when it launched its 2004 F-150. The F-150 has been the top-selling truck for 22 years, but the Chevrolet Silverado and Dodge Ram are challenging its leadership position. To retain its position, Ford launched the 2004 F-150 with the biggest ad blitz in its history. In the first two months of the campaign, Ford spent over $60 million in advertising, nearly 90 percent of which went to television. On average, each male between the ages of 25 and 49 saw the F-150 ad 30 times during the 60-day launch period. The online campaign employed pop-up ads in major auto-related websites, as well as "portal roadblocks." Portal roadblocks involve the simultaneous display of ads on multiple sites. The online roadblock campaign reinforced the F-150's "rugged and tough" image. Ford also used radio, print, outdoor, and direct-mail ads to support the launch.

Marketing Evolution, an online marketing research company, conducted a cross-media optimization study (XMOS). XMOS uses a combination of time series and factorial experimental designs to isolate the effects of different media messages such as radio and online ads. XMOS employs an experimental design in which matched markets and ads are used to create identical "exposed" and "control" groups. XMOS translates campaign goals into survey questions and uses the participants' responses to quantify each branding metric. Typically, XMOS measures three core branding metrics: brand awareness (unaided and aided), brand image, and intent to take action (pur-

chase of the product). In addition, XMOS measures actual sales to analyze both the branding and the sales effects.

XMOS assessed the F-150 campaign's effectiveness by surveying over 10,000 consumers and partitioning them into various exposure groups based on the experimental design. Then, by linking sales data to attitudinal branding metrics, XMOS isolated the impacts of different promotional elements, such as magazine ads, online banners, and TV commercials. XMOS even facilitated examining the impact of promotional sponsorships of events like the Texas Rodeo, which had the F-150 on display. The sophisticated experimental design employed by XMOS enabled the assessment of both individual and combined effects of the various components of the promotional campaign.

The results showed that brand recall rose 26 percent over the six-month campaign. There was a large improvement in brand image over the course of the campaign. Ford's F-150 campaign created strong branding results across the board. The results also revealed variability in advertising's impact on branding metrics across the different media. For instance, although all types of ads significantly influenced branding metrics, television ads were the most effective at achieving high levels on the so-called "upper funnel" metrics, such as brand recall and image.

Marketing Evolution examined the incremental sales impact of online advertising by comparing the purchases of a group of customers exposed to the advertising with those of an unexposed (control) group. The results showed that sales of the F-150 were 20 percent higher in the exposed group than in the control group. In sum, the incremental impact caused by online advertisements accounted for 6 percent of total vehicle sales.[d]

Some modified designs are quite sophisticated and are capable of measuring the relative effectiveness of multiple treatments within the same study (such as four versions of a television commercial for a product) or the influence of different levels of more than one independent variable (three different price levels in combination with two types of promotion). Such designs are sometimes called *statistical designs* because they require somewhat complex data analysis procedures for sorting out the separate effects of multiple independent variables or treatment levels. Interested readers can refer to this textbook's website for more discussion on these designs.

SUMMARY

Experimentation is research conducted to examine causal associations between variables under controlled conditions. Three conditions must be satisfied for inferring that one variable is the cause of another: (1) temporal ordering of variables—if variable 1 is inferred to have a causal effect on variable 2, variable 1 must occur first; (2) evidence of association—the data on the two variables must show a definite relationship; and (3) control of other causal factors—accounting for all extraneous influences on the two variables and their relationships.

There are two approaches to conducting experimental research: laboratory experiments and field experiments. A laboratory experiment uses an artificial setting under tightly controlled conditions. It generally offers better internal validity (assurance that the results obtained are solely due to the experimental manipulation) than a field experiment, which uses a natural setting with as much control as possible. A key drawback of laboratory experiments is that the results obtained may not be generalizable beyond the experimental setting, thereby lowering external validity. Choosing which approach to use depends on time, cost, exposure to competition, and nature of the manipulation.

There are six standard threats to the internal validity of experiments: the history, maturation, pretesting, instrument variation, selection, and mortality effects. These threats also indirectly affect external validity because generalizing results that lack internal validity is meaningless. Direct threats to external validity include reactive bias, pretest-manipulation interaction bias, and nonrepresentative-sample bias.

Not all threats to internal and external validity are necessarily present in every experiment. Factors such as whether an experiment is a laboratory or a field experiment and whether the units of observation are consumers or stores play a role in determining which threats are serious.

This chapter covered two broad classes of experimental designs: pre-experimental and true experimental designs. Pre-experimental designs offer little or no control over extraneous factors. The least rigorous of pre-experimental designs is the one-group, after-only design. This design not only lacks control of extraneous factors but also has no explicit benchmark against which to compare the experimental results.

An improvement over the preceding design is the one-group, before-after design, which provides a benchmark in the form of premeasurement. But causal inferences from studies employing one-group, before-after designs are still quite risky because there is no control over many of the various validity threats.

A third pre-experimental design is the two-group, ex post facto design. This design provides an unexposed control group against which the experimental group can be compared. Unfortunately, the two groups are essentially self-selected and are formed after the experimental manipulation is introduced. It reduces one's confidence in causal inferences stemming from the use of this design. Causal inferences from studies using pre-experimental designs are tentative at best.

True experimental designs differ from pre-experimental designs in two key ways: (1) they have one or more control groups (established before the start of an experiment) and (2) the various experimental and control groups are always formed through random assignment of the initial sample of units. Random assignment theoretically ensures equivalence among the groups on all characteristics, so that any selection effect can be ruled out. A commonly used true experimental design is the two-group, before-after design. This design is sound except for one major problem inherent in the design itself—namely, the threat of pretest-manipulation interaction bias when consumers are involved.

As we have seen, researchers wishing to use experimentation have a varied palette of designs to work with. Ultimately the choice falls to the design that best matches the requirements set forth by whomever is sponsoring the research.

ACE self-test

REVIEW AND DISCUSSION QUESTIONS

1. Distinguish between laboratory and field experiments, pointing out the relative strengths and weaknesses of each.

2. Apart from validity considerations, what factors play a role in the choice between laboratory and field experiments?

3. Briefly describe simulated test-markets and their strengths.

4. "Instrument variation effect will not be a problem as long as the researcher is very careful and consistent." Discuss the extent to which this statement is likely to be true.

5. Can the mortality effect lower external validity in any way? Why or why not?

6. Would the internal validity of a laboratory experiment using the one-group, before-after design be higher than that of a field experiment using the same design? Explain your answer.

7. "Pre-experimental designs are helpful in generating hypotheses about causal relationships between variables." Discuss this statement.

8. In what ways does a true experimental design differ from a pre-experimental design?

APPLICATION EXERCISES

1. Toys & Games is a toy store located in a shopping mall. Toys & Games ran a major in-store promotion (consisting of special displays and price reductions) during the last quarter (October to December) of each of the past five years. Every year, without fail, its sales in the last quarter were at least 25 percent higher than sales in any of the previous quarters. Thus the store manager is seriously thinking about expanding the in-store promotion to at least one other quarter each year. What advice would you give the store manager? Discuss your answer from the perspective of the three conditions for inferring causality. Is this experiment a laboratory or a field experiment? Does it involve consumers or stores? Go through the list of internal and external validity threats we discussed and indicate which are and which are not likely to be serious in this experiment.

2. A food products company has designed a new and improved container for its brand of peanut butter, which will reduce waste and maintain freshness over a longer period of time. However, this container will increase the product's price by 30 percent. The company wants to ascertain whether and to what extent the new and improved container will affect sales of its peanut butter. Propose an appropriate experimental approach that can provide the information desired. Defend your answer.

3. ABC Company sells a line of packaged food products. It recently test-marketed a new frozen dessert. This product achieved a 5 percent share of the frozen-dessert market in the test area within a period of six months. On the basis of this result, the firm decided to introduce the frozen dessert nationally because, in the opinion of ABC's marketing manager, "New food products typically achieve only a 2 to 3 percent market share at the end of the year they are introduced." What specific experimental design and causal inference are implied in this scenario? What is your evaluation of the validity of the implied causal inference? Explain your answer.

4. A national retail store chain has 1,500 stores dispersed throughout the country. The chain's management wants to test the relative impact of two different, special in-store promotional displays (X_1 and X_2) on individual stores' sales. It also wants to know whether not having any special in-store promotional display is necessarily worse than having X_1 or X_2. Create and describe an appropriate true experimental design capable of meeting management's information needs.

5. Suppose you are the marketing manager for Nabisco. You are interested in finding consumer reactions to the taste of your cookie relative to other brands and the effect of increasing your price by 25 percent. Design an experiment to test the taste of your cookie relative to that of the leading competitor. Also design an experiment to test the effects of the price increase.

 ## INTERNET EXERCISES

1. Go to the homepage of the Virtual Customer Center at MIT (mitsloan.mit.edu/vc) and examine one of the various experimental studies presented at the website. Assess what the independent variables are, the levels within each variable, and the dependent variable. What are the advantages and disadvantages of Web-based experimentation?

2. A grocery store in a certain town plans to run a full-page ad in the town's newspaper offering either a double-coupon or a triple-coupon deal; that is, the store would redeem manufacturers' coupons at two or three times their face value. The firm has a comprehensive database of its customers, including e-mails. How will you develop a Web-based experiment to help the grocery firm?

 ## CASE 8.1 THE POLAROID I-ZONE CAMERA[1]
(http://www.i-zone.com/izone/index.jsp)

The new-product development team at Polaroid was excited about a new version of a product concept that was under development. It involved an instant pocket camera that took mini, 1- to 1.5-inch pictures—about the size of a postage stamp. The camera would be targeted toward teens as a fun way to express themselves by decorating lockers, notebooks, and other belongings; collecting them; or sharing them with friends. The concept for the film was that it would come in two different types: regular instant and instant with a sticky backing to adhere the photos to belongings. The team was making arrangements for concept testing, with the anticipation that a new version of the product would be introduced to the market in a short period of time.

Polaroid Corporation

Polaroid Corporation is the worldwide leader in instant imaging. The only manufacturer of traditional chemical-based instant cameras and film in the United States, Polaroid supplies instant photographic cameras and films; digital-imaging hardware, software, and media; identification systems; and sunglasses to markets worldwide. Leveraging its widely recognized brand name, global distribution network, and technical expertise, it has built its strategy for growth around the revitalization of its core imaging business. Central to its success is the introduction of new products and product line extensions penetrating new demographic segments, such as children, teens, and young adults. Its success is also based on further reducing the time it takes to bring new products to market and increasing the efficiency of the entire process.

Polaroid New-Product Development and Testing

During 1999, Polaroid developed a new-product concept for an instant camera and film for personal photography marketed to teens. The first version of the pocket camera, the Xiao, was made available in Japan as a regional test in cooperation with Tomy, a Japanese toy company. Marketed as the world's smallest instant camera and film, the product line was extended in 2000 to include a number of new colors. The development of a third version for global marketing was under way. Research for this version was conducted with the help of the Virtual Customer Initiative (VCI) at the Massachusetts Institute of Technology (MIT).[2]

In order to determine the most attractive options for the next version of the camera, additional research was conducted. During the early stages of its development, researchers identified several different product features with the most promise of adoption by teen consumers: picture quality, number of steps in the picture-taking process, picture removal method, light selection method, style of cover, and camera opening.[3] (The different options for each feature are presented in Table 1.) They also included results of a consumer research study conducted for the Polaroid i-Zone Pocket Camera team by Meghan McArdle as her MIT master's thesis.[4] The research was conducted through the VCI under the supervision of Dr. John Hauser at MIT's Sloan School of Management, in collaboration with MIT's Center for Innovation in Product Development. Consumer data were collected using two parallel data collection regimes—one a mall intercept with central-location interviewing and one with Web-based interviewing, via a website designed specifically for the purpose of data collection.[5] Although the response rates varied, the basic managerial implications were quite similar. Meghan McArdle and the Web designer, Limor Weisberg, studied the websites that were popular with the target market. They then tried to create a new design that would appeal to that target market. It included a unique series of simulated "demos" of different product features, animated so that the respondents could better understand the camera in use. The demos were cleverly designed and very important for clearly conveying key usage information. The "picture quality"

TABLE 1
Options for the Six Camera Features

Product Features	Option A	Option B
Picture quality	Good	Average
Picture taking	*1-step action:* Press the button to take the picture.	*2-step action:* Select scenery setting, then press the button to take the picture.
Picture removal method	Picture comes out automatically.	Picture must be manually removed.
Light selection method	*Feedback:* Light settings selector must be moved until an indicator light comes on, indicating the best picture.	*3 settings:* Slide indicator to one of three different settings without feedback on best picture setting.
Style cover	Can switch the outside cover to a new style or cover.	Fixed cover that cannot be switched.
Opening camera	A protective sleeve must be slid back from over the lens.	Fixed cover that does not cover the lens.

feature was a real challenge. Polaroid, with the help of Meghan and Limor, developed a demonstration of final picture quality that would display well on the Web.

The use of Web-based technology for data collection offers an attractive research method because it is both an efficient means to reduce the time to market and a cost-effective way to assess the desirability of different features of a new-product design without having to first build the product. The need to reach young teens in an ethically appropriate manner, however, added time and expense to the research. It required a complicated recruitment process to obtain parental permission and assure privacy and security, because these issues were a high priority for those involved with the research. Polaroid product development managers specifically ruled out going directly to teens, for obvious privacy reasons, so teens were recruited to participate while they were with a parent at one of five mall locations located across the United States. A unique user ID and password were set up for each respondent to access the study's website and complete the questionnaire.

The desirability of the different product feature options was assessed using three techniques. First, a straight comparison of different features was conducted, in which respondents were asked to pick which option

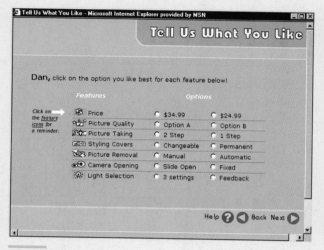

Exhibit 1
Straight Comparison Task
The image included in this figure is open-source GNU licensed and can be used freely. GNU Lesser General Public License is available at www.mitsloan.mit.edu/vc. Screen shot reprinted with permission from Microsoft Corporation.

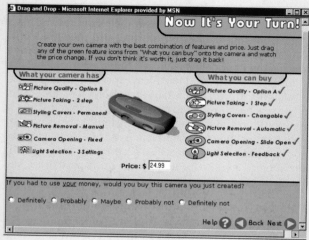

Exhibit 3
Drag-and-Drop Exercise
The image included in this figure is open-source GNU licensed and can be used freely. GNU Lesser General Public License is available at www.mitsloan.mit.edu/vc. Screen shot reprinted with permission from Microsoft Corporation.

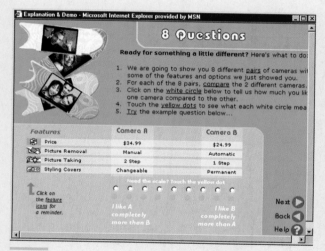

Exhibit 2
Sample Conjoint Analysis Page
The image included in this figure is open-source GNU licensed and can be used freely. GNU Lesser General Public License is available at www.mitsloan.mit.edu/vc. Screen shot reprinted with permission from Microsoft Corporation.

they preferred for each feature. Exhibit 1 presents an image of the screen associated with the straight comparison task. Second, the tradeoffs of different combinations of options for the camera were assessed using a technique called *conjoint analysis*.[6] This involved respondents' being shown two versions of the product, after which they were asked to indicate their relative preference for one version over the other. Exhibit 2 presents an image of one of the screens associated with the conjoint analysis. In total, respondents were asked to indicate

their relative preference for a total of eight paired comparisons. Finally, an experimental drag-and-drop task was used. This provided respondents with an interesting and interactive activity in which they could express what they really wanted, unconstrained by the limitations associated with the first two tasks.[7] In the drag-and-drop exercise, the respondents were shown a baseline camera with a starting price of $24.99 and a list of options consistent with the options they were shown throughout the survey. They were then provided with the list of six options that they could opt to "buy." They would then "buy" an option by dragging the corresponding icon onto the camera. The price changed accordingly with each added option. Exhibit 3 presents an image of the screen associated with the drag-and-drop exercise. After respondents completed the task of designing their own version, they were asked if they would purchase the camera with their own money. The results of the study confirmed the direction of the feature-set options, which included a sleek design and changeable faceplates.

Rollout of the i-Zone Instant Pocket Camera

After the results of the research confirmed the most desirable features for the camera design, the Polaroid i-Zone Instant Pocket Camera and film were introduced. The third version of the new product was introduced in 2001 as a smaller, sleeker, customizable version of earlier models, with changeable faceplates. It sold for $24.99 and was offered with good picture quality, one-step picture-taking action, manual picture removal, three-setting light selection, and a fixed-style cover and opening.

CASE QUESTIONS

1. Do you consider the study experimental? If so, what type? Explain your answers.

2. Identify the causal and effect variables. Does the design meet the necessary conditions for causality? Justify your answers.

3. Identify and describe threats to internal and external validity in this type of study.

4. What are the strategic implications of using this method of marketing research?

CASE NOTES

1. www.i-zone.com/izone/index.jsp; www.polaroid.com/global/detail.jsp?PRODUCT%3C%3Eprd_id=845524441759921&FOLDER%3C%3Efolder_id=2534374302023757&bmUID=1103233246889&bmLocale=en_US. Courtesy of Polaroid Corporation.

2. Focusing on the Internet as a medium, the Virtual Customer Initiative (VC) encourages the development of methods that can be used throughout the product development process to make customer-driven design decisions using techniques like Voice of the Customer (VOC) and conjoint analysis. Additional information about the program is available at www.mitsloan.mit.edu/vc/.

3. Researchers conducted this analysis based on two sources of information: (1) the new-product development team's rank ordering of a set of 10 initial features in terms of appeal to teen consumers and (2) tapes of previous focus groups conducted with teens on the topic.

4. Additional detail is available from Meghan P. McArdle (2000), "Internet-based Rapid Customer Feedback for Design Feature Tradeoff Analyses," submitted to the Sloan School of Management and the Department of Mechanical Engineering in Partial Fulfillment of the Requirements for the Degrees of Master of Science in Management and Master of Science in Mechanical Engineering at the Massachusetts Institute of Technology, June 2000. ©2000 Massachusetts Institute of Technology.

5. A demonstration of the exercise can be viewed by accessing and responding to the questions at http://conjoint.mit.edu/demos/camera/PagesUD/logon-demo.html.

6. For additional information about conjoint analysis, see Chapter 15.

7. It was also a test of a novel Internet survey methodology for research purposes.

This case was written by Jeanne L. Munger (University of Southern Maine) in collaboration with the textbook authors, as a basis for class discussion rather than to illustrate either effective or ineffective marketing practice.

CASE 8.2 LANDS' END
(www.landsend.com)

With sales revenues over $1.3 billion, Lands' End Inc. is one of the leading catalogue companies in the United States. It markets traditionally styled casual clothing, shoes, and accessories for men, women, and children, along with items for the home. With approximately 269 million full-price catalogues mailed worldwide during the year 2000, the company exported products to more than 185 countries. The company is known for offering quality merchandise at competitive prices, backed by an unconditional guarantee. Roughly three-quarters of catalogue orders are placed by telephone, with the remainder from the Internet, mail, and fax.

Growth in Internet Sales

Lands' End enjoys a strong presence on the Internet, with merchandise sales growing from $61 million in 1999 to $138 million in 2000 to an impressive $218 million in 2001. In fact, www.landsend.com has been widely recognized as an outstanding website to shop. The National Retail Federation identified landsend.com as the largest seller of apparel online, and *Fortune* magazine[1] named it as a notable site to shop, based on level of comfort and shopping convenience. It offers the full line of Lands' End products year round, using a dynamic, innovative Internet shopping experience designed to attract new customers and better serve existing customers.

Personal Shopper Service

One of its recent innovations has been My Personal Shopper (MPS), which debuted in November 2000. Much like the services of an expert personal shopper, MPS provides product suggestions that best match a shopper's unique preferences. It is designed to save shoppers time and effort when selecting clothing online, through the use of conjoint analysis—the first use of this technique by an online retailer.

The first step asks consumers to select men's or women's items. In the second step, consumers complete a set of personal profile questions (see Exhibit 1). The third step is for consumers to simply complete a short questionnaire by noting their preferences in a series of six pairs of outfits using a five-item scale (see Exhibit 2). The fourth step is to identify consumers' aversions to fabrics, colors, and styles (see Exhibit 3).

The information is then used to sort through the more than 90,000 apparel options available at www.landsend.com, to immediately recommend the most suitable items based on the shopper's preferences (see Exhibit 4). Consumers can obtain recommendations for work or leisure occasions from a wide variety of clothing product lines. The analysis incorporates preferences for different color combinations, contemporary or classical styles, and levels of formality for both men and women. In addition to this, women specify their body shape in terms of the proportionality of their waist, hip, and bust measurements.

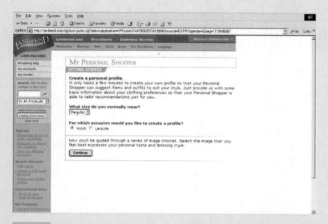

Exhibit 1
Personal Profile Questions
© 2005 Lands' End, Inc. Used with permission. Screen shot reprinted with permission from Microsoft Corporation.

Exhibit 2
Outfit Preference
© 2005 Lands' End, Inc. Used with permission. Screen shot reprinted with permission from Microsoft Corporation.

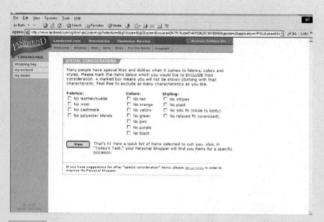

Exhibit 3
Special Considerations
© 2005 Lands' End, Inc. Used with permission. Screen shot reprinted with permission from Microsoft Corporation.

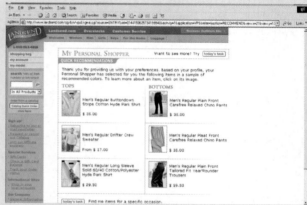

Exhibit 4
Quick Recommendations
© 2005 Lands' End, Inc. Used with permission. Screen shot reprinted with permission from Microsoft Corporation.

CASE QUESTIONS

1. Suppose Lands' End is interested in assessing the effectiveness of its My Personal Shopper service (MPS). Construct a true experiment to assess the effectiveness of MPS. What are some alternative experimental approaches that Lands' End could use?

2. In the experiments you proposed in response to the previous question, identify the dependent and independent variables. For each experiment, explain how you would examine the results to determine whether the MPS service provides value to consumers.

3. Assess the extent to which the personal shopper program incorporates all important attributes of the process of purchasing men's or women's clothing. Can you suggest additional attributes that might be involved?

CASE NOTE

1. It was named by *Fortune*'s *Technology Guide* for the 2000/2001 holiday season.

This case was written by Jeanne L. Munger (University of Southern Maine) in collaboration with the textbook authors, as a basis for class discussion rather than to illustrate either effective or ineffective marketing practice.

Data Collection: Measurement Instruments and Sampling

Part Three

Chapter Objectives

After reading and understanding the material in this chapter, you should be able to:

- Identify the four levels of measurement under which numbers generated through a survey can be classified.

- Distinguish among attributes, behavioral variables, beliefs, and attitudes.

- List and describe five methods for inferring people's attitudes.

- Discuss the various dimensions on which rating scales can vary.

- Apply the formats of Likert, semantic-differential, and Stapel scales, and discuss how the data generated by these scales are analyzed and interpreted.

- Define the validity, reliability, and sensitivity of a scale.

The Most Reputable Companies in the United States[1]

Johnson & Johnson, 3M, Coca-Cola, Procter & Gamble, United Parcel Service, Microsoft, and Sony were found to be the nation's most reputable by a Harris Interactive (www.harrisinteractive.com) U.S.-based survey. The top 10 corporations are listed in the following table.

Rank	Company	Reputation Quotient Score
1	Johnson & Johnson	79.81
2	3M	79.07
3	The Coca-Cola Company	78.90
4	Procter & Gamble	78.26
5	United Parcel Service (UPS)	78.24
6	Microsoft Corporation	78.00
7	Sony Corporation	77.95
8	FedEx	77.49
9	General Mills	77.42
10	Honda Motor Co.	76.15

The survey was based on a lengthy nomination phase in which more than 10,000 respondents (4,063 by telephone and 5,975 online) were interviewed to identify the top 60 reputable firms. More than 21,000 online respondents were then asked to rate one or two companies on 20 attributes using a seven-point

scale. On average, each company was rated by 600 respondents. The various attributes form six dimensions:

- Emotional Appeal
  1. Good feeling about the company
  2. Admire and respect the company
  3. Trust the company

- Products and Services
  4. Stands behind products/services
  5. Offers high-quality products/services
  6. Develops innovative products/services
  7. Offers products/services that are good value

- Workplace Environment
  8. Is well managed
  9. Looks like a good company to work for
  10. Looks like it has good employees

- Social Responsibility
  11. Supports good causes
  12. Environmentally responsible
  13. Treats people well

- Vision and Leadership
  14. Has excellent leadership
  15. Has a clear vision for the future
  16. Recognizes/takes advantage of market opportunities

- Financial Performance
  17. Record of profitability
  18. Looks like a low-risk investment
  19. Strong prospects for future growth
  20. Tends to outperform its competitors

The summed score on these 20 items formed the reputation score reported in the table. ■

The key to the assessment of reputations of and attitudes toward top companies is the use of sound measurement techniques. This chapter focuses on measuring or quantifying customer responses to different types of survey questions, with particular emphasis on data dealing with people's feelings, opinions, and the like. A typical definition of **measurement** is the assignment of numbers to responses, based on a set of guidelines.

Measurement is the assignment of numbers to responses, based on a set of guidelines.

Assigning numbers to responses has two potential benefits. First, we can more efficiently and economically summarize quantified responses from a large sample than we can nonquantified responses. Second, we can manipulate quantified responses by using a variety of mathematical techniques. The results of the data analyses can provide rich insights that may go undiscovered if we examine merely unquantified responses. Despite these attractive advantages, however, assigning numbers to survey responses in a meaningful fashion is no easy task. It is especially difficult in global marketing research.

In global research, we need to be concerned about whether the scales are comparable across countries.[2] As we'll see shortly, depending on the nature of the questions and the responses being quantified, the numbers assigned may not possess all the mathematical properties commonly attributed to the number system. Therefore, we need a thorough understanding of what the scaled responses represent to determine the types of analyses we can legitimately perform with the collected data.[3] The next section describes four types of scales representing different levels of quantified responses and the numerical properties of each.

Measurement Levels

Let's briefly review the nature of the number system. Any set of numbers—say, 3, 6, 9, 12, 24, and 36—has certain basic properties. First, the numbers follow a rank order; thus 9 is greater than 3, 12 is less than 24, and so on. Second, the differences, or intervals, between pairs of numbers can be compared. Thus the interval between 6 and 3 is the same as the interval between 9 and 6; the interval between 36 and 24 is twice the interval between 12 and 6; and so on. Third, we can divide one number by another and interpret the resulting ratio as being indicative of the relative magnitudes of the two numbers. Thus 6 is twice as large as 3 because $6/3 = 2$, 12 is one-third as large as 36 because $36/3 = 12$, and so on. We can compute and interpret ratios of numbers because the number system has a unique zero point. In other words, all elements within the number system are measured from the same starting point—namely, zero.

Although the three properties of the number system are obvious and invariably taken for granted, they are of special significance in the context of quantifying survey responses because it is not always appropriate to interpret quantified responses as if they were numbers. Quantified responses fall into one of four measurement levels (also known as *scales of measurement*): nominal, ordinal, interval, and ratio, with varying properties. We will examine each level of measurement next.

Nominal–Scaled Responses

On a **nominal scale,** numbers are no more than labels and are used solely to identify different categories of responses.

In a **nominal scale,** numbers are no more than labels and are used solely to identify different categories of responses. The following examples illustrate:

What is your gender?

1. ❑ Male
2. ❑ Female

Which one of the following media influences your purchasing decisions the most?

1. ❑ Television
2. ❑ Radio
3. ❑ Newspapers
4. ❑ Magazines
5. ❑ Internet

The numbers accompanying the response categories in these questions have none of the three properties described earlier. They do not imply any particular rank ordering of the responses. Moreover, the intervals between and the ratios of pairs of these numbers reveal nothing about the nature of the responses. That these numbers form no more than a nominal scale is easily demonstrated by the fact that any set of numbers can be used to represent the response categories. For example, the following numbers would serve to describe the responses just as well as the numbers previously used:

265	Male		600	Television
575	Female		755	Radio
			523	Newspapers
			524	Magazines
			525	Internet

The **mode** is the most frequent category.

Central tendency is a number depicting the "middle" position in a given range or distribution of numbers.

An **ordinal scale** is more powerful than a nominal scale in that the numbers possess the property of rank order.

The only permissible mathematical operation with nominal-scaled responses is counting the number of responses falling within each category. After counting, we can report, for instance, that 75 percent of the respondents checked category 600 in answering the media question, and hence 600 is the **mode**—the most frequently checked response category. Determining any measure of **central tendency**—a number depicting the "middle" position in a given range or distribution of numbers—other than the mode is inappropriate when response categories form only a nominal scale.

Ordinal–Scaled Responses

An **ordinal scale** is more powerful than a nominal scale in that the numbers possess the property of rank order. Consider the following question:

How long do you spend reading newspapers on a typical weekday?

1. ❑ Less than 5 minutes
2. ❑ 5 minutes to less than 15 minutes
3. ❑ 15 minutes to less than 30 minutes
4. ❑ 30 minutes or more

In addition to serving as labels, the scale values of 1, 2, 3, and 4 assigned to the response categories provide an indication of the extent of newspaper reading. For instance, a respondent checking category 4 spends more time reading newspapers than one checking category 3; however, the numbers do not indicate *how much* more time the former spends than the latter. A respondent who spends 15 minutes a day and another who spends 25 minutes a day will both check category 3. Because the exact reading times cannot be inferred from the scale values, the intervals between them have no meaningful interpretation. Stated differently, given the nature of the response categories, any set of four numbers can be used as scale values, as long as they go from lowest to highest. For example, a set of scale values such as 10, 15, 25, 40 is equivalent in this case to the set 1, 2, 3, 4.

Two measures of central tendency are meaningful for ordinal-scaled responses: their mode as well as their **median;** that is, the category into which the 50th percentile response falls when all responses are arranged from lowest to highest (or highest to lowest). To illustrate, consider the following distribution of responses to the question about reading newspapers:

> The **median** is the category into which the 50th percentile response falls when all responses are arranged from lowest to highest (or highest to lowest).

Response Category	Percentage of Respondents Checking Category
1	40
2	25
3	25
4	10

In this case, the mode is category 1, and the median is category 2.

Interval–Scaled Responses

An **interval scale** has all the properties of an ordinal scale, but in addition, the differences between scale values can be meaningfully interpreted. This characteristic makes interval-scaled responses more powerful than ordinal-scaled responses. Strictly speaking, variables such as attitudes, opinions, and preferences cannot be quantified to yield exact interval scales. Nevertheless, responses to questions like the following are frequently assumed to form an interval scale.

> An **interval scale** has all the properties of an ordinal scale, but the differences between scale values can be meaningfully interpreted.

> **How likely are you to buy a new automobile within the next six months? (Please check the most appropriate category.)**
> 1. ❑ Will definitely not buy
> 2. ❑ Extremely unlikely to buy
> 3. ❑ Unlikely to buy
> 4. ❑ Likely to buy
> 5. ❑ Extremely likely to buy
> 6. ❑ Will definitely buy

The values assigned to this set of responses run from 1 through 6 (these numbers could also be in reverse order) and, strictly speaking, form only an ordinal scale. But they are considered to be interval scaled under the assumption that respondents will be likely to treat the differences between adjacent response categories as equal, especially because the categories are physically separated by equal distances.

Unfortunately, verifying that respondents' mental or psychological perceptions of the differences between adjacent response categories are equal is very difficult, if not impossible. Nevertheless, such scales are more often than not treated as having interval properties in marketing research practice.

The **mean** is the simple average of various numbers.

The **standard deviation** (a measure of dispersion) is the degree of deviation of numbers from their mean.

Numbers forming an interval scale, in addition to possessing ordinal-scale attributes, permit computation of the mean and standard deviation. The **mean** is the simple average of the various numbers. The **standard deviation** (a measure of dispersion) is the degree of deviation of the numbers from their mean. Suppose we present the question about likelihood of buying a new automobile to a sample of 200 respondents and obtain the response distribution presented in the table to the left.

The mode and the median for the distribution are 3 and 4, respectively. The mean response turns out to be 3.8, computed as follows:

Response Category	Number (Percentage) of Respondents Checking Category
1	10 (5%)
2	10 (5%)
3	70 (35%)
4	60 (30%)
5	20 (10%)
6	30 (15%)
	200 (100%)

$$[(1 \times 10) + (2 \times 10) + (3 \times 70) + (4 \times 60) + (5 \times 20) + (6 \times 30)]/200$$
$$= (10 + 20 + 210 + 240 + 100 + 180)/200$$
$$= 3.80$$

Thus the mean likelihood of purchase for the total sample is precisely at the 3.8 mark on the 1-to-6 scale. The computation and interpretation of the mean are legitimate because of the assumption that the unit of measurement remains constant throughout the scale.

Now suppose we administer the same question to a different sample of 200—say, a sample of respondents with lower income levels than the earlier sample—and obtain the responses shown in the table to the left.

In contrast to the first sample's mean of 3.8 on the 6-point scale, the mean for the second sample is only 1.9:

Response Category	Number (Percentage) of Respondents Checking Category
1	120 (60%)
2	40 (20%)
3	10 (5%)
4	10 (5%)
5	10 (5%)
6	10 (5%)
	200 (100%)

$$[(1 \times 120) + (2 \times 40) + (3 \times 10) + (4 \times 10) + (5 \times 10) + (6 \times 10)]/200$$
$$= (120 + 80 + 30 + 40 + 50 + 60)/200$$
$$= 1.90$$

Although 3.8 is twice as large as 1.9, we cannot say that the first sample is twice as likely to buy a new automobile within the next six months as the second sample. Even though the unit of measurement remains constant throughout an interval scale, its starting, or zero, point is arbitrary.

The ratio of two values on an interval scale is also arbitrary and has no meaningful interpretation, because it depends on the scale's starting point. To illustrate, suppose we number the six response categories 0 through 5 instead of 1 through 6. We still have an interval scale, but it has a different starting point. Exhibit 9.1 shows the impact of this change on the mean responses of the two samples. From the exhibit we see that the ratio of sample mean values on scale A is 3.8/1.9 = 2.0. The ratio of sample mean values on scale B, though, is 2.8/0.9 = 3.1.

As Exhibit 9.1 demonstrates, with the new starting point for the interval scale, the first sample on the average is now more than three times as likely to buy a new

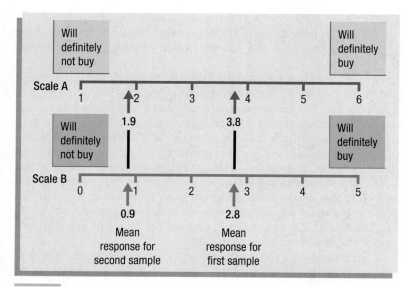

Exhibit 9.1
Impact of Arbitrariness of an Interval Scale's Starting Point

automobile as is the second. This conclusion is obviously ludicrous, because the answers obtained from the two samples and the relative positions of their mean responses on the scale have not changed. Although this point is subtle, it is extremely important, because there is usually a strong temptation to compute and interpret ratios of quantified responses that are no more than interval scaled. For instance, you have probably heard claims like "Users of our brand are twice as satisfied as users of competitors' brands" and "Homeowners are four times as strongly opposed to a property tax increase as renters." Such claims, even when based on data from well-conducted surveys, are suspect because scales used to measure respondents' feelings, opinions, and other internal variables are invariably only interval scales.

Ratio–Scaled Responses

Quantified responses forming a ratio scale are the most analytically versatile. **Ratio scales** possess all the properties of an interval scale, and the ratios of numbers on these scales have meaningful interpretations. Data on certain demographic or descriptive attributes, if they are obtained through open-ended questions, will have ratio-scaled properties. Consider the following questions:

> What is your annual income before taxes? $_____
> How far is your workplace from your home? _____ miles

A **ratio scale** possesses all the properties of an interval scale, and the ratios of numbers on such a scale have meaningful interpretations.

Answers to these questions have a natural, unambiguous starting point—namely, zero. Because the starting point is not chosen arbitrarily, as in the case of an interval scale, computing and interpreting ratios make sense. For instance, we can say that a respondent with an annual income of $40,000 earns twice as much as one with an annual income of $20,000.

In summary, quantified responses fall into one of four levels or scales of measurement: nominal, ordinal, interval, or ratio. Each scale possesses the attributes of the scales below it. In other words, ratio scales have the properties of interval scales, which in turn have the properties of ordinal scales, and so on. The permissible data analyses and inferences depend on the scale level of the data.

One final point before we examine the classes of variables typically encountered in marketing research and the levels of measurement appropriate for them: data with only nominal or ordinal properties are classified as **nonmetric data,** whereas data with interval or ratio properties are classified as **metric data.** The difference between these two types of data is that the intervals between numbers have precise meaning for metric data but not for nonmetric data.

Nonmetric data are data with only nominal or ordinal properties.

Metric data are data with interval or ratio properties.

Classes of Variables

An **attribute** is a personal or demographic characteristic, such as education level, age, size of household, or number of children.

Behavioral variables relate to such behaviors as frequency of visits to a store or extent of magazine readership.

A **belief** relates to knowledge and what respondents consider (correctly or incorrectly) to be true.

An **attitude** is similar to a belief, except that it also reflects a respondent's evaluative judgment.

The nature of a variable plays a key role in determining the most powerful scale on which it can be measured meaningfully. Virtually all variables encountered in survey research can be classified within one of four categories: attributes, behavior, beliefs, and attitudes.[4] **Attributes** are personal or demographic characteristics, such as education level, age, size of household, or number of children. **Behavioral variables** relate to such behaviors as frequency of visits to a store or extent of magazine readership. **Beliefs** relate to knowledge and are what respondents consider (correctly or incorrectly) to be true; for example, do respondents believe that banning print advertisements for cigarettes will lower lung cancer deaths? **Attitudes** are similar to beliefs, except that they also reflect respondents' evaluative judgments; for instance, do respondents feel print advertisements for cigarettes should be banned?

Although both beliefs and attitudes pertain to a person's mental state, an attitude can be viewed as stemming from a belief (or set of beliefs) that a person holds. For instance, a person may develop a negative attitude toward cigarette advertisements on the basis of a belief that lung cancer is a major problem and that banning cigarette advertisements will lower lung cancer deaths. Another person who has the same beliefs but in addition feels strongly that the Constitution guarantees advertisers freedom of expression may develop a neutral (rather than a negative) attitude toward cigarette advertisements. Given that beliefs and attitudes are intertwined, formal definitions of attitudes often include beliefs as an integral component, as discussed next.

The term *attitude* has been defined in a number of different ways. Our purpose here is not to present the various definitions and discuss their diversity. Rather, it is primarily to review scaling techniques suitable for measuring attitudes and, more generally, any internal disposition that can affect an individual's behavior. Fortunately, even the seemingly different definitions of attitudes share

One approach for determining the effectiveness of an antismoking campaign is to conduct surveys that measure people's smoking-related attitudes and behaviors before and after launching the campaign.

certain common threads. They all depict attitudes as underlying mental states capable of influencing a person's choice of actions and maintaining consistency across those actions. These common threads imply that attitudes can be interpreted quite broadly. Therefore, the general principles underlying attitude-scaling techniques should also be useful in measuring other internal variables, such as beliefs, opinions, preferences, motives, and purchase intentions. Indeed, virtually all consumer behavior textbooks portray attitudes as being multifaceted and consisting of three components: cognitive (knowledge, beliefs); affective (liking, preference); and behavioral (action tendency, purchase intention).[5] Thus, in measuring attitudes, we actually measure several internal variables making up the three components.

Attributes and behavioral variables are similar in that they are less ambiguous and more readily measurable than the other two types of variables. Therefore, choosing the most appropriate levels of measurement for them, based on the degree of detail desired by the researcher, is somewhat easier. For instance, consider income level, an attribute of respondents. If the researcher desires metric data on income, he or she can use a ratio scale of measurement; that is, ask an open-ended income question. However, if the researcher is interested in nonmetric data (the relative income levels of respondents), the scale of measurement can be ordinal and consist of a multiple-category income question. Similarly, consider people's smoking habits, a behavioral variable. Depending on how much detail the researcher desires, data on smoking can be obtained on a nominal scale (by asking whether or not a respondent smokes), an ordinal scale (by asking a suitable multiple-category question), or a ratio scale (by asking an open-ended question to ascertain the number of cigarettes smoked per day).

Measurement of beliefs and attitudes, however, is not quite as simple. Because beliefs and attitudes are more cognitive and emotional than factual, they are more nebulous than attributes or behavior. Defining them, let alone measuring them precisely, is difficult.[6] To understand this difficulty, variables that cannot be directly observed have to be defined both conceptually and operationally. Research in Use 9.1 is a good illustration of issues surrounding measurement of one such variable: brand equity.

For example, conceptually, *attitude* may be a predisposition to respond favorably or unfavorably to a stimulus object. However, operationally, a person's attitude toward a particular retail store may be measured in the following fashion: it is the total of the person's expressed degree of agreement—on a 5-point, "strongly agree" to "strongly disagree" scale—with each of a set of 20 evaluative statements about various aspects of the retail store.

Obtaining accurate, unambiguous measures of unobservable variables, such as beliefs and attitudes, is generally difficult. Interestingly, from a measurement standpoint, unobservable variables are typically neither nominal nor ratio. They usually have ordinal or interval properties and fall in the gray area between nonmetric and metric measurements.

Attitude Scaling

Attitudes are widely believed to be a key determinant of behavior, although some authors suggest that behavior can also lead to changed attitudes. For instance, when a person with a mildly positive attitude toward Apple computers buys an Apple computer, his or her attitude may become much more positive following the purchase, perhaps to justify the purchase. In any event, firms and institutions are constantly interested in the attitudes of various constituencies.

For example, General Motors may be interested in the attitudes of consumers toward its automobiles, the attitudes of employees toward its working environment, and the attitudes of shareholders toward its business performance. United Way may want to assess the public's attitude toward charitable organizations in general and toward United Way in particular. How can General Motors, United Way, and other organizations measure the attitudes of relevant constituencies? A variety of methods are available for this purpose. Before we discuss the methods, however, we should point out that attitude measurement as a whole is indirect. In other words, attitudes can only be inferred and cannot be directly ascertained.

Several measurable responses can offer clues about people's attitudes:[7]

1. Measures in which inferences are drawn from self-reports of beliefs, feelings, behavior, and so forth, toward an object or class of objects

2. Measures in which inferences are drawn from observed overt behavior toward the object

3. Measures in which inferences are drawn from the individual's reaction to, or interpretations of, partially structured material relevant to the object

4. Measures in which inferences are drawn from performance on objective tasks in which functioning may be influenced by disposition toward the object

5. Measures in which inferences are drawn from physiological reactions to the object

The major focus of this chapter will be on self-report, or so-called paper-and-pencil, methods—category 1—because they are by far the most widely used in attitude-scaling studies. However, we will first briefly review the other four types of methods.

Observing Overt Behavior

We commonly assume that a person's behavior concerning an object will be consistent with his or her attitudes toward it. This assumption has found empirical support.[8] Nevertheless, the notion of consistency between attitudes and behavior seems almost intuitive. For instance, a consumer with an unfavorable attitude toward a certain brand of automobile is more likely than not to buy a competing brand. A television viewer with a strongly negative image of a particular firm may visibly frown on seeing a commercial touting the firm's products. The assumed link between attitude and behavior is the rationale behind inferring the former from observing the latter.

Observation of overt behavior is useful when other attitude measurement methods are inconvenient or infeasible. For instance, an observation study can be used to ascertain the attitudes of very young children toward a variety of toys. Children, in groups or individually, can be left in a room containing the stimulus set of toys, and their behavior—how long and how enthusiastically they play with each toy—can be observed. Inferences about the children's attitudes toward each toy can be made from those observations. The use of one-way mirrors to observe focus groups (as we saw in Chapter 7) is another example of this approach to gaining insight into people's attitudes.

As you might suspect, observation of behavior can yield at best only rough estimates of attitudes. A number of factors other than attitudes can influence behavior. To illustrate, a homemaker may buy a cheap brand of detergent, despite an unfavorable attitude toward it, because a more expensive brand that she or he

Measuring Brand Equity

One of the most popular marketing concepts to emerge in recent times is that of brand equity. *Brand equity* has been defined in a number of different ways, resulting in many ways of measuring it. Practitioners and academicians seem to agree that brand equity represents the "added value" a brand imparts to a product. This added value can be measured by many different means, as illustrated by the following three examples.

EquiTrend Fall 2004 Online Survey by Harris Interactive

Harris Interactive (www.harrisinteractive.com) asked its online survey participants to evaluate 1,031 brands in 35 categories, with everyone evaluating 20 "core brands" and 60 brands randomly selected from a list of 1,031 brands. In all, 24,046 consumers aged 15 and over participated in the study. EquiTrend's equity scores are composite scores derived from consumers' ratings on five different scales—familiarity, quality, purchase intent, brand expectations, and distinctiveness—with each scale having its own rating format. For instance,

quality was measured using a 10-point scale, with 0 being "very poor quality," 5 being "very acceptable quality," and 8 or above being "world class." The table below summarizes the results from the EquiTrend 2004 study for the top 10 online brands.

Brand Keys Customer Loyalty Index

Brand Keys (www.brandkeys.com), a marketing research company based in New York, takes a different approach to measuring brand equity. For Brand Keys president Robert Passikoff, customer loyalty is an important measure of brand value and therefore a good indicator of brand equity. The loyalty index is derived by probing customers' relationships with 203 brands in 32 categories. Specifically, the company identifies and obtains ratings on key drivers that bond customers with their favorite brands within each category. The drivers include such measures as satisfaction with the brands, evaluation of competitive brands, interest in buying the brands, and so forth. According to the Brand Keys 2004 study, regional brands New Balance (based in Boston)

EquiTrend "Online Top 10" Brands (out of 42 brands in the category)

Brand	Rank	Brand Equity	Quality	Familiarity (%)	Purchase Intent	Brand Expectations	Distinctiveness
Google	1	69.3	7.43	85	8.23	7.44	6.65
Yahoo!	2	68.0	7.20	93	7.98	7.07	6.36
Microsoft.com	3	63.2	6.88	88	6.42	6.42	6.22
HistoryChannel.com	4	62.7	7.20	79	6.97	6.97	6.59
Barnes & Noble.com	5	61.8	7.03	75	6.69	6.69	5.79
Hallmark.com	6	61.6	7.14	68	6.85	6.85	5.91
Amazon	7	61.5	6.94	77	6.69	6.69	6.33
Discovery.com	8	60.7	7.11	62	6.97	6.97	6.18
eBay	9	60.3	6.89	85	6.24	6.24	6.97
BestBuy.com	10	59.9	6.76	78	6.41	6.41	5.53

really likes is not available. A teenager who hates cigarettes may still smoke them because of peer pressure. Thus the validity of attitudes inferred solely from overt behavior may be questionable. (Validity of attitude measures is discussed later.) Furthermore, this approach can become quite expensive, because it requires the services of highly skilled and qualified observers.

and Skechers (based in Manhattan Beach, California) have performed very well in a crowded market and are tied for first place in terms of brand value within the athletic shoe category. The secret behind their success apparently lies in their superior ability to retain loyal customers relative to other, better-known brands.

It is worthwhile to note that, although New Balance and Skechers may score high on loyalty, because of their small market shares relative to their famous competitors, they may not score high on familiarity and, therefore, not on brand equity either as measured by EquiTrend. Nike and Reebok are likely to score higher on EquiTrend's measure by virtue of their higher popularity and hence familiarity (which is a key component of EquiTrend's measure).

Interbrand's Brand Valuation

Interbrand (www.interbrand.com), a division of Diversified Agency Services (www.dasglobal.com), an operating company for Omnicom Group, is well known for its valuation of brands. Based on public documents,

Interbrand first compiles the total revenue from products or services that carry the brand name and forecasts the projected revenue for the next five years. It then estimates the percentage of the revenue that can be directly attributed to the brand name. This percentage is estimated based on data about many factors, such as brand awareness and brand preference. Finally, Interbrand estimates a "risk profile" for the brand based on the brand's strength and uses that information to estimate the discounted value of the brand. Brand strength itself is a composite measure reflecting a variety of factors, such as the brand's market, stability, leadership, trend, support, and protection. The higher the brand strength, the lower the discount rate, and vice versa. The table below shows Interbrand's top 10 brands for 2002, 2003, and 2004.

Many researchers and practitioners are continuing to address issues surrounding equity measurement. The meaning and measurement of brand equity depends on its purpose and its use in the decision-making process.[a]

Interbrand's Top 10 Brands

2002	2003	2004
Coca-Cola ($69.64 billion)	Coca-Cola ($70.45 billion)	Coca-Cola ($67.4 billion)
Microsoft ($64.09 billion)	Microsoft ($65.17 billion)	Microsoft ($61.37 billion)
IBM ($51.19 billion)	IBM ($51.77 billion)	IBM ($53.79 billion)
GE ($41.31 billion)	GE ($42.34 billion)	GE ($44.11 billion)
Intel ($30.86 billion)	Intel ($31.11 billion)	Intel ($33.50 billion)
Nokia ($29.97 billion)	Nokia ($29.44 billion)	Disney ($27.11 billion)
Disney ($29.26 billion)	Disney ($28.04 billion)	McDonald's ($25.00 billion)
McDonald's ($26.37 billion)	McDonald's ($24.70 billion)	Intel ($33.50 billion)
Marlboro ($24.15 billion)	Marlboro ($22.18 billion)	Toyota ($22.67 billion)
Mercedes ($21.01 billion)	Mercedes ($21.37 billion)	Marlboro ($22.13 billion)

Analyzing Reactions to Partially Structured Stimuli

As its name implies, the approach of analyzing reactions to partially structured stimuli involves asking respondents to react to, or describe in some fashion, an incomplete, vague stimulus. The responses obtained are analyzed by trained professionals to reveal the respondents' attitudes. The underlying rationale is that a person's response to an object or a situation depicted by a vague stimulus will necessarily be shaped by his or her attitudes. The various projective techniques we examined in Chapter 7—word association test, sentence completion test, TAT, cartoon test—are examples of methods employing partially structured stimuli. Therefore, these techniques can be used to infer attitudes. The advantages and disadvantages of projective techniques, as well as several illustrative applications, are given in Chapter 7 and hence will not be repeated here.

Evaluating Performance on Objective Tasks

To evaluate performance on objective tasks, respondents are asked to complete an ostensibly objective, well-defined task. The nature of their performance is then analyzed to infer their attitudes. To illustrate, consider the attitudes of a rural community toward attracting manufacturing firms to locate within the community. One way to use the performance-on-objective-tasks approach to gauge the community's attitudes toward industrialization is as follows. A representative sample of residents is asked to read carefully (or even memorize) an essay containing numerous facts and figures and presenting a balanced view of the pros and cons of industrializing rural communities. After a period of time, the respondents are quizzed on the essay's content. The specific parts of the essay they remember and how well they remember them will offer clues about the community's attitudes concerning industrialization. For instance, sound memory of a disproportionately large amount of unfavorable information about industrialization will signal a negative attitude toward increased industrialization.

Examples we discussed under structured, disguised questionnaires in Chapter 6 are also illustrations of the performance-on-objective-tasks approach. A major drawback of this approach is the difficulty of constructing appropriate objective tasks and meaningfully interpreting performance on those tasks.

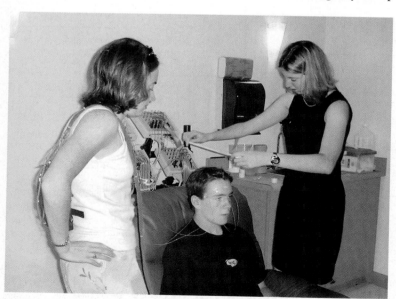

Preparations being made to monitor a young consumer's brainwave activity; researchers can infer consumers' reaction to visual stimuli (for instance, ads or product packaging) from such physiological measurements.

Monitoring Physiological Responses

Monitoring physiological responses is based on the premise that a person's emotional reactions to a stimulus will be accompanied by corresponding involuntary physiological changes. For example, a feeling of fear or anxiety can induce physiological reactions such as shivering, perspiration, and increased heartbeat. Mechanical and electronic instruments like the galvanic skin response (GSR) meter (to measure changes in the electrical resistance of the skin caused by changes in the amount of perspiration) and pupillometer (to measure the extent of pupil dilation in response to a visual stimulus) are available to measure physiological reactions from which internal emotions can be inferred.

Other physiological measurements include eye-tracking equipment and response latency measures (such as VOPAN), which we discussed under mechanical observation techniques in Chapter 6.

Physiological measurements, however, have a serious drawback, because they measure merely emotional arousal rather than attitudes. They cannot by themselves reveal whether the source of the arousal is a positive or a negative emotion. For instance, a respondent who is annoyed by a test advertisement and one who is favorably impressed by it may be equally interested in it and hence display identical pupil dilations as measured by a pupillometer. Consequently, physiological responses may serve as no more than measures of the attention-getting power or excitement-generating potential of such marketing stimuli as product advertisements and packages.

One marketing research firm specializing in physiological measurements based on eye-tracking technology is Perception Research Services International. The following excerpt from a brochure describing the firm's services emphasizes the inappropriateness of inferring attitudes solely on the basis of physiological measures:

> Eye tracking is an addition to, not a substitute for, the data provided by traditional question and answer procedures. Eye tracking provides an indication of two stages in the communications process:
>
> - Attention
> - Involvement
>
> To examine the remaining dimensions, it is necessary to uncover opinions, attitudes, and inclinations which reflect if the material generates a favorable impression of the brand and encourages trial and/or usage.[9]

More and more organizations are realizing the importance of assessing customer experiences over a product's life cycle. Measuring these experiences involves tapping a number of different areas (see Research in Use 9.2).

Self-Report Measures of Attitudes

As mentioned earlier, attitudes can only be inferred and cannot be directly observed or measured. Nevertheless, self-report measures are somewhat more straightforward than the other four categories of methods. This method involves asking respondents relatively direct questions concerning attitudes toward whatever is of interest to the researcher. The questions are typically in the form of rating scales on which respondents check off appropriate positions that best reflect their feelings.[10]

Use of Rating Scales in Self-Report Measurements

Rating scales can take a variety of physical forms. There are several key dimensions on which rating scales and the nature of the data they yield vary: graphic versus itemized formats; comparative versus noncomparative assessments; forced versus nonforced response choices; balanced versus unbalanced response choices; labeled versus unlabeled response choices; number of scale positions; and measurement level of data obtained. We will now briefly discuss each of these dimensions using a hypothetical scenario in which the management of eBay wants to measure overall consumer attitudes toward eBay.

Measuring Customer Experiences

Increasingly, organizations are trying to measure customer experiences to create a customer-based view of strategy. This is what Bruce Corner, COO of Symmetrics Marketing Corporation, has to say about measurement of customer relationships:

> Building and managing relationships with prospects and customers is a difficult job. It requires a comprehensive strategy encompassing the entire customer life cycle from attracting the "right" segments of prospects to delivering on the brand promise to churn management. Every stage in the life cycle (i.e., attraction, sales effectiveness, loyalty management, and churn management) requires effective metrics to guide managers in their most critical responsibility—allocating resources in a way that maximizes shareholder value.

How do we capture customer experiences over the life cycle?

Measures of Attraction

- Brand recognition
- Brand recall
- Brand's uniqueness
- Brand personality
- Brand's perceived values
- Feelings toward the brand

Measures of Sales Effectiveness

- Income statement
- The fit between segment's perception of brand strengths and company's offerings—uptake of target programs and promotions
- Customer lifetime value
- Customer-level ROI
- Customer acquisition rate
- Share of high-value customers

Measures of Loyalty Management

- Attitudes toward the brand
- Relationship depth
- Share of the wallet
- Spending from repeat customers
- Number of accounts per customer
- Actual buying behaviors
- Tier movement among customers
- Customer retention/turnover/tenure

Measures of Churn Management

- Reasons for defections

The ultimate goal of measuring customer experiences is to acquire, retain, and develop the most valuable customers. Only by measuring all aspects of customer experiences can companies hope to be successful in customer relationship strategy. The lesson is measurement matters.[b]

Graphic Versus Itemized Formats

A graphic rating scale presents a continuum, in the form of a straight line, along which a theoretically infinite number of ratings is possible.

A **graphic rating scale** presents a continuum, in the form of a straight line, along which a theoretically infinite number of ratings is possible. The implicit rationale for using a graphic rating scale is that it allows detection of fine shades of difference in attitudes. A true, or pure, graphic rating scale resembles the following question:

> **Indicate your overall opinion about eBay by placing a ✓ mark at an appropriate position on the line below.**
>
> **Very bad**   **Very good**

To quantify responses to this question, we measure the physical distance between the left extreme position and the response position on the line; the greater the distance, the more favorable the attitude toward eBay.

A potential difficulty in using a graphic rating scale is that coding and analysis will require a substantial amount of time, because we first have to measure physical distances on the scale for each respondent. An even more serious drawback is that respondents may be incapable of mentally perceiving fine shades of difference in attitudes, let alone accurately translating their perceptions into measurable physical distances. In other words, although graphic rating scales are in theory capable of facilitating precise attitude measurements, whether they can be meaningfully used in practice is arguable. Consequently, graphic rating scales (at least the pure variety) are not widely used in marketing research surveys.

Itemized rating scales have a set of distinct response categories; any suggestion of an attitude continuum underlying the categories is implicit. They essentially take the form of multiple-category questions. Typical itemized rating scale formats are illustrated by the following questions:

An **itemized rating scale** has a set of distinct response categories; any suggestion of an attitude continuum underlying the categories is implicit.

Indicate your overall opinion about eBay by checking one of the following categories.

Very bad	Bad	Neither bad nor good	Good	Very good
❑	❑	❑	❑	❑
1	2	3	4	5

Which of the following best describes your overall opinion of eBay?

Terrible	Poor	Fair	Good	Very good	Excellent
❑	❑	❑	❑	❑	❑

Although less refined than a graphic rating scale, an itemized rating scale should be easier to respond to and more meaningful from the respondent's perspective. Also, coding and analysis of the raw data should be somewhat less laborious. As you might expect, itemized rating scales are much more widely used than the graphic type.

To gain the benefits of both types of scales, we can also use a combination format. The scale in the following question illustrates such a format.

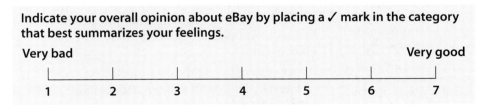

Indicate your overall opinion about eBay by placing a ✓ mark in the category that best summarizes your feelings.

Very bad   Very good

| 1 | 2 | 3 | 4 | 5 | 6 | 7 |

This scale resembles a graphic scale because its horizontal line signifies an underlying continuum. Yet the scale has a distinct set of response categories.

Comparative Versus Noncomparative Assessments

Contrast the set of questions in the previous section with the set of two questions shown at the top of the next page.

> **What is your overall rating of eBay compared with other auction websites?**
>
> | Much worse | Worse | About the same | Better | Much better |
> |---|---|---|---|---|
> | ❏ | ❏ | ❏ | ❏ | ❏ |
>
> **Rank the following by placing a 1 beside the auction site you think is best overall, a 2 beside the auction site you think is second best, and so on.**
>
> Yahoo! Auctions _____
>
> Amazon.com Auctions _____
>
> Bidz.com _____
>
> eBay _____
>
> uBid _____

A key difference between the two sets is that questions in the latter set explicitly ask respondents to compare eBay with other auction sites. Whereas the questions in the first set seek absolute or noncomparative ratings, those in the second set seek relative or comparative ratings. Which type of rating scale is better? This question has no clear-cut answer other than: It depends.

A **comparative rating scale** provides all respondents with a common frame of reference. In contrast, a **noncomparative rating scale** implicitly permits respondents to use any frame of reference, or even none at all. A comparative rating scale, by virtue of its common frame of reference, allows the researcher to be confident that all respondents are answering the same question. However, in the context of measuring attitudes, a standard frame of reference imposed by the researcher may not necessarily be meaningful to all respondents (some respondents may have had no exposure to or experience with the stated comparison norm). Under such circumstances, the validity of the comparative ratings may be questionable.

The choice between comparative and noncomparative formats must therefore be situation specific. Depending on the nature of potential respondents and their realm of experience with the attitude objects about which ratings are desired, the researcher must decide which format is likely to be most appropriate.

Forced Versus Nonforced Response Choices

A **forced-choice scale** does not give respondents the option to express a neutral, or middle-ground, attitude. A **nonforced-choice scale** does give respondents the option to express a neutral attitude. The following questions have nonforced-choice scales.

A **comparative rating scale** provides all respondents with a common frame of reference.

A **noncomparative rating scale** implicitly permits respondents to use any frame of reference, or even none at all.

A **forced-choice scale** does not give respondents the option to express a neutral or middle ground.

A **nonforced-choice scale** gives respondents the option to express a neutral attitude.

> **Indicate your overall opinion about eBay by checking one of the following categories.**
>
> | Very bad | Bad | Neither bad nor good | Good | Very good |
> |---|---|---|---|---|
> | ❏ | ❏ | ❏ | ❏ | ❏ |
> | 1 | 2 | 3 | 4 | 5 |
>
> **What is your overall rating of eBay compared with other auction sites?**
>
> | Much worse | Worse | About the same | Better | Much better |
> |---|---|---|---|---|
> | ❏ | ❏ | ❏ | ❏ | ❏ |

In general, an itemized rating scale with an odd number of response categories will have a neutral position, represented by the category falling exactly in the middle (one possible exception is a scale with unbalanced response choices, which is discussed later). By the same token, a scale with an even number of categories will typically force respondents to take a definite position on either the positive or the negative side of the scale, as illustrated by the following questions:

Indicate your overall opinion about eBay by placing a ✓ mark in the category that best summarizes your feelings.

Very bad					Very good
❏	❏	❏	❏	❏	❏
1	2	3	4	5	6

What is your overall rating of eBay compared with other auction sites?

Much worse	Worse	Better	Much better
❏	❏	❏	❏

The issue of whether scales with forced response choices are better than those with nonforced response choices has no unambiguous answer. Intuitively, a prudent choice is to include a neutral position by having an odd number of response choices to accommodate respondents with no definite attitudes toward the subject matter. However, even provision of an odd number of categories, with a neutral category in the middle, may not guarantee that a scale does not force respondents, and maybe the researcher should provide a separate "not applicable" or "no opinion" category. Scales with an odd number of categories appear to be more widely used than those with an even number of categories. But a neutral position may tempt certain respondents, especially those who are reluctant to reveal their true responses, to select it as a fake response. Therefore, scales with an even number of categories deserve serious consideration when the topic to be studied is such that few respondents are likely to have a strictly neutral attitude toward it. Just as in comparative versus noncomparative rating scales, the choice between a forced and a nonforced format must be made after carefully considering the characteristics unique to the situation.[11]

Balanced Versus Unbalanced Response Choices

The balanced-versus-unbalanced dimension is relevant in constructing itemized rating scales. A **balanced scale** is one that has an equal number of positive/favorable and negative/unfavorable response choices, as in the following questions:

A **balanced scale** has an equal number of positive/favorable and negative/unfavorable response choices.

Indicate your overall opinion about eBay by checking one of the following categories.

Very bad	Bad	Neither bad nor good	Good	Very good
❏	❏	❏	❏	❏
1	2	3	4	5

What is your overall rating of eBay compared with other auction sites?

Much worse	Worse	About the same	Better	Much better
❏	❏	❏	❏	❏

Itemized rating scales in general should be balanced in order to reduce response biases.

One exception to this recommendation is a situation in which the true attitudes of respondents are likely to be predominantly one-sided, either positive or negative. When this situation is anticipated, we should use an **unbalanced scale** with a larger number of response choices on the side of the scale where the overall attitude of the respondent sample is likely to fall. For instance, if a rating scale is used to determine the importance of various automobile attributes in influencing the final purchase, respondents may not use the choices at the low-importance end of the scale as freely as those at the high-importance end. Using a balanced scale under these circumstances could lead to most responses' falling into just a few categories at one end of the scale. Such a scale will not be very sensitive (sensitivity of scales is described later). The following question illustrates an unbalanced rating scale that can be used if respondents' opinions about eBay are anticipated to be predominantly positive.

> An **unbalanced scale** has a larger number of response choices on the side of the scale where the overall attitude of the respondent sample is likely to fall.

Which of the following best describes your overall opinion of eBay?

Terrible	Poor	Fair	Good	Very good	Excellent
❑	❑	❑	❑	❑	❑

Labeled Versus Unlabeled Response Choices

> An **anchor label** defines one of the two extremes of a rating scale.

Rating scales will usually have a pair of **anchor labels,** which define their two extremes. However, a researcher has considerable latitude in deciding whether to include one or more intermediate labels and whether those labels should be in the form of words, numbers, or both.

No rules exist for determining the number and types of labels to include in a scale. Intuitively, however, when generating a simple and appropriate label for an intermediate category is difficult, leaving the category unlabeled is better than making up an ill-fitting label for it. To illustrate, consider the following question:

Indicate your overall opinion about eBay by placing a ✓ mark in the category that best summarizes your feelings.

Very bad									Very good
❑	❑	❑	❑	❑	❑	❑	❑	❑	❑
1	2	3	4	5	6	7	8	9	10

To come up with meaningful verbal labels for the unlabeled categories in this question is likely to be very difficult, if not impossible; hence, the best approach is not to have verbal labels for those categories. Moreover, when the researcher plans to treat the response categories as being interval scaled (as is presumably the case in this question), the use of inappropriate verbal labels can cast doubt on the assumption of interval data.[12] According to one study that examined the impact of category labels, even labels such as "reasonably poor" and "reasonably good," or "pleasant" and "unpleasant," were not perceived by respondents to be equidistant from the middle, "neutral" position.[13] Thus verbal labels should be used cautiously and sparingly when the quantified ratings are to have interval-scale properties (as is necessary for a number of statistical analysis techniques to be discussed in later chapters).

Numerical labels, although easier to generate than verbal labels, must also be used and interpreted cautiously. Placing numbers on a rating scale can be helpful in suggesting to respondents the notion of equal distances between adjacent response categories. Herein lies a hidden danger, however, when the scale categories already have verbal labels that suggest no more than an ordinal scale. Sequentially numbering the categories on such a scale can result in the researcher's erroneously interpreting as interval data what are really only ordinal data.

Another consideration in determining whether to use verbal labels, numerical labels, or both is the likely audience for the final research report. For instance, suppose the research report is to be presented to a group of eBay managers, and we are considering the following two alternative scales for inclusion in a survey of customers:

Indicate your overall opinion about eBay by placing a ✓ mark in the category that best summarizes your feelings.

Very bad									Very good
❑	❑	❑	❑	❑	❑	❑	❑	❑	❑
1	2	3	4	5	6	7	8	9	10

Which of the following best describes your overall opinion of eBay?

Poor	Fair	Good	Very good	Excellent
❑	❑	❑	❑	❑

Let's examine how we would summarize for managers the results of using these alternative rating scales. If we used the first rating scale, our summary might read something like this: "On a scale of 1 to 10 (ranging from 'very bad' to 'very good'), eBay's average customer rating is 6.8." If we used the second rating scale, our summary might read as follows: "Of the customers surveyed, 20 percent rated eBay as 'excellent,' 40 percent rated it as 'very good,' 30 percent rated it as 'good,' 5 percent rated it as 'fair,' and 5 percent rated it as 'poor.'" Intuitively, the latter summary is likely to be more informative for the managers than the former. Therefore, a scale having a small number of categories with verbal labels may at times be more appropriate than a seemingly more precise scale having a greater number of sequentially numbered categories.

When conducting research in many different international markets, we must make sure a survey is consistent (with category labels that convey the same meaning) across languages and cultures. One researcher found that the use of "totally satisfied" instead of "very satisfied" (similarly, "totally dissatisfied" instead of "very dissatisfied" at the other end of the scale) produced more reliable results in nine European and five Asian countries.[14]

One final point concerning category labels. Although our discussion has focused on verbal and numerical labels, other types of labels, such as picture labels, are also used to help respondents understand the categories and distinguish among them. Picture labels can be especially useful in surveying samples of children or nonreaders, for instance. Exhibit 9.2 gives examples of scales with picture labels used by one marketing research firm to measure children's reactions to commercials.

Number of Scale Positions

The number of points or categories to include in a rating scale is another area with no rigid rules. However, rating scales used in most surveys typically have between five and nine categories. Logically, more precise measurements should

**Exhibit 9.2
Rating Scales with Picture
Labels**

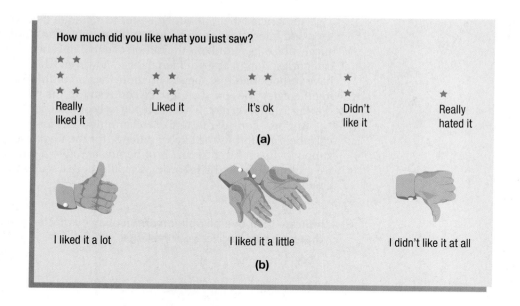

result as the number of scale positions increases. Of course, a scale with a large number of positions will not be meaningful if respondents are unable to make fine mental distinctions with respect to whatever is being measured. Therefore, the nature of the variable as well as the capabilities of potential respondents must be taken into account when deciding on the number of scale positions to use.

It is important to use rating scales that make the most sense to the target population. This is an important consideration in international marketing research. One researcher conducting a satisfaction study found that Germans are most familiar with a 1-to-6 rating scale, with 1 indicating "totally satisfied" and 6 indicating "totally dissatisfied." The Japanese are most familiar with a 100-point scale. Moreover, the researcher found that Germans consistently provide a lower rating than Italians do. And Italians rate every attribute as being more important than Spaniards do.[15] A "somewhat satisfied" rating means a stronger commitment to the French than to Britons, for whom the category indicates a less enthusiastic response.[16] In a recent study, researchers found that variation of meanings assigned to satisfaction category labels and the ratings were due to differences in customer characteristics.[17] Another factor to consider is whether the variable will be measured by a single-item scale represented by just one question (like those we have seen thus far) or by summing response values obtained from a number of questions, that is, by using a multiple-item scale (we will discuss multiple-item scales in a subsequent section). The literature suggests that, for accurate measurements, more scale positions are needed when a single-item scale is used than when a multiple-item scale is used.[18]

Measurement Level of Data Obtained

The **measurement level** indicates how powerful the data are—whether they are nominal, ordinal, interval, or ratio.

Measurement level refers to how powerful the data are—whether they are nominal, ordinal, interval, or ratio. The type of question and the type of rating scale used have a major bearing on the measurement level of the data generated. To illustrate this point, let's consider the questions and rating scales in Table 9.1. In this exhibit, questions 1 through 6 are ones we have seen while discussing the previous dimensions of rating scales. Questions 7 and 8 are new and have been included to illustrate other available options for ascertaining customers' perceptions of eBay.

> **TABLE 9.1**
> **Different Types of Rating Scales**
>
> 1. Indicate your overall opinion about eBay by placing a √ mark at an appropriate position on the line below.
>
> | Very bad | | Very good |
> |---|---|---|
>
> 2. Indicate your overall opinion about eBay by placing a √ mark in the category that best summarizes your feelings.
>
>   Very
>   bad
>
> | ❑ | ❑ | ❑ | ❑ | ❑ | ❑ | ❑ | ❑ | ❑ | ❑ |
> |---|---|---|---|---|---|---|---|---|---|
> | 1 | 2 | 3 | 4 | 5 | 6 | 7 | 8 | 9 | 10 |
>
>   Very
>   good
>
> 3. Indicate your overall opinion about eBay by checking one of the following categories.
>
> | Very bad | Bad | Neither bad nor good | Good | Very good |
> |---|---|---|---|---|
> | ❑ | ❑ | ❑ | ❑ | ❑ |
> | 1 | 2 | 3 | 4 | 5 |
>
> 4. Which of the following best describes your overall opinion of eBay?
>
> | Terrible | Poor | Fair | Good | Very good | Excellent |
> |---|---|---|---|---|---|
> | ❑ | ❑ | ❑ | ❑ | ❑ | ❑ |
>
> 5. What is your overall rating of eBay compared with other auction sites?
>
> | Much worse | Worse | About the same | Better | Much better |
> |---|---|---|---|---|
> | ❑ | ❑ | ❑ | ❑ | ❑ |
>
> 6. Rank the following by placing a 1 beside the auction site that you think is best overall, a 2 beside the auction site that you think is second best, and so on.
>
>   _____ Yahoo! Auctions
>   _____ Amazon.com Auctions
>   _____ Bidz.com
>   _____ eBay
>   _____ uBid
>
> 7. In each of the following pairs, which auction site do you think is better? (Please check one online auction site within each pair.)
>
>   _____ Amazon.com Auctions   or   _____ eBay
>   _____ eBay   or   _____ Yahoo! Auctions
>   _____ Bidz.com   or   _____ eBay
>   _____ eBay   or   _____ uBid
>
> 8. Allocate a total of 100 points among the following online auction sites, depending on how favorably you feel toward each; the more highly you think of each auction site, the more points you should allocate to it. (Please check that the allocated points add up to 100.)
>
>   Yahoo! Auctions   _____ points
>   Amazon.com Auctions _____ points
>   Bidz.com   _____ points
>   eBay   _____ points
>   uBid   _____ points
>   ___100___

A **constant-sum scale** has a natural starting point (zero) and asks respondents to allocate a given set of points among several attitude objects.

First, let's consider question 8, asking respondents to allocate 100 points among the five auction sites. The scale implied in this question is commonly known as a **constant-sum scale,** and it has a natural starting point (zero). In question 8, the lowest possible rating for each auction site is zero, which is nonarbitrary and remains the same across all respondents. Constant-sum scales, by virtue of their fixed starting point, have ratio-scale properties. Thus a respondent's opinion of eBay can be said to be twice as favorable as her or his opinion of Yahoo! Auctions if she or he allocates, say, 50 points to eBay and 25 points to Yahoo! Auctions. The graphic rating scale in question 1 also has ratio-scale properties, because responses on it are quantified as physical distances (such as inches), which necessarily have a fixed zero point.

Now examine question 7, asking respondents to select one auction site from each of several pairs of sites. What measurement level is achieved in this case? For each pair of auction sites, a respondent can be classified as either one who "prefers eBay" or one who "does not prefer eBay." At first glance, this classification resembles a nominal scale. However, the two categories are actually ordinal; the "prefers eBay" category connotes a more favorable attitude toward eBay than the "does not prefer eBay" category.

A **paired-comparison rating scale** consists of a question seeking comparative evaluations of two objects at a time.

Questions seeking comparative evaluations of two objects at a time are sometimes called **paired-comparison rating scales.** These scales are frequently used in marketing research, especially in studies involving consumer evaluations of physical products or product concepts.[19] Although a respondent's task in comparing two objects at a time is seemingly simple, using paired-comparison rating scales to assess attitudes toward each of several objects has a serious drawback: even when the number of objects to be evaluated is modest, a disproportionately large number of pairs have to be compared. For example, assessment of six objects requires 15 paired comparisons. In addition, the number of paired comparisons rises sharply even with a slight increase in the number of objects. (When the number of objects to be evaluated is n, the number of possible paired comparisons is given by $n(n-1)/2$.) However, for a small number of objects, the paired-comparison approach can be easily implemented to derive a rank ordering of the objects.

Now let's examine the measurement levels implied by the remaining questions (2 through 6) in Table 9.1. Data to be generated by question 6 will clearly be ordinal, because the numerical responses in this case are by definition no more than ranks. The measurement levels implied by questions 2 through 5, strictly speaking, fall in the gray area between ordinal and interval scales. However, in practice we often assume they have interval properties.

In summary, there is no such thing as the ideal scale format. We should choose one carefully after we consider the characteristics and requirements unique to the research setting—the nature of the variable to be measured, the extent to which potential respondents are capable of making refined mental judgments concerning the variable, and the types of analyses the researcher intends to perform on the data to be collected.[20]

Commonly Used Multiple-Item Scales

A **single-item scale** attempts to measure feelings through just one rating scale.

A **single-item scale,** as its name implies, attempts to measure feelings through just one rating scale. For example, the rating scales in questions 1 through 5 in Table 9.1, used separately, are single-item scales. In contrast, a **multiple-item scale** contains a number of statements pertaining to the attitude object, each with a rating scale attached to it. The combined rating, usually obtained by summing the ratings on the individual items, is treated as a measure of attitude toward the object. Multiple-item scales are frequently used in marketing research to measure attitudes.

A **multiple-item scale** contains a number of statements pertaining to the attitude object, each with a rating scale attached to it; the combined rating, usually obtained by summing the ratings on the individual items, is treated as a measure of attitude toward the object.

A Likert scale consists of a series of evaluative statements (or items) concerning an attitude object; respondents are asked to rate the object on each statement (or item) using a five-point agree/disagree scale.

Likert Scale

Based on a format originally developed by Rensis Likert,[21] the **Likert scale** consists of a series of evaluative statements (or items) concerning an attitude object. Each statement has a five-point agree/disagree scale. The number of statements included in the scale may vary from study to study, depending on how many relevant characteristics the attitude object has. However, a typical Likert scale has about 20 to 30 statements.

Table 9.2 presents six illustrative statements from a Likert scale. Online auction sites like eBay can use them to measure customer attitudes. Two points concerning the statements in Table 9.2 are worthy of special note. First, the response categories have verbal labels but no numerical labels. After the scale has been administered, however, we assign numbers to the responses to generate a quantified measure of attitudes. Typically we use 1 through 5, although other sets of numbers (such as +2, +1, 0, −1, −2) can also be used.

Second, whereas statements 1, 3, and 4 are favorable toward the site, the others are unfavorable, another typical feature of statements making up a Likert scale. Typical instructions for responding to a Likert scale—say, one that pertains to eBay—are as follows:

Instructions. For each of the following statements, check one of the five categories depending on how strongly you feel the statement applies to eBay. If you strongly agree that the statement is descriptive of eBay, check the rightmost category. If you strongly disagree that the statement is descriptive of eBay, check the leftmost category. If your feelings are less strong, check a category between the two extremes that best reflects your feelings.

Summing numerical ratings on all the statements making up the scale allows us to measure overall attitudes. However, because some statements will be favorable and others unfavorable, numbers must be assigned to the scale categories in such a way that a high (or low) numerical rating on each statement always represents

TABLE 9.2
Likert Scale Items

	Strongly Disagree	Disagree	Neither Agree nor Disagree	Agree	Strongly Agree
1. This online auction site contains an abundance of exhibits.	_____	_____	_____	_____	_____
2. User registration is complex at this site.	_____	_____	_____	_____	_____
3. The auction site's commission is reasonable.	_____	_____	_____	_____	_____
4. The auction site responds to complaints quickly.	_____	_____	_____	_____	_____
5. The auction site is not careful with personal information.	_____	_____	_____	_____	_____
6. The auction site's support system is confusing.	_____	_____	_____	_____	_____

the same attitude direction. In other words, the "strongly agree" category attached to favorable statements and the "strongly disagree" category attached to unfavorable statements must correspond (for example, the number 5, if a 1-to-5 numbering scheme is used).

The overall usefulness of a Likert scale depends on the statements making up the final scale. To capture all relevant aspects, the statements must be sufficiently varied. In addition, they must be unambiguous, to minimize erratic fluctuations in the responses. Last, but by no means least, each statement must be sensitive enough to discriminate among respondents with differing attitudes. For instance, consider the statement "eBay is a very large online auction site in the United States." Customers with favorable attitudes toward eBay, as well as those with unfavorable attitudes, are bound to agree strongly with this statement. Consequently, such statements must be eliminated from the final scale because they will contribute little to the measurement of true attitudes.

As the foregoing discussion implies, designing a good Likert scale requires first generating a large pool of statements relevant to the measurement of an attitude and then eliminating from the pool statements that are vague or non-discriminating.[22] Although a comprehensive discussion of this process is beyond our scope, let's look at an example to gain an intuitive understanding of it.

Suppose eBay wants to develop a 20-item scale to measure customer attitudes toward different online auction sites. The first step is to develop a large number of items—say, 100—similar to the six statements shown in Table 9.2. There are no rules for generating the initial pool of items, except that they should reflect the entire range of factors likely to influence customer attitudes. Managerial judgment and exploratory research, such as an informal online chat with online auction site employees, online customer focus groups, and interviews with individual customers, can help generate a broad range of items. A procedure similar to the one outlined next can reduce the initial 100-item pool to a final 20-item instrument.

We administer a questionnaire containing the initial 100 items, each with five possible response categories ranging from "strongly agree" to "strongly disagree," to a representative sample of customers. We ask these customers to rate eBay (or any other online auction site) on each statement by checking one of the five response categories. We number the categories 1 through 5, with higher numbers reflecting more favorable perceptions. With 100 items, a respondent's total score (summed across all items) ranges from 100 to 500. Further, because the initial item pool should reflect various aspects relevant to customer attitudes, we can view the total score as a rough indication of the respondent's overall attitude: the higher the score, the more favorable the attitude. This total score condenses the initial pool of items into an appropriately concise scale.

To illustrate, consider the following total scores of two respondents, A and B, as well as their scores on two individual items, i and j:

Respondent	Score on Item i	Score on Item j	Total Score
A	3	4	428
B	3	1	256

On the basis of the total scores, A has a more favorable attitude than B. By looking at their scores on items i and j, we see that item i is a poor discriminator and item j is a good discriminator between the two respondents. Item j is thus likely to be a better indicator of attitudes and hence more useful in a multiple-item scale. If we extend this insight across all statements and respondents, we see that items on which respondents' scores correlate strongly with the respondents' total scores are better candidates for inclusion in the final scale than other items. Therefore, of the 100 initial items, the 20 items with the highest correlations between individual scores and total scores are chosen to form the final scale.

This scale development process can be quite laborious if it is to be done in an organized fashion. Nevertheless, such a systematic approach is essential for constructing a valid, reliable, and sensitive Likert scale.

We can use the final scale measuring customer attitude toward different online auction sites as follows. We administer a questionnaire containing the 20-item scale to an appropriate sample of respondents and compute their total scores. With 20 items, each using a five-point scale, the total scores will range from 20 to 100; the higher the respondents' scores, the more favorable their attitudes. We can also compare the average total scores (across all respondents) for the various online auction sites to get a feeling for customers' relative attitudes toward them.

For instance, if uBid and Yahoo! Auctions have average total scores of 40 and 80, respectively, we can infer that customer attitudes toward Yahoo! Auctions are more favorable than toward uBid. However, we cannot infer that customer attitudes toward Yahoo! Auctions are twice as favorable as those toward uBid, because the scores on each scale item, and hence the total scores, have only interval-scale properties. We can also use the 20-item scale to monitor customer attitudes toward different online auction sites over time, by administering it to representative samples of customers at different times and examining the changes in average attitude scores for each online auction site.

A **semantic-differential scale** is similar to the Likert scale in that it consists of a series of items to be rated by respondents; however, the items are presented as bipolar adjectival phrases or words that are placed as anchor labels of a seven-category scale with no other numerical or verbal labels.

Semantic–Differential Scale

The format for the semantic-differential scale originated from work done over four decades ago by Charles Osgood, George Suci, and Percy Tannenbaum to investigate the perceived meanings of words and concepts.[23] The **semantic-differential scale** is similar to the Likert scale in that it consists of a series of items to be rated by respondents. However, there are some key differences, as the six semantic-differential scale items in Exhibit 9.3 demonstrate.

Exhibit 9.3 highlights three basic features of a typical semantic-differential scale, as listed on the next page.

1. Abundance of exhibits — — — — — — — Scarcity of exhibits
2. Complex user registration — — — — — — — Simple user registration
3. Low commission — — — — — — — High commission
4. Good response to complaints — — — — — — — Poor response to complaints
5. Poor protection of personal information — — — — — — — Good protection of personal information
6. Confusing support system — — — — — — — Clear support system

Exhibit 9.3
Semantic-Differential Scale Items

1. It consists of a series of bipolar adjectival words or phrases (rather than complete statements, as in a Likert scale) that pertain to the attitude object.

2. Each pair of opposite adjectives is separated by a seven-category scale, with neither numerical labels nor verbal labels other than the anchor labels.

3. Although some individual scales have favorable descriptors on the right-hand side, the other scales are reversed, with favorable descriptors appearing on the left-hand side. The rationale for the reversals is similar to the rationale for having a mixture of favorable and unfavorable statements in a Likert scale.

Typical instructions for responding to a semantic-differential scale—say, one that pertains to eBay—are as follows:

Instructions. Listed below are a number of rating scales, each containing a range of seven categories separated by a pair of opposite descriptive phrases. For each scale, check one category that best summarizes your feelings about eBay. If you feel that one of the two phrases is a totally accurate description of eBay, check the category closest to that phrase. If you feel that neither phrase is a totally accurate description of eBay, check a category between the two extremes that best reflects your feelings.

We can compute overall attitude scores for each respondent through a procedure similar to the one used with Likert scales. We code the seven categories numerically—say, 1 through 7 (making sure to reverse code items that are reversed)—and obtain overall attitude scores by summing the coded responses on the individual items. We interpret these scores the same way we did for the Likert scale.

A more common application of the semantic-differential scale, however, is to develop a pictorial profile of the attitude objects based on the mean ratings on the individual items. Exhibit 9.4 presents hypothetical pictorial profiles for two online auction sites. To facilitate interpretation of the profiles, researchers usually place all the favorable descriptors on the same side of these diagrams.

According to Exhibit 9.4, customers apparently have a more favorable overall attitude toward online auction site ABC than toward online auction site XYZ. Notice that the overall profile for ABC is in general closer to the left end (the more

**Exhibit 9.4
Pictorial Profiles Based on
Semantic-Differential Ratings**

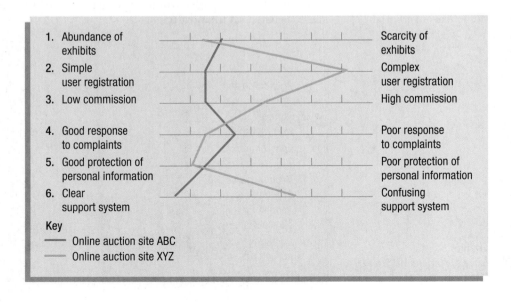

Key
— Online auction site ABC
— Online auction site XYZ

favorable end) of the scales. When we look at specific items, we see that ABC has a significant edge over XYZ with respect to user registration and support systems; it is also perceived to be superior with respect to commissions. Online auction site XYZ is perceived to be better than ABC in terms of exhibits availability, response to complaints, and protection of personal information; however, ABC does not appear to be at a significant disadvantage along these dimensions.

The semantic-differential scale has considerable practical appeal because profiles like those in Exhibit 9.4 can pinpoint a particular firm's relative strengths and weaknesses as perceived by customers. The profiles can thus have useful, immediate managerial implications. Not surprisingly, the semantic differential is the most widely used attitude-scaling technique in marketing research. Generating a useful and comprehensive set of adjectival pairs such as is necessary for an effective semantic-differential scale is not always as easy as it may seem. The constraints and caveats mentioned in the context of developing effective Likert scales are relevant here as well.

Stapel Scale

A **Stapel scale** is a variation of the semantic-differential scale; however, each item consists of just one word or phrase on which respondents rate the attitude object using a ten-item scale with just numerical labels.

The **Stapel scale** is really a variation of the semantic-differential scale. The format of a typical Stapel scale is illustrated by the six items presented in Table 9.3. Notice that the items in Tables 9.2 and 9.3, as well as in Exhibit 9.3, correspond to the same online auction site traits. A comparison of these sets of items should reveal the key format differences among the Likert, semantic-differential, and Stapel scales.

The Stapel scale has four distinctive features:

1. Each item has only one word or phrase indicating the dimension it represents.
2. Each item has 10 response categories.

TABLE 9.3
Stapel Scale

Abundance of Exhibits	Complex User Registration	Low Commission	Poor Protection Good Response to Complaints	Confusing of Personal Information	Support System
+5	+5	+5	+5	+5	+5
+4	+4	+4	+4	+4	+4
+3	+3	+3	+3	+3	+3
+2	+2	+2	+2	+2	+2
+1	+1	+1	+1	+1	+1
−1	−1	−1	−1	−1	−1
−2	−2	−2	−2	−2	−2
−3	−3	−3	−3	−3	−3
−4	−4	−4	−4	−4	−4
−5	−5	−5	−5	−5	−5

3. Each of the items is a forced-choice scale because it has an even number of categories.

4. The response categories have numerical labels but no verbal labels.

Typical instructions for responding to a Stapel scale—say, one that pertains to eBay—are as follows:

Instructions. In the following items, select a *plus* number for words that you think describe eBay accurately. The more accurately you think the word describes eBay, the larger the *plus* number you should choose. Select a *minus* number for words you think do not describe eBay accurately. The less accurately you think a word describes eBay, the larger the *minus* number you should choose. Therefore, you can select any number, from +5 for words you think are very accurate to –5 for words you think are very inaccurate.

We can analyze data obtained through Stapel scales by using procedures similar to those we discussed under semantic-differential scales. We compute overall attitude scores for the respondents by summing their ratings on the individual items. Alternatively, we can construct pictorial profiles of the attitude objects from the mean (or median) respondent ratings on each item.

One apparent advantage of the Stapel scale is that we do not have to develop complete statements or come up with pairs of bipolar words or phrases—tasks that can be very tedious. Nevertheless, the Stapel scale is not as widely used as the other two types, perhaps because its format and instructions appear to be relatively more complex. However, this reason for the infrequent use of the Stapel scale is speculative. Therefore, the final choice of a particular scale format should be based on practical considerations unique to the research setting.

A couple of final comments concerning the multiple-item scales discussed here are in order. First, the overall attitude scores generated through them are no more than interval scaled. Therefore, although such scores can be used to compare the attitudes of different groups of individuals at a given time or to track changes in the attitudes of the same group of respondents over time, computing and interpreting their ratios are inappropriate. Second, the three standard scale formats discussed do not exhaust all possibilities. Because each multiple-item scale is merely a collection of many single-item scales, one can create a large variety of multiple-item scale formats by varying the structure of the individual rating scales along one or more of the dimensions we discussed earlier, in the section "Self-Report Measures of Attitudes." Which format is the best depends on the circumstances surrounding the research setting.

Even though multiple-item scales require more effort to construct and use, they are capable of producing much better measures of attitudes than single-item scales. The next section briefly examines the strengths of multiple-item scales from a measurement standpoint.

Strengths of Multiple–Item Scales

Although a single-item scale is capable of offering clues about respondents' overall feelings toward an object, it is a rather crude measure. To understand why, we must consider three criteria on which the adequacy of attitude scales should be judged: validity, reliability, and sensitivity. We will now define and discuss these criteria and indicate why multiple-item scales are better than single-item scales along each criterion.

Validity

Validity is the extent to which a rating scale truly reflects the underlying variable it is attempting to measure.

The **validity** of a scale is the extent to which it is a true reflection of the underlying variable it is attempting to measure. Alternatively, it is the extent to which the scale fully captures all aspects of the construct to be measured. Single-item attitude scales are typically deficient on this criterion because, as we have already seen, attitudes are multifaceted. A number of different factors concerning an object or issue can contribute to how a person feels about it. For instance, a person's attitude toward eBay is likely to be shaped by what he or she knows and feels about eBay's website layout, availability of exhibits, safety of trade, privacy of personal information, ease of use and registration, support systems, and other such factors. When a researcher attempts to ascertain respondents' attitudes solely through a single-item rating scale, there is invariably doubt about whether the scale is trustworthy. Therefore, a carefully designed multiple-item scale containing numerous items, each intended to tap the respondent's position on a key facet of the attitude object, is likely to be a more valid measure. Several different types of validity are outlined next.

Content (face) validity represents the extent to which the content of a measurement scale seems to tap all relevant facets of an issue that can influence respondents' attitudes.

■ Content Validity
Also known as *face validity*, the criterion of **content validity** represents the extent to which the content of a measurement scale seems to tap all relevant facets of an issue that can influence respondents' attitudes. To illustrate, consider a scale intended to measure the job satisfaction of industrial salespeople and made up of multiple items dealing with pay, promotional opportunities, and the quality of supervision. This scale lacks content validity because it lacks items dealing with certain key aspects of a salesperson's job, such as traveling and visiting with customers. Content validity of an attitude scale is a sort of overall criterion, but it can be assessed only through a researcher's subjective judgment. In global research, we should also be concerned about the equivalence of constructs across countries. This requires asking questions such as: Are we studying the same phenomena in Brazil, India, and Britain?[24] V. Kumar and Anish Nagpal propose four types of equivalence, as shown in Exhibit 9.5.

Construct validity assesses the nature of the underlying variable or construct measured by the scale, by examining the scale's convergent and discriminant validity.

■ Construct Validity
Construct validity assesses the nature of the underlying variable or construct measured by the scale. We can assess it quantitatively by computing its correlations with measures of other constructs that we would expect to be strongly associated with the attitude and with measures of constructs that we would not expect to be closely tied to the attitude. Strong correlations in the former case are indicative of what is commonly termed *convergent validity,* and weak correlations in the latter case are indicative of *discriminant validity.* For a scale to have high construct validity, it must possess both convergent and discriminant validity. A scale purporting to measure attitudes toward abortion can be said to have high construct validity if, for instance, it has relatively strong correlations with measures of attitudes toward respect for life in general (reflecting high convergent validity) and relatively weak correlations with attitudes toward civil rights (reflecting high discriminant validity).

Predictive validity answers the question: How well does the attitude measure provided by the scale predict some other variable or characteristic that it is supposed to influence?

■ Predictive Validity
As its name implies, **predictive validity** answers the question: How well does the attitude measure provided by the scale predict some other variable or characteristic that it is supposed to influence? For example, a scale measuring attitudes toward eBay will have high predictive validity if respondents with relatively high scores on it are found to patronize eBay more frequently than respondents with relatively low scores on the scale.

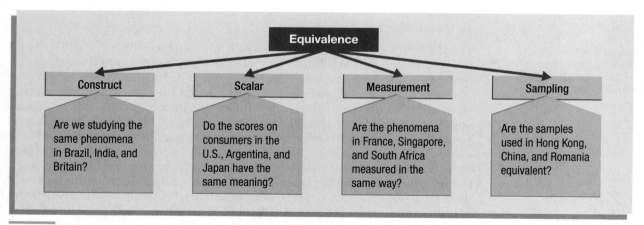

Exhibit 9.5
Types of Equivalence
Source: Reproduced from V. Kumar and Anish Nagpal, "Segmenting Global Markets: Look Before You Leap," *Marketing Research* (Spring 2001): 12.
© 2001 by the American Marketing Association. Reprinted by permission of the American Marketing Association. All rights reserved.

Reliability measures how consistent or stable the ratings generated by the scale are likely to be.

Reliability

The **reliability** of an attitude scale measures how consistent or stable the ratings generated by the scale are likely to be. Whereas validity focuses on whether a scale truly measures the construct (and not something else), reliability focuses on whether the scale consistently measures the concept. Clearly, a good attitude scale must be both valid and reliable. Indeed, unless a scale is reasonably consistent, it cannot be viewed as a true, trustworthy measure of whatever it purports to measure. In this sense, reliability is a necessary, although not sufficient, condition for validity.

Scale reliability can be measured through several different criteria. Two popular criteria are test-retest reliability and split-half reliability.[25]

Test-retest reliability measures the stability of ratings over time and relies on administering the scale to the same group of respondents at two different times.

■ **Test–Retest Reliability**   **Test-retest reliability** measures the stability of ratings over time and relies on administering the scale to the same group of respondents at two different times. The scale can be considered to have high test-retest reliability if the ratings generated through the two measurements correlate strongly and hence are consistent.

The time interval between the two measurements is crucial for test-retest reliability to be a meaningful indicator of a scale's stability. The interval must be long enough so that respondents' ratings during the second measurement are not influenced by their memory of the ratings they gave on the first measurement. But the interval must not be so long that the underlying attitudes change between measurements. Unfortunately, no clear guideline exists for determining an optimal time interval. A rule of thumb, however, is to allow an interval of about two to four weeks between measurements; attitudes, which are often viewed as being deeply rooted, are unlikely to change during such a short interval.

Split-half reliability measures the degree of consistency across items within a scale and can be assessed only for multiple-item scales.

■ **Split–Half Reliability**   **Split-half reliability** measures the degree of consistency across items within a scale and can be assessed only for multiple-item scales. It requires splitting the scale items randomly into two sets, with an equal number of items in each set, and examining the correlation between respondents' total scores derived from the two sets of items.

For example, consider a 20-item scale designed to measure customer attitudes toward online banking services. Suppose each item in this scale has five response categories, numbered 1 through 5. After this scale has been administered to a sample of customers, the 20 scale items can be randomly divided into two sets of 10 items. For each respondent, the total score in each set will be between 10 (10 scale items times the lowest scale value of 1) and 50 (10 scale items times the highest scale value of 5). If the 20 scale items are measuring the same underlying construct—namely, customer attitudes toward online banking services—a respondent whose total score for the first set of items is, for instance, 38 should have a total score close to 38 for the second set as well. Likewise, comparison of the total score for the two sets across respondents should show a consistent pattern of association; the stronger the association, the higher the split-half reliability of the scale.[26]

Note that the two illustrative methods of assessing a scale's reliability actually focus on two separate dimensions of reliability. Test-retest reliability is a measure of *stability* of the scale items and the degree to which scores obtained through the scale remain *the same from measurement to measurement over time*. Split-half reliability is a measure of their *equivalency* or *internal consistency* and the degree to which scores obtained through randomly split halves of the scale correlate with others *within the same measurement*. Both dimensions are important for the scale's overall reliability.

Ratings on a single-item scale are more susceptible to erratic or random fluctuations (thereby lowering reliability) than summed ratings obtained from a multiple-item scale. Summing the ratings across a number of items has the effect of neutralizing random fluctuations; positive errors in a respondent's ratings on certain items may be offset by negative errors in his or her ratings on other items.[27] Therefore, multiple-item scales are generally more reliable than single-item scales.[28]

Sensitivity

Sensitivity is closely tied to reliability and focuses specifically on a scale's ability to detect subtle differences in the attitudes being measured.

The **sensitivity** of an attitude scale is closely tied to its reliability and focuses specifically on its ability to detect subtle differences in the attitudes being measured. A highly sensitive attitude scale should be able to discriminate between respondents who differ even slightly in their attitudes toward something. Alternatively, it should be able to uncover minute changes in the same respondents' attitudes over time.

This description of sensitivity implies that reliability is a prerequisite. When an attitude scale is unreliable, one cannot be sure whether differences in attitude scores reflect real differences in attitudes or are merely random fluctuations. Therefore, a scale must be reliable to be sensitive.

Another requirement for a sensitive scale is that it should have a sufficient range of numbers to facilitate detection of fine variations in attitudes (which we touched on earlier in the chapter). Although a single-item scale can theoretically have a large number of rating position questions (for example, questions 1 and 2 in Table 9.1), respondents may not be capable of making such fine judgments. In this regard, multiple-item scales have a definite advantage. Even when individual items have only a limited number of response categories, the total scores obtained by summing responses across all items will span a wide range. For example, suppose a multiple-item attitude scale consists of 10 items, each with seven response categories, numbered 1 through 7. Respondents' total scores on this 10-item scale can range from 10 to 70. From these total scores we can classify respondents into categories reflecting finer distinctions than would be reflected if only a single-item, seven-point scale were used. Our discussion has shown the reasons that a multiple-item scale is far superior to a single-item scale for measuring attitudes.

SUMMARY

The process of measurement in survey research involves quantifying responses by assigning appropriate numbers to them. However, numbers assigned to survey responses may not possess all the properties commonly attributed to the number system. How closely quantified responses resemble the number system depends on whether they are nominal, ordinal, interval, or ratio scaled. Nominal-scaled responses have virtually none of the properties of the number system; ratio-scaled responses have all of them; and ordinal- and interval-scaled responses fall in between. Nominal- and ordinal-scaled responses are called *nonmetric data* because the concept of differences, or distances between numbers, is meaningless for such scales. Interval- and ratio-scaled responses, by virtue of the distance property they possess, are labeled *metric data.*

Virtually all variables encountered in marketing research surveys can be classified as attributes, behaviors, beliefs, or attitudes. Of these four, beliefs and attitudes, whose measurement is the primary focus of this chapter, are relatively more difficult to measure. Scales used to measure beliefs and attitudes are often assumed to have interval properties.

Attitudes have been defined in a number of different ways, but the various definitions seem to agree that attitudes are multifaceted and relate to certain inner dispositions of people. These general traits of attitudes have two important implications for their measurement. First, attitudes can be inferred only from indirect measurements. Second, to be effective, an attitude measurement procedure attempts to tap the various facets capable of influencing overall attitudes.

Five broad, indirect methods for measuring attitudes are available: observing overt behavior, analyzing reactions to partially structured stimuli, evaluating performance on objective tasks, monitoring physiological responses, and using self-report measures. The last method is the most direct of the five approaches and also the most widely used.

Self-report measures of attitudes typically involve the use of rating scales. A researcher can choose from a wide variety of rating scales, which differ on such dimensions as graphic versus itemized formats, comparative versus noncomparative assessments, forced versus nonforced response choices, balanced versus unbalanced response choices, labeled versus unlabeled response choices, number of scale positions, and measurement level of the data obtained. The choice of an appropriate format for a research project must take into account the nature of the variable to be measured, respondents' ability to make mental judgments, and the types of analyses to be performed on the collected data.

Three popular multiple-item attitude scales are the Likert, semantic-differential, and Stapel scales. Of the three, the semantic-differential scale is the most widely used, perhaps because of its practical appeal and the visually effective profile diagrams that can be constructed from the data generated. Despite the format differences across the three scales, there are apparently no significant differences in the attitudes inferred from the data generated through them. Therefore, a researcher can choose the scale format that best meets the practical requirements of the situation.

To be useful, attitude scales must satisfy three crucial criteria: validity, reliability, and sensitivity. Validity refers to whether a scale truly and fully measures an attitude. It can be assessed in several different ways, including examination of a scale's content or face validity, construct validity (convergent and discriminant validity), and predictive validity. Reliability focuses on the consistency or stability of scores generated by a scale. Two commonly used criteria for reliability assessment are test-retest reliability and split-half reliability. Sensitivity of an attitude scale is the extent to which it is capable of discriminating among respondents with different attitudes. In general, multiple-item scales are better than single-item scales on all three criteria.

REVIEW AND DISCUSSION QUESTIONS

ACE self-test

1. Discuss the advantages and limitations of quantifying survey responses.

2. What are the four key levels of measurement? What mathematical operations are and are not permissible on data from each type of scale?

3. Briefly discuss, with concrete examples, whether attitudes are more difficult or less difficult to measure than behaviors.

4. What is meant when we say that attitudes are multifaceted? Support your explanation with a specific example.

5. Other than self-report measures, what are the four general methods for inferring attitudes? For each method, state one limitation that you consider to be most serious.

6. When should an itemized rating scale have unbalanced choices? Why?

7. Define *scale validity, reliability,* and *sensitivity.*

8. Briefly describe the various methods of validity assessment.

9. Can an attitude scale be sensitive if it is not reliable? Why or why not?

10. Explain why a multiple-item scale is a more sensitive measure of attitudes than a single-item scale.

APPLICATION EXERCISES

1. Suppose a restaurant in your city wants to ascertain the image it has among its patrons. Construct a five-item scale to measure the perceived image of the restaurant, using each of the three multiple-item scale formats we discussed. Make sure that the five items in each format correspond to the same five dimensions.

2. From a survey of users and nonusers of its products, a local telephone firm came up with the following inferences:

   a. On the average, users are only half as old as nonusers.

   b. The image that users have of our company is twice as positive as that of nonusers.

   Critically evaluate the meaningfulness and legitimacy of these inferences.

 ## INTERNET EXERCISE

Kraft introduced Easy Mac, a single-serving microwave version of its classic macaroni and cheese brand, in October 1998. The company was hoping to leverage the consumer's desire for speed and convenience. However, the product captured only a 2.5 percent share of the market in the first year, far less than the expected 5 percent. A tracking study by Millward Brown, a marketing research company, showed that users' perceptions were very different from those of nonusers. Fifty percent of the users said the product tasted good, compared with only 20 percent of the nonusers. Kraft brand managers concluded that the problem was with communication, not with the product, and the company decided to modify its advertising campaign. A series of focus groups was conducted to understand the usage. Mothers preferred the product because it allowed older children to prepare a meal for themselves. Kraft and its advertising agency, Foote Cone & Belding Worldwide (FCB), decided to move away from the traditional consumer benefit of convenience to a more specific benefit: "Older kids can make it themselves." FCB created several slice-of-life vignettes and tested them in a series of focus groups consisting of mothers. Kraft launched its new advertising campaign in January 2000. Sales climbed 30 percent, making it the most successful line extension ever.[29]

1. Given these issues, develop a questionnaire to better understand current consumer perceptions of Easy Mac and attitudes toward Kraft, using online software (see www.surveytime.com or www.infopoll.com).

2. Do you think it would be important to get information from both users and nonusers? Explain your answer.

3. After developing the questionnaire, justify your choice of scales (Likert, semantic-differential, balanced versus unbalanced, and so on) for measuring the constructs of interest (for instance, quality, convenience, usage).

 ## CASE 9.1 DON'S AUTO DETAILING

Don's Auto Detailing is a full-service car wash and detailing center in the Boston area. The only other major car wash and detailing center in the immediate area is located about 6 miles from Don's. Don Johnson, owner and manager, founded the company four years ago with an initial investment of $1 million, consisting of $200,000 in personal funds and $800,000 in borrowed capital. After barely breaking even in the first two years of operation, the business made a net profit of $60,000 in the third year. It incurred a loss of $15,000, however, in the fourth year. Don noticed that the loss was primarily the result of a 20 percent drop in the number of cars serviced by Don's Auto Detailing during the past year.

The Car Wash Industry

According to the most recent U.S. Census information, car washes are a lucrative business; according to that census, there were nearly 14,000 car wash facilities in the United States, with total revenues of over $6 billion.[1] The number of facilities has remained the same since the last census in 1997, while the total revenues have decreased more than 5 percent. In the Massachusetts area, there are 279 establishments.[2] Industry growth is stagnant as a result of the current trends of franchising and larger companies' buying out smaller establishments.[3]

Within the car wash service market, consumers are able to choose from several service options. Among these are coin-operated self-service facilities, automatic facilities, full-service conveyor facilities, and automobile detailers. The different types are all substitutes for one another, which causes competition among different types of providers within the same area. Because any ordinary individual can perform the act of cleaning a car, full-service washing and detailing services are at the luxury end of the industry. Therefore, these operations are dependent on consumers' discretionary income, which varies depending on economic conditions. For example, an economic slowdown, when discretionary income decreases, negatively affects full-service operations. Similarly, during economic booms, discretionary income increases, and operations are favorably affected.

Don's Research Needs

Alarmed by this sharp decline in business, Don hired a small local firm, Burgess Consulting, to conduct some marketing research to help him assess the situation. Although he believed that increased competition was the primary reason for the decline in revenues, Don was concerned about whether or not his advertising strategy was partly responsible. All television advertising was aired on a local channel affiliated with CBS. Radio spots were divided equally among the top stations in the area in three formats: country and western, top 40, and easy listening. Discount coupons were also distributed, primarily through coupon books that contained similar offers from a number of area retailers. Don asked that Burgess analyze the following issues and make recommendations for improving Don's Auto Detailing's performance:

1. The nature of and recent trends in the car detailing industry.

2. The demographic and other relevant characteristics of Don's Auto Detailing's customers.

3. Customers' perceptions and evaluation of the services provided by Don's Auto Detailing.

4. The effectiveness of Don's Auto Detailing's current promotional expenditures of $25,000 per year, which amount to approximately 3 percent of sales. These expenditures are split among television (50 percent), radio (30 percent), and discount coupons (20 percent).

Secondary Marketing Research Findings

After examining a variety of publications and articles pertaining to the auto detailing industry, Burgess Consulting uncovered several key insights. A significant trend in the industry is a major shift in the type of car wash operation frequented by customers. Car wash users prefer the addition of gasoline and accessibility to a convenience store. Large gas stations are installing automatic facilities in many retail outlets and offering free or discounted washes with the purchase of gasoline. As a result, convenience stores and gas stations are the fastest-growing sectors of the car wash industry.[4] Therefore, full-service outlets like Don's Auto Detailing are under increasing competitive pressure.

The customers' wants and needs have also changed. Over the years, most car washes have been full service, which means that they perform interior as well as exterior cleaning at the same time. Full-service car washes, however, do not give customers the option to choose only one cleaning service of the two. As a result, the number of self-service and automatic facilities has increased steadily to address this market need.

Other consumer behavior issues were of interest. For example, the majority of car wash customers base their loyalty to a particular car wash on convenience, price, and effectiveness of the wash. Furthermore, car wash users are usually turned off by long lines and waiting times, although some customers have a higher tolerance for waits than others. In general, car wash users would like their cars to be serviced as quickly as possible.

Full-service auto detailers also face several uncontrollable factors that can significantly affect their profitability. One primary factor is the weather. Auto detailers typically shut down when it rains or snows, yet they are expected to be fully operational as soon as the weather improves. Such variability can adversely affect labor productivity, cash flow, and profits. Another critical factor affecting the industry is the highly seasonal nature of its business. Peak times are between November and March, when temperatures are low. Warm weather brings increasing competition from do-it-yourselfers.

Customer Survey

To address the company-specific issues that Don raised, Burgess Consulting decided to survey a sample of Don's Auto Detailing's customers. A two-page questionnaire (shown in Exhibit 1) was designed. The actual questionnaire was printed on two sides of a single sheet of legal-size paper, with questions 1 through 8 appearing on the front side of the questionnaire and questions 9 through 18 on the back side.

Customers had to wait at least 10 minutes before their car would be ready. Therefore, Burgess Consulting asked the cashier, who was stationed in the customer waiting area, to distribute the questionnaire to customers, to fill out while they waited. Specifically, the cashier was instructed to hand out a questionnaire to every tenth customer during the first two weeks of April. A total of 280 questionnaires were handed out during operating hours over a period of 14 days. Each customer receiving a questionnaire was asked to complete and drop it off in a box next to the cashier's window. At the end of the survey period, the box contained a total of 256 completed questionnaires. The remaining 24 questionnaires were presumably discarded by the customers who received them. Burgess Consulting has coded the data from the 256 questionnaires and is getting ready to analyze them to address the specific issues that Don raised.

CASE QUESTIONS

1. Critically evaluate the questionnaire designed by Burgess Consulting. What changes, if any, would you recommend, and why?

2. For each question in Exhibit 1, indicate the level of measurement for the collected data (nominal, ordinal, interval, or ratio).

Exhibit 1
Survey Questionnaire

To help us serve you better, please take a few minutes to fill out this short questionnaire. Thank you for your help.

1. How often do you usually have your car washed?
   _____ Less than once a month
   _____ Once a month
   _____ Two times a month
   _____ Three times a month
   _____ Four or more times a month

2. How often do you usually have your car waxed?
   _____ Less than once a month
   _____ Once a month
   _____ Two times a month
   _____ Three times a month
   _____ Four or more times a month

3. How often do you usually wash and/or wax your car yourself?
   _____ Less than once a month
   _____ Once a month
   _____ Two times a month
   _____ Three times a month
   _____ Four or more times a month

4. How long has it been since you last brought your car to Don's Auto Detailing?
   _____ Less than a week
   _____ One to less than two weeks
   _____ Two to less than three weeks
   _____ Three to less than four weeks
   _____ Four weeks or more

5. How far away from Don's Auto Detailing do you live?
   _____ Less than one mile
   _____ One to less than three miles
   _____ Three to less than five miles
   _____ Five miles or more

6. How old is your car that is now being washed/waxed at Don's Auto Detailing?
   _____ Less than one year
   _____ One to less than two years
   _____ Two to less than three years
   _____ Three to less than four years
   _____ Four years or more

7. In the past three months, have you used any car wash other than Don's Auto Detailing?
   _____ Yes   _____ No

8. How long are you willing to wait to have your car professionally washed/waxed? _____ minutes

9. Indicate the extent to which you disagree or agree with the following statements. For each statement, circle "1" if you strongly disagree, circle "7" if you strongly agree, or circle an appropriate number in between if your feelings are less strong.

	Strongly Disagree						Strongly Agree
a. The washing/waxing job done by Don's Auto Detailing is excellent.	1	2	3	4	5	6	7
b. The service performance of Don's Auto Detailing is consistent from one visit to the next.	1	2	3	4	5	6	7
c. The prices charged for Don's Auto Detailing's services are reasonable.	1	2	3	4	5	6	7
d. The time taken by Don's Auto Detailing to provide its services is reasonable.	1	2	3	4	5	6	7
e. The customer waiting area at Don's Auto Detailing is comfortable.	1	2	3	4	5	6	7
f. I would recommend Don's Auto Detailing to anyone looking for a professional car wash.	1	2	3	4	5	6	7
g. I would rate Don's Auto Detailing as being excellent overall.	1	2	3	4	5	6	7

10. What is your age?
    _____ 16–20   _____ 31–40
    _____ 21–25   _____ 41–50
    _____ 26–30   _____ 51 or older

11. What is your sex?
    _____ Male   _____ Female

12. What is your primary occupation? _____

13. What is your marital status?
    _____ Married   _____ Single (Please skip to question 15)

14. If married, what is your annual household income?
    _____ Under $10,000
    _____ $10,000–$19,999
    _____ $20,000–$29,999
    _____ $30,000 or more (Please skip to question 16)

15. If single, what is your annual personal income?
    _____ Under $10,000
    _____ $10,000–$19,999
    _____ $20,000–$29,999
    _____ $30,000 or more

16. What newspaper do you read most often? _____

17. What radio station do you listen to most often? _____

18. What TV station do you watch most often? _____

Thank you very much!

CASE NOTES

1. Based on 2002 U.S. Census data about North American Industrial Classification System (NAICS) category 811192. Taken from www.census.gov/epcd/ec97/industry/E811192.HTM.
2. Based on NAICS category 811192 in 2002 (www.census.gov/econ/census02/data/ma/MA000_81.HTM#N81).

3. Julie C. Mead, "Doing Business with Car Washers," *Newsday*, July 3, 2000, 8.
4. According to the International Carwash Association.

This case was written by Jeanne L. Munger (University of Southern Maine) in collaboration with the textbook authors, as a basis for class discussion rather than to illustrate either effective or ineffective marketing practice.

CASE 9.2 RUBY'S CYBER CAFÉ

Ruby's Cyber Café is located in Portland, Maine, within walking distance of a variety of businesses and tourist attractions in the Old Port region. Fred Ladd, who graduated with a bachelor's degree in business administration several years ago, owns the café. It is open from 9:00 A.M. to 8:00 P.M. daily and offers the use of a total of 13 PCs and 2 iMacs, all with the most current system software. The café provides Internet access using the most current high-speed connections, making for very fast surfing. Well known for its fine food and high-speed Internet access, the café attracts local business-people, residents, university students, and tourists alike. Ruby's Cyber Café's sales revenue has been growing at a rate that Ladd considers quite satisfactory. Of late, however, he has been somewhat concerned about rumors that another cyber café is set to open in the same geographic area within the next year or two.

Cyber Cafés

Cyber cafés were introduced in the late 1990s as a result of the booming popularity of Internet use in home and business environments. Blending aspects of a gourmet coffee bar with high-speed access to the Internet, cyber cafés are open to anyone looking for a place to relax, pass the time, make friends, and explore the developing world of online communication. The provision of food and beverages is but one aspect of the business, albeit an important one for creating the right ambiance. Patrons can enjoy a range of coffees, teas, soft drinks, alcoholic beverages, and light meals while they utilize state-of-the-art computer technology. Relying heavily on a relaxed atmosphere and a leisure environment, cyber cafés provide a relaxing and nonintimidating point of contact with others.

Some larger cyber cafés offer additional services. Businesses can arrange for customized training sessions on topics such as Internet awareness, Internet strategy, Web design, and Web development. Typically provided by freelance expert-specialists, courses are tailored to the businesses' needs and ensure high-quality personal attention to those who attend. Cyber café premises are also rented out for seminars, film and fashion shoots, art exhibits, and other special events involving the Internet. Facilities often provide live audio and video linkups. Some well-known cyber cafés also sell a variety of logo merchandise, such as T-shirts, pens, pencils, bags, disc holders, and mouse pads.

The Questionnaire

As a first step in designing an effective strategy to offset any potential threat from another new café, Ladd decided to conduct a survey of his current customers to gain insight into their demographic characteristics and their perceptions of and loyalty toward Ruby's Cyber Café.

Ladd designed a brief questionnaire that was handed out to café patrons before they paid their bill. Eight hundred seventy-eight questionnaires were distributed to all customers who came to Ruby's Cyber Café during a one-week period in July. If a party of two or more customers arrived, just one questionnaire was handed out, and the party "head" was asked to complete it. As an incentive for participation, the questionnaire offered $2 off the bill in return for its completion.

Of the 878 questionnaires distributed, 625 were filled out completely. In addition, on every questionnaire, regardless of whether or not it was completed by a customer, Ladd or one of his assistants recorded three pieces of data: time of day, number of individuals in the party to which the questionnaire was handed out, and total food bill for the party. These data were recorded on a part of the questionnaire labeled "For Office Use Only." The questions on the survey instrument are shown in Exhibit 1.

CASE QUESTIONS

1. Critically evaluate the questionnaire designed by Fred Ladd. What changes, if any, would you recommend, and why?
2. For each question in Exhibit 1 (including question 12), indicate the level of measurement for the collected data (nominal, ordinal, interval, or ratio).

This case was written by Jeanne L. Munger (University of Southern Maine) in collaboration with the textbook authors, as a basis for class discussion rather than to illustrate either effective or ineffective marketing practice.

Exhibit 1
Ruby's Cyber Café Survey Questionnaire

1. How far did you travel to reach this café today?
   _____ 0 to 3 miles
   _____ 4 to 6 miles
   _____ 7 to 9 miles
   _____ 10 or more miles

2. How many times have you been to this café before today?
   _____ I have not been here before
   _____ 1 to 3 times
   _____ 4 to 6 times
   _____ 7 to 9 times
   _____ 10 or more times

3. Do you plan to come to this café again with in a month?
   _____ Yes   _____ No   _____ Don't know

4. How did you first learn about Ruby's Cyber Café?
   _____ On the Internet
   _____ Radio advertisement
   _____ Newspaper advertisement
   _____ TV commercial
   _____ From a friend or relative
   _____ From a business associate
   _____ Drove by and saw the café
   _____ Other

5. What was the primary reason for your coming to Ruby's Cyber Café today?
   _____ To check e-mail
   _____ For access to computer software
   _____ To play games
   _____ For a meal
   _____ For a drink
   _____ To socialize with others

6. Rank the following attributes 1 through 9 in terms of which attribute you feel Ruby's Cyber Café is best on, which attribute it is second best on, and so on.
   _____ Speed of Internet access
   _____ Variety of software
   _____ Up-to-date computer technology
   _____ Menu variety
   _____ Food quality
   _____ Location
   _____ Prices
   _____ Service
   _____ Decor/atmosphere

7. Rank the following attributes 1 through 9 in terms of which attribute is most important to you in selecting a cyber café, which attribute is next important, and so on.
   _____ Speed of Internet access
   _____ Variety of software
   _____ Up-to-date computer technology
   _____ Menu variety
   _____ Food quality
   _____ Location
   _____ Prices
   _____ Service
   _____ Decor/atmosphere

8. Compared with other cyber cafés you have visited during the past several months, how would you rate Ruby's Cyber Café along the following dimensions? (Please circle the appropriate number for each dimension.).

Fast Internet access	1	2	3	4	5	Slow Internet access
Lots of software	1	2	3	4	5	Not enough software
Up-to-date technology	1	2	3	4	5	Dated technology
Expensive	1	2	3	4	5	Inexpensive
Friendly	1	2	3	4	5	Unfriendly
Quiet	1	2	3	4	5	Noisy
Good service	1	2	3	4	5	Bad service
Pleasing atmosphere	1	2	3	4	5	Unpleasing atmosphere
Excellent food	1	2	3	4	5	Terrible food

9. Your sex is:
   _____ Male   _____ Female

10. Your age is:
   _____ 22 or under
   _____ 23 to 30
   _____ 31 to 45
   _____ 46 to 60
   _____ 61 or over

11. The highest educational level you have attained is:
   _____ Less than high school
   _____ High school diploma
   _____ Bachelor's degree
   _____ Master's degree
   _____ Doctorate

12. For Office Use Only
   (a) _____   (b) _____   (c) _____

10 Questionnaire Design

Circuit City: BizRate Customer Satisfaction Survey

Realizing that customer satisfaction is a key driver of business success, companies are employing multifaceted methods to measure in-store satisfaction. Circuit City (www.circuitcity.com) is no exception. Circuit City operates over 600 stores in the United States and employs mystery shopping, exit interviews, focus groups, and telephone surveys to measure customer satisfaction. In 2000 the company tapped BizRate.com, a popular comparison shopping site, to measure nationwide in-store and online shopping experiences.

Shopzilla.com, a newly formed shopping-site arm of BizRate.com, makes available to potential customers previous shoppers' ratings about their satisfaction with a variety of online retailers. Shopzilla.com has a powerful search engine that covers products such as clothing, electronics, and DVDs from around 45,000 retailers. Shopzilla.com obtains results faster and offers more products than the original BizRate.com site, which continues to be available. Shoppers can also compare merchants across 15 service dimensions.

Overall Satisfaction Ratings	
Would shop here again	8.6 out of 10
Overall rating	8.6 out of 10
Preordering Satisfaction	
Ease of finding	8.7 out of 10
Selection of products	8.5 out of 10
Clarity of product information	8.5 out of 10
Price	8.6 out of 10
Look and design of site	8.6 out of 10
Shipping charges	8.9 out of 10
Variety of shipping options	8.8 out of 10
Charges stated clearly	9.0 out of 10
Postfulfillment Satisfaction	
Availability of product	8.9 out of 10
Order tracking	8.8 out of 10
On-time delivery	8.9 out of 10
Product met expectations	8.8 out of 10
Customer support	8.2 out of 10

Source: Courtesy of BizRate.com (www.bizrate.com).

Courtesy of Shopzilla.

Circuit City has extended this survey to offline (in-store) customers. Checkout receipts invite customers to visit a specially designed website (www.cc.bizrate.com) to complete an online survey of shopping experience. To encourage customers to complete the survey, they are automatically registered in Circuit City's "Customer First" Sweepstakes to win valuable prizes from Circuit City.

BizRate.com solicits feedback from Circuit City customers on a number of key attributes, including on-time delivery, product selection, price, posted privacy policies, and website navigation, as well as shipping and handling. BizRate.com evaluates shopping experiences on a scale of 1 to 10 on ten shopping dimensions. Results as of April 2005 are shown in the table on page 278.

Although BizRate.com ratings are free of pressure from merchandisers, it is difficult to tell what the numbers mean. According to Preston Gralla, author of *The Complete Idiot's Guide to Online Shopping*, "What's an 8.4 versus a 9.5?"[1] Not knowing what it means may limit the value of such surveys.

The point is that the surveys play an important role in managerial decision making, and therefore a well-designed questionnaire can go a long way toward getting high-quality customer feedback. ■

As we saw in Chapter 6, questioning and observation methods are the two basic approaches available for gathering primary data. Of the two, questioning is used much more frequently in research projects involving primary-data collection. Furthermore, although data collection instruments are needed in both methods, designing an instrument for a questionnaire study is far more difficult than designing one for an observation study. Researchers as well as users of marketing research must develop an appreciation for the difficulties of constructing a good questionnaire and the potential dangers of using a poorly designed one. The primary focus of this chapter is therefore on designing questionnaires. We will briefly discuss constructing observation forms at the end of the chapter.

Questionnaire Design

A **questionnaire** is a set of questions designed to generate the data necessary to accomplish a research project's objectives.

A **questionnaire** is simply a set of questions designed to generate the data necessary for accomplishing a research project's objectives. As we demonstrated in earlier chapters, primary data may be needed in exploratory as well as conclusive research projects. Primary-data collection in exploratory research projects is accomplished in an informal, flexible fashion. Indeed, seldom is a standard questionnaire needed in such projects; rather, all that is normally required is a checklist of items to be investigated. Therefore, questionnaire design considerations are not as basic to exploratory research projects as they are to conclusive research projects. The bulk of the material covered here relates to constructing standard questionnaires (those to be used in conclusive research projects), although some of the guidelines discussed may be relevant for exploratory questioning as well.

Complexity of Questionnaire Design

Designing a questionnaire may appear to be simple, especially to those who have not designed one before. After all, you might think, once you have a clear notion of the information desired, it should be easy to formulate appropriate questions and arrange them in the form of an instrument. But experienced researchers will quickly point out that nothing is further from the truth. Indeed, even the adage "Practice makes perfect" does not hold when it comes to designing questionnaires. Perhaps "Practice makes almost perfect" is the best a researcher can hope for in questionnaire construction.

No rules can guarantee a flawless questionnaire. As numerous illustrations in this chapter will demonstrate, even questionnaires constructed by skilled researchers may have drawbacks. For example, consider the following question that appeared in a mail questionnaire from a presumably experienced researcher:

> **Do you consider the many marketing research texts available to be adequate for most of your business majors at the undergraduate level?**
>
> _____ Yes   _____ No
>
> **If no, briefly, why not?**

At first glance, there appears to be nothing wrong with this question. However, a closer examination reveals potential problems. It is subject to varying interpretations by different respondents and may be difficult to answer meaningfully. For instance, what exactly do the words *many, adequate,* and *most* refer to in this question? Will one respondent's interpretation of "many" (or "adequate" or "most") be the same as that of another? If Jane Smith feels there are three "adequate" texts, should she answer yes or no? What if she feels there are six "adequate" texts? Several such issues can be raised concerning the meaningfulness of this question.

One positive feature of the question is the inclusion of "If no, briefly, why not?" This part at least offers respondents an opportunity for an open-ended answer if they are unsure of their response. However, open-ended answers, in addition to creating potential coding problems, may just point out the difficulty respondents had in answering the question, rather than provide data pertaining directly to the purpose of the research.

The intent of this illustration is not to criticize the researcher who wrote the question, but to emphasize the complexity of designing questionnaires. Generally, an outsider can easily find some fault with even the most carefully thought-out question. Yet the same outsider may be at a loss to construct a flawless question to replace the one being criticized. Even seasoned researchers may discover questionnaire flaws only after data collection occurs.

In summary, even carefully designed questionnaires are not immune to questionnaire errors. So a research project in which questionnaire design is taken lightly will most likely be worthless. As the next section shows, the questionnaire is a critical determinant of data accuracy—that is, the extent to which the collected data are error free and trustworthy.

A Questionnaire's Impact on Data Accuracy

The questionnaire is the main channel through which data are obtained from respondents and transferred to researchers in conclusive research projects employing personal interviews or mail, telephone, or online surveys. This channel has a dual communication role: (1) it must communicate to the respondent what the researcher is asking for, and (2) it must communicate to the researcher what the respondent has to say. The accuracy of data gathered through questionnaires will be greatly influenced by the amount of distortion, or "noise," that occurs in the two types of communication. Unless a set of questions faithfully reflects a researcher's data requirements, and unless those questions are interpreted and answered correctly by respondents, the accuracy of the collected data will suffer. A sloppy questionnaire can lead to a great deal of distortion in the communication from researcher to respondents, and vice versa.

An additional source of potential distortion in questionnaire studies using face-to-face or telephone interviews is the entry of an intermediary— the interviewer—into the communication channel between researcher and respondent. A poorly designed questionnaire, such as one that confuses an interviewer or is subject to varying interpretations by different interviewers, is an open invitation for the interviewer to bias the data being collected.

Exhibit 10.1 shows the vital position occupied by the questionnaire in the link between researcher and

Trained interviewers who communicate questions clearly and record answers correctly are essential for ensuring data accuracy.

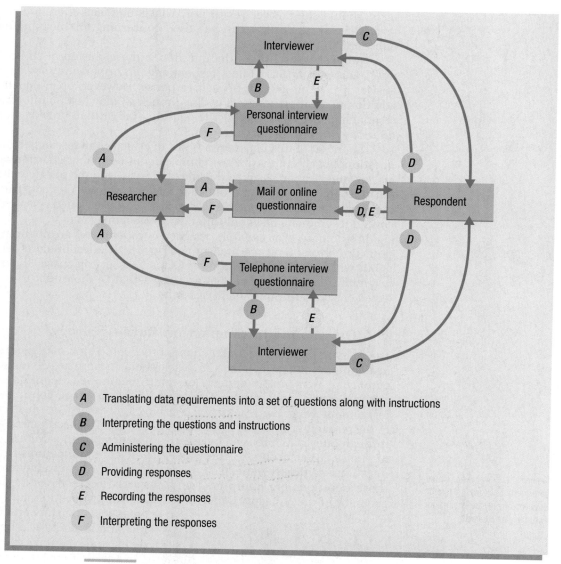

A   Translating data requirements into a set of questions along with instructions

B   Interpreting the questions and instructions

C   Administering the questionnaire

D   Providing responses

E   Recording the responses

F   Interpreting the responses

Exhibit 10.1
Questionnaire: Link Between Researcher and Respondents

respondent. The communication flows represented by the arrows in this figure are of major concern when constructing questionnaires. Lack of adequate attention to questionnaire design will lead to distortions in these communication flows, generating data of doubtful accuracy.

Although there are no rules for developing a flawless questionnaire, the collective experience of numerous researchers offers a broad set of guidelines for minimizing the likelihood and severity of data validity problems. Several excellent books have been written on the subject of questionnaire design.[2] Therefore, we need not and cannot cover all the issues of questionnaire design in a mere chapter. Rather, we will focus here on discussing the key tasks a researcher must perform to design a good questionnaire.

The Questionnaire Design Process

The process of drawing up a questionnaire is a sequence of interrelated tasks. This section provides an overview of the process; subsequent sections describe each task in detail. Exhibit 10.2 shows the key questionnaire design tasks and the relationships among them.

The logical starting point for constructing a questionnaire is to translate the data requirements of a project into a set of rough questions. Of course, as pointed out in earlier chapters, an important prerequisite for identifying the appropriate types of data to be collected is a clear and correct definition of the research problem, objectives, or hypotheses. Next, certain critical checks of the rough draft have to be made: Does each question have the most appropriate form (for instance, structured versus nonstructured)? Is each question relevant and properly worded to obtain meaningful, valid responses? Is the sequencing of the questions likely to introduce any bias? Are the layout and appearance of the questionnaire conducive to accurate and easy data collection?

Each of these checks will invariably suggest changes in the rough draft. Moreover, the questionnaire features involved in these checks are interrelated, in that changes in one may call for corresponding changes in others. For instance, a change in question sequencing may also require changes in the form and wording of questions. The point to remember is that questionnaire design is an iterative process. Numerous loops through the various checks may be needed before a suitable draft of the questionnaire is available for pretesting, which is another critical task. Depending on the number and the magnitude of changes resulting from pretesting, the task may have to be repeated—in some cases, several times—before a final draft of the questionnaire is ready.

The general process outlined in Exhibit 10.2 is relevant for designing questionnaires to be used in face-to-face, telephone, mail, or Internet surveys. Nevertheless, the type of questionnaire administration method will normally impose unique requirements on certain questionnaire features. We'll point out these requirements in the following sections.

Question Form

There are basically two forms of questions: nonstructured (open-ended) questions and structured (fixed-response) questions (see Chapter 6). Here we will emphasize variations of the two basic forms and discuss when and how they can be most effectively used in a questionnaire.

Nonstructured Questions

Although nonstructured questions permit free responses, not all of them may require lengthy or wordy responses. Consider the following illustrative questions:

How old are you? _____

What do you like most about owning your own home? _____

_____

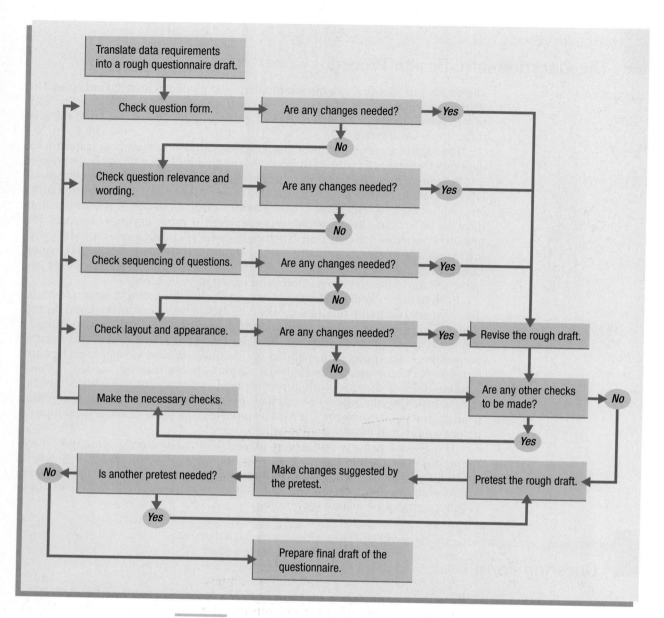

Exhibit 10.2
The Questionnaire Design Process

Will you please describe your thoughts about a person who shoplifts items from a grocery store to keep from going hungry? _____

_____

_____

_____

All three questions are nonstructured. However, the effort, time, and space required to answer them obviously vary considerably. Questions like the last one may be inappropriate for questionnaires to be used in conclusive research projects; the large samples typically required in such projects will make data collection, coding, and analysis particularly difficult. But open-ended questions like the first two, especially the age question, can be effectively used even in the large-scale studies, because responses to them will be relatively short. Hence, not all open-ended questions must be avoided in standard questionnaires intended for a large sample of respondents.

Depending on the types of information desired from a conclusive research project, one may at times need to leave certain questions open ended, provided the expected responses are likely to be brief. For example, compare the data to be obtained by asking the open-ended age question we just saw with data to be obtained through a structured question like this one:

In which of the following categories does your age fall?

_____ Less than 18

_____ 18 to 30

_____ 31 to 45

_____ 46 to 60

_____ Over 60

The open-ended question will generate refined data (the exact ages of respondents), whereas the structured question will only give a rough indication of respondents' ages. Depending on the types of analyses needed to provide the information desired in a project, refined data and hence appropriate open-ended questions may be necessary.[3] Chapter 9 discussed different types of data, and Chapters 12 through 15 discuss their impact on the choice of analysis procedures.

Some researchers also recommend starting a face-to-face or telephone interview with a general open-ended question to put the respondent at ease and kindle interest in the study.[4] For example, an interview dealing with home computers might begin with a question such as "What are your feelings about how the numerous electronic products available today are affecting people's lifestyle?" The respondent can then be introduced to the main questionnaire with a statement such as "That's very interesting. Our interview deals with home computers."

Beginning an interview with an open-ended question is worthwhile if it will be easy to answer and aid in smooth completion of the rest of the interview. Sometimes a general open-ended question may also help during an interview to ensure smooth transition from one major topic to another (such as from purchase to use of a product). For such open-ended questions to accomplish their intended purpose, they must be chosen carefully and be unlikely to embarrass or present difficulties to the respondent. Assuming that a suitable nonstructured question is available for starting an interview, it can be used without the constraints that would normally preclude its use in a large-scale survey. In other words, neither coding nor analyzing the responses to the question is necessary.

Structured Questions

A **dichotomous question** offers just two answer choices, typically in a yes/no format.

Structured questions are of two basic forms: dichotomous and multiple-category. A **dichotomous question** offers just two answer choices, typically in a yes/no format.

Do you smoke cigarettes?

_____ Yes   _____ No

Have you ever watched CNN Headline News?

_____ Yes   _____ No

A **multiple-category question** has more than two answer choices.

Questions with more than two answer choices are **multiple-category questions.** A number of variations of the multiple-category question are possible.[5] Consider the following illustrative questions:

Approximately how many long-distance telephone calls do you make per week?

_____ 0 to 1 call

_____ 2 to 3 calls

_____ 4 to 5 calls

_____ 6 to 7 calls

_____ More than 7 calls

In your opinion, which product category is the most suited to purchase on the Internet?

_____ Automobiles

_____ Books

_____ Electronic items (TVs, video cameras, VCR and DVD players)

_____ Videos, CDs

_____ Computer-related items

_____ Travel (airline tickets, car rental, hotel reservations)

What do you like about Bank of America's online banking service?

_____ 24-hour service

_____ Transaction privacy

_____ No need to travel—do it from home

_____ Paying bills online—no need to mail bills

_____ Other _____ (Please specify)

Although these questions are all multiple-category questions, they differ in distinct ways that have important implications for response quality. We will discuss the differences and their implications under the following headings: response category sequence, response category content, and number of response categories.

■ **Response Category Sequence**   The response categories in the question about long-distance telephone calls follow a natural sequence. In fact, no alternative sequence, other than presenting the categories in reverse order, will be meaningful. However, for the other two questions, the specific response categories under each can be presented in any order. This distinction is important because the sequence of presentation can, by itself, influence a respondent's choice, especially when the respondent is not quite sure how to answer a question.

Researchers have found, for instance, that categories in the middle have greater drawing power than the ones at the extremes if the categories involve numbers (such as the question on long-distance telephone calls). When the categories are in the form of words, phrases, or statements, the categories at the extremes have greater drawing power.[6]

It may not be possible to entirely eliminate the biases stemming from response category sequence. However, some precautions can be taken to minimize such biases. An approach frequently followed is response category sequence rotation, which means rotating the sequence of categories from one questionnaire to the next. The assumption underlying this procedure is that any possible response bias arising from using a particular sequence will be neutralized across all respondents.

The ease and effectiveness with which sequence rotation can be accomplished depends on the nature of the response choices. As we just saw, the only sequence rotation possible when response categories follow a natural order is a complete reversal of the sequence. Unfortunately, even reversing the response sequence in half the questionnaires, an approach known as the *split-ballot technique,* may not effectively neutralize potential response position bias.

Response category rotation is also somewhat more difficult in a mail survey than in face-to-face or telephone interviews. When an interviewer is asking a multiple-category question, he or she can be instructed to start with a different response category in each interview and follow the listed sequence until the starting category is reached. For instance, in the question dealing with purchasing on the Internet, the interviewer can be instructed to start with "Automobiles" and end with "Travel" in one interview, start with "Books" and end with "Automobiles" in the next interview, and so on. When questionnaires are administered through automated computer interviewing or the Internet (as we saw in Chapter 6), one may be able to rotate the response categories automatically from interview to interview.

Response category rotation in mail questionnaires will require printing and mailing different versions of the same questionnaire, which may not always be feasible due to the additional expenses involved.

Clearly, even as subtle a feature as the sequence in which response categories are presented can result in biased data. Nevertheless, depending on the nature of the response categories and the type of questionnaire administration method to be used, potential biases may be minimized. A prudent procedure is to take as many precautions as is feasible.

■ **Response Category Content** What should be included in the response choices for a multiple-category question? The nature of the variable the question is attempting to investigate, as well as the type of data desired, will have a bearing on category content. However, as a general rule, the response choices must be collectively exhaustive; that is, taken together, they should provide for every possible answer a respondent might give. The response choices should also be mutually exclusive; that is, they should not overlap.

For questions dealing with a respondent's attributes (such as age) or behavior (such as number of long-distance calls made per week), we can easily construct response categories that are collectively exhaustive and mutually exclusive. We simply determine the total range of possible answers (which will usually be in the form of numbers) and divide the range into as many suitable categories as the researcher's data requirements dictate. (The number of categories is discussed in the next subsection.) A case in point is the question on long-distance telephone calls presented earlier.

Constructing structured-response categories for questions dealing with respondents' attitudes, beliefs, opinions, and motives (reasons for behavior) is

Structured multiple-category questions about issues that some respondents may not be able to answer should include a "don't know" or "no opinion" category to prevent erroneous responses.

not quite so easy. The range of possible answers to such questions will seldom be clear-cut, nor will wording the categories to reflect potential responses accurately. For example, questions like "What do you think of our president's foreign policy?" or "Why do consumers fail to use manufacturers' coupons when buying products?" will be more difficult to cast into a structured format than a question like "How many years of formal education have you completed?"

Converting open-ended questions about attitudes, beliefs, and the like into structured questions may require some exploratory research, just to get a feeling for the range and content of responses. Even if such preliminary research is conducted, however, an "other" category should be included, just in case the structured responses listed are not collectively exhaustive. Inclusion of an "other" category, like the one in the question dealing with online banking service, will make a question partially nonstructured. But a partially nonstructured question is better than a fully structured question when it is not certain that the response choices provided are collectively exhaustive (for example, the question about purchasing on the Internet). Otherwise, a respondent whose intended answer does not fit any of the listed alternatives will be forced to give an nvalid response or no response at all. In either case, the quality of the data collected will be adversely affected.

Another potential reason why response choices to a multiple-category question may not be collectively exhaustive is failure to include a "don't know" or "no opinion" category. When there is a possibility that some respondents may have no basis for answering a question, failure to provide a "don't know" or "no opinion" response choice will most likely lower data accuracy. As evidence for this statement, in a study in which researchers sought respondents' opinions about a fictitious public agency, many respondents actually expressed opinions about it. This finding led the researchers to conclude, "Clearly, respondents will express an opinion about issues of which they have no knowledge. Such a response occurred even in a situation involving relatively limited pressure to respond."[7] These researchers also found that inclusion of a "don't know" category reduced the occurrence of uninformed, hence invalid, responses. Look again at the question dealing with Internet purchasing and decide whether an "other" response choice should be added. Also reexamine the other two examples of multiple-category questions. Would you recommend any modifications to them?

In addition to being collectively exhaustive, response choices must be mutually exclusive. In other words, a respondent's answer must fit one, and only one, response category. In the following question, for instance, the response choices are collectively exhaustive but not mutually exclusive:

On the average, how many cans of cola do you drink per week?

_____ 0 to 3 cans

_____ 3 to 6 cans

_____ More than 6 cans

Changing the 3 in the second category to a 4 will make the response choices mutually exclusive.

Now refer to the question "What do you like about Bank of America's online banking service?" and its response choices, presented earlier. The meanings of the response choices are distinct and nonoverlapping. However, they overlap in another sense: respondents' answers to the question may fall into more than one of the listed alternatives. From the way the question is currently set up, whether the researcher expects each respondent to check only one category is not clear. Consequently, although some respondents will check just one response, others will check several, even if all of them like more than one attribute of Bank of America's online banking service.

Two options are available to ensure that all respondents interpret the question in the same way:

1. Modify the question to read, "Which one of the following do you like most about Bank of America's online banking service?" With this revision each respondent would, or should, check only one response category.

2. Augment the question to read, "What do you like about Bank of America's online banking service? (Please check as many categories as apply.)"

A researcher choosing the second option must realize, however, that coding and analyzing multiple responses may be somewhat cumbersome.[8] Which of the two revisions should be made depends on the nature of the researcher's data requirements.

▪ **Number of Response Categories** Multiple-category questions fall between dichotomous questions and open-ended questions in terms of the variety of responses they permit. Consider a question dealing with income. If the researcher wants to know only whether a respondent's income is above a certain amount, a dichotomous question will suffice. At the other extreme, if a respondent's exact income is to be ascertained, an open-ended question will be necessary. Frequently, however, a project's data requirements will be between the two extremes, and the researcher will have to decide on the number of response categories to provide. Although no rules exist for determining the optimal number of categories, the following considerations are worth taking into account.

One useful approach for deciding on the number, as well as content, of response categories is to examine past studies similar to the one being contemplated. This approach can be especially beneficial if one goal is to compare the data to be generated with available secondary data. To illustrate, suppose a study of Internet users is to be conducted to determine how their demographic characteristics compare with those of the general public. Data on the general public's demographic characteristics are readily available through publications of the U.S. Census Bureau. Therefore, a beneficial procedure would be to make the form of the study questions (including the number of response choices) consistent with census classifications.

Another important consideration is the type of questionnaire administration method to be used. Having too many response choices to each of numerous multiple-category questions can cause problems in a mail questionnaire. The increased questionnaire length may not only increase mailing costs but also discourage potential respondents from filling out and returning questionnaires. The best solution under these circumstances is to list only the most likely responses (perhaps determined through exploratory research) along with an "other" category.[9]

Multiple-category questions may pose a somewhat different set of problems in personal and telephone interviews, especially when the categories have to be read aloud to the respondents. One obvious drawback of having too many response choices when the interviewer has to read them aloud is increased interview time, which in turn may irritate the respondent. Another drawback is the very real possibility that the respondent will not remember all the alternatives by the time the interviewer gets to the end of the list. As a result, the answer may be biased in favor of alternatives mentioned at the very beginning or the very end. One option for tackling these problems is not to read response categories at all—that is, to ask an open-ended question but have a collectively exhaustive list of response choices printed on the questionnaire, so that coding will be easy and fast. Online surveys minimize these problems, as it is easier to control the presentation of categories.

Unfortunately, the option of not reading the response choices aloud may not always be feasible. For example, in studies dealing with advertisements, researchers may wish to measure aided recall of ads by respondents. Aided recall requires that all alternatives (for instance, all ads appearing in a certain issue of a magazine) be mentioned to the respondent. The researcher can guide aided recall adequately and efficiently in a personal interview by, for instance, handing the respondent a card listing all the alternatives and asking him or her to respond after looking through the list. This technique will obviously not be possible in a telephone interview. Thus the nature of the questions to be asked may dictate the type of questionnaire administration method to use. For instance, a complex magazine readership and advertising recall study may leave the researcher no choice but to select personal interviewing or online surveys, which, as we saw in Chapter 6, are the two most versatile questionnaire administration methods.

Question Relevance and Wording

One of the most critical tasks after drawing up a rough questionnaire draft is to ensure the relevance of every question in it. Each question must be carefully examined to determine whether the data to be generated will be pertinent to the purpose of the research. Although this piece of advice seems obvious (after all, who would want to ask an irrelevant question?), it is frequently overlooked, especially by inexperienced questionnaire designers.

A worthwhile issue to raise concerning each question on the rough draft is: Can the research objectives be fulfilled *without* asking this question? If the answer is yes, the question should be deleted. The only exceptions are general open-ended questions that might be asked at the start of an interview to kindle the respondents' interest or put them at ease, or a question asked during the interview to aid transition from one topic to another. If the answer is anything other than a yes, the question may still be a candidate for revision or deletion and must be further examined with respect to criteria like those discussed next.

Can the Respondent Answer the Question?

Even when a question is apparently relevant, it will be useless if respondents are unlikely to have a meaningful basis for answering it. For instance, consider the following question taken from a mail questionnaire eliciting professors' perceptions about marketing education and marketing students:

> **In your opinion, how many students in your marketing courses are potentially successful marketing managers?**
>
> 10 percent _____
>
> 20 percent _____
>
> 30 percent _____
>
> _____ percent

This question deals with professors' perceptions of their students and is therefore relevant to the study. But many respondents will be at a loss to answer it meaningfully. In other words, the data sought are likely to be beyond many respondents' realm of experience. By the way, see whether you think this question has any other drawbacks.

Another frequent reason for respondents' inability to answer a question, even when the information it seeks is within their realm of experience, is lack of memory. Most people can readily recall the number of traffic accidents they were involved in during the past year or even the past several years. However, most people will have difficulty remembering the number of times they have been to a McDonald's within the past year; they can recall those within the previous week, perhaps, but not within the past year. Ability to remember a past event depends on the time elapsed since its occurrence as well as the importance of the event to the respondent. The latter factor is crucial, because what may be extremely important to the researcher may be trivial to the respondent.

For instance, consider the following question taken from a questionnaire used by a marketing research firm in conducting a face-to-face survey of female household heads:

How much has your family spent in the last 12 months on cookware? $_____

No doubt this question was important to the research firm and its client. But how many respondents would have been able to remember the amount they spent on cookware during the previous 12 months? Our guess is very few, if any. Yet many of them would have answered some amount, the accuracy of which, of course, would have been highly questionable.

Writing a questionnaire for international markets creates another set of problems. V. Kumar and Anish Nagpal caution that the same word can have different meanings in different cultures. Therefore, we should clearly understand word equivalence when writing a questionnaire for different markets.[10] For example, "very satisfied" may be interpreted differently by diverse cultures. In Japan, China, and non-English-speaking European countries, the word *very* is equivalent to *somewhat*. To create equivalence, we should replace "very satisfied" with "totally satisfied."[11]

Good question writers, rather than becoming blinded by what is important to the researcher or research user, must put themselves in the respondent's shoes when evaluating a question's potential value. Questions that might seem meaningless or difficult from the respondent's standpoint must be modified or deleted.

Will the Respondent Answer the Question?

When a question deals with a sensitive issue or is embarrassing, respondents may refuse to answer it, even if they have sufficient information to respond accurately. Worse still, they may actually provide less-than-truthful responses. Questions about personal financial matters or sexual behavior are examples of sensitive questions. Such questions also run the risk of irritating respondents. Therefore, unless absolutely essential, they should not be included in a questionnaire. In studies for which data on sensitive issues are crucial, the researcher may have to use disguised techniques (like those discussed in Chapter 6).

The relevance of a question, the respondents' ability to answer it, and their willingness to answer it can all be affected by its wording. Writing questions capable of generating relevant and valid data is perhaps the most critical and most difficult part of designing a questionnaire. Unfortunately, there is no magic wand we can wave to produce the best question to fit each research objective. In short, the wording of a question and its influence on responses may be so situation specific and complex as to defy any universal set of guidelines. For this reason, and also because of space limitations, we will not cover all the issues of question wording here; books dealing specifically with questionnaire design offer excellent discussions. Rather, in the following sections we will examine several examples to highlight some of the most frequent errors stemming from question wording and the ways such errors can be minimized.

Avoiding Double-Barreled Questions

Suppose the following question is to be used in a survey of the general public:

Do you feel firms today are concerned about their employees and customers?

_____ Yes   _____ No   _____ No opinion

A **double-barreled question** raises several separate issues but provides only one set of responses.

This question is a classic example of a **double-barreled question,** one that raises several separate issues but provides only one set of responses.

Answers to double-barreled questions are very difficult to interpret. For instance, suppose a respondent answers no to this question. A no response can be interpreted three different ways:

- The respondent believes that firms are concerned about neither employees nor customers.
- The respondent believes that firms are concerned about employees but not about customers.
- The respondent believes that firms are not concerned about employees but that they are concerned about customers.

Which of these interpretations is accurate? Only the respondent will know for sure. A yes or a no opinion response to this question may be equally difficult to interpret.

If meaningful, easy-to-interpret data are to be obtained, a double-barreled question must be reworded to focus on one specific issue at a time and provide an unambiguous set of response choices. This revision is usually accomplished by breaking it up into several questions. Thus our illustrative question can be reworded as two separate questions:

Do you feel firms today are concerned about their employees?

_____ Yes   _____ No   _____ No opinion

Do you feel firms today are concerned about their customers?

_____ Yes   _____ No   _____ No opinion

A **leading (loaded) question** steers respondents toward a certain answer, regardless of what their true responses are.

Avoiding Leading Questions

A **leading question,** also known as a **loaded question,** is one that may steer respondents toward a certain answer, regardless of what their true responses might be. The following questions illustrate:

Don't you think offshore drilling for oil is environmentally unsound?

_____ Yes   _____ No   _____ No opinion

Do you think the quality of products on the market today is as high as it used to be 10 years ago?

_____ Yes   _____ No   _____ No opinion

Of course, not all respondents may be led to a certain answer by questions like these. Respondents who have definite feelings about the environmental impact of offshore drilling or about the quality of products currently on the market are unlikely to be swayed by the way the questions are worded. However, other respondents, including those who really have no opinion, are likely to be tempted to answer yes to the first question and no to the second. Invalid data will result if those respondents yield to the temptation.

The risk of asking leading questions is especially great when the focus of research is on people's attitudes, beliefs, or opinions. A researcher might end up unknowingly designing leading questions by failing to remain objective during the questionnaire design process—that is, by wording questions in such a way as to bias potential responses in favor of his or her own preconceived notions about the issues being studied. A conscious effort to construct questions in as neutral a fashion as possible is a prerequisite for obtaining unbiased data. The two leading questions we saw earlier can be modified for neutrality as follows:

What is your feeling about the environmental impact of offshore drilling for oil?

_____ Offshore drilling is environmentally sound.

_____ Offshore drilling is environmentally unsound.

_____ No opinion

How do you feel about the quality of products on the market today compared with the quality of products on the market 10 years ago?

_____ Product quality is better now than 10 years ago.

_____ Product quality is worse now than 10 years ago.

_____ Product quality is the same now as 10 years ago.

_____ No opinion

Avoiding One-Sided Questions

A **one-sided question** presents only one aspect of the issue on which respondents' reactions are being sought.

As their name implies, **one-sided questions** present only one aspect of the issue on which respondents' reactions are being sought. One-sided questions can bias the response, often very subtly. Consider the following questions (notice that the first question is a modified version of a double-barreled question presented earlier):

Do you feel firms today are concerned about their employees?

_____ Yes   _____ No   _____ No opinion

Would you agree or disagree that deregulation of the airline industry has benefited consumers?

_____ Agree   _____ Disagree   _____ No opinion

To appreciate why these questions are one-sided, and hence may lead to biased responses, look at the following rewordings of the same questions:

> **Do you feel that firms today are concerned or unconcerned about their employees?**
>
> _____ Concerned   _____ Unconcerned   _____ No opinion
>
> **Do you feel deregulation of the airline industry has benefited consumers, has had no impact on consumers, or has hurt consumers?**
>
> _____ Has benefited consumers
>
> _____ Has had no impact on consumers
>
> _____ Has hurt consumers
>
> _____ No opinion

The reworded questions are more neutral in that they make explicit all sides of the issues involved.

Certain respondents may have a tendency to agree with whatever opinion is presented by one-sided questions. This phenomenon is referred to as **yea-saying,** and the resulting bias is known as **acquiescence bias,** which results from a respondent's tendency to agree with whatever side is presented by one-sided questions.

The rationale behind presenting all sides of an issue is that the respondent will at least have something to think about instead of blindly answering yes or agreeing with whatever the question suggests. Presenting all sides of an issue should reduce erroneous responses.

The **split-ballot technique,** mentioned in our earlier discussion about rotating response choices in a multiple-category question, has also been suggested as a means of neutralizing possible acquiescence bias.[12] The split-ballot technique usually involves two versions of the same questionnaire, with one version having questions presenting one side of the issues and the second version having questions presenting the other side. In using this technique to nullify acquiescence bias, researchers prepare two versions of the questionnaire, one presenting one side of the issues being researched and the second presenting the other side. (Although the split-ballot technique usually creates only two versions of the same questionnaire, as many versions can be created as there are alternatives to be presented.) Researchers randomly split the respondent sample into two comparable halves and administer one version of the questionnaire to each half. When the data are merged, any acquiescence bias should cancel out.

Although the split-ballot technique appears elegant, it has two primary limitations. First, preparing different versions of the questionnaire can become complicated and quite expensive if several different versions are needed. Second, if responses to the same question vary widely across the different versions, combining the responses to yield an average response might not be meaningful, in which case the question will be essentially useless. Therefore, the split-ballot technique is recommended only when stating all sides of an issue within the same question is likely to make the question too complex or awkward.

A variation of one-sidedness can occur in multiple-category questions when the alternatives presented are loaded toward one side, as in the following example:

Acquiescence bias (yea-saying) is the bias resulting from a respondent's tendency to agree with whatever side is presented by one-sided questions.

The **split-ballot technique** usually involves two versions of the same questionnaire, with one version having questions presenting one side of the issues and the second version having questions presenting the other side.

How important is price to you in buying a new car?

_____ More important than any other factor

_____ Extremely important

_____ Important

_____ Somewhat important

_____ Unimportant

The alternatives listed are unbalanced: four out of the five suggest that price is an important criterion.[13]

To understand the potential bias that unbalanced alternatives may subtly introduce, consider the following balanced version of the same question. The balanced alternatives in this version offer a wider choice to respondents who do not consider price to be a critical factor.

How important is price to you in buying a new car?

_____ Very important

_____ Relatively important

_____ Neither important nor unimportant

_____ Relatively unimportant

_____ Very unimportant

▎Avoiding Questions with Implicit Assumptions

In a **question with implicit assumptions,** the responses can be greatly influenced by what respondents assume in answering it.

The responses to some questions can be greatly influenced by what respondents assume in answering them. **Questions with implicit assumptions** do not provide or imply the same frame of reference to all respondents. Thus the question should state explicitly what respondents should assume rather than let them make their own assumptions. Suppose the following question is part of a questionnaire to be mailed to a city's residents:

Are you favorable, indifferent, or unfavorable toward a 10 percent increase in city taxes?

_____ Favorable   _____ Indifferent   _____ Unfavorable

A respondent's answer to this question will differ depending on whether he or she has accurate information, inaccurate information, or no information about why the 10 percent tax increase is needed. The researcher must provide a common frame of reference to all respondents to obtain meaningful responses and draw valid inferences from them. To assume that all respondents have the same accurate background information pertaining to the question is dangerous. The question can be improved as follows:

Are you favorable, indifferent, or unfavorable toward a 10 percent increase in city taxes to repair potholes in the city's streets?

_____ Favorable   _____ Indifferent   _____ Unfavorable

Implicit assumptions may be embedded in a question in more ways than one. Consider the following question:

Do you drink coffee while watching football, baseball, and so on?

_____ Yes   _____ No

This question makes several implicit assumptions. First, from the respondent's standpoint, it is not clear whether "watching football, baseball" applies to doing so at home on TV, outside the home, or both. Therefore, the answer is likely to vary depending on what a respondent assumes. Second, exactly what "and so on" includes is unclear. Does it, for example, include or exclude sporting events other than ball games? Again, the question is subject to varying interpretations by different respondents. Third, the question apparently assumes that the respondent is a coffee drinker. Whether this implicit assumption is a problem depends on what questions were asked before this particular one.

We can remedy the first two problems, concerning vagueness of the question, by rewording the question as follows:

During which of the following activities do you drink coffee? (Check as many as apply.)

_____ **Attending ball games**

_____ **Attending sporting events other than ball games**

_____ **Watching ball games on TV**

_____ **Watching sporting events other than ball games on TV**

The number and types of response categories included in this question depend on the researcher's specific objectives. But the important point is that the reworded format has much less room for varying assumptions across respondents.

Now let's turn to the apparent assumption that the respondent is a coffee drinker. The question will obviously be irrelevant to respondents who do not drink coffee at all. One way to avoid asking this question of such respondents is to use a filter question. A **filter question** is meant to qualify respondents for a subsequent question or to ensure the question is within their realm of experience. A possible filter question in our example is "Do you ever drink coffee?" Only those who answer yes will be asked the question about activities during which they drink coffee.

A **filter question** qualifies respondents for a subsequent question or to ensure that the question is within their realm of experience.

One note of caution concerning filter questions is that too many of them can sharply increase questionnaire length and interview time. They should therefore be used sparingly, perhaps only when needed to qualify respondents for the entire interview or to avoid asking a question of an ineligible respondent (such as asking respondents the ages of their children before ascertaining whether they have children). Under other circumstances, any potential problem of lack of question relevance can be overcome by simply adding a special response category (in lieu of a separate filter question) to be checked by respondents if the question does not apply. For instance, in the multiple-category version of the question on coffee drinking, the following response choice can be provided at the top of the list:

_____ **I do not drink coffee. (Skip to the next question.)**

The following question is yet another illustration of a question that is vague as a result of the question writer's failure to make explicit exactly what key words include or refer to:

How often do you eat eggs for breakfast?
_____ Frequently
_____ Occasionally
_____ Rarely
_____ Never

The problem with this question is that different respondents may attach different meanings to the first three response choices. For instance, one respondent's notion of "occasionally" may be what another respondent would term "rarely." When such varying interpretations are possible, the meaningfulness of the data collected will be questionable. One way to guard against errors due to misinterpretation is to revise the question as follows:

On the average, how many days per week do you eat eggs for breakfast?
_____ Every day
_____ 5 or 6 days
_____ 3 or 4 days
_____ 1 or 2 days
_____ Less than 1 day per week
_____ Never eat eggs for breakfast

Of course, the question writer may not always be able to come up with categories as clearly spelled out as in this instance. But the point is that, to the extent possible, the question writer must choose words and categories that will be interpreted the same way by all respondents.

Avoiding Complex Questions

Words that a question writer understands perfectly may be unfamiliar or sound complicated to the respondent. Using such words in a question will make it a **complex question,** as the following example shows:

In a **complex question,** words that the question writer understands perfectly may be unfamiliar or sound complicated to the respondent.

In which of the following do you typically invest your liquid assets?
_____ Insured accounts
_____ Stock market
_____ Insured accounts and stock market
_____ Other accounts

If this question is posed to respondents drawn from the general public, many of them may not know what "liquid assets" means, and some may even be unfamiliar with terms like *stock market.* Nevertheless, most will probably give some response so as not to reveal their ignorance. We obviously cannot place much trust in data obtained from respondents who answer a question without understanding it. The important point is to use simple words when possible in writing questions and to make sure respondents can easily understand them. However, this guideline cannot be used rigidly.

In trying to cast a question in the simplest possible terms, the writer must also ensure that it does not become complicated because of increased length. Stated differently, in the interest of keeping questions relatively short, complex words may be used as long as potential respondents are likely to be familiar with them. A sample of business executives (Charles Schwab's potential target), for example, should have no difficulty understanding the terms *liquid assets* and *stock market*. In fact, when the respondents are knowledgeable, spelling out such terms in simple words may be viewed as an insult.

In short, whether a question is perceived as simple or complex depends not only on its wording but also on the type of respondent sample to which it will be posed. A good question writer must be sensitive to respondents' capabilities and design questions that neither go over their head nor talk down to them.

Another type of complex question is one that demands too much effort from respondents. An example of such a question is as follows:

Of the total number of miles you drove during the past month, approximately what percentage was traveled while driving to and from work?
_____ percent

This question is complex, not because it is difficult to understand, but because it is hard to answer. A respondent has to expend a lot of mental effort to answer it. An approach to simplifying it somewhat is to break it into two questions: one focusing on the total number of miles driven and the other focusing on the number of miles driven to and from work. The researcher can then compute the desired percentage figure during the data analysis stage. Whenever feasible, one should ask several simple questions rather than one complex question. The less work respondents have to do, the more willing they will be to answer a question, and the lower their chance will be of making response errors.

Despite our lengthy treatment of question wording, we have merely scratched the surface of this topic. However, our discussion of the various types of faulty questions—double-barreled questions, leading questions, one-sided questions, questions with implicit assumptions, and complex questions—does illustrate the most common wording problems and highlights the dangers of not remedying them. Some of these same problems, or variations of them, are bound to be present in most rough questionnaire drafts.

Question wording requires special care in the context of international marketing research. Researchers conducting multinational studies need to take several steps to ensure that the translation into the local language is done correctly. First, a professional who is fluent in both the languages should translate the original questionnaire. Second, a different translator must translate the local-language questionnaire back to the original version. In the third step, researchers should compare the original version and the translated original version to ensure that they are identical in meaning. In the fourth step, the local-language version should also be checked by the marketing research professionals in the country of interest. Finally, the local-language version should be pretested to make sure the questionnaire serves the intended purpose.[14]

Sequencing of Questions

Questions must be arranged in a logical sequence to minimize data errors and facilitate easy and smooth administration of the questionnaire. Terra Friedrichs, founder of Product Management Associates, a research firm based in Acton, Massachusetts, points out that effective sequencing of questions is one of the most critical aspects of international survey research.[15] The ordering of specific questions in a given situation, of course, depends on characteristics unique to that situation. However, the broad guidelines presented in this section should be helpful in virtually all situations.

Position of Demographic and Sensitive Questions

Classification data are useful in obtaining a profile of the respondent sample and in cross-classifying responses to other questions that pertain directly to the study objectives.

Place questions about respondents' personal or demographic characteristics (e.g., age, education level, income, and so on) at the end of a questionnaire. These questions are included in virtually all questionnaires because they provide **classification data** useful in obtaining a profile of the respondent sample and in cross-classifying responses to other questions that pertain directly to the study objectives. However, asking these questions at the beginning may irritate some respondents and affect their willingness to complete the rest of the survey. The only situation in which demographic questions should be asked at the beginning is when they are to serve as filter questions to qualify respondents for the survey. (This situation will arise when respondents are chosen through quota sampling, discussed in Chapter 11).

Sensitive questions, likely to embarrass respondents or put them in an awkward position, should also be placed near the end of the questionnaire. This placement is especially critical if the questionnaire is to be administered through face-to-face or telephone interviews. Good rapport between interviewer and respondent is essential for obtaining truthful responses to sensitive or threatening questions. Hence, a delay in asking sensitive questions will offer the interviewer additional time to build rapport with the respondent. Placing sensitive questions toward the end of a questionnaire has another advantage: even if the respondent refuses to answer such questions, data gathered through earlier questions may still be useful. But asking sensitive questions at the beginning may cause the entire interview to be lost. Sensitive questions may not even be possible in many international markets. For instance, China, in 1999, passed new regulations on conducting marketing research and collecting sensitive personal information.[16]

Ask simple questions as early as possible. This guideline is a corollary to the preceding guidelines. Easy-to-answer questions can get the questionnaire administration process off to a smooth start (even in the case of mail and online questionnaires, which are self-administered). They also help pave the way for more difficult questions.

Arrangement of Related Questions

When a questionnaire addresses a variety of topics, it is advisable to cluster questions that focus on the same topic. Skipping from topic to topic in a haphazard fashion may confuse respondents, break their train of thought, and cause errors in the data. In other words, grouping questions into meaningful clusters can increase respondents' ease in answering the questions and reduce the chance of response errors. For instance, in a survey of business executives' views on the economy, competition, and employee turnover, a prudent approach is to divide the questionnaire into three parts, with questions in each part linked to a single topic.

Funnel and Inverted–Funnel Sequences

Move from general to specific questions within a topic. This approach, also known as using a **funnel sequence,**[17] begins with a very general question on a topic, gradually leading up to a narrowly focused question on the same topic. Employing a funnel sequence is advisable in virtually all situations (with one exception, which we will consider a little later). But it is essential in situations in which asking specific questions first can bias the answers to later questions.

To illustrate, consider the following sequence of multiple-category questions. (*Note:* To conserve space, only illustrative answer categories have been shown for each question.)

> A **funnel sequence** begins with a very general question on a topic, gradually leading up to a narrowly focused question on the same topic.

---

1. **Which of the following types of TV shows do you watch? (Check as many categories as apply.)**

   _____ News shows   _____ Quiz shows   _____ Game shows

2. **Which of the following types of TV shows do you like the most? (Check as many categories as apply.)**

   _____ News shows   _____ Quiz shows   _____ Game shows

3. **Which of the following specific shows did you watch during the past seven days? (Check "Yes" or "No" for each show listed.)**

   CBS Evening News   _____ Yes _____ No
   Who Wants to Be a Millionaire   _____ Yes _____ No
   Wheel of Fortune   _____ Yes _____ No

These three questions follow a funnel sequence. Reversing this sequence (asking first about the specific shows watched during the past seven days) may bias responses to the questions on the types of shows watched and liked most. In other words, respondents may intentionally or unintentionally give more weight to the types of shows similar to the specific ones they recalled watching during the past seven days.

Although a funnel sequence is generally the recommended format for ordering questions pertaining to the same topic, it may not always be appropriate. An **inverted-funnel sequence** may be better when respondents do not have clearly formulated views about a topic or when they need to have a common frame of reference in responding to general questions on the topic.[18] For example, consider a consumer survey to measure the image of NetGrocer.com, one of numerous dot-com companies of similar size within the dot-com industry. Given the proliferation of such companies, many respondents may be at a loss to readily express what they feel about any particular company, including NetGrocer.com. Furthermore, if they are first asked a general-image question (for example, "What is your overall impression of NetGrocer.com?"), they may not all use the same frame of reference in answering it. For instance, some may base their responses on NetGrocer.com's website, whereas others may base their responses on NetGrocer.com's products. Therefore, it would be preferable to ask the respondents what they think of specific attributes of NetGrocer.com (website, products, customer service, and so on) before asking them for their overall opinion. This inverted-funnel sequence may help jog respondents' memories and provide them with a common set of criteria on which to base their overall opinion.

> An **inverted-funnel sequence** begins with specific questions on a topic, gradually leading to a more general question on the same topic.

Skip Patterns

In a **skip pattern,** questions that are not relevant to certain respondents are skipped.

Ensure that question sequencing is conducive to clear and simple **skip patterns.** Questions that are not relevant to certain respondents must be skipped. Consequently, the number of questions asked and the sequence in which they are asked may vary across respondents and give rise to different skip patterns. Proper sequencing of questionnaire items is essential to avoid complicated skip patterns that may confuse interviewers and respondents.

To better understand this guideline, examine Exhibit 10.3, which contains part of a mail questionnaire. The five questions appear straightforward at first glance. Notice, however, that questions 13 and 14 require the respondent to first determine whether these questions should even be answered. Making respondents screen themselves for a question by using "if" statements has two undesirable features: (1) respondents have to do extra work to decide whether or not to answer the question, and (2) too many ifs in the filter part of the question (as in question 14) may confuse respondents and cause errors. Although question wording is crucial in preventing these potential problems, question sequencing is equally important, as discussed next.

Exhibit 10.4 presents a modified version of the partial questionnaire in Exhibit 10.3. The revised question sequencing and the corresponding wording changes have simplified the questionnaire. The "if" filters requiring a certain amount of effort from respondents to screen themselves have been replaced with simpler "go to" instructions at appropriate places. Furthermore, the question sequencing appears more logical than in the original version. Moving question 11 in the original version to the position of question 13 in the revised version offers a major benefit: questions dealing with the same issue are now closer together. Although all the questions deal with respondents' place of residence, questions 11, 11a, and 12 deal with the state of the residence, and questions 13, 14, and 15 involve the type of residence. The questions also follow a funnel sequence: state questions first, followed by building questions.

Exhibit 10.3
Question Sequence Needing Improvement

11. Do you own or rent your current place of residence?
    ________ Own ________ Rent

12. How long have you lived in this state?
    ________ Less than one year
    ________ One year to less than five years
    ________ 5 years or more

13. If you have lived outside this state, in which state did you live immediately before moving here?
    ____

14. If you have lived in this state 5 years or more and if you currently rent your residence, do you intend to buy a home within the next two years?
    ________ Yes ________ No ________ Don't know

15. How long have you lived in your current place of residence?
    ________ Less than one year
    ________ One year to less than 5 years
    ________ 5 years or more

Exhibit 10.4
Improved Question Sequence

11. Have you always lived in this state?

_____ Yes (Go to Question 12)   _____ No (Go to Question 11a)

11a. In which state did you live immediately before moving into this state? _____

12. How long have you lived in this state?

_____ Less than one year

_____ One year to less than 5 years

_____ 5 years or more

13. Do you own or rent the place where you live?

_____ Own (Go to Question 15)   _____ Rent (Go to Question 14)

14. Do you intend to buy a home within the next two years?

_____ Yes   _____ No   _____ Don't know

15. How long have you lived in your current place of residence?

_____ Less than one year

_____ One year to less than 5 years

_____ 5 years or more

The preceding observations about Exhibit 10.4 carry an important message for questionnaire designers: just following the various question wording and sequencing guidelines outlined earlier (ask simple questions, cluster similar questions) can be very helpful in devising skip patterns that are clear and simple.

You have probably noticed that the skip patterns in Exhibits 10.3 and 10.4 are not equivalent. Specifically, in the original version, only respondents who currently rent and have lived in the state for five years or more are required to answer question 14. In the revised version, however, all respondents who currently rent are required to answer question 14. Is this revision a problem? Not really, for three reasons. First, question 14 is appropriate and meaningful to all respondents who currently rent. Second, and perhaps more important, introducing an additional filter to qualify current renters on the basis of length of residence within the state will unduly complicate the questionnaire. Third, the researcher can still selectively ascertain the home-buying intentions of only those renters who have lived in the state for five years or more by cross-tabulating the responses to questions 12 and 14 (more on cross-tabulation in Chapter 13).

The point is that, in the interest of keeping a questionnaire simple and minimizing potential confusion, filters are best used only when a subsequent question is likely to be meaningless or embarrassing to certain respondents. Alternatively, keeping the number of filter questions to a minimum, through appropriate wording and sequencing of questions, can facilitate questionnaire administration and reduce the chances of error.

Questionnaire Appearance and Layout

The way a questionnaire looks and the way questions are laid out within it can influence the degree of respondent cooperation as well as the quality of the data collected. Appearance and layout are especially critical in mail and online surveys, because the questionnaire has to sell itself. A professionally done, attractive questionnaire can increase the chances of respondent cooperation.

Designing online surveys poses some special challenges. In an online environment, marketing stimuli and measurement instruments appearing on a computer screen may look different to different respondents because the size and type of monitor, the resolution, and color all affect the appearance of an online survey. Furthermore, respondents rely on keystrokes and mouse clicks to answer questions, which is different from how traditional written and spoken surveys are answered.[19]

An uncluttered questionnaire—one with clear instructions, adequate separation between questions, properly located answer spaces, and so on—will significantly lower the chances of error.[20] To illustrate, consider the following two versions of the same question:

Version 1

How old are you?

_____ **Less than 18** _____ **18 to 25** _____ **26 to 40** _____ **Over 40**

Version 2

How old are you?

_____ **Less than 18**

_____ **18 to 25**

_____ **26 to 40**

_____ **Over 40**

Version 2 is laid out better than version 1. Also, it is less likely to lead to the error of inadvertently checking the wrong category. Clearly, it is worthwhile to pay careful attention to questionnaire layout before data collection begins. Yet layout considerations are often overlooked, especially by those new to questionnaire design.

A detailed discussion of such questionnaire features as type of paper, type of printing, and paper size is not given here but can be found elsewhere.[21] In general, a questionnaire must appear attractive, neat, and uncluttered. It must also be convenient to handle, easy to read, and simple to fill out.

An important consideration in deciding how a questionnaire should look is cost. As you might expect, making a questionnaire look professional and eye catching can be expensive. However, cost is usually more of a constraint on appearance (quality of paper and printing) than on layout (arrangement of questions and answer categories). Therefore, a limited budget is not an excuse for a cluttered and confusing questionnaire.

We turn next to pretesting, which can point out potential problems with questionnaire layout and with question wording and sequencing.

Pretesting

Pretesting is administering a questionnaire to a limited number of potential respondents and other individuals capable of pointing out design flaws. It is indispensable because even the most diligent questionnaire designer may make mistakes that can be detected only through an external evaluation. Although

Pretesting is administering a questionnaire to a limited number of potential respondents and other individuals capable of pointing out design flaws.

most researchers recognize the importance of pretesting, it is often improperly conducted or even misused.

A common misuse of pretesting stems from viewing the process as a substitute for careful thought and attention in the earlier stages of questionnaire design. This view can lead to a false sense of security about the soundness of a questionnaire. Pretesting must be viewed as a tool for shedding light on specific features or issues in a questionnaire that the researcher is particularly concerned about.

To assume that pretest respondents will be able to uncover all the potential limitations of a questionnaire is incorrect. As a matter of fact, one study found that pretest respondents failed to detect even glaring errors, especially those concerning questions with loaded and ambiguous terms. According to the authors of the study, "In case of ambiguity, a respondent may not realize that more than one meaning can be associated with a particular term. Because the error arises from different meanings being used by different respondents, a single respondent would be unlikely to bring this error to the attention of the interviewer."[22]

All errors stemming from differences in interpretation across respondents will go undetected in a pretest unless the researcher scrutinizes the questionnaire beforehand, identifies potential trouble spots, and specifically probes the pretest respondents about those trouble spots. Stated differently, a researcher who considers a questionnaire to be sound simply because pretest respondents filled it out completely without any apparent difficulty is making a big mistake.

There are no standard specifications for the number and nature of pretests to conduct in a given situation. Generally, however, one pretest should be conducted using personal interviews, regardless of the administration methods that will ultimately be used, because being face to face with respondents may suggest problem areas or points of confusion that may otherwise go unnoticed.[23] Also, a second pretest conducted using the proposed questionnaire administration method is normally recommended. The purpose of this pretest is to detect problems that may be unique to the way the questionnaire is to be administered. Finally, when a questionnaire draft is substantially modified from the results of any pretest, one or more additional pretests may be necessary before the questionnaire is finalized.

How many respondents should the pretest sample include? Pretest sample size is a subjective decision that depends on a variety of factors, such as how confident the researcher is that the questionnaire is sound and how much time and money are available. In general, however, it is better to pretest the questionnaire systematically by having specific objectives in mind. It is better to do extensive probing of respondents in a relatively small sample than to pretest on a relatively large sample by simply asking respondents to fill the questionnaire out. In other words, the potential usefulness of pretesting will depend more on quality than on quantity.

The composition of pretest respondents should be similar to that of respondents who will ultimately participate in the study. However, pretesting need not be limited to such respondents. Other individuals capable of providing valuable insights include the researcher's colleagues as well as potential users of the data to be gathered.[24] Pretesting the questionnaire on them can be extremely valuable, as they are likely to look at the questionnaire more critically than the typical survey respondent. In fact, a worthwhile approach is to first obtain feedback from such expert respondents and modify the questionnaire draft as necessary before pretesting it on survey respondents.

Questionnaires for Computerized and Online Interviewing

In **computerized interviewing,** the questionnaire appears on a monitor, and the responses are entered directly into computer memory.

In **online interviewing,** respondents selected from a database are invited to visit a website to respond to an electronic form of a survey.

Marketing research companies have long used **computerized interviewing,** in which the questionnaire appears on a monitor and the responses are entered directly into computer memory. Examples of computerized interviewing include centralized telephone interviewing with the aid of PC monitors and questionnaires filled out by respondents using computer kiosks placed strategically in shopping malls. Recent technological advances are leading to increased use of **online interviewing,** in which respondents selected from a database are invited to visit a website to respond to an electronic form of a survey.[25]

Although questionnaires used in computerized interviewing and online interviewing are stored in computer memory, they still have to be designed first, bearing in mind the guidelines and caveats discussed thus far.[26] Also, properly programming the questionnaire into computer memory requires additional time and expense. Nevertheless, in addition to eliminating the need for printed questionnaires and enabling instant analysis of the collected data, computerized and online interviewing offer several attractive questionnaire features not possible in the past. The following list illustrates these features:

- *Randomizing response choices.* For multiple-category questions in which category sequence may influence response choice, the computer can be programmed to randomize the order of presentation of the categories separately for each respondent. Randomization provides neutralization of any response bias stemming from the way response categories are ordered.

- *Checking for response consistency.* The computer can be programmed to check for consistency between the response given to a question at hand and responses given to certain key questions asked earlier. As soon as any inconsistency is detected, the PC screen can bring it to the respondent's attention and give him or her an opportunity to correct the inconsistency. In this way, the accuracy of the collected data can be improved.

- *Incorporating complex skip patterns.* Earlier in the chapter, we saw that complex skip patterns—such as "If your answer to question 5 is 'Yes' and your answer to question 7 is 'No,' skip to question 10; otherwise, go to question 9"— can confuse respondents or interviewers and hence should be avoided. However, computerized or online interviewing can handle even very complex skip patterns. The computer can easily check as many "if" statements and previous responses as necessary, decide which question should be asked next, and pose that question on the screen almost instantaneously.

- *Personalization.* Once a respondent's name is entered into the computer keyboard at the start of an interview, that name can be automatically inserted into key questions and instructions throughout the questionnaire, to provide a degree of personalization that would be very time consuming to achieve in noncomputerized interviewing. Personalization can add greatly to the rapport established with the respondent.

- *Drawing questions from computer libraries.* Developing a questionnaire for online and computerized interviewing has become simpler with the availability of Web-based questionnaire design software. A questionnaire writer simply clicks and drags a standard questionnaire from an online library and modifies it as necessary to create a desired questionnaire.[27] SurveyZ.com, an online marketing research company, offers survey templates for many different marketing applications.

SurveyTime.com (also known as SurveyZ.com) Develops Customer Satisfaction Survey for Microsoft[28] Microsoft conducted an online survey targeted at developers whose companies manufacture, distribute, sell, service, or support computer-related products or services. An online survey was ideal for this group. Microsoft had access to the developers because they had registered for products and developer seminars or with Microsoft for developer assistance. Lisa Wilmore, the manager of the project, expected that developers would respond well to the online survey because they typically spend a large portion of their time at the computer and have online access.

The survey met several criteria for an effective online survey: (1) it was well targeted, (2) it was of interest to the prospective respondents, and (3) there was an incentive attached. When the survey was administered, a coupon redeemable at Amazon.com was offered.

This survey began by qualifying the respondents, eliminating individuals who were either currently unemployed; were not with companies that manufacture, distribute, sell, service, or support computer-related products or services; or were not actually working as developers.

Overall metrics for satisfaction were then asked, including overall satisfaction with Microsoft, likelihood of recommending Microsoft products to a friend or colleague, and likelihood of repurchasing Microsoft products. Price and value evaluations were made next, followed by a detailed evaluation of relationships with Microsoft employees—whether face to face, over the telephone, through Microsoft conferences and seminars, or via websites, e-mail, or regular mail.

Section topics were then addressed, including an evaluation of company reputation, programs, specific Microsoft developers' network services, and support for developers.

The survey concluded by profiling the developer's use of products, specific development platforms, and interest in new technology areas.

When the survey was deployed, there was an immediate response, with nearly 1,000 completed surveys received within 48 hours. Most of these responses were received in the first four hours the survey was active. The survey was considered a great success.

A step-by-step approach for developing an online survey using SurveyZ.com is described at the end of this chapter. The website also contains tips for constructing an effective questionnaire.[29] ◀

- *Adding new response categories.* Consider a multiple-category question with an "other" category. In computerized and online interviewing, when a prespecified number of respondents provide the same open-ended response to the "other" category, that response can be automatically converted into an explicit checkoff category by adding it to the set of prespecified categories. The addition of such new categories may help reduce the time required for subsequent interviews. In fact, the greatest advantage of online interviewing is the ability to intervene during the data collection process and make necessary changes to the questionnaire to get better responses.

The preceding features are by no means an exhaustive list of the increased capabilities offered by computerized and online interviewing. The questionnaire designer's and computer programmer's ingenuity are the only limits on the creative ways such interviewing can be used to overcome some of the limitations of traditional interviewing. It is important to note, however, some of the drawbacks that are inherent in computerized and online interviewing. The size and type of monitor, resolution and color palette, scrolling mechanism, bandwidth, modem connection (cable modem, DSL, or telephone), network connection (ISP provider), and network traffic will affect the appearance of online surveys.[30] We must remember that the computer cannot design a questionnaire; design is still a human responsibility. Computerized or online interviewing is therefore not a panacea for questionnaire design.

Designing Cover Letters for Mail and Online Surveys

The **cover letter** tells potential respondents what the study is about and, more critically, convinces them of the importance of participating in it.

Among the factors likely to have a major impact on whether a mail questionnaire is filled out and returned is the cover letter accompanying it. The primary purpose of a **cover letter** is to win the cooperation of respondents. Studies have shown that what the cover letter says and how it says it can affect the response rate to a mail survey.[31] Therefore, a researcher planning to use a mail questionnaire must spend some time and effort designing an effective cover letter.

A good cover letter should tell potential respondents what the study is about and, more critically, convince them of the importance of participating in it. The cover letter should also be concise and objective; it should not bias the respondent in any way. Several of the guidelines mentioned in connection with wording, appearance, and layout of questionnaires are relevant to designing cover letters as well.[32]

Exhibit 10.5 presents an illustrative cover letter and a list of its key features. The numbers identifying different sections of the cover letter correspond to the features listed below it. Notice that virtually all the features either directly or indirectly attempt to impress on respondents the need to cooperate. However, not all these features need to be incorporated in every cover letter. In fact, a cover letter containing every listed feature can at times be self-defeating; it may become, or at least appear to be, so lengthy that some respondents may lose interest in reading it. Exhibit 10.5 aims merely to show the variety of ways respondents can be encouraged to participate in a survey. An effective cover letter must possess at least several, but not necessarily all, of the illustrated attributes.

The guidelines for designing cover letters for mail surveys are also relevant for online surveys. Winning respondents' cooperation is just as critical in online surveys as it is in mail surveys. Persuading potential respondents to visit the website containing an online survey requires a convincing and succinct online invitation as well as a clear and enticing e-mail subject. An effective online invitation should have features similar to those of a good mail-survey cover letter.

Openers for Personal and Telephone Interviews

Just as cover letters are important in mail surveys, good introductory statements are essential to securing respondent cooperation in personal and telephone interviews. Openers in these interviews need not, and perhaps should not, be as lengthy as a typical cover letter. But they should usually include the following features:

- An appropriate salutation, such as "Good morning! I'm Ralph Johnston with Marketing Research Associates Company."
- A brief statement about the project and its purpose, such as "We're conducting a survey of heads of household regarding their feelings about modern home appliances."
- An indication of how long the interview might last, such as "This survey should take no more than 10 minutes."
- A polite request for permission to conduct the interview, such as "May I please talk to the male or female head of your household for a few minutes?"

MAIL SURVEYS COMPANY
12345 Easy Street
Mytown, California 90000   (17)

(1) Dear Mr. Stockton,   (Date)

(2) ———— Will you do us a favor?   (3)   (3)   (4)   (1)   (4)

(1) We are conducting a nationwide survey among executives and managers in the automotive
industries. The purpose of this research is to find out the opinion of yourself and other experts on
(5) the advantages and disadvantages of using e-commerce in conducting business-to-business
(6) transactions. Your answers will enable e-commerce managers to understand the requirements of   (3)
current and potential users, and this in turn will help them to design better e-commerce applications.
(7)

Your name appeared in a scientifically selected random sample. Your answers are very
(11) important to the accuracy of our research, whether or not your company is an extensive user of e-   (5)
commerce applications.   (8)   (6)

(9) ———— It will take only a short time to answer the simple questions on the enclosed questionnaire
and to return it in the stamped reply envelope.   (10)   (3)

(12) ———— Of course all answers are confidential and will be used only in combination with those of
other automotive executives and managers from all over the United States.   (4)

(13) ———— If you are interested in receiving a report on the findings of this research, just write your
name and address at the end of this questionnaire, or if you prefer, request the results of the survey
on e-commerce in a separate letter. We will be glad to send you a complimentary report when
ready.   (12)

(14) ———— Please return the completed questionnaire at your earliest convenience. Thank you for your   (15)
help.

Sincerely,

Stanley M. Black   (1)

Stanley M. Black
Director of Research   (16)

(18) P.S.   The enclosed amazon.com coupon is just a token of our appreciation. It may brighten the day
of a child you know.

Key

1. Personal communication
2. Asking a favor
3. Importance of research
4. Importance of the recipient
5. Importance of the replies in general
6. Importance of the replies where the reader is not qualified to answer most questions

7. How the recipient may benefit from this research
8. Completing the questionnaire will take only a short time
9. The questionnaire can be answered easily
10. A stamped reply envelope is enclosed
11. How recipient was selected
12. Answers are anonymous or confidential

13. Offer to send report on results of survey
14. Note of urgency
15. Appreciation of sender
16. Importance of sender
17. Importance of the sender's organization
18. Description and purpose of incentive

Exhibit 10.5
Illustrative Cover Letter and Key Features
Adapted from Paul R. Erdos, *Professional Mail Surveys*, rev. ed. (Melbourne, FL: Krieger Publishing, 1983), 102–103. Used by permission.

Openers for personal and telephone interviews should be carefully constructed and be an integral part of the questionnaire to ensure consistency across interviews and across interviewers. Lack of consistency in openers can result in unnecessary distortions and biases in the data to be collected. And just as a suitable opener is important for getting the interview off to a good start, common courtesy demands that the questionnaire end with an appropriate thank-you statement.

Designing Observation Forms

As mentioned at the beginning of the chapter, designing observation forms is somewhat easier than constructing questionnaires. Nevertheless, the quality of data gathered through observation depends on the clarity of the instructions given and the tasks assigned to the observers. A standard form is not necessary when a study involves nonstructured observation; the observer simply makes mental and written notes about whatever is being observed. In these studies, the training and skills of the observer are critical for generating relevant and objective information.

When structured observation is involved, however, a standard form that clearly states the specific observations to be made and provides for efficient

Exhibit 10.6
Observation Form for Recording Characteristics and Behavior of Customers Stopping at a Special Display

Observation number _____

AS SOON AS YOU OBSERVE ANY ADULT CUSTOMER (ANY CUSTOMER WHO APPEARS TO BE 18 YEARS OF AGE OR MORE) STOPPING AT THE DISPLAY, START YOUR STOPWATCH AND RECORD THE FOLLOWING:

1. Sex of the customer:
   _____ Male   _____ Female

2. Approximate age of the customer:
   _____ 18–30
   _____ 31–50
   _____ Over 50

3. Number of individuals accompanying the customer: _____
   (IF NONE, GO ON TO ITEM 4.)
   a. How many of the accompanying individuals are adults? _____
   b. How many are cildren? _____

4. Does the customer touch or handle the product?
   _____ Yes   _____ No

5. Do any of the accompanying *adults* touch or handle the product?
   _____ Yes   _____ No   _____ No accompanying adult

6. Do the customer or accompanying adults, if any, leave the display with one or more units of the displayed product?
   _____ Yes   _____ No
   How many *total* units? _____

STOP YOUR STOPWATCH WHEN THE CUSTOMER *AND* ACCOMPANYING ADULTS, IF ANY, LEAVE THE DISPLAY AREA. RECORD BELOW THE TOTAL TIME SPENT AT THE DISPLAY.
   _____ Minutes   _____ Seconds

GO TO A NEW OBSERVATION FORM AND RECORD INFORMATION FOR THE NEXT ADULT WHO STOPS AT THE DISPLAY.

recording of those observations is desirable. Several of the guidelines concerning such aspects as wording, sequencing, and layout, which we discussed under questionnaire design, are germane to constructing observation forms as well. After all, a structured-observation form is basically a questionnaire that the observer fills out. A cluttered or confusing observation form can cause problems for the observer and result in erroneous data.

Exhibit 10.6 illustrates a form that can be used in a structured-observation study to ascertain the impact on customers of a special in-store display. The primary purpose of Exhibit 10.6 is to show what a structured-observation form might look like. It is not to be viewed as an exhaustive list of items to be observed to evaluate a special display's impact. As in the case of a questionnaire, the content of an observation form—that is, the various observation tasks and items it includes—should be based on well-defined objectives and specific information requirements in a given setting.

Creating an Online Questionnaire Using SurveyZ.com*

Login Screen

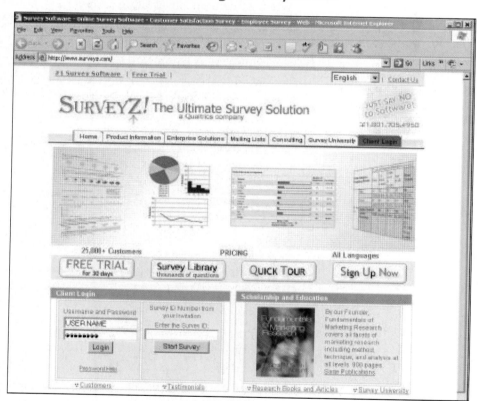

Setting up an Account (first–time users)

1. From the home page, click "Free Trial" on the far left side under the member login boxes.

2. Complete the required information, selecting a user name and password for your personal account.

3. *Enter the PassKey code provided with your textbook to upgrade your account.*

*Courtesy of SurveyZ.com. Screen shots reprinted by permission from Microsoft Corporation.

4. Read and check the terms and conditions box.

5. Indicate your willingness to be part of a survey panel.

6. Click "Register Now" at the bottom of the page when complete.

7. When finished, you will receive notification that you are registered and that an e-mail has been generated to confirm the account setup. (The e-mail will contain your user name and password.)

8. You will then be prompted for your password to log in.

9. Once logged into the system, you will be taken to the survey page to build your first survey.

Already Registered

1. Enter your user name and password in the member login boxes.

2. Click "LOGIN."

3. The first page will contain a list of the surveys you have previously created.

4. To begin a new survey, you can choose an existing survey or select "Create New Survey" in the upper-right-hand corner of the survey box.

Create a Survey

Note: First-time users will want to review the question types before starting the survey. To view the options, simply click "Question Types" at the far right on the home page, under "Build Your Survey Online."

Step 1
Click "Use Survey Creation Wizard."

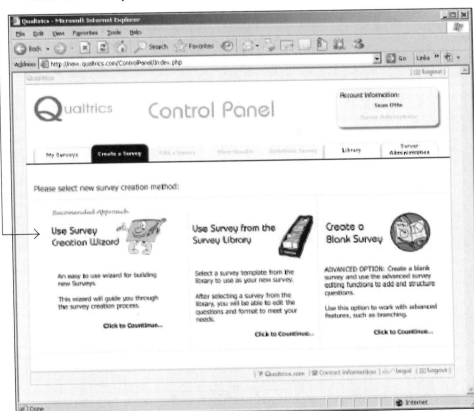

Step 2
a. Enter a title for your survey.
b. Enter a survey description.
c. Make sure you are selected as the user.

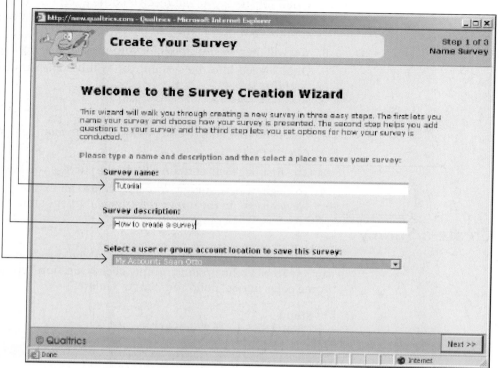

Step 3
Select between two options:
a. Single Question—every question is presented on a different web page
b. Multiple Question—every question is presented on the same web page
   unless you force a page break

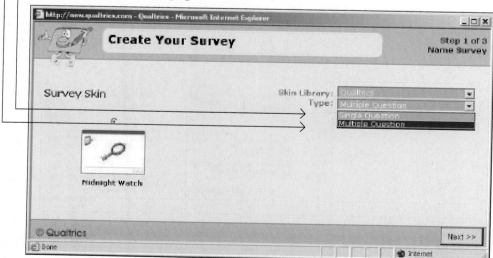

Step 4

This screen confirms that you have created the survey and are now adding questions to the survey.

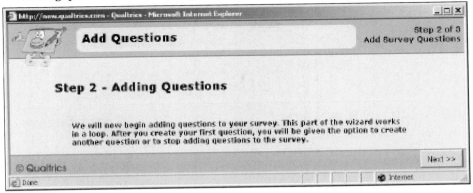

Add Questions to a Survey

Step 1

Select a **question category** from the drop-down box on the left.

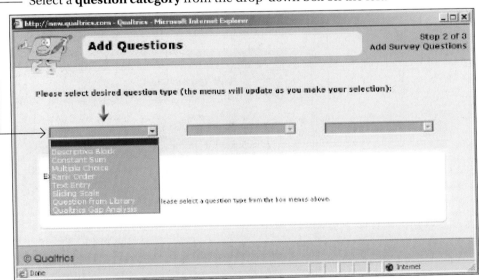

Step 2
Select a **question type** from the drop-down box in the middle.

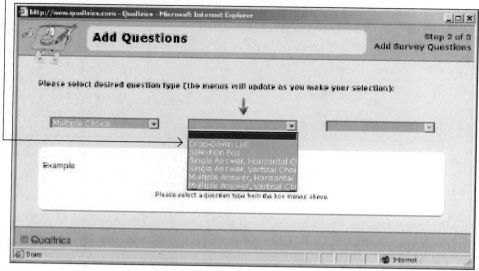

Step 3
Select the **question medium**—graphic or text choice.

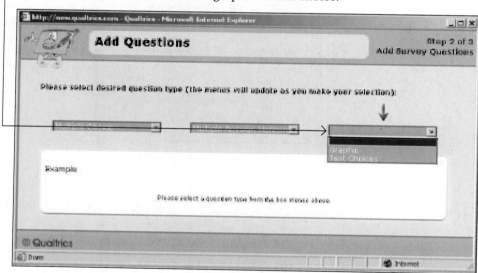

Step 4

Upon completion, an example of the question chosen will be shown.

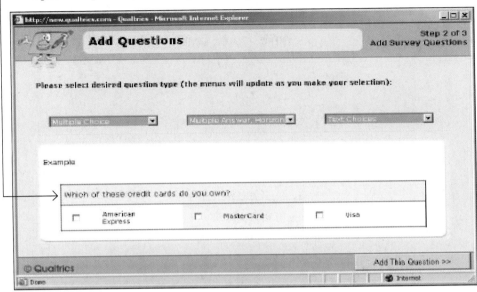

Step 5

Add your question text and answer text.

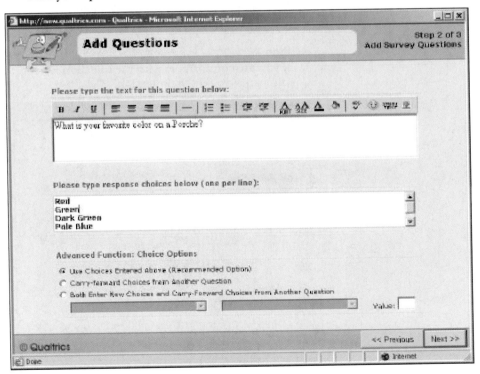

Step 6
Select any additional options as necessary.

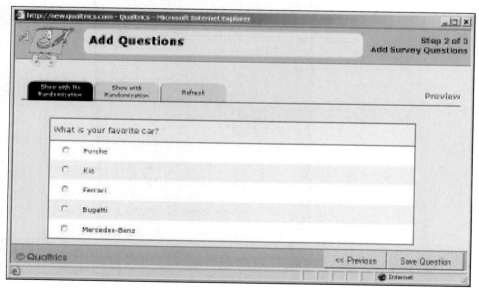

Step 7
If you are comfortable with the question, select "Save Question." If not, select "Previous" to edit the question.

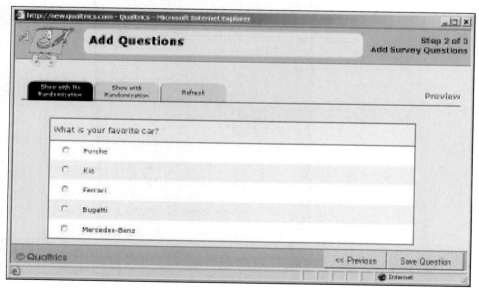

Step 8

From this screen you can **edit questions** in the survey and **add** additional questions.

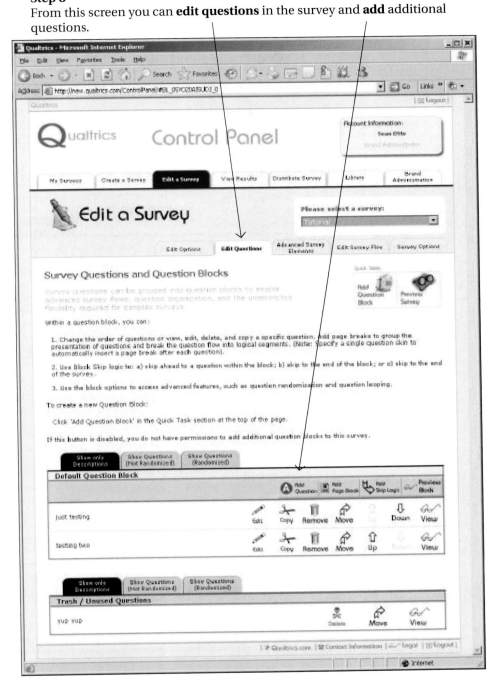

Distribute a Survey

Step 1
a. Select "Distribute Survey" on the top set of tabs.
b. Cut and paste the **default link** into an email and send it off.

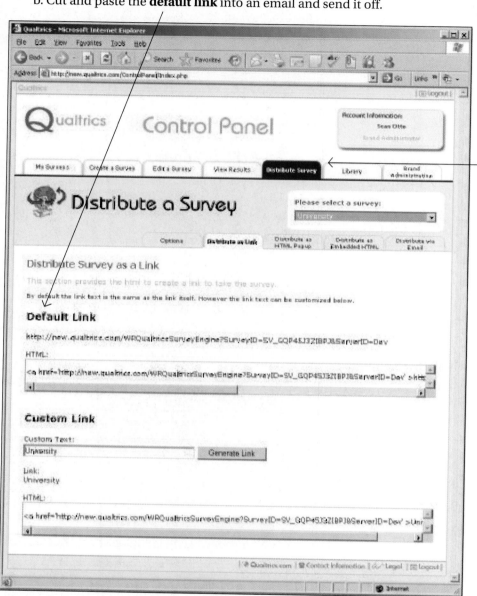

Step 2
Select "Distribute via Email" to upload and distribute a mailing list.

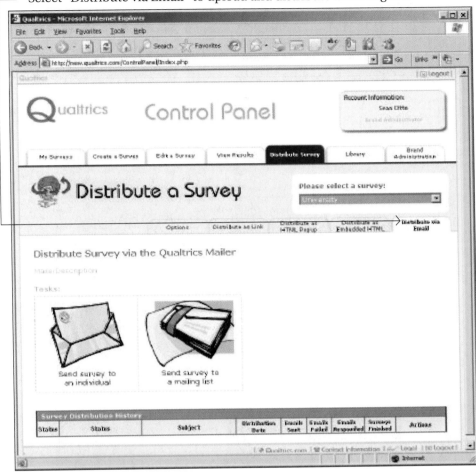

Survey Results

Step 1
Select the survey for which you wish to view results.

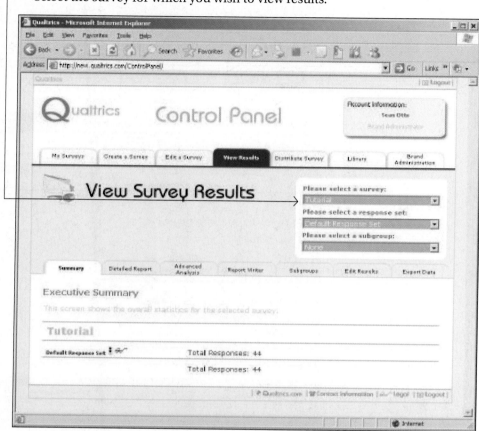

Step 2
Select "Export Data," and select the file type you'd prefer.

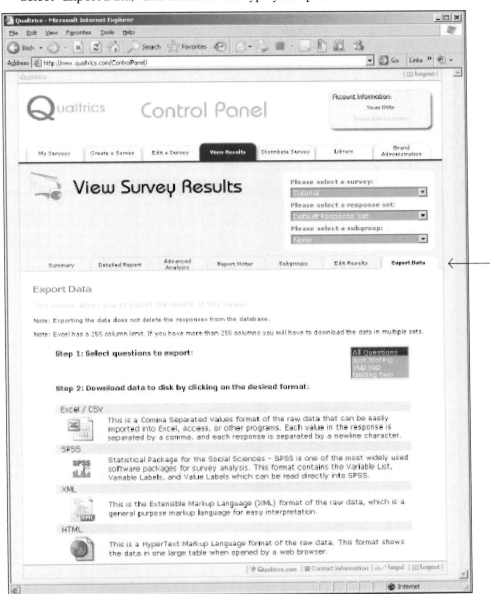

Step 3
Select "Detailed Report" and "Comprehensive" to view your data.

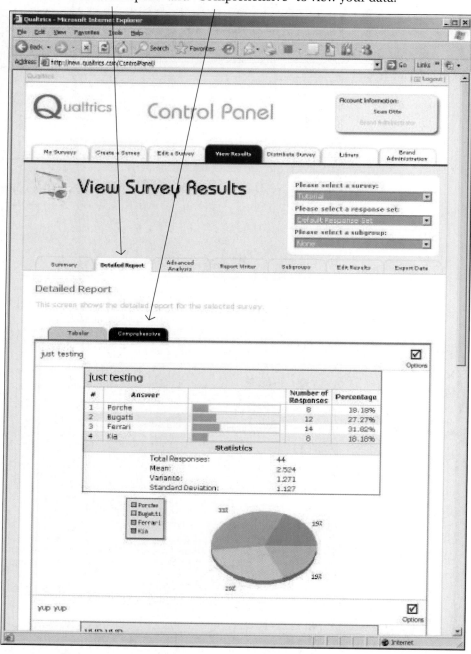

Step 4
For **advanced analysis,** select the "View Results" tab, and then select "Add."

SUMMARY

Constructing questionnaires is not an easy undertaking. Even seasoned researchers at times inadvertently overlook design flaws. Devoting adequate time and effort to questionnaire design is therefore critical. The quality and the ultimate usefulness of data to be gathered through a survey are vitally dependent on how good the questionnaire is.

No standard methodology exists for designing questionnaires; however, we can regard the design as a sequential process consisting of interrelated steps. Once the data requirements of a project are clearly defined, they can be transformed into a corresponding set of rough questions. The rough draft must then go through one or more iterations involving a variety of checks.

A key decision to be made concerning each question is whether it should be open ended or structured. Open-ended questions are generally not recommended for surveys of large samples. However, they can be used as warmup questions or as transition questions to aid the smooth flow of the interview. Structured questions can be dichotomous or multiple-category questions. The categories in a multiple-category question must be collectively exhaustive and mutually exclusive. One should also rotate the categories, if feasible. The number of response categories to include depends on the nature of the research objectives, the data requirements, and the type of questionnaire administration method to be used.

The relevance of each question must be carefully examined and irrelevant questions dropped. This guideline is especially important because there is a normal tendency to include more questions than are really needed. Also, questions that a respondent cannot answer meaningfully or will not answer truthfully should be eliminated if they cannot be suitably rephrased.

Question wording is perhaps the most critical determinant of data accuracy. Unfortunately, the essentials for wording questions properly cannot be reduced to a neat, concise set of rules. However, even unseasoned researchers can spot wording problems by putting themselves in the respondent's shoes and critically examining each question. Attention must be paid to identifying problem questions, such as double-barreled questions, leading questions, one-sided questions, questions with implicit assumptions, and complex questions. Question wording requires even more attention in international research involving data collection in multiple countries.

The sequencing of questions is another determinant of data accuracy. Questions must be arranged in a logical sequence. The following principles should generally be heeded, unless certain exceptional situations demand otherwise. Questions that are personal, sensitive, or difficult to answer should be placed as far into the questionnaire as possible. Questions related to the same topic should appear together. Questions within a topic should go from general to specific (follow a funnel sequence). Question skip patterns should be simple and kept to a minimum.

Questionnaire appearance and layout, if ignored, can lead to confusion and coding errors. In mail and online surveys, these elements can also have a significant impact on respondents' willingness to cooperate.

Pretesting involves administering a questionnaire to a limited number of respondents to uncover and correct any faults before the final draft is prepared. A researcher's colleagues and potential users of the data to be generated are valuable critics at this stage. Resources permitting, a questionnaire should be pretested on survey respondents at least twice: once through personal interviews involving in-depth probing and a second time using an administration procedure similar to the one proposed for the study. For pretesting to be most effective, the researcher should have already identified specific items likely to be potential trouble spots in the questionnaire and should probe for information capable of shedding light on those items.

Computerized interviewing and online surveys, which are becoming increasingly popular, offer a number of questionnaire design benefits that are difficult if not impossible to achieve under conventional modes of interviewing. These benefits include capabilities for randomizing response choices, checking for response consistency, incorporating complex skip patterns, personalization, drawing questions from computer libraries, and adding new response categories on the basis of interviews already completed.

An element unique to mail and online surveys, and critical for obtaining high response rates, is the cover letter. Above all else, a good cover letter should convince respondents to cooperate and do so in a concise and objective fashion. Personal and telephone interviews also require appropriate, concise openers.

Studies involving structured observation typically use standard data collection forms. Although these forms are somewhat easier to construct than questionnaires, they must be designed with care. Several of the guidelines presented for designing questionnaires are also relevant for designing observation forms.

REVIEW AND DISCUSSION QUESTIONS

1. "Designing a questionnaire for a conclusive research project is more difficult than designing one for an exploratory research project." Discuss this statement.

2. Give two examples to illustrate why the steps involved in questionnaire design are interrelated.

3. Under what circumstances could you use nonstructured questions in a conclusive research study?

4. What factors should be considered in deciding on the number of categories to include in a multiple-category question?

5. Explain why you agree or disagree with the following statement: "As long as a question pertains to at least one of the research objectives, it must be included in the questionnaire."

6. What is a filter question? When are such questions most appropriate?

7. What is meant by a funnel sequence? Is it always beneficial in a questionnaire? Why or why not?

8. Using Exhibit 10.1 as a guide, briefly discuss the major ways in which a questionnaire may result in inaccurate data.

9. State and briefly describe the questionnaire design benefits offered by computerized interviewing.

10. In what ways do the design and use of an online questionnaire differ from those of other types of questionnaires?

APPLICATION EXERCISES

1. Suppose you want to ascertain the extent to which students in your class are paying for their educational expenses through their own earnings. Assuming that you want to ask just one question, how would you phrase it in each of the following forms: open-ended, dichotomous, and multiple-category? In what ways would the type of data obtained through each form differ?

2. Make up an example of your own to illustrate each of the following: (a) a double-barreled question; (b) a leading question; and (c) a question with an implicit assumption. In each case, suggest a revised question that will reduce potential bias.

3. 3M, a $16 billion company, is known for its innovative culture. The company enjoys a strong position in the home and leisure business, with well-known brands such as Scotch, Scotch-Brite, O-Cel-O, Post-it, Scotchgard, and 3M. Despite strength in three home care market segments (plain sponges, scouring pads, and scrub sponges), 3M did not have a presence in the wool soap pad segment, a niche dominated by titans SOS and Brillo. 3M conducted eight focus groups with consumers around the country. The research revealed that the standard steel wool pads scratched consumers' expensive cookware. This finding produced the idea for Scotch-Brite Never Scratch Soap Pads. 3M made Scotch-Brite from gentler minerals than those used by Brillo and SOS, thus reducing the odds of damaging cookware. Develop a questionnaire to assess consumer perceptions of the effectiveness of the new product relative to the competition (Brillo and SOS).

INTERNET EXERCISES

1. Go to CNN's website (www.cnn.com) and evaluate the QuickVote question of the day. Could this question have been phrased better? If yes, provide the new phrasing.

2. Go to BizRate's website (www.bizrate.com) and evaluate its online questionnaire (see the opening vignette).

CASE 10.1 THIS STUDY BROUGHT TO YOU BY …

Janet Raines was recently hired by Brown's Marketing Insight, a prominent marketing research firm, as an assistant research analyst. Janet was asked by her boss, Anna Brown, to assist in the development of a survey to assess factors that influence employee satisfaction. Being a well-trained researcher, Janet began by searching for secondary data on the topic. In her search, she came across an article discussing a study conducted by InsightExpress, an online marketing research firm.

The InsightExpress study was conducted to determine what factors contributed to increased happiness and productivity among office workers. Because this was exactly the topic Janet had been asked to investigate, she decided to read the article in detail. The article turned out to be a press release from Microsoft. According to the press release, one of the key factors influencing workers' productivity and happiness was the level of "quality and comfort of mice and keyboards."[1] Eight out of 10 computer users according to the survey believed that "high-quality mice and keyboards have an important impact on their productivity at work." Also reported was that 60 percent of the respondents believed that having high-quality mice and keyboards would boost morale. When asked which company produced the highest-quality mice and keyboards, Microsoft was the company "most associated" with quality.

The remainder of the press release went on to discuss how Microsoft has focused on developing high-quality peripherals, such as mice and keyboards. Microsoft hardware is an industry leader in offering products that enhance consumer comfort. The press release also pointed out that the respondents were unaware of Microsoft's involvement in the research.

Janet took the findings from the InsightExpress study and included them in her memo to Anna Brown reporting the results of her secondary-data analysis. Anna called Janet into her office and asked her about the InsightExpress study. Janet explained that she found the results in a press release from Microsoft and that it did state that Microsoft had sponsored the study. Anna asked Janet if she was comfortable relying on the results of that study. Janet decided that she should investigate the findings further before relying on them to use in her own research. She told Anna that she would investigate further before committing to using those results.

Once again Janet went back to secondary-data sources and found that a recent *Wall Street Journal* article had discussed the findings of the InsightExpress study. According to the article, Microsoft did include in the press release that it had sponsored this research but failed to disclose to readers that it was disclosing only partial results of the survey. According to the article, a spokesperson for InsightExpress stated that, because the sponsoring company owns the results, it is not required to publish the full results.[2] Microsoft also failed to disclose that many of the questions were written in such a manner that the choice favorable to Microsoft's desired result was obvious. For example, when asked which company was associated with high-quality peripherals the choices were: Microsoft, Belkin, Kensington, and Logitech. Because the other three companies listed in the choice set were not as well known, it was almost a given that Microsoft would be chosen.

As for the main banner-head finding that 60 percent of office workers thought that having high-quality mice and keyboards would contribute significantly to morale, the questionnaire item that generated that result was a loaded question. The respondents were asked, "Which piece of office equipment would boost morale?" The choices were a footrest, a handset for your phone, a desk

EMPLOYEE SATISFACTION QUESTIONNAIRE

Assess the importance of the following attributes in selecting an employer to work for. Please circle the number that corresponds to your response.

	Very Important 1	Important 2	Neutral 3	Unimportant 4	Very Unimportant 5
1. Pay	1	2	3	4	5
2. Career mobility	1	2	3	4	5
3. Well-known employer, such as IBM	1	2	3	4	5
4. Comfortable work environment	1	2	3	4	5

Please circle the number that corresponds with your level of agreement or disagreement with the following statements.

	Strongly Agree	Agree	Neutral	Disagree	Strongly Disagree
5. I like a job that is challenging.	1	2	3	4	5
6. I change jobs every few years.	1	2	3	4	5
7. An employer should be fair.	1	2	3	4	5
8. Employers with fitness facilities can help employees lead healthy lives.	1	2	3	4	5
9. An employer should be caring and trustworthy.	1	2	3	4	5
10. I like a fast lifestyle.	1	2	3	4	5

11. Don't you think companies that pay well will have satisfied employees? _____ Yes _____ No

12. Do you feel companies today are concerned about their employees' welfare? _____ Yes _____ No

13. Gender
    1. Male
    2. Female

14. Which of the following categories best describes your annual household income?
    01   Less than $10,000
    02      $10 to $40,000
    03      $40 to $70,000
    04      $70 to $100,000
    05      $100,000 or more

Thank you very much for your participation.

lamp, or comfortable mice and keyboards with state-of-the-art features and functionality. Given these choices, it was not surprising that the overwhelming choice was the mice and keyboards, which allowed Microsoft to highlight its hardware products

In essence the study was designed in such a manner that the responses favored Microsoft. Although Janet was not surprised by the findings, given that Microsoft had sponsored the research, she was unsure whether that meant that the results were necessarily invalid. Many firms sponsor research, the results of which are used in other studies or picked up by the media and used by consumers in purchase decisions. Janet wondered if or how she could use the results of the study in her own research. She made an appointment with Anna to discuss her concerns.

Anna understood the dilemma that Janet was facing. She told Janet that many companies in a wide variety of industries do sponsor research and that research is valuable and informative. But, as this Microsoft example illustrates, sponsored research often does require higher levels of scrutiny to assess the validity of the findings. Anna felt that, in this case, what was not reported in the press release was as important as what was reported. Yet often readers of these press releases have no access to the original questionnaire and cannot evaluate the findings. Anna pointed out that Janet was correct in being concerned about relying on results from this type of secondary-data research. She then asked Janet to design a questionnaire for a primary-data collection study that would hopefully yield more valid results about the factors influencing employee satisfaction. After pondering this assignment for a while and reflecting on the findings of the Microsoft-sponsored research, Janet developed a first draft of the questionnaire shown on page 326.

CASE QUESTIONS

1. In the questionnaire prepared by Janet, identify all questions that are likely to produce biased, erroneous, or irrelevant answers (questions that are leading, loaded, double-barreled, and so on). Discuss the nature of the problem with each such question and propose a revised question that overcomes the problem.

2. In general, how would the information generated by the proposed survey compare with that of the Microsoft-sponsored survey in terms of comprehensiveness and usefulness for understanding the drivers of employee satisfaction?

CASE NOTES

1. "Reliable Mice and Keyboards Boost Workplace Morale," *PR Newswire*, February 18, 2005.
2. Carl Bialik, "When Considering Surveys on Business, Follow the Money," Wall Street Journal Online, online.wsj.com/public/article_print/0,,SB111219863592293188,00.html (accessed March 31, 2005).

This case was written by Catharine Curran-Kelly (University of Massachusetts at Dartmouth) in collaboration with the textbook authors, as a basis for class discussion rather than to illustrate either effective or ineffective marketing practice.

CASE 10.2 BURDINES-MACY'S

Burdines is a division of Federated Department Stores, Inc., the nation's leading operator of upscale department stores. Recently, all Burdines-Macy's stores have been converted to Macy's. Burdines is adept at tailoring its merchandise offerings to the needs of individual stores. The Latin American tourist in Miami, the Palm Beach seasonal socialite, and the conservative midwestern retiree living on the Gulf Coast all find unique selections of merchandise and specific sizes available to them at the Burdines in their area.

The Burdines Competitive Advantage

Burdines has based its brand identity on its image as "The Florida Store" and operates exclusively within that state. The stores are light and bright, with open skylights and images of sailboats, dolphins, seashells, the ocean, and palm trees. In-store merchandising supports a tropical theme, with the use of lots of coral, turquoise, and white colors. This identity is further supported outside the store, with well-recognized local community outreach programs. Burdines has gained success through the strategy of marketing solely in Florida.

The fact that Burdines knows its consumers better than department store competitors do is widely recognized within the industry. The following quotes from respected retail experts, reported in the *Miami Herald*,[1] reflect these sentiments:

"Burdines has always understood how to merchandise for our climate and our population," said Arthur Weiner, an Aventura retail consultant. "It's very hard for a retailer from outside this state to come into Florida and understand the ethnicity, weather and the change of seasons."

"Burdines today is synonymous with Florida," said Kurt Barnard, president of Barnard's Retail Marketing Report, a national retail consulting firm. "It's a part of Florida and Florida is a part of Burdines. There is a kind of organic affinity there."

"It really has been a remarkable brand for us in the state of Florida," said James Zimmerman, chairman and chief executive of Federated. "They have a vision for their customer and are very focused on taking care of that customer."

Burdines's ability to be attuned to its customers is further exemplified by its highly focused merchandise offerings. For example, in the fall, when competing department stores are stocking the racks with coats, wool sweaters, long sleeves, and heavy clothing, Burdines features more seasonably suitable items, such as bathing suits, shorts, cotton sweaters, short sleeves, and lighter-weight clothing. Burdines's competitive position is founded on the notion that no one else was based in Florida and knew the consumer the way it did. Burdines deliberately built its image on the fact that it was the hometown store and supported that in all of its marketing efforts.

The Gift Headquarters

Burdines recently developed a new marketing program called "Gift Headquarters." Because competition was heating up from a variety of retail formats—specialty stores, including The Limited and Gap; discount stores, including Target; outlet stores; and department stores from other parts of the country—Burdines developed the strategy to bolster its position as the market leader in Florida. Gifts represented a product category that both fit well with its competitive position and provided growth opportunity in higher-margin items. Furthermore, as a full-service department store, Burdines had a variety of existing services that could be pulled together to make a compelling gift offering to customers.

The Gift Headquarters program involved several unique elements. Leveraging the overwhelmingly positive perception of Burdines' exchange/return policy, the gift receipt, a sales receipt that doesn't include the price, was designed to make returns hassle free. Burdines also instituted an electronic gift card for purchase in a variety of denominations. Similar to a gift certificate, the electronic gift card could be used by the recipient to make future purchases in the store, thus providing a thoughtful gift that guaranteed revenue from the sale of the card and future traffic into the store. Finally, the stores' existing gift-wrap services rounded out the program. The Gift Headquarters program seemed an ideal method for leveraging the image of the store while generating additional high-margin sales and future traffic into the store.

Research on the Gift Headquarters Strategy

To gain insights into how Burdines customers view its Gift Headquarters strategy, a marketing research project was completed. First, it involved the completion of a total of 60 in-depth interviews to better understand consumer responses to the program. These were conducted at three separate locations: Dadeland, West Dade International, and Aventura.

In addition to providing useful information for the development of the questionnaire, the interviews confirmed the strong image of Burdines. The following is a selection of quotes in response to the question "When you think of Burdines, what comes to your mind?"

> "I remember the slogan 'The Florida Store'" (female, age 25, financial analyst)

> "Fashion, good lighting, and good customer service" (female, age 28, credit analyst)

> "The most exquisite things, the most beautiful things" (female, age 54, homemaker)

> "I love the Bridal Shows that they put on. I have never seen such well-prepared and detail-oriented people . . ." (female, age 50, homemaker)

Other, more general responses were equally positive:

> "I purchased a watch for my wife and I found it at Burdines for the best price . . ." (male, age 26, college student)

> "Burdines, they have the best shoe selection, better selection of clothes . . ." (female, age 23, college student)

> ". . . they have a lot of sales and a variety of designer clothes with a great atmosphere" (female, age 25)

When asked if Burdines was her Gift Headquarters, one respondent replied enthusiastically, "Yes, no doubt about it. I have been shopping here all my life!" (female, age 54).

The input from the interviews was used to develop a closed-ended questionnaire (see Exhibit 1). A total of 389 questionnaires were completed in the same three locations: Dadeland, West Dade International, and Aventura. A free Burdines calculator was distributed to each respondent as an incentive to complete the survey. A summary of the demographics for respondents follows:

Gender: female (65%), male (35%)

Age: under 18 (8%), 18–29 (38%), 30–44 (29%), 45–64 (20%), 65 and up (5%)

Ethnic background: Hispanic (63%), Caucasian (19%), African American (7%), Asian (4%), Native American (2%), Other (5%)

Marital status: married (46%), not married (54%)

Income: <$20,000 (10%), $20–29,000 (13%), $30–39,000 (13%), $40–49,000 (15%), $50–74,000 (22%), $75,000 and above (27%)

Residency: Permanent Florida resident (85%), nonresident (10%), seasonal (5%)

Charge cards: Burdines charge card holder (61%), nonholder (39%)

CASE QUESTIONS

1. Were the in-depth interviews helpful? Why or why not?

2. Discuss the extent to which the design of the questionnaire in Exhibit 1 reflects the insights provided by the in-depth interviews.

3. Assess how well the questionnaire addresses information pertaining to the effectiveness of the Gift Headquarters program.

4. What changes would you recommend to the existing questionnaire? Justify your recommendations.

CASE NOTE

1. "Miami-Based Burdines Department Store Focuses on Florida Strategy," *Miami Herald*, September 28, 1998.

This case was written by Jeanne L. Munger (University of Southern Maine) in collaboration with the textbook authors, as a basis for class discussion rather than to illustrate either effective or ineffective marketing practice.

ID#: _____   Store: _____   Time: _____
Interviewer: _____

Burdines
THE FLORIDA STORE

Burdines is very pleased to have you as a customer and values your opinion. In order to serve you better, we would appreciate your assistance in completing this brief survey. Please fill out this questionnaire and return it for a FREE BURDINES CALCULATOR.

In the past 12 months, about how many times have you shopped at a department store? _____

In the past 12 months, about how many times have you shopped at Burdines? _____

About how much did you spend on a gift purchases this past holiday season? Please indicate your best estimate in dollars. $ _____

About what percentage of this amount did you spend at Burdines? _____ %

Think about the last 10 times you purchased a gift for holidays such as Christmas, Mother's Day, Father's Day, and Valentine's Day. How many times did you purchase gifts from the following stores? (Please write the number of times by each blank, total should add to ten)
_____ Burdines
_____ Macy's
_____ Other Department Stores (e.g. JCPenney, Dillards)
_____ Discount Stores (e.g. Target)
_____ Other
Total = 10

To what extent do you agree that Burdines is your Gift Headquarters? (check one box)

1	2	3	4	5
Strongly Disagree	Disagree	Neither Agree nor Disagree	Agree	Strongly Agree

Have you seen any Burdines advertising promoting them as the Gift Headquarters?

1	0
Yes	No

If yes, where did you see or hear this advertising? (Check all that apply)

Television	Radio	Newspaper	Direct Mail	Internet
1	2	3	4	5

Which of the following services are you aware of that are provided by Burdines? (Please check all that apply)
Have you ever used any of the following services? (Please check all that you have used)
Please rate the services you have used by circling one number for each. (1 = Poor 5 = Excellent)

	Aware	Used It	Poor				Excellent
Gift Wrap	☐	☐	1	2	3	4	5
Return/Exchange Policy	☐	☐	1	2	3	4	5
Electronic Gift Card	☐	☐	1	2	3	4	5
Gift Receipt	☐	☐	1	2	3	4	5

IF YOU ARE AWARE OF THE GIFT RECEIPT:
Where did you find out about the gift receipt?

Sales Associate	Radio	Newspaper	Direct Mail
1	2	3	4

Please turn page

Exhibit 1
Burdines Survey

Please check one box for each statement that best represents your opinion.

	Poor				Excellent
Overall satisfaction	1	2	3	4	5
Customer service	1	2	3	4	5
Store cleanliness	1	2	3	4	5
Knowledgeable sales associates	1	2	3	4	5
Display of merchandise	1	2	3	4	5
Variety/Selection of merchandise	1	2	3	4	5
Value for the money	1	2	3	4	5

	Very Unlikely				Very Likely
How likely would you be to recommend Burdines as a place to shop for a gift to a friend?	1	2	3	4	5
How likely are you to return to Burdines?	1	2	3	4	5

These last few questions are for classification purposes only.

Gender: ☐ 1 Male   ☐ 2 Female

What age group are you in?

☐ 1 Under 18   ☐ 2 18–29   ☐ 3 30–44   ☐ 4 45–64   ☐ 5 65 and older

Ethnic Background:

☐ 1 African American   ☐ 2 Asian   ☐ 3 Caucasian   ☐ 4 Hispanic

☐ 5 Native American   ☐ 6 Other

Marital Status

☐ 1 Married   ☐ 2 Single, never married   ☐ 3 Divorced/Widowed/Separated

Do you have any children under 18 living with you?   ☐ 1 Yes   ☐ 0 No

Are you a:

☐ 1 Permanent Florida Resident   ☐ 2 Seasonal Florida Resident   ☐ 3 Not a Florida Resident

Do you have a Burdines Charge Card?   ☐ 1 Yes   ☐ 0 No

What is your household income?

☐ 1 Less than $20,000   ☐ 2 $20,000–29,999   ☐ 3 $30,000–39,999

☐ 4 $40,000–49,999   ☐ 5 $50,000–74,999   ☐ 6 $75,000 and above

Thank you for your time!!!

Exhibit 1
Burdines Survey (continued)
Source: Courtesy of Burdines, The Florida Store.

Sampling Foundations

Gallup on Sampling: Gallup China

E**very** three years since 1994, the Gallup Organization has been conducting a Nationwide Study of Consumer Attitudes and Lifestyles in China. This Gallup China research program was unique in that its sample covers, and represents with statistical precision, the entire adult population (age 18 and older) of the People's Republic of China. A total of 3,597 hour-long, in-person, in-home interviews were conducted across China from June to November 2004. Interviewing was conducted in every administrative region of mainland China—that is, in each of its 22 provinces, 3 municipalities, and 5 autonomous regions.

Chapter Objectives

After reading and understanding the material in this chapter, you should be able to:

- Define and distinguish between sampling and census studies.

- Discuss when to use a probability versus a nonprobability sampling method, and implement the different methods.

- Explain sampling error and sampling distribution.

- Construct confidence intervals for population means and proportions.

- List the factors to consider in determining sample size and compute the required sample size to achieve a specific degree of precision at a desired confidence level.

The strict probability-based sample was drawn in the following stages:

1. 12,500 counties, cities, and urban districts were divided into 50 strata based on their geographic location, degree of economic development, and proportion of nonagricultural population.

2. One primary sampling unit (PSU), consisting of either a county or a city, was selected from each stratum, based on probability proportional to population size.

3. Within each PSU, the populations of all neighborhoods and villages were compiled. From this listing, four neighborhoods or villages were selected with probability proportional to size.

4. From each of these four neighborhoods or villages, five households were selected at random.

5. One respondent was selected from each selected household according to the Kish method. This research procedure, designed to ensure proper representation in the sample of all age groups by both genders, involves first recording on a grid the ages and genders of each of a selected household's adults. The respondent to be interviewed is then selected according to a prescribed systematic procedure.

6. If the designated respondent was not at home or could not be reached, a second or, if needed, a third adult family member was selected systematically from among the household members remaining on the grid. If contact with the designated respondent could not be made after a total of three separate visits to the household, an interview with a respondent in a substitute household in the same locale was permitted. (Two substitute households were kept in reserve for each of the five assigned households in the interviewing area.)

The same basic selection procedure, based on probability selection according to population size, was also used for each of the augmented (oversampled) 10-city subsamples.

In Beijing, Shanghai, and Guangzhou, a minimum of 400 interviews were conducted (Beijing, 402; Shanghai, 422; Guangzhou, 411; three-city total, 1,235). In oversampled cities 4 through 10 (Chongqing, Tianjin, Shenyang, Wuhan, Nanjing, Chengdu, and Xian), 807 interviews were conducted. Nationwide, among other areas classified as urban, 523 interviews were conducted, bringing the total of all urban-sector interviews to 2,565. Finally, nationwide, 1,032 interviews were conducted in areas classified as rural.

To correct for the effects of deliberate oversampling of urban areas, postweighting was applied so that the final data were statistically accurate and projectable to the total adult population of China within plus or minus 2 percentage points.[1] ■

Consider the following research studies:

Harris Interactive (www.harrisinteractive.com). The Harris Poll is a weekly study that monitors the reactions of the American public to a variety of economic, political, and social issues. The importance and popularity of this survey are evident from its wide citation in newspapers and on radio and TV. Each Harris Poll is based on a nationally representative online survey of 1,000 adults age 18 or over.[2]

ACNielsen (www.acnielsen.com). The ACNielsen ScanTrack index offers valuable scanner-based sales and brand share data on a regular basis to manufacturers of a wide variety of consumer products, such as food, drugs, and cosmetics. These sales and brand share estimates are gathered weekly from a representative sample of more than 4,800 stores representing over 800 retailers in 52 major markets.[3]

One important feature common to most research studies emerges from these research studies and the Gallup survey in the opening vignette: insights and inferences that are crucial to decision makers can be based on data from a sample of units. The size of the sample is quite small compared to that of the total group of units of interest to the decision makers. What is termed *sampling* is the starting point of the inferential process involved in marketing research studies.

Sampling Versus Census Studies

Sampling is the selection of a fraction of the total number of units of interest to decision makers for the ultimate purpose of being able to draw general conclusions about the entire body of units. The entire body of units of interest to decision makers in a situation is known as the **population,** or **universe.** A listing of population units from which a sample is chosen is known as a **sampling frame.**

To clarify the distinction between population and sampling frame, let's consider the following scenario. A university offering a graduate program in business wants to conduct a study to determine the criteria that prospective students use to evaluate different graduate business programs. In this scenario, the population can be defined as "all individuals with an interest in pursuing a graduate degree in business within the next year." How can we identify such individuals?

One approach is to contact the organization that administers the Graduate Management Admission Test (GMAT) and obtain from it a list of individuals who took the test during the past 12 months. Such a list constitutes a sampling frame. Note that this sampling frame will contain most, but not all, of the individuals implied in the definition of the population (some individuals who did not take the GMAT during the past 12 months, and therefore are excluded from the sampling frame, may nevertheless be interested in pursuing a graduate business degree). However, because generating an exhaustive list of population units is often impractical or prohibitively expensive, sampling frames that are more readily obtainable and are good approximations of the population are frequently used to select samples.

In marketing research studies, the term *population* is not restricted to people per se. Rather, it is used to denote any group of units—human or nonhuman—about which researchers or decision makers want to make inferences. For instance, the implied population in the studies conducted to determine the

Sampling is the selection of a fraction of the total number of units of interest to decision makers.

The **population** (or **universe**) consists of the entire body of units of interest to decision makers in a situation.

The **sampling frame** is a listing of population units from which a sample is chosen.

Nielsen ScanTrack index is a collection of nonhuman units—all grocery, drug, and similar stores. There are basically two ways to draw inferences from a population: (1) a **census study,** drawing inferences from the entire body of units of interest; and (2) a **sampling study,** drawing inferences from a sample drawn from the population.

A **census study** involves drawing inferences from the entire body of units of interest.

In a **sampling study,** inferences are drawn from a sample taken from the population.

The basic reason why sampling is an important component of most marketing research projects is that a study based on a sample of units has distinct advantages over a census study, which involves obtaining data from every unit in a population. For instance, a census study would be involved in determining the Nielsen ScanTrack index if data for the index were to be collected from all stores selling the categories of products to which the index pertains. Now let's examine the advantages of a sampling study over a census study.

Advantages of Sampling

One main advantage of a sampling study is its lower cost relative to a census study. A key factor that directly affects the data collection and data analysis costs in any research project is the number of units studied. Regardless of whether the data collection method in a research project involves a personal interview survey, a telephone survey, a mail survey, an Internet survey, or an observation, the more units from which data are obtained, the greater are the data collection costs and the data analysis costs (because of the larger volume of data to be analyzed). In most real-life research projects, the population sizes are prohibitively large and the money allocated for research too limited for conducting census studies. The 2000 U.S. Census is estimated to have cost around $4 to $5 billion.

Sampling error is the difference between a statistic value, which is generated through a sampling procedure and the parameter value, which can be determined only through a census study.

A second advantage of a sampling study over a census study is the reduced time needed for a research project. Given a set of limited resources for conducting research (money, fieldworkers to collect the data, facilities to code and analyze the data), the research will take longer to complete if it involves a census study than it will for a sampling study. Data that are not obtained on a timely basis may not be relevant for decision making; worse still, the use of such data may result in erroneous decisions.

Data collected in research studies can be in the form of responses from people or from nonhuman units, such as grocery stores (for example, sales data from checkout scanners).

By now you are probably wondering, "Well, a census study is more expensive and time consuming than a sampling study; but isn't it more *accurate* than a sampling study because it obtains data from each and every unit within a population?" Surprisingly, the answer to that question is "Not necessarily." By definition, a census study involves looking at every unit in a population. However, the accuracy of data obtained from a study depends not only on the number of population units included in it, but also on a host of other factors related to the process of collecting the data.

The total error associated with a research project may contain one or both of the following: sampling error and nonsampling error. Exhibit 11.1 summarizes the three types of nonsampling errors and their potential causes. Exhibit 11.2 compares nonsampling errors in telephone and online surveys.

1. **Sampling error** is the difference between a statistical value that is generated through a sampling procedure and the population parameter value that can be determined only through an accurate census of the population. Sampling error will occur in any

Nonsampling Error
(Any error other than sampling error)

Sampling Frame Error (Sampling frame not representative of ideal population)	Nonresponse Error (Final sample not representative of planned sample)	Data Error (Distortions in collected data and mistakes in data coding, analysis, or interpretation)
Potential Causes ▶ Incomplete sampling frame that overrepresents some population segments and underrepresents others ▶ Sampling frame that contains irrelevant units	**Potential Causes** ▶ Mail surveys: Certain types of sample units more likely to respond than others ▶ Telephone and personal interview surveys: Not-at-home problem and respondent refusal problem	**Potential Causes** ▶ Respondents' reluctance/inability to give accurate answers ▶ Ill-trained interviewers ▶ Unscrupulous interviewers ▶ Poorly designed questionnaire ▶ Mistakes in coding data ▶ Erroneous analysis ▶ Incorrect/inappropriate interpretation of results

Exhibit 11.1
Types and Potential Causes of Nonsampling Errors

Nonsampling error is any error in a research study other than sampling error.

project involving a sampling study, merely because only a sample of the population is studied. (We will discuss sampling error in detail later in this chapter.)

2. **Nonsampling error** is any error in a research study other than sampling error (which arises purely because a sample, rather than the entire population, is studied). Nonsampling errors may occur during the process of data collection and analysis. Nonsampling errors can arise from a multitude of factors, such as poor questionnaire construction, ill-trained fieldworkers, errors on the part of respondents, and errors in coding responses. The best way for researchers to minimize nonsampling errors is to have adequate control over the entire process of data gathering, coding, and analysis—for example, by using properly trained fieldworkers, giving them proper instructions, and

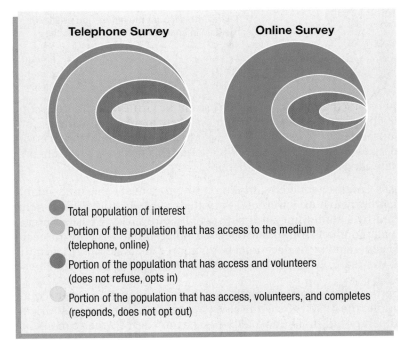

Telephone Survey   Online Survey

⬤ Total population of interest

⬤ Portion of the population that has access to the medium (telephone, online)

⬤ Portion of the population that has access and volunteers (does not refuse, opts in)

⬤ Portion of the population that has access, volunteers, and completes (responds, does not opt out)

Exhibit 11.2
Nonsampling Errors and Coverage: U.S. Telephone and Online Surveys

Source: Taken from Thomas W. Miller, "Can We Trust the Data of Online Research," *Marketing Research* (Summer 2001), Vol. 13, No. 2, p. 31.© 2001 by the American Marketing Association. Reprinted by permission of the American Marketing Association. All rights reserved.

TABLE 11.1
Summary of Potential Errors in Research Projects

Type of Error	Ways to Minimize Error
Sampling Error	
(Occurs when a sample, rather than the entire population, is studied)	Increasing the sample size Using a statistically efficient sampling plan (making the sample as representative of the population as possible)
Nonsampling Error	
Sampling frame error (Occurs when the sampling frame is not representative of the ideal population)	Starting with a complete sampling frame Modifying the sampling frame to make it representative of the ideal population (e.g., using plus-one dialing in telephone surveys)
Nonresponse error (Occurs when the final sample is not representative of the planned sample)	Mail surveys: Increasing response rates through the use of incentives, followup mailings, etc. (*Caution:* Increase in response rate per se may not reduce nonresponse error.)
	Telephone and personal interview surveys: Making callbacks and spreading out the time blocks during which interviews are conducted
Data error (Occurs because of distortions in the data collected, as well as mistakes in data coding, analysis, or interpretation)	Ensuring that the questionnaire is good (is simple, unbiased, etc.)
	Proper selection, training, and supervision of interviewers
	Keeping the interviewers' task simple and making it clear to them
	Giving adequate compensation to the interviewers
	Using sound editing and coding procedures
	Taking into account the nature and quality of the data in analyzing and interpreting them

closely supervising their work. A sampling study, by virtue of its limited scope compared with a census study, is much more likely to offer a researcher control over nonsampling errors. Table 11.1 describes the different types of errors and summarizes strategies for controlling them. This textbook's website presents nonsampling errors in greater detail.

In most cases, a well-conducted sampling study, in spite of some unavoidable sampling error, is likely to have lower total error than a census study. This conclusion is supported by a somewhat surprising activity of the U.S. Census Bureau: the bureau actually conducts some controlled sampling studies to verify the accuracy of the data generated by its decennial population census studies. In fact, the Census Bureau wanted to use statistical sampling instead of a nationwide head count in 2000.

Many experts believe the national census undercounts hard-to-count areas. For example, the 1990 census missed 4.4 percent of the nation's African Americans, 5.0 percent of its Latinos, 12.2 percent of Native Americans living on reservations, and 0.7 percent of whites. However, the Census Bureau's attempt to use sampling, even though it had widespread support among experts, was struck down by the U.S. Supreme Court because sampling violates the Census Act.[4] Experts in marketing, statistics, and population studies continue to believe that the 2000 census undercounted hard-to-reach segments of the population by as much as 40 percent. Although the U.S. Supreme Court ruled that sampling cannot be used for determining U.S. congressional districts, the Court has not ruled out the use of sampling for allocating federal funds. In fact, the Census Bureau plans to conduct sample surveys following the actual head count. The response rate of 67 percent for the 2000 Census exceeded the 1990 census response rate of 65 percent and far exceeded the expected response rate of 61 percent.[5]

In addition to the cost, time, and accuracy advantages we have discussed so far, sampling studies have another indirect benefit over census studies in situations involving human populations. Because of the increasing use of research studies by a variety of institutions, greater numbers of people are likely to be asked to participate in surveys. Consequently, fresh respondents—those who have not participated in any research surveys—are becoming harder to find than ever before. Hence, in the interest of conserving the available pool of fresh respondents in the long run, a sampling study is preferable over a census study.

When Census Studies Are Appropriate

Although census studies have several important limitations, we do not mean to say that they should never be conducted in marketing situations. Notice that the cost, time, and accuracy drawbacks of a census study will not be significant *if the population is small* or *if it can be accessed easily.*[6] For example, populations such as "all neurosurgeons in the Chicago metropolitan area," "all savings and loan associations in Arkansas," and "all manufacturers who have a need for gold in its raw form" are unlikely to contain a large number of units. In research projects involving small populations, a census is certainly feasible from a cost, time, and accuracy standpoint. Whether or not a census study is *necessary* depends on the extent of variability among the population units with respect to the variables about which data are required.

In summary, two conditions must be met for a census study to be appropriate: (1) the feasibility condition and (2) the necessity condition. A census study will be feasible whenever a population is relatively small or can be accessed easily. A census study will be necessary only when the population units are extremely varied—that is, when each population unit is likely to be very different from all the other units. Consequently, the use of census studies in marketing is usually limited to industrial or institutional customer populations, situations in which marketers may be interested in studying relatively small but highly varied populations.

The Internet now allows wider reach to the population in a relatively short period of time. BizRate.com, a leading comparison shopping site, contains offerings from more than 2,000 merchants. It reaches all online buyers of participating merchants with a request to complete an online survey on point-of-sale and fulfillment experiences. The Internet technology allows companies to reach diverse online buyers with ease. The cost of reaching and collecting data from such a diverse population is also relatively small, as long as the technology is in place.[7]

Probability Versus Nonprobability Sampling

Probability sampling is an objective procedure in which the probability of selection is known in advance for each population unit.

The rest of this chapter covers various methods for picking a sample of units from a given population. Let's preview two basic sampling methods available to researchers: probability sampling and nonprobability sampling.

Probability sampling is an objective procedure in which the probability of selection is known in advance for each population unit. A researcher using a probability sampling method does not play a role in determining which specific population units are chosen to be part of a sample; that is, the researcher has no say in deciding whether or not each individual population unit is included in the sample. In probability sampling, the researcher merely specifies some *objective scheme* for choosing units from a population. Once the scheme has been laid out, the selection of the sample units is independent of the personal preferences or biases of the researcher. Each population unit is assigned an objective probability of being selected on the basis of the specified sampling scheme. (The probability of selection may or may not be the same for all population units, as we will see later in the chapter.) The Gallup Organization, for example, offers a business

Exhibit 11.3
Classification of Sampling Methods

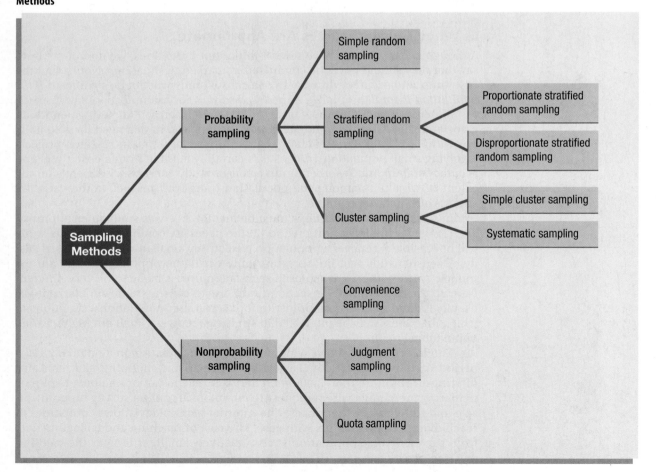

service called the Gallup Omnibus. The service is a national survey conducted every two to four weeks using personal in-home interviews. Questions that are custom-designed to fit the requirements of individual clients can be included in the national survey in any desired month of the year. The survey's results are projectable to the adult (18 years and older) civilian population of the United States.[8] An intuitive explanation of sampling in general and probability sampling in particular is given in Research in Use 11.1, which describes Gallup's sampling approach in the United States.

Nonprobability sampling is a subjective procedure in which the probability of selection for each population unit is unknown beforehand. It is more judgmental than objective in the sense that the selection of individual population units is not done on a strictly chance basis; a researcher's subjective judgment does play a role in determining which specific population units get included in the sample. Hence, determining an objective probability of selection for each population unit beforehand is impossible.

A researcher conducting a sampling study has a choice from among a variety of probability and nonprobability methods. Exhibit 11.3 presents a classification of the basic types of probability and nonprobability sampling. The sections below provide an overview of probability and nonprobability sampling methods.

> **Nonprobability sampling** is a subjective procedure in which the probability of selection for each population unit is unknown beforehand.

▮ Probability Sampling

Sophisticated probability sampling techniques are used especially by large commercial marketing research firms that maintain national samples or panels that can be readily accessed for conducting periodic research surveys. The sample for the Gallup China survey is chosen through an elaborate probability sampling plan, as described in the opening vignette.

Simple random sampling is the most straightforward form of probability sampling. The more advanced probability sampling methods are stratified, cluster, and systematic sampling. The following subsections provide a detailed discussion of each of these methods.

▮ **Simple Random Sampling** **Simple random sampling** is a procedure in which every possible sample of a certain size within a population has a known and equal probability of being chosen as the study sample. It is the most basic type of probability sampling. The actual selection of a simple random sample can be done by randomly picking the desired number of units from the population. This procedure is statistically equivalent to first identifying all possible samples of the desired size and then picking one of those samples at random.

> In **simple random sampling**, every possible sample of a certain size within a population has a known and equal probability of being chosen as the study sample.

Many spreadsheet programs, including Excel and Lotus, have pseudo-random-number generators that can readily provide a set of random numbers, which can be used in selecting a simple random sample from a numbered population list. Computer-based selection of sample units is particularly helpful in telephone surveys requiring a random sample of respondents. Such surveys can make use of random-digit dialing, in which telephone numbers are randomly selected and dialed by a computer.

▮ **Stratified Random Sampling** **Stratified random sampling** is a probability sampling procedure in which the chosen sample is forced to contain units from each of the segments, or strata, of the population. In simple random sampling, for a given sample size, any combination of population units is just as likely to become the actual sample as any other combination of the same size. Hence, the

> In **stratified random sampling**, the chosen sample is forced to contain units from each of the segments, or strata, of the population.

Gallup on Sampling: How Polls Are Conducted in the United States

The Sampling Issue

Probability sampling is the fundamental basis for all survey research. For national Gallup polls, in other words, the objective is to present the opinions of a sample of people that reveal exactly the same opinions that would have been obtained had it been possible to interview all adult Americans in the country.

Selecting a Random Sample

By necessity, the earliest polls were conducted in person, with Gallup interviewers fanning out across the country, knocking on Americans' doors. This was the standard method of interviewing for nearly 50 years, from about 1935 to the mid-1980s, and it was a demonstrably reliable method.

By 1986, a sufficient proportion of American households had at least one telephone, making telephone interviewing a viable and substantially less expensive alternative to the in-person method. By the end of the 1980s, the vast majority of Gallup's national surveys were being conducted by telephone. Gallup proceeds with several steps to put together its poll, with the objective of allowing every American household and every American adult to have an equal chance of falling into the sample:

> First we clearly identify and describe the population that a given poll is attempting to represent. If we were doing a poll about baseball fans on behalf of the sports page of a major newspaper, the target population might simply be all Americans aged 18 and older who say they are fans of the sport of baseball. If the poll was being conducted on behalf of major-league baseball, however, the target audience required by the client might be more specific, such as people aged twelve and older who watch at least five hours' worth of major-league baseball games on television, or in person, each week.

In the case of Gallup polls that track elections and the major political, social, and economic questions of the day, the target audience is generally referred to as "national adults." Strictly speaking, the target audience is all adults, age 18 and over, living in telephone households within the continental United States. In effect, it is the civilian, noninstitutionalized population. College students living on campus, armed forces personnel living on military bases, prisoners, hospital patients, and others living in group institutions are not represented in Gallup's sampling frame. Clearly these exclusions represent some diminishment in coverage of the population, but because of the practical difficulties involved in attempting to reach the institutionalized population, it is a compromise Gallup usually needs to make.

> Next, we choose or design a method that will enable us to sample our target population randomly. In the case of the Gallup Poll, we start with a list of all household telephone numbers in the continental United States. This complicated process really starts with a computerized list of all telephone exchanges in America, along with estimates of the number of residential households those exchanges have attached to them. The computer, using a procedure called random digit dialing (RDD), actually creates phone numbers from those exchanges, then generates telephone samples from those. In essence, this procedure creates a list of all possible household phone numbers in America and then selects a subset of numbers from that list for Gallup to call.
>
> It is important to go through this complicated procedure because estimates indicate that about 30% of American residential phones are unlisted. Although it would be much simpler if we used phone books to obtain all listed phone numbers in America and sampled from them (much as you would if you simply took every 38th number from your local phone book), we would miss out on unlisted phone numbers, and introduce a possible bias into the sample.

The typical sample size for a Gallup poll designed to represent this general population is 1,000 national adults.[a]

actual study sample may turn out to be a skewed sample that does not adequately represent the population. The example discussed next illustrates this possibility.

> **EXAMPLE** Suppose the administrators of Kirkwood University want to determine their students' attitudes about various aspects of the university. Kirkwood University's student body, which is the population of interest here, contains 10,000 students—3,000 freshmen, 3,000 sophomores, 2,000 juniors, and 2,000 seniors—and we want to select a sample of 500 students for the attitude survey. If we use simple random sampling to pick 500 students, there is no guarantee the chosen sample will adequately represent the four classification segments of the student body. In fact, simple random sampling may yield a sample in which all 500 students are from the same student classification group. In this case, the sample will be extremely skewed. Such a skewed sample is not desirable, because we cannot use it to generalize the survey results to the entire student body.

The **statistical efficiency** of a sampling procedure reflects the precision of the population estimate generated by it; for a given sample size, a sampling procedure that generates a more precise estimate than another is statistically more efficient.

In **proportionate stratified random sampling**, the sample consists of units selected from each population stratum in proportion to the total number of units in the stratum.

In **disproportionate stratified random sampling**, the sample consists of units selected from each population stratum according to how varied the units within the stratum are.

A sampling approach that prevents the chosen sample from being skewed is stratified random sampling. Stratified random sampling will be *statistically more efficient* than simple random sampling because it will provide a more accurate population estimate of the variable of interest. The **statistical efficiency** of a sampling procedure reflects the precision of the population estimate generated by it; for a given sample size, a sampling procedure that generates a more precise estimate than another is statistically more efficient.

Two different types of stratified random sampling are possible: proportionate and disproportionate. In **proportionate stratified random sampling,** the sample consists of units selected from each population stratum in proportion to the total number of units in the stratum. Table 11.2 illustrates the proportionate allocation of the total sample of 500 students in the Kirkwood University example. After the total sample is allocated, each population stratum is treated as a subpopulation, and a simple random sample of the specified number of units is chosen from each subpopulation to make up the total study sample.

In **disproportionate stratified random sampling,** the sample consists of units selected from each population stratum according to how varied the units within the stratum are. If one stratum contains more diverse units, and hence exhibits a greater degree of variability than another stratum of the same size, a larger number of units should be chosen from the former than from the latter. Disproportionate stratified random sampling is appropriate in such a situation.

For a given sample size, disproportionate stratified sampling will provide a better representation of the total population than proportionate stratified random sampling. This representation is accomplished by sampling more than proportionately from those strata that are more diverse than other strata. Disproportionate stratified random sampling will be *statistically more efficient* than proportionate stratified random sampling because, for the same sample size, it will provide a more precise population estimate of the variable of interest. Therefore, if the degrees of variability across the strata are different and known, disproportionate rather than proportionate stratified random sampling must be used.[9]

ACNielsen Company uses a form of disproportionate stratified random sampling in selecting stores that provide the data for the Nielsen Retail Index.

TABLE 11.2
Proportionate Allocation of Total Sample of Kirkwood University Students

Population Strata	Number of Population Units		Number of Sample Units Allocated
Freshmen	3,000	30%	$500 \times .30 = 150$
Sophomores	3,000	30%	$500 \times .30 = 150$
Juniors	2,000	20%	$500 \times .20 = 100$
Seniors	2,000	20%	$500 \times .20 = 100$
Total	10,000	100%	500

Exhibit 11.4 illustrates the disproportionate sampling plan that Nielsen uses. Notice that chain and large independent stores are sampled more than would be proportionate to their sizes. Notice also that the "take ratio," the selection probability of a store in each stratum, varies from stratum to stratum.

In **cluster sampling,** clusters of population units are selected at random and then all or some of the units in the chosen clusters are studied.

■ **Cluster Sampling**   **Cluster sampling** is a probability sampling procedure in which clusters of population units are selected at random, and then all or some units in the chosen clusters are studied. In a stratified random sampling, after partitioning the population into strata, a sample of population units is randomly selected from each stratum. This approach requires a sampling frame for each stratum. A sampling frame of all population units is also needed for choosing a sample through simple random sampling. An adequate sampling frame of individual population units may not always be readily available, and in this case cluster sampling is helpful.

For example, suppose a researcher wants to conduct personal interviews with a random sample of households in a Metropolitan Statistical Area (MSA). In this scenario, a complete sampling frame of households in the MSA might be unavailable and prohibitively expensive to compile. However, a complete listing of census tracts in the MSA (in which each census tract represents a cluster of households) should be readily available from the U.S. Census reports. Therefore, the researcher can randomly select a sample of census tracts from a sampling frame of census tracts and then interview all or some of the households in the chosen census tracts. This sampling approach is a form of cluster sampling.

Even when such a sampling frame is available, if the frame can be conveniently divided into a series of representative clusters, a cluster sampling approach may be easier to use than a simple or stratified random sampling approach.

Exhibit 11.4
Disproportionate Stratified Random Sampling Used by ACNielsen Company
Copyright © ACNielsen Company. Reprinted by permission.

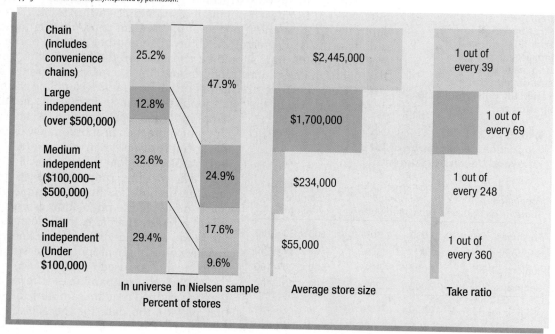

Systematic Sampling In **systematic sampling,** the researcher selects the first unit randomly and the remaining units systematically. As its name implies, systematic sampling is an organized procedure, selecting a sample from a list containing all the population units. Specifically, it requires these steps:

1. Determine the sampling interval k:

$$k = \frac{\text{Number of units in the population}}{\text{Number of units desired in the sample}}$$

2. Choose randomly *one unit* between the first and kth units in the population list.

3. The randomly chosen unit and every kth unit thereafter are designated as part of the sample.

To illustrate the procedure, let's consider a sampling frame of 1,000 units (numbered 1 through 1,000) from which we select a sample of 50 units. The sampling interval k is $1{,}000/50 = 20$. To select the first unit in our sample, we randomly pick one number between 1 and 20, say, 17. Thus our sample consists of the population units numbered 17, 37, 57, . . . , 997. Notice that only the starting unit for the sample (unit 17) is randomly selected; the rest are "systematically" selected from the population list. The starting unit completely determines the rest of the sample.

The most obvious attraction of systematic sampling is its simplicity relative to the other methods we have seen: given a population list, we require only one random number to select a sample from it. A less obvious benefit of systematic sampling is that, in most practical applications, its statistical efficiency is no lower than that of simple random sampling. This benefit of systematic sampling, coupled with its simplicity, makes it very appealing from a researcher's standpoint.

Practical Considerations: Probability Sampling Methods Not all probability sampling methods may be equally practical in any research project. Table 11.3 summarizes the strengths and weaknesses of the various probability sampling methods in terms of their statistical efficiency and their feasibility, as reflected by the amount of information about the population that is required and the effort involved in selecting units for the sample. Clearly, none of the methods can be considered best in terms of relative statistical efficiency and feasibility. The choice of the most appropriate sampling technique for a research project must be based on a careful evaluation of the nature of the population, the degree of precision desired for the estimates, and the amount of resources available for the research.

Nonprobability Sampling Methods

Recall that nonprobability sampling is a subjective procedure in which the probability of selection for the population units cannot be determined. The selection of sample units from a population is not done on a strictly chance basis, as it is in probability sampling. An important feature of nonprobability sampling is that it offers researchers greater freedom and flexibility in selecting the individual population units than does probability sampling. Before examining this feature, let's first discuss the basic types of nonprobability sampling methods.

Convenience Sampling In **convenience sampling,** a researcher's convenience forms the basis for selecting a sample of units. All of us have been and

TABLE 11.3
Comparison of Probability Sampling Methods

Method	Statistical Efficiency	Required Information About Population	Selection of Sample Units
Simple random sampling	Less efficient than stratified random sampling	List of all population units	Each unit picked randomly
Stratified Random Sampling			
Proportionate	More efficient than simple random sampling	List of all population units; data on relevant characteristic for stratifying population	Each unit picked randomly
Disproportionate	More efficient than simple and proportionate stratified random sampling	List of all population units; data on relevant characteristic for stratifying populations; knowledge about degree of variability within each stratum	Each unit picked randomly
Cluster Sampling			
Simple cluster	Less efficient than simple random sampling *unless* each cluster adequately represents population	List of clusters of population units	Only clusters picked (census is randomly conducted of each chosen cluster)
Systematic	As efficient as simple random sampling when population units are in random order; as efficient as proportionate stratified random sampling when population units are arranged according to a relevant population characteristic; may be less efficient than simple random sampling if there is periodicity in the population list (e.g., if every kth unit is a male)	List of all population units	Only the first unit picked randomly (the remaining units are picked systematically according to the sampling interval)

continue to be exposed to numerous applications of convenience sampling during our daily routines. For instance, you have probably come across several situations similar to the one in the following example.

> **EXAMPLE** The administrators of your college have just announced a sharp increase in tuition fees for the next year, citing rapidly increasing administrative costs as the main reason for the increase. This announcement is covered in the evening news program on your local TV station. The TV reporter covering this news item says, "While some of the students feel that the 10 percent fee hike is justified, most of them consider it to be unfair." Then, as apparent support for this conclusion, the reporter is shown on campus talking to several students, one at a time, about their reactions to the proposed tuition fee increase.

The use of responses from a sample of individuals is evident in this example. However, in contrast to the methods of probability sampling, notice that in this case the "researcher"—namely, the TV news reporter—is apparently willing to make some inferences on the basis of inputs from whatever sample was *conveniently available*. The researcher made no effort to locate and use inputs from a representative sample of units.

This form of sampling has become very popular in online research. An online version of convenience sampling is known as *intercept sampling* or *pop-up surveying*. Many Internet service providers use pop-up surveys when a user accesses a particular page or completes a transaction. However, participation is entirely voluntary, and the resulting sample is, in effect, a convenience sample—a nonprobability sample that is obtained on the basis of the researcher's convenience rather than randomly from a well-defined sampling frame.

In **judgment sampling**, the researcher exerts some effort in selecting a sample deemed to be most appropriate for the study.

■ **Judgment Sampling**   Judgment sampling is similar to convenience sampling, except that it is more refined. In convenience sampling, a researcher exerts no effort to obtain a representative sample. Such effort is expended in judgment sampling.[10] **Judgment sampling** (or *purposive sampling*) is thus a procedure in which a researcher exerts some effort in selecting a sample that he or she believes is most appropriate for a study.

Let's take another look at the TV news story example. If the TV news reporter were to seek out officers from various student organizations and obtain their reactions to the proposed fee hike, instead of merely interviewing a conveniently available sample of students, she or he would be using a judgment sampling procedure. Whether a judgment sample is more representative of the ideal population than a convenience sample will depend on how sound the judgment of the researcher is in selecting the sample units. To the extent that officers of student organizations may be well informed about the feelings of the general student body, a judgment sample of student officers may be more representative than a convenience sample of students. In practical situations, the researcher will, or should, be knowledgeable about the nature of the relevant or ideal population for a study, Hence, although a judgment sample will require greater researcher effort, it will generally be more appropriate than a convenience sample.

In **quota sampling**, a prespecified quota of units is selected from each population segment, or cell, based on the judgment of the researchers or decision makers.

■ **Quota Sampling**   **Quota sampling** involves sampling a quota of units to be selected from each population cell, based on the judgment of the researchers or decision makers. It is the most refined form of nonprobability sampling and is often used in practice, especially in studies involving personal interviewing. Quota sampling resembles stratified random sampling and possesses certain features of judgment and convenience sampling as well. It requires the following steps:

1. Divide the population into segments (typically referred to as *cells*) based on certain control characteristics.
2. Determine the quota of units for each cell (quotas are determined by the researchers or decision makers).
3. Instruct the interviewers to fill the quotas assigned to the cells.

Quota sampling does not require prior knowledge about the cell to which each population unit belongs. It allows a researcher to use two or more control characteristics in defining the population cells. The benefit is that a researcher can control a quota sample's representativeness on several relevant population characteristics. However, quota sampling does have some potential limitations. First, it lacks the statistical precision and generalizability that probability sampling procedures possess. Second, increasing the number of control characteristics to improve a sample's representativeness can sharply lower quota sampling's flexibility and make it prohibitively expensive to locate the respondents needed to fill the various cell quotas. Third, even if several control characteristics are used in designing a quota sample, the sample that is actually obtained may still be biased if the quotas are not filled as planned or if some important control characteristics are not included.

Sampling Error and Sampling Distribution

From data collected from a cross section of families living in a city, we can estimate the mean income of the population of families in the city, the proportion of families with microwave ovens, and the like. However, unless we conduct a census study of all the families in the city, we cannot pinpoint the actual mean family income, the exact proportion of families with microwave ovens, and so on. The reason we cannot do so is the presence of sampling error, discussed next.

Sampling Error

The **parameter** is the actual, or true, population mean value or population proportion for any variable (income, product ownership, and so on).

A **statistic** is an estimate of a parameter from sample data.

The actual, or true, population mean value or population proportion for any variable (such as income or product ownership) is referred to as a **parameter.** An estimate of a parameter from sample data is referred to as a **statistic.** Whenever a sampling procedure is used to estimate a population parameter, there may be some discrepancy between the sample statistic and the actual (but unknown) parameter value, no matter how objectively and carefully the sample is chosen. Such a discrepancy is commonly called *sampling error.* Sampling error is thus the difference between a statistic value, which is generated through a sampling procedure, and the parameter value, which can be determined only through a census study.

Knowledge of the magnitude of the sampling error is essential for ascertaining how precisely the population parameter can be estimated from a sample statistic value. But we cannot accurately determine the magnitude of the sampling error associated with a sampling process for two reasons. First, we do not know the true population parameter value (if we already did, there would be no need for any sampling study). Second, the sample statistic value itself may vary from sample to sample within the same population. Hence, we can only estimate the average amount of sampling error associated with a given sampling procedure. An important statistical concept that is critical for estimating sampling error is sampling distribution, discussed next.

Sampling Distribution

Consider a population consisting of just 10 families. Suppose the 10 families' annual expenditures for eating out are as shown in Table 11.4. Here the population mean expenditure for eating out (the population *parameter* value) is $275. Suppose we want to estimate the population parameter on the basis of data from a simple random sample of just two families.

There are 45 possible samples of size 2 in this population. For any sample, the value of the sample mean expenditure for eating out (the sample statistic value) will depend on the families included in it. Table 11.5 contains a partial list of the various samples of size 2, along with their sample mean expenditures for eating out. Notice that the sample mean values span a range—from $75 to

TABLE 11.4
Expenditures for Eating out for a Hypothetical Population

Family Number	Annual Expenditure for Eating Out ($)
1	50
2	100
3	150
4	200
5	250
6	300
7	350
8	400
9	450
10	500

TABLE 11.5
Partial List of Possible Samples and Sample Means

Samples of Two Families	Sample Mean Values ($)
1, 2	75
1, 6; 2, 5; 3, 4	175
1, 10; 2, 9; 3, 8; 4, 7; 5, 6	275
5, 10; 6, 9; 7, 8	375
9, 10	475

A **sampling distribution** is a representation of the sample statistic values obtained from every conceivable sample of a certain size, chosen from a population by using a specified sampling procedure, along with the relative frequency of occurrence of those statistic values.

$475—and that some mean values (such as $275) occur more frequently than others, because a greater number of samples yield those mean values. Thus, theoretically, if we were to pick samples of size 2 over and over again from this population and compute the sample mean value each time, we would observe a range of mean values, with certain values showing up more often than others. This phenomenon underlies the sampling distribution concept. A **sampling distribution** is a representation of the sample statistic values obtained from every conceivable sample of a certain size, chosen from a population by using a specified sampling procedure, along with the relative frequency of occurrence of those statistic values.

Exhibit 11.5 represents the sampling distribution associated with a simple random sampling procedure for picking samples of 2 families from our population of 10 families. The horizontal axis in this exhibit portrays the actual range of sample mean values, and each vertical bar indicates the relative frequency of occurrence of a corresponding sample mean value. For instance, if we pick many samples of size 2 and compute the sample mean for each, approximately 3/45 (or about 6.7 percent) of those values will be $175. In other words, three independent samples yield a sample mean value of $175 (see Table 11.5). Each of the three independent samples has the same probability of being selected (namely, 1/45). Therefore, the relative frequency (or probability) of occurrence for a sample mean value of $175 can be computed in the following way:

$$\frac{1}{45} + \frac{1}{45} + \frac{1}{45} = \frac{3}{45}$$

We emphasize that the sampling distribution concept is a theoretical concept in the sense that in real life we will pick only *one* random sample rather than a large number of random samples that are needed to construct a sampling distribution. Nevertheless, an understanding of this concept is essential because it forms the basis for estimating a population parameter from a sample statistic value. The nature of the sampling distribution associated with a sampling procedure is the key to estimating the sampling error generated by the procedure.

The sampling distribution in Exhibit 11.5 has two noticeable features:

1. The most frequently occurring sample mean values cluster around the population parameter value of $275.

2. Extreme sample mean values, although possible, are not very likely to occur.

These features are common to all sampling distributions. Repeated selection of random samples from the same population will yield sample statistic values such that the closer a value is to the population parameter value, the more often it will occur.

Exhibit 11.5
Sampling Distribution (Bar Chart) for Simple Random Samples of Two Units

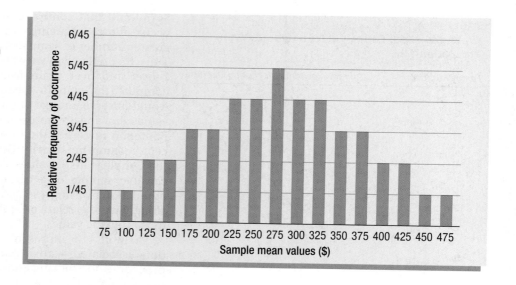

In our hypothetical illustration, the population size of 10 families is relatively small and hence restricts the total number of possible sample mean values. For this reason, the sampling distribution shown in Exhibit 11.5 is discrete and has a somewhat spiked appearance. If the population size is larger and more varied (as is normally the case in real life), a greater variety of sample compositions, and hence a greater variety of sample mean values, will be possible. Consequently, the sampling distribution will contain a much larger number of vertical bars and will have a denser appearance than the one shown in Exhibit 11.5.

When an infinite number of sample compositions are possible, the range of sample mean values can be considered to be *continuous* rather than *discrete;* that is, the sample mean can be considered as being able to take on any value in the range, rather than only certain specific values, such as $75, $100, and $125 in our example. The sampling distribution for a continuous variable is usually shown as a *histogram* (rather than as a diagram, as in Exhibit 11.5, which indicates the probability of occurrence of every possible value of the variable). An example of a histogram representing the sampling distribution of the sample mean is shown in Exhibit 11.6. In Exhibit 11.6, the height of each rectangle denotes the total frequency of occurrence of all sample mean values included within the range defined by the two vertical sides of the rectangle. Thus the histogram portrays the frequency of occurrence for different ranges of sample mean values rather than for each possible sample mean value. However, notice that the probability distribution diagram in Exhibit 11.5 and the histogram in Exhibit 11.6 have the same general shape. Indeed, the histogram can be approximated by a bell-shaped curve, as shown by the solid curve in Exhibit 11.6. Such a smooth curve is sometimes called the *theoretical* sampling distribution.

According to the **central limit theorem,** when the sample size is sufficiently large, the sampling distribution associated with a sampling procedure displays the properties of a normal probability distribution.

The sampling distribution curve has an important characteristic based on a theorem called the **central limit theorem:** for a sufficiently large sample size (in practice, a sample size of 30 or more), the sampling distribution curve for sample means associated with a sampling procedure will be centered on the population parameter value and will have all the properties of a *normal probability distribution* (the so-called normal curve).[11] This characteristic remains consistent regardless of how the values of the original variable are distributed in the population. In other words, regardless of the shape of the population distribution of a variable,

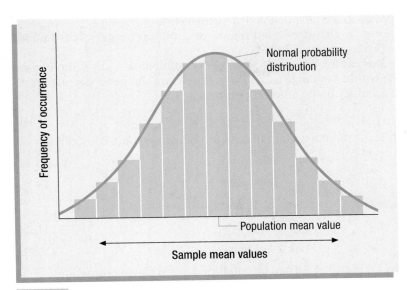

the sample mean values will be "normally" distributed as long as the sample size is adequate ($n = 30$ or more). This property is useful in making inferences about the population on the basis of sample data, as discussed next.

Following conventional notation, let's use the symbol μ to represent the true population mean value, the symbol $\bar{x}$ to represent a sample mean value, and the symbol $\sigma_{\bar{x}}$ to represent the *standard deviation of the different sample mean values* that will be obtained through repeated selection of samples from the same population. We can interpret $\sigma_{\bar{x}}$ as an average amount of sampling error associated with the sampling procedure. Traditionally, it is referred to as the **standard error** of the mean.

Exhibit 11.6
Sampling Distribution Shown as a Histogram

The **standard error** of a statistic (mean or proportion) represents the standard deviation of the different sample statistic values that will be obtained through repeated selection of samples from the same population; it can be interpreted as an average amount of sampling error associated with the sampling procedure.

If the theoretical sampling distribution behaves like the normal probability distribution, we can make a statement like the following:

> If we repeatedly pick random samples of a given size from a population, we can predict that a certain percentage (say, q percent) of the sample mean values will be within the range given by $\mu \pm z_q \sigma_{\bar{x}}$,

where z_q is the standard normal-deviate value corresponding to q percent. The z-values can be read from a normal probability table like the one shown in Appendix 1. Alternatively, we can make the following statement:

> If we pick one random sample of a given size from a population, we can predict with q percent confidence (or certainty) that the mean value for that sample will be within the range given by $\mu \pm z_q \sigma_{\bar{x}}$.

This latter statement forms the basis for estimating confidence intervals for population parameter values.

Estimating Confidence Intervals

The preceding section illustrates that we can make certain confidence statements about sample statistic values, given that the population parameter value (μ) and the standard error ($\sigma_{\bar{x}}$) are known. However, in practice, neither μ nor $\sigma_{\bar{x}}$ is known. Moreover, our purpose is to predict, with a certain degree of confidence, the range of values or the confidence interval within which the population parameter is likely to be, given data from just one random sample. We can accomplish this purpose by drawing on the theoretical principles discussed in the preceding sections and by making some approximations.

Finding Confidence Intervals for Population Mean Values

The z-value corresponding to a *two-tailed* q-value of 95 percent is 1.96 (see Appendix 1). Notice the emphasis on *two-tailed;* this term underscores that a confidence interval is symmetric about the mean (or proportion), and therefore the

z-value corresponds to the tail portion of a normal curve covering an area equivalent to $(100 - q) \div 2$. This two-tailed nature of confidence intervals is implied throughout the discussion hereafter.

Now, as we saw earlier, we can be 95 percent confident that any sample mean value ($\bar{x}$) will be within the range $\mu \pm 1.96\sigma_{\bar{x}}$; that is, we can be 95 percent confident about the accuracy of the following expression:

$$\mu - 1.96\sigma_{\bar{x}} \leq \bar{x} \leq \mu + 1.96\sigma_{\bar{x}} \tag{11.1}$$

Expression 11.1 can be rewritten in the form of two separate components:

$$\mu - 1.96\sigma_{\bar{x}} \leq \bar{x} \tag{11.1a}$$

$$\mu + 1.96\sigma_{\bar{x}} \geq \bar{x} \tag{11.1b}$$

Let us now rewrite expressions 11.1a and 11.1b as follows:

$$\mu \leq \bar{x} + 1.96\sigma_{\bar{x}} \tag{11.2a}$$

$$\mu \geq \bar{x} - 1.96\sigma_{\bar{x}} \tag{11.2b}$$

Expressions 11.2a and 11.2b can be combined into a single expression:

$$\bar{x} - 1.96\sigma_{\bar{x}} \leq \mu \leq \bar{x} + 1.96\sigma_{\bar{x}} \tag{11.2}$$

In comparing equation 11.2 and expression 11.1, notice that $\bar{x}$ and μ have switched places. Thus the preceding algebraic manipulations have resulted in the derivation of the confidence interval. Specifically, we have derived a lower and an upper bound within which we can be 95 percent confident that the population parameter (μ) will fall. This interval is really the type of confidence interval we are looking for. Unfortunately, expression 11.2 has one drawback from a practical standpoint: we do not know the value of $\sigma_{\bar{x}}$. However, from statistical theory we can obtain an approximate estimate of the standard error of the sample mean (conventionally denoted as $s_{\bar{x}}$) if we know the standard deviation (s) of the data obtained from the units in our random sample.

The equation for the *standard deviation* is as follows:[12]

$$s = \sqrt{\frac{\sum_{i=1}^{n}(x_i - \bar{x})^2}{n - 1}}$$

where

n = number of units in the sample

x_i = data obtained from each sample unit i

$\bar{x}$ = sample mean value, given by $\dfrac{\sum_{i=1}^{n} x_i}{n}$

There is a simple relationship between $s_{\bar{x}}$ and s, namely,

$$s_{\bar{x}} = \frac{s}{\sqrt{n}}$$

Thus, given $\bar{x}$ and $s_{\bar{x}}$ (both of which can be computed by using sample data), we can construct a 95 percent confidence interval for the population mean, as follows:

$$\bar{x} - 1.96\,s_{\bar{x}} \leq \mu \leq \bar{x} + 1.96\,s_{\bar{x}}$$

In other words, we can be 95 percent confident (or 95 percent certain) that the population parameter we are looking for will be in the range given by $\bar{x} \pm 1.96\ s_{\bar{x}}$. It was no accident that we picked a value of 95 percent for q in he preceding illustration. Most practical applications of sampling use a 95 percent confidence interval. However, we can use the same procedure to construct other kinds of confidence intervals; we simply choose an appropriate z_q-value (from the normal probability table) corresponding to whatever confidence level we may desire. For instance, a 99 percent confidence interval for the population mean is given by $\bar{x} \pm 2.575\ s_{\bar{x}}$, because the z-value corresponding to a confidence level of 99 percent is 2.575 (Appendix 1). We can similarly construct a 90 percent confidence interval by using a z-value of 1.645.

Let's look at a numerical problem to illustrate the construction of confidence intervals.

Problem. A simple random sample of 100 men's clothing stores was chosen from the population of such stores in a city. The average annual sales of men's suits in this sample was 1,278 units, and the standard deviation of sales was 399 units. Construct a 95 percent confidence interval for the average annual sales of men's suits in the *population* of stores.

In this problem, $n = 100$, $\bar{x} = 1{,}278$ units, and $s = 399$ units. Thus

$$s_{\bar{x}} = \frac{s}{\sqrt{n}} = \frac{399}{\sqrt{100}} = 39.9\ \text{units}$$

The 95 percent confidence interval is

$\bar{x} \pm 1.96\ s_{\bar{x}} = 1{,}278 \pm (1.96)(39.9) = 1{,}278 \pm 78.204 = 1{,}278 \pm 78$, approximately.

From the sample data, we can be 95 percent confident that the average annual sales of men's suits, across *all* men's clothing stores in the population, are between 1,200 and 1,356 units.

A key factor influencing sample size is the degree of variability among units in the population of interest: the greater the variability, the larger the sample size should be.

American Demographics Survey: Estimation of Maximum Sampling Error

According to *American Demographics*:

> Surveys conducted on *American Demographics'* behalf are nationally representative and have a sample size of approximately 1,000 randomly selected respondents. With a sample of this size, sampling error (the variability that occurs because only a sample of the population is studied rather than the entire population) is reduced to plus or minus 3 percentage points at a 95 percent confidence level. For example, if a survey shows that 55 percent of respondents buy widgets once a month, we can be certain that if the survey were repeated indefinitely, the results would show that between 52 percent and 58 percent of respondents buy widgets once a month in 95 percent of the follow-up surveys.

The error of ±3 percent in this example is the maximum sampling error associated with any percentage estimate obtained from a sample of 1,000 at a 95 percent confidence level. Let's see how the ±3 percent is derived. The standard deviation, and hence standard error (which is a measure of sampling error), will be highest when $p = .5$, or 50 percent. Thus the maximum sampling error in the *American Demographics* magazine example can be derived by estimating the standard error when $p = .5$ and computing the ± term associated with a 95 percent confidence interval:

$$\text{Maximum standard error} = \sqrt{\frac{(.5)\,(1 - .5)}{1,000}} = \sqrt{\frac{.25}{1,000}}$$
$$= .0158, \text{ or } 1.58\%$$

At the customary confidence level of 95 percent, a standard error of 1.58 percent implies a sampling error of $\pm(1.96)(1.58) = \pm3.09$ percent, or approximately ±3 percent. For percentage estimates that are greater or lower than 50 percent, the error will be lower than 3 percent. Therefore, 3 percent represents the upper bound on sampling error associated with any percentage estimate from that sample.[b]

Finding Confidence Intervals for Population Proportions

The parameters of interest in some research projects may include population *proportions* (for example, proportion of households that own DVDs in a city or proportion of firms in a region that employ more than 50 people). In such instances, we must construct confidence intervals for population proportions from sample data. The procedure is quite similar to the one we discussed for population mean values. However, the following notation is customary for confidence intervals for population proportions:

π = true population proportion (i.e., the parameter value)

p = proportion obtained from a single sample (i.e., the statistic value)

s_p = estimate of the standard error of the sample proportion

The 95 percent confidence interval for the population proportion is given by

$$p - 1.96s_p \leq \pi \leq p + 1.96s_p \qquad (11.3)$$

where

$$p = \frac{\text{Number of sample units having a certain feature}}{\text{Total number of sample units } (n)}$$

and

$$s_p = \sqrt{\frac{p(1-p)}{n}}$$

Notice that we need to know only the sample proportion and the sample size to be able to estimate the standard error s_p. Research in Use 11.2 illustrates the estimation of maximum sampling error in an *American Demographics* magazine survey.

> *Problem.* A simple random sample of 100 grocery stores was chosen from *all* grocery stores in a city. Only 64 of the 100 stores carried potted plants; that is, the proportion of stores in the sample that carried potted plants was .64. Construct a 95 percent confidence interval for the *population* proportion of stores carrying potted plants.

In this problem, $n = 100$ and $p = .64$. So

$$s_p = \sqrt{\frac{p(1-p)}{n}}$$

$$= \sqrt{\frac{(.64)(.36)}{100}} = .048$$

The 95 percent confidence interval, then, is

$$p \pm 1.96\, s_p = .64 \pm (1.96)(.048)$$

$$= .64 \pm .09408$$

$$= .64 \pm .09, \text{ approximately.}$$

This confidence interval can also be expressed in *percentage* terms: 64% ± 9%. In other words, we can be 95 percent confident that between 55 and 73 percent of all grocery stores in the city carry potted plants.

A final point about confidence interval estimation is worth noting: quantitative generalizations about the population on the basis of sample data, in the form of confidence interval estimates, are permitted only if probability sampling is used. Hence, studies using nonprobability sampling can only lead to qualitative statements, in the form of hunches or hypotheses, about the population.

Determining Sample Size

A basic purpose of sampling is to estimate population parameter values as accurately as possible. We have already seen that we cannot know for sure what a population parameter value is unless we do a census study. The only way to "predict" a parameter value from sample data is to come up with an estimate in the form of a confidence interval, usually the 95 percent confidence interval. For a given confidence level, the tighter, or more compact, the confidence interval, the more precise, and hence the more useful, the interval estimate will be.

For instance, consider two sampling studies, A and B, that are conducted to estimate the proportion of a target market that has tried a recently introduced product. Suppose the results of the two studies are as follows. From study A, we can be 95 percent confident that the proportion of all target customers who have tried the product is between .48 and .52; from study B, we can be 95 percent confident that the proportion of all target customers who have tried the product is between .35 and .65. Notice that the two confidence intervals imply that the sample proportion obtained through each study is the same, .50.

If you are a product manager, which of these two studies will you consider more useful for decision-making purposes? Study A is apparently superior because the interval estimate derived from study A is more precise. It implies that you can be reasonably certain that about half your target market has tried your new product, thereby providing you with a precise evaluation of the effectiveness of your marketing strategy for your product. The interval estimate obtained from study B contains little, if any, useful information. It merely indicates that you can be reasonably certain that the proportion of your target market that has tried your new product can be as low as .35 or as high as .65. This information is not really helpful in evaluating the effectiveness of the marketing strategy to launch the product.

In short, to be managerially useful, the term that is subtracted from and added to the sample statistic value (namely, the ± term) must be as small as possible. This point has key implications regarding certain factors that play a role in sample size determination, as discussed next.

Factors Influencing Sample Size

Let's examine the composition of the ± term that is used in the construction of confidence intervals. This term is $z_q s_{\bar{x}}$ when we are dealing with population mean values, and it is $z_q s_p$ when we are dealing with population proportions. We know that $s_{\bar{x}}$ = (sample standard deviation) ÷ $\sqrt{n}$. The expression for s_p is $\sqrt{p(1-p)} \div \sqrt{n}$; however, $\sqrt{p(1-p)}$ is simply the sample standard deviation for a proportion. Hence, regardless of whether we are interested in constructing confidence intervals for population means or population proportions, the general expression for the ± term is

$$z_q \times \frac{\text{sample standard deviation}}{\sqrt{n}}$$

where z_q is the standard normal deviate corresponding to the desired confidence level and n is the sample size.

This expression for the ± term is central in determining how compact or how wide a confidence interval will be. Simply by examining this expression, we can gain some insights about factors that play a role in determining the sample size for a study.

First, the desired degree of compactness of the confidence interval—usually known as the desired *precision level*—plays a role in determining sample size. Other things remaining the same, the greater the desired precision level, the smaller the acceptable magnitude for the ± term and hence the larger the sample size should be.

Given a certain desired precision level, the larger the values of z_q, the larger the sample size should be. In other words, if the numerator of the expression is large, the denominator must be correspondingly large to keep the magnitude of the expression small. Thus a second factor that must be considered in determining sample size is the z_q-value, or the desired confidence level, on which the value of z_q depends. Other things remaining the same, the more confidence we want to have in the interval estimate, the larger the z_q-value will be, and hence the larger the sample size should be. For instance, the z-values associated with the 95 and 99 percent confidence levels are 1.96 and 2.575, respectively. Thus, if we desire a 99 percent confidence interval (rather than a 95 percent confidence interval) but want it to have the same width, or degree of precision, as a 95 percent confidence interval, we need to pick a larger sample than what we would need for constructing the 95 percent confidence interval.

The sample standard deviation is another key variable in the expression for the ± term. What does a large or a small standard deviation mean? Standard deviation is a summary measure of how much the data provided by individual sample units differ from the overall central tendency of the total sample (the sample mean or proportion). The standard deviation of a sample is a measure of how diverse or similar the individual units that make up the sample are; the larger the standard deviation, the greater is the diversity of the units included in the sample. Because a simple random sample is supposed to be an objective representation of the population, we can view the sample standard deviation as being an approximate measure of the extent of variability or similarity of units in the population itself. Hence, a third factor that must be considered in determining sample size is the *degree of variability* across the population units. Other things remaining the same, the greater the degree of variability within the population, the larger the sample size should be.

Last, but not least, the *resources available* for conducting a study must also be considered in determining sample size. The time and money available are quite critical because, in practice, they place an upper limit on sample size. After all, if resources are unlimited, we can simply pick the largest possible sample, or even do a census study, and not worry about determining sample size. Such an ideal situation rarely, if ever, exists in real life, however. Although decision makers may desire a certain level of confidence in research results and want the results to have a specified degree of precision, the fulfillment of their desires is often constrained by a lack of resources. In many real-life situations, the available budget becomes the sole determinant of sample size.

Methods for Determining Sample Size

How does the researcher determine numerical values for sample sizes in different situations? First, the researcher must make certain assumptions and provide the following inputs:

1. The desired *precision level;* that is, the magnitude of the ± term that the researcher (or decision maker) is willing to tolerate. For example, a decision maker may want to estimate the mean age of a target market within a margin of ±4 years or to estimate the percentage of a population that owns microwave ovens within a margin of error of ±5 percent.

2. The desired *confidence level;* that is, the degree of confidence the decision maker wants to have in the interval estimate.

3. An *estimate* of the degree of variability in the population, expressed in the form of a standard deviation.

Given a desired precision level (customarily denoted as H to signify *half-interval*—one-half of the confidence interval range), a desired confidence level (q), and an estimate of the standard deviation (s), we can write the following equation:

$$H = \frac{z_q s}{\sqrt{n}}$$

(11.4)

We can square both sides of equation 11.4 and rewrite it as follows:

$$n = \frac{z_q^2 s^2}{H^2} \tag{11.5}$$

Equation 11.5 can be used to determine sample size, regardless of whether the objective is to estimate a population mean or a population proportion. The following problem demonstrates its application in a situation involving estimation of a population mean.

> *Problem.* A marketing manager of a frozen-foods firm wants to estimate within ±$10 the average annual amount that families in a certain city spend on frozen foods per year and to have 99 percent confidence in the estimate. He estimates that the standard deviation of annual family expenditures on frozen foods is about $100. How many families must be chosen for this study?

In this problem, $H = \$10$, $s = \$100$, and $z_q = 2.575$ (corresponding to a confidence level of 99 percent). Notice that H and s are expressed in the *same* units, namely, dollars; H and s must be specified in the same units before solving any problem of this kind. We can solve for the value of n by using equation 11.5:

$$n = \frac{(2.575)^2 \, (100)^2}{(10)^2} = 663 \text{ families, approximately.}$$

Although the preceding numerical solution to our problem is straightforward, there is a critical hidden catch relating to the estimate of the standard deviation of expenditures on frozen foods. How did the manager obtain this estimate? If it is merely an educated guess, how much trust can we place in its accuracy? What impact will this guessed value have on the sample size estimate? The impact can be great. For instance, even if the manager's estimate falls short of the true standard deviation by a mere $10 (if the true value of the standard deviation is $110 instead of the assumed value of $100), the actual sample size required will be approximately 802 families, and hence the estimated sample size of 663 will be off by 139 families.

The point is that the estimated sample size is very sensitive to even minor errors in the assumed value of the standard deviation. In many real-life situations, in which estimates of standard deviations are often based merely on intuition, using equation 11.5 to estimate sample size is meaningless.

Can a manager or a researcher do better than estimate the standard deviation through subjective judgment? Better estimates are available under certain circumstances:

1. If a study similar to the one being contemplated has been done in the past, the researcher may be able to use the standard deviation obtained from that study.

2. If enough time and money are available, a pilot study using, say, 30 or so units can be conducted simply to estimate the standard deviation of the variable.

3. If the minimum and maximum values of the variable in the population are known, and if the variable values for the population units can be assumed to be normally distributed, the standard deviation can be estimated as follows:

$$s = \frac{\text{Maximum value} - \text{Minimum value}}{6}$$

This equation is derived as follows. Given a group of numbers that are normally distributed, almost all the numbers will be included in the interval formed by the group mean ±3 standard deviations. In other words, the difference between the largest and smallest numbers in the group should be approximately equal to 6 standard deviations.

Although the three circumstances outlined here may yield better estimates of the standard deviation than those based on subjective judgment, a researcher would be wise to bear in mind that such estimates are still only approximations and cannot be expected to be totally error free.

Now let's consider sample size determination in situations with estimates of population proportions. As mentioned earlier, equation 11.5 can be used to determine sample size when the objective is to estimate a population proportion. However, estimating the standard deviation for this parameter is perhaps even more complex than estimating the standard deviation for a population mean. By definition, the standard deviation of a proportion is expressed in terms of the proportion itself; that is, $s = \sqrt{p(1 - p)}$. Hence, to estimate s, we need to estimate p, which is what the study, when completed, is supposed to find out.

Of course, if resources permit, we can conduct a pilot study to estimate p and then use that estimate to determine the sample size for the final study. However, a more meaningful approach in problems involving proportions is to determine an upper limit for the sample size that can guarantee an interval estimate that has the desired precision level *and* confidence level. How can we determine this upper limit? If we examine the general sample size formula given by equation 11.5, we see that for given values of H and z_q, n will take on its maximum value when s assumes its maximum value. For proportions, the value of s is largest when $p = .5$, and that largest value is given by

$$s = \sqrt{.5\,(1 - .5)}$$
$$= \sqrt{(.5)\,(.5)}$$
$$= .5$$

Hence, we can compute the upper limit for sample size, n_{max}, by using the following equation:

$$n_{max} = \frac{.25z_q^2}{H^2} \tag{11.6}$$

Problem. A sporting goods marketer wants to estimate the proportion of tennis players among high school students in the United States. The marketer wants the estimate to be accurate within ±0.02 and wants to have 95 percent confidence in the interval estimate. A pilot telephone survey of 50 high school students showed that 20 of them played tennis. Estimate the required sample size for the final study from the given data. What should the sample size be if the desired precision and confidence levels are to be *guaranteed*?

In this problem, $H = .02$ and $z_q = 1.96$. An estimate of s (from the pilot survey) is

$$s = \sqrt{20/50\,(1 - 20/50)}$$
$$= \sqrt{(.4)\,(.6)}$$
$$= \sqrt{.24}$$

Thus,

$$n = \frac{z_q^2 s^2}{H^2}$$

$$= \frac{(1.96)^2 (\sqrt{.24})^2}{(.02)^2}$$

$$= 2,305 \text{ students, approximately}$$

The maximum sample size is

$$n_{max} = \frac{.25 z_q^2}{H^2}$$

$$= 2,401 \text{ students}$$

By this time, you have probably noticed that one important factor—the available resources—is conspicuously absent in the sample size formulas we discussed. However, available resources often modify the estimated sample sizes. If resources are plentiful, the sample sizes that are estimated using the formulas should be feasible. However, if resources are limited, we may not be able to pick as large a sample as dictated by a sample size formula. For instance, if the required sample size for a study is 1,500 units but resources are available for only 1,000 units, the researcher has no choice other than to pick 1,000 units. Under such circumstances, the sample size is dictated by the available resources, and the researcher or decision maker will simply have to accept a lower precision level (a higher value for H) or a lower confidence level (a lower value for z_q) than desired.

Another point worth noting about the sample size formula is that its application involves using data on just one study variable or question. Specifically, the estimate of the standard deviation (s) employed in the formula is for a single variable (such as annual expenditures on frozen foods or ownership of microwave ovens). In practice, researchers are typically interested in measuring multiple variables through the same study. When a study involves more than one variable, an estimate of the standard deviation of the most important variable (one for which the most precise estimate is desired) can be used in the formula. Alternatively, an estimate of the standard deviation for the variable expected to have the greatest variation (and have the highest standard deviation) can be used. For a given confidence level, this approach will yield a sample size that is adequate to achieve or exceed the desired precision level for all variables. When the study variables are to be measured as proportions, a sample size that will guarantee the desired precision level for all the variables can be estimated by using the formula for n_{max} given by equation 11.6.

A final point for consideration in determining the sample size for some studies with special populations (such as households with Palm Pilots or families with children under five years of age) is the incidence rate of the special characteristic in question. The **incidence rate** of a characteristic is the proportion of the general population possessing that characteristic. Suppose the computed sample size for a study of households with Palm Pilots is 200, with an estimated one-half of the households in the general population owning Palm Pilots (the incidence rate is .5). The actual size of the sample from the general population to yield a sample of 200 households with Palm Pilots is 200/.5 = 400 households. In general, when the incidence rate is I and the required sample size is n, the actual sample size n' is given by

The **incidence rate** is the proportion of the general population possessing the characteristic of interest.

$$n' = \frac{n}{I}$$

Adjusting the required sample size is not needed when an adequate sampling frame of the special population is readily available; that is, if there is no need to select units from the general population and determine whether they are relevant for the study.

SUMMARY

Most marketing research projects use sampling, the first step in the process of making inferences about a total group of units known as a population. A population of interest to a researcher can be a collection of human or nonhuman units. A census study is one in which every population unit is examined.

When a research population is relatively large, a sampling study is likely to be less expensive, faster, and more accurate than a census study. Furthermore, given the rapidly increasing number of research surveys of human populations, sampling studies can help minimize the depletion of the pool of fresh respondents.

Census studies have a place in marketing research projects when they may be both feasible and necessary. The feasibility and necessity conditions for conducting a census study will be satisfied by a population that is relatively small and contains units that are distinctly different from one another.

In probability sampling, the selection of individual population units is independent of a researcher's judgment or biases. In nonprobability sampling, a researcher's subjective judgment plays a role in the selection of individual population units. Simple random sampling is the most basic form of probability sampling. It assigns an equal probability of selection to every possible sample of a given size in a population. However, the actual selection of a simple random sample can be done by randomly picking the desired number of units from the population. This procedure is statistically equivalent to first identifying all possible samples of the desired size and then picking one of those samples at random.

Probability sampling techniques other than simple random sampling include stratified random sampling (proportionate and disproportionate), cluster sampling, and systematic sampling. In stratified random sampling, the chosen sample is forced to contain units from each segment, or stratum, of the population. The sample selected from each stratum can be in proportion to the total number of units in the stratum. In disproportionate stratified random sampling, the sample consists of units selected from each population stratum according to how varied the units within the stratum are.

Convenience sampling and judgment sampling are two very basic forms of nonprobability sampling. Whereas convenience sampling is done purely on the basis of a researcher's convenience, judgment sampling involves some effort to select a representative sample.

Quota sampling is a refined form of nonprobability sampling that has some features of stratified random sampling, although it also involves the use of judgment in selecting the sample units. Nevertheless, a quota sample may still suffer from serious biases owing to non-representativeness on dimensions that are not explicitly included as controls. The relative flexibility of quota sampling and its ability to provide reasonably representative samples have made it a popular technique.

The choice between probability and nonprobability sampling for a study hinges on the study's objectives as well as on the resources available for conducting the study.

Every sampling procedure has an associated sampling distribution. The sampling distribution shows how a sample statistic varies across random samples of a given size chosen from the same population. The nature of the distribution associated with a sampling procedure determines the extent of its sampling error. The sampling error can be quantified as the standard deviation of the sample statistic value obtained through repeated sampling; this quantified estimate is known as the standard error.

According to the central limit theorem, when the sample size is sufficiently large, the sampling distribution associated with a sampling procedure displays the properties of a normal probability distribution. This theorem allows us to construct confidence intervals for a population parameter value (mean or proportion) from a sample statistic value.

Quantitative generalizations about the population on the basis of sample data, in the form of confidence interval estimates, are permitted only if probability sampling is used. Hence, studies using nonprobability sampling can lead only to hunches or hypotheses about the population.

The sample size for a study must be based on the desired precision level, the desired confidence level, the degree of variability in the population to be studied, and the available resources. Formulas can be used to determine the required sample size for a study. However, because accurately estimating the standard deviation prior to conducting a study is difficult, caution must be exercised in using sample size formulas. Moreover, the sample size formulas we discussed do not directly take into account the resources available for a study. In addition, when the focus of a study is on population units with a special characteristic, the required sample size may have to be increased by taking into account the incidence rate of the characteristic.

REVIEW AND DISCUSSION QUESTIONS

1. Distinguish between a sample study and a census study, and describe the advantages of the former over the latter.

2. Discuss why stratified random sampling will produce more accurate population estimates than will simple random sampling.

3. Using an appropriate example, illustrate the distinction between proportionate and disproportionate stratified random sampling.

4. Describe a hypothetical situation that would be ideal for using (a) cluster sampling and (b) systematic sampling. Justify your answer.

5. Briefly discuss the various nonprobability sampling methods.

6. Briefly describe the advantages and limitations of nonprobability sampling relative to probability sampling.

7. Briefly discuss the distinction between *parameter* and *statistic,* using a suitable example, and define *sampling error.*

8. Define *sampling distribution.* What properties does a sampling distribution curve associated with a random sampling procedure have? Be specific.

9. State the four factors to be considered in determining the sample size for any study, and indicate in what way each factor influences sample size.

10. Define the *incidence rate* of a characteristic and illustrate its role in sample size determination.

APPLICATION EXERCISES

1. A simple random sample of 900 undergraduate students at Exmont University had an average grade point ratio of 2.3, with a standard deviation of 2. The sample was chosen randomly by a computer from a university record containing the names and grade point ratios of all undergraduate students at Exmont. The sample mean and the standard deviation were also calculated and reported by the computer.

   a. Construct a 95 percent confidence interval for the average grade point ratio of Exmont's undergraduate population.

   b. If you were asked to start from scratch and estimate the average grade point ratio parameter, would you use the same procedure as in part a? Would you use a different procedure? Explain your answer. (*Hint:* Consider the pros and cons of a census study versus a sampling study.)

2. A marketer wants to be 95 percent confident that the per capita family income in a certain area is at least $12,000 before deciding to locate a retail outlet in the area. A simple random sample of 81 families chosen from the area had a mean income of $13,000, with a standard deviation of $4,500.

   a. Should the marketer locate a retail store in the area?

   b. Would your answer be different if the marketer raised the minimum per capita income requirement from $12,000 to $12,500? Why or why not?

3. Firm XYZ introduced a new product in a test-market area. Six months after the product had been introduced, a random telephone survey of 500 households in the area indicated that 150 had tried the product.

   a. Construct a 95 percent confidence interval for the percentage of all households in the test area that tried the new product.

   b. Suppose XYZ's goal is "to ensure that at least 50 percent of the households in the test area try our new product within 12 months after introduction." What recommendations would you make to XYZ from the results in part a?

4. J. R. Soper, a presidential candidate, does not want to campaign in any state in which she is not almost certain (99 percent confident) that at least 30 percent of all registered voters already favor her. A random telephone survey of 1,000 registered voters in state A showed that 320 favored Soper. Should Soper campaign in state A?

5. A charitable organization is considering whether to launch a fund-raising telethon. However, before making a "go or no-go" decision, the organization wants to conduct a national telephone survey of households to estimate the average contribution a household will make in response to the telethon. The organization wants to be 95 percent confident

in the interval estimate derived from the survey, and it desires the estimate to be within ±$20. The standard deviation of charitable contributions in response to similar telethons in the past is about $125. How many households should the organization interview in its telephone survey?

6. ABC Company wants to conduct a study to estimate, within ±10 percent, the percentage of households in Texas that have digital camcorders. Moreover, ABC wants to have 99 percent confidence in the interval estimate. A pilot study of 250 households in typical Texas communities found that 50 had digital camcorders. What sample size should ABC use for its study? What should the sample size be if ABC Company wants to guarantee an interval estimate within ±5 percent at a 99 percent confidence level?

7. A study conducted in 1990 showed that family expenditures on travel and entertainment ranged from a low of $500 to a high of $3,500 per year. Although the range of current family expenditures on travel and entertainment is likely to be the same as in 1990, the mean expenditure is likely to have changed substantially. Suppose you want to estimate the current mean expenditure within ±$10, and you desire a confidence level of 95 percent for your estimate. How many families would you interview regarding their travel and entertainment expenditures?

8. A firm planning a phased launch for a new product wishes to estimate the average family purchases of the new product within a precision level of 3 units and with 90 percent confidence. From the data of other territories, the regional manager estimates the standard deviation to be 20 units per family. Calculate the minimum sample size if the desired precision and confidence levels are to be achieved.

9. A researcher wishes to estimate the proportion of travelers visiting a gift shop at a major airport terminal. From experience in other airports, 20 out of every 100 travelers visit such stores. Estimate the required sample size if the researcher wants to be accurate within ±0.05 and wants to be 95 percent confident of the estimate. What should the sample size be if the desired precision and confidence intervals are to be guaranteed?

10. For each of the following situations, suggest a specific sampling plan—probability, nonprobability, or perhaps a combination of the two—and justify your selection. Also briefly describe how the sample should be selected in each situation.

a. A political candidate for the U.S. Senate is in a very tight race with her opponent. Election Day is 10 weeks away, and this candidate wants to get a weekly reading of how many registered voters prefer her to her opponent.

b. A large, independent discount department store carries 20,000 different products. The manager of the store wants to know whether store customers are experiencing any difficulty in locating the products they are looking for.

c. The president of an electronic products firm wants to know what the field of computer chip technology will look like five years from now.

d. The school district in a metropolitan area has 30 elementary schools spread across the area. The superintendent of the school district wants to ascertain the opinions of parents in the area about the quality of the elementary school education their children are receiving.

11. The management of a large shopping mall has designed a study "to determine the perceptions and likes/dislikes of the mall's customers concerning various aspects of the mall." The study design calls for a sample of 600 adult customers (300 males and 300 females) chosen by contacting every 10th adult customer who comes in through the mall's main entrance between 2:00 P.M. and 8:00 P.M., Monday through Saturday, of a randomly chosen week. Which of the various sampling procedures would adequately describe the proposed sampling plan? How representative is the sample likely to be of the ideal population of interest in this situation? Explain your answers.

INTERNET EXERCISES

1. Go to www.cnn.com. Go to the QuickVote section and click on "View Results" to view the poll of the day. What is the question of the day? What type of scale is used by the QuickVote? How many said yes and how many no? Describe the sampling procedure used by QuickVote. Can we generalize the results to all Internet users? to the U.S. population?

2. Go to www.gallup.com. Select a poll of interest to you and briefly describe the results (you may need to register for a free trial of Gallup Poll on Demand). What survey methods did Gallup use to conduct the poll? What sampling method did Gallup use? What is the maximum margin of sampling error? Can we generalize the findings to a larger population of interest? If so, which population would that be?

CASE 11.1 NIKE CHAINSAW AD (PART B)
(www.nike.com)

Assume you are a research associate who reports to the research director at Nike, and you are reviewing the results of an important survey that has just been tabulated. The survey was developed to assess customer reactions to the controversial Nike advertisement that appeared during NBC's coverage of the Olympic Games in Sydney, Australia. The research was conducted by a subsidiary (QuickTake) of Greenfield Online (www.greenfieldonline. com). The results were based on a sample of 150 respondents. Some of your colleagues are concerned that the results of the survey may not be representative of the population of consumers who viewed the television advertisement.

Company Background

As the largest athletic apparel and footwear marketer in the world, Nike, Inc., is involved principally in the design, development, and worldwide marketing of high-quality footwear, apparel, equipment, and accessory products. Although a large percentage of the products are worn for everyday purposes, Nike's footwear products are designed mainly for specific athletic use. Nike also sells active sports apparel, athletic bags, and accessories covering these activities. Although Nike products are produced by independent contract manufacturers throughout the world, Nike is responsible for all marketing activities for the brand. The Nike brand is known throughout the world, with its products marketed in approximately 140 countries in addition to the United States. Nike products are available through thousands of individual retail stores around the world.

The Chainsaw Ad

The ad was one of three in a series, all intended as humorous spots. It opens with a spooky scene of the front of a remote cabin and cuts to a scene of Suzy Favor Hamilton getting ready for a bath. While she combs her hair, she gazes into the bathroom mirror and sees a Freddie Krueger type behind her, wearing a mask and brandishing a chainsaw. In a series of quick scene changes, the homicidal maniac pursues his target, breaking the mirror with the chainsaw, cutting through a door, and pursuing the frightened Suzy through the woods. The only dialogue is Suzy's bloodcurdling screams and heavy breathing. The spot ends with the exhausted pursuer falling to his knees and the Olympic runner making her way into the distant woods. The ad closes with the tag line "Why sport? You'll live longer" and the Nike swoosh logo.

Presumably the ad was designed with teenage boys in mind; they spend 60 percent of all sneakers dollars.[1] Response to the ad, however, was quite negative; because NBC received over 2,000 complaints, it pulled the ad after it had aired for only a few days. The ad was so controversial that it was the focus of both favorable and unfavorable discussion in a variety of media.

Sampling for the Survey

As you review the survey results, consider the extent to which the sampling method used was appropriate. Note that, through QuickTake's relationships with firms such as DoubleClick, Engage, and 24/7 Real Media, the survey was sent out to the Internet population. (Refer to Tables 1, 2, and 3 for summary demographics.) QuickTake considered its sample to be the "general Internet user" who was surveyed while online when he or she clicked on the banner with a chance to win a cash prize. All respondents were screened to be 18 years or older. The banners were run across roughly 2,500 websites of the following types: automotive, business, travel, commerce, entertainment, technology, and health. Because the sampling methods have an impact on how to interpret the results, it is important to understand the nature of the sample used.

CASE QUESTIONS

1. Describe the current sample and sampling method. Are they appropriate?

2. What sampling procedure should Nike use to assess as accurately as possible customer reaction to the chainsaw ad?

CASE NOTE

1. According to Chana R. Schoenberger, "Sneaker Attack," *Forbes*, October 30, 2000.

This case was written by Jeanne L. Munger (University of Southern Maine) in collaboration with the textbook authors, as a basis for class discussion rather than to illustrate either effective or ineffective marketing practice.

TABLE 1
Age and Gender of Those Offended by the Ad

What gender/age below best describes you?	Number of Respondents	Percentage
1 Male 18–24	6	16.22
2 Male 25–34	7	18.92
3 Male 35–44	3	8.11
4 Male 45–54	3	8.11
5 Male 55+	3	8.11
6 Female 18–24	6	16.22
7 Female 25–34	3	8.11
8 Female 35–44	3	8.11
9 Female 45–54	2	5.41
10 Female 55+	1	2.70
Total	37	

TABLE 2
Annual Household Income of Sample

What is your annual household income before taxes?	Number of Respondents	Percentage
1 Less than $15,000	19	12.67
2 $15,000 to $30,000	26	17.33
3 $30,001 to $45,000	35	23.33
4 $45,001 to $60,000	24	16.00
5 $60,001 to $75,000	20	13.33
6 $75,001 to $90,000	5	3.33
7 $90,001 to $105,000	9	6.00
8 $105,001 to $125,000	4	2.67
9 $125,001 to $150,000	5	3.33
10 $150,001 to $200,000	2	1.33
11 More than $200,000	1	0.67
Total	150	

TABLE 3
Marital Status of Sample

What is your current marital status?	Number of Respondents	Percentage
1 Single	66	44.00
2 Married	56	37.33
3 Divorced	23	15.33
4 Widowed	5	3.33
Total	150	

CASE 11.2 EXIT POLLS: THE 2000 AND 2004 PRESIDENTIAL ELECTIONS

Pollster Harry O'Neill, vice chairman of Roper Starch Worldwide, summarized the 2000 U.S. presidential election results when he stated, "From all of the pre-election polls, I thought that it was going to be a close election, a two- or three-point election. Never did I think it would be a .00001 election."[1] Although the networks initially called Gore the winner, then announced Bush the winner, they finally reasoned that the results were too close to call. With news sources calling the wrong presidential winner in 2000, the 2004 coverage was much more cautious. CNN used a combination of research methods including public polling, trends, interviews and independent studies to predict who would win the Bush-Kerry race in each state and then tallied the electoral votes. The reports made it clear that the results of the studies were applicable only if the election were to be held at that moment and that they were not predictive of what might happen on Election Day.[2]

Election Polling

During the elections, the media typically rely on polling to project results. According to the Brookings Institution Center for Media and Public Affairs, which has been analyzing election coverage by the networks, emphasis on poll results has increased.[3] In fact, voter exit poll results have become a central theme of news reports on the night of a major election.

Election polling involves interviewing voters as they leave the polls. Voters are asked their party affiliation, whom they voted for, which issues were important in their selection of a candidate—personal qualities, the economy, jobs—and demographic characteristics such as gender, age, and income. In addition to being used to project the winners, this information is used to develop profiles of voters for each candidate. It is commonplace for news anchors and reporters to discuss which of these characteristics distinguish voters for each candidate, especially for the candidates of the two major political parties.

The major media all get their polling information from the same source, Voter News Service (VNS), a polling consortium funded by ABC, CBS, CNN, Fox, NBC, and the Associated Press. VNS collects information—from exit polls, actual vote returns from sample precincts, and actual county vote tabulations—to be used in statistical models for projecting results. Output from the models is made available to the member news organizations. Each major network interprets the information independently in making its own projections.

2000 Results

On November 7, 2000, the night of the heavily contested 2000 presidential election, it became obvious that heavily contested Florida would determine the winner. With 45 exit poll locations in the state, VNS indicated that Gore was ahead by 6.5 percentage points. At around 7:50 P.M., VNS and all of its members called the election for Gore based on the results of the exit polls at 38 of the 45 Florida precincts and actual votes from a small number of locations. VNS, in a statement released to the press, said,

> The exit poll gave Gore a small lead but no member nor VNS thought that it was enough to call the race with confidence. However, when reports of actual votes from sample or model precincts came in, they supported the survey results and allowed the race to be called.[4]

2004 Results

Even when reported with caution, various news media polls taken the weekend prior to the 2004 election resulted in conflicting predictions, with some placing Kerry ahead of Bush and others placing Bush ahead of Kerry. The CBS/New York Times and Pew Research surveys found Bush leading by 3 points, which turned out to be consistent with the election results the following week. However, USA Today/CNN/Gallup's survey declared Kerry to be pulling ahead in Florida by 3 percentage points (he actually lost there by 5 percentage points). Similarly, Bush was predicted to win Pennsylvania by 4 points but was disappointed when he actually lost there by 2 points.[5]

CASE QUESTIONS

1. What kinds of samples did the networks rely on to call the election for Gore in 2000? What was the sampling frame for the exit polls?

2. How do you explain the variance in the results of the poll and the final results (in both 2000 and 2004)? What types of error might account for this variance?

CASE NOTES

1. A transcript of the interview between Bill Moult and Harry O'Neill is contained in "A Pollster's View of the 2000 Election," *Inside Business,* December 4, 2000.
2. "Report Suggests Changes in Exit Poll Methodology," www.cnn.com (accessed February 8, 2005).
3. Stephen Hess, Brookings Institution, interview on *Inside Politics,* CNN, October 30, 2000.
4. "Voter News Service Scrutinized," Associated Press Online, November 17, 2000.
5. John Mercurio and Molly Levinson, "CNN Analysis: Eight States Too Close to Call," www.cnn.com (accessed February 8, 2005); Mark Memmott, "Predictions Burn Pollsters, Pundits—Again," www.usatoday.com (accessed February 8, 2005); Alaina Potrikus, "Zogby Projected Victory by Kerry; Exit Polls Erred, but Pollster Defends Pre-Election Surveys Pointing to Bush," *Post-Standard/Herald-Journal,* November 4, 2004; "It's Really Close: Online Survey Shows Kerry with Two-Point Lead; Telephone Survey Shows Four-Point Bush Lead," *PR Newswire,* November 1, 2004; "Enter Pollsters, Exit Judgment?" *Economic Times,* April 26, 2004.

This case was written by Jeanne L. Munger (University of Southern Maine) in collaboration with the textbook authors, as a basis for class discussion rather than to illustrate either effective or ineffective marketing practice.

Data Analysis

Part Four

Quality Control and Initial Analysis of Data

Chapter Objectives

After reading and understanding the material in this chapter, you should be able to:

- Define editing and distinguish between a field edit and an office edit.

- Define coding and outline the steps it involves.

- Compute measures of central tendency and of dispersion of the data for each variable in a data set.

- State the potential uses of frequency distributions or one-way tables.

*Vignette written by Charles L. Colby, president of Rockbridge Associates, Inc. (www .rockresearch.com). Reprinted by permission of Charles L. Colby.

Data Analysis at Rockbridge Associates: From Data Integrity to Hypothesis Testing*

Data integrity is the foundation for successful marketing research. It would not matter how well we defined the problem, wrote the survey questions, reported the findings, or offered creative recommendations if there was doubt about the underlying accuracy of the data itself.

One area where Rockbridge ensures integrity is in the collection and processing of the data. We implement a number of quality control checks to ensure accuracy. For example, we still collect some data on paper forms, such as mail surveys, and we need to prepare these data in electronic form so they can be tabulated. To ensure accuracy, we key enter all of the data twice and compare the two files, eliminating virtually all errors. Most of our data are entered directly into an electronic database, including telephone surveys, which are scripted by Computer Assisted Telephone Interviewing (CATI) software, and Web surveys. We do a lot of careful checking of the programming for these surveys and also pretest them to ensure that the data are captured correctly. When we collect data by telephone, we also monitor the interviewing extensively and call back respondents to validate that the interview was completed properly.

Most of our questionnaires rely on questions that are close-ended, meaning they use predefined answer categories. Our computerized interviewing software ensures the integrity of these questions by blocking entry of responses that are illogical or inconsistent. Some of our questions are open-ended and qualitative in nature, such as "Why do you feel this way?" These questions are assigned numerical codes for tabulation purposes, a process that takes some careful preparation by an experienced analyst or coding supervisor.

We tabulate all of our survey results in a "banner format," which neatly breaks out all of the survey questions by various analysis groups (such as demographic categories we wish to study). These tabulations are usually checked by an analyst for accuracy and often compared to a separate tabulation using different software.

The importance of the data preparation process, and how it affects credibility, can be illustrated with a real example. I have seen a study where a single case was incorrectly keyed but not discovered until late in the process, causing the numbers to be revised by less than one-half of 1 percentage point. Even though the change was minor, it caused the users to question the accuracy of the study in general and to disregard all of its information.

Data integrity also stems from how the results are interpreted and explained to management. As anyone will learn in a statistics or marketing research course, all samples have a natural margin of error that is measurable. It is important to conduct hypothesis testing to ensure that our observations are likely to be part of a real story and not an aberration that results from the randomness of the sample. An experienced researcher knows to be careful about reporting small differences as a key finding without first conducting an appropriate statistical test.

The most common application of hypothesis testing is in gauging differences between groups. For example, we may look at the percent satisfied between males and females or the percent who can identify a brand name in three different time periods to see if change has occurred. To facilitate hypothesis testing, we program statistical tests between groups in our tabulations, usually a T-test.

We win business and grow relationships by being creative and doing a good job consulting on marketing strategy. But at the same time, everyone on the Rockbridge team has to be preoccupied with the most minute details of data preparation to ensure our credibility as a source. ∎

Although certain fieldwork errors can be prevented through such precautionary measures as proper questionnaire design and adequate interviewer training, unanticipated errors do occur. Failure to quickly discover and remedy those errors will result in meaningless or misleading data.

For example, one of the textbook authors participated in a descriptive research project consisting of a personal interview survey of a quota sample of 500 adult respondents. The purpose of the project was to obtain data on such lifestyle variables as leisure time activities, reading habits, and television viewing behavior. Several seemingly professional interviewers were recruited to gather the data. Gender was one of the quota controls, and the interviewers were instructed to divide their interviews equally between males and females. The questionnaire, although lengthy, was fairly structured and straightforward. Moreover, the interviewers expressed no difficulties or complaints during data collection. As a result, the researchers in charge grew complacent and made only a cursory examination of interviewers' quota sheets to verify that adequate progress was being made toward filling the gender quotas. The questionnaires were not scrutinized until well after all of them had been returned.

A careful examination of the questionnaire data revealed that 25 questionnaires had both male and female checked under the item "Respondent's Gender." Yet the interviewers had been assigned quotas of 50 percent male and 50 percent female respondents, and these quotas had apparently been adhered to. Additional investigation traced all 25 questionnaires to the same interviewer, who, unfortunately, had moved out of the area by that time. Therefore, the only clue to these strange responses was the following additional notation the interviewer had made on one of the questionnaires:

❑ **Male**   **Husband; answered most of the questions**
❑ **Female**   **Wife; answered certain leisure activity questions**

Evidently this interviewer did not restrict the interview to just one person in households where both husband and wife were willing to participate in the survey. Conducting part of the interview with a male and part with a female was a serious error, and all 25 interviews had to be discarded. However, this mistake might have been an honest one, as the formal quota sampling instructions asked the interviewers to contact 50 percent males and 50 percent females (apparently interpreted by this particular interviewer as "make initial contact with"). The point is that, regardless of whether the mistake was an honest one, it could and should have been caught and corrected much earlier than it was. Discovering fieldwork errors and attempting to correct them early in the project is discussed in the next section.

Editing

Editing is the process of examining completed data collection forms and taking whatever corrective action is needed to ensure the data are of high quality.

Editing is the process of examining completed data collection forms and taking whatever corrective action is needed to ensure the data are of high quality. Editing is a quality control check that is performed when the data are still in raw form. It is essential for detecting and correcting data collection problems before it is too late. To illustrate, the problem that occurred in the lifestyle research study could have been minimized and perhaps completely solved by a preliminary edit, also known as a field edit.

Field Edit

A **preliminary** or **field edit** is a quick examination of completed data collection forms, usually on the same day they are filled out.

A **preliminary** or **field edit** is a quick examination of completed data collection forms, usually on the same day they are filled out. In the lifestyle research study, even a cursory examination of completed questionnaires immediately after the researcher received them from the interviewers would have pinpointed the interviewer who was checking both male and female on some questionnaires. The errant interviewer could then have been reinstructed about the quota sampling

A field edit is useful for detecting and correcting interviewing deficiencies before they turn into major problems.

requirements and asked to repeat the defective interviews using correct proce-dures. Even if repeating the interviews was not feasible, the mistake could have been prevented in subsequent interviews, and the number of wasted interviews would have been much lower than 25.

A field edit has two objectives: to ensure that proper procedures are being followed in selecting respondents, interviewing them, and recording their re-sponses; and to remedy fieldwork deficiencies before they turn into major prob-lems. Obviously, speed is crucial for an effective field edit: it must be done while the study is still in progress, preferably at the end of each interviewing day and especially at the end of the first day of interviewing. Indeed, in central-location, computer-based telephone or Internet interviewing, some field editing can and should be done by a supervisor as the interviews are taking place.

Typical problems that a field edit can reveal include inappropriate respon-dents (as in the lifestyle research study); incomplete interviews (one or several questions left unanswered for no apparent reason); and illegible or unclear responses (especially in the case of open-ended questions). Upon uncovering problems of this nature, the field editor, who is usually the person in charge of supervising the fieldwork, must immediately seek an explanation from the inter-viewer, when the interview is still fresh in the interviewer's mind.

Office Edit

A final or office edit is conducted after all the field-edited data collection forms are received in a central location.

A **final** or **office edit** verifies response consistency and accuracy, makes necessary corrections, and determines whether some or all parts of a data collection form should be discarded. Thus this second stage of editing is conducted after all the field-edited data collection forms are received in a central location. In computer-based telephone or Internet interviewing, there are typically no physical ques-tionnaires, and interviewers store the collected data directly in computer memory. Final editing of such data can be done with the aid of a computer (we discuss this topic later).

An office edit is more thorough than a field edit, and the task of an office editor is somewhat more complex than that of a field editor. The following cases illustrate the types of problems an office editor may have to deal with.

Case 1. A respondent said he was 18 years old but indicated that he had a Ph.D. when asked for his highest level of education.

Case 2. On a questionnaire containing a mixture of positive and negative Likert scale items, a respondent "strongly agreed" with all of them.

Case 3. In response to the question "What is the most expensive purchase you have made within the past month?" three respondents gave the following answers: respondent 1, "a new car"; respondent 2, "a vacation in Hawaii"; respondent 3, "water, gas, and electricity for my household use."

In case 1, the responses to the age and education questions appear to be inconsistent. Case 2 involves a set of responses that are too consistent. Because the questionnaire contained a mixture of positive and negative items, a respondent who agreed with all such items was obviously being frivolous or inattentive to providing valid answers. In this case, the office editor may have no alternative but to throw the entire questionnaire out.[1]

Case 3 depicts a different type of editing problem—namely, consistency or comparability of responses to the same question across questionnaires. Although the answers given by all three respondents are legitimate, they appear to be based on different frames of reference. The major issue facing the office editor is deciding how these diverse responses should be coded (coding is discussed in detail in the next section). One way to improve the question would be to reword it, because it is not specific as to type of purchase (necessity versus luxury). The specific information objectives of the study play a critical role in coding responses. In fact, before beginning the editing process, the researcher should establish a detailed set of guidelines, preferably in writing, for interpreting and categorizing open-ended responses.

This sample of editing problems is certainly not exhaustive. Exhibit 12.1 contains a more comprehensive list of problems that an editor should look for and deal with when they do occur. Notice that several of these problems can be handled at the field-editing stage.

Preventing Errors

A few final points about editing should be discussed. First, a number of potential editing problems can be avoided through careful planning before fieldwork begins. Preventing ambiguous, inappropriate, or incorrect responses is better than attempting to correct data errors after they occur. Editing is not a panacea for all data quality problems, and it is a serious mistake to view it as such.

Second, when the collected data are already in computer memory in the case of Internet or computer-assisted interviews, editing can be done thoroughly and efficiently. Editing tasks that are difficult or impossible to accomplish manually, especially in large-scale surveys, can be done easily through computer editing. For instance, a computer can be programmed to check for such patterns as response values falling within prespecified ranges, responses to key questions being consistent with those to related questions, and a respondent's pattern of answers deviating substantially from the average pattern. Problem responses and respondents can thus be brought to the office editor's attention quickly.

Third, the role that editing can play in improving data quality is much more restricted in mail surveys than in personal interview or telephone surveys. A mail survey researcher has little control over data collection once the questionnaires are mailed out. Therefore, the only editing possible in mail surveys is a limited office edit.

Exhibit 12.1
A List of Problems That Editing Can Help Uncover
Source: John A. Sonquist, William C. Dunkelberg, *Survey and Opinion Research: Procedures for Processing and Analysis*, ©1977, pp. 43–44. Reprinted by permission of Pearson Education.

1. Improper field procedures.
   a. Wrong questionnaire form used.
   b. Interview inadvertently not taken.

2. Incomplete interviews.
   a. Questions not asked.
   b. Directions not followed (proper segments of the questionnaire were not administered).

3. Improperly conducted interviews.
   a. The wrong respondent interviewed (e.g., son instead of father).
   b. Questions misinterpreted by interviewer or respondent.
   c. Evidence of bias or influencing of answers.
   d. Failure to probe for adequate answers or the use of poor probes.
   e. Interviewer apparently does not understand what types of responses constitute an answer to the actual question asked; or does not understand what the objective of the question is, and thus accepts an improper frame of reference for the respondent's answer.
   f. Interviewer's illegible writing and/or style.
   g. Interviewer recorded information which identified a respondent whose anonymity should have been protected.
   h. Other evidence of need for training or instructions to be given to interviewer (e.g., failure to write down probes, wrong abbreviations, failure to follow directions).

4. Technical problems with the questionnaire or interview.
   a. Space was not provided for needed information.
   b. The presence of unanticipated or unusually frequent extreme responses to questions, indicating a possible need for rewording of certain questions.
   c. Inappropriate or unworkable interviewer instructions not detected in the pretest.
   d. The order in which questions were asked introduces confusion, resentment, or bias into the respondent's answers.

5. Respondent rapport problems.
   a. Frequent refusal to answer certain questions.
   b. Reports of abnormal termination of the interview (or presence of hostility) due to sensitive questions.
   c. Evidence that respondent and interviewer are playing the "game" of "What answer do you want me to give?"
   d. Evidence that the presence of other people in the interview situation is causing problems.

6. Consistency problems that can be isolated and reconciled.
   a. Contradictory answers (e.g., reports no savings in one section of the interview but reports interest from bank accounts in another section).
   b. Misclassification (e.g., mortgage debt improperly reported as installment debt).
   c. Impossible answers (e.g., reports paying $600 for a new Edsel in 1970—the car should have been recorded as a "used" car; or weekly income reported on the income-per-month line).
   d. Unreasonable (and probably erroneous) responses (e.g., reports borrowing $2,000 for two years to buy a car but reported monthly payments multiplied by 24 months are less than $2,000; or house value is reported as being $90,000 while income is $2,000 per year and the respondent claims less than a high school education).

Finally, the process of editing is not limited to evaluating data collected through questionnaires. Editing can also check the quality of data collected through observation. For example, ACNielsen Company offers an information service called ScanTrack, which is based on retail sales data collected electronically from a panel of grocery stores equipped with computerized optical scanners. Once a week, sales data from these stores are sent to Nielsen on tape. Before a store is included in Nielsen's panel, the data tapes are monitored and subjected to a rigorous, computerized editing process to ensure the data are trustworthy. Research in Use 12.1 describes this editing process.

In most survey research projects, the process of editing, especially the office edit, goes hand in hand with the process of coding, to which we now turn.

Coding

Coding broadly refers to the set of all tasks associated with transforming edited responses into a form that is ready for analysis.

Coding broadly refers to the set of all tasks associated with transforming edited responses into a form that is ready for analysis. Our emphasis here will be on questionnaires used in conclusive research projects, which invariably rely on large sample sizes and computer data analyses. Exploratory research projects are characterized by fairly informal data collection and analysis procedures. Hence, a formal coding process is typically not necessary in such projects.

We can view coding as the following sequence of steps:

1. Transforming responses to each question into a set of meaningful categories
2. Assigning numerical codes to the categories
3. Creating a data set suitable for computer analysis

In discussing these steps, we will illustrate with a research study (hereafter referred to as "National Insurance Company—Service Quality Assessment") conducted by one of the authors. The primary purpose of this study was to ascertain how customers perceived National's quality of service and to identify areas for improvement. A four-page questionnaire was mailed to a random sample of 1,000 policyholders from National's customer base. Completed questionnaires were received from 285 respondents. The questionnaire appears in Exhibit 12.2; we will use it to illustrate the various coding steps.

Transforming Responses into Meaningful Categories

How difficult and time consuming this step is depends on the degree to which the questionnaire is structured. A structured question is precategorized; that is, it has a set of fixed-response categories. Responses to a nonstructured or open-ended question have to be grouped into a meaningful and manageable set of categories, a task that can be laborious if respondents' answers vary widely.[2]

Consider the questionnaire presented in Exhibit 12.2. The questions listed are completely structured, with one exception: question 6 in the final section is open-ended, asking respondents for ways they can be served better. Very few gave suggestions, so the open-ended question did not pose a major coding difficulty. A large number of respondents answering the open-ended question, however, would have strongly suggested that the questionnaire was not well designed to tap all aspects of service quality and cover the bulk of the respondents. In other words, a well-designed questionnaire is unlikely to pose any major coding problems.

Questions in section 2, although open-ended, sought a numerical response. Numerical responses are already coded in quantified form and need not be

ACNielsen Company: Computerized Editing of ScanTrack Data

Nielsen New Store Quality Edit

Certain idiosyncrasies in vendor scanning systems create data problems. Nielsen statisticians have developed a series of computerized data edit routines that are run for every store each week to determine whether such idiosyncrasies have affected the data. The logic of these edit routines is based on thousands of hours of comprehensive review and research of actual scanning data problems encountered over the years. For the first several weeks during which Nielsen receives a scanning tape from a retailer, the data are thoroughly checked for consistency and completeness. Nielsen's computerized New Store Quality Edit procedure provides a comprehensive analysis of all UPC data contained on the tape to ensure that the scanning data accurately represent the sales for that particular store.

To check for data completeness, the UPCs on each tape are grouped into more than 1,000 product modules. The scan sales for each module are accumulated, and modules with sales of zero are checked to determine whether the scan data are missing or the store does not carry items in those modules.

The 1,000 product modules are collapsed into 80 product categories to check further on the completeness of data from new stores. Each category's share of total scan sales is calculated. These shares are then compared with market norms calculated from other stores in the same geographical area. Categories that deviate markedly from these norms are analyzed further to determine whether the deviations are caused by a scanning problem.

Finally, the total scan dollar sales on the tape are compared with the total Accumulated Commodity Volume (ACV) of the store, a figure provided by the retailer's accounting system. This ensures that the size of the store, as measured with the scanning data, is consistent with the size as measured from an outside source, in order to produce a complete scan sales assessment.

These tests are conducted for as long as it takes to ensure that the scanning data received from each store are complete and accurate. Throughout the evaluation process, as questions arise, Nielsen data analysts are in contact with the retailer's data processing center, or Nielsen field personnel visit the store to examine deviations in the scanning data.

Nielsen Store Usability Edit

Once a store passes the initial quality evaluation and is being used in the Nielsen reporting sample, each weekly tape received is subjected to a thorough evaluation for data accuracy and completeness. The computerized Store Usability Edit procedure systematically examines all scan data on the tape by comparing current data with data from previous weeks in the same store.

The procedure begins by taking the 80 product categories mentioned earlier and further collapsing these into 10 broad "super groups" such as frozen food, health and beauty aids, and so on. The total dollar sales and UPC counts for each super group are calculated and compared by group. Averages are calculated using the previous eight weeks' scan sales from each store. If sales and UPC counts for each group fall within a certain statistical range of the average, the data for the store are automatically accepted for use in the sample. If the sales for any product group fall outside the acceptable range, diagnostic work begins to determine the cause for the unusual sales.

To assist Nielsen data analysts in investigating questionable figures, data for individual product categories comprising the super group are automatically printed. Local merchandising is checked to determine if a promotion or some other market event affected the figures. A UPC item exception report is also produced, listing UPCs with abnormally high sales or selling prices that could be contributing to the problem. Based on this research, a decision is made about whether the out-of-range data reflect actual market activity or a scanning problem.

If further analysis is required, a more complete UPC-by-UPC analysis is performed by comparing one week's questionable data with data from the previous week. Detailed item frequency distributions are constructed for each week, and statistical tests of difference are performed to determine whether the basic item structure for the two weeks is the same. An examination of UPCs common to both weeks, as well as items that appear one week and not the other, helps identify data other than the seven days of sales data studied. This detailed analysis helps identify the type of problem. Appropriate action is taken to correct the data, or a decision is made not to use it in the sample.

The Store Usability Edit system provides for a continuous comprehensive check on scan data quality for all stores used in the Nielsen sample. The computerized nature of the system makes such detailed editing of millions of records of data each week possible. Careful attention to input data quality results in a more reliable and accurate output reporting system.[a]

Exhibit 12.2

Questionnaire Used in the Survey of Policyholders of National Insurance Company

Note: The labels for the five dimensions in Sections 1 and 2 did not appear in the original questionnaire. They are included here to indicate the dimension to which each question pertains.

Section 1

Directions: The following set of statements relates to your feelings about National Insurance Company. For each statement, please show the extent to which you believe National has the feature described by the statement. Circling a "1" means that you strongly disagree that National has that feature, and circling a "7" means that you strongly agree. You may circle any of the numbers in between that show how strong your feelings are. There are no right or wrong answers—all we are interested in is a number that best shows your perceptions about National.

	Strongly disagree					Strongly agree	

Reliability

1. When National promises to do something, it does so. 1 2 3 4 5 6 7

2. When you have a problem, National shows a sincere interest in solving it. 1 2 3 4 5 6 7

3. National performs the service right the first time. 1 2 3 4 5 6 7

4. National provides its services at the time it promises to do so. 1 2 3 4 5 6 7

5. National maintains error-free records. 1 2 3 4 5 6 7

Empathy

6. National treats you with care. 1 2 3 4 5 6 7

7. National has operating hours convenient to all its policyholders. 1 2 3 4 5 6 7

8. National has employees who give you personal attention. 1 2 3 4 5 6 7

	Strongly disagree					Strongly agree	

9. National has your best interests in mind. 1 2 3 4 5 6 7

10. Employees of National understand your specific needs. 1 2 3 4 5 6 7

Tangibles

11. National has modern-looking equipment. 1 2 3 4 5 6 7

12. National's physical facilities are visually appealing. 1 2 3 4 5 6 7

13. National's employees are neat-appearing. 1 2 3 4 5 6 7

14. Materials associated with service (such as pamphlets or statements) are clear. 1 2 3 4 5 6 7

Responsiveness

15. Employees of National tell you exactly when services will be performed. 1 2 3 4 5 6 7

16. Employees of National give you prompt service. 1 2 3 4 5 6 7

17. Employees of National are always willing to help you. 1 2 3 4 5 6 7

18. Employees of National are never too busy to respond to your requests. 1 2 3 4 5 6 7

Assurance

19. The behavior of employees of National instills confidence in you. 1 2 3 4 5 6 7

20. You feel safe in your transactions with National. 1 2 3 4 5 6 7

21. Employees of National are consistently courteous with you. 1 2 3 4 5 6 7

22. Employees of National have the knowledge to answer your questions. 1 2 3 4 5 6 7

(Continued on next page.)

Section 2

Directions: Listed below are five features pertaining to insurance companies and the service they offer. We would like to know how important each of these features is to you when you evaluate an insurance company's quality of service. Please allocate a total of 100 points among the five features according to your impression about how important each feature is to you—the more important a feature is to you, the more points you should allocate to it. Please ensure that the points you allocate to the five features add up to 100.

Tangibles

1. The appearance of the insurance company's physical facilities, equipment, personnel, and communication materials   _____ points

Reliability

2. The insurance company's ability to perform the promised service dependably and accurately   _____ points

Responsiveness

3. The insurance company's willingness to help policyholders and provide prompt service   _____ points

Assurance

4. The knowledge and courtesy of the insurance company's employees and their ability to convey trust and confidence   _____ points

Empathy

5. The caring, individualized attention the insurance company provides to its policyholders   _____ points

Total points allocated   **100 points**

Section 3

For questions in this section, please circle the number that corresponds to your answer.

1. On a scale of 1 to 10, how would you rate the overall quality of service provided by National?

Extremely poor									**Extremely good**
1	2	3	4	5	6	7	8	9	10

2. Would you recommend National to a friend interested in insurance services?

Yes   1

No   2

3. How long have you been using the services of National?

Less than 1 year	1
1 to less than 2 years	2
2 to less than 5 years	3
5 years or more	4

4. Have you recently had a problem with the service you received from National?

Yes   1

No   2

5. If you did have a problem, was it resolved to your satisfaction?

Yes   1

No   2

Section 4

The following information is solely for statistical purposes and will be kept confidential. Please circle the number that corresponds to your answer.

1. Your gender is:

Male	1
Female	2

2. Your marital status is:

Single	1
Married	2
Widowed	3
Divorced	4

3. Your age is:

Under 25	1
25–44	2
45–64	3
65 or over	4

4. Your total annual family income is:

Under $10,000	1
$10,000–$19,999	2
$20,000–$29,999	3
$30,000–$49,999	4
$50,000–$64,999	5
$65,000 or over	6

5. The highest level of schooling you have completed is:

High school or less	1
Some college	2
College graduate	3
Graduate school	4

6. What can we do to serve you better?

_____

_____

_____

_____

_____

_____

_____

Thank you very much!

collapsed into a set of categories. In fact, collapsing numerical responses into fewer categories will generally lead to a loss of information and hence is not usually advisable.

A special problem in coding responses to open-ended as well as structured questions relates to the treatment of "don't know" responses. A "don't know" might be a legitimate response if the respondent could not honestly answer the question. Or it might represent an interviewing failure; that is, the respondent had an answer but for some reason did not divulge it. An editor/coder must ascertain which of these two interpretations of "don't know" is correct. Unfortunately, this task is not easy, except in certain cases. For instance, a "don't know" answer to the question "Do you have any credit cards?" is most likely an interviewing failure. But a "don't know" answer to the question "Do you favor or oppose spending public funds to support certified abortion clinics?" may or may not be an interviewing failure.

There are no rules for the best way to treat "don't know" responses. One approach is to infer an actual response; that is, make an educated guess about what the answer might have been on the basis of the answers to other questions. For example, a respondent's likely income bracket might be subjectively estimated from his or her age, education level, and occupation. However, this approach is fraught with questionable assumptions and hence is of dubious validity. A safer and more defensible approach is to simply classify "don't know" as a separate response category for each question. If a legitimate "don't know" can be distinguished from one that is an interviewing failure, the researcher should report the latter separately as a missing value, a topic discussed next.

A **missing-value category**, as its name implies, codes questions for which answers should have been obtained but for some reason were not. A missing value can stem from a respondent's refusal to answer a question, an interviewer's failure to ask a question or record an answer, or a "don't know" that does not seem legitimate. Sound questionnaire design, tight control over fieldwork, and a thorough field edit can help reduce, but not necessarily eliminate, the occurrence of missing values. Questions plagued by a large number of missing values, however, invariably indicate a poorly designed questionnaire or shoddy fieldwork. In such a case, researchers should be careful during subsequent analysis and interpretation of the data gathered.

> A **missing-value category** codes questions for which answers should have been obtained but for some reason were not.

Assigning Numerical Codes

The next stage in the coding process is to assign appropriate numerical codes to responses that are not already in quantified form. The purpose of numerical coding is to facilitate computer manipulation and analysis of the responses. In Exhibit 12.2 the response categories in questions 2, 3, 4, and 5 in section 3 and questions 1 through 5 in section 4 need to be assigned numerical codes.

We covered the assignment of numbers to responses at length in Chapter 9 and will not repeat it here. Nevertheless, we reemphasize that the scale or measurement level reflected by the numerical codes depends on the way a question is asked and the nature of the variable it is attempting to measure. Table 12.1 summarizes the measurement levels achieved by responses to the various questions in Exhibit 12.2. The researcher must keep these measurement levels in mind while analyzing and interpreting the quantified responses.

Exhibit 12.3 shows a portion of a spreadsheet used to record the data generated in the survey of policyholders of National Insurance Company. This example uses SPSS, but Excel is another program that serves this purpose. (Please see Appendix 6 for data analysis using Excel.) Each row of numbers on this spreadsheet represents all the answers given by one respondent.

TABLE 12.1
Measurement Levels of the Responses to the Questions Used in the Survey of Policyholders of National Insurance Company

Question Number	Construct Measured by Question	Measurement Level of Response
Section 1, Q1–Q5	Reliability	Interval
Section 1, Q6–Q10	Empathy	Interval
Section 1, Q11–Q14	Tangibles	Interval
Section 1, Q15–Q18	Responsiveness	Interval
Section 1, Q19–Q22	Assurance	Interval
Section 2, Q1–Q5	Importance of features	Ratio
Section 3, Q1	Overall quality of service	Interval
Section 3, Q2	Recommend service to others	Nominal; may be treated as ordinal, as "1" is better than "2"
Section 3, Q3	Length of service usage	Ordinal
Section 3, Q4	Problem with service	Nominal; may be treated as ordinal, as "2" is better than "1"
Section 3, Q5	Problem resolved to satisfaction	Nominal; may be treated as ordinal, as "1" is better than "2"
Section 4, Q1	Gender	Nominal
Section 4, Q2	Marital status	Nominal
Section 4, Q3	Age	Ordinal
Section 4, Q4	Income	Ordinal
Section 4, Q5	Education	Ordinal

A detailed set of instructions, preferably in writing, is essential to avoid errors in coding data. Table 12.2 lists the coding instructions pertaining to the questionnaire in Exhibit 12.2 and the spreadsheet in Exhibit 12.3.

To see the interrelationships among the survey questionnaire (Exhibit 12.2), the coding instructions (Table 12.2), and the data spreadsheets (Exhibit 12.3), consider respondent 3 and try to infer his or her responses from the numerical codes in the spreadsheets. You should notice that respondent 3 circled 7 for question 1, section 1 (p1, column 1); circled 7 for question 2, section 1 (p2, column 2); circled 6 for question 10, section 1 (p10, column 10); and so on.

Two features pertaining to Table 12.2 are noteworthy. First, each survey question has just one corresponding variable. The reason is that each question in the survey of policyholders of National had one, and only one, possible response. Second, the entries in the Variable Name column were the symbols used in the survey of policyholders to identify the respective variables during computer analysis. Because variable names are no more than identification labels, they can be chosen

national Insurance - SPSS Data Editor

File Edit View Data Transform Analyze Graphs Utilities Window Help

1 : p1   7

	p1	p2	p3	p4	p5	p6	p7	p8	p9	p10
1	7	7	7	7	7	7	7	7	7	7
2	1	1	1	1	1	2	2	1	1	1
3	7	7	4	7	5	6	6	6	7	6
4	6	6	7	7	7	7	6	7	7	7
5	6	6	6	6	7	7	5	5	6	6

Data View Variable View

national Insurance - SPSS Data Editor

File Edit View Data Transform Analyze Graphs Utilities Window Help

	Name	Type	Width	Decimals	Label	Values	Missing	Columns	
1	p1	Numeric	1	0		None	None	8	Rigl
2	p2	Numeric	1	0		None	None	8	Rigl
3	p3	Numeric	1	0		None	None	8	Rigl
4	p4	Numeric	1	0		None	None	8	Rigl
5	p5	Numeric	1	0		None	None	8	Rigl
6	p6	Numeric	1	0		None	None	8	Rigl
7	p7	Numeric	1	0		None	None	8	Rigl

Data View Variable View

Exhibit 12.3
Illustrative Spreadsheets Used in the Survey of Policyholders of National Insurance (Data View and Variable View)

to fit a researcher's preferences, as long as they do not violate any restrictions imposed by the specific computer program to be used.

The one-question/one-variable feature is not universal. A question allowing multiple responses will need as many variables as there are possible responses. The following question is a case in point:

Which of the following countries have you visited during the past 12 months?

_____ Canada

_____ England

_____ France

_____ Germany

_____ Japan

_____ Mexico

As few as zero or as many as six categories can be checked in response to this question. Simply assigning a series of numerical codes to the six response categories (say, 1 through 6) and treating them as pertaining to a single variable will be inadequate for coding purposes because this question is, in effect, asking respondents six separate questions: "Did you visit Canada during the past 12 months?" "Did you visit England during the past 12 months?" and so on. Therefore, we will need six variables, each relating to a specific country and having two possible values—for example, 1 = No and 2 = Yes. Furthermore, six columns must be set aside in the spreadsheet (or computer **data records**) to record responses to this question.[3] Similarly, "rank-order" questions like the question that follows require as many variables (and columns) as there are objects to be ranked.

A **data record** contains all the coded data pertaining to a single sample unit.

TABLE 12.2
Coding Instructions for the Questionnaire Used in the Survey of Policyholders of National Insurance Company

Column Numbers on Spreadsheet	Description of Item to Be Coded	Question Number	Variable Name	Range of Permissible Numerical Codes*
9	Responsiveness, Assurance	Q1–Q22		7 = strongly agree)
23	Tangibles	Section 2, Q1	tanimp	0–100 points
24	Reliability	Section 2, Q2	relimp	0–100 points
25	Responsiveness	Section 2, Q3	resimp	0–100 points
26	Assurance	Section 2, Q4	asrimp	0–100 points
27	Empathy	Section 2, Q5	empimp	0–100 points
28	Overall service quality	Section 3, Q1	OQ	1–10 (1 = extremely poor; 10 = extremely good)
29	Recommend company	Section 3, Q2	rec	1–2 (1 = yes; 2 = no)
30	Length of service	Section 3, Q3	use	1–4 (1 = less than 1 year; 2 = 1 to less than 2 years; 3 = 2 to less than 5 years; 4 = 5 years or more)
31	Service problem	Section 3, Q4	prob	1–2 (1 = yes; 2 = no)
32	Problem resolved	Section 3, Q5	resolve	1–2 (1 = yes; 2 = no)
33	Gender	Section 4, Q1	gender	1–2 (1 = male; 2 = female)
34	Marital status	Section 4, Q2	mstat	1–4 (1 = single; 2 = married; 3 = widowed; 4 = divorced)
35	Age	Section 4, Q3	age	1–4 (1 = under 25; 2 = 25–44; 3 = 45–64; 4 = 65 or over)
36	Annual income	Section 4, Q4	inc	1–6 (1 = under $10,000; 2 = $10,000–$19,999; 3 = $20,000–$29,999; 4 = $30,000–$49,999; 5 = $50,000–$64,999; 6 = $65,000 or over)
37	Education	Section 4, Q5	ed	1–4 (1 = high school or less; 2 = some college; 3 = college graduate; 4 = graduate school)

*When any variable has a missing value, leave the corresponding column or cell blank.

Please rank the following fast-food restaurants by placing a 1 beside the restaurant you think is best overall, a 2 beside the restaurant you think is second best, and so on.

_____ **Burger King**

_____ **McDonald's**

_____ **Wendy's**

_____ **Whataburger**

TABLE 12.3
Structure of a Data Sheet

Observations	Variables					
	1	2	...	j	...	m
1	x_{11}	x_{12}	...	x_{1j}	...	x_{1m}
2	x_{21}	x_{22}	...	x_{2j}	...	x_{2m}
.	.	.	.	.	.	.
.	.	.	.	.	.	.
.	.	.	.	.	.	.
i	x_{i1}	x_{i2}	...	x_{ij}	...	x_{im}
.	.	.	.	.	.	.
.	.	.	.	.	.	.
.	.	.	.	.	.	.
n	x_{n1}	x_{n2}	...	x_{nj}	...	x_{nm}

A **data set** or **data file** is an organized collection of data records.

A **case** or **observation** is each sample unit for which data are available within a data set.

Raw variables are variables directly defined by the questionnaire data.

Transformed (or **recoded**) **variables** are new variables constructed from data on raw variables.

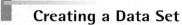

Creating a Data Set

A **data set,** also known as a **data file,** is an organized collection of data records. Each sample unit within the data set is called a **case,** or **observation.** If the sample size is n (the number of observations = n) and the total number of variables embedded in the questionnaire is m, the resulting data set is an $n \times m$ matrix of numbers, as illustrated by Table 12.3. Coded data are transferred to a computer in a format similar to that in Table 12.3. Each x_{ij} in the table is a number and represents the coded response for the ith sample unit on the jth variable.

A researcher may sometimes want to modify the data on certain variables to create new variables for inclusion in the data analysis. To understand this process, let's once again look at Exhibit 12.2. Each question in Exhibit 12.2 represents a distinct variable. Question 1 in section 1, for instance, represents reliability as measured by the statement "When National promises to do something, it does so." Question 2 in section 1 also represents reliability, but as measured by the statement "When you have a problem, National shows a sincere interest in solving it." Variables like these are directly defined by the questionnaire data, and hence we call them **raw variables.** New variables constructed from data on raw variables are called **transformed** or **recoded variables.**

To illustrate, suppose we want to construct an overall scale of "Reliability" from a set of five rating scales. To create a new transformed variable, Reliability, consider the following five rating scales that appeared in the survey of policyholders:

Please indicate your impression of National Insurance Company on each of the following attributes on a scale of 1 ("Strongly disagree") to 7 ("Strongly agree").

Reliability	Strongly disagree						Strongly agree
1. When National promises to do something, it does so.	1	2	3	4	5	6	7
2. When you have a problem, National shows a sincere interest in solving it.	1	2	3	4	5	6	7
3. National performs the service right the first time.	1	2	3	4	5	6	7
4. National provides its services at the time it promises to do so.	1	2	3	4	5	6	7
5. National maintains error-free records.	1	2	3	4	5	6	7

Coding the ratings on these attributes would require five raw variables, say, $p1$, $p2$, $p3$, $p4$, and $p5$. All five questions measure one construct: reliability. One approach for ascertaining customers' overall reliability rating of National consists of the following steps:

1. Compute the average score—say, Reliable—for each individual customer by averaging the sum of her or his ratings on the five attributes. That is,

Reliable = $(p1 + p2 + p3 + p4 + p5)/5$

2. Compute the mean value of Reliable across all customers to obtain their overall impressions.

In this approach, "Reliable" is a transformed or recoded variable, and a legitimate component of data analysis. We can use transformed variables in subsequent data analyses to gain more useful insights from the collected data.

Variable transformations are accomplished after data on raw variables have been coded and stored. Virtually all standard computer programs are capable of creating transformed variables. However, the researcher must specify the necessary transformations. The creation of transformed variables will increase the size of the data set. For example, if we create one transformed variable by using the data set in Table 12.3, one more column of numbers will appear in it. Thus an expanded data set in the form of an $n \times (m + 1)$ matrix will result. Exhibit 12.4 contains a summary of steps used in creating a new variable using SPSS and displays SPSS dialogue boxes for the preceding example.

Exhibit 12.4
SPSS—Transforming Raw Data: National Insurance Company

Create a new variable, "Reliable," from a set of five rating scales p1, p2, p3, p4, and p5.

Reliable = (p1 + p2 + p3 + p4 + p5)/5

The following steps should be followed to create a new variable in SPSS:

1. Select TRANSFORM.

2. Click on COMPUTE.

3. Type "reliable" in TARGET VARIABLE box.

4. Click on parentheses () and move it to the NUMERIC EXPRESSIONS box.

5. Click on "p1" and move it inside the parentheses in the NUMERIC EXPRESSIONS box.

6. Click on the "+" sign.

7. Click on "p2" and move it to the NUMERIC EXPRESSIONS box and then click on the "+" sign.

8. Repeat this for "p3," "p4," and "p5," and then divide the whole expression by 5.

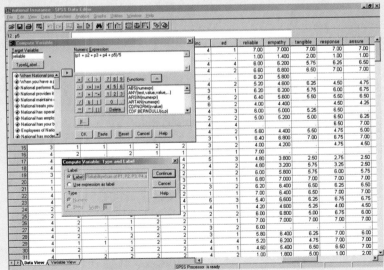

9. Click on "Type & LABEL" under the TARGET VARIABLE box and type Overall Reliability—constructed from the 5 rating scales" in the LABEL box.

10. Click OK.

SPSS will create a new column for "Reliable."
The column will contain the average of all the five rating scales, p1, p2, p3, p4, and p5.
The frames shown above demonstrate this.

Preliminary Data Analysis: Basic Descriptive Statistics

Before analyzing a data set using sophisticated techniques, a researcher should get a feeling for what the data are like. The purpose of preliminary data analysis is to reveal features of the basic composition of the data collected. It can also provide useful insights pertaining to the research objectives and suggest meaningful approaches for further analysis of the data.

Preliminary data analysis examines the central tendency and the dispersion of the data on each variable in the data set. The measurement level of a variable—that is, whether the variable is nominal, ordinal, interval, or ratio—has a bearing on which measures of central tendency and dispersion will be appropriate for it. Table 12.4 summarizes the measures commonly used for different types of variables.

Note that Table 12.4 lists the same measures of central tendency and dispersion for interval and ratio data. Almost no statistical techniques have been developed specifically for ratio data; therefore, we always analyze those data using techniques developed for interval data. Ratio data, of course, have all the properties of interval data. Furthermore, the measures listed in Table 12.4 for nominal and ordinal data can be computed for interval and ratio data as well. Similarly, nominal data measures are permissible for ordinal data.

Measures of Central Tendency

The most common measures of central tendency are the mode, median, and mean.

The **mode** is the most frequently occurring value for a variable.

■ **Mode**　The **mode** is the most frequently occurring value for a variable in a data set. It is an appropriate measure for data that are grouped into categories.

TABLE 12.4
Measures of Central Tendency and Dispersion for Different Types of Variables

Measurement Level of Data Pertaining to Variable	Measures of Central Tendency	Measures of Dispersion
Nominal	Mode: Most frequently occuring response	Strictly speaking, the concept of dispersion is not meaningful for nominal data, but an idea about the distribution of responses can be obtained by examining their relative frequencies of occurrence.
Ordinal	Median: 50th percentile response	Range: Defined by the highest and lowest response values; interquartile range = difference between the 75th and 25th percentile responses
Interval	Mean: Arithmetic average of response values	Standard deviation: As defined in Chapter 9
Ratio	Mean: Arithmetic average of response values	Standard deviation: As defined in Chapter 9

TABLE 12.5
How Long Have You Been Using the Services of National? Computing Mode

Length of Service (USE)	Assigned Value	Count/Frequency
Less than 1 year	1	36
1 to less than 2 years	2	16
2 to less than 5 years	3	26
5 years or more	4	193 ◄——— (Mode = 4, most frequently occurring value)
Total		271

In SPSS

1. Select ANALYZE
2. Click DESCRIPTIVE STATISTICS
3. Select FREQUENCIES
4. Move the variable "USE" to the Variable(s) box
5. Click STATISTICS box
6. Select MODE
7. Click CONTINUE
8. Click OK

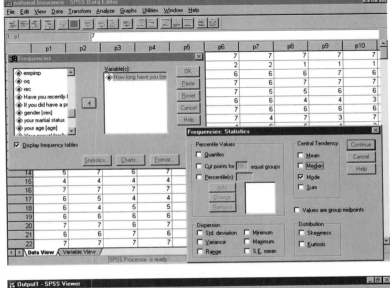

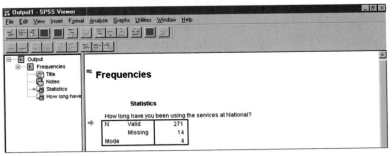

Returning to our illustration of National Insurance Company, consider the question "How long have you been using the services of National?" The results are shown in Table 12.5. The response "5 years or more" occurred 193 times. Because this occurred the most frequently, it is the mode. Table 12.5 details the steps for carrying out this analysis in SPSS and also displays the SPSS output.

The **median** is the category into which the 50th percentile response falls when all responses are arranged from lowest to highest (or highest to lowest).

▪ **Median** The **median** is the category into which the 50th percentile response falls when all responses are arranged from lowest to highest (or highest

---

TABLE 12.6
Length of Time Service Used: Responses from 20 Customers

How long have you been using the services of National?

4	3	4	1	4	4	4	4	4	4	3
4	4	3	4	4	4	3	1	1		

1 = Less than 1 year; 2 = 1 to less than 2 years; 3 = 2 to less than 5 years; 4 = 5 years or more

Arranging the 20 values in ascending order:

1	1	1	3	3	3	3	4	4	**4**	**4**
4	4	4	4	4	4	4	4	4		

Because the sample size = 20, there are two middle values: 4 and 4. The median is therefore the average of the two middle values = 4.

---

to lowest). It is the middle value that divides the sample into two approximately equal parts. Consider again the question "How long have you been using the services of National?" Table 12.6 presents data for 20 respondents. Arranging the data in ascending order, we identify two middle values: 4 and 4. The median is the average of the two values. Because both these values are 4, the median of this sample is 4. Table 12.7 presents SPSS output for the whole sample. The measurement of a variable must be at least ordinal for computing the median (see Chapter 9).

The **mean** is the simple average of the various responses pertaining to a variable.

■ **Mean**   The **mean** is the simple average of the various responses pertaining to a variable. It is by far the most widely used and easiest measure to work with. We compute it by summing all the values and dividing by the number of valid cases. For computing the mean, the variables must at least have interval measurement properties (see Chapter 9).

The mean uses all the data pertaining to a variable; therefore, information is not lost as it is in computing the median or the mode. However, a few extreme responses or "outliers," if present in a data set, can dominate the mean and result in a distorted picture of central tendency. Consider the question used in the National Insurance Company example "On a scale of 1 to 10, how would you rate the overall quality of service provided by National?" The results are shown in Table 12.8. The mean is 7.80, the mode is 10.00, and the median is 9.00.

Measures of Dispersion

Measures of dispersion describe how the responses are clustered around the mean or a central value.

Measures of dispersion describe how the data are clustered around the mean or a central value. Along with measures of central tendency, measures of dispersion provide a richer description of the data. The most commonly used measures of dispersion are range and standard deviation. These measures are appropriate only if the level of measurement is interval or ratio (see Chapter 9).

Range is a measure of dispersion of responses; we calculate it as the difference between the largest and smallest response values.

■ **Range**   The **range** is the difference between the largest and the smallest value. It is the simplest measure of dispersion. Although easy to compute, the range is influenced by extreme values (outliers) and provides only a rough estimate of variability. In the National example, the highest overall service quality rating marked by a respondent was 10, and the lowest was 1. The range is simply the difference between the highest and the lowest value, 9.

TABLE 12.7
Length of Time Service Used: Computing Median

In SPSS

1. Select ANALYZE
2. Click DESCRIPTIVE STATISTICS
3. Select FREQUENCIES
4. Move the variable "USE" to the Variable(s) box
5. Click STATISTICS box
6. Select MEDIAN
7. Click CONTINUE
8. Click OK

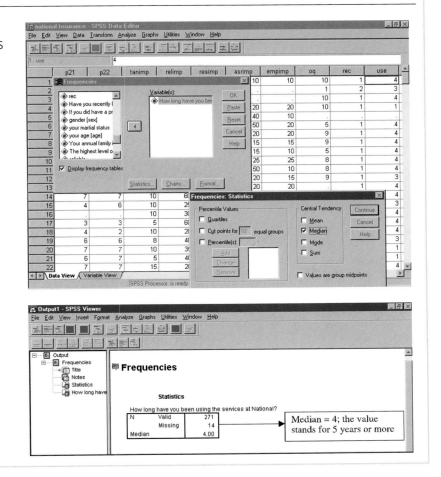

Variance is a measure of dispersion of responses around their mean; we calculate it as the average of squared deviations about the mean.

Standard deviation is a measure of dispersion of responses around their mean; we calculate it as the square root of the variance.

■ **Variance and Standard Deviation** The **variance** of a set of data is a measure of deviation of the data around the arithmetic mean. We calculate it as the average of squared deviations about the mean. The **standard deviation,** which is the square root of the variance, is the most popular measure of variability. The standard deviation is easy to interpret because it is expressed in the same units as the mean. The standard deviation is defined as follows:

$$s = \sqrt{\frac{\sum_{i=1}^{n}(x_i - \bar{x})^2}{n-1}}$$

where

n = number of units

x_i = data obtained from each sample unit i

$\bar{x}$ = sample mean value, given by $\dfrac{\sum_{i=1}^{n}(x_i)}{n}$

TABLE 12.8
Overall Quality of Service: Computing Mean

On a scale of 1 to 10, how would you rate the overall quality of service provided by National?

Extremely poor									Extremely good
1	2	3	4	5	6	7	8	9	10

In SPSS

1. Select ANALYZE
2. Click DESCRIPTIVE STATISTICS
3. Select FREQUENCIES
4. Move the variable "OQ-Labeled as OVERALL SERVICE QUALITY" to the Variable(s) box
5. Click STATISTICS box
6. Select MEAN, MEDIAN, AND MODE
7. Click CONTINUE
8. Click OK

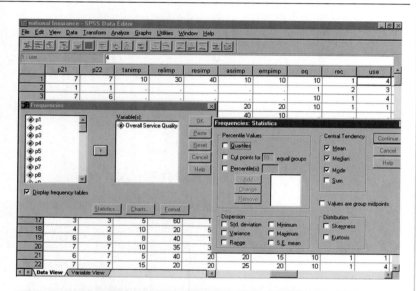

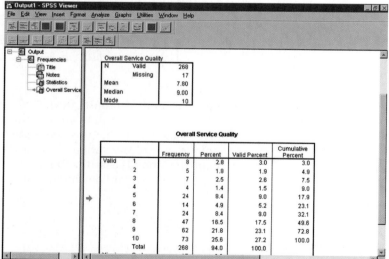

Because the level of measurement is interval, we can compute mean, median, and mode.

Like the arithmetic mean, the standard deviation is also influenced by extreme values and should not be used if the distribution of responses to a question is highly skewed. Marketing researchers rely on standard deviation most often in descriptive and inferential statistics. It is worthwhile to recall from Chapter 11 that, in a normal distribution (bell-shaped and symmetric) curve, $\bar{x} \pm 1s$ contains 68 percent of the data values, $\bar{x} \pm 2s$ contains 95 percent of the data values, and $\bar{x} \pm 3s$ contains 99.7 percent of the data values. Table 12.9 shows how to compute the range, variance, and standard deviation in SPSS for the overall National service quality question presented earlier.

A simple way to uncover the central tendency or dispersion of data for virtually any variable is to construct a one-way table for it, as we discuss next.

Frequency Distribution: One–Way Tabulation

A **one-way table** shows the distribution of data pertaining to categories of a single variable.

A **one-way table** is a table showing the distribution of data pertaining to categories of a single variable. Virtually all computer analysis packages are capable of generating the frequency distribution for any variable in a data set. Table 12.10 contains the one-way tables for one of the variables in the National Insurance Company survey: length of time service used (USE—ordinal scaled). One-way tables are particularly appropriate for examining data on nominal- and ordinal-

---

TABLE 12.9
Overall Quality of Service: Computing Range, Variance, and Standard Deviation

In SPSS

1. Select ANALYZE
2. Click DESCRIPTIVE STATISTICS
3. Select FREQUENCIES
4. Move the variable "OQ-Labeled as OVERALL SERVICE QUALITY" to the Variable(s) box
5. Click STATISTICS box
6. Select STANDARD DEVIATION, VARIANCE, and RANGE
7. Click CONTINUE
8. Click OK

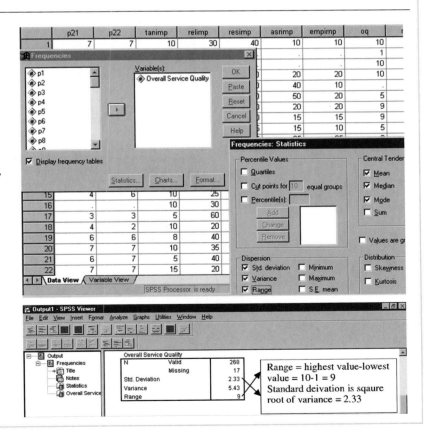

Range = highest value-lowest value = 10-1 = 9
Standard deivation is sqaure root of variance = 2.33

TABLE 12.10
Length of Time Service Used: Frequency Distribution

In SPSS

1. Select ANALYZE
2. Click DESCRIPTIVE STATISTICS
3. Select FREQUENCIES
4. Move the variable "USE" to the Variable(s) box
5. Click CHARTS box
6. Select BAR CHARTS
7. Click CONTINUE
8. Click OK

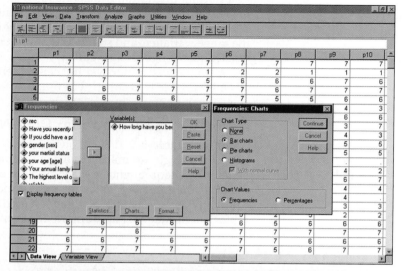

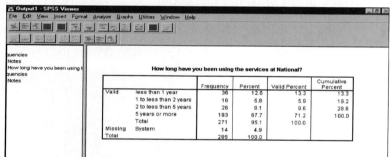

How long have you been using the services at National?

		Frequency	Percent	Valid Percent	Cumulative Percent
Valid	less than 1 year	36	12.6	13.3	13.3
	1 to less than 2 years	16	5.6	5.9	19.2
	2 to less than 5 years	26	9.1	9.6	28.8
	5 years or more	193	67.7	71.2	100.0
	Total	271	95.1	100.0	
Missing	System	14	4.9		
Total		285	100.0		

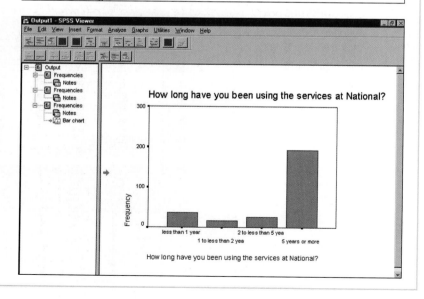

scaled variables because they normally have only a limited set of discrete-response categories.

In addition to revealing the general nature of the data, one-way tables offer some very specific benefits. First, they are helpful in detecting certain types of coding errors. Human errors can occur at various stages of the coding process. For instance, in the survey of National Insurance Company, an initial tabulation of data on the variable USE (length of time service used) revealed two responses under category 8, although the variable should have had only four categories, numbered 1 through 4. Tracing this error back through the coding process and questionnaires showed that response category 3 checked by two respondents had been erroneously coded as 8. Thus, in general, preliminary one-way tabulation can facilitate data cleaning (as it is sometimes called) by pointing out glaring coding errors. However, we cannot detect less obvious errors—for example, mistakenly coding a 2 as a 3 when 3 is also a legitimate response category, as in the case of USE—by examining one-way tables.

Second, one-way tables can provide valuable insights through comparisons with other relevant distributions. They can be especially helpful in understanding the composition of the respondent group and in looking for evidence of non-response error. For instance, comparing the frequency distribution of respondents on key demographic variables with appropriate distributions for the population as a whole or for nonrespondents will indicate how representative the collected data are.

Another useful technique is to compare one-way tables across similar variables within a given survey or across the same variable measured at different times. Research in Use 12.2 demonstrates comparing frequency results of one study with those of prior studies.

Consider another illustration. A newspaper readership study asked respondents to indicate how often they read various syndicated columns in the newspaper. The response frequency distributions for three of the newspaper columns are presented in Table 12.11. Mere visual inspection of the one-way tabulations for the three columns is quite revealing. Bill Clinton's column is a clear winner, followed by Anthony Lewis's column and Paul Krugman's column, in that order.

Third, one-way tables can suggest potentially useful variable transformations. Consider the one-way table for the variable USE in Table 12.10. A large proportion of the responses are piled up toward one end of the range of data obtained. In other words, the variable USE has a **skewed response distribution.**[4] Variables with skewed response distributions can be troublesome in that they may not satisfy all the requirements of statistical analysis techniques to be used

In a **skewed response distribution,** a large proportion of the responses are piled up toward one end of the range of data obtained.

TABLE 12.11
Some One-Way Tables for Newspaper Readership Study

| | RESPONSE DISTRIBUTIONS | | | | | |
| | Bill Clinton's Column | | Anthony Lewis's Column | | Paul Krugman's Column | |
Response Category	Number	Percentage	Number	Percentage	Number	Percentage
Usually read	228	76	108	36	42	14
Occasionally read	45	15	60	20	66	22
Rarely or never read	27	9	132	44	192	64
Total	300	100%	300	100%	300	100%

The Government's Role in Curbing Indecency in the Media: Conservatives and Liberals Switch Their Position

Pew Research Center (www.pewresearch .org), an independent research group, conducted a nationwide survey of Americans' attitudes toward curbing indecent material in the media. It is commonly believed that liberals want bigger government and that the opposite is true for conservatives. However, this is not so when it comes to some sensitive family/social issues. The survey reveals the tug of war between Americans' feelings about the role of government and the desire to curb indecency in the media.

The study asked respondents, "What presents the greater danger: harmful content or undue government restrictions?"

A significant majority of conservative Republicans (57 percent) said that harmful content in the media poses a greater danger than undue government restrictions. A resounding 72 percent of liberal Democrats said that undue government restrictions posed a greater danger than harmful content in the media. In essence, liberal Democrats do not want government interference. It is also interesting to note that, in general, respondents saw a greater danger in undue government restrictions than in harmful content in the media.

The study also asked respondents the following question:

Your opinion of movie, TV industry
1. Favorable
2. Unfavorable
3. Don't know

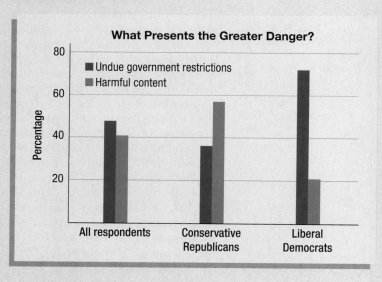

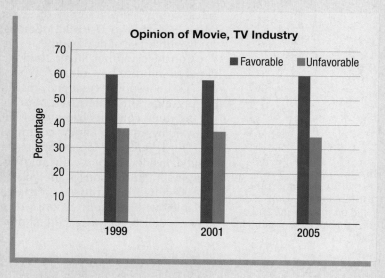

subsequently. Such variables may have to be transformed into new variables that more closely fit those requirements.

To illustrate transformations, let's focus for a moment on USE (length of time service used, measured in years). One objective of the survey of National's customers was to see whether length of time service used was associated with willingness to recommend National to a friend (REC). The appropriate analysis technique for accomplishing this objective is chi-square contingency analysis (this technique is discussed in Chapter 13). Chi-square analysis requires a sufficient number of responses in each response category. The variable USE was deficient in this regard because it

Despite criticisms about sex and violence in the media, the respondents' opinions of the movie/TV industry have changed very little since the 1993 survey.

Respondents, although expressing some reservations about undue government restrictions, also expressed support for some regulatory proposals. As the chart shows, conservative Republicans showed stronger support than liberal Democrats. The results seem to reflect the political divide about the issues.[b]

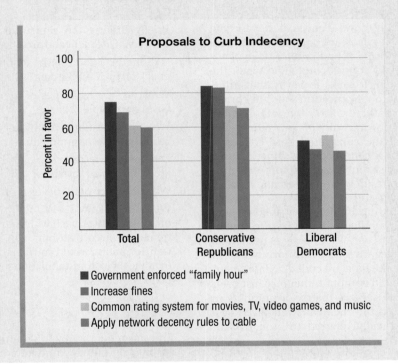

Proposals to Curb Indecency

had relatively few responses in categories 1 and 2. The nature of its one-way table suggested collapsing the first two categories into a single category. The resulting transformed variable had just three categories (less than 2 years, 2 to less than 5 years, and 5 years or more), with each containing an adequate number of responses.

In summary, one-way tabulations, although not as sophisticated as other data analysis techniques, can be just as insightful. Indeed, using complex techniques to analyze data without first understanding what the data look like may produce meaningless results and lead to erroneous conclusions. Even such a simple task as computing the mean value for a variable, without having a good idea about the variable's response distribution, can be meaningless.

The following example, cited by Robert L. Lavidge, president of Elrick and Lavidge, a marketing research firm, further emphasizes the danger inherent in ignoring the nature of the distribution of data:

> Consider the test of a new sauce product. On the average, consumers wanted it neither really hot nor really mild. The mean rating of the test participants was quite close to the middle of the scale, which had "very mild" and "very

hot" as its bipolar adjectives. This happened to fit the client's preconceived notion. However, examination of the distribution of the ratings revealed the existence of a large proportion of consumers who wanted the sauce to be mild and an equally large proportion who wanted it to be hot. Relatively few wanted the in-between product, which would have been suggested by looking at the mean rating alone.[5]

In short, a clear understanding of the distribution of responses can help a researcher avoid erroneous inferences.

SUMMARY

Editing performs a quality control check of the raw data through inspection and necessary corrections of completed data collection forms. A preliminary stage of editing, known as the field edit, is conducted when the data are being collected. It seeks to verify that interviewers are following proper procedures and to correct any fieldwork problems before it is too late. A more comprehensive edit, known as the final, or office, edit, is conducted after all the completed data collection forms are returned to a central office. Office editors check for response consistencies, decide on appropriate ways to handle "don't know" responses and missing values, and classify open-ended responses.

The process of coding immediately follows, and often overlaps with, the office edit. It classifies open-ended responses into categories and assigns numerical values to response categories that are not already in quantified form. Once the data are coded, a data set, or data file, can be created in computer memory just prior to data analysis. A data set is a matrix of numbers in which each row contains the coded answers given by a single respondent (typically referred to as a *case* or *observation*).

It is good practice to conduct a preliminary analysis to get an initial idea about the nature of the data. Preliminary analysis involves obtaining and examining the central tendency and the dispersion of the data for all variables (including transformed variables) of interest. Choosing the most appropriate measure of central tendency and dispersion depends on whether the variables are nominal, ordinal, interval, or ratio.

A relatively simple way to ascertain what the data look like is a one-way tabulation; that is, the frequency distribution of responses for each variable. One-way tables reveal the general nature of the data and help detect certain types of coding errors; compare the distribution of data on a variable with other relevant distributions, such as the overall population distribution and the distributions of similar variables; and suggest meaningful variable transformations.

REVIEW AND DISCUSSION QUESTIONS

ACE
self-test

1. Briefly discuss the similarities of and differences between a field edit and an office edit.

2. "Editing plays no role in acting as a quality control check on mail survey data." Discuss this statement.

3. What are the two types of "don't know" responses? Give an example of each.

4. Why do questions permitting multiple responses require special attention during coding?

5. Define these terms: *case, data record, data set.* What are transformed variables?

6. What are three potential uses of one-way tabulation?

7. What is a skewed distribution? Suppose that two ordinal variables, each with eight categories, have extremely skewed distributions. What type of variable transformation would you create for the two variables to make their cross-tabulation meaningful? Briefly explain your answer.

SPSS EXERCISES

1. Transform the variable USE in the survey of National Insurance Company into an appropriate three-category new variable (excluding the missing value category) that reflects varying ranges of length of time service used (call the new variable NUSE). Use SPSS or Excel to perform the analysis. Explain your rationale.

2. Construct a one-way table for the new variable (NUSE). Use SPSS or Excel to perform the analysis.

3. Jill Baxter, vice president of customer service for National Insurance Company, and her assistant, Tom Kurtis, want you to develop and briefly discuss the demographic profile of the survey respondents. Use SPSS or Excel to perform the analysis.

4. Jill Baxter and Tom Kurtis want to find out National's average service perception rating along each of the five dimensions. They also want to know which are the most and the least critical service dimensions, as perceived by customers. Perform the necessary statistical analyses (using either SPSS or Excel) and report the findings in statistical and managerial terms.

CASE 12.1 PUMA
(www.puma.com)

Having a business platform in the U.S. market for athletic shoes and apparel is important to the success of a global brand. Companies that establish their brands successfully in the U.S. market signal the potential of their brand to retailers in other countries. Puma is gaining momentum in that market. U.S. sales were just shy of $100 million in 2000, with footwear accounting for 70 percent and apparel 30 percent of total sales. But with a 0.48 percent market share in contrast to market leader Nike's 47 percent share, Puma aims to use innovation rather than size to set itself apart from competitors.

Background

A global company with origins in Germany, Puma AG Rudolf Dassler Sport is a recognized leader in the design, development, and marketing of athletic foot-wear, apparel, equipment, and sports-related accessories. The company is known for fostering fresh ideas and a youthful outlook, both of which are attributed to its top executive, Jochen Zeitz. In 1993, at age 30, Zeitz was named chairman and CEO of Puma AG, thus becoming the youngest chairperson in German history to head a company listed on that country's stock exchange. Under his leadership, Puma has realized solid financial growth.

Executives at Puma mix influences from sports, lifestyle, and fashion to create a unique personality for the brand. They recognize the importance of striking a fine balance. If Puma were all fashion, it would be swallowed up by the fashion brands. If it were all sport, it would be swallowed up by the sports brands. But the consumer also buys the product based on whether it fits his or her individual lifestyle. An understanding of the market's lifestyle, a sharp sense of fashion appeal, and a 50-year sports heritage make for a blend that distinguishes Puma in the marketplace. Puma has successfully managed to reposition itself as a hip lifestyle and fashion brand.

Puma's Marketing Strategy

Roughly 50 percent of global sporting goods sales, the youth market represents the most important demographic segment of the industry. Yet it is a fickle market.

Not so long ago, teens were enamored of athletic superstars like Michael Jordan, Shaquille O'Neal, and Scotty Pippen, and followed suit by buying the brands those celebrities endorsed. Teens today are looking more for footwear and apparel that express their individuality rather than their adoration of a particular superstar. All of that spells trouble for the athletic shoe business that has become addicted to "the star." In fact, Puma executives believe they must keep Puma's name and image such that it isn't found everywhere, because then it will lose its appeal. Furthermore, Puma has a focused plan to keep the brand "cool" by keeping it from being over exposed to any one set of customers. And because it isn't the biggest company in the industry, it needs to maintain its distinctly cool Puma persona.

Puma executives believe it is important for the brand to stay cool and be relevant in the mind of the edgy consumer. For that reason, Puma conducts periodic research to stay at the forefront of what its market desires in the product. One such questionnaire is presented in Exhibit 1 on the next page. The survey was developed by QuickTake.com to demonstrate its research capabilities.

CASE QUESTIONS

1. Set up an SPSS data template for the questionnaire presented in Exhibit 1. *Hint:* Refer to Tables 12.1 and 12.2 and Exhibit 12.3 in the chapter.

2. Describe the type of measurement scale used in each item in the Puma questionnaire. (Is each question nominal, ordinal, interval, or ratio?) Justify your responses.

3. What is the appropriate measurement of central tendency for each question? Why?

4. Identify the median and modal values for each question.

5. Which of the survey questions have skewed distributions? Justify your answer and indicate how you would create a transformed variable for each of those questions to reduce the degree of skewness.

This case was written by Jeanne L. Munger (University of Southern Maine) in collaboration with the textbook authors, as a basis for class discussion rather than to illustrate either effective or ineffective marketing practice.

Exhibit 1
Puma Questionnaire Frequency Statistics
Source: Courtesy of Greenfield Online.

Possible Answers	Response Count	Response Percentage
1. Have you ever heard of Puma brand athletic shoes?		
1. Yes	93	83.04
2. No	16	14.29
3. Don't know	3	2.68
Total	112	
2. What attributes do you associate with the Puma brand of athletic shoes? (Select all that apply.)		
1. Sporty	83	86.46
2. Classic lifestyles	11	11.46
3. Funky yet functional	15	15.63
4. Grunge-like	12	12.50
5. Masculine	34	35.42
6. Feminine	13	13.54
Total	96	
3. Of the attributes you selected in the previous question, which one do you associate with Puma athletic shoes the most? (Pick one only.)		
1. Sporty	72	75.00
2. Classic lifestyles	2	2.08
3. Funky yet functional	9	9.38
4. Grunge-like	7	7.29
5. Masculine	5	5.21
6. Feminine	1	1.04
Total	96	
4. If the attributes most important to you were available in Puma brand athletic shoes, would you purchase them if the price were fair?		
1. Yes	72	75.00
2. No	4	4.17
3. Don't know	20	20.83
Total	96	

Possible Answers	Response Count	Response Percentage
5. What is your age?		
1. 17 or younger	0	0
2. 18 to 24	33	29.46
3. 25 to 34	31	27.68
4. 35 to 44	23	20.54
5. 45 to 54	15	13.39
6. 55 or older	10	8.93
Total	112	
6. What is your gender?		
1. Male	58	51.79
2. Female	54	48.21
Total	112	
7. What is your race?		
1. Caucasian	69	61.61
2. African American	7	6.25
3. Asian	16	14.29
4. Hispanic	4	3.57
5. Other	16	14.29
Total	112	
8. What is your annual household income?		
1. Less than $15,000	24	21.43
2. $15,000 to $30,000	19	16.96
3. $30,001 to $45,000	22	19.64
4. $45,001 to $60,000	16	14.29
5. $60,001 to $75,000	10	8.93
6. $75,001 to $90,000	8	7.14
7. $90,001 to $105,000	3	2.68
8. $105,001 to $125,000	1	0.89
9. $125,001 to $150,000	3	2.68
10. $150,001 to $200,000	1	0.89
11. $200,001 to $250,000	1	0.89
12. $250,001 to $300,000	1	0.89
13. More than $300,000	3	2.68
Total	112	

CASE 12.2 ROCKBRIDGE ASSOCIATES: NATIONAL TECHNOLOGY READINESS SURVEY (PART A)[1]

(www.rockresearch.com)

Tom Duggan, recently hired as an assistant research analyst for Bank of Nations, is considering how best to analyze the data from the National Technology Readiness Survey (NTRS), a survey conducted by Rockbridge Associates, Inc., a marketing research firm located in Great Falls, Virginia. A report based on the NTRS was brought to Tom's attention by Anna Malone, his boss and leader of Bank of Nations' online banking team. Anna asked Tom to examine the NTRS carefully and come up with insights that would be helpful in designing a new marketing campaign for the bank's online banking division.

Bank Background

Through a series of mergers over the last few years, Bank of Nations has become the second largest bank in the United States. Bank of Nations' aggressive growth strategy has focused not only on traditional banking but also on online banking. Its online banking services have achieved the highest penetration rate in the United States, with 40 percent of Bank of Nations households now using online banking, whereas the national average is 31 percent. Although Bank of Nations is clearly ahead of the competition, the bank's top management has set an aggressive growth target for its online banking division—achieving a penetration rate of at least 50 percent by 2010.

Online banking offers both customers and the bank significant advantages over traditional banking. For customers there are several clear benefits: 24-7 account access with the ability to instantly track transactions, check account balances, and pay bills. For the bank, online banking yields significant cost savings. In addition, satisfaction scores for online banking customers were higher than for traditional banking customers. A key question facing the bank—and Tom Duggan—is how to identify the next set of customers who are most likely to adopt online banking. Tom feels that understanding the profile of customers most likely to adopt online banking will be helpful in designing the most appropriate marketing campaign for achieving the bank's 50 percent target penetration rate.

The NTRS

The NTRS is an extensive survey of a representative cross section of the adult population (18 years of age and over) in the United States. Based on a sample of 1,000 respondents, the NTRS covers a variety of issues pertaining to technology-related attitudes and behaviors. The survey also asks several questions about the respondents' demographics. The NTRS report that Anna gave Tom included an abbreviated version of the complete survey, as well as an SPSS data set containing the responses to the survey questions. Exhibit 1 shows the abbreviated NTRS survey. To get an initial feel for the survey data, Tom picks four of the survey questions at random and analyzes the frequency distributions for those questions using an SPSS program. Exhibit 2 contains the SPSS output from Tom's analysis. Tom now realizes that, to get the best set of insights from the survey data, he should first understand and evaluate the survey questions in a more systematic fashion and then conduct a more thorough analysis.

CASE QUESTIONS

1. Describe the type of measurement scale used in each of the questions in Exhibit 1. (Is each question nominal, ordinal, interval, or ratio?) Justify your responses.

2. What is the appropriate measurement of central tendency for each question? Why?

3. Set up an SPSS data template for the questionnaire presented in Exhibit 1. *Hint:* Refer to Tables 12.1 and 12.2 and Exhibit 12.3 in the chapter.

4. Based on the SPSS output from Tom's preliminary analysis (Exhibit 2), determine the mode, median, and/or mean values for each of Tom's four selected questions.

CASE NOTE

1. Reprinted by permission of Rockbridge Associates, Great Falls, VA.

This case was written by Catharine Curran-Kelly (University of Massachusetts at Dartmouth) in collaboration with the textbook authors, as a basis for class discussion rather than to illustrate either effective or ineffective marketing practice. The authors thank Rockbridge Associates, Inc., and their staff for providing access to the NTRS survey and data.

Exhibit 1
National Technology Readiness Survey (NTRS)

This questionnaire is based on a more comprehensive copyrighted National Technology Readiness Survey (NTRS).
© 2004 by Rockbridge Associates, Inc., and Professor A. Parasuraman. Adapted with permission.

[Note: Words shown in ALL CAPS are interviewer instructions or codes that are NOT to be read aloud by the interviewer,]

Hello, my name is _____, and I am calling on behalf of Rockbridge Associates, a marketing research firm in Great Falls, Virginia. We are conducting research on the role of technology in people's lives and are interested in your opinions. We are talking to a random cross-section of people, including those who use technology and those who do not use it much. This is not a sales call, and all of your responses will remain confidential. This call may be monitored for quality assurance purposes.

DO NOT READ. GENDER   1. ☐ MALE   2. ☐ FEMALE

1. We are interested in your views on how technology influences your life. I will read you a series of statements. For each one, please tell me whether you "strongly agree," "somewhat agree," are "neutral," "somewhat disagree," or "strongly disagree." [REPEAT SCALE AS OFTEN AS NEEDED. READ STATEMENTS.]
   1 Strongly disagree
   2 Somewhat disagree
   3 Neutral
   4 Somewhat agree
   5 Strongly agree
   8 Don't know
   9 Refused

   [RANDOMIZE LIST.]
   a. You like computer programs that allow you to tailor things to fit your own needs.
   b. You find new technologies to be mentally stimulating.
   c. When you get technology support from a provider of a high-tech product service, you sometimes feel as if you are being taken advantage of by someone who knows more than you do.
   d. If you provide information to a machine or over the Internet, you can never be sure it really gets to the right place.
   e. Other people come to you for advice on new technologies.
   f. In general, you are among the first in your circle of friends to acquire new technology when it appears.
   g. You can usually figure out new high-tech products and services without help from others.
   h. You do not consider it safe to do any kind of financial business online.
   i. You worry that information you send over the Internet will be seen by other people.
   j. It is embarrassing when you have trouble with a high-tech gadget while people are watching.

2. We would like to learn more about your usage of technology. First of all, do you have a computer at home?
   1 YES   2 NO   9 Don't know/Refused

3. [ASK OF EVERYONE, EVEN IF NO COMPUTER.] Do you currently have Internet access that you pay for at home?
   1 YES   2 NO   9 Don't know/Refused

4. Do you access the Internet from home from a regular phone line, or do you have some form of high speed access like DSL, or cable modem?
   1 REGULAR PHONE LINE
   2 HIGH SPEED
   3 BOTH
   4 OTHER: SPECIFY: _____
   8 Don't know
   9 Refused

5. About how many years ago was it that you *first* signed up for any kind of online service or Internet access for your home. [IF NECESSARY, READ CATEGORIES.]
   1 Within the past year
   2 Past 2 years
   3 Past 3 years
   4 Past 4 years
   5 Past 5 years
   6 Past 6 years
   7 Past 7 years
   8 Past 8 years
   9 Past 9 years
   10 Past 10 or more years
   99 Don't know

6. About how many hours a week do you personally access the Internet for personal reasons? [IF NEEDED: Do not count times spent using the Internet solely for your work.] [WHOLE NUMBERS ONLY, NO RANGES] _____ HOURS
   DK DON'T KNOW   REF REFUSED

7. What types of things have you yourself done for personal purposes, either at home, at work, or elsewhere on the Internet in the past year? Have you: [READ.]
   1 YES   2 NO   6 DON'T KNOW   9 REFUSED
   a. Booked travel arrangements online?
   b. Purchased an item costing over $100 online?
   c. Bought or sold stock or securities online?
   d. Checked information on your bank account online?
   e. Moved money between bank accounts, made deposits, or made withdrawals online?
   f. Applied for a credit card online?
   g. Paid a bill online at the website of the company that billed you?
   h. Taken a course taught online?
   i. Purchased an item from another person, such as through an auction site or classifieds online?

Exhibit 1 (continued)
National Technology Readiness Survey (NTRS)

8. [ASK IF ANSWER TO Q7d OR Q7e IS YES.] You said you do some online banking. How satisfied are you overall with your online banking services? Would you say: [READ. IF MORE THAN ONE BANK, ASK: Please answer for the service you use the most.]
   1 Extremely dissatisfied?
   2 Very dissatisfied?
   3 Somewhat dissatisfied?
   4 Neither satisfied nor dissatisfied?
   5 Somewhat satisfied?
   6 Very satisfied?
   7 Extremely satisfied?
   8 Don't know/Refused

9. What is your age? [ENTER WHOLE NUMBER, REF = 999]
   _____ YEARS

10. What is your marital status? Is it: [READ.]
    1 Married?
    2 Single, never married?
    3 Divorced or separated?
    4 Widowed?
    5 OTHER; SPECIFY _____
    9 Don't know/Refused

11. How many children do you have in your household who are 18 or younger? _____
    Don't know/Refused = 999

12. What is you employment status? Are you: [READ. STOP IF RESPONDENT SAYS YES.]
    1 Employed or in business full time?
    2 Employed or in business part time?
    3 Not employed and not seeking work?
    4 Not employed but seeking work?
    9 Don't know/Refused

13. Are you in a technology related profession, such as computing, programming, systems engineering, systems consulting, or technology sales?
    1 YES   2 NO   9 DON'T KNOW/REFUSED

14. What is the highest level of education that you have completed? Is it: [READ CATEGORIES IF NEEDED. STOP IF RESPONDENT SAYS YES OR GIVES ANSWER.]
    1 Less that high school degree?
    2 High school graduate or GED?
    3 Some college or two year degree?
    4 Four-year college degree?
    5 Masters or professional degree?
    6 Doctorate?
    7 Postdoctorate
    8 OTHER; SPECIFY: _____
    9 Don't know/Refused

15. What is your ethnic background? Is it: [READ.]
    1 White?
    2 African American?
    3 Hispanic?
    4 Asian?
    5 Another background?
    9 Don't know/Refused

16. Which of the following categories best describes your annual household income, before taxes? [READ. STOP IF RESPONDENT SAYS YES OR GIVES ANSWER.]
    01 Less than $10,000
    02 $10,000 but less than $20,000
    03 $20,000 but less than $30,000
    04 $30,000 but less then $40,000
    05 $40,000 but less than $50,000
    06 $50,000 but less than $75,000
    07 $75,000 but less than $100,000
    08 $100,000 but less than$150,000
    09 $150,000 but less than $200,000
    10 $200,000 or more
    99 Don't know/Refused

Thank You!

Exhibit 2
Preliminary Analysis Output

Have you: Bought or sold stocks or securities online?

		Frequency	Percentage	Valid Percentage	Cumulative Percentage
Valid	YES	100	10.0	12.1	12.1
	NO	726	72.6	87.9	100.0
	Total	826	82.6	100.0	
Missing	DK	1	.1		
	REF	1	.1		
	System	172	17.2		
	Total	174	17.4		
Total		1,000	100.0		

Have you: Checked information on your bank account online?

		Frequency	Percentage	Valid Percentage	Cumulative Percentage
Valid	YES	457	45.7	55.3	55.3
	NO	369	36.9	44.7	100.0
	Total	826	82.6	100.0	
Missing	DK	1	.1		
	REF	1	.1		
	System	172	17.2		
	Total	174	17.4		
Total		1,000	100.0		

You said you do some online banking. How satisfied . . . ?

		Frequency	Percentage	Valid Percentage	Cumulative Percentage
Valid	Extremely dissatisfied	4	.4	.9	.9
	Very dissatisfied	4	.4	.4	1.8
	Somewhat dissatidied	12	1.2	2.7	4.5
	Neither satisified nor disatisfied	20	2.0	4.5	9.0
	Somewhat satisfied	90	9.0	20.2	29.1
	Very satsfied	181	18.1	40.6	69.7
	Extremely satisfied	135	13.5	30.3	100.0
	Total	446	44.6	100.0	
Missing	DK/REF	15	1.5		
	System	539	53.9		
	Total	554	55.4		
Total		1,000	100.0		

Exhibit 2 (continued)
Preliminary Analysis Output

How many children do you have in your household who are 18 or younger?

		Frequency	Percentage	Valid Percentage	Cumulative Percentage
Valid	0	610	61.0	61.9	61.9
	1	157	51.7	15.9	77.9
	2	140	14.0	14.2	92.1
	3	56	5.6	5.7	97.8
	4	13	1.3	1.3	99.1
	5	8	.8	.8	99.9
	6	1	.1	.1	100.0
	Total	985	98.5	100.0	
Missing	DK/REF	15	1.5		
Total		1,000	100.0		

Hypothesis Testing

Chapter Objectives

After reading and understanding the material in this chapter, you should be able to:

- Distinguish between descriptive and inferential analysis.

- State the null and alternative hypotheses pertaining to a variety of decision situations requiring formal hypothesis testing.

- Define Type I and Type II errors and state the relationship between them.

- Define the significance level and power of a hypothesis test.

- Lay out the steps involved in conducting a hypothesis test.

- Interpret two-way tabulation and chi-square contingency tests.

- Use the appropriate test pertaining to hypotheses involving a single mean, a single proportion, two means (when the two samples are independent and when they are dependent), and two proportions.

Hypothesis Testing: Key to Actionable Strategies*

Generally, we start all research projects with in-depth interviews of the business heads generating hypotheses or hunches about the topic being researched. At the end of these meetings, it's often important to stress with the business heads that these are just hypotheses that need to be validated with research. The reason is that often these hypotheses are viewed to be facts without any evidence to support them—corporate assumptions. The fact that the business leaders articulated them can further engrain their beliefs.

*Written and reprinted by permission of Dave Moxley, President, Customer Knowledge Consulting.

It may seem obvious, but other benefits of involving the business leaders in the early hypothesis generation phase are to

1. Ensure you are asking all the necessary questions to collect the data for testing relevant assumptions.
2. Increase business buy-in to the process as a full project partner, thereby dramatically increasing the likelihood of subsequent market action.
3. Improve the image of the research function as an integrated and valued contributor to the strategic direction and tactical program implementation of the business.

From my experience, one example of an early assumption (and a testable hypothesis) was that bankers assumed high-income earners are more profitable (i.e., carry higher balances and fees) than low-income earners. Another example was that clients who carefully balance their checkbooks every month and minimize fees due to overdrafts are unprofitable checking account customers. These are examples of oversimplified or incorrect assumptions that need to be subjected to more formal hypotheses testing.

In these examples, the first step is to build cross-tabulation reports of profitability versus income or profitability versus checking or savings account balancing. Often the conclusion is that no relationship exists or, if one does, it is not statistically significant enough to warrant taking action. Though the process might seem tedious at times, you will conclude there must be other factors in play. By continuing to generate additional hypotheses, a meaningful and actionable business discovery can be made. Discoveries such as this can help gain a competitive advantage. Furthermore, this advantage can be sustainable and dramatic because the unique knowledge can assist an organization to better isolate, communicate, and serve customers in new or more efficient ways.

In another case, we found that older clients (compared to younger clients) were more likely to diminish CD balances by large amounts. This was nonintuitive because conventional wisdom suggested that older clients have a larger portfolio of assets and seek less risky investments. This triggered a small qualitative marketing research validation project that determined high-balance CD prospects were the target group for competitive financial planners selling mutual funds. The result was a dramatic change in the marketing strategy for this segment. ■

Descriptive analysis consists of computing measures of central tendency and dispersion, as well as constructing one-way tables; it helps the researcher summarize the general nature of the study variables.

The data analysis procedures discussed in Chapter 12—computing measures of central tendency and dispersion, as well as constructing one-way tables—help the researcher summarize the general nature of the study variables and the interrelationships among them. Such procedures constitute **descriptive analysis** and can provide valuable insights, as demonstrated by the examples in the previous chapter. In fact, certain research studies may require no more than descriptive analysis of the data.

Descriptive Versus Inferential Analysis

Inferential analysis is data analysis aimed at testing specific hypotheses.

In some studies, however, we must go beyond descriptive analysis to verify specific statements, or hypotheses, about the populations of interest. Data analysis aimed at testing specific hypotheses is usually called **inferential analysis.** This chapter describes the general procedure involved in hypothesis testing, discusses the role of hypothesis testing in data analysis, and outlines several hypothesis tests frequently encountered in marketing.

Overview of Hypothesis Testing

A useful starting point for discussing hypothesis testing is to consider the following situations, which illustrate critical questions typically faced by decision makers.

SCENARIO 1 Karen, product manager for a Web-enabled cellular phone service (cell phones that allow users to access the Internet and e-mail), is wondering whether to introduce the service into a new market area. A recent survey of a random sample of 400 households in that market showed a mean income per household of $30,000. On the basis of past experience and comprehensive studies in current market areas, Karen strongly believes that the product line will be adequately profitable only in markets where the mean household income (across all households) is greater than $29,000. Should Karen introduce the service into the new market?

SCENARIO 2 Tom, advertising manager for BMW, is in the process of deciding which of two short online films, X or Y, he should use to attract a younger audience. Both films feature BMW cars and Hollywood stars in an action story in which BMW cars play a prominent role (www.bmwfilms.com). Tom is not sure which movie will be more effective in attracting their target market, consisting of the 18-to-30 age group. Tom commissioned an experiment in which a random sample of 400 respondents who clicked on Google.com participated. There, respondents (all of whom were screened to ensure they were 18 to 30 years old) were randomly directed to view either film X or film Y. A sample of 200 respondents was exposed to each film. After viewing, the respondents were asked to rate the likeability of the film. Of the 200 respondents who saw film X, 40 liked it. Thus 20 percent liked film X, whereas 25 percent liked film Y. Can Tom conclude that film Y will be more effective in attracting the 18-to-30 age group?

What features do scenarios 1 and 2 have in common? Clearly, to reach a final decision, both Karen and Tom have to make a general inference from sample data. However, making generalizations from sample data is a feature implicit in virtually all conclusive research projects and hence is not unique to scenarios 1 and 2. As we saw in Chapter 11 on sampling, the purpose of any sampling study is to learn *something* about the population.

A more distinctive feature of scenarios 1 and 2, one that is more directly relevant to hypothesis testing, is that each implies a criterion on which the final decision depends. In scenario 1, the criterion is the mean income across all households in the new market area under consideration. Specifically, if the mean population household income is greater than $29,000, Karen should introduce the service into the new market. In scenario 2, the criterion is the relative degrees of awareness likely to be created by the two BMW films in the population of everyone in the 18-to-30 age group. Specifically, Tom should conclude that BMW

Managers frequently have to decide which of several alternative marketing stimuli (such as television commercials) is likely to have the strongest impact on consumers. Hypothesis testing offers a systematic basis for evaluating such alternatives and choosing the best one.

film Y is more effective than film X only if the anticipated population awareness rate for Y is greater than that for X.

Stated differently, Karen's decision making in scenario 1 is equivalent to either accepting or rejecting the following hypothesis: "The population mean household income in the new market area is greater than $29,000." Similarly, Tom's decision making in scenario 2 is equivalent to either accepting or rejecting the following hypothesis: "The potential awareness rate that film Y can generate among the population of the 18-to-30 age group is greater than that which film X can generate." A situation calling for formal hypothesis testing will usually stipulate a specific criterion for choosing between alternative inferences or courses of action. However, as we will see later, certain types of hypothesis tests may not have a criterion as clear-cut as those in scenarios 1 and 2. Furthermore, in many real-life situations, final decisions may depend on several factors, rather than on a single, clear-cut criterion. We have intentionally simplified scenarios 1 and 2 to highlight the defining features of hypothesis testing.

Null and Alternative Hypotheses

After recognizing that a particular decision requires formal hypothesis testing, the first step is to state a null hypothesis and an alternative hypothesis. We will use the symbols H_o and H_a to denote the null and alternative hypotheses, respectively. Before discussing the specific meanings of H_o and H_a, we make one general comment about stating hypotheses: hypotheses always pertain to *population* parameters or characteristics rather than to *sample* characteristics. It is the population, *not* the sample, about which we want to make an inference from limited data. Although this point might seem obvious, it is easy to become confused about it when formally stating and interpreting hypotheses.

The null and alternative hypotheses complement each other; they are mutually exclusive and collectively exhaustive. In other words, the two hypotheses are stated in such a way that H_a will not be accepted if the sample evidence strongly supports H_o. Similarly, H_a will be accepted if the sample evidence is strong enough to reject H_o. In scenario 1, with μ denoting the population mean household income, the two hypotheses are as follows:

$$H_o: \mu \leq \$29,000$$

$$H_a: \mu > \$29,000$$

You are probably wondering how to decide which hypothesis is the null (H_o) and which is the alternative (H_a). The null hypothesis should be stated more conservatively; that is, failure to reject H_o from the sample evidence should preserve the status quo. Notice that in scenario 1 the product line will not be introduced into the new market area (status quo will be maintained) if H_o is not rejected. If a decision is such that one of the two hypotheses implies a strict equality (for instance ($\mu = \$29,000$), that hypothesis should always be treated as H_o.

Type I and Type II Errors

We cannot be entirely certain whether a null hypothesis is true or false unless we conduct a census of the population. In the absence of a census study, we try to determine whether the null hypothesis should be accepted or rejected based on evidence from the sample. Such evidence can at times lead to wrong inferences about the population, however, because of possible sampling error. Specifically, the sample evidence might suggest that H_o should be rejected when it is actually true or that H_o should not be rejected when it is actually false. The resulting mistakes are called Type I and Type II errors, respectively. A **Type I error** is committed if the null hypothesis is rejected when it is true, whereas a **Type II error** is committed if the null hypothesis is *not* rejected when it is false.

> A Type I error is committed if the null hypothesis is rejected when it is true.

> A Type II error is committed if the null hypothesis is *not* rejected when it is false.

Although we cannot entirely avoid Type I and Type II errors, we can lower the risk of their occurrence to an acceptable level. Virtually all hypothesis-testing procedures place a limit on the probability of committing a Type I error. The researcher or decision maker specifies this limit, and as we will see a little later, it forms the basis for deciding when to reject H_o and when not to do so.

Significance Level

The significance level associated with a hypothesis-testing procedure is the maximum probability of rejecting H_o with that procedure when H_o is actually true. The term *significance level* refers to the upper-bound probability of a Type I error. We use the symbol α, the Greek letter alpha, to denote the significance level. The complement of the significance level, $1 - \alpha$, is the *confidence level.*

> The significance level refers to the upper-bound probability of a Type I error.

> The confidence level is the complement of the significance level (i.e., $1 -$ significance level).

> The power of a hypothesis test is the probability of rejecting H_o when H_o is false.

The symbol β, the Greek letter beta, denotes the probability of committing a Type II error. The quantity $1 - \beta$, which is the probability of avoiding a Type II error, is called the *power of the test,* or simply *power.* The **power** of a hypothesis test is the probability of rejecting H_o when H_o is false.

Table 13.1 summarizes the key concepts and terms in hypothesis testing. Although the researcher can and typically does specify α, β is difficult to constrain because its value depends on the actual (but unknown) value of the population parameter. Moreover, an inverse relationship exists between α and β. In other words, as we lower the probability of a Type I error, the probability of a Type II error goes up (power decreases). Therefore, it is difficult to limit *both* α and β within prespecified levels. We discuss the relationship of β (and hence of power) to α and the population parameter value further on this textbook's website.

Now let's examine the role played by the significance level in deciding when to reject H_o. In scenario 1, suppose Karen does not want to allow more than a 5 percent chance of rejecting H_o when $\mu \leq \$29,000$ ($\alpha = .05$). In other words, she does not want to reject H_o unless the sample evidence is overwhelmingly against it. The significance level is the key in deciding what type of evidence we can consider "overwhelmingly against" H_o.

Recall from Chapter 11 that mean values of samples selected repeatedly from a given population will fall on either side of the population mean and form a distribution (called the *sampling distribution*) around it. Intuitively, sample mean ($\bar{x}$) values greater than $\$29,000$—that is, $\bar{x}$-values on the right-hand side of the sampling distribution centered on $\mu = \$29,000$—suggest that H_o may be false. More important, the farther to the right $\bar{x}$ is, the stronger is the evidence against H_o. Therefore, beyond some critical $\bar{x}$-value—say,

TABLE 13.1
Summary of Errors Involved in Hypothesis Testing

Inference Based on Sample Data	Real State of Affairs	
	H_o Is True	H_o Is False
H_o is true	Correct decision Confidence level $= 1 - \alpha$	Type II error P (Type II error) $= \beta$
H_o is false	Type I error Significance level $= \alpha$*	Correct decision Power $= 1 - \beta$

*Term α represents the maximum probability of committing a Type I error.

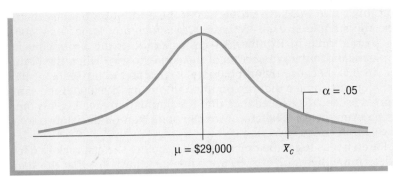

$\bar{x}_c$—Karen should be able to conclude that the evidence is overwhelmingly against H_0. Specifically, she should choose $\bar{x}_c$ such that any sample whose mean exceeds $\bar{x}_c$ has less than a 5 percent chance of having come from a population whose mean is \$29,000 or less. This criterion is shown graphically in Exhibit 13.1.

How do we select an appropriate significance level (or confidence level) for a hypothesis test? For instance, in

Exhibit 13.1
Identifying the Critical Sample Mean Value

scenario 1, how or why did Karen choose a significance level of .05? The choice of a particular significance level is subjective and depends on the nature of the problem as well as on the degree of risk the decision maker is willing to take. The following example illustrates this point.

EXAMPLE Consider two firms, Apple Computer and GoVideo, each considering introducing a new product that differs radically from its current product line. Apple Computer has a well-established customer base and enjoys a distinct reputation for its existing product line. In contrast, GoVideo is a relative newcomer in the world of consumer electronics and does not have a well-established image for its present products. Which of these two firms should be more cautious in making a decision to introduce the new product?

Intuitively, we believe that Apple Computer should be more cautious, because it apparently has more to lose than GoVideo by making a hasty go-ahead decision. Stated differently, Apple Computer perhaps should set a lower significance level (or a higher confidence level) than GoVideo if both firms are to make a "go or no-go" decision on the basis of a suitable hypothesis test using sample data pertaining to potential customer acceptance of the new product. Thus different significance levels for the two firms (for instance, $\alpha = .01$ for Apple and $\alpha = .20$ for GoVideo) would be quite appropriate in this situation. Of course, the willingness of the two firms' management to assume risk also plays a role: generally, the more risk averse management is, the lower the significance level should be.

In summary, the choice of a suitable significance level for a hypothesis test is, or should be, situation specific. There is no standard significance level that is equally appropriate under all circumstances. In other words, although many hypothesis tests use seemingly standard significance levels of .01, .05, or .10, there is nothing sacred about these numbers. It is not wrong to use a significance level of, say, .20 or .30 if the circumstances warrant it.

Decision Rule for Rejecting the Null Hypothesis

A **decision rule** is a guideline that specifies the sample evidence necessary to reject the null hypothesis.

A **decision rule** is a guideline that specifies the sample evidence necessary to reject the null hypothesis. In scenario 1, for instance, Karen needs a decision rule specifying a *critical* sample mean income level ($\bar{x}_c$) such that, if the actual sample mean ($\bar{x}$) exceeds that level, she can reject H_0. The critical value to be incorporated in the decision rule depends on the significance level (α) specified for the hypothesis test. Suppose Karen does not want to allow more than a 5 percent chance of rejecting H_0 when the population mean is actually less than or equal to \$29,000 (that is, she sets the value of α at .05). Exhibit 13.1 shows the sampling distribution curve associated with a population mean of \$29,000. Recall from

Chapter 11 that this curve will have properties of the normal probability distribution because the sample size in scenario 1 is sufficiently large ($n = 400$). Therefore, the shaded area in Exhibit 13.1 corresponds to the probability of obtaining sample means in the tail portion of the curve ($\bar{x} > \bar{x}_c$) when the population mean is $29,000. Because this probability is specified to be .05 ($\alpha = .05$), there is only a 5 percent chance that the population mean is $29,000 if the sample mean obtained exceeds $\bar{x}_c$ (the chance that the population mean is *less than* $29,000 would be even lower). Therefore, we can state Karen's decision rule as "Reject H_o if the sample mean exceeds $\bar{x}_c$."

Of course, Karen needs to set the exact value of $\bar{x}_c$ before she can make a decision. She can determine the value of $\bar{x}_c$ by applying her knowledge that the sampling distribution in this situation is a normal probability distribution.

Specifically, every mean $\bar{x}$ has a corresponding, equivalent standard normal deviate z, given by

$$z = \frac{\bar{x} - \mu}{\sigma_{\bar{x}}} \tag{13.1}$$

where $\sigma_{\bar{x}}$ is the standard deviation associated with the sampling distribution curve. When $\sigma_{\bar{x}}$ is unknown, it is approximately estimated by $s_{\bar{x}}$, the standard error of the sample mean, given by

$$s_{\bar{x}} = s/\sqrt{n}$$

where s is the sample standard deviation and n is the sample size. Therefore, the expression for z can be modified as follows:

$$z = \frac{\bar{x} - \mu}{s_{\bar{x}}} \tag{13.2}$$

Rearranging the terms in equation 13.2 gives

$$\bar{x} = \mu + z\, s_{\bar{x}} \tag{13.3}$$

Substituting $\bar{x}_c$ for $\bar{x}$ and z_c for z in equation 13.3 yields

$$\bar{x}_c = \mu + z_c s_{\bar{x}} \tag{13.4}$$

where z_c is the standard normal deviate corresponding to the critical sample mean, $\bar{x}_c$. That is, z_c is a critical z-value that corresponds to a significance level of α under the standard normal curve. The areas, or probabilities, under different sections of the standard normal curve and their corresponding z-values are tabulated in Appendix 1 at the end of the book. The value of z_c corresponding to a specified α-level appears in the table in Appendix 1.

Now let's return to scenario 1. Suppose the standard deviation of household income for the sample of 400 households is $8,000. The standard error of the mean ($s_{\bar{x}}$) is given by

$$s_{\bar{x}} = \frac{s}{\sqrt{n}} = \frac{\$8,000}{\sqrt{400}} = \frac{\$8,000}{20} = \$400$$

We can now compute the critical mean household income $\bar{x}_c$ through the following two steps:

1. Determine the critical z-value z_c such that the area to its right under the standard normal curve is α, which is .05 in this case. From Appendix 1, $z_c = 1.645$.
2. Substitute the values of z_c, s, and μ (under the assumption that H_o is "just" true) into equation 13.4 and solve for $\bar{x}_c$.

A note about the term *just true* is needed here. When H_o is stated as an inequality (as it is in scenario 1), it can be true for a *range* of population parameter values. It is "just" true, or "barely" true, when the population parameter is exactly equal to the hypothesized value. Furthermore, the probability of committing a Type I error is greatest when H_o is just true. Therefore, calculating the value of $\bar{x}_c$ when H_o is just true guarantees that the probability of committing a Type I error will be no more than the specified significance level (α).

In scenario 1, H_o is just true when $\mu = \$29,000$. From equation 13.4,

$$\bar{x}_c = \mu + z_c\, s_{\bar{x}} = \$29,000 + 1.645 \times \$400$$

$$= \$29,000 + \$658$$

$$= \$29,658$$

Karen can state her decision rule as follows: "If the sample mean household income is greater than \$29,658, reject the null hypothesis and introduce the Web-enabled cell phone service into the new market area." She could also state the same decision rule in terms of z-values, as follows: "If the z-value corresponding to the sample mean household income is greater than 1.645, reject the null hypothesis and introduce the service into the new market area." In general, we use the latter format to specify the decision rule for rejecting H_o, because it is cast in terms of a standard test statistic. The **test statistic** is a standard variable whose value is computed from sample data and compared with a critical value (obtained from an appropriate probability table) to determine whether or not to reject the null hypothesis.

A **test statistic** is a standard variable whose value is computed from sample data and compared with a critical value (obtained from an appropriate probability table) to determine whether or not to reject the null hypothesis.

Every hypothesis test has a corresponding test statistic, which depends on the sampling distribution involved. Because the sampling distribution in scenario 1 has the properties of the normal probability distribution, the appropriate test statistic is the z-variable. The value of the test statistic is simply the z-value corresponding to $\bar{x} = \$30,000$. From equation 13.2,

$$z = \frac{\bar{x} - \mu}{s_{\bar{x}}} = \frac{\$30,000 - 29,000}{\$400}$$

$$= \frac{\$1,000}{\$400} = 2.5$$

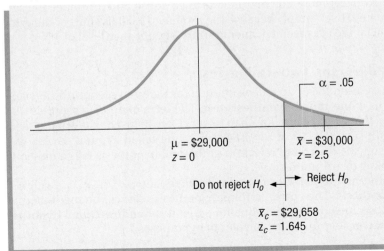

μ = \$29,000
z = 0

$\bar{x}$ = \$30,000
z = 2.5

α = .05

Do not reject H_o ← → Reject H_o

$\bar{x}_c$ = \$29,658
z_c = 1.645

Clearly Karen should reject H_o from the sample evidence, because $\bar{x} > \bar{x}_c$ and $z > z_c$. In other words, she should introduce the service into the new market area. If she does so, the probability of her committing a Type I error will be less than .05, as shown in Exhibit 13.2.

The intuitive notion underlying this hypothesis test is embedded in the following question: "What are the chances that a sample mean income as high as \$30,000 (or a test statistic value as high as 2.5) will have occurred when the true population mean income is \$29,000 or less?" The answer to this question in scenario 1 is "Less than 5 percent, the

Income data gathered from a sample of households in an area of interest can be analyzed through an appropriate hypothesis-testing procedure to help a marketer decide whether to introduce an expensive new product into that area.

subjectively selected significance level." Therefore, from the sample evidence, the hypothesis that the population mean income is $29,000 or less is not tenable and we should reject it.

The probability of obtaining an $\bar{x}$-value as high as $30,000 or more when μ is only $29,000 is given by the area under the distribution curve to the right of $z = 2.5$. From Appendix 1 this probability is only .0062. This value is sometimes called the *actual* significance level, or the *p-value*, of the test, to distinguish it from α, which is the preset, maximum significance level. The actual significance level of .0062 in this case means that the odds are less than 62 out of 10,000 that the sample mean income of $30,000 would have occurred entirely due to chance (when the population mean income is $29,000 or less).

For decision makers facing "go or no-go" decisions (such as whether a new service should be introduced or an online product film should be introduced), the actual significance level provides an estimate of the risk involved in erroneously making a go decision. Therefore, rather than making their "go or no-go" decisions on the basis of a prespecified "standard" significance level—say, .05—they can examine the actual significance level and then decide whether they are willing to tolerate that level of risk of making an unwarranted go decision. For instance, suppose the test statistic value (*z*-value) were 1.0 instead of 2.5 in scenario 1. From Appendix 1 the actual significance level, or *p*-value, corresponding to $z = 1.0$ is .1587 (that is, the area under the normal probability curve to the right of $z = 1.0$ is .1587). This *p*-value implies that there is about a 16 percent chance that we would have obtained a test statistic value as high as 1.00 when the population mean was only $29,000. In other words, there is about a 16 percent chance that Karen would be making a mistake if she decided to introduce the service on the basis of the sample evidence. If Karen finds this level of risk, a probability of a Type I error of .16, acceptable, she may decide to go ahead and introduce the service rather than hold back simply because the *z*-value of 1.0 falls short of the critical value of 1.645 at the prespecified, and arbitrary, significance level of .05.

One-Tailed Versus Two-Tailed Tests

The procedure we used to set up a decision rule for Karen in scenario 1 involved what is known as a **one-tailed hypothesis test.** The term *one-tailed* signifies that all $\bar{x}$- or *z*-values that would cause Karen to reject H_o are in just one tail of the sampling distribution ($\bar{x} > \$29,658$ or $z > 1.645$). In a one-tailed hypothesis test, values of the test statistic leading to rejection of the null hypothesis fall in only one tail of the sampling distribution curve.

Whenever the null hypothesis contains an inequality ($\leq$ or $\geq$), we call it a **directional hypothesis.** The corresponding hypothesis test will be one-tailed. If the null hypothesis includes a strict equality ($=$), it is a **nondirectional hypothesis.** For instance, consider the following pair of hypotheses:

$$H_o: \mu = \$29,000$$

$$H_a: \mu \neq \$29,000$$

In a **one-tailed hypothesis test,** values of the test statistic leading to rejection of the null hypothesis fall in only one tail of the sampling distribution curve.

The null hypothesis is said to be **directional** when it contains an inequality ($\leq$ or $\geq$). The null hypothesis is said to be **nondirectional** when it includes a strict equality ($=$).

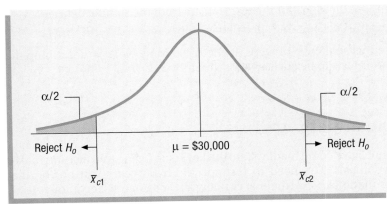

Exhibit 13.3
Critical Sample Mean Values for a Two-Tailed Test

In a **two-tailed hypothesis test,** values of the test statistic leading to rejection of the null hypothesis fall in both tails of the sampling distribution curve.

Intuitively, both very high and very low values of $\bar{x}$ should lead to rejection of H_o. Therefore, the decision rule for rejecting H_o will have *two* critical $\bar{x}$-values: one below \$29,000 (say, $\bar{x}_{c1}$) and the other above \$29,000 (say, $\bar{x}_{c2}$). The decision rule will be "Reject H_o if $\bar{x} < \bar{x}_{c1}$ *or* if $\bar{x} > \bar{x}_{c2}$." As Exhibit 13.3 shows, $\bar{x}$-values in either tail of the curve imply that H_o should be rejected.

A **two-tailed hypothesis test** is one in which values of the test statistic leading to rejection of the null hypothesis fall in both tails of the sampling distribution curve. A two-tailed hypothesis test has one special implication: the significance level specified for the test must be allocated equally to each tail of the sampling distribution curve. In other words, when the significance level is α, the two critical test statistic values must be established in such a way that the tail portion of the sampling distribution curve beyond each critical value corresponds to a probability of $\alpha/2$. This allocation is illustrated in Exhibit 13.3. We will look at a more detailed example involving a two-tailed hypothesis test later.

In practice, whether a hypothesis test should be one-tailed or two-tailed depends on the nature of the problem. A one-tailed test is appropriate when the decision maker's interest centers primarily on one side of the issue. For example, is the proportion of customers preferring our brand over competitors' brands greater than .3? Is customer response to our coupon campaign greater in city A than in city B? Is our current advertisement less effective than the proposed new advertisement? A two-tailed test is appropriate when the decision maker has no a priori reason to focus on one side of the issue. For example, is the average useful life for our appliance as perceived by consumers different from the objectively determined average life of 10 years? Is test market C different from test market D in terms of average household incomes? Is the satisfaction level of salespeople over 30 years of age different from that of salespeople 30 years of age or younger?

Steps in Conducting a Hypothesis Test

Up to this point, we have discussed several key terms and concepts pertaining to hypothesis testing. In particular, the calculations we have performed for scenario 1 illustrate how a hypothesis test is conducted. The procedures followed in those calculations are representative of hypothesis testing in general. In summary, the sequence of tasks involved in a typical hypothesis test are as follows:

Step 1. Set up H_o and H_a.

Step 2. Identify the nature of the sampling distribution curve and specify the appropriate test statistic. *Note:* In scenario 1, the sampling distribution was the normal curve, and the test statistic was the z-variable. But, as we will see later, depending on the specific problem, the appropriate sampling distribution and test statistic will vary.

Step 3. Determine whether the hypothesis test is one-tailed or two-tailed.

Step 4. Taking into account the specified significance level, determine the critical value *(two* critical values for a two-tailed test) for the test statistic from the appropriate statistical table.

Step 5. State the decision rule for rejecting H_o.

Step 6. Compute the value for the test statistic from the sample data.

Step 7. Using the decision rule specified in step 5, reject either H_o or H_a.

We will use this sequence of steps as the basic framework in describing the various hypothesis tests to be covered subsequently.

Role of Hypothesis Testing in Data Analysis

In scenarios 1 and 2, we could readily state the key issue facing the decision maker as a formal hypothesis. The need to test specific hypotheses will not be that apparent in all situations. Nevertheless, virtually all data analysis techniques to be discussed in the next two chapters rely on hypothesis testing, at least indirectly. In other words, we view hypothesis testing as an integral (although not always formally stated) part of most analysis procedures that go beyond merely describing the nature of the data. Therefore, at this point we will review certain key determinants of the appropriate analysis technique (and hence the appropriate hypothesis test) to use in a given situation.

Two factors are crucial in choosing an appropriate analysis procedure: the number of variables to be analyzed and the nature of the data collected on each variable. Analysis procedures are broadly classified as being univariate or multivariate. As the terms imply, **univariate analysis** is appropriate when just one variable is the focus of the analysis, and **multivariate analysis** is appropriate when two or more variables are to be analyzed simultaneously. (The label *bivariate analysis* rather than *multivariate* is often used when the analysis considers just two variables.)

The second factor affecting the choice of analysis techniques is the nature of the data collected. Particularly relevant in this regard is the measurement level of the data; that is, whether they are nominal, ordinal, interval, or ratio. As we discussed in Chapters 9 and 12, nominal and ordinal (nonmetric) data are not as powerful or versatile as interval and ratio (metric) data. Therefore, we can perform only relatively crude statistical analyses with nonmetric data.

The types of analyses and hypothesis tests appropriate for nonmetric data are typically labeled **nonparametric procedures.** Statistical procedures that are nonparametric require only minimal assumptions about the nature of the data, especially with respect to their measurement level and the shape of their distribution. Analysis techniques suitable for metric data are said to be **parametric procedures.** The use of most parametric methods requires data with at least interval-scale properties and a distribution that resembles the normal probability distribution.[1]

In short, as a general rule, nonparametric procedures are appropriate for nominal and ordinal data, and parametric procedures are appropriate only for interval and ratio data. For more details on nonparametric tests, we refer you to this textbook's website.[2]

Univariate analysis is appropriate when just one variable is the focus of the analysis.

Multivariate analysis is appropriate when two or more variables are to be analyzed simultaneously.

Nonparametric procedures are analysis techniques suitable for nonmetric data

Parametric procedures are analysis techniques suitable for metric data.

Specific Hypothesis Tests

This section deals with some hypothesis tests that are used quite frequently. Table 13.2 presents an overview of the specific hypothesis tests we will discuss.[3] The first technique we will look at is a cross-tabulation procedure, also known as the chi-square contingency test.

Cross-Tabulations: Chi-Square Contingency Test

The objectives of most research studies include an examination of relationships among key variables. Two-way tabulation is a useful preliminary step in understanding the nature of the association between a pair of variables. A *two-way table* is a table showing the number of responses in each category of one variable falling into the categories of a second variable.

For two-way tabulation to be meaningful, the data on each variable must be coded into a fixed set of categories, and the number of categories should not be large. Therefore, two-way tables are particularly appropriate for categorical (nominal- or ordinal-scaled) variables. Of course, two-way tables are also appropriate for interval- or ratio-scaled variables that have been transformed into ordinal-scaled variables with a limited number of categories.

Constructing a two-way table means breaking down the number of responses in each category of one variable into the categories of the second variable. This process is the simplest form of *cross-tabulation*, the simultaneous tabulation of data on two or more variables. Standard software programs capable of cross-tabulating data on any combination of variables in a data set are readily available.

TABLE 13.2
Univariate Hypothesis Tests

Type of Test	Primary Purpose of Test	Illustrative Research Question Test Is Designed to Answer
Chi-square contingency test	When the association between two categorical (nominal or ordinal) variables is to be examined	Is there a significant relationship between customers' highest level of schooling (education, measured, say, as a four-category ordinal variable) and whether they would recommend Sprint PCS to a friend (measured as an ordinal variable)?
Test for a single mean	To test hypotheses that compare the population mean of a variable to a prespecified value	Is the average waiting time for customers at Ace Supermarket's checkouts significantly greater than 10 minutes?
Test for a single proportion	To test hypotheses that compare the population proportion of a variable to a prespecified value	Is the proportion of households using broadband Internet service in Dallas significantly less than .3?
Test of two means	To test hypotheses that compare the population mean of a variable for two separate populations	Is the average per-household expenditure on eating out significantly higher in Detroit than in Des Moines?
Test of two means when samples are dependent	To test hypotheses that compare two population means of the same variable when the data for the test are collected from the same set of sample units	On the basis of data collected from a panel of households before and after the special ad campaign for Suds detergent, is the mean purchase volume of Suds per household significantly higher after the campaign than before?
Tests of two proportions	To test hypotheses that compare the population proportion of a variable for two separate populations	Is the proportion of two-income households significantly lower in midwestern states than in northeastern states?

Are consumers more apt to buy a new cell phone if it has Bluetooth wireless than if it does not? Cross-tabulations and chi-square contingency tests are techniques that can be used to answer this question, as well as others dealing with the association between two categorical variables.

The **chi-square contingency test** is widely used for determining whether there is a statistically significant relationship between two categorical (nominal or ordinal) variables.

The **chi-square contingency test** is a widely used technique for determining whether there is a statistically significant relationship between two categorical (nominal or ordinal) variables. (Although the chi-square test requires only nominal data, it can also be used to analyze associations between two ordinal-scaled variables or one nominal- and one ordinal-scaled variable.) A mere visual inspection of a two-way tabulation of data can suggest whether or not the variables are associated with each other. The chi-square contingency test is a means of formally checking the relationship between such variables. To illustrate the chi-square contingency test, let's consider the following example.

EXAMPLE The marketing manager of a telecommunications company is reviewing the results of a study of potential users of a new cell phone. The study used a random sample of 200 respondents and was conducted in a metropolitan area representative of the company's target market area. The marketing manager is intrigued by one table, which is a cross-tabulation of data on whether target consumers would buy the phone (yes or no) and whether or not the phone has Bluetooth wireless technology for easy transfer of data, pictures, and text. In other words, are consumers more likely to buy a new cell phone if it has the Bluetooth wireless technology feature than if it does not (yes or no)? Table 13.3 presents this cross-tabulation. Can the marketing manager infer that an association exists between availability of Bluetooth wireless technology and buying the cell phone?

The percentage breakdowns in Table 13.3 do suggest an association between the two variables. And the association does appear to be somewhat intriguing, with more respondents willing to buy the cell phone when it has Bluetooth technology than when it does not. However, is this result trustworthy, or could the association have occurred in this sample purely by chance? A chi-square contingency test of the following hypotheses can answer this question.

TABLE 13.3
Two-Way Tabulation of Bluetooth Wireless Technology Feature and Whether Customers Would Buy Cell Phone

Bluetooth Feature	Would Buy Cell Phone		
	Yes	No	Total
Yes	80 (80%)	20 (20%)	100
No	20 (20%)	80 (80%)	100
Total	100 (100%)	100 (100%)	200

H_o: There is no association between the Bluetooth technology feature and buying the cell phone (the two variables are independent of each other).

H_a: There is some association between the Bluetooth technology feature and buying the cell phone (the two variables are not independent of each other).

Conducting the Test

Computing the test statistic in the chi-square contingency test requires comparing the actual, or observed, cell frequencies in the cross-tabulation (also called the contingency table in this context) with a corresponding set of expected cell frequencies. The expected cell frequencies are generated under the assumption that the null hypothesis is true. In other words, they are generated by asking the following question: "How would the total sample have partitioned itself into the various cells if the two variables were truly unrelated in the population?" The expected cell frequency (E_{ij}) for any cell defined by the ith row and jth column in the contingency table is given by

$$E_{ij} = \frac{n_i\, n_j}{n}$$

where n_i and n_j are the marginal frequencies; that is, the total number of sample units in category i of the row variable and category j of the column variable, respectively.

The rationale for this expression is based on probability theory and is quite intuitive. The probability that any given respondent within the sample will be in category i of the row variable is n_i/n. Similarly, the probability that this same respondent will be in category j of the column variable is n_j/n. Therefore, if the row and column variables are independent, the joint probability of the respondent being in both row category i and column category j is given by $(n_i/n)(n_j/n)$. For the total sample of n respondents, the expected value (number of respondents) we should find in cell ij if H_o is true is given by $(n)(n_i/n)(n_j/n)$, which simplifies to $n_i n_j/n$.

Using this expression, we can compute an E_{ij}-value for each cell. For instance, the expected frequency for the first-row, first-column cell is given by

$$E_{ij} = \frac{100 \times 100}{200} = 50$$

Table 13.4 contains the expected cell frequencies corresponding to the various cells in Table 13.3. The row (as well as column) totals in Table 13.4 are identical for both the observed and the expected frequencies. This feature is always true and is helpful in verifying whether the expected cell frequencies have been computed correctly.

We obtain the value of the *chi-square test statistic* in a contingency test by the following formula:

$$\chi^2 = \sum_{i=1}^{r} \sum_{j=1}^{c} \frac{(O_{ij} - E_{ij})^2}{E_{ij}}$$

where r and c are the number of rows and columns, respectively, in the contingency table. The number of degrees of freedom (d.f.) associated with this chi-square statistic are given by the product $(r-1)(c-1)$. In our example,

$$\text{d.f.} = (2-1)(2-1) = 1$$

TABLE 13.4
Observed and Expected Cell Frequencies for Bluetooth Technology and Whether Customers Would Buy Cell Phone

Bluetooth Technology	Would Buy Cell Phone		
	Yes	No	Total
Yes	80 (50)	20 (50)	100
No	20 (50)	80 (50)	100
Total	100	100	200

Note: In each cell ij, the number without parentheses is the observed cell frequency (O_{ij}), and the number in parentheses is the expected cell frequency (E_{ij}).

Assuming a significance level of .05, the critical chi-square (χ_c^2) value from Appendix 2 for 1 degree of freedom is 3.84. Furthermore, a chi-square contingency test of independence between two variables is always a one-tailed test. Therefore, the decision rule is "Reject H_o if $\chi^2 > 3.84$." The computed value of the test statistic is

$$\chi^2 = \frac{(80-50)^2}{50} + \frac{(20-50)^2}{50} + \frac{(80-50)^2}{50} + \frac{(80-50)^2}{50}$$

$$= 72.00$$

Because the computed chi-square value is greater than the critical value of 3.84, we can reject the null hypothesis. In other words, the apparent relationship between "Bluetooth technology" and "would buy the cell phone" revealed by the sample data is unlikely to have occurred because of chance. In fact, the *actual* significance level associated with a chi-square value of 72 is *less than* .001 (from Appendix 2). Thus the chances of getting a chi-square value as high as 72 when there is no relationship between Bluetooth techonology and purchase of cell phones are less than 1 in 1,000.

That the chi-square contingency test requires only categorical data for ascertaining whether two variables are associated is a great advantage and has contributed to its wide use. However, for the test to be meaningful, we must have a minimum expected cell frequency (minimum E_{ij}). A commonly suggested rule of thumb is that no cell should have an expected frequency of less than 1, and no more than one-fifth of the cells should have expected frequencies of less than 5. Too many low expected frequencies will artificially inflate the computed chi-square value and may lead to the rejection of H_o when such a result is not warranted.

In practical terms, the minimum expected frequency requirement implies that the test may not be meaningful when the observed *marginal* frequencies of one or both variables (the n_i- or n_j-values) are very small for certain categories. In some cases, however, we may be able to combine adjacent variable categories in such a way that the collapsed category has a large enough marginal frequency.

Cross–Tabulation Using SPSS for National Insurance Company

One crucial issue in the customer survey of National Insurance Company was how a customer's education was associated with whether or not she or he would recommend National to a friend. Table 13.5 summarizes the results of cross-tabulating two variables in National's customer survey (the example was introduced in Chapter 12): a four-category "education" variable (high school or less, some college, college graduate, and graduate school) and a two-category "Would you recommend National to a friend interested in insurance services?" variable (yes and no). The results are also shown graphically in Table 13.5. Several key features of Table 13.5 deserve to be highlighted.

First, notice that the two-way table is based on a total sample of only 259 respondents. This total occurs because 26 of the 285 responding customers did not answer the question dealing with education. An important general caveat underlies this feature: the total sample size available for cross-tabulating two variables is constrained by the variable with the larger number of missing values (this maximum, effective sample size may be further reduced by missing values on the other variable). Therefore, even if just one of the two variables has a large number of missing values, the resulting two-way table may be misleading. Under such circumstances, the researcher should exercise caution in interpreting the table, especially if respondents with missing values on the variable in question are likely to differ markedly from other respondents in other ways as well.

TABLE 13.5
Association Between Education and Customer's Willingness to Recommend National to a Friend

For Two-Way Tabulation

1. Select ANALYZE on the SPSS menu
2. Click on DESCRIPTIVE STATISTICS
3. Select CROSS-TABS
4. Move the "highest level of schooling" to ROW(S) box
5. Move "rec" variable to COLUMN(S) box
6. Click on CELLS
7. Select OBSERVED and ROW PERCENTAGES
8. Click CONTINUE
9. Click OK

Notes:
COUNT represents the actual number of customers in each cell.

The percentages are based on the corresponding row totals.

The TOTAL COUNT is less than the sample size of 285 because of the 26 missing values for the two variables under consideration.

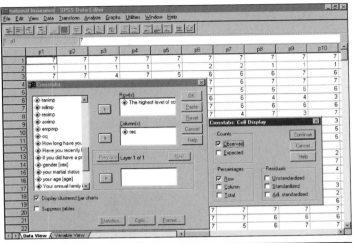

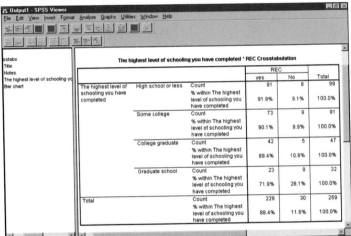

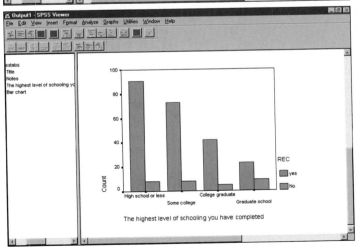

Second, as Table 13.5 shows, we customarily report the responses falling within each cell as raw frequencies as well as percentages. Percentages are easy to compare and hence are helpful in gaining insight into the relationships among the variables being cross-tabulated. A simple glance at the cell percentages in Table 13.5 (both the tabular format and the bar charts) reveals that 91.9 percent of the customers in the "high school or less" education category, 90.1 percent of those in the "some college" category, 89.4 percent of those in the "college graduate" category, and 71.9 percent of those in the "graduate school" category said "yes" to recommending National to a friend. Thus the lower the educational level of a customer, the more likely she or he will recommend National to a friend. In other words, there is an inverse, or negative, association between a customer's education level and recommending National to a friend.

Third, the cell frequencies in Table 13.5 are expressed as percentages of row totals rather than as column totals. An important question here is: In which direction (row or column) is it most meaningful to compute percentages for the cell frequencies? A general, intuitively appealing guideline is *to compute percentages in the direction of the presumed causal variable.*[4] In other words, when we can logically view one of the two variables being cross-tabulated as a *possible cause* of the other, we should base the percentages on the response totals in corresponding categories of the causal variable. Note the emphasis on *possible cause.* Cross-tabulation of data gathered through descriptive research can only suggest, but not prove, cause and effect between variables.

Let's examine Table 13.5 in light of this guideline. To view a customer's education as influencing her or his decision to recommend National to a friend, rather than the other way around, seems more logical. Therefore, Table 13.5 was constructed to reflect row percentages with the probable causal variable on the left and the effect variable on the top.

The general guideline for computing percentages in two-way tables has one potential problem: it may not always be clear which of the two variables is the likely causal variable. For instance, consider a cross-tabulation of data on firms' competitive positions (coded as weak, average, or strong) and their spending on marketing research (coded as low, medium, or high). A firm's competitive position may affect how much it spends on marketing research (weaker firms may believe they have less to spend and hence may allocate little or nothing to marketing research). In contrast, a firm's expenditures on marketing research may influence its relative competitive strength (firms may be competitively weak *because* of their failure to spend enough on marketing research). Thus the general guideline will not be helpful when there is no clear basis for presuming a particular direction of causality between the variables. In such cases, a researcher should compute and report percentages in both directions.

Research in Use 13.1 presents and briefly describes an SPSS procedure for performing cross-tabulation and chi-square analysis.

Precautions in Interpreting Two-Way Tables

Two-way tabulation, although helpful in uncovering relationships, has a few pitfalls that can easily lead a careless researcher to unwarranted conclusions. A frequent temptation when a two-way table shows evidence of a relationship, especially when one of the two variables is presumed to influence the other, is to view it as conclusive evidence of a *causal* relationship. Researchers must resist this temptation, however, because to infer causation from association is risky unless such evidence stems from a controlled experimental study. Two-way tables can, at best, only *suggest* the possibility of a causal relationship.

National Insurance Company Study Cross-Tabulation: Chi-Square Test Using SPSS

We will work with the National Insurance Company example presented in Chapter 12 to illustrate cross-tabulation analysis. Jill Baxter, vice president of customer service for National Insurance Company, and her assistant, Tom Kurtis, manager of customer service, examined the two-way tabulation presented in Table 13.5 and are wondering whether there is a statistically significant relationship between customers' educational attainment and their willingness to recommend National to a friend. They need to conduct a chi-square contingency test to reach a conclusion.

The hypotheses are as follows:

H_o: There is no association between educational level and willingness to recommend National to a friend (the two variables are independent of each other).

H_a: There is some association between educational level and willingness to recommend National to a friend (the two variables are not independent of each other).

SPSS dialog boxes for conducting a chi-square test are shown below. The actual significance level (p-value) of .019 (under the label "Asymp. Sig. [2-sided]") in the computer output implies that the chances of getting a chi-square value as high as 10.007 when there is no relationship between education and recommendation are less than 19 in 1,000. In other words, the apparent relationship between education and recommendation revealed by the sample data is unlikely to have occurred because of chance. Jill and Tom can safely reject the null hypothesis.

 For Chi-Square Assessment

1. Select ANALYZE
2. Click on DESCRIPTIVE STATISTICS
3. Select CROSS-TABS
4. Move the variable "highest level of schooling" to ROW(s) box
5. Move "rec" COLUMN(S) box
6. Click on "STATISTICS"
7. Select CHI-SQUARE, CONTINGENCY COEFFICIENT, and CRAMER'S V
8. Click on CELLS
9. Select OBSERVED and EXPECTED FREQUENCIES
10. Click CONTINUE
11. Click OK

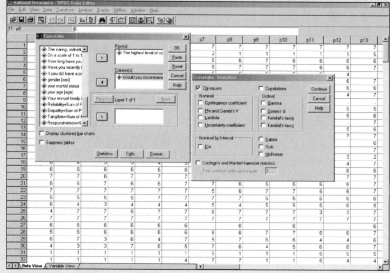

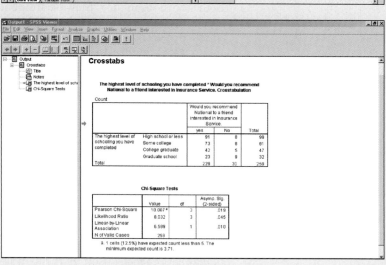

Are joggers less likely to contract heart disease than nonjoggers? A two-way tabulation of data on jogging behaviors and heart conditions of a sample of people can shed light on this question. However, the total sample size and the individual cell sizes in the table must be sufficiently large to avoid making incorrect choices.

Another caveat in interpreting two-way tables is to watch out for small cell sizes and be wary of percentages that are unaccompanied by the raw totals on which they are based. Consider the following two-way table based on a survey of 200 hospital patients:

	Patients Who	
	Jog	*Do Not Jog*
Patients with heart disease	20%	40%
Patients without heart disease	80%	60%
	100%	100%

This table appears to confirm what is commonly believed to be true: joggers are less likely than nonjoggers to contract heart disease. Specifically, the table shows that joggers are only half as likely (20 percent versus 40 percent) to contract heart disease. But assume for a moment that you have no prior knowledge of a possible link between jogging and lowered risk of contracting heart disease. Would you now infer that joggers are half as likely as nonjoggers to contract heart disease? You should not do so before ascertaining how many in the sample of 200 were joggers. For instance, even if there were only five joggers in the sample and only one of them had heart disease, the percentages in the first column would be correct. But you could not put much trust in those figures. So, before you jump to conclusions about results from two-way tables (especially when the evidence is consistent with your preconceived notions), ensure that the individual cell sizes, in addition to the overall sample size, are sufficiently large.

Finally, and perhaps most important, two-way tables, by definition, are constructed by using data on just two variables at a time. Although this feature makes the tables easy to interpret, it also increases the risk of drawing erroneous inferences, because the relationship between two variables may often depend on *other* variables. For example, the nature and the extent of association between students' intelligence levels and their test grades in a course may depend on factors such as course content, effort exerted by the students, and test format. Making inferences about the association between intelligence levels and test grades without taking into account such outside factors is risky. In situations in which a pair of variables being cross-tabulated may be influenced by other variables, the evidence presented by the two-way table may tell just part of the story. Similarly, an apparent *absence* of association between two cross-tabulated variables does not necessarily mean they are unrelated. Critical variables excluded from the table may be masking a relationship that really does exist, as illustrated by the following example.

EXAMPLE Suppose we survey a sample of 400 grocery stores and gather data for a certain brand of detergent on three variables: unit sales, promotional expenditures, and price. On the basis of these data, we classify the stores as above or below the median on each of the three variables. In other words, we label each store as "above the median" or "below the median" with respect to the detergent's sales, with respect to promotional expenditures for it, and with respect to its price. The cross-tabulations of these categorical data are shown in Table 13.6.

Let's examine Table 13.6(a), the two-way tabulation of sales and promotional expenditures. This table shows no association between promotional expenditures and sales, a rather unusual finding. Because price can also influence sales, the particular set of prices used by the sample of stores may be masking the association

TABLE 13.6
Associations Among Sales, Promotional Expenditures, and Price

(a) Sales Versus Promotional Expenditures

| | Sales | | |
Promotional Expenditures	Above the Median	Below the Median	All Firms
Above the median	100 (50%)	100 (50%)	200 (100%)
Below the median	100 (50%)	100 (50%)	200 (100%)

(b) Sales Versus Promotional Expenditures and Price

| | | Sales | | |
Promotional Expenditures	Price	Above the Median	Below the Median	All Firms
Above the median	Above the median	40 (33%)	80 (67%)	120 (100%)
	Below the median	60 (75%)	20 (25%)	80 (100%)
Below the median	Above the median	20 (25%)	60 (75%)	80 (100%)
	Below the median	80 (67%)	40 (33%)	120 (100%)

between promotional expenditures and sales. Table 13.6(b), which is a three-way table incorporating price, confirms such a masking effect. From the numbers in the first and third rows of this table (both rows relating to stores having above-median prices), we see that stores with above-median promotional expenditures are more likely to enjoy above-median sales than other stores (33 versus 25 percent). The second and fourth rows (both relating to stores with below-median prices) suggest a similar conclusion: stores with higher promotional expenditures are more likely to enjoy higher sales (75 versus 67 percent). In short, when price is held constant, there is a direct association between promotional expenditures and sales. Thus incorporation of price as a third variable into the original two-way table has helped reveal an important relationship that would otherwise have gone unnoticed.

The illustrations in Table 13.6 imply that the larger the number of variables included in the cross-tabulated data, the smaller the risk of making erroneous inferences. In other words, three-way tables are better than two-way tables; four-way tables (having four variables cross-tabulated simultaneously) are better than three-way tables; and so on. Unfortunately, although theoretically sound, this rule is not always easy to implement. Even a modest increase in the number of variables included in a cross-tabulation will sharply increase the number of cells in the table. This increase will, in turn, reduce the number of sample units per cell, because the total sample size is fixed. As we pointed out earlier, drawing inferences from tables with small cell sizes can be dangerous.

Furthermore, even assuming the total sample size is large enough to warrant our going beyond two-way tabulation, it may not always be easy to identify the most appropriate third variable to add to the table. When several variables seem to be equally worthy of inclusion as the third variable, a researcher may be tempted to construct all possible three-way tables to see which variable is most useful. This approach is generally not recommended, however, because it will usually be laborious and may amount to no more than an aimless fishing expedition.

That cross-tabulations may quickly become unwieldy and meaningless emphasizes the need to plan ahead and map out a systematic analysis strategy well in advance. Sound exploratory research, including a thorough review of past studies related to the topic being researched, is extremely useful in developing hypotheses about the nature of the variables of interest and the relationships among them. Such hypotheses, at least in the form of informal hunches, are essential in deciding which two-way tables to construct and which of those to expand by incorporating other relevant variables. Moreover, recognizing that an apparent relationship may be spurious—or that an apparent lack of relationship may be suspect—is not possible without the benefit of prior hypotheses. In short, a researcher with no hypotheses who hopes to gain insights through cross-tabulations is like a ship without a compass hoping to get from point A to point B. If the ship ever gets to point B, it will only be after following numerous miscues and wasting countless resources.

Test for a Single Mean

We already examined in detail one instance in which the focus was on hypotheses about a single mean. Specifically, in scenario 1 described earlier, we tested the following hypotheses:

$$H_o: \mu \leq \$29,000$$

$$H_a: \mu > \$29,000$$

Therefore, we do not need to repeat the entire procedure here. Some clarification is needed, however, concerning the proper test statistic and the critical value to use when conducting tests involving single means. Recall that, in scenario 1, the test statistic we used was the z-statistic (standard normal deviate). Our use of the z-statistic was actually an approximation, because the theoretically correct sampling distribution for sample means is the t-distribution, and the appropriate test statistic is the t-statistic. Fortunately, when the sample size is 30 or more, the t-distribution closely resembles the standard normal curve. Hence, our use of the z-statistic in scenario 1 was justified.

If the sample size in scenario 1 were, say, only 25 instead of 400, the z-statistic would no longer be appropriate. The correct test statistic is the t-statistic, defined as

$$t = \frac{\bar{x} - \mu}{s_{\bar{x}}}$$

Also, the critical test statistic value (t_c) must be obtained from a t-table (Appendix 3 at the end of this book). The value of t_c depends not only on α but also on the number of degrees of freedom. The t-statistic associated with a single sample mean has $n - 1$ degrees of freedom, where n is the sample size.

To illustrate the use of the t-statistic, let's rework some of the steps in the problem for scenario 1, assuming $n = 25$, $\bar{x} = \$30,000$ (as before), and $s = \$8,000$ (as before). From the t-table in Appendix 3, $t_c = 1.71$ for $\alpha = .05$ and d.f. = 24. Hence, the decision rule is "Reject H_o if $t > 1.71$." Now let's compute the value of t from the sample data.

$$t = \frac{30,000 - 29,000}{8,000/\sqrt{25}} = \frac{1,000}{1,600} = .625$$

Because the computed value of t is less than 1.71, H_o *cannot* be rejected. In other words, Karen should not introduce the product line into the new market area.

Notice that this conclusion contradicts the one we arrived at earlier after performing a z-test in the same situation (except for the larger sample size). However, bear in mind that, by failing to reject H_o based on the t-test, we may be committing a Type II error. Indeed, in general, when everything else remains the same, the smaller the sample size, the higher will be the β-probability, the lower will be the power, and the less likely it is that H_o will be rejected. Because traditional hypothesis-testing procedures limit only the probability of committing a Type I error, we have to be cautious in interpreting a finding that H_o cannot be rejected on the basis of a small-sample-size hypothesis test.

Test for a Single Proportion

EXAMPLE Ms. Jones is marketing vice president for Peripherals, Inc., a firm that sells a variety of personal computer accessories under the brand name Comp-Ease. She is wondering whether she should yield to a request from Mr. Berry, the advertising manager, for a substantial increase in the firm's advertising budget. Mr. Berry has just surveyed a random sample of 100 personal computer owners and found that only 20 had heard of the Comp-Ease name. In making his plea for an increased advertising budget, Mr. Berry described the sample awareness rate of .2 as being "shamefully low." Ms. Jones, however, believes the .2 awareness rate is not all that bad, especially because the Comp-Ease line was introduced only recently. In any case, she is reluctant to increase the advertising budget unless Mr. Berry can show "beyond a reasonable doubt" (with less than a 5 percent chance of error) that the true awareness rate for the Comp-Ease name across all personal computer owners is less than .3. Should Ms. Jones increase the advertising budget on the basis of Mr. Berry's survey results?

The key decision in this scenario boils down to testing the following hypotheses about the population proportion (π is the symbol for population proportion) of personal computer owners who are aware of the Comp-Ease name:

$$H_o: \pi \geq .3$$

$$H_a: \pi < .3$$

The theoretically correct sampling distribution for sample proportions is the binomial distribution. However, for a sufficiently large sample size, the binomial distribution resembles the normal distribution, and the z-statistic can be used as the test statistic. How large a sample size is "sufficiently large"? A rule of thumb is that n must be large enough to make each of the following quantities equal to at least 10: $n\pi$ and $n(1 - \pi)$, where the value of π is its value when H_o is just true. In our scenario, $n = 100$ and $\pi = .3$. Hence, $n\pi$ and $n(1 - \pi)$ are both greater than 10, and the z-statistic, as defined below, can be used as the test statistic.

$$z = \frac{p - \pi}{\sqrt{\pi(1 - \pi)/n}}$$

where p is the sample proportion. Notice that the denominator of this expression is really the standard error of the sample proportion. However, in contrast to the standard error in the test for the mean, where we had to approximate $\sigma_{\bar{x}}$ by $s_{\bar{x}}$ (which, of course, can be determined only after the sample standard deviation is computed), we know the standard error of the proportion exactly once we specify π and n.

Because only small values of p relative to π (or relatively large *negative* values of z) will lead to the rejection of the H_o stated earlier, this hypothesis test is one-tailed, as shown in Exhibit 13.4. The critical test statistic value (z_c) is negative, because the shaded tail corresponding to rejection of H_o is on the left-hand side of the sampling distribution centered on $\pi = .3$, or $z = 0$ (the z-value at the center of a normal

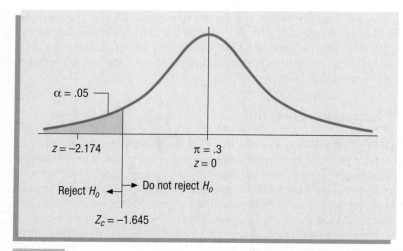

$\alpha = .05$

$z = -2.174$

$\pi = .3$
$z = 0$

Reject H_o ← → Do not reject H_o

$Z_c = -1.645$

Exhibit 13.4
Hypothesis Test Related to Proportion of Personal Computer Owners

probability distribution is always zero; z-values on the left-hand side of the distribution are all negative, and those on the right-hand side are all positive). From Appendix 1, $z_c = -1.645$ for $\alpha = .05$. The appropriate decision rule here is "Reject H_o if $z < -1.645$." Using $p = .2$, $\pi = .3$, and $n = 100$, we can compute the value of z:

$$z = \frac{.2 - .3}{\sqrt{(.3)(.7)/100}} = \frac{-.1}{.046} = -2.174$$

Because $-2.174 < -1.645$, we reject H_o; the sample awareness rate of .2 is too low to support the hypothesis that the population awareness rate is .3 or more. The actual significance level (p-value) corresponding to $z = -2.174$ is approximately .015 (from Appendix 1). This level of significance implies that the odds are lower than 15 in 1,000 that the sample awareness rate of .2 would have occurred entirely by chance (that is, when the population awareness rate is .3 or higher). In other words, Mr. Berry apparently has a legitimate request, and Ms. Jones should increase the advertising budget.

Test of Two Means

EXAMPLE A health service agency has designed a public service campaign to promote physical fitness and the importance of regular exercise. Because the campaign is a major one, the agency wants to make sure of its potential effectiveness before running it on a national scale. To conduct a controlled test of the campaign's effectiveness, the agency has identified two similar cities: city 1 will serve as the test city, and city 2 will serve as a control city. A preliminary random survey of 300 adults in city 1 and 200 adults in city 2 was conducted to measure the average time per day a typical adult in each city spent on some form of exercise. The survey showed that this average was 30 minutes per day (with a standard deviation of 22 minutes) in city 1 and 35 minutes per day (with a standard deviation of 25 minutes) in city 2. From these results, can the agency conclude confidently that the two cities are well matched for the controlled test? The agency does not want to allow more than a 5 percent chance of inferring that the cities are *not* matched when they truly are matched.

This situation is typical of those that require testing hypotheses with two means. Let's denote the population means in city 1 and city 2 as μ_1 and μ_2, respectively. We can summarize the survey results in the two cities as follows, using our customary notation:

City 1: $n_1 = 300$ $\quad \bar{x}_1 = 30$ $\quad s_1 = 22$

City 2: $n_2 = 200$ $\quad \bar{x}_2 = 35$ $\quad s_2 = 25$

The hypotheses are

$$H_o: \mu_1 = \mu_2 \quad \text{or} \quad \mu_1 - \mu_2 = 0$$
$$H_a: \mu_1 \neq \mu_2 \quad \text{or} \quad \mu_1 - \mu_2 \neq 0$$

In a two-means hypothesis test, when the sample sizes are sufficiently large ($n_1 > 30$ and $n_2 > 30$), the sampling distribution for the difference between sample means resembles the normal probability distribution, and the test statistic is the z-statistic, given by

$$z = \frac{(\bar{x}_1 - \bar{x}_2) - (\mu_1 - \mu_2)}{\sqrt{s_1^2/n_1 + s_2^2/n_2}}$$

Both n_1 and n_2 are greater than 30 in our example. The z-statistic can therefore be used as the test statistic.

Because the null hypothesis is in the form of a strict equality, the hypothesis test is two-tailed, and hence we have to identify two critical values of z, one for each tail of the sampling distribution. The probability corresponding to each tail is .025, because $\alpha = .05$. From Appendix 1, the z-value associated with a tail probability of .025 is 1.96. The decision rule is "Reject H_o if $z < -1.96$ or if $z > 1.96$."

Now let's compute the value of z from the survey results and under the customary assumption that the null hypothesis is true ($\mu_1 - \mu_2 = 0$).

$$z = \frac{(30 - 35) - (0)}{\sqrt{(22)^2/300 + (25)^2/200}} = \frac{-5}{\sqrt{1.61 + 3.13}}$$

$$= \frac{-5}{\sqrt{4.74}} = \frac{-5}{2.18} = -2.29$$

Because $z < -1.96$, we should reject H_o. Therefore, the health service agency cannot confidently assume that the current levels of exercising activity of residents in the two cities are identical. Exhibit 13.5 gives a pictorial summary of this hypothesis test.

In addition to the assumption of a large sample size, the use of the z-statistic in a hypothesis test with two means requires us to assume *independent samples*; that is, the samples must be chosen independently of each other. Thus, for example, the z-test is not appropriate for checking whether there is a statistically significant difference between two mean values obtained at *different times* from the same sample. Under such circumstances, a different hypothesis-testing procedure, which we will discuss a little later, should be used.

Furthermore, just as in the case of a single-mean hypothesis test, when one or both sample sizes are small ($n_1 < 30$ or $n_2 < 30$), a t-test rather than a z-test should be conducted. Using the t-statistic in a two-means hypothesis test requires us to make two additional assumptions, however:

1. The two populations from which the samples are selected are each normally distributed with respect to the variable.

2. The two populations have equal variances.

We usually take these assumptions for granted. Ideally, however, we should verify them to ensure that conducting a t-test is legitimate.[5]

Exhibit 13.5
Hypothesis Test Related to Mean Exercising in Two Cities

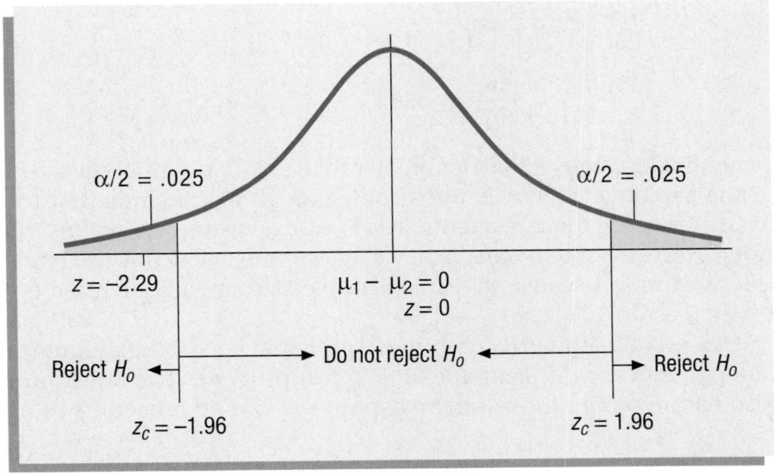

$\alpha/2 = .025$

$\alpha/2 = .025$

$z = -2.29$

$\mu_1 - \mu_2 = 0$
$z = 0$

Reject H_o ← → Do not reject H_o ← → Reject H_o

$z_c = -1.96$

$z_c = 1.96$

When the two preceding assumptions, along with the assumption of independent samples, are satisfied, the appropriate test statistic is

$$t = \frac{(\bar{x}_1 - \bar{x}_2) - (\mu_1 - \mu_2)}{s^*\left(\sqrt{1/n_1 + 1/n_2}\right)}$$

with d.f. $= n_1 + n_2 - 2$. In this expression, s^* is the *pooled standard deviation*, given by

$$s^* = \sqrt{\frac{(n_1 - 1)s_1^2 + (n_2 - 1)s_2^2}{n_1 + n_2 - 2}}$$

The procedure for conducting the t-test is quite similar to the one for conducting the z-test. To illustrate the use of the t-statistic, let's assume that the sample sizes for city 1 and city 2 in the health service agency survey were only 20 and 10, respectively, but that means and standard deviations were the same as before. Thus

$$n_1 = 20 \qquad \bar{x}_1 = 30 \qquad s_1 = 22$$
$$n_2 = 10 \qquad \bar{x}_2 = 35 \qquad s_2 = 25$$

The degrees of freedom for the t-statistic are

$$\text{d.f.} = n_1 + n_2 - 2 = 20 + 10 - 2 = 28$$

From Appendix 3, the critical value of t with 28 degrees of freedom for a tail probability of .025 is 2.05. Therefore, the decision rule is "Reject H_o if $t < -2.05$ or if $t > 2.05$." The pooled standard deviation is

$$s^* = \sqrt{\frac{(20 - 1)(22)^2 + (10 - 1)(25)^2}{20 + 10 - 2}}$$

$$= \sqrt{\frac{9196 + 5625}{28}} = \sqrt{\frac{14821}{28}}$$

$$= \sqrt{529} \text{ (approximately)} = 23$$

So the test statistic is

$$t = \frac{(30 - 25) - (0)}{23\left(\sqrt{1/20 + 1/10}\right)} = \frac{-5}{23\left(\sqrt{.05 + .1}\right)}$$

$$= \frac{-5}{23(.39)} = \frac{-5}{8.97} = -.56$$

Because t is neither less than -2.05 nor greater than 2.05, we cannot reject H_o. In other words, the sample evidence is not strong enough to conclude that the two cities differ in terms of their residents' levels of exercising activity. As we pointed out under t-tests for single means, however, we must view this inference with a good deal of caution because the small sample sizes greatly increase the possibility of a Type II error.

Research in Use 13.2 illustrates a computer-conducted test of the difference between two independent means using the SPSS t-Test program. The t-Test program in SPSS also has an option for using the hypothesis-testing procedure to be discussed next.

Test of Two Means When Samples Are Dependent

The testing procedures in the preceding section can be used only when the two samples do not overlap and are chosen independently of each other. However, marketers often need to check for significant differences between two mean values when the samples are not independent. For instance, "On the basis of a survey of husband-wife households, is there a significant difference between the mean attitude score of husbands and that of wives toward our product?" Here, although there is a sample of husbands and a sample of wives, the two samples are not independent because they are from the *same sample of households*. Marketers also may want to check differences between two mean values when the two sets of data are from the *same sample of respondents* (the same individuals). For example, "On the basis of data from a panel of women, is the mean frequency of use for our product among the women significantly higher after the coupon campaign than before?" In both cases, a modified hypothesis-testing procedure is necessary, as discussed next. The following example illustrates yet another situation that calls for the modified procedure.

> **EXAMPLE** A retail chain ran a special promotion in a representative sample of 10 of its stores, hoping to boost sales substantially. Weekly sales per store before and after the introduction of the special promotion are shown in Table 13.7. The key question now is whether the sample evidence in Table 13.7 is strong enough to support management's a priori hunch that the special promotion would lead to a significant increase in sales.

For this example, the "before" and "after" sales data (X_{bi} and X_{ai}, respectively) are clearly not independent, because they are from the same sample of stores. The hypothesis-testing procedure in situations like these calls for first computing *difference* scores for pairs of related sample data; in our example, these differences are the X_{di} values in the last column of Table 13.7. This step essentially collapses what appear to be two-sample data into a set of single-sample difference scores. The rest of the procedure is similar to the hypothesis-testing procedure for a single mean.

Let μ_d represent the population *mean change* in sales per store. Because management had an a priori expectation that the special promotion would be effective, that expectation should be consistent with the alternative hypothesis (the null hypothesis, the one that should be stated more conservatively, is that the special promotion did not improve sales). Therefore,

$$H_o: \mu_d \leq 0$$
$$H_a: \mu_d > 0$$

The sample estimate of μ_d is $\bar{x}_d$, given by

$$\bar{x}_d = \frac{\sum\limits_{i=1}^{n} X_{di}}{n}$$

TABLE 13.7
Sales per Store Before and After a Promotional Campaign

Store Number (i)	Sales per Store ($\times$ \$1,000)		
	Before Promotion (X_{bi})	After Promotion (X_{ai})	Change in Sales ($\times$ \$1,000) ($X_{di} = X_{ai} - X_{bi}$)
1	250	260	10
2	235	240	5
3	150	151	1
4	145	140	−5
5	120	124	4
6	98	100	2
7	75	70	−5
8	85	95	10
9	180	200	20
10	212	220	8
Total			50

National Insurance Company Study: Perceived Service Quality Differences Between Males and Females

Test of Two Means Using the SPSS T-TEST Program

The questionnaire used in the National Insurance Company study mentioned in Chapter 12 included a number of questions to assess customers' perceptions of the company's services. One of those questions asked customers to rate the overall quality of the company's services on a scale of 1 to 10, wherein 1 was labeled "Extremely Poor" and 10 was labeled "Extremely Good." The company was interested in determining whether or not male and female customers differed significantly in terms of their mean ratings on this scale. The ratings provided by the two groups of customers were analyzed using the SPSS T-Test program, and the following output was obtained. SPSS dialog boxes are shown below.

On the 10-point scale, males gave a mean rating of approximately 7.87, whereas females gave a mean rating of approximately 7.83. The output contains two actual significance levels or p-values (one under the "Sig." column and the other labeled "Sig. [two-tailed]"). The first one is a summary of a test (which has an F-value as the test statistic) conducted by the program to see if the variances for the two groups can be assumed to be equal. The p-value of .210 indicates that the null hypothesis of equal variances for the two groups cannot be rejected at the customary significance level of .05. In fact, the p-value of .210 implies that the odds are greater than 21 to 100 that any observed difference (which happens to be quite small, as reflected by the similar standard deviations shown in the upper half of the output) occurred entirely from chance. Therefore, computing a pooled estimate of the standard deviation (the $s*$ value defined in the chapter) is appropriate.

The t-value based on such an estimate and the associated degrees of freedom and p-value are reported under the columns labeled "t" and "Sig. (two-tailed)" of the output. The p-value implies that the odds are 88 to 100 that a difference of magnitude of .04 (7.87 − 7.83) could have occurred from chance. Therefore, the null hypothesis of no difference between the two groups cannot be rejected at the customary significance level of .05.

The second row of the output is similar to the first row except for the fact that the program computed the standard deviation used in figuring the t-value by using a formula that does not assume equality of variances for the two groups. This row (rather than the first row) should be examined if the F-value (for testing the equality of variances) turns out to be statistically significant (the null hypothesis of equality of variances is rejected).

Group Statistics

	Gender	N	Mean	Standard Deviation	Standard Error Mean
OQ	Male	137	7.87	2.26	.19
	Female	126	7.83	2.31	.21

In SPSS

1. Select ANALYZE from the menu
2. Click COMPARE MEANS
3. Select INDEPENDENT-SAMPLES T-TEST
4. Move "OQ–Overall Service Quality" to the "TEST VARIABLE(S)" box
5. Move "gender" to "GROUPING VARIABLE" box
6. DEFINE GROUPS (SEX = 1 for male and 2 for female)
7. Click OK

Independent Samples Test

OQ	Levene's Test for Equality of Variances		T-Test for Equality of Means						95% Confidence Interval of the Difference	
	F	Sig.	t	d.f.	Sig. (two-tailed)	Mean Difference	Standard Error Difference		Lower	Upper
Equal variances assumed	1.579	.210	.154	261	.878	.04	.281		−.511	.597
Equal variances not assumed			.153	258.11	.878	.04	.282		−.511	.598

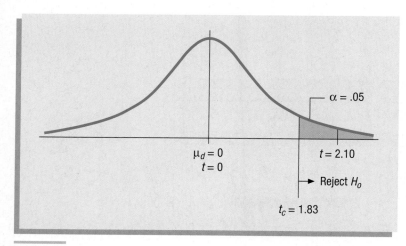

Exhibit 13.6
Hypothesis Test Related to Change in Weekly Sales per Store

where n is the sample size. In our example, the summation in the numerator is the total of the difference scores in the last column in Table 13.7 (50) and $n = 10$. Therefore, $\bar{x}_d = 5$.

The sampling distribution for $\bar{x}_d$ is the t-distribution, and the test statistic is

$$t = \frac{\bar{x}_d - \mu}{s / \sqrt{n}}$$

with $(n - 1)$ degrees of freedom, and where s is the standard deviation of the difference scores and is given by

$$s = \sqrt{\frac{\sum_{i=1}^{n} (X_{di} - \bar{x}_d)^2}{n - 1}}$$

Given the way H_o and H_a are stated, only relatively high values of $\bar{x}_d$ (or t) will lead to the rejection of H_o. Hence, the hypothesis test is one-tailed, as shown in Exhibit 13.6, in which we have assumed a significance level of .05. From Appendix 3, the critical value of t with $n - 1 = 9$ degrees of freedom, for a one-tailed probability of .05, is 1.83. The decision rule, then, is "Reject H_o if $t > 1.83$."

The standard deviation of the difference scores (s) in our example turns out to be 7.53. We can now compute the value of the test statistic:

$$t = \frac{\bar{x}_d - \mu}{s / \sqrt{n}} = \frac{5 - 0}{7.53 / \sqrt{10}}$$

$$= \frac{5}{2.38} = 2.10$$

Because $t > 1.83$, we reject H_o and conclude that the mean change in sales per store was significantly greater than zero. In other words, the special promotion was indeed effective.

Test of Two Proportions

We will use the data in scenario 2 (described earlier in the chapter) to illustrate hypothesis tests with two proportions. Recall that Tom, the advertising manager for BMW, is wondering whether BMW film Y will be more effective than film X in attracting a younger audience (18-to-30 age group). The subjects were randomly directed to view either film X or film Y. Subsequent surveys showed that the sample likeability rates for films Y and X were 25 percent and 20 percent, respectively.

Using the subscript 1 for symbols pertaining to film Y and the subscript 2 for symbols pertaining to film X, we can summarize scenario 2 as follows:

Sample sizes: $n_1 = 200$ $n_2 = 200$

Sample proportions: $p_1 = .25$ $p_2 = .20$

The hypotheses are

$$H_o: \pi_1 \leq \pi_2 \quad \text{or} \quad \pi_1 - \pi_2 \leq 0$$
$$H_a: \pi_1 > \pi_2 \quad \text{or} \quad \pi_1 - \pi_2 > 0$$

When the two samples are sufficiently large in a test of two proportions, we can assume the sampling distribution of the difference between sample proportions to be the normal probability distribution, and the z-test is appropriate. A rule of thumb for ensuring that the sample sizes are adequate is to verify that each of the following quantities is at least 10: n_1p_1, $n_1(1 - p_1)$ and n_2p_2, $n_2(1 - p_2)$. The data in scenario 2 satisfy these requirements. Hence, the z-test is appropriate. The test statistic is given by

$$z = \frac{(p_1 - p_2) - (\pi_1 - \pi_2)}{\sigma_{p1-p2}}$$

where $\sigma_{p1 - p2}$ is the population standard error for the difference between proportions.

Because $\sigma_{p1 - p2}$ is invariably unknown, it is estimated by the sample standard error $(s_{p1 - p2})$, as follows:

$$s_{p1-p2} = \sqrt{PQ\,(1/n_1 + 1/n_2)}$$

where P is the weighted proportion across both samples and Q is its complement:

$$P = \frac{n_1p_1 + n_2p_2}{n_1 + n_2}$$

$$Q = 1 - P$$

The null hypothesis in scenario 2 will be rejected only for certain positive values of the quantity $p_1 - p_2$. Therefore, the hypothesis test is one-tailed. Assuming the customary significance level of .05, the critical value of z (from Appendix 1) is 1.645. The decision rule is "Reject H_o if $z > 1.645$."

To compute the value of z from the sample data, we first have to compute P and Q, then $s_{p1 - p2}$ and z.

$$P = \frac{200(.25) + 200(.2)}{200 + 200} = \frac{50 + 40}{400} = \frac{90}{400} = .225$$

$$Q = 1 - .225 = .775$$

$$s_{p1-p2} = \sqrt{(.225)(.775)(1/200 + 1/200)}$$

$$= \sqrt{(.225)(.775)(1/100)} = \sqrt{.00174} = 0.42$$

Exhibit 13.7
Hypothesis Test Related to Likeability Generated by Two Online BMW Films

$$z = \frac{(.25 - .20) - (0)}{.042} = \frac{.05}{.042} = 1.19$$

Because $z < 1.645$, we *cannot* reject H_o. Therefore, the sample evidence is not strong enough to suggest that film Y will be more effective than film X. The results of our hypothesis test in scenario 2 are pictured in Exhibit 13.7.

One final point concerning the various hypothesis tests we have examined is noteworthy: a hypothesis test is often labeled in terms of the test statistic it involves. For instance, the test for a single mean when the sample size is sufficiently large uses the z-statistic (standard normal deviate). Therefore, we often refer to this test itself as a z-test. Likewise, the test for a single mean when the sample size is small is a t-test.

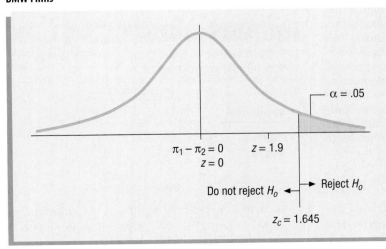

SUMMARY

An analysis procedure that goes beyond merely describing what the sample data look like is called *inferential analysis,* and it invariably involves some form of hypothesis testing. Situations calling for hypothesis testing will have a prespecified criterion on which a final decision, or inference, hinges. This criterion plays a key role in the formal statement of the null and alternative hypotheses.

Two kinds of errors are possible in testing hypotheses about population characteristics based on sample data: a Type I error, which refers to rejecting the null hypothesis when it is actually true, and a Type II error, which refers to failing to reject the null hypothesis when it is false. Traditional hypothesis-testing procedures place an upper bound on the probability of a Type I error—called the significance level α—but do not explicitly control Type II error. When α is lowered, however, the probability of a Type II error (called β) will increase, and power $(1 - \beta)$, which represents protection against a Type II error, will decrease.

The general procedure for testing hypotheses consists of the following steps:

1. Set up H_o and H_a (in accordance with the guidelines stated in the chapter).

2. Identify the nature of the sampling distribution curve and specify the appropriate test statistic.

3. Determine whether the hypothesis test is one-tailed or two-tailed (in general, a test will be one-tailed when H_o does not involve a strict equality).

4. Specify the critical values for the test statistic, depending on the preset significance level.

5. State the decision rule for rejecting H_o.

6. Compute the value of the test statistic from sample data.

7. Compare the test statistic value with the critical values and decide whether or not to reject H_o.

Hypothesis testing is an integral, although sometimes an implicit, part of virtually all statistical analyses that go beyond mere data description. Therefore, factors that affect the choice of an appropriate analysis technique are also germane to selecting suitable hypothesis tests. Two such factors are crucial: number of variables and measurement level of the data. Analyses and hypothesis tests pertaining to just one variable are univariate; those pertaining to two or more variables are multivariate (they are sometimes described as bivariate when just two variables are involved). Nonparametric tests are used when the data are nonmetric (nominal or ordinal), and parametric tests are used when the data are metric (interval or ratio).

This chapter discussed several hypothesis tests; the first is nonparametric, and the rest are parametric. The specific tests covered are as follows:

- The chi-square contingency test for determining whether two nonmetric variables are related to each other

- The z-test for a single mean when the sample size is large

- The t-test for a single mean when the sample size is small

- The z-test for a single proportion (valid only when the sample size is large)

- The z-test for two means when both samples are large

- The t-test for two means when either sample is small

- The t-test for two means when the samples are dependent

- The z-test for two proportions (valid only when both samples are large)

The risk of committing a Type II error is especially high in t-tests involving small sample sizes.

ACE
self-test

REVIEW AND DISCUSSION QUESTIONS

1. Can data gathered through a descriptive research project be useful in conducting inferential analysis? Why or why not? (Refer to Chapter 3 to refresh your memory about what is meant by descriptive research.)

2. What are Type I and Type II errors? Explain the relationship between these two types of errors.

3. What will happen to the probability of committing a Type II error when the significance level is increased from, say, .05 to .1?

4. "Hypothesis-testing procedures, given their statistical rigor, are free of decision maker subjectivity." Discuss this statement.

5. What are the potential limitations of the chi-square contingency test?

APPLICATION EXERCISES

1. From a survey of 1,000 families, the following two-way table was constructed:

	Owned Product X	
Income Level	Yes	No
High	200	150
Medium	175	100
Low	125	250
	500	500

Is there a statistically significant relationship between income level and ownership of product X at the 95 percent confidence level?

2. A random sample of 500 consumers in a certain county consisted of 300 males and 200 females. Of the males in the sample, 150 were smokers, and of the females, 75 were smokers. On the basis of this evidence, is there a statistically significant relationship (at the 95 percent confidence level) between the sex of consumers in this county and whether or not they smoke?

3. A computer retailer in a large city wanted to see whether the purchase of Apple computers by families was associated with whether or not families had children living at home. A random survey of 900 families in the city showed that 300 had children living at home. The survey also showed that 40 percent of the families with children owned Apple computers, whereas 30 percent of the families without children owned Apple computers. Is there a statistically significant association between children living at home and Apple computer ownership (assume a significance level of .01)?

4. Miller Cereal Company has been running an advertising campaign for one of its brands for quite some time. It wants to continue running the campaign only if at least 20 percent of the target audience is now aware of the brand; otherwise, it wants to discontinue the campaign. A just-completed survey of a random sample of 500 customers in the target audience showed that 90 were aware of the advertised brand. Should Miller Cereal Company discontinue the advertising campaign on the basis of this evidence? Assume that, if the company does decide to discontinue the campaign, it wants to be 95 percent confident that it is making the correct decision.

5. XYZ Company wants to advertise its product in a magazine only if the average age of the magazine's readership is greater than 40. A random sample of 625 readers had an average age of 41, with a standard deviation of 20. Suppose the firm does not want more than a 5 percent chance of making the mistake of advertising in the magazine when the magazine is really inappropriate. Set up and test a suitable pair of hypotheses, and indicate whether the firm should advertise in the magazine.

6. ABC Company is currently selling brand Z through 3,000 retail outlets across the United States. To strengthen Z's market position, ABC's objective is to make it the highest-selling brand in each of the 3,000 outlets. To achieve this goal, one of ABC's options is to cut the retail selling price of Z. However, it wants to cut the retail price only if analysis of last year's sales indicates that Z is not the highest-selling brand in more than 50 percent of the stores. In its decision making based on this sample information, ABC does not want more than a 5 percent chance of cutting price when Z is indeed the highest-selling brand in at least 50 percent of the 3,000 stores. Suppose ABC picks a random sample of 400 stores and finds that Z is not the highest-selling brand in 210 of them. Should the price be cut based on this sample information?

7. A firm wanted to see if there was a significant difference between two neighboring communities in terms of the mean number of members per household. A random survey of 100 households in the first community showed that the mean household size was 3 with a standard deviation of 5. In the second community, a random survey of 90 households showed that the mean household size was 4 with a standard deviation of 6. Assuming a significance level of .01, test the hypothesis that the two communities are statistically equivalent with respect to household size.

8. A sample of 400 female consumers of a product had a mean age of 33 with a standard deviation of 5, and a sample of 500 male consumers had a mean age of 32 with a standard deviation of 3. Can the mean ages of the female and male populations of consumers be considered significantly different at a significance level of .05?

9. A new product was promoted to two similar target markets using two *different* advertising media: medium 1 was used for market 1, and medium 2 was used for market 2. After the promotional campaign was over, a random sample of 200 people was surveyed from market 1 and a random sample of 300 people was surveyed from market 2. Of the market 1 sample, 154 were aware of the new product, whereas 210 of the market 2 sample were aware of the new product. Using this evidence, test the *null* hypothesis that the effectiveness of medium 1 is equal to that of medium 2 in terms of generating awareness among consumers (at the .05 significance level).

SPSS EXERCISES

1. Tom and Jill of National Insurance Company wanted to see whether there is a relationship between customers' willingness to recommend National to a friend and the following:

   a. Age
   b. Marital status
   c. Income

   Perform cross-tabulations and report the findings in statistical and managerial terms.

2. Tom and Jill of National Insurance Company were wondering whether there is a significant relationship between recommending National to a friend and overall perception of service quality. Conduct the appropriate analysis and indicate what inference Tom and Jill can draw from the results.

CASE 13.1 ROCKBRIDGE ASSOCIATES: NATIONAL TECHNOLOGY READINESS SURVEY (PART B)[1]
(www.rockresearch.com)

Tom Duggan, a newly hired research analyst for Bank of Nations, was part of the bank's online banking team headed by Anna Malone. His team was charged with increasing the bank's online banking penetration rate from the current 40 percent among Bank of Nations' customers to 50 percent by the year 2010. Anna asked Tom to examine a report based on the National Technology Readiness Survey (NTRS)—a survey conducted by Rockbridge Associates, Inc., a marketing research firm located in Great Falls, Virginia—and suggest some ideas for a new marketing campaign that the team had to develop for the bank's online services.

The NTRS is an extensive survey of a representative cross-section of the U.S. adult population (18 years of age and over). Based on a sample of 1,000 respondents, this survey covers a variety of issues pertaining to people's technology-related attitudes and behaviors. The survey also asks several questions about the respondents' demographics. The NTRS report that Anna gave Tom included an abbreviated version of the complete survey, as well as an SPSS data set containing the responses to the survey questions. Exhibit 1 in Case 12.2 (Chapter 12) contains the abbreviated NTRS survey.

After conducting some preliminary analysis to get an initial feel for the survey data (results of this analysis are summarized in Exhibit 2 in Case 12.2), Tom studied the NTRS in greater detail to identify questions that might be helpful in developing the marketing campaign for the bank's online services. A set of 10 items in the first question of the survey (Q1a through Q1j) related to the respondents' feelings and attitudes about technology in general. Tom felt that these questions, along with questions about technology-based products and services the respondents already had at home (for instance, Q2 and Q3), about respondents' online activities (for instance, Q7a through Q7i), respondents' overall satisfaction with online banking services (Q8), and respondents' demographics (the question about the respondents' gender at the beginning of the survey and Q9 through Q16) would all be useful in profiling the types of customers who are likely to be the most attractive prospects for online banking services.

As a starting point for exploring the differences and associations between responses to the various questions, Tom analyzed the survey data to see if having a computer at home (Q2) made any difference in respondents' views about (1) computer programs that allow people to tailor things to fit their needs (Q1a) and (2) respondents' general satisfaction with online banking services (Q8). Specifically, Tom conducted an independent-samples t-test using the SPSS program, to examine the significance of the differences in mean values of the responses to Q1a and Q8 for respondents with and without computers at home. Exhibit 1 presents the SPSS output from this analysis. Tom is now wondering what other types of analyses he should conduct to gain a more comprehensive set of insights that would be useful in developing the bank's marketing campaign.

CASE QUESTIONS

1. Interpret the SPSS output shown in Exhibit 1 to shed light on the two issues that Tom wanted to explore in his preliminary analysis.

2. Tom wants to determine whether there is any significant difference between respondents with and without home computers in terms of their overall attitudes toward technology (based on responses to Q1a through Q1j, rather than just Q1a, as in Exhibit 1). To assist Tom in this analysis, do the following:

   a. Create an overall "technology readiness" (TR) variable by combining the responses to Q1a through Q1j. (*Hint*: Review the section on constructing transformed [recoded] variables in Chapter 12. Please note that five of the ten items in Q1a through Q1j are "negative" items. Identify these items and reverse-code them in the data set [reassign the scale values for these items as follows: $5 = 1, 4 = 2, 3 = 3, 2 = 4,$ and $1 = 5$] before combining them with the remaining five positive items.)

   b. Conduct an independent-samples t-test to see if the mean TR score for respondents with home computers is significantly different from the mean TR score for respondents without home computers. Interpret the results.

3. Conduct appropriate SPSS analyses to see if mean TR scores are different for

   a. Males versus females

   b. Those with high school degrees or less versus those with more than high school degrees

   c. Those 30 years of age or less versus those over 30

   d. Those with a household income less than $40,000 versus those with a household income of $40,000 or more

   e. Those who have conducted some online banking (answered "yes" to Q7d or Q7e, or both) versus those who have not. (*Hint*: For the analyses involving education, age, income, and online banking, you need first to construct the appropriate two-category transformed variables.)

4. What other types of analyses would you recommend to Tom? Conduct those analyses and interpret the results.

5. Putting yourself in Tom's place, write a memo to Anna Malone summarizing the insights from the various analyses and containing your recommendations for the marketing campaign.

CASE NOTE

1. Reprinted by permission of Rockbridge Associates, Great Falls, VA.

This case was written by Catharine Curran-Kelly (University of Massachusetts at Dartmouth) in collaboration with the textbook authors, as a basis for class discussion rather than to illustrate either effective or ineffective marketing practice. The authors thank Rockbridge Associates, Inc., and their staff for providing access to the NTRS survey and data.

Exhibit 1
T-Test

Group Statistics

	We would like to learn more about your usage …	N	Mean	Std. Deviation	Std. Error Mean
You like computer programs that allow you to tailor things to fit your own needs.	YES	798	4.25	1.046	.037
	NO	169	3.37	1.499	.115
You said you do some online banking. How satisfied … ?	YES	428	5.86	1.128	.055
	NO	18	5.56	1.149	.271

Independent Samples Test

		Levene's Test for Equality of Variances		T-Test for Equality of Means					95% Confidence Interval of the Difference	
		F	Sig.	t	d.f.	Sig. (2-tailed)	Mean Difference	Std. Error Difference	Lower	Upper
You like computer programs that allow you to tailor things to fit your own needs.	Equal variances assumed	74.412	.000	9.121	965	.000	.879	.096	.690	1.068
	Equal variances not assumed			7.258	203.995	.000	.879	.121	.640	1.117
You said you do some online banking. How satisfied … ?	Equal variances assumed	.474	.491	1.129	444	.259	.307	.271	−.227	.840
	Equal variances not assumed			1.110	18.404	.281	.307	.276	−.273	.886

CASE 13.2 THE PANKEY INSTITUTE (PART A)
(www.pankey.org)

Christian B. Sager, executive director of the Pankey Institute, commissioned a research study to assess overall satisfaction with the continuous education services the organization provides to dentists. The overriding objective was to gain insight into the factors that affected participants' decisions to return to the Pankey Institute for coursework beyond the first training program.

Background

Founded in 1972, the Pankey Institute promotes excellence in dentistry and helps dentists educate their patients about the availability and benefits of comprehensive oral care. Through its educational programs, Pankey has a three-pronged focus: enhancement of clinical skills, development of professional practice management skills, and fostering of good interpersonal relations. The overall mission and objectives of the Pankey Institute are clearly articulated on its website, www.pankey.org:

> Simply put, we help dentists and other dental professionals achieve excellence and fulfillment through educational programs that systematically develop personal and professional growth, and lead to greater education of the patients they serve. Our objectives are:
>
> - To provide the most advanced clinical training available and a curriculum for successful practice management.
>
> - To foster a philosophy that encourages improved relationships and communication among all dental professionals and the patients they serve.
>
> - To steadfastly advocate the integrity, quality and value inherent in a fee-for-service practice subscribing to the Principles and Practices of Optimal Care, which we define as treatment regimes that are appropriate, individualized, relationship-based, and comprehensive in nature.

Today, the Pankey Institute is acknowledged as one of the world's most prestigious centers of advanced dental education. The institute is structured uniquely, and courses are laid out as building blocks of the concepts and principles that make up optimal dentistry. The curriculum starts with a core course and builds to very complex treatment planning. All courses are one week in duration, beginning on a Sunday and ending with a midday Friday wrap-up. Each class has at least a 7:1 student-teacher ratio and is no larger than 24 students, with in-house faculty members and at least three visiting faculty members who are full-time practicing dentists from across the country.

Coursework is broken into a set of several programs of study, termed "Continuum Levels." The foundational program is Continuum Level 1, which focuses on the new-patient experience, including the new-patient exam and evaluation. Because almost everything that subsequently happens between the doctor and patient is based on that first experience, a good initial interaction with the patient is highlighted as critical to the development of a trusting doctor-patient relationship. Continuum Level 1 emphasizes the recognition of differences among patients and the importance of an individualized approach to each patient. In addition to basic dental practices, this is where the dentist develops his or her vision, a clarifying process that continues throughout one's tenure with the Pankey Institute.

Subsequent coursework builds on Continuum Level 1 as its foundation, covering increasingly difficult dental issues from Continuum Levels 2 to 4. The two that have most recently been added are Continuum Levels 5 and 6, where the most difficult cases are addressed.

The Questionnaire

The design of the questionnaire was undertaken with two objectives in mind. (A condensed version of the questionnaire appears in Exhibit 1.) The primary objective was to compare the dentists who attended two or more courses at the Pankey Institute with those who had attended only Continuum Level 1 in terms of their profile, attitudes, and preferences. In addition to guiding the identification and prioritization of issues pertinent to the study's primary objective, the results would also be used to investigate the possibility of expanding the range of services provided by the Pankey Institute to its existing base of clients.

Several questions were included to assess the extent to which the program should devote more time to dental procedures, managing the dental practice, or hands-on learning of clinical procedures. Other questions were included to determine the relevance of the clinical procedures and the extent to which they would contribute to the practice of the attendee and the ease with which they could be applied.

A number of items were included to measure perceptions of the instructors and staff, and the quality of different aspects of the program. Another set of questions was designed to obtain feedback on the price of the course itself, the total course expense (including the cost of travel and lost work days), and overall value for the money. A final set of questions addressed other noncurriculum issues, such as meals, lodging, and general perceptions of the institute's location in Miami, Florida.

Initial Analysis of the Results

Christian Sager was enthusiastic to learn the results of the study, and once the data were collected, he set out to better understand several aspects of overall satisfaction with the program: perceived quality and enjoyment of the program, evaluations of instructors, attitudes about the curriculum, perceived price and value, and evaluations of the staff and facilities. He was also interested in the profiles of different user groups, and personal preferences and situational factors affecting repeat attendance at the institute.

Initial data reduction of the 15 questions Q1–Q5, Q6a–c, Q7–Q10, and Q12–Q14 resulted in the identification of five factors: enjoyment, value for the money, newness of material, environment/staff, and applicability of material. Four items loaded on the enjoyment factor: "I enjoyed the course"; "I liked the visiting instructors"; "I liked the in-house instructors"; and "Overall, I enjoyed the week at Pankey." Three items loaded on the value for the money factor: "The price for the course was very reasonable"; "Compared to other continuing education courses that I have taken, the Pankey course was a good value for the money"; and "The total course expense (including the cost of travel and lost work days) was worth the money." Two items loaded on the newness of material factor: "A lot of the course material was new to me" and "Some of the material was difficult to comprehend." Three items loaded on the environment/staff factor: "All of the instructors were experts"; "The support staff were all very helpful"; and

"The dental equipment was state-of-the-art." Three items loaded on the applicability of material factor: "More of the course should have been devoted to (a) dental procedures, (b) managing the dental practice, and (c) hands-on learning of clinical procedures."

Mr. Sager was initially interested in aspects relating to the demographic variables that were captured on the questionnaire. The specific demographic items related to sex, age, type of practice, whether or not the practice was in a major metropolitan area, and geographic location of the practice. He also wanted to investigate the effects of gender and practice location on each of the five factors identified in the data reduction. There was a lot of work ahead, but he looked forward to the insights that would emerge from the results.

CASE QUESTIONS

1. Examine the relationships, if any, among key demographic variables that you believe might be related to one another. Justify your choice of variables. (*Hint:* Conduct cross-tabulation analyses and assess the statistical significance of the chi-square statistic.)

2. Examine the effects of gender and practice location on the various factors identified through the data reduction stage. (*Hint:* Use *t*-tests where appropriate.)

This case was written by Jeanne L. Munger (University of Southern Maine) in collaboration with the textbook authors, as a basis for class discussion rather than to illustrate either effective or ineffective marketing practice.

Exhibit 1
Pankey Institute Survey (abbreviated version)
Source: Courtesy of the Panky Dental Institute.

The first few questions pertain to the facilities, personnel and the last course you attended at the institute. Please indicate the extent of your agreement or disagreement with each statement by marking a number between 1 and 4 (1 = strongly disagree; 4 = strongly agree).

	SD	D	A	SA
1. All of the instructors were experts.	❑	❑	❑	❑
2. The support staff were all very helpful.	❑	❑	❑	❑
3. The dental equipment was state-of-the-art.	❑	❑	❑	❑
4. A lot of the course material was new to me.	❑	❑	❑	❑
5. Some of the material was difficult to comprehend.	❑	❑	❑	❑
6. More of the course should have been devoted to:	❑	❑	❑	❑
a. ❑ dental procedures.				
b. ❑ managing a dental practice.				
c. ❑ hands-on learning of clinical procedures.				
7. I enjoyed the course.	❑	❑	❑	❑
8. I liked the visiting instructors.	❑	❑	❑	❑
9. I liked the in-house instructors.	❑	❑	❑	❑
10. Overall, I enjoyed the week at Pankey.	❑	❑	❑	❑

Exhibit 1 (continued)
Pankey Institute Survey (abbreviated version)

11. Please mark the last Continuum that you attended.

❏ C-I   ❏ C-II   ❏ C-III

❏ C-IV   ❏ C-V   ❏ C-VI

The next set of questions focuses on the applicability of the *last course* to your practice and the value of this course to you. Please indicate the extent of your agreement or disagreement with each statement by marking a number between 1 and 4 (1 = strongly disagree; 4 = strongly agree).

	SD	D	A	SA
12. The price of the course was very reasonable.	❏	❏	❏	❏
13. Compared to other continuing education courses that I have taken, the Pankey course was a good value for my money.	❏	❏	❏	❏
14. The total course expense (including the cost of travel and lost workdays) was worth the money.	❏	❏	❏	❏
15. I was very satisfied with the course.	❏	❏	❏	❏

The following questions address a variety of issues other than the curriculum at Pankey. Please indicate the extent to which your expectations were met or not met using the following scale.

	Worse than expected		As expected		Better than expected
16. Meals provided were:	❏	❏	❏	❏	❏
17. Lodging accommodations were:	❏	❏	❏	❏	❏
18. My experience (in Miami) outside of the Institue was:	❏	❏	❏	❏	❏
19. My experience at the Institute was:	❏	❏	❏	❏	❏

Finally, just for classification purposes:

20. What is your gender?   ❏ Female   ❏ Male

21. What is your age?

❏ Under 35 years   ❏ 35–44 years   ❏ 45–54 years   ❏ 55 years and over

22. What type of practice do you have?

❏ Individual practice   ❏ Group practice   ❏ Other_____

23. Is your practice located in a major metropolitan area? (check one)

❏ No   ❏ Yes

THANK YOU FOR YOUR HELP. YOUR ANSWERS WILL HELP THE PANKEY INSTITUTE PROVIDE BETTER PROGRAMS AND SERVICES.

14

Examining Associations: Correlation and Regression

Did You Know That . . .

College degree, color, and race make a difference in home refinancing? A study of broker fees showed that borrowers without a college degree pay an average of $1,472 more than applicants with a college degree. The study also found that, when all factors other than race were held constant, African Americans on average paid $500 more than whites, and Hispanics paid $275 more than whites. These conclusions were based on results of regression analysis of refinancing data, to determine whether various borrower characteristics had a bearing on the amount of broker fees and closing costs paid by the borrowers.[1]

- Disaster-area declarations are related to electoral votes? A study of data from 1989 to 2003 pertaining to all states declared as disaster areas (making them eligible for disaster relief from the government) revealed that the importance of a state to the U.S. presidential race was associated with its chances of being declared a disaster area. The study used regression analysis to examine the impact of a state's actual need for disaster relief (estimated from insurance company figures and declarations of damage from the National Climatic Data Center) and the state's number of electoral votes (representing the state's importance in the

Chapter Objectives

After reading and understanding the material in this chapter, you should be able to:

- Compute the Spearman correlation coefficient between ordinal scaled variables and determine whether or not it is statistically significant.

- Compute the Pearson correlation coefficient between two variables and assess its statistical significance.

- Explain simple regression analysis and state the distinction between a dependent variable and an independent variable.

- Describe common indicators for checking the usefulness of a regression equation.

- Discuss practical applications of regression equations and precautions for their use.

- Interpret the results of a multiple regression analysis.

437

presidential race). The results showed that, after controlling for actual need for disaster relief, a battleground state with 20 electoral votes received 50 percent more disaster declarations than a state with just 3 electoral votes.[2]

- **The presence of an NFL team boosts rental costs?** A regression analysis of city characteristics and rental costs found that apartment rents in the central areas of cities that had a National Football League (NFL) team were 8 percent higher than in comparable cities without an NFL team. The presence of an NFL team also increased property tax receipts. The study showed that, in 22 of the 25 cities with an NFL team, the potential increase in revenues due to higher property taxes more than offset the subsidies those cities provided to their NFL team.[3]

- **An extra bathroom or bedroom adds to a home's sales value?** A study examining real estate values involved regression analysis of various physical characteristics and selling prices of 28,828 properties spread over a wide geographic area. The study revealed several interesting findings: an additional bedroom adds about 4 percent to a home's price; an additional full bathroom adds about 24 percent; a garage adds about 12.9 percent; a location on the water adds about 8 percent; an in-ground pool adds about 8 percent; and an above-ground pool adds no value.[4] ■

The previous chapter covered cross-tabulation (the chi-square contingency test, measuring the association between two nominal or ordinal variables) and hypothesis tests for investigating the statistical significance of differences between the means or proportions pertaining to one variable. This chapter investigates associations between two or more variables. Table 14.1 lists the techniques discussed in this chapter, indicates when they are appropriate, and illustrates their potential applications. (Certain other multivariate techniques are covered in the next chapter.) The first technique we will look at is the Spearman correlation coefficient, a measure of association between two ordinal variables.

Spearman Correlation Coefficient

The chi-square contingency test discussed in Chapter 13 can be used to examine the association between variables whose categories are ordinal. However, a more powerful measure of association between two ordinal variables, called the *Spearman correlation coefficient* (r_s), can be computed when the data are refined enough to rank the sample units 1 through n on each variable. Consider the following example.

> **EXAMPLE** Over the past several years, an industrial marketing firm has been hiring all its salespeople from among the graduates of 10 business schools in the vicinity of its headquarters. To ascertain whether any association exists between the relative prestige of the 10 schools and the performance of the graduates hired from each, the firm's sales managers developed a subjective ranking of the perceived prestige levels of the 10 schools and the performance levels of the groups of graduates recruited from them. These rankings are shown in the second and third columns of Table 14.2. What is the degree of association between the prestige levels of the schools and the sales performance levels of their graduates hired by this company?

TABLE 14.1
Overview of Techniques for Examining Associations

Technique	When the Technique Is Appropriate	Illustrative Research Questions the Technique Can Answer
Spearman correlation coefficient	When the degree of association between two sets of ranks (pertaining to two variables) is to be examined	Is there a significant relationship between salespeople's motivation level and the quality of their performance? (Assume the data on motivation and quality of performance are in the form of ranks—say, 1 through 20—for 20 sales-people who were evaluated subjectively by their super-visor on each variable.)
Pearson correlation coefficient	When the degree of association between two metric-scaled (interval or ratio) variables is to be examined	Is there a significant relationship between customers' age (measured in actual years) and their perceptions of our company (measured on a scale of 1 to 7)?
Simple regression analysis	When a mathematical function or equation linking two metric-scaled (interval or ratio) variables is to be constructed under the assumption that values of one of the two variables is dependent on the values of the other	Are sales (measured in dollars) significantly affected by advertising expenditures (measured in dollars)? What proportion of the variation in sales is accounted for by variation in advertising expenditures? How sensitive are sales to changes in advertising expenditures?
Multiple regression analysis	Same as under simple regression analysis, except that more than two variables are involved wherein one variable is assumed to be dependent on the others	Are sales significantly affected by advertising expenditures and price (where all three variables are measured in dollars)? What proportion of the variation in sales is accounted for by advertising and price? How sensitive are sales to changes in advertising and price?

The **Spearman correlation coefficient** is a measure of association between two ordinal variables.

A **Spearman correlation coefficient** is a measure of association between two sets of ranks. It is an appropriate measure for answering the question posed in this situation. The formula for computing it is as follows:

$$r_s = 1 - \frac{6 \sum_{i=1}^{n} d_i^2}{n(n^2 - 1)}$$

where d_i is the difference between the ith sample unit's ranks on the two variables and n is the total sample size. Notice that $r_s = 1$ when the sum of the d_i^2 values is zero; that is, when the two sets of ranks are identical.[5] The range of possible values for r_s is $+1$ (perfect direct association) to -1 (perfect inverse association), with a value of 0 signifying no association.

As shown in the last column of Table 14.2, the value of $\sum d_i^2$ in our example is 56. Therefore,

$$r_s = 1 - \frac{(6)(56)}{10(100 - 1)} = 1 - .339 = .661$$

The r_s-value of .661 suggests at least a moderate association between the two sets of ranks. Is this association statistically significant? To answer this question, we assume the 10 schools are a random sample from a population of business schools and test these hypotheses:

$$H_o: \rho_s = 0$$

$$H_a: \rho_s \neq 0$$

TABLE 14.2
Association Between School Prestige and Performance of Graduates

Business School (i)	Ranking of School's Prestige (SP_i)	Ranking of Performance of School's Graduates (GP_i)	Difference Between Ranks $(d_i = SP_i - GP_i)$	Squared Difference (d_i^2)
1	10	8	2	4
2	7	3	4	16
3	9	7	2	4
4	1	2	1	1
5	6	9	−3	9
6	2	4	−2	4
7	3	5	−2	4
8	8	10	−2	4
9	5	6	1	1
10	4	1	3	9

$$\sum_{i=1}^{10} d_i^2 = 56$$

where ρ_s is the population correlation coefficient between the two sets of ranks. When $n \geq 10$, the following test statistic will have a t-distribution with $n - 2$ degrees of freedom:

$$t = r_s \sqrt{\frac{n-2}{1-r_s^2}}$$

This hypothesis test is a two-tailed test. Assuming a significance level of .05, the critical values of t for 8 degrees of freedom (d.f. $= n - 2 = 10 - 2 = 8$) are $+2.31$ and -2.31. Hence, the decision rule is "Reject H_o if $t > 2.31$ or if $t < -2.31$." In the present example,

$$t = .661\sqrt{\frac{10-2}{1-(.661)^2}} = .661\sqrt{\frac{8}{1-.437}} = (.661)(3.770) = 2.49$$

Because $t > 2.31$, we reject H_o and conclude that there is a true association between the prestige of business schools and the job performance of its graduates. In other words, the sample correlation of .661 is unlikely to have occurred because of chance.

Note that the basis for determining r_s is the computation of differences between pairs of ranks, an operation that is apparently inconsistent with the notion that it is inappropriate to place any meaning on the magnitude of the difference between numbers forming only an ordinal scale. Indeed, in computing r_s, we are implicitly assuming that the differences between ranks on the two variables can be meaningfully compared. If they cannot, the Spearman correlation coefficient may be misleading.

Pearson Correlation Coefficient

The **Pearson correlation coefficient (product moment correlation)** measures the degree of association between variables that are interval or ratio scaled.

A **scatter diagram** is a two-dimensional graph in which data on two metric-scaled (interval or ratio) variables are plotted.

The **Pearson correlation coefficient** (also known as the **Pearson product moment correlation**) is the degree of association between variables that are interval or ratio scaled. It is a more refined measure than the ones discussed so far. The Pearson correlation coefficient is insightful in its own right and also plays a key role in advanced multivariate analysis procedures.

To illustrate the computation and interpretation of the Pearson correlation coefficient, let's consider some data gathered by a firm selling Bright detergent in numerous market areas nationwide. Table 14.3 contains data from a sample of 20 market areas for the following variables: the revenues generated by sales of Bright during a one-month period, the advertising expenditures for Bright during that period, and the number of competing detergent brands being sold in each market area.

Notice that the data in Table 14.3 are metric data; indeed, all three variables are ratio scaled. Therefore, as a first step in understanding the association between any two of the variables, we can plot the corresponding data on a two-dimensional graph. Such a plot is called a **scatter diagram,** and it can indicate how closely and in what fashion the variables are associated. Exhibit 14.1 shows a scatter diagram of the sales and advertising data; Exhibit 14.2 shows a plot of sales versus number of competing brands.

The scatter diagram in Exhibit 14.1 clearly shows a direct relationship between dollar sales and advertising expenditures: in general, the higher the advertising expenditures, the higher the sales. Also, the swarm of points in the diagram seems to follow a linear trend. We will say more about this linear trend later, when we discuss regression analysis. Here we note that the existence of a linear scatter is a prerequisite for the Pearson correlation coefficient to be meaningful, because it is designed only to capture the extent of linear association between variables.

Two other key assumptions that must be met, especially for making statistical inferences based on the Pearson correlation coefficient, are the following:

1. The two variables have a bivariate normal distribution. In other words, the population is such that all units with a given value of one variable have values on the second variable that are normally distributed.

2. The variance of the normal distribution of one variable remains the same across all values of the second variable.

These assumptions are hard to verify by using sample data and are often taken for granted.[6]

TABLE 14.3
Data Gathered by Marketer of Bright Detergent

Market Area	Dollar Sales of Bright ($ thousands)	Advertising Expenditures for Bright ($ hundreds)	Number of Competing Detergents
1	5	5	15
2	10	13	8
3	6	5	14
4	20	15	5
5	15	10	9
6	9	9	10
7	11	5	12
8	18	13	4
9	22	17	6
10	7	6	13
11	24	19	2
12	14	12	8
13	16	15	6
14	17	14	7
15	23	18	1
16	8	7	11
17	12	10	10
18	13	12	7
19	21	16	7
20	19	16	3

Exhibit 14.1
Scatter Diagram of Sales and Advertising Data

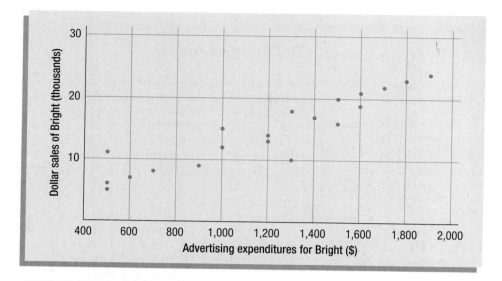

Exhibit 14.2
Scatter Diagram of Sales and Number of Competing Brands Data

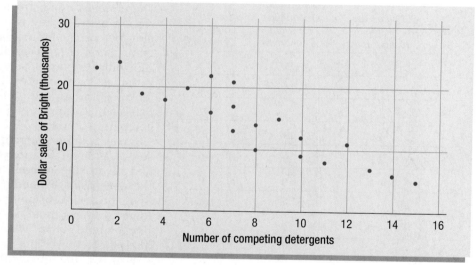

The scatter diagram in Exhibit 14.2 also displays an underlying linear association between sales and number of competing brands. Notice, however, that this trend is an inverse one; that is, in general, the greater the number of competing brands, the lower the sales of Bright. Exhibit 14.2 thus suggests a fairly strong, but negative, association between sales and number of competing brands.

The direction and the degree of association between two variables shown graphically by a scatter diagram like those in Exhibits 14.1 and 14.2 can be quantified in a single number, which is the Pearson correlation coefficient.

When the two variables are labeled X and Y, the Pearson correlation coefficient (r_{xy}) between them is given by

$$r_{xy} = \frac{\sum_{i=1}^{n} (X_i - \overline{X})(Y_i - \overline{Y})}{(n-1)\, s_x s_y}$$

where n is the sample size (total number of data points), X_i and Y_i are values for any sample unit i, $\overline{X}$ and $\overline{Y}$ are means, and s_x and s_y are standard deviations. The derivation of this formula and a discussion of the rationale underlying its interpretation are provided on this textbook's website.

We can easily calculate correlation coefficients by using readily available computer packages once a data set (like the one in Table 14.3) has been created. But if we want to calculate correlation coefficients by hand, a shortcut formula that is easier to use than the expression given here is available in basic statistics and regression textbooks.[7]

Pearson correlation coefficients, like Spearman coefficients, can range from $+1$ to -1. The sign of a correlation coefficient indicates the direction of association, whereas its magnitude indicates the strength of association. In our example, the correlation between sales and advertising turns out to be .927. This value reaffirms the strong positive association suggested by the scatter diagram in Exhibit 14.1. Consistent with our interpretation of the scatter diagram in Exhibit 14.2, the correlation between sales and number of competing brands is $-.909$ (a strong inverse association).

The sample correlation coefficient r can itself serve as the test statistic in conducting a two-tailed test of the following hypotheses:

$$H_o: \rho = 0$$

$$H_a: \rho \neq 0$$

where ρ is the population correlation coefficient. The degrees of freedom associated with r are $n - 1$, and its critical values are listed in Appendix 4. In our example, for $\alpha = .05$ and 19 degrees of freedom (d.f. $= n - 1 = 19$), the critical values are $r_c = +.433$ and $r_c = -.433$. The decision rule is "Reject H_o if $r > .433$ or if $r < .433$." Applying this decision rule to the .927 correlation between sales and advertising and to the $-.909$ correlation between sales and number of competing brands, we should reject H_o in both cases.

Although Pearson correlation coefficients are extremely helpful in uncovering bivariate associations, there are two important caveats concerning their use. First, a low sample correlation (or a failure to reject H_o) does not necessarily mean there is no association; it implies only an absence of linear association. Exhibit 14.3 illustrates this point. The scatter diagram in this figure clearly shows a strong U-shaped relationship between X and Y. Yet the Pearson correlation coefficient in this case will be close to zero because there is no discernible linear trend when the

Exhibit 14.3
Scatter Diagram Showing a Nonlinear Association Between Variables

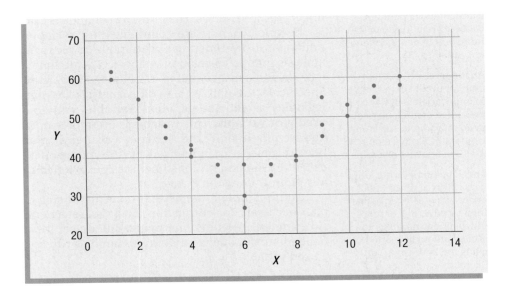

data points are considered together. The moral: even if the Pearson correlation coefficient is very small or not statistically significant, we should explore the possible presence of a nonlinear association, especially when intuitive or theoretical considerations suggest that the variables may be related. Perhaps the simplest way to explore a nonlinear association is to plot and visually examine a scatter diagram.

Second, as pointed out earlier in this book, the existence of a correlation by itself is not sufficient for us to infer causation between variables. For instance, the correlation of .927 between sales and advertising does not necessarily imply that increased advertising expenditures will lead to increased sales, although it is tempting to draw such a conclusion. The only thing this correlation says is that the data on the two variables follow a very similar pattern in the 20 market studies. But this pattern may be a result of a causal linkage going from sales to advertising, rather than the other way around. For example, anticipation of a certain level of sales in each market may have dictated a correspondingly low or high advertising expenditure level. Thus, unless all other relevant factors are controlled or accounted for, to infer a certain direction of causality between variables simply on the basis of a correlation coefficient is dangerous. Research in Use 14.1 describes the procedure for computing the Pearson correlation coefficient using SPSS for the National Insurance Company data.

Simple Regression Analysis

Simple regression analysis generates a mathematical relationship (called the *regression equation*) between one variable designated as the dependent variable (*Y*) and another designated as the independent variable (*X*).

Multiple regression analysis generates a mathematical relationship (called the *regression equation*) between a designated dependent variable (*Y*) and two or more designated independent variables (*X*s).

An **independent** (**explanatory** or **predictor**) **variable** in multivariate analysis is presumed to influence a dependent variable and is conventionally plotted along the *X*-axis in a scatter diagram.

The **dependent** (**criterion**) **variable** in multivariate analysis is presumed to be influenced by one or more independent variables and is conventionally plotted along the *Y*-axis in a scatter diagram.

Simple regression analysis is somewhat similar to the procedure for computing the Pearson correlation coefficient between two variables. A technique called **multiple regression analysis** is similar to simple regression analysis, but it examines associations among more than two variables. We will cover multiple regression analysis in the next section, after laying the foundation for the general regression technique in this section.

Correlation and regression analyses have a lot in common. Nevertheless, there are a few subtle differences between the two in terms of purpose and assumptions. First, whereas correlation analysis focuses on summarizing the degree and direction of association between variables as a single number, the purpose of regression analysis is to generate a mathematical function or equation linking those variables. The resulting equation is called a *regression equation*.

Second, when we are examining the association between two variables, the notion of a presumed causal variable is much more germane to regression analysis than to correlation analysis. (Recall that we introduced the concept of a presumed causal variable in Chapter 13 while discussing cross-tabulations.) Specifically, in simple regression analysis we must designate one of the two variables as the **independent variable,** also known as an **explanatory** or **predictor variable.** This variable is often presumed to be a cause of the other, and we plot it along the *X*-axis in a scatter diagram. The second variable, the one we believe is influenced by the independent variable, is appropriately called the **dependent,** or sometimes the **criterion, variable** and it is traditionally plotted along the *Y*-axis.

Third, although the assumptions about statistical properties of the input data necessary for correlation analysis are generally also required for regression analysis, there is one major difference: in regression analysis, only the dependent variable is random; we implicitly treat the independent variable as a fixed variable.[8]

Deriving a Regression Equation

A scatter diagram is useful for developing a conceptual understanding of the process involved in constructing a regression equation. We will once again use the data on sales and advertising and the corresponding scatter diagram in Exhibit 14.1. Suppose management has reason to presume that advertising is the likely causal variable for sales; that is, advertising expenditures for Bright detergent in the 20 market areas were not influenced by past or anticipated sales of Bright. Advertising is hence the independent variable and is plotted along the X-axis in Exhibit 14.4. Sales, the implied dependent variable, are plotted along the Y-axis. We can summarize the resulting scatter diagram's linear trend by constructing an appropriate upward-sloping straight line through it. Any straight line constructed on a two-dimensional graph can be mathematically represented by the following type of equation linking the X and Y variables:

$$Y = a + bX$$

where a and b are constants. An equation of this form is what regression analysis of data is intended to generate.

How do we construct an appropriate straight line through the scatter diagram? One obvious approach is to visually scan the scatter diagram and subjectively construct a line that appears to fit it. The problem with this approach, however, is that it is unlikely to produce one unique line; several different lines may seem to fit the scatter diagram equally well, as Exhibit 14.4 demonstrates. Clearly, then, we need a more objective procedure to identify the best-fitting line. We discuss one widely used procedure, called the *least squares approach,* on this textbook's website.

Statistical packages available on most computers (for example, SPSS or Excel) are capable of performing least squares regression analysis. They can provide the values of a and b, as well as a variety of statistics for evaluating the regression equation. Exhibit 14.5 shows the computer output (produced by an SPSS program) for the regression analysis of sales and advertising data.

We have not yet discussed all the regression analysis concepts necessary for fully understanding this output. Hence, we will refer to Exhibit 14.5 as we cover

Exhibit 14.4
Several Subjectively Constructed Regression Lines

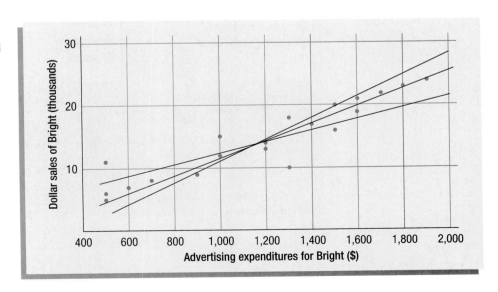

National Insurance Company: Computing Pearson Correlation Among Service Quality Constructs Using SPSS

Jill Baxter, vice president of customer service for National Insurance Company, and her assistant, Tom Kurtis, manager of customer service, are interested in the correlations between respondents' overall service quality perceptions (on the 10-point scale) and their average ratings along each of the five dimensions.

In SSPS

1. Click ANALYZE
2. Select CORRELATE
3. Select BIVARIATE

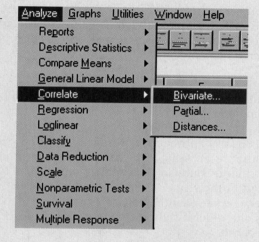

For Bivariate Correlations

4. Move oq, reliable, empathy, tangible, response, and assure to VARIABLES box
5. Click OK

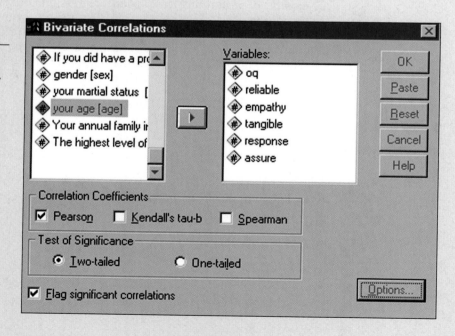

Tom has used SPSS to conduct a correlational analysis. Tom lays out the steps he followed and the correlational output.

Each of the five service quality measures (reliability, empathy, tangibles, responsiveness, and assurance) is significantly related to overall quality (OQ) at the .001 level of significance (shown below). Responsiveness has the strongest correlation (.863), and tangibles has the weakest correlation (.504), although all the correlations are strong enough to be meaningful.

Correlations

		OQ	Reliable	Empathy	Tangible	Response	Assurance
OQ	Pearson correlation	1	.846*	.822*	.504*	.863*	.859*
	Sig. (2-tailed)	—	.000	.000	.000	.000	.000
	N	268	251	250	217	260	254
Reliable	Pearson correlation	.846*	1	.826*	.581*	.867*	.842*
	Sig. (2-tailed)	.000	—	.000	.000	.000	.000
	N	251	254	256	217	249	243
Empathy	Pearson correlation	.822*	.826*	1	.648*	.882*	.873*
	Sig. (2-tailed)	.000	.000	—	.000	.000	.000
	N	250	256	262	216	250	243
Tangible	Pearson correlation	.504*	.581*	.648*	1	.607*	.567*
	Sig. (2-tailed)	.000	.000	.000	—	.000	.000
	N	217	217	216	219	219	213
Response	Pearson correlation	.863*	.867*	.882*	.607*	1	.921*
	Sig. (2-tailed)	.000	.000	.000	.000	—	.000
	N	260	249	250	219	262	253
Assurance	Pearson correlation	.859*	.842*	.873*	.567*	.921*	1
	Sig. (2-tailed)	.000	.000	.000	.000	.000	—
	N	254	243	243	213	253	256

*Correlation is significant at the .01 level (two-tailed).

Exhibit 14.5
SPSS Computer Output or Simple Regression Analysis of Sales and Advertising Data

Model Summary

Model	R	R Square	Adjusted R Square	Std. Error of the Estimate
1	.927[a]	.860	.852	2.28

[a] **Predictors:** (constant), advertising expenditures for Bright ($)

ANOVA[b]

Model		Sum of Squares	d.f.	Mean Square	F	Sig.
1	Regression	571.646	1	571.646	110.221	.000[a]
	Residual	93.354	18	5.186		
	Total	665.000	19			

[a] **Predictors:** (constant), advertising expenditures for Bright ($)
[b] **Dependent variable:** dollar sales of Bright ($ thousands)

Coefficients[a]

Model		Unstandardized Coefficients B	Std. Error	Standardized Coefficients Beta	t	Sig.
1	(Constant)	.163	1.457		.112	.912
	Advertising expenditures for Bright (hundreds of dollars)	1.210	.115	.927	10.499	.000

[a] **Dependent variable:** dollar sales of Bright ($ thousands)

each concept. For now, let's simply get the values of a and b from the exhibit. The number corresponding to advertising expenditures in the column labeled "B" is the value of b. The number immediately above that number is the value of a. Thus

$$a = .163$$

$$b = 1.210$$

The Y-intercept represents the predicted value of the dependent variable when all independent variables are set to zero.

The slope corresponding to an independent variable represents the change in the predicted value of the dependent variable for a one-unit change in the independent variable, assuming all other variables likely to influence the dependent variable remain the same.

The regression equation is

$$\hat{Y}_i = .163 + 1.210X_i$$

where $\hat{Y}_i$ is the value of sales (in thousands of dollars) *predicted* by the regression equation for an advertising expenditure level of X_i (in hundreds of dollars).

When $X_i = 0$, $\hat{Y}_i = .163$, which is the constant a. The a in a regression equation is known as the **Y-intercept** and represents the predicted value of the dependent variable corresponding to a value of zero for the independent variable.

The constant b, representing the coefficient of X_i, is known as the **slope** of the regression equation. The slope has a very important interpretation: *it represents* *the change in the predicted value of the dependent variable for a one-unit change in the independent variable*, assuming that all other variables likely to influence the dependent variable remain the same. In our example, because sales are measured in thousands of dollars and advertising expenditures are measured in hundreds of dollars, the value of 1.210 for b implies the following: if advertising expenditures are increased (or decreased) by $100 (which constitutes one unit of advertising), sales can be predicted to increase (or decrease) by $1,210 (which constitutes 1.210 units of sales), assuming no other relevant factor changes.

Evaluating the Regression Equation

The least squares procedure will yield the best possible straight line and corresponding regression equation for a given data set. However, when the data observed in a scatter diagram are widely dispersed rather than falling within a relatively narrow linear band that follows an upward- or downward-sloping trend, the usefulness of the resulting regression equation is questionable.

To illustrate, consider the two scatter diagrams shown in Exhibit 14.6. Suppose a least squares analysis of either diagram results in the same regression equation (the same a- and b-values). But intuitively the regression equation stemming from the scatter diagram in Exhibit 14.6(a) will be more trustworthy and valuable than one stemming from the diagram in Exhibit 14.6(b). Clearly, then, we need objective criteria for evaluating the *goodness* of the regression equation. One such criterion is called the **coefficient of determination,** denoted by R^2. The coefficient of determination is a global measure of how much better predictions of the dependent variable made with the aid of the regression equation are than those made without it.

For a given value of X, what is the best prediction of Y without using the regression equation? The best prediction should be $\overline{Y}$, the mean value of the dependent variable. Although $\overline{Y}$ will greatly underpredict some actual values and greatly overpredict others, on the average (over a number of such predictions), the overpredictions and underpredictions will cancel out.

For any given value of X_i, the deviation between the actual and the mean values of Y—that is, $(Y_i - \overline{Y})$—is called the total deviation in Y. The sum of the total squared deviations—that is, $(Y_i - \overline{Y})^2$ added across all data points in the scatter

The **coefficient of determination** is a global measure of how much better predictions of the dependent variable made with the aid of the regression equation are than those made without.

Exhibit 14.6
Two Identical Regression Lines Based on Different Scatter Diagrams

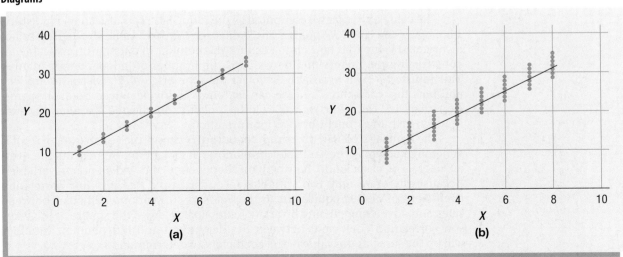

diagram—is a measure of the variation in Y about its mean value. This sum is the *total sum of squares,* denoted by SS_T. Part of SS_T can be accounted for when an appropriate regression equation is available. The variance thus explained is called the *regression sum of squares,* SS_R. The variance left unexplained by the regression equation is called the *error,* or *residual sum of squares,* SS_E.

The least squares procedure fits a straight line through the scatter diagram such that SS_E has the smallest possible value. Because SS_T is fixed by the input data on Y, the SS_R corresponding to the best-fit line will have the highest possible value. Intuitively, the higher the value of SS_R for a given value of SS_T, the better the regression equation should be. Therefore, a good way to see whether a regression equation is trustworthy is to examine the ratio between SS_R and SS_T, which is exactly what the coefficient of determination R^2 accomplishes.

$$R^2 = \frac{\text{Variance explained by the regression equation}}{\text{Total variance}} = \frac{SS_R}{SS_T}$$

The right-hand half of the computer output in Exhibit 14.5 contains the values of SS_R and SS_E under the heading "Sum of Squares." They are

$$SS_R = 571.646$$

$$SS_E = 93.354$$

$$SS_T = SS_R + SS_E = 665$$

$$R^2 = \frac{SS_R}{SS_T} = \frac{571.646}{665} = .860$$

Thus, from the regression equation in our example, advertising expenditures can be said to explain about 86 percent of the total variance in sales.

The range of possible values for R^2 is from 0 to 1. The R^2 for a regression equation corresponding to a scatter diagram that displays no apparent upward- (or downward-) sloping linear trend will be close to zero. When the scatter diagram forms a perfectly horizontal swarm of points, the regression line will coincide with a horizontal line constructed at $Y = \overline{Y}$. Predictions based on such a regression line will, of course, be no better than those given by $\overline{Y}$, and hence R^2 will be zero. What will R^2 be when all the data points in a scatter diagram fall exactly on a downward- or upward-sloping straight line? In such a case, SS_E will be 0, SS_R will be the same as SS_T, and R^2 will be 1.

The value of R^2 that we computed as the ratio SS_R/SS_T is also shown in Exhibit 14.5, below the label "*R* Square." The "Adjusted *R* Square" value shown next to it is a corrected value that takes into account the number of data points available for constructing the regression line vis-à-vis the number of independent variables. The adjusted R^2 will invariably be lower than the original R^2. Discussion of why and how this correction is made can be found in any advanced book on regression analysis.[9] Hereafter, we will examine only the unadjusted R^2-values because they have a more straightforward interpretation.

The item labeled R in the computer output is simply the square root of R^2. It is generally known as the multiple correlation coefficient and represents the overall degree of association between the dependent and independent variables. Because there are only two variables in our example, the multiple correlation coefficient of .927 is equivalent to the Pearson correlation coefficient between sales and advertising. In any bivariate regression analysis, the square of the Pearson correlation coefficient between the dependent and independent variables will be the same as the value of the coefficient of determination.

■ **Testing the Significance of R²** The R^2-value is an important measure of how trustworthy a regression equation is: the higher the R^2-value, the more trustworthy the equation is. Nevertheless, the regression equation and its R^2-value are based only on sample data. Thus, depending on the nature of the data, we can sometimes obtain a high R^2-value when there is really no association between the dependent and independent variables in the population. For instance, suppose we obtained data on sales and advertising expenditures from a sample of just two markets chosen at random from a population of all such markets. A scatter diagram of these data will consist of just two points. We can fit a straight line through these points no matter where they are on the two-dimensional graph. Thus R^2 will be 1, because the fit will be perfect. But we cannot trust this regression line to be an accurate representation of any underlying association between sales and advertising. Thus a high R^2-value by itself is necessary but not sufficient to conclude that a regression equation is trustworthy.

We need a suitable test to verify whether a nonzero R^2-value stemming from a sample regression line truly reflects an underlying linear association in the population. We can check whether a sample R^2-value is significantly greater than zero by computing the following F-statistic:

$$F = \frac{SS_R/k}{SS_E/(n-k-1)}$$

where k is the number of independent variables included in the equation and n is the sample size (the number of data points).

To determine the critical value of F, we need to specify two types of degrees of freedom associated with the F-statistic: the numerator degrees of freedom, given by k, and the denominator degrees of freedom, given by $n-k-1$. Critical values of F are given in Appendix 5 for the customary significance level (α) of .05. In our example, $k = 1$ and $n - k - 1 = 18$. For these numerator and denominator degrees of freedom, the critical value of F from Appendix 5 is 4.41. The decision rule implied in this F-test is to reject the null hypothesis that R^2 is not significantly greater than zero if the computed F-statistic value is greater than its critical value.

The computed F-statistic value in our example is given by

$$F = \frac{571.646/1}{93.354/18} = \frac{571.646}{5.186} = 110.221$$

Because this F is greater than the critical F, we can infer that the R^2-value of .860 is statistically significant; it is unlikely to have occurred because of some idiosyncrasy in the sample data.

Now that we have covered the mechanics of conducting an F-test, let's formally define a couple of other important concepts implicit in the test, concepts that will be helpful in understanding certain other techniques, to be covered later. One such concept is the *mean square*, which is simply a sum-of-squares value divided by its corresponding degrees of freedom. Both the numerator of the F-statistic (SS_R/k) and its denominator ($SS_E/n-k-1$) are thus mean squares. Specifically, SS_R/k is the regression mean square, and we can interpret it as the average sum of the squared variations explained per independent variable. The term $SS_E/n-k-1$ is the error mean square (or residual mean square), and we can roughly interpret this as the average sum of the squared variations (per data point) left unexplained by the regression equation. With these interpretations, you can see why a high regression mean square and a low error mean square, and the resulting high F-value, will tend to support an inference that the R^2-value is statistically significant. The mean square values and the corresponding F-value are provided by the computer output (see Exhibit 14.5).

The square root of the error mean square is called the *standard error of the regression*. Conceptually, it is a sort of standard deviation of the portion of the variation in the dependent variable left unexplained by the independent variable (or variables, in a multiple regression equation). The conventional notation used for the standard error associated with a simple regression equation is $s_{y/x}$. It is given by

$$s_{y/x} = \sqrt{\frac{SS_E}{n - k - 1}}$$

The value of the standard error ($s_{y/x}$) is shown in Exhibit 14.5 (under "Std. Error of the Estimate") as 2.28, which is the square root of the error mean square value of 5.186. The concept of standard error is crucial in constructing confidence intervals around the predictions made by a regression equation. It is also relevant for evaluating whether the slope is significantly different from zero, as we discuss next.

■ **Testing the Significance of the Slope** An important element of evaluating the usefulness of a regression equation is checking whether the coefficient associated with an independent variable is significantly different from zero. A regression equation based on sample data (namely, $\hat{Y}_i = a + bX_i$) is a crude reflection of an underlying population regression equation, $\hat{Y}_i = \alpha + \beta X_i$, which can be constructed if data from all the population units are available. In other words, the slope b is merely a sample estimate of the population parameter β. Determining the statistical significance of the slope means testing the following hypotheses:

$$H_o: \beta = 0$$

$$H_a: \beta \neq 0$$

The appropriate test statistic here is a t-statistic, defined as

$$t = \frac{b - \beta}{s_b}$$

where S_b is the standard error associated with b and is given by

$$S_b = \sqrt{\frac{s_{y/x}^2}{(n - 1) s_x^2}}$$

where s_x is the standard deviation of the independent variable whose slope we are evaluating. The degrees of freedom for the t-statistic are $n - k - 1$ (d.f. $= 18$ in our example), and the hypothesis test is two-tailed. The critical values of t from Appendix 3 for a significance level of .05 are $+2.10$ and -2.10. Therefore, we should reject H_o if $t > 2.10$ or if $t < -2.10$.

Before computing t, we need to determine S_b. The standard deviation of advertising (s_x) turns out to be 4.534. Hence,

$$S_b = \sqrt{\frac{(2.28)^2}{(20 - 1)(4.534)^2}} = .115$$

This value is shown under "Std. Error" in the computer output in Exhibit 14.5. Thus

$$t = \frac{b - \beta}{s_b} = \frac{1.210 - 0}{.115} = 10.499$$

Advertising expenditures, number of competing brands, amount of shelf space allocated to a brand, and price are potential independent variables for a regression analysis intended to predict brand sales (dependent variable).

Because $t > 2.10$, we can reject H_o and conclude that the slope of 1.210 is significantly different from zero.

In simple regression analysis, the t-test for checking the significance of b is equivalent to the F-test for checking the significance of R^2. Indeed, the t-statistic value is simply the square root of the F-statistic value associated with R^2 (you can verify this statement in our example). You can also see the equivalence of the two tests by picturing the nature of the true regression line when b is zero: the line will be perfectly horizontal, implying that R^2 should be zero. Similarly, when the true R^2 is zero, β should also be zero. In multiple regression analysis, however, there is one overall F-test but several t-tests, one for each b-value. Therefore, the notion of equivalence between the F-test for R^2 and the t-tests is not very meaningful (we discuss this topic more fully later).

One final comment concerning the computer output in Exhibit 14.5: the number under the heading "Beta" is not the value of the true regression line's slope, β. Rather, it is simply the standardized regression coefficient; that is, the b-value when the data on all the variables are standardized (reduced to a mean of 0 and a standard deviation of 1) before performing the least squares regression analysis. One problem with looking at the regression coefficients is that they depend on the scale of the variables. If advertising expenditures had been measured in thousands of dollars (instead of in hundreds), the regression coefficients would have been much smaller. For this reason, many researchers prefer to use standardized coefficients (reported under column "Beta" in the SPSS output in Exhibit 14.5) that would have been obtained if the regression had been on standardized variables. Standardized regression coefficients are useful in multiple regression analysis because we can compare their magnitudes across independent variables to gain insight into the relative influence of each on the dependent variable. Consequently, the higher the value of the standardized regression coefficient, the greater the relative importance of that variable vis-à-vis the other independent variables in the regression equation.

Practical Applications of Regression Equations

We have covered quite a few details about constructing, interpreting, and evaluating regression equations. Now let's pause to look at some practical applications of simple regression equations before we discuss multiple regression equations.

Let's assume a regression equation is trustworthy; that is, it has a high enough and statistically significant R^2-value. (There is no rule telling us what R^2-value can be considered high enough; for practical purposes, however, R^2-values of around .7 or higher are usually adequate.) The regression equation can be helpful in two ways.

First, the regression coefficient, or slope, can indicate how sensitive the dependent variable is to changes in the independent variable. To illustrate, suppose the firm marketing Bright detergent currently spends \$2,000 on advertising the detergent in a particular market. It is considering a 20 percent reduction in its advertising budget and wants to know by how much sales revenue might decline in this market as a result. The information the firm desires can be obtained from the slope b of the regression equation we derived:

$$b = 1.210$$

which, taking into account the units of measurement of X and Y, means sales revenue will decline by $1,210 for every $100 reduction in advertising expenditures. Also, the proposed reduction in advertising expenditures $= \$2,000 \times .2 = \$400$. Therefore,

$$\text{Anticipated decline in sales revenue} = \frac{1,210 \times 400}{100} = \$4,840$$

Second, the regression equation is a forecasting tool for predicting the value of the dependent variable for a given value of the independent variable. For example, suppose the firm marketing Bright wants to forecast sales revenue from a market in which it intends to spend $750 on advertising the detergent. We obtain the needed forecast by simply substituting the value of 7.50 for X_i (recall that advertising expenditures are expressed in hundreds of dollars in the regression equation) into the regression equation and solving for $\hat{Y}_i$.

$$\hat{Y}_i = .163 + 1.210X_i = .163 + 1.210(7.5) = .163 + 9.075 = 9.238$$

Because sales revenue is expressed in thousands of dollars in the regression equation, the forecast in dollars is given by

$$9.238 \times \$1,000 = \$9,238$$

Most practical applications of regression analysis revolve around some form of forecasting. Not all applications are for forecasting sales, however.[10] The examples in Research in Use 14.2 demonstrate a wide variety of circumstances in which regression analysis can provide valuable insights.

Precautions in Using Regression Analysis

The wide popularity of regression analysis and the ready access to computer programs capable of performing it offer a strong temptation to researchers to rush into using the technique without ascertaining whether it is appropriate and without giving much thought to its pitfalls. However, potential users of regression analysis must be aware of several key limitations that, if ignored, can result in erroneous inferences.[11] This section discusses the limitations in the context of simple regression analysis; the same limitations apply to multiple regression analysis (to be discussed in the next section).

First, just as in the case of correlation analysis, regression analysis is capable of capturing only linear associations between dependent and independent variables. The regression technique we have covered is not appropriate when the scatter diagram does not display a meaningful linear trend.[12]

Second, a regression equation with a significant R^2-value does not necessarily imply a cause-and-effect association between the independent and dependent variables. This point is particularly noteworthy; the convention of labeling one variable "dependent" and the other "independent" may persuade careless researchers that the former is definitely caused by the latter when the regression results are statistically significant. But the fact is that a particular direction of causality between two variables must stem from prior knowledge and theoretical

Regression Applications: Illustrative Scenarios Calling for Regression Analysis

Scenario	Possible Dependent Variable	Possible Independent Variable
Curtis is a construction industry lobbyist in an economically depressed area of the country. His current charge is to convince local government officials to vote in favor of several tax concessions for the construction industry. He is wondering whether he can generate any concrete evidence to show that increased construction activity (presumably spurred by the proposed tax concessions) would greatly benefit the state.	Number of people unemployed or the unemployment rate; data on this variable may be gathered from a sample of areas from around the country.	Number of construction permits issued or number of ongoing construction projects; data on this variable should be gathered from the same sample.
Carol, chief librarian at a major university, is eager to increase the number of students borrowing books from the library, as well as the number of books borrowed per student. However, she feels she needs some persuasive evidence to show how increased book borrowing might benefit students.	Cumulative grade point ratio; data on this variable should be gathered for a sample of students who have borrowed books in the past.	Number of books borrowed; assuming that the library has records of the books borrowed by students, data on this variable can be obtained from those records for the same sample of students.
Jack, an officer in an association in charge of putting together and promoting industrial trade shows, is wondering about the nature and extent of the impact of number of exhibitors on trade show attendance.	Number of people visiting a trade show; from the association's past records; data on this variable can be obtained for a representative sample of trade shows.	Number of exhibitors in a trade show; the necessary data can be obtained from past records.

considerations rather than from mathematical manipulation of data on the variables. Thus the researcher, not the regression technique, specifies which is the dependent and which is the independent variable.

To illustrate, consider the second scenario in Research in Use 14.2. Suppose Carol, the librarian, conducts a regression analysis of data on cumulative grade point ratio (dependent variable) and number of books borrowed (independent variable) and obtains a statistically significant R^2-value of .9. Does this result mean that high grade point ratios are a result of increased borrowing from the library? The inference does not necessarily follow. Although Carol may be tempted to make such an inference, there is another plausible explanation for the regression results: students borrowing a large number of books may have done so because they were studious and had high grade point ratios to begin with. In other words, Carol can switch the dependent and independent variables in the regression equation and still obtain a high R^2-value.

Third, a regression equation may not yield a trustworthy prediction of the dependent variable when the value of the independent variable at which the prediction is desired is outside the range of values used in constructing the equation. For example, the range of advertising expenditures used in deriving the regression equation for Bright detergent's sales was $500 to $1,900. We take a risk in using this regression equation to predict sales revenue corresponding to an advertising expenditure level of, say, $50 or $2,500. We do not know whether the scatter diagram would follow the same linear trend if it were extended at either end by

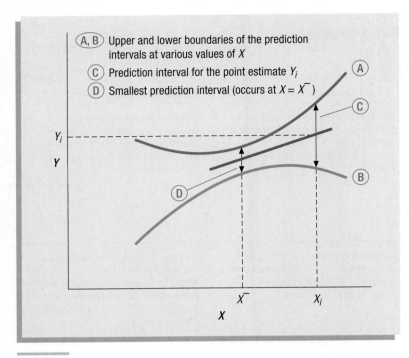

A, B Upper and lower boundaries of the prediction intervals at various values of X

C Prediction interval for the point estimate Y_i

D Smallest prediction interval (occurs at $X = \bar{X}$)

Exhibit 14.7
Prediction Intervals Corresponding to a Regression Line

plotting new data points. In fact, even within the original range of independent variable values, prediction errors will increase as we move away from the sample mean ($\bar{X}$) value in either direction.

The regression equation's prediction for a given value of the independent variable is merely a point estimate. We can construct a prediction interval (similar to the 95 percent confidence intervals discussed in Chapter 11) around each such estimate. A 95 percent prediction interval, for instance, is the range of values within which we can be 95 percent confident that the actual value of the dependent variable (corresponding to the given value of the independent variable) will fall. Formulas needed to construct prediction intervals are available in many statistics textbooks.[13] The resulting intervals at various levels of the independent variable form a sort of hourglass shape, as shown in Exhibit 14.7.

Fourth, a regression equation based on relatively few data points cannot be trusted. As we saw earlier, a simple regression equation based on just two data points will have an R^2-value of 1, no matter where those points are. Sample size and hence the number of data points available are especially critical in multiple regression analysis. Including too many independent variables when the sample size is small will lead to an artificially high R^2-value. A rule of thumb is to have at least 10 sample units for every independent variable included in the equation.

Fifth, the ranges of data on the dependent and independent variables can affect the meaningfulness of a regression equation. The ranges for both variables must be sufficiently wide if the regression equation is to be useful. Deriving a meaningful regression line when data on either variable span only a narrow range will be difficult.

Multiple Regression Analysis

Multiple regression analysis is useful when more than one independent variable is likely to be associated with a dependent variable and when ascertaining the contribution of all such independent variables in accounting for variation in the dependent variable is necessary. We can write a multiple regression equation with k independent variables as follows:

$$\hat{Y}_i = a + b_1 X_{1i} + b_2 X_{2i} + \ldots + b_k X_{ki}$$

where $\hat{Y}_i$ is the predicted value of the dependent variable for some unit i; X_{1i}, X_{2i}, $\ldots$, X_{ki} are values of the independent variables for unit i; b_1, b_2, $\ldots$, b_k are the regression coefficients (slopes) for the corresponding independent variables; and a is the Y-intercept representing the prediction for Y when all independent variables are set to zero. The slopes b_1 through b_k have the same interpretation as in simple regression analysis. For instance, b_k represents the change in Y per unit change in X_k, assuming the values of all other variables remain the same.

The Y-intercept and slopes are determined by using a least squares procedure similar to the one we discussed for simple regression analysis. We can readily obtain their values by using standard computer packages once a data set (like the one in Table 14.3) has been created. Research in Use 14.3 describes the procedure for conducting multiple regression analysis using SPSS for the National Insurance Company data.

Advertising expenditures for Bright detergent were the only independent variable in the regression equation discussed in the preceding section. But, as we saw when we discussed correlation analysis, number of competing brands was also strongly associated with Bright's sales. Therefore, examining a regression equation with both advertising and number of competing brands as independent variables may be interesting. The SPSS output for the multiple regression analysis of the data set in Table 14.3 is shown in Exhibit 14.8.

Exhibit 14.8
SPSS Computer Output for a Multiple Regression Analysis of the Data in Table 14.3

Model Summary

Model	R	R Square	Adjusted R Square	Std. Error of the Estimate
1	.934[a]	.873	.858	2.23

[a] **Predictors:** (constant), number of competing detergents, advertising expenditures for Bright ($ hundreds)

ANOVA[b]

Model		Sum of Squares	d.f.	Mean Square	F	Sig.
1	Regression	580.373	2	290.187	58.293	.000[a]
	Residual	84.627	17	4.978		
	Total	665.000	19			

[a] **Predictors:** (constant), number of competing detergents, advertising expenditures for Bright ($ hundreds)
[b] **Dependent variable:** dollar sales of Bright ($ thousands)

Coefficients[a]

Model		Unstandardized Coefficients B	Unstandardized Coefficients Std. Error	Standardized Coefficients Beta	t	Sig.
1	(Constant)	8.854	6.717		1.318	.205
	Advertising expenditures for Bright ($ hundreds)	.808	.324	.619	2.496	.023
	Number of competing detergents	−.498	.376	−.328	−1.324	.203

[a] **Dependent variable:** dollar sales of Bright ($ thousands)

National Insurance Company:
Multiple Regression Using SPSS

Jill and Tom are interested in conducting a multiple regression analysis in which overall service quality perception is the dependent variable and the average ratings along the five dimensions are the independent variables. SPSS dialog boxes are shown below.

In SSPS

1. Click ANALYZE
2. Select REGRESSION
3. Click LINEAR

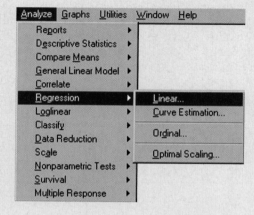

For Linear Regression

4. Move oq to DEPENDENT box
5. Move reliable, empathy, tangible, response, and assure to INDEPENDENT(S) box
6. Click OK

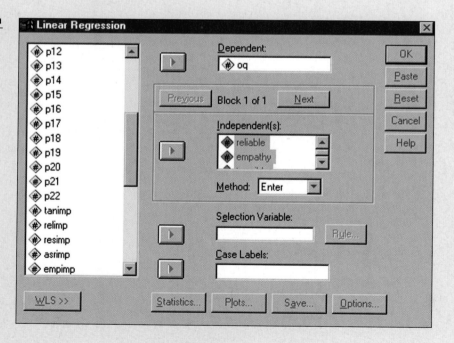

SPSS output is shown below. Note that all variables except empathy are significantly related to overall service quality (as indicated by the t-test of significance in the far right column). The R^2 of .810 indicates a strong relationship between these variables and overall quality.

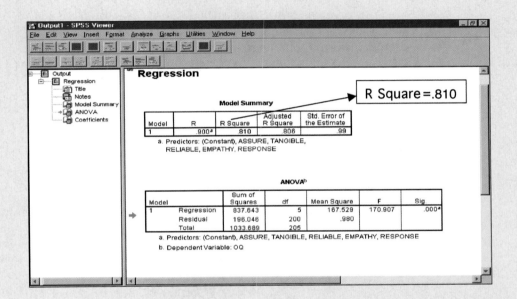

Regression

Coefficients*

| Model | Understandardized Coefficients | | Standardized Coefficients | | |
	B	Std. Error	Beta	t	Sig.
1 (Constant)	.263	.394		.668	.505
RELIABILITY	.505	.101	.327	5.003	.000
EMPATHY	.123	.115	.076	1.075	.284
TANGIBLES	−.198	.085	−.093	−2.333	.021
RESPONSIVENESS	.247	.133	.167	1.858	.065
ASSURANCE	.685	.135	.428	5.053	.000

*Dependent variable: oq.

Advertising expenditures and number of competing detergent brands are the independent variables. Except for the addition of one row corresponding to number of competing detergent brands, the format of this computer output is the same as the format of the simple regression analysis output (Exhibit 14.5). Using Y to represent sales (in thousands of dollars), X_1 to represent advertising expenditures (in hundreds of dollars), and X_2 to represent number of competing detergent brands (in actual number of competing detergent brands), we can write the regression equation as

$$\hat{Y} = 8.854 + .808X_1 - .498X_2$$

In this equation, the subscript i is omitted from the variables for simplicity. Also, we obtain the values of a (8.854), b_1 (.808), and b_2 (−.498) directly from the computer output. The negative sign of b_2 stems from the inverse relationship between sales of Bright and number of competing brands (see Exhibit 14.2).

The R^2-value for this multiple regression equation is .873. Thus advertising expenditures and number of competing brands together account for a little more than 87 percent of the total variation in sales of Bright. The F-statistic value for this R^2 is 58.293, with degrees of freedom $k = 2$ for the numerator and $n - k - 1 = 17$ for the denominator. The critical F-value for a significance level of .05 is 3.59 (from Appendix 5). Because the calculated F-value is greater than the critical value, we can infer that the R^2-value is statistically significant and that the regression equation is trustworthy.

A statistically significant R^2-value in multiple regression analysis does not necessarily mean that all regression coefficients (b) are significantly different from zero. Each b-value must be checked separately for statistical significance, using a t-test similar to the one for checking the significance of a simple regression coefficient. Because there are two independent variables in our multiple regression equation, we must test two sets of hypotheses:

$$H_o: \beta_1 = 0 \quad \text{and} \quad H_a: \beta_1 \neq 0$$

and

$$H_o: \beta_2 = 0 \quad \text{and} \quad H_a: \beta_2 \neq 0$$

The value of the t-statistic for each regression coefficient is shown in the computer output in Exhibit 14.8. The degrees of freedom for the t-statistic are $n - k - 1 = 17$. Assuming a significance level of .05, the critical values for t for a two-tailed hypothesis test are 2.11 and −2.11 (from Appendix 3). The t-value for b_2 is negative.

Comparing these t-values with the critical t-values, b_1 is significantly different from zero, but b_2 is not. In other words, according to our multiple regression results, although advertising apparently has a significant association with sales, the number of competing brands does not. This finding is somewhat puzzling because, as we saw earlier, the Pearson correlation coefficient between sales and number of competing brands is quite high (−.909) and statistically significant. The explanation for this apparent anomaly lies in the fact that the two independent variables are strongly associated with each other, as we see by scanning the last two columns in the data set shown in Table 14.3. When independent variables in a multiple regression equation are highly correlated among themselves, the problem of **multicollinearity** is said to exist. Interpretation of individual regression coefficients is very difficult and can be misleading when multicollinearity is present, as we will see in the next section.

Multicollinearity exists when independent variables in a multiple regression equation are highly correlated among themselves.

Implications of Multicollinearity

Multicollinearity is a frequently encountered problem. We must check for its presence before we interpret a multiple regression equation. Most computer packages provide a matrix of correlations among all variables as part of the regression analysis output. Exhibit 14.9 contains the matrix of correlations printed by the SPSS program used to derive the multiple regression equation for sales of Bright.

The high correlation between advertising expenditures and number of competing brands in Exhibit 14.9 implies that interpreting their regression coefficients is risky. Every user of the multiple regression technique must examine such a correlation matrix and exercise caution in interpreting the coefficient (slope) of any independent variable that is strongly associated with one or more other independent variables.

A comprehensive discussion of the rationale underlying the difficulty in interpreting regression coefficients when multicollinearity exists can be found elsewhere.[14] However, we can intuitively see why there is difficulty if we reexamine the general interpretation of a regression coefficient: it is the change in the dependent variable per unit change in the independent variable, *assuming all other variables remain the same*. The emphasized words here refer to a condition that cannot be met when there is multicollinearity. In other words, a high correlation between two independent variables implies that a change in one will be accompanied by a corresponding change in the other. Hence, we will have difficulty sorting out the individual contributions of the independent variables in accounting for variations in the dependent variable.[15]

Exhibit 14.9
SSPS Computer Output for a Pairwise Correlation Analysis of the Data in Table 14.3

Correlations		Dollar Sales of Bright (thousands of dollars)	Advertising Expenditures for Bright (hundreds of dollars)	Number of Competing Detergents
Dollar sales of Bright ($ thousands)	Pearson correlation	1.000	.927	−.909**
	Sig. (2-tailed)	—	.000	.000
	N	20	20	20
Advertising expenditures for Bright ($ hundreds)	Pearson correlation	.927**	1.000	.937**
	Sig. (2-tailed)	.000	—	.000
	N	20	20	20
Number of competing detergents	Pearson correlation	−.909**	.937**	1.000
	Sig. (2-tailed)	.000	.000	—
	N	20	20	20

** Correlation is significant at the 0.01 level (2-tailed).

The simple and multiple regression analyses of the data related to Bright detergent yielded two different values for the regression coefficient of advertising expenditures. It was 1.210 in the simple regression analysis (Exhibit 14.5) and .808 in the multiple regression analysis (Exhibit 14.8), despite the fact that the same set of data on sales and advertising was used in both cases. The lower *b*-value in the multiple regression analysis is due to advertising's high correlation with number of competing brands. Neither the regression coefficient of .808 for advertising expenditures nor the regression coefficient of $-.498$ for number of competing brands has a clear-cut interpretation because of the extensive overlap between the two variables. Had the correlation between them been weak, advertising's regression coefficient in the multiple regression analysis would have been close to its original value of 1.210. Moreover, we could have meaningfully interpreted the standardized regres-sion coefficients (listed under the heading "Beta" in the computer output) for number of competing brands and advertising expenditures. Specifically, if number of competing brands and advertising expenditures were only weakly correlated, the relative magnitudes of their standardized regression coefficients (.328 for number of competing brands and .619 for advertising expenditures) would imply that advertising expenditures were almost twice as important as number of competing brands in accounting for the variation in Bright's sales.

The presence of multicollinearity does not necessarily mean the regression equation is useless. As long as the R^2-value is high and statistically significant, we can still use the equation for predicting *Y* if we are given values for all the independent variables. One caveat, however, is that the relative values of the independent variables must be consistent with the general pattern of values in the data set used to derive the multiple regression equation.

For instance, consider the multiple regression equation derived for sales of Bright. The input data on advertising and number of competing brands (Table 14.3) are never both high or low. For this reason, the two variables have a strong negative correlation. If we want to predict Bright's sales for a pair of new values of the independent variables, one of them must be high and the other low for the prediction to be meaningful. Thus, for example, the equation's prediction of sales when advertising is $650 and number of competing brands is two is unlikely to be trustworthy; both values are low compared to the range of values in the data set.

Multicollinearity is not the only potential limitation of multiple regression analysis. The precautions we discussed under simple regression analysis apply to multiple regression analysis as well, and they must be heeded to avoid making misleading inferences. These precautions include (1) bearing in mind that regression analysis captures only the extent of linear relationship between dependent and independent variables; (2) not inferring cause-and-effect associations solely from statistically significant regression results; (3) exercising caution in predicting the dependent variable for independent variable values that fall outside the ranges used in constructing the regression equation; (4) ensuring that there are enough data points (a rule of thumb is to have at least 10 data points for each independent variable); and (5) ensuring that the ranges of data on all variables are sufficiently wide.

A few final remarks about regression analysis are in order. Despite the rather extensive treatment of the technique in this chapter, we covered only the fundamentals necessary to give you a basic understanding of it, including its capabilities and limitations. Students wishing to gain a comprehensive understanding of regression analysis will benefit from additional reading.[16]

SUMMARY

This chapter deals with procedures for ascertaining and interpreting associations between variables. The Spearman correlation coefficient r_s is a measure of association when the data on variables are ordinal and in the form of ranks of the sample units on each variable. This coefficient will range from $+1$ to -1, with a value of zero signifying no correlation. Its statistical significance can be verified by conducting a t-test.

The Pearson correlation coefficient is a widely used measure of association between metric (interval or ratio) variables. It is a number ranging from $+1$ to -1 and summarizes the degree of compactness as well as the direction of a scatter diagram, which is a plot of the data on the variables. Whether this correlation coefficient is significantly different from zero can be determined easily given its value, the sample size, and a desired significance level. A limitation of the Pearson correlation coefficient is that it can capture only the degree of linear association between variables. Furthermore, evidence of a strong correlation by itself does not constitute evidence of causality in any particular direction.

Simple regression analysis is similar to correlation analysis, except that it generates a mathematical relationship (called the *regression equation*) between one variable designated as the dependent variable (Y) and another designated as the independent variable (X). An independent variable is typically assumed to influence the dependent variable in some fashion. The regression equation, $\hat{Y}_i = a + bX_i$, is derived by fitting a straight line through the scatter diagram to minimize the error sum of squares (SS_E). This procedure is called the *least squares technique* and is available in several computer packages. The constant a is called the Y-intercept, and the regression coefficient b is called the *slope*. The slope has an important interpretation: it is the change in the predicted value of Y per unit change in X when all other variables likely to influence X remain the same.

Several indicators are available to check the usefulness of a regression equation. One that is commonly examined is the coefficient of determination R^2. The value of R^2 can range from 0 to 1 and is a measure of the proportion of the total variance in Y that is accounted for by predictions made by the regression equation. The higher the R^2-value, the better the regression equation is. The statistical significance of R^2 can be checked by using an F-test. The square root of R^2 is called the *multiple correlation coefficient*. In bivariate regression analysis, the multiple correlation coefficient is the same as the Pearson correlation coefficient. A related measure of goodness of a regression equation is the standard error of the regression $s_{y/x}$, which is a sort of average variation in Y left unexplained by the regression equation. The smaller the value of $s_{y/x}$, the better the regression equation is.

Another way to evaluate a regression equation is to see whether the slope is significantly different from zero. A t-test is employed for this purpose. The F-test for the significance of R^2 and the t-test for the significance of b are equivalent in simple regression analysis.

Two practical applications of simple regression analysis are to ascertain changes in the dependent variable when the independent variable changes by a specified amount and to predict the value of the dependent variable for a given value of the independent variable. In interpreting and using the regression equation, however, researchers must keep several potential pitfalls in mind. Regression analysis by itself cannot establish causality between variables. Regression equations based on nonlinear scatter diagrams, on a limited number of data points, or on data spanning relatively narrow ranges are unlikely to be meaningful. Also, it is risky to make predictions of the dependent variables for values of the independent variable that fall outside the range of data used in deriving the regression equation.

Multiple regression analysis is a logical extension of simple regression analysis and involves two or more independent variables. The analytical procedures and the interpretation of the results are quite similar in both cases. The limitations of simple regression analysis apply to multiple regression analysis as well. A key difference between the two techniques is that statistical significance of the R^2-value of a multiple regression equation (based on an F-test) does not automatically mean that all the regression coefficients (b-values) are significantly different from zero. Each regression coefficient must be individually evaluated by using a t-test. Furthermore, a potentially serious problem in multiple regression analysis is multicollinearity, the presence of strong correlations among independent variables. When multicollinearity exists, caution must be exercised in interpreting the values of individual regression coefficients.

ACE
self-test

REVIEW AND DISCUSSION QUESTIONS

1. What are the key differences between simple regression and correlation analyses?

2. Clearly summarize in a sentence or two what the least squares approach to regression analysis does. (*Hint:* Go to this textbook's website for details on the least squares approach.)

3. What is the distinction between simple and multiple regression analyses?

4. What is multicollinearity? What implications does the presence of multicollinearity have for the interpretation and use of a regression equation?

APPLICATION EXERCISES

1. Ace Chemicals, Inc. (ACI), selected 15 of its customer firms at random and rank ordered them from highest (rank 1) to lowest (rank 15) on the basis of the volume of their purchases from ACI. It then rank ordered the same 15 firms according to how formalized their purchasing operations were (rank for most formalized = 1 and rank for least formalized = 15). For the firms ranked 1 through 15 in terms of purchase volume, the following ranks reflect the degree of formalized purchasing operations: 3, 4, 2, 1, 5, 8, 13, 7, 6, 11, 9, 10, 15, 12, 14. Compute the Spearman correlation coefficient between customer purchase volume from ACI and formalization of customers' purchasing operations. Use SPSS to derive the Spearman correlation coefficient. How do you interpret this correlation coefficient? Is this correlation coefficient statistically significant? Why or why not?

2. The sales manager of a firm administered a standard, multiple-item job satisfaction scale to a sample of the firm's sales force. The manager then correlated the satisfaction scores with the ages of the salespeople in the sample. The Pearson correlation coefficient between satisfaction and age turned out to be .08. On the basis of this evidence, the sales manager came to the following conclusions: "A salesperson's age has little to do with his or her satisfaction. Furthermore, as salespeople get older, they continue to have the same average levels of job satisfaction." Do you agree or disagree with the sales manager's conclusions? Explain your answer.

3. Using SPSS, compute the Pearson correlation coefficient for the data in question 1. How does this coefficient compare with the Spearman correlation coefficient computed earlier? From this comparison, what inference can you make about marketing researchers' frequent assumption that ordinal data have interval properties?

4. Exhibit 14.10 shows the SPSS output for the simple regression analysis of the data on sales (expressed in thousands of dollars) and number of competing detergents given in Table 14.3. Notice that the format of Exhibit 14.10 is identical to that of Exhibit 14.5. Use the output of Exhibit 14.10 to answer the following questions:

   a. Identify the Y-intercept and slope values, and interpret those values.
   b. Write the regression equation linking predicted sales of Bright and the number of competing detergent brands.
   c. What is the R^2-value associated with the regression equation? Is it statistically significant? Why or why not?
   d. Verify that $R^2 = SS_R/SS_T$ and give a verbal interpretation of the R^2-value.
   e. Circle the number representing the Pearson correlation coefficient between the two variables.
   f. Verify that the square root of the error mean square is the standard error of the regression.
   g. Is the slope of the regression equation statistically significant? Why or why not?
   h. Use the implied regression equation to predict sales for Bright in a market in which it will have 19 competing detergent brands. Is this prediction meaningful? Explain your answer.
   i. Bright currently has five competing detergent brands in a certain market area. The firm expects five additional competing brands to enter the market in the near future. What impact will the new detergent brands have on Bright's monthly dollar sales in this market area? What precautions should you take in interpreting the estimated impact?

5. The results for a regression analysis of a dependent variable (Y) and two independent variables $(X_1$ and $X_2)$ from a sample of 30 observations are shown in the table below.

   a. Is the R^2-value statistically significant? Why or why not?

Means	$\bar{Y} = 3{,}000$	$\bar{X}_1 = 100$	$\bar{X}_2 = 150$
Standard deviations	$S_y = 25$	$S_{x_1} = 30$	$S_{x_2} = 20$
Correlation coefficients	$r_{yx_1} = .75$	$r_{yx_2} = .95$	$r_{x_1x_2} = .8$
Estimated regression equation		$\hat{y} = 1{,}000 + 5X_1 + 10X_2$	
$R^2 = .85$		F-value associated with $R^2 = 5.78$	

Exhibit 14.10
SPSS Computer Output for a
Simple Regression Analysis of
Sales and Number of Competing
Brands

Model Summary

Model	R	R Square	Adjusted R Square	Std. Error of the Estimate
1	.909[a]	.826	.816	2.53

[a] **Predictors:** (constant), number of competing detergents

ANOVA[b]

Model		Sum of Squares	d.f.	Mean Square	F	Sig.
1	Regression	549.348	1	549.348	85.500	.000[a]
	Residual	115.652	18	6.425		
	Total	665.000	19			

[a] **Predictors:** (constant), number of competing detergents
[b] **Dependent variable:** dollar sales of Bright ($ thousands)

Coefficients[a]

Model		Unstandardized Coefficients		Standardized Coefficients	t	Sig.
		B	Std. Error	Beta		
1	(Constant)	25.377	1.306	—	19.435	.000
	Number of competing detergents	−1.377	.149	−.909	−9.247	.000

[a] **Dependent variable:** dollar sales of Bright ($ thousands)

b. Can you meaningfully determine the change in Y when X_1 is increased by one unit? If you can, what is the change in Y? If you cannot, why not?

c. What proportion of the variance of Y is not explained by the regression equation? What does this result say about how good the regression equation is?

💿 SPSS EXERCISES

1. Jill Baxter, vice president of customer service for National Insurance Company, and her assistant, Tom Kurtis, want you to analyze the correlations among the five items of reliability (questions 1 through 5, labeled p1, p2, p3, p4, and p5) and overall service quality perceptions, labeled oq (on the 10-point scale). What are the correlations among the five reliability items and overall service quality? Are these correlations statistically significant? Use SPSS or Excel to perform the analysis.

2. Jill and Tom are wondering how the various items of reliability (questions 1 through 5, labeled p1, p2, p3, p4, and p5) are related to overall service quality perceptions, labeled oq. Conduct a multiple regression analysis wherein overall service quality perception (oq) is the dependent variable and the five items of reliability (p1, p2, p3, p4, and p5) are the independent variables. What specific inferences can you make from the results of the analysis? Examine the standardized regression coefficients and comment on the relative influence of each independent variable on the dependent variable.

CASE 14.1 ATHENAEUM BOOKSELLERS (PART A)

The retail book business is highly competitive, and Constantine Karvonides knew, when he first took the helm at Athenaeum Booksellers, that, to compete with large national bookstore chains, he would need to develop a strong product offering with high levels of service. He had just commissioned a research study to gauge the level of customer satisfaction with current operations and was looking over some of the results, trying to get a sense of how customers perceived the store.

Background

Homer Karvonides first opened Athenaeum Booksellers in downtown San Francisco 35 years ago, and his son Constantine took it over during the last 5 years. Homer stayed on in an advisory role because he had a good sense of local customers' changing needs and had built strong loyalty among them, knowing many of them on a first-name basis.

Athenaeum is located in a high-traffic area, with convenient access to major commercial thoroughfares and ample parking. The store offers extended shopping hours, generally 9:00 A.M. to 11:00 P.M., seven days a week. The store is approximately 40,000 square feet and features an extensive selection of books ranging from 100,000 to 120,000 titles. Athenaeum's merchandising strategy is to be the authoritative community bookstore that carries a dominant selection of titles in all subjects, including an extensive assortment from small independent publishers and university presses. The comprehensive title selection is diverse and reflects the interests of both the local community and visitors to the area. Athenaeum also offers a broader range of books online, which customers can have shipped to the store or directly to their home. Constantine Karvonides believes that the tremendous selection, including many otherwise hard-to-find titles, helps build customer loyalty to Athenaeum. Athenaeum's close connection to customers also strengthens its market position and increases its perceived value.

Exhibit 1
Book Store: Correlations

Variables: visually appealing performance (VAPER); availability of books on discount performance (ABDPER); convenient store hours performance (CSHPER); low price performance (LOPRIPER); overall perceived value (VALUE)

Correlations

		VAPER	ABDPER	CSHPER	LOPRIPER	VALUE
VAPER	Pearson Correlation	1	−.301**	.370**	−.016	−.028
	Sig. (2-tailed)	—	.000	.000	.846	.743
	N	142	142	142	142	142
ABDPER	Pearson Correlation	−.301**	1	−.341**	.100	.328**
	Sig. (2-tailed)	.000	—	.000	.238	.000
	N	142	142	142	142	142
CSHPER	Pearson Correlation	.370**	−.341**	1	.411**	.323**
	Sig. (2-tailed)	.000	.000	—	.000	.000
	N	142	142	142	142	142
LOPRIPER	Pearson Correlation	−.016	.100	.411**	1	.504**
	Sig. (2-tailed)	.846	.238	.000	—	.000
	N	142	142	142	142	142
VALUE	Pearson Correlation	−.028	.328**	.323**	.504**	1
	Sig. (2-tailed)	.743	.000	.000	.000	—
	N	142	142	142	142	142

** Correlation is significant at the 0.01 level (2-tailed).

Besides its comprehensive title base, Athenaeum Booksellers offers a café, a children's section, a music department, a magazine section, and a calendar of ongoing events, including author appearances and children's activities, which make it an active part of the community. Athenaeum creates a comfortable atmosphere with ample public reading space. The café offers coffee, tea, sandwiches, and bakery items; listening stations for customers to preview compact discs; and public restrooms. The café further enhances the ambience of the bookstore as a community meeting place. In addition, the company continues to develop and introduce new offerings to meet customers' changing tastes and needs. These offerings and services have helped make the store a neighborhood institution.

Exhibit 2
Book Store: Multiple Regression

Dependent variable: overall satisfaction (OSAT)

Independent variables: overall perceived value (VALUE); convenient store hours performance (CSHPER); low price performance (LOPRIPER); visually appealing performance (VAPER); availability of books on discount performance (ABDPER)

Model Summary

Model	R	R Square	Adjusted R Square	Std. Error of the Estimate
1	.809[a]	.655	.642	.343

[a] **Predictors:** (constant), VALUE, VAPER, CSHPER, LOPRIPER, ABDPER

ANOVA[b]

Model		Sum of Squares	d.f.	Mean Square	F	Sig.
1	Regression	30.376	5	6.075	51.672	.000[a]
	Residual	15.990	136	.118		
	Total	46.366	141			

[a] **Predictors:** (constant), VALUE, VAPER, CSHPER, LOPRIPER, ABDPER
[b] **Dependent variable:** OSAT

Coefficients[a]

Model		Unstandardized Coefficients		Standardized Coefficients		
		B	Std. Error	Beta	t	Sig.
1	(Constant)	−.886	.436		−2.030	.044
	VAPER	6.502E-02	.043	.085	1.511	.133
	ABDPER	.155	.031	.314	5.040	.000
	CSHPER	.590	.099	.405	5.949	.000
	LOPRIPER	.133	.041	.201	3.241	.001
	VALUE	.201	.038	.341	5.224	.000

[a] **Dependent variable:** OSAT

Athenaeum also offers Bookreaders Advantage memberships, which entitle the customer to receive a 10 percent discount in the company's stores and a 5 percent discount at the Athenaeum.com website. Bookreaders Advantage also offers other benefits and invitations to members-only events.

The Survey

The survey, designed by a local research firm, was used to assess consumer satisfaction with a number of different aspects of Athenaeum bookstores. (A copy of the survey is presented at the end of this case.) The survey was administered to individuals who visited the store over a one-week period. It was administered each day of the week at different times of the day to obtain a good cross-section of different customers. A total of 142 usable surveys were completed, and the research director of the firm had conducted some preliminary analysis of the data using SPSS software. (Exhibits 1 and 2 show output from the analyses.) He brought the output of certain correlation and regression analyses to Constantine Karvonides.

CASE QUESTIONS

1. Help Constantine Karvonides interpret the correlation results provided in Exhibit 1.[1] He is given the correlations among the following six variables: visually appealing performance (VAPER); availability of books on discount performance (ABDPER); convenient store hours performance (CSHPER); low prices performance (LOPRIPER); and overall perceived value (VALUE). Interpret the correlations in terms of whether or not they are significant, the size of the effect, the direction of the effect, and managerial relevance.

2. Help Constantine Karvonides interpret the regression results provided in Exhibit 2. The dependent variable is overall satisfaction (OSAT). The independent variables are overall perceived value (VALUE); convenient store hours performance (CSHPER); low price performance (LOPRIPER); visually appealing performance (VAPER); and availability of books on discount performance (ABDPER). Interpret the regression analysis in terms of the overall significance of the model and the percentage of variance explained. Also assess the effects of each individual independent variable in terms of its significance, overall relative size of effect (standardized beta) and the direction of the effect.

CASE NOTE

1. The data in this case are real, but the name of the company is disguised.

This case was written by Jeanne L. Munger (University of Southern Maine) in collaboration with the textbook authors, as a basis for class discussion rather than to illustrate either effective or ineffective marketing practice.

Customer Satisfaction Survey

Please take a few minutes to complete this questionnaire. Thank you in advance for your time.

Section I: *Please indicate the <u>importance</u> of the item and your <u>satisfaction</u> with that item in regards to the Athenaeum Booksellers.*

Importance Scale
1 = Very Unimportant
2 = Unimportant
3 = Neutral
4 = Important
5 = Very Important

Performance Scale
1 = Very Poor
2 = Poor
3 = Neutral
4 = Good
5 = Very Good

Importance					Item	Performance				
1	2	3	4	5	**Visually Appealing**	1	2	3	4	5
1	2	3	4	5	**Wide Selection**	1	2	3	4	5
1	2	3	4	5	**Knowledgeable Staff**	1	2	3	4	5
1	2	3	4	5	**Ease of Finding Books**	1	2	3	4	5
1	2	3	4	5	**Availability of Books on Discount**	1	2	3	4	5
1	2	3	4	5	**Friendly Service**	1	2	3	4	5

1	2	3	4	5	*Availability of Magazines/Papers*	1	2	3	4	5
1	2	3	4	5	*Availability of Tables/Couches*	1	2	3	4	5
1	2	3	4	5	*Restaurant/Coffee Service*	1	2	3	4	5
1	2	3	4	5	*Convenient Store Hours*	1	2	3	4	5
1	2	3	4	5	*Cleanliness*	1	2	3	4	5
1	2	3	4	5	*Low Prices*	1	2	3	4	5

Please indicate your overall satisfaction with Athenaeum Booksellers:

Very Dissatisfied   1   2   3   4   5   **Very Satisfied**

Based on your experience at Athenaeum, how likely are you to visit Athenaeum again?

Very Unlikely   1   2   3   4   5   **Very Likely**

Overall, rate the value of product and service you received at Athenaeum for the money paid:

Poor Value   1   2   3   4   5   **Excellent Value**

Would you recommend Athenaeum to a friend?

_____ Yes;   _____ Not sure;   _____ No.

Have you ever used the Internet to purchase a book (online purchase)?

_____ No **(please go to Section II)**

_____ Yes; please specify the website _____

How do you rate your buying experience on the Internet?

Very Bad   1   2   3   4   5   **Very Good**

How likely are you to buy books on the Internet in the future?

Very Unlikely   1   2   3   4   5   **Very Likely**

Have you visited www.athenaeum.com (the website)?

_____ Yes;   _____ No **(please go to Section II)**

How do you rate the www.athenaeum.com website?

Very Bad   1   2   3   4   5   **Very Good**

How likely are you to visit www.athenaeum.com (the website) to buy books in the future?

Very Unlikely   1   2   3   4   5   **Very Likely**

Section II: *Please place an "X" in the appropriate place.*

Gender: _____ Female;   _____ Male.

Age: ____ Under 20; ____20–24; ____ 25–29; ____ 30–39; ____ 40–49; ____ 50–59; ____ 601.

Marital status: ____ Single; ____ Married; ____ Divorced/Separated; ____ Widowed.

Education: ____ High school or less; ____ Some college or technical school;

_____ College graduate; ____ Post-graduate.

Income: ____ Less than $20,000; ____ $20,000–$29,999; ____ $30,000–$39,999;

____ $40,000–$49,999; ____ $50,000–$74,999; ____ $75,0001.

Number of children in your household: ____ None; ____ 1; ____ 2; ____ 3; ____ 4 or more.

Thank you for your input. It is greatly appreciated.

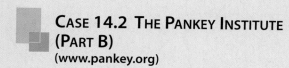

CASE 14.2 THE PANKEY INSTITUTE (PART B)
(www.pankey.org)

Christian B. Sager, executive director of the Pankey Institute, commissioned a research study to assess various aspects of the continuing education services that the organization provides to dentists. After completing an initial analysis,[1] Mr. Sager was now involved in the second phase of data analysis, whose overriding objective was to gain insight into the factors that affected participants' decisions to return to the Pankey Institute for coursework beyond the first training program. The second phase of the process involved an analysis of the association between the different factors identified through initial data reduction techniques.

Background

Founded in 1972, the Pankey Institute promotes excellence in dentistry and helps dentists educate their patients about the availability and benefits of comprehensive oral care. The Pankey Institute is acknowledged as one of the world's most prestigious centers of advanced dental education. The institute provides a series of courses that are laid out as building blocks of the concepts and principles that make up optimal dentistry.

Analyzing the Results

A factor analysis of a subset of 15 questions had identified five factors: enjoyment, value for the money, newness of material, environment/staff, and applicability of material. These variables are provided in the data set as TENJOY, TVALUE, TNEW, TENVIRON, and TAPPLY. Mr. Sager expected that additional analysis would reveal associations among these factors. He expected that level of enjoyment was positively correlated with value for the money, environment/staff, and applicability of the material, but he wasn't certain how it would correlate with newness of the material. Although he had heard some comments from dentists that they enjoyed exposure to the new material, he wasn't certain how the more difficult content would influence the other factors. He also wanted to determine the impact of each factor on overall satisfaction with the program, measured by the item "I was very satisfied with the course."

Christian Sager was eager to learn the results of the second phase of the analyses. A lot of work had already been completed, but he looked forward to the insights that would emerge from this phase of analysis.

CASE QUESTIONS

1. Using the data set provided, examine the associations among the various factors. (*Hint:* Use correlation analysis on TENJOY, TVALUE, TNEW, TENVIRON, and TAPPLY.)

2. Examine the effects of the various factors (TENJOY, TVALUE, TNEW, TENVIRON, and TAPPLY) on overall satisfaction (question 15, labeled q15 in the data set). (*Hint:* Use regression analysis.)

CASE NOTE

1. A more complete discussion of the Pankey Institute, along with a condensed version of the questionnaire, appears in Case 13.2, "The Pankey Institute (Part A)."

This case was written by Jeanne L. Munger (University of Southern Maine) in collaboration with the textbook authors, as a basis for class discussion rather than to illustrate either effective or ineffective marketing practice.

Overview of Other Multivariate Techniques and Data Mining

Virtual Consumer Initiative

Focusing on the use of the Internet as a medium, MIT's Virtual Customer Initiative (VC), led by MIT professor John Hauser, encourages the creation of methods that can be used to develop new products using customer input. VC uses Web-based methodologies, such as Web-based conjoint analysis, to increase the speed of integrating customer data into product development decisions. The Web-based conjoint method, which involves assessing consumer preferences for alternative features, is suitable for a wide variety of applications. Several demonstrations based on actual studies (crossover vehicle, ski resort, camera, and laptop bag) are provided on the website (http://mitsloan.mit.edu/vc/).

- *Crossover Vehicle.* This study ascertained consumer preferences for various features of a crossover vehicle. Consumers selected design options for seven different features: seating capacity, cargo space, fuel economy, horsepower, acceleration, towing capacity, and price.[1]

MIT's Sloan School of Management.

Chapter Objectives

After reading and understanding the material in this chapter, you should be able to:

- Distinguish between dependence and interdependence techniques.

- Discuss ANOVA and interpret the results of ANOVA.

- Interpret interaction effect in a factorial ANOVA.

- Identify two key purposes of discriminant analysis.

- Discuss factor analysis and interpret a factor-loading matrix.

- Distinguish between cluster analysis and discriminant analysis.

- State the purpose of multidimensional scaling and use the results from such an analysis.

- State the purpose of conjoint analysis and use the results from such an analysis.

- Define data mining and discuss its applications.

- Explain the concepts behind these data mining methods: market basket analysis, classification, scoring models, and forecasting/prediction

- Describe new trends in data mining: text, audio, and video mining.

- *Ski Resort.* This study assessed consumer preferences for six different features of a ski resort: price, distance, level of crowding, type of ski terrain, snow conditions, and availability of nightlife and activities.[2]

- *Camera.* The camera study determined teens' preferences for six different features of an instant camera: picture quality, number of steps in the picture-taking process, picture removal process, light selection method, style of cover, and camera opening. As a result, the Polaroid i-Zone Instant Pocket Camera was developed and introduced in 2001 as a smaller, sleeker, customizable version of earlier models with changeable faceplates. Selling for $24.99, it featured the preferred options of good picture quality, one-step picture-taking action, manual picture removal, three-setting light selection, and a fixed-style cover and opening.[3]

- *Laptop Bag.* This study evaluated consumer preferences for various configurations of features in a laptop computer bag. It assessed 10 different features: price, size, color, and various options, including a logo, briefcase handle, PDA (Palm Pilot) holder, cell phone holder, mesh pocket for water bottle or keys, type of Velcro closure, and heavy-duty reinforcement of the bottom. Based on the findings, the product was made available as a build-to-order messenger, laptop, or lifestyle bag. Consumers can now access www.timbuk2.com to build their own custom bag from three different styles, with various options to choose from. They select from various sizes, fabrics, colors, custom features, and accessories. The bag is made to order and shipped out to the consumer within two to five working days.[4] ■

The preceding chapter discussed a variety of techniques for examining associations, including regression analysis, a very widely used multivariate procedure. There are many other multivariate techniques, some of which are relatively new and becoming increasingly popular. This chapter introduces several of these methods and attempts to provide you with an intuitive understanding of each.

Dependence and Interdependence Techniques

With the **dependence technique,** one variable is designated as the dependent variable, and the rest are treated as independent variables.

With the **interdependence technique,** there are no dependent and independent variable designations; all variables are treated equally in a search for underlying patterns of relationships.

Multivariate techniques are broadly classified into dependence and interdependence techniques. With a **dependence technique,** one variable is designated as the dependent variable, and the rest are treated as independent variables. Regression analysis is an example of a dependence technique. With an **interdependence technique,** there are no dependent and independent variable designations; rather, all variables are treated equally in a search for underlying patterns of relationships.

Table 15.1 provides an overview of commonly used dependence and interdependence techniques. The techniques differ in terms of the form of the input data or the purpose of the analysis. Of these techniques, regression analysis was discussed in Chapter 14, and the remaining techniques are covered in this chapter. Because they are rather complex, our coverage of them will be basic.

TABLE 15.1
Overview of Multivariate Techniques

Type of Technique	Usual Form of the Input Data	Primary Purpose of the Technique
Dependence Techniques		
Regression analysis	Dependent variable, metric Independent variables, metric	To ascertain the relative importance of independent variables in explaining variation in the dependent variable; also to predict dependent variable values for given values of the independent variables
Analysis of variance (ANOVA)	Dependent variable, metric Independent variables, nonmetric	To see whether different levels (treatments) of independent variables have significantly different impacts on the dependent variable
Discriminant analysis	Dependent variable, nonmetric Independent variables, metric	To identify independent variables that are critical in distinguishing between subsamples defined by the dependent variable categories; also to aid in classifying new units into one of the subsample categories
Interdependence Techniques		
Factor analysis	Metric	To reduce data on a large number of variables to a relatively small set of factors; also to identify key constructs underlying the original set of measured variables
Cluster analysis	Metric	To identify natural clusters of objects on the basis of the objects' similarities on a variety of characteristics
Multidimensional scaling	Nonmetric (similarity ranks based on comparison of actual objects)	To identify key dimensions underlying respondent evaluations of products, brands, stores, etc.; also to determine the relative positions of the objects in multidimensional space
Conjoint analysis	Nonmetric (preference ranks based on comparisons of hypothetical stimuli formed by systematically varying selected attribute levels)	To derive utility values that respondents implicitly assign to various levels of key attributes used in evaluating objects; the utility values themselves aid in ascertaining the relative importance of the attributes and the potential attractiveness of descriptive profiles defined by different combinations of attributes

Analysis of Variance

Analysis of variance (ANOVA) is a technique for detecting relationships between a metric-scaled dependent variable and one or more categorical (nominal or ordinal) independent variables.

Treatment refers to each specific level at which an independent variable is set in an ANOVA procedure.

Analysis of variance (ANOVA) is closely related to regression analysis in that it, too, attempts to examine the relationship between dependent and independent variables. There is, however, one basic difference between the two techniques: whereas both dependent and independent variables are metric (interval or ratio) in regression analysis, only the dependent variable is metric in analysis of variance; the independent variable is categorical (nominal or ordinal). ANOVA is therefore especially appropriate in situations in which the independent variable is set at certain specific levels (called **treatments** in an ANOVA context) and metric measurements of the dependent variable are obtained at each of those levels. Not surprisingly, researchers often use ANOVA procedures to analyze data from marketing experiments employing designs like those covered in Chapter 8. For instance, ANOVA would be appropriate for an experiment in which we select different groups of stores in which to examine various amounts of in-store promotion for a brand and measure the results on some criterion variable (such as sales of the brand). Let's look at a specific example to understand what ANOVA does.

EXAMPLE   A grocery store chain wanted to evaluate the price sensitivity of sales of its store brand of orange juice. Twenty-four of the chain's stores in a certain region were chosen at random to participate in an experimental study using the following three treatments:

1. Store brand sold at the regular price
2. Store brand sold at 50 cents off the regular price
3. Store brand sold at 75 cents off the regular price

Eight of the 24 stores were randomly assigned to the first treatment, another 8 were randomly assigned to the second treatment, and the rest were assigned to the third treatment. Researchers monitored sales of the store brand of orange juice for a week in each store. Table 15.2 summarizes the data that were gathered.

The experimental design implied in this study is the *completely randomized design* described in Chapter 8. Using X's to denote treatments and O's to denote measurements, we can symbolically represent this experimental design as follows:

$$
\begin{array}{lll}
EG_1(R) & X_1 & O_1 \\
EG_2(R) & X_2 & O_2 \\
EG_3(R) & X_3 & O_3
\end{array}
$$

Price is the independent variable (nonmetric, with three categories) in Table 15.2. Unit sales, which is ratio scaled, is the dependent variable. The basic question now is whether the cents-off treatments had any significant impact on sales. One way to check this question is to look for evidence of significant differences in mean sales between *pairs* of treatment groups, using the t-test procedure discussed in Chapter 13. A problem with this approach is that a separate t-test is required for each possible pair of treatments. We would have to conduct three t-tests in our example, a potentially cumbersome and statistically inaccurate procedure. The task would be even more laborious with more treatment levels. ANOVA is a more appropriate approach to use when we want to compare multiple

TABLE 15.2
Unit Sales Data Under Different Pricing Treatments

Treatment	Regular Price $(j = 1)$	50 Cents Off $(j = 2)$	75 Cents Off $(j = 3)$
Unit sales in each store (Y_{ij})	37	46	46
	38	43	49
	40	43	48
	40	45	48
	38	45	47
	38	43	48
	40	44	49
	39	44	49
Number of stores (n_j)	8	8	8
Mean sales $(\bar{y}_{.j})$	38.75	44.13	48.00

sample means. It provides a one-shot, global test for detecting significant differences between treatment group means.

When there are k treatment groups or samples, ANOVA can aid in testing the following hypotheses:

$$H_o: \mu_1 = \mu_2 = \cdots = \mu_k$$

H_a: At least one μ is different from one or more of the others.

Here μ represents the mean of the dependent variable in the populations represented by the corresponding treatment groups. The test statistic in this case is an F-statistic based on the concept of partitioning the total sum of squares, introduced while discussing regression analysis in Chapter 14. The following general notation is helpful in developing an understanding of what the F-statistic in ANOVA represents:

Y_{ij} = Dependent variable value for sample unit i in treatment group j

$\overline{Y}_{\cdot j}$ = Mean value for treatment group j

$\overline{Y}_{\cdot\cdot}$ = Grand mean value (across all units in all treatment groups)

n_j = Number of sample units in treatment group j

The total deviation of any sample unit's value from the grand mean is $(Y_{ij} - \overline{Y}_{\cdot\cdot})$. This total deviation can be written as

$$(Y_{ij} - \overline{Y}_{\cdot\cdot}) = (Y_{ij} - \overline{Y}_{\cdot j}) + (\overline{Y}_{\cdot j} - \overline{Y}_{\cdot\cdot})$$

With the above expression as a starting point, it can be shown that

$$(Y_{ij} - \overline{Y}_{\cdot\cdot})^2 = (Y_{ij} - \overline{Y}_{\cdot j})^2 + (\overline{Y}_{\cdot j} - \overline{Y}_{\cdot\cdot})^2 \tag{15.1}$$

Summing equation 15.1 across all units in any treatment group j yields

$$\sum_{i=1}^{n_j} (Y_{ij} - \overline{Y}_{\cdot\cdot})^2 = \sum_{i=1}^{n_j} (Y_{ij} - \overline{Y}_{\cdot j})^2 + n_j(\overline{Y}_{\cdot j} - \overline{Y}_{\cdot\cdot})^2 \tag{15.2}$$

Now summing equation 15.2 across all treatments yields

$$\sum_{j=1}^{k} \sum_{i=1}^{n_j} (Y_{ij} - \overline{Y}_{\cdot\cdot})^2 = \sum_{j=1}^{k} \sum_{i=1}^{n_j} (Y_{ij} - \overline{Y}_{\cdot j})^2 + \sum_{j=1}^{k} n_j (\overline{Y}_{\cdot j} - \overline{Y}_{\cdot\cdot})^2 \tag{15.3}$$

The left-hand term in equation 15.3 is the *total sum of squares* (SS_T) representing the variation across all units and all treatments. The first term on the right-hand side is called the *within sum of squares* (SS_W). It is a measure of variation in dependent variable values within the treatment groups. The second term on the right-hand side is called the *between sum of squares*, or sum of squares attributable to the *treatments* (SS_{TR}). Term SS_{TR} is a weighted measure of variation in values between treatment groups.

It follows that $SS_T = SS_{TR} + SS_W$. Notice the similarity between this expression and the expression $SS_T = SS_R + SS_E$ that we derived in Chapter 14's regression analysis discussion. The treatment sum of squares (SS_{TR}) is analogous to the explained variation (SS_R) under regression analysis, and the within sum of squares (SS_W) is analogous to the residual (or unexplained) variation (SS_E). Intuitively, if the experimental treatments (independent variable) had little impact on the Y-values (dependent variable), we would expect SS_{TR} to be small. For a given value of SS_T, a small SS_{TR} would imply a large SS_W. Just as in regression analysis, a comparison of SS_{TR} and SS_W, taking into account their appropriate degrees of freedom, is the basis for the F-statistic in ANOVA.

When there are k treatments, the degrees of freedom associated with SS_{TR} and SS_W are $(k - 1)$ and $(n - k)$, respectively, where n is the total number of units across all treatments. Therefore,

$$F = \frac{SS_{TR}/k - 1}{SS_W/n - k}$$

The numerator and denominator of F are mean squares, corresponding to the variation due to the treatments and chance variation due to sampling, respectively. To see whether the experimental treatments had a significant impact on the dependent measure, we can check the computed value of F against an appropriate critical value from the F-table. We reject hypothesis H_o if the computed value exceeds the critical value.

Returning to the data in Table 15.2, let's conduct an ANOVA to see whether at least one of the treatment means (shown in the last row of the table) is significantly different from one or more others. Although we can compute the necessary F-value by hand, using the formulas just derived, it is more convenient to use one of the readily available computer packages for this purpose. Given the raw dependent variable values for each treatment (the Y_{ij}-values), a computer program can perform ANOVA efficiently and provide a rich variety of output information. The computer output resulting from analyzing the raw data in Table 15.2 by using the SPSS ANOVA program is shown in Exhibit 15.1.

The name TREAT was used for the dependent variable in the computer program (shown in the third row of the lower panel in Exhibit 15.1). A tabular array like the one in Exhibit 15.1, showing various sums of squares, degrees of freedom,

Exhibit 15.1
SPSS Computer Output for ANOVA Analysis of the Data in Table 15.2

Between-Subjects Factors

		Value Label	N
Treatment group	1	Regular price	8
	2	50 cents off	8
	3	75 cents off	8

Tests of Between-Subjects Effects

Dependent variable: SALES

Source	Type III Sum of Squares	d.f.	Mean Square	F	Sig.
Corrected Model	345.250[a]	2	172.625	137.445	.000
Intercept	45675.375	1	45675.375	36367.123	.000
TREAT	345.250	2	172.625	137.445	.000
Error	26.375	21	1.256		
Total	46047.000	24			
Corrected Total	371.625	23			

[a] R squared = .929 (Adjusted R squared = .922)

mean squares, *F*-values, and their corresponding significance levels, is usually called an *ANOVA table*. Its format resembles the formats we saw in the regression analysis computer outputs (Exhibits 14.5 and 14.8).

The number 137.445 shown under *F* in the row labeled "TREAT" (sometimes labeled as *between groups* to reflect the assessment of differences between the treatment groups) in Exhibit 15.1 is the computed *F*-value we are looking for. It is the ratio of the mean square value of 172.625 associated with TREAT (that is, $SS_{TR}/k - 1$) and the mean square value of 1.256 associated with "Error" (that is, $SS_W/n - k$). The critical *F*-value with 2 numerator degrees of freedom and 21 denominator degrees of freedom at the traditional significance level of .05 is only 3.47 (from Appendix 5). We should therefore reject H_o and conclude that at least one of the treatment means is significantly different from one or more others.

Indeed, in this case we need not even have determined the critical value of *F* to arrive at the above conclusion, because the ANOVA output shows the actual significance level of the *F*-test value .000 under the column "Sig." This value means there is less than a .001 probability of obtaining an *F*-value as high as 137.445 by chance when TREAT has no impact on sales. In other words, there is less than 1 chance in 1,000 of committing a Type I error by rejecting H_o on the basis of the available evidence.

Some additional explanation of the output in Exhibit 15.1 is in order. Perhaps you are wondering why there are two identical rows of numbers (the first and third rows) in the computer output. Although there was just one independent variable in our illustration, we can examine the impact of two or more independent variables by using ANOVA. The row labeled "Corrected Model" refers to results aggregated over *all* independent variables considered in a given situation. Because TREAT was the only independent variable in this case, numbers in the first and third rows of the computer output are the same. (Had there been more than one independent variable, there would have been additional rows of numbers under the row corresponding to TREAT, one row for each additional variable.) Furthermore, because our example involves only one independent variable, no interaction effect occurs. The "Error" (sometimes labeled as "Residual") row corresponds to variance in the dependent variable not accounted for by the independent variables and their interactions. So, the sum of squares and degrees of freedom in the "Corrected Model" and "Error" rows must add to the corresponding numbers in the "Corrected Total" row (verify this result in Exhibit 15.1). In an experimental design, we are not concerned with interpreting the "Intercept" row. The R^2 number (.929) indicates that changes in treatment account for 92.9 percent of changes in sales.

Now that we know that TREAT had a significant impact on sales, which specific treatment group means are significantly different? Visual inspection of the three treatment group means suggests that each may differ significantly from the other two. An extension of the ANOVA technique called *constructing and evaluating contrasts* is available to verify the statistical significance of differences between any pair of treatment means. We will not cover the details of this extension.[5] Most computer programs for performing ANOVA offer an option for evaluating specific treatment differences.

The similarity between the expressions for the total sum of squares (SS_T) under ANOVA and regression analysis was pointed out earlier. Research in Use 15.1 describes the application of SPSS to analyze some of the National Insurance Company data using the ANOVA procedure.

National Insurance Company: Impact of Educational Level on Overall Perceived Quality

Jill Baxter, vice president of customer service for National Insurance Company, and her assistant, Tom Kurtis, manager of customer service, were wondering whether there were any significant differences in perceived quality across consumer groups with varying educational backgrounds.

The chart they were studying showed some meaningful differences between the groups. Customers with a high school education or less seemed to think highly of National compared with customers with a graduate school education. Examining averages is not enough to conclude that there are significant differences between the groups. Therefore, Jill asked Tom to perform an ANOVA to compare between-group variation to within-group variation. The SPSS dialog boxes for performing an ANOVA are shown at the right.

The significance level associated with the F-value is .002. Jill and Tom should therefore reject H_o and conclude that at least one of the group means is significantly different from one or more others. The value .002 means that there is less than a .002 probability of obtaining an F-value as high as 5.218 by chance when ED has no impact on OQ. In other words, there are fewer than 2 chances in 1,000 of committing a Type I error by rejecting H_o on the basis of the available evidence.

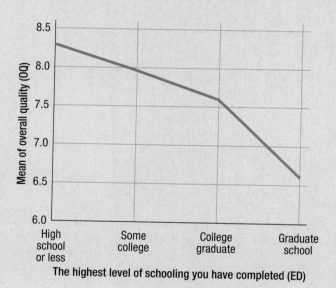

The highest level of schooling you have completed (ED)

Factorial ANOVA

Factorial ANOVA is used to analyze data from a factorial design experiment; that is, one intended to investigate the impact of *more than one* categorical independent variable on a metric-scaled dependent variable.

The **factorial ANOVA** is used to analyze data from a factorial design experiment; that is, one intended to investigate the impact of *more than one* categorical independent variable on a metric-scaled dependent variable. A factorial design is thus a multivariate design. We will review and illustrate this design using our grocery chain example. Suppose we want to investigate the impact of an in-store point-of-purchase display on unit sales of orange juice, in addition to the pricing factor already described. Also, suppose that the presence and the absence of the point-of-purchase display are the two treatment levels for this new factor. When we consider the two factors simultaneously, six *combinations* of treatment levels are

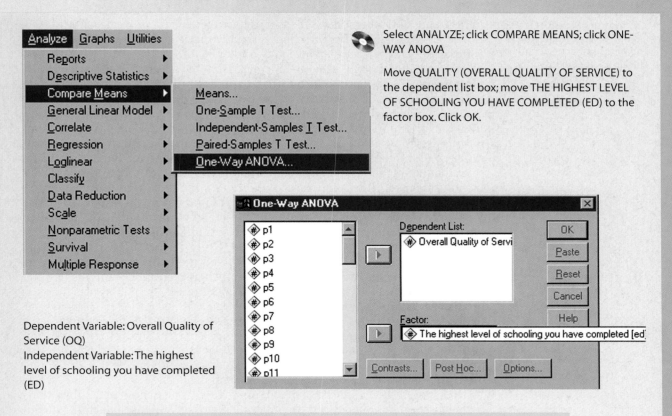

Select ANALYZE; click COMPARE MEANS; click ONE-WAY ANOVA

Move QUALITY (OVERALL QUALITY OF SERVICE) to the dependent list box; move THE HIGHEST LEVEL OF SCHOOLING YOU HAVE COMPLETED (ED) to the factor box. Click OK.

Dependent Variable: Overall Quality of Service (OQ)
Independent Variable: The highest level of schooling you have completed (ED)

ANOVA

Impact of Education on Overall Quality

OQ	Sum of Squares	d.f.	Mean Square	F	Sig.
Between groups	77.538	3	25.846	5.218	.002
Within groups	1273.022	257	4.953		
Total	1350.559	260			

possible: presence or absence of the point-of-purchase display with each of the three pricing treatments (regular price, 50 cents off, and 75 cents off). We can now allocate sample stores to the six treatment levels, and we can monitor and analyze unit sales to gain insight into the impact of the two factors.

When numerous factors, each with several levels, are involved in a factorial design, the number of possible combination levels and hence treatment groups can be high, and the cost of studying a subsample of units under each combination level may be prohibitive. Fortunately, procedures are available to let us systematically select and study just a few of the levels and still gain insight into the impact of all the factors.[6]

In our example we can, of course, use two separate one-way designs: one to study the impact of price and the other to study the impact of the point-of-purchase display. However, a major limitation of this approach is that it will not

An **interaction effect** is said to be present when the relative impact of treatment levels of one factor varies across treatment levels of another factor.

indicate possible interaction effects of the two factors on unit sales. An **interaction effect** is said to be present when the relative impact of treatment levels of one factor varies across treatment levels of another factor.

For instance, suppose that the increases in unit sales due to the price reductions are much more pronounced when the point-of-purchase display is present than when it is absent. In this case, the two factors (price and point-of-purchase display) are said to interact with each other in influencing the dependent variable (unit sales). Exhibit 15.2(a) illustrates this interaction effect. Here price reductions have a positive impact on unit sales under both display and no-display treatments. This impact reflects a *main* effect due to the price factor. Similarly, the unit sales that are higher in the display treatment than those in the no-display treatments (under all three price levels) reflect a *main* effect due to the point-of-purchase display factor. The *steeper* increases in unit sales (in response to price reductions) under the display treatment and the resulting nonparallel sales trend lines reflect the *interaction* effect due to the joint influence of price and point-of-purchase display.

Exhibit 15.2(b) depicts a situation in which there are main effects but no interaction effect. Price reductions result in higher sales under both display and no-display treatments, and the display treatment results in higher sales than the no-display treatment under all three price levels. However, the increases in sales due to price reductions are the same for the display and no-display treatments (the slopes of corresponding sections of the two sales trend lines are equal). Moreover, the increases in sales due to having a display are the same for the three price treatments; that is, the gap between the two sales trend lines is the same at all three price levels. Therefore, there is no interaction effect.

In factorial ANOVA, the sum of the squares across all treatment combinations (six such combinations in our example), denoted as SS_{TR}, is split into sums of squares attributable to each treatment variable separately and to interactions between treatment variables. If we label the treatment variables in a two-way ANOVA as *A* and *B*, we can represent the partitioning of the total sum of squares as follows:

$$SS_T = SS_{TR} + SS_e$$
$$= SS_A + SS_B + SS_{AB} + SS_e$$

where SS_A and SS_B correspond to the main effects of the two treatments, SS_{AB} corresponds to the interaction effect between them, and SS_e is the error sum of squares.

Exhibit 15.2
Illustrations of Main and Interaction Effects

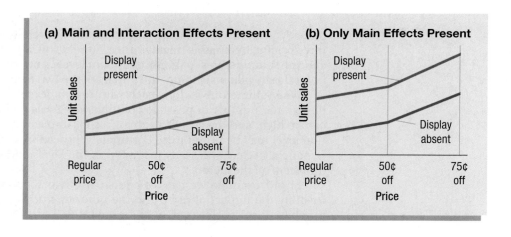

(a) Main and Interaction Effects Present

(b) Only Main Effects Present

The computer output for a factorial ANOVA will indicate the value of each SS component in the expression for SS_T along with its associated degrees of freedom and mean square value. It will also provide separate F-values for ascertaining the significance of each main effect and the interaction effect. Research in Use 15.2 describes results from a study in which main and interaction effects were investigated by using the SPSS ANOVA program.

Discriminant Analysis

Discriminant analysis is a technique for identifying the distinguishing features of prespecified subgroups of units that are formed on the basis of some categorical dependent variable.

Discriminant analysis identifies the distinguishing features of prespecified subgroups of units that are formed on the basis of some dependent variable (such as heavy, moderate, and light users of a product; homeowners and renters; viewers and nonviewers of a television program). Thus the dependent variable in discriminant analysis is categorical, and there are as many prespecified subgroups as there are categories. The independent variables are typically metric scaled. The purpose of discriminant analysis includes classifying new units into one of the subgroups given the new units' values on the independent variables.

To illustrate discriminant analysis, consider the following example.

EXAMPLE   A computer manufacturer wants to see whether household income (X_1) and number of years of formal education of the household head (X_2) are useful in clearly distinguishing households owning personal computers from those not owning personal computers. If X_1 and X_2 seem to be crucial determinants of personal computer ownership, the firm also wishes to be able to determine whether a prospective customer household is likely to buy a personal computer given the household's values on X_1 and X_2. The firm has gathered data on X_1 and X_2 for two random samples of households: an owner sample and a nonowner sample. These data are plotted on the two-dimensional graph shown in Exhibit 15.3.

Exhibit 15.3
Scatter Plot of Income and Education Data for Personal Computer Owners and Nonowners

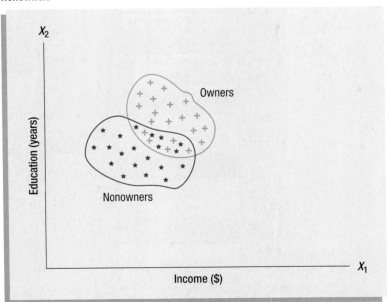

Two enclosed areas are shown in Exhibit 15.3, one containing primarily households with personal computers and the other containing primarily households without personal computers. Although the two areas overlap, the extent of overlap does not seem substantial. Intuitively, this exhibit implies that income and education are good discriminators between households with and without personal computers. Minimal overlap between groups, as in Exhibit 15.3, is a critical requirement if discriminant analysis is to be fruitful.

The task of discriminant analysis now is to utilize the two groups of data points (1) to quantify the relative importance of X_1 and X_2 in discriminating between the two sets of households and (2) to develop a criterion for classifying prospective households as potential owner or nonowner households. The key to accomplishing this twofold

Bank Customer Perceptions Study: Factorial ANOVA with Main and Interaction Effects

A large bank in the United States conducted a mail survey of its customers to assess their perceptions of various aspects of the bank's services. A question in the concluding section of the survey asked respondents to rate the overall quality of service provided by the bank on a scale of 1 ("extremely poor") to 10 ("extremely good"). The bank's management was interested in ascertaining whether (1) male and female customers differed in their overall perceptions; (2) customers' perceptions differed according to their age; and (3) gender and age interacted in influencing perceptions. Data were available on gender (coded as a two-category vari-

able) and age (coded as a three-category variable: under 35 years; 35–64 years; and over 64 years).

To generate the information sought, management conducted a two-way factorial ANOVA. In this ANOVA, gender and age were the two categorical independent variables, and overall quality rating was the metric-scaled dependent variable. The total sample size for the analysis was 474. The computer output from the SPSS ANOVA program follows.

As the computer output shows, the main effects of both GENDER and AGE as well as their interaction effect on QUALITY are highly significant. Notice that the actual significance levels (shown in the last column of the output) for the effects of AGE, GENDER, and AGE-GENDER interaction are all below the customary significance level of .05. The mean quality ratings (generated by the SPSS ANOVA program) for different subgroups of respondents are summarized in the table (numbers under the column "N" are sample sizes for the subgroups). The means for the six GENDER-AGE combinations are also portrayed graphically in the accompanying figure.

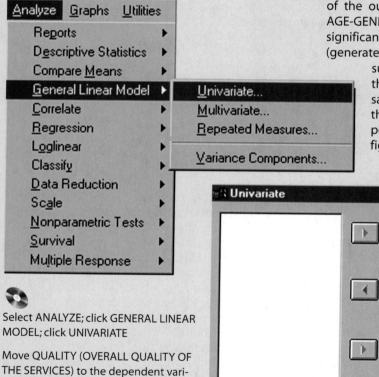

Select ANALYZE; click GENERAL LINEAR MODEL; click UNIVARIATE

Move QUALITY (OVERALL QUALITY OF THE SERVICES) to the dependent variable box; move GENDER and AGE to fixed factor(s) box. Click OK.

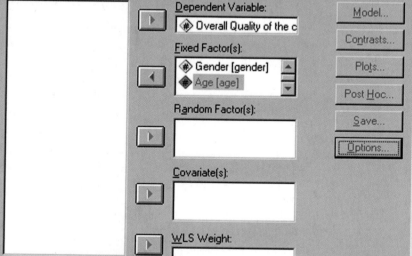

Between-Subjects Factors

		Value Label	N
GENDER	1	Male	252
	2	Female	222
AGE	1	<35	134
	2	35–64	167
	3	>64	173

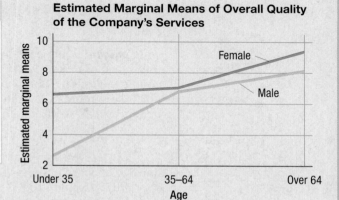

Estimated Marginal Means of Overall Quality of the Company's Services

The figure shows a main effect for gender (females have more favorable perceptions than males), a main effect for age (the older the customers, the more favorable their perceptions), and a gender-age interaction effect (notice the nonparallel quality perception trend lines for males and females). The interaction effect here shows that the difference in quality perceptions between males and females varies by age: the difference is most pronounced for the under-35 age group and least pronounced for the 35–64 age group.

Descriptive Statistics

Dependent Variable: QUALITY (Overall quality of the company's services)

GENDER	AGE	Mean	Std. Deviation	N
1 Male	1 <35	2.54	1.31	79
	2 35–64	6.72	1.17	88
	3 >64	8.08	.82	85
	Total	5.87	2.57	252
2 Female	1 <35	6.49	1.39	55
	2 35–64	6.95	.58	79
	3 >64	9.36	.48	88
	Total	7.79	1.53	222
Total	1 <35	4.16	2.36	134
	2 35–64	6.83	.94	167
	3 >64	8.73	.93	173
	Total	6.77	2.35	474

Tests of Between-Subjects Effects

Dependent Variable: QUALITY (Overall quality of the company's service)

Source	Type III Sum of Squares	d.f.	Mean Square	F	Sig.
Corrected Model	2156.112[a]	5	431.222	438.891	.000
Intercept	20665.912	1	20665.912	21033.424	.000
GENDER	382.436	1	382.436	389.237	.000
AGE	1311.623	2	655.811	667.4741	.000
GENDER * AGE	260.433	2	130.216	132.532	.000
Error	459.823	468	.983		
Total	24341.000	474			
Corrected Total	2615.935	473			

[a] R squared = .824 (Adjusted R squared = .822)

task is to develop an appropriate discriminant function, which is simply a linear combination of X_1 and X_2, specified as

$$v_1X_1 + v_2X_2$$

where v_1 and v_2 are constants called *discriminant weights*, or *coefficients*. Given the values of v_1 and v_2 (we will see shortly how these are determined), we can compute a number summarizing the linear combination for each sample household. This number is called a household's *discriminant score*, which we will denote as its Y-score. For any household h,

$$Y_h = v_1X_{1h} + v_2X_{2h}$$

Now let's turn to the determination of v_1 and v_2. Theoretically, an infinite number of combinations of v_1- and v_2-values are possible. Furthermore, depending on these values, the Y-scores for the sample households will vary. Discriminant analysis selects v_1 and v_2 such that the variation in the Y-scores *between* the two groups of households is made as large as possible relative to variation in the Y-scores *within* them. In other words, v_1 and v_2 are chosen to maximize the ratio of between to within sums of squares corresponding to Y-scores. The discriminant function is thus the linear combination of the independent variables that offers the best separation (least overlap) of Y-scores between the prespecified groups.

Exhibit 15.4 provides a graphical interpretation of a discriminant function of the form $v_1X_1 + v_2X_2$. It is a family of parallel straight lines in a two-dimensional graph with X_1 and X_2 as axes. Each straight line in the family corresponds to a specific Y-score. Therefore, the Y-scores of data points on the same straight line will be identical, but Y-scores of data points on different straight lines will vary. In fact, we can measure the Y-scores along a line perpendicular to the family of lines representing the discriminant function. This perpendicular line, called the *discriminant axis*, represents the dimension along which maximum separation between the two groups occurs. Stated differently, projections on the discriminant axis of the data points corresponding to the two groups will be clustered together within each group and spread apart between groups.

Exhibit 15.4
Discriminant Function and
Discriminant Scores

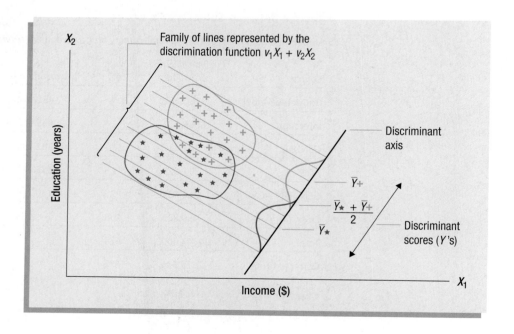

Using the Discriminant Function

The weights v_1 and v_2 can be interpreted as signifying the relative importance of X_1 and X_2 in being able to discriminate between the two groups, provided both independent variables are measured in the same units. When the measurement units are different (as in our example), we must obtain standardized weights—say, v_1^* and v_2^*—as follows:

$$v_1^* = v_1 s_1$$

$$v_2^* = v_2 s_2$$

where s_1 and s_2 are pooled standard deviations for X_1 and X_2, respectively. The pooled standard deviation s_k for any variable X_k can be computed by using the following formula in which the subscripts 1 and 2 refer to the two samples:

$$S_k = \sqrt{\frac{(n_1 - 1)\, s_{k1}^2 + (n_2 - 1)\, s_{k2}^2}{n_1 + n_2 - 2}}$$

Use of this formula requires the assumption of equal X_k variances in the populations implied by the two samples.

The two extreme situations depicted in Exhibit 15.5 graphically demonstrate the correspondence between the discriminant weights and the relative importance of the two independent variables in the discriminant function.

Classification of a new household with the discriminant function is quite straightforward. Given X_1- and X_2-values for a new unit, we compute a Y-score for it by using the discriminant function.

$$Y_{\text{new}} = v_1 X_{1,\text{new}} + v_2 X_{2,\text{new}}$$

We then compare Y_{new} with the mean discriminant scores, $\overline{Y}_*$ and $\overline{Y}_+$, for the two groups, which we compute as follows (the subscript $+$ refers to personal computer owner households and the subscript $*$ refers to nonowner households):

$$\overline{Y}_* = v_1 \overline{X}_{1,}{}^* + v_2 \overline{X}_{2,}{}^*$$

$$\overline{Y}_+ = v_1 \overline{X}_{1,+} + v_2 \overline{X}_{2,+}$$

We assign the new household to the owner group if Y_{new} is closer to $\overline{Y}_+$ than to $\overline{Y}_*$; if not, we assign it to the nonowner group. Another way of stating this assignment criterion is as follows: compare Y_{new} with a critical discriminant score Y_{cri}, defined as shown on the next page.

Exhibit 15.5
Relative Importance of Independent Variables in a Discriminant Function

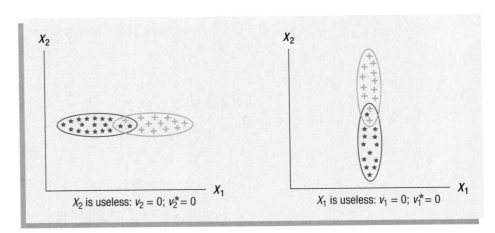

X_2 is useless: $v_2 = 0$; $v_2^* = 0$

X_1 is useless: $v_1 = 0$; $v_1^* = 0$

$$Y_{\text{cri}} = \frac{\overline{Y}_* + \overline{Y}_+}{2}$$

If $Y_{\text{new}} > Y_{\text{cri}}$, assign the household to the owner group; if not, assign it to the nonowner group. This allocation rule implicitly assumes that the cost of misallocation is the same for both groups. In other words, erroneously classifying a potential owner as a nonowner will cost the same as classifying a potential nonowner as an owner. When the costs of misallocation are different, we need a more sophisticated classification criterion (not discussed here).[7] The middle line in the family of lines in Exhibit 15.4 is the critical discriminant line.

To illustrate the use of a discriminant function, suppose the data collected by the computer manufacturer on households with and without personal computers, and the results of analyzing such data, are as follows:

	Owner Households	Nonowner Households
Sample sizes	$n_+ = 20$	$n_* = 20$
Sample means	$\overline{X}_{1+} = \$30{,}000$	$\overline{X}_{1*} = \$20{,}000$
	$\overline{X}_{2+} = 18$ years	$\overline{X}_{2*} = 16$ years
Standard deviations	$s_{1+} = \$6{,}000$	$s_{1*} = \$5{,}000$
	$s_{2+} = 4$ years	$s_{2*} = 6$ years
Discriminant weights	$v_1 = .009; v_2 = 3.25$	
Discriminant function	$.009X_1 + 3.25X_2$	

Programs are available in several computer packages (such as SPSS) for deriving a discriminant function given the prespecified groupings of the sample units and data on the independent variables for each of those units.

In addition to wanting to know the relative importance of income (X_1) and education (X_2) in discriminating between personal computer owner and nonowner households, the firm wishes to classify a prospective household with $X_1 = \$28{,}000$ and $X_2 = 15$ years into one of the two groups. Because X_1 and X_2 are measured in different units, the discriminant weights v_1 and v_2 must be standardized through multiplication by the corresponding pooled standard deviations s_1 and s_2:

$$s_1 = \sqrt{\frac{(n_+ - 1)s_{1+}^2 + (n_* - 1)s_{1*}^2}{n_+ + n_* - 2}}$$

$$= \sqrt{\frac{(19)(\$6000)^2 + (19)(\$5000)^2}{38}} = \$5{,}522.68$$

$$s_2 = \sqrt{\frac{(n_+ - 1)s_{2+}^2 + (n_* - 1)s_{2*}^2}{n_+ + n_* - 2}}$$

$$= \sqrt{\frac{(19)(4)^2 + (19)(6)^2}{38}} = 5.10 \text{ years}$$

$$v_1{}^* = v_1 s_1 = (.009)(5{,}522.68) = 49.70$$

$$v_2{}^* = v_2 s_2 = (3.25)(5.10) = 16.52$$

Comparing v_1^* with v_2^*, we can say that household income is about three times as important as education of the household head in distinguishing between personal computer owner and nonowner households.

To classify the prospective household, we need to determine its Y-score and compare it with Y_{cri}.

$$Y_{new} = v_1 X_{1, new} + v_2 X_{2, new}$$

$$= (.009)(28,000) + (3.25)(15)$$

$$= 252 + 48.75 = 300.75$$

$$\overline{Y}_+ = (.009)(30,000) + (3.25)(18)$$

$$= 270 + 58.5 = 328.5$$

$$\overline{Y}_* = (.009)(20,000) + (3.25)(16)$$

$$= 180 + 52 = 232$$

$$Y_{cri} = \frac{\overline{Y}_+ + \overline{Y}_*}{2} = \frac{328.5 + 232}{2} = 280.25$$

Because $Y_{new} > Y_{cri}$, we should classify the prospective household as a potential owner of a personal computer.

Evaluating a Discriminant Function

In the preceding discussion of discriminant analysis, we did not consider the issue of how trustworthy the resulting discriminant function is. However, tests are available for checking the statistical significance of a discriminant function as well as its discriminant weights. These tests are similar to those we discussed for regression analysis. Because both regression analysis and discriminant analysis form linear combinations of independent variables, the potential limitations of regression analysis and the precautions to be taken in interpreting its results apply to discriminant analysis as well.

For a discriminant function that is statistically significant, an intuitive way to evaluate its practical usefulness is to construct and examine what is usually called a *confusion matrix*. A confusion matrix indicates the degree of correspondence, or lack thereof, between the actual groupings of the sample units and the predicted groupings obtained by classifying the same units through the discriminant function. The confusion matrix corresponding to our illustration (Exhibit 15.4) is shown in Table 15.3.

Numbers on the diagonal going down from left to right in the confusion matrix refer to sample units correctly classified. A summary indicator of a discriminant function's predictive ability is the following ratio, called the *hit rate*:

$$\frac{\text{Total number of correctly classified units}}{\text{Total sample size}}$$

The hit rate for the confusion matrix in Table 15.3 is

$$\frac{17 + 16}{20 + 20} = \frac{33}{40} = .825$$

Thus our illustrative discriminant function is able to correctly classify 82.5 percent of all sample households.

TABLE 15.3
Confusion Matrix Corresponding to Exhibit 15.4

Actual Groupings	Predicted Groupings	
	Households With Personal Computers	Households Without Personal Computers
Households with personal computers	17	3
Households without personal computers	4	16

Note that the hit rate calculated here is based on the same set of sample units used to construct the discriminant function. Hence, it is likely to be somewhat biased in favor of the function. A more stringent way to measure a discriminant function's predictive ability is to construct the function by using part (say, one-half or two-thirds) of the sample and compute the hit rate on the basis of predictions for the units in the remainder of the sample. Our ability to use this approach depends, of course, on how large the sample size is.

How good is the hit rate (prediction accuracy) of 82.5 percent? The answer depends on how accurately we can classify the units by chance, which is a function of the relative sizes of the two actual groups. In our example, both groups are the same size, implying that the a priori probability of any sample unit's being a personal computer owner is .5. Also, our objective is to classify the units into owners and nonowners. So, suppose we toss a fair coin for each unit and classify the unit as a personal computer owner if we observe heads and as a nonowner if we observe tails. We will be correct 50 percent of the time, and therefore our prediction accuracy by chance will be 50 percent. Therefore, the hit rate of 82.5 percent for our discriminant function appears to be quite good.

What if the two groups are not the same size? For instance, suppose that the owner group is three times as large as the nonowner group ($n_+ = 30$ and $n_* = 10$). Now the a priori probability of a sample unit's being a personal computer owner is .75. Therefore, if we want to classify each unit as either an owner or a nonowner without the aid of a discriminant function, we can use the following procedure. For each unit, draw a random number between 1 and 100. If the number is between 1 and 75, classify the unit as an owner; if not, classify the unit as a nonowner. The accuracy of chance prediction in this case can be shown to be

$$p^2 + (1-p)^2$$

where p is the proportion of units in one group and $(1-p)$ is the proportion of units in the other. When $p = .75$, the chance prediction accuracy is $(.75)^2 + (.25)^2 = .625$, or 62.5 percent. A hit rate of 82.5 percent compared with a chance prediction accuracy of 62.5 percent is still not bad, although it is worse than when the two groups are of equal size; that is, $p = .5$ (verify that the chance prediction accuracy is 50 percent when $p = .5$).

In general, the more dissimilar the sizes of the two original groups, the lower the ability of a discriminant function to outperform a chance classification scheme that relies merely on the relative group sizes. Such a chance classification scheme implies the use of what is usually called the *proportional chance criterion*. There is another chance classification scheme that uses the so-called *maximum chance criterion*, in which all the units are classified into the larger of the two a priori groups. Thus, when a sample of 40 units has 30 owners and 10 nonowners, classifying all 40 units as owners will result in a maximum prediction accuracy of 75 percent. The maximum chance criterion is unrealistic, however, because putting all units into just one group defeats the very purpose of identifying distinct group memberships.

Final Remarks

Our treatment of discriminant analysis has centered on situations in which the total sample is divided into two groups on the basis of some prespecified criterion. However, discriminant analysis is not limited to two-group situations. The rationale underlying multiple-group discriminant analysis is similar to that underlying the two-group case, although details of the technique are much more complex.

Discriminant functions are not restricted to just two independent variables either. The sole reason for including only two independent variables in our discussion was to keep it simple and facilitate graphical interpretation of what the technique does. Discriminant functions can and often do contain more than two independent variables. The general form for a discriminant function with k variables is

$$v_1X_1 + v_2X_2 + \ldots + v_kX_k$$

The potential for applying discriminant analysis is great, given marketers' ever-present need to define customer segments, identify critical characteristics capable of distinguishing among them, and classify prospective customers into appropriate segments.

Factor Analysis

Factor analysis is a data and variable reduction technique that attempts to partition a given set of variables into groups (called *factors*) of maximally correlated variables.

Factor analysis is essentially a data and variable reduction technique that attempts to partition a given set of variables into groups of maximally correlated variables. For metric-scaled data on a large number of variables, factor analysis generates a smaller number of variables, called *factors,* which capture as much information as possible from the original data set. We typically begin by examining a matrix of pairwise correlations among the original variables and explore ways to combine them into factors such that each factor represents primarily a group of maximally correlated variables. We will not cover the mechanics of analyzing correlations to derive the factors here;[8] rather, we will focus on providing an intuitive understanding of what factor analysis does and how its results can be interpreted and used.

An Intuitive Explanation

To examine the procedure of factor analysis, let's first consider this hypothetical situation.

> **EXAMPLE** Star Brands, Inc. (SBI), a manufacturer of a variety of home appliances and electronic products, recently conducted a survey of customers owning Star products. The purpose of the survey was to find out how customers felt about SBI in general and about specific Star products in particular. The survey involved numerous evaluative statements that respondents answered by using a 7-point scale on which the higher the number, the more favorable the evaluation.

We discussed a variety of rating scales in Chapter 9. Recall that data obtained through rating scales are typically assumed to have interval-scale properties. Factor analysis requires data that are at least interval scaled. Although it typically involves simultaneously analyzing data on a large number of statements (variables), let's consider only the following two statements from the SBI survey to graphically illustrate the rationale underlying the technique:

1. I have been satisfied with the Star products I have purchased.
2. When I have to purchase a home appliance in the future, it will likely be a Star product.

Customer ratings on each statement can be considered as data on a single variable. Let S_1 and S_2 denote the variables implicit in the two statements. A plot of the survey data on S_1 and S_2 is shown in Exhibit 15.6. Clearly, S_1 and S_2 are highly correlated. In other words, ratings on the two statements are largely redundant, because they apparently represent very similar customer sentiments.

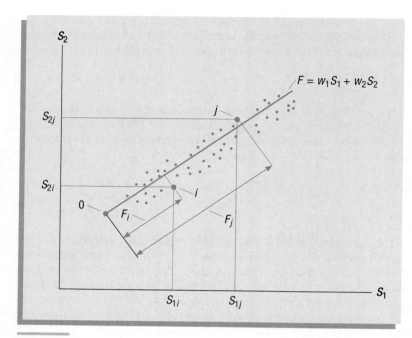

Exhibit 15.6
Situation in Which Factor Analysis Will Be Beneficial:
S_1 **and** S_2 **Highly Correlated**

Therefore, we should be able to combine them into ratings along just one dimension with no significant loss of information embedded in the raw data set. This combination is exactly what factor analysis of the data on S_1 and S_2 will accomplish. The straight line labeled F in Exhibit 15.6 is a factor representing the dimension along which measurements can be made for all sample units from an arbitrary origin, such as point 0 shown on the line. These measurements are called *factor scores*. Two such factor scores, F_i and F_j, are shown in the exhibit for respondents i and j.

What does a comparison of the factor scores for respondents i and j with their ratings on S_1 and S_2 reveal? Clearly, the higher a respondent's rating on S_1 or S_2, the higher the respondent's factor score is, in an almost proportionate fashion. Exhibit 15.6 further suggests that the close correspondence between the two original sets of ratings and the factor scores can be generalized to the entire sample. In factor analysis, the terms S_1 and S_2 are said to have *high factor loadings* on F. A *factor loading* is the Pearson correlation coefficient between an original variable and a factor.

In short, having data on just F for the sample respondents is virtually as good as having separate ratings on S_1 and S_2. What Exhibit 15.6 demonstrates graphically for just two variables is the foundation underlying factor analysis, which can be generalized to more than two variables. Given data on a large number of variables, *at least some of which are highly correlated with one another*, factor analysis can provide a more parsimonious set of factors with little loss of information. The emphasis on correlations among the original variables in the preceding sentence is noteworthy: factor analysis will do little good if the original variables are poorly correlated.

This limitation of factor analysis is demonstrated in Exhibit 15.7, in which S_1 and S_2 are poorly correlated. Poor association between factor scores and S_1 and S_2 ratings is illustrated by the fact that all data points along line ab (with S_1 ratings ranging from S_{1a} to S_{1b} and S_2 ratings ranging from S_{2a} to S_{2b}) will have the same factor score, F_{ab}.

The factor scores along dimension F in Exhibit 15.7 do not correlate strongly with the data on either S_1 or S_2. The factor F thus does a poor job of capturing the essence of the original data set. We can make F parallel to the S_1 axis, as shown by line FS_1, so that the factor scores will correspond perfectly with the S_1 ratings. Unfortunately, factor scores along FS_1 will reflect nothing about the ratings on S_2. We would have to construct another perpendicular factor, such as FS_2, to capture the S_2 ratings. But by doing so, we would defeat the purpose of factor analysis—namely, data and variable reduction. Obviously, using the original two variables themselves is sensible if two factors are needed to fully capture the gist of the raw data. Thus factor analysis is not always guaranteed to accomplish its intended purpose.

Returning to Exhibit 15.6, what interpretation can we place on factor F? Mathematically, it is a linear combination that accounts for almost all the variation in S_1 and S_2:

$$F = w_1 S_1 + w_2 S_2$$

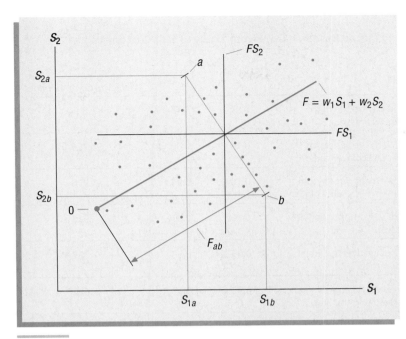

where w_1 and w_2 are weights determined by the factor analysis procedure. But does this have any *substantive* meaning? In other words, because F is a new, combined variable, what *name* can we give it?

The issue of naming factors is subjective and hence somewhat controversial. Invariably, users of factor analysis simply choose a label on the basis of any common thread running through the original variables that have high loadings on it. Thus naming a factor can be difficult when variables with high loadings on it have little in common, which is not an unusual occurrence in factor analysis applications and thus is a potential limitation of the technique. In our illustration, S_1 represents satisfaction with Star products, and S_2 represents likelihood of future purchases of Star products. Hence, F is perhaps *trust* in Star products.

Factor Analysis Output and Its Interpretation

Most statistical software packages, such as SPSS, can perform factor analysis. These packages typically conduct the analysis after standardizing the variables (converting each to a mean of 0 and variance of 1). The primary output of factor analysis is a *factor-loading matrix*. To illustrate this matrix, let's assume that a factor analysis is conducted on ratings on a 7-point scale given by owners of Star DVD players on six statements included in the SBI survey. These statements (designated as variables X_1 through X_6) and their factor-loading matrix are shown in Table 15.4. Table 15.4 implies that two factors (F_1 and F_2) have been constructed by analyzing data on variables X_1 through X_6. In general, as many factors as there are variables can be derived from an original data set. Software packages allow factor analysis users to specify the number of factors to be extracted. Of course, the smaller the number of factors that can adequately reflect the information in the original data set, the better.

One feature of factor analysis that is crucial in interpreting its results is that the factors themselves are *independent*. In other words, the technique constructs factors in such a way that the correlation between any pair of extracted factors will be zero, and there is no overlap or redundancy of information among the factors.

The numbers in Table 15.4 under the column heading "Factors" through the sixth row are factor loadings. Thus, for instance, the correlation coefficient between X_1 and F_1 is .89, and that between X_1 and F_2 is .15. Recall from Chapter 14 that the squared correlation coefficient between two variables is the proportion of variance in one accounted for by the other. Therefore, $(.89)^2$ is the variance in X_1 accounted for by F_1, and $(.15)^2$ is the variance in X_1 accounted for by F_2. Because there is no duplication of information between F_1 and F_2, the variance in X_1 extracted by both factors considered together is $(.89)^2 + (.15)^2 = .815$. This value is called the *achieved communality* for X_1. The achieved communality for any original variable represents the proportion of variance in it accounted for by all the

TABLE 15.4
Factor-Loading Matrix Based on Data from Study of Star Customers

	Factors		
Factor Loadings	F_1	F_2	*Achieved Communalities*
X_1: I did not mind paying the high price for my Star DVD player.	0.89	0.15	.815
X_2: I am pleased with the variety of things that a Star DVD player can do.	0.16	0.86	.766
X_3: I hardly ever worry about anything going wrong with my Star DVD player.	0.18	0.94	.916
X_4: My friends are very impressed with the Star DVD player.	0.96	0.06	.926
X_5: The Star DVD player has the latest technology built into it.	0.09	0.88	.782
X_6: No other brand of DVD player even comes close to matching the Star.	0.92	0.17	.875
Eigenvalues: Standardized variance explained by each factor	2.626	2.454	
Proportion of the total variance explained by each factor	0.438	0.409	

extracted factors. The achieved communalities for all six variables are listed in the last column of Table 15.4.

We derive achieved communalities for the original variables by summing the squared factor loadings corresponding to each variable. These values shed light on the extent to which a reduced set of factors reflects the data on each original variable. The two factors in our example account for more than 75 percent of the variance in each of the six variables, suggesting that the factor analysis has been quite effective.

Numbers in the row labeled "Eigenvalues" in Table 15.4 summarize the amount of information captured by each factor. The *eigenvalue* of any factor is the total standardized variance accounted for by that factor. Eigenvalues of the extracted factors are given by summing the squared factor loadings corresponding to each factor. The total standardized variance in the original data set is simply the number of variables, because each variable has a variance of 1. The total standardized variance in our example is 6. Therefore, the proportion of variance extracted by F_1 is its eigenvalue divided by 6, or $2.626/6 = .438$. Similarly, the proportion of the total variance extracted by F_2 is .409. These proportions are shown in the last row of Table 15.4. The proportion of the total original variance extracted by the two factors together is .847 (or 84.7 percent). This result is another indication that the factor analysis has been quite effective.[9]

Now let's turn to interpretation of F_1 and F_2. The first factor is strongly correlated with X_1, X_4, and X_6, and weakly correlated with X_2, X_3, and X_5. The second factor is strongly correlated with X_2, X_3, and X_5, and weakly correlated with X_1, X_4, and X_6. These results are somewhat fortunate; factor loadings will not always be so clean as to suggest that key variables making up one factor have little in common with another factor.[10] What do X_1, X_4, and X_6 have in common? Not minding the product's high price (X_1), impressing friends with the product (X_4), and viewing the product as being greatly superior to competing products (X_6) suggest that the common dimension underlying them can be called a *prestige* factor. Similarly, satisfaction with the product's capabilities (X_2), lack of worry about the product's failing (X_3), and believing the product is technologically up to date (X_5) imply that F_2 can perhaps be labeled a *performance* factor. However, as we pointed out earlier, these labels are subjective and may be challenged by others as being inappropriate.

Not all factor loadings have to be positive, as in Table 15.4. After all, they are correlation coefficients and can range from -1 to $+1$. The features that the original variables are measuring and the nature of the interrelationships among them will have an impact on the signs of the factor loadings. For instance, if a statement such as "Star DVD players are technologically behind the times" had been included in the SBI survey, its loading on factor F_2 in Table 15.4 would most likely have been negative. Intuitively, a negative factor loading means that the variable represents something contrary to what the overall factor dimension represents.

▌Potential Applications

Factor analysis has several applications. First, we can use it to develop concise, but comprehensive, multiple-item scales for measuring various marketing constructs. This application is perhaps the most frequent one, judging from published research reports and articles. In Chapter 9 we saw that the process of developing a multiple-item scale (a Likert or semantic-differential scale for measuring attitudes) typically starts with generating a large set of statements related to a topic. Factor analysis can help reduce the set of statements to a concise instrument and at the same time ensure that the retained statements adequately reflect critical aspects of the construct being measured. The following scenario illustrates this application.

> **SCENARIO** A public utility company wants to develop a 15-item scale to measure its customers' attitudes toward nuclear power. The company has already generated an initial pool of 100 items concerning nuclear power. Further, it has data on these items in the form of ratings obtained through a pilot survey of customers.

One approach to constructing the final 15-item scale is to use factor analysis in the following fashion. As we stated in Chapter 9, attitudes are generally believed to have three distinct dimensions: cognitive, affective, and behavioral. We can therefore conduct a factor analysis of the initial pool of 100 items and extract three factors from it. An examination of the resulting factor-loading matrix and the key items making up each factor can indicate whether the three attitude dimensions are adequately covered by the initial set of items. If they are, we can choose the 5 items with the highest loadings on each factor for the final 15-item scale.[11]

A second application of factor analysis is to illuminate the nature of distinct dimensions underlying an existing data set and hence offer managerial insights that may not emerge otherwise—insights that can be helpful in developing market segmentation and marketing mix strategies. For instance, the factor-loading matrix pertaining to the SBI survey data (Table 15.4) implies that prestige and performance may be two critical criteria underlying customer evaluations of Star DVD players. This finding, in turn, suggests that SBI may benefit by building its promotional strategy for Star DVD players around the themes of prestige and performance.

Third, the ability of factor analysis to convert a large volume of data into a set of factor scores on a limited number of *uncorrelated* factors makes the technique ideal for use in conjunction with other analysis procedures, such as multiple regression and discriminant analysis. Suppose 20 closely related independent variables are to be included in a multiple regression equation. Two potential problems here are multicollinearity and the lack of a sufficient number of observations. An effective way to circumvent both problems is to perform a factor analysis of the 20 independent variables. Because the variables are closely related, just a few factors—say, four—should capture most of the information in the independent variable data set. The four uncorrelated factors can be treated as independent variables, and their factor scores can be used as raw data for the multiple regression analysis.

Cluster Analysis

Cluster analysis segments objects, such as customers, market areas, or products, into groups, so that objects within each group are similar to one another on a variety of characteristics.

As its name implies, the basic purpose of **cluster analysis** is to segment objects, such as customers, market areas, or products, into groups, so that members within each group are similar to one another on a variety of characteristics. Cluster analysis is potentially valuable in market segmentation studies in which the objective is to identify distinct customer groups. This technique strives to identify natural groupings of objects on the basis of their values on a number of variables, without designating any of them as a dependent variable. The following example illustrates this point.

> **EXAMPLE**   A firm offering recreational services wants to enter a new region of the country. It recently surveyed a large sample of households in this region and gathered data on more than 100 characteristics, including demographics, expenditures on recreation, leisure time activities, and interests of household members. The firm wants to identify one or several household segments that are likely to be most responsive to its advertising and services.

One way for the firm to identify such segments is to conduct a cluster analysis of the data it has gathered. The results of this analysis will reveal clusters of households, each of which contains households that have similar data on the measured characteristics and each of which differs markedly from other clusters. Examining the composition of individual clusters will aid the firm in deciding which clusters to target and how best to reach them through its advertising.[12]

Cluster analysis differs from discriminant analysis, even though both techniques deal with partitioning a collection of objects into groups so that each group contains similar objects. In discriminant analysis, the researcher prespecifies the groups on the basis of a dependent variable. The technique then examines the ability of a set of independent variables to distinguish effectively among the various groups. In cluster analysis, the groups are not prespecified. Instead, the technique itself generates the groups on the basis of similarity of the objects on a number of variables.

How does cluster analysis work? Several clustering procedures are available, each based on a somewhat different set of complex computer routines.[13] But the basic principle underlying them is the same, and they all measure the similarity between objects on the basis of their values on the various characteristics. Similarity between objects is often ascertained through some *distance measure*, which can best be illustrated in the context of a situation involving just two clustering characteristics. Suppose data are available for a sample of individuals on the following two variables:

• The extent to which they participate in outdoor sporting events (X1)
• The extent to which they watch outdoor sporting events on TV (X2)

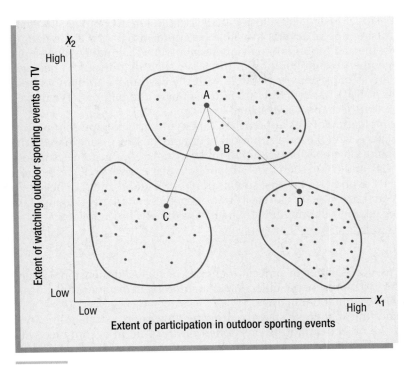

Exhibit 15.8
Clusters Formed by Using Data on Two Characteristics

Data on X_1 and X_2 are plotted on a two-dimensional graph in Exhibit 15.8. Each point in Exhibit 15.8 represents one individual. The physical distance between any pair of points is *inversely* related to how similar the corresponding individuals are when their X_1- and X_2-values are considered together. Thus individual A is more like B than like either C or D. From a comparison of all such interpoint distances, Exhibit 15.8 reveals three distinct clusters.

Constructing clusters from a scatter plot—that is, determining how many distinct clusters there are and to which cluster each data point should be assigned—is an iterative, trial-and-error process. To construct clusters efficiently and systematically, we must use computer algorithms. These start with some arbitrary cluster boundaries and progressively modify them until the average interpoint distances with-in clusters are as small as possible relative to average distances between clusters. This logic—minimizing interpoint distances within clusters and maximizing them across clusters—also applies to situations in which a large number of variables form the basis for clustering. We can use cluster analysis not only for segmenting customers but also for segmenting objects such as geographic market areas or brands within a product category.

Multidimensional Scaling

Multidimensional scaling is intended to infer the underlying dimensions from a series of similarity or preference judgments provided by customers about objects (products, brands, and so on) within a given set.

Whereas cluster analysis groups objects according to similarities inferred from data on prespecified dimensions, **multidimensional scaling** does somewhat the reverse, uncovering key dimensions underlying customers' evaluations while working from a series of similarity or preference judgments provided by customers about products or brands within a given set. It is most often used in marketing to identify the relative positions of competing brands, stores, and the like, as perceived by customers. Data on perceived similarities or preferences can be nonmetric, in the form of ranks, or metric, in the form of more refined ratings. Multidimensional scaling approaches are available for analyzing nonmetric as well as metric input data; we can also analyze data on similarities and preferences separately or on both simultaneously.[14] To get an intuitive idea of what multidimensional scaling does, we will use a simple example involving analysis of similarities provided in the form of ranks.

EXAMPLE A customer is asked to consider a set of six SUVs and describe how similar each SUV is to the others. Specifically, the customer is asked to compare *pairs* of SUVs and rank the pairs from most similar to least similar. Because there are six SUVs, 15 distinct pairs of SUVs are possible. The customer's rankings appear in Table 15.5.

Multidimensional scaling, like cluster analysis, is an iterative process that can be carried out using one of several available computer programs. If the data in Table 15.5 are subjected to multidimensional scaling, the technique will attempt to generate a geometric configuration of the SUVs such that distances between pairs of SUVs are as consistent as possible with the customer's similarity ranks; that is, the pair of SUVs ranked 15th are farthest apart, the pair of SUVs ranked 14th are the next farthest apart, and so on.

An important feature of this approach is that it attempts to represent objects in a geometric space, with the lowest number of dimensions necessary to make the resulting configuration consistent with the similarity ranks. For instance, suppose three objects, A, B, and C, are such that a respondent perceives A and B to be most similar (rank = 1), B and C to be least similar (rank = 3), and A and C to be somewhere in between (rank = 2). We can easily transform these similarity rankings into a corresponding geometric configuration in just *one* dimension, as follows:

$$B \qquad A \qquad\qquad\qquad\qquad\qquad\qquad C$$

However, as the number of objects increases, a higher-dimensional space may be necessary to represent the objects so that interobject distances are consistent with perceived similarity rankings.

Conceptually, this technique starts by arraying objects on a straight line (one dimension). If the object cannot be positioned on this line in accordance with perceived similarities between them, it adds another perpendicular line and moves the objects around in two-dimensional space to see whether a configuration that is reasonably consistent with the similarity rankings can be obtained. If it cannot be obtained, the technique adds a third dimension, reconfigures the objects in three-dimensional space, and so on. Exhibit 15.9 shows a two-dimensional configuration of the six SUVs in which the inter-SUV distances are consistent with the input ranking shown in Table 15.5.

Ignoring for the moment the point marked "Ideal SUV," what insight does Exhibit 15.9 offer? To answer this question, we must know what the two dimensions represent. Labeling the dimensions is quite subjective, however, and hence is a potential problem area. It requires us to inspect the relative positions of the objects along each dimension and infer what the dimension is most likely to represent on the basis of our prior knowledge about the objects themselves.

TABLE 15.5
Similarity Rankings of Six 2005 SUVs

	Lexus LX 470	Land Rover LR3	Mercedes-Benz M-Class	Acura MDX	Infiniti FX45	BMW X5
Lexus LX 470		15	14	12	11	13
Land Rover LR3			1	4	7	2
Mercedes-Benz M-Class				5	8	3
Acura MDX					10	6
Infiniti FX45						9

Note: The numbers are ranks indicating perceived similarities between pairs of SUVs; the smaller the number, the more similar the pair of SUVs.

**Exhibit 15.9
Multidimensional Map of 2005
SUVs Based on Similarity
Rankings**

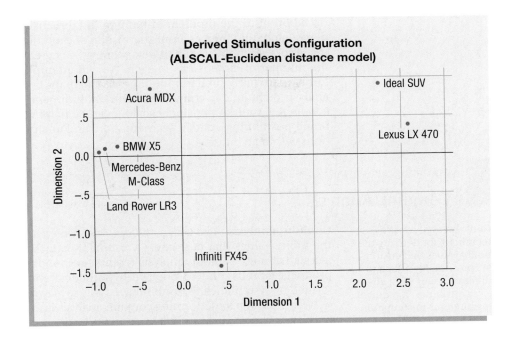

When the six SUVs in our example are arrayed along the horizontal dimension (dimension 1), the Infiniti FX45 is closest to the origin, and the Lexus LX 470 is farthest from the origin. From what we know about the SUVs, we can perhaps label dimension 1 as *value,* with value increasing from left to right along the dimension. Likewise, dimension 2 can be interpreted as representing *quality,* with quality increasing from bottom to top. (Remember, however, that someone else looking at the same map may come up with a different set of labels for the two dimensions. Also, in some cases it may be impossible to interpret certain dimensions meaningfully.)

Thus, from Exhibit 15.9, which summarizes the results of applying multidimensional scaling to the customer's similarity rankings, we can infer that this particular customer implicitly used value and quality as key criteria in comparing the six SUVs. These criteria may therefore be critical influences on the customer's choice of SUVs.

Now let's look at the position marked "Ideal SUV" in Exhibit 15.9. As its name suggests, this label signifies a hypothetical SUV best able to meet the customer's specific needs. We can derive the position of the ideal SUV by including it in the set of SUVs initially compared by the customer—in other words, by asking the customer to make pairwise comparisons among *seven* SUVs (six actual and one ideal). From the position of the ideal SUV in Exhibit 15.9, the Lexus LX 470 would appear to be most attractive and the Infiniti FX45 least attractive to the customer. Insights like these will suggest changes in strategy and the dimensions along which such changes must be made to move a particular SUV closer to a customer's ideal.

The SUV configuration shown in Exhibit 15.9 is derived from just one customer's perceived similarities among the SUVs and hence does not necessarily reflect the perceptions of other customers. For the same set of SUVs, another customer's similarity rankings may produce an entirely different multidimensional map. Herein lies another practical limitation of multidimensional scaling (in addition to the problem of naming the dimensions): we may not be able to derive global inferences from the results of multidimensional scaling when the maps corresponding to different customers vary greatly, especially with respect to the number of dimensions in each. We can attempt to identify *segments* of customers with fairly similar multidimensional maps by using an appropriate cluster analysis technique in conjunction with multidimensional scaling. When properly conducted, multidimensional scaling can be helpful in areas such as product or brand positioning, market segmentation, and analysis of competing firms' positions within an industry.

Conjoint Analysis

Conjoint analysis is a technique for deriving the utility values that customers presumably attach to different levels of an object's attributes. It requires respondents to compare hypothetical profiles of products, brands, and so on.

Conjoint analysis (also called *conjoint measurement*) is a technique for deriving the utility values that customers presumably attach to different levels of an object's attributes. Conjoint analysis requires respondents to compare hypothetical products, brands, and so on. The hypothetical stimuli are descriptive profiles formed by systematically combining varying levels of certain key attributes.

The first step in performing conjoint analysis is to construct several descriptive profiles or hypothetical stimuli by combining different levels of selected attributes. Suppose we want to assess the role played by the following attributes in customer evaluations of personal computers: price, processor speed, and hard drive capacity. Also suppose we are particularly interested in evaluating three levels of price ($299, $649, and $999); two levels of processor speed (2.6 GHz and 2.8 GHz); and four levels of hard drive capacity (80 GB, 120 GB, 160 GB, and 200 GB). With these levels for the three attributes, a total of 24 different descriptive profiles of personal computers are possible (3 levels of price × 2 levels of processor speed × 4 levels of hard drive capacity).

One approach to obtaining customer-preference ranking data suitable for conjoint analysis is called the *two-factors-at-a-time*, or *tradeoff*, *approach*. In this approach, we ask customers to rank their preferences for various combinations of attribute levels, considering just a pair of attributes at a time. Considering price and processor speed in our example, customers are asked to rank the six possible combinations of levels according to their preferences (most preferred = 1 and least preferred = 6). We can obtain similar sets of preference ranks for the price–hard drive capacity and speed–hard drive capacity attribute pairs.

Another way to obtain customer-preference ranking data is to use a *full-profile approach*. Here we ask customers to rank order their preferences for the 24 different profiles representing all possible combinations of the three attributes. For each approach, Research in Use 15.3 presents illustrations of instructions and stimuli that are typically used in gathering data for conjoint analysis.

The two-factors-at-a-time approach is easier for customers to comprehend and respond to, especially when numerous attributes are included in the analysis. This approach is somewhat unrealistic, however, because it presents only partial stimuli to respondents. Hence, there is some question about how meaningful the preference ranks will be. The full-profile approach is more realistic but may overwhelm respondents when the number of attributes is large.[15] The full-profile approach, however, seems to work well in an Internet setting.[16]

The output of conjoint analysis is a set of *utility values* corresponding to each attribute. The higher the utility value for a certain level of an attribute, the greater a customer's preference is for descriptive profiles containing that level. For

Personal Computer Study

Instructions and Stimuli for Data Collection in Conjoint Analysis: Two-Factors-at-a-Time Approach

We would like to know what your relative preferences are concerning personal computer features and how much of one feature you are willing to trade off for another feature. The table to the right has six blank boxes representing different combinations of price and memory for personal computers. Please indicate your relative preferences for the different combinations by simply writing the number 1 in the box that represents your *most preferred* price-memory combination, then writing the number 2 in the box that represents your *second most preferred* price-memory combination, and so on, until you have assigned the number 6 to your least preferred combination.

		Price	
Processing Speed	$299	$649	$999
2.6 GHx	☐	☐	☐
2.8 GHz	☐	☐	☐

Note: This rating procedure would be repeated for the 12 price-versatility combinations and the 8 memory-versatility combinations.

Full-Profile Approach

Here are 24 cards representing different combinations of price, processing speed, and hard drive capacity levels of personal computers. Please study each card and place it in one of three categories— (a) definitely prefer; (b) indifferent; or (c) definitely not prefer—according to how much you prefer a personal computer that has the features listed on the card. After you have allocated all 24 cards across the three categories, rank order the cards *within each category* from "most preferred" to "least preferred."

PERSONAL COMPUTER— DESKTOP	PERSONAL COMPUTER— DESKTOP	PERSONAL COMPUTER— DESKTOP	PERSONAL COMPUTER— DESKTOP
Price $299	Price $299	Price $299	Price $299
Speed 2.6 GHz	Speed 2.6 GHz	Speed 2.6 GHz	Speed 2.6 GHz
Hard Drive 80 GB	Hard Drive 120 GB	Hard Drive 160 GB	Hard Drive 200 GB

Note: Only 4 of the 24 cards are shown. Also, the stack of cards will typically be shuffled to randomize the order before being given to each respondent.

instance, assume that the utility values plotted in Exhibit 15.10 are generated by a conjoint analysis of preference rankings given by one customer. This exhibit offers several interesting insights. As we would expect, the utility of price decreases for the higher price levels, whereas the utilities for processor speed and hard drive capacity go up with increases in their attribute levels. We can ascertain the relative importance of the three attributes by computing and comparing their respective *ranges* of utility values.

Range for price = 0.8 − 0.3 = 0.5

Range for processor speed = 0.9 − 0.6 = 0.3

Range for hard drive capacity = 0.8 − 0.4 = 0.4

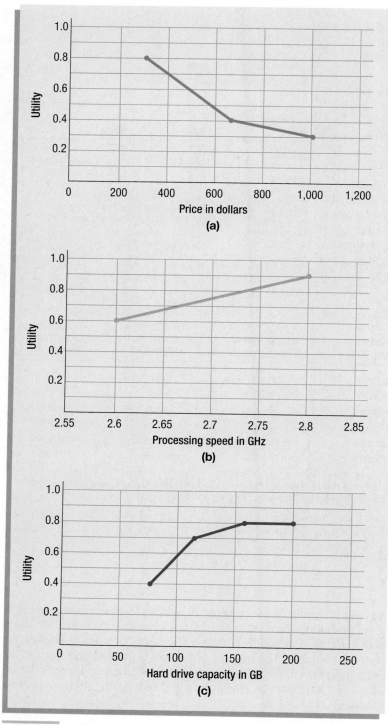

Price in dollars

(a)

Processing speed in GHz

(b)

Hard drive capacity in GB

(c)

Exhibit 15.10
Utility Values for Three Personal
Computer Attributes

Intuitively, a wide range of utility values should signify that customer preferences are quite sensitive to changes in the levels of the attribute. Hence, in our illustration price is most critical, hard drive capacity is next most critical, and processor speed is least critical in influencing customer preferences for personal computers.

The utility values in Exhibit 15.10 can also be used to compare the potential attractiveness of different personal computer configurations. For instance, is a personal computer with a 2.6 GHz processor speed, a 120 GB hard drive, and a cost of $649 likely to be more attractive to the customer than one with a 2.8 GHz processor speed, a 160 GB hard drive, and a cost of $999? We can answer this question by computing the total utility of the two hypothetical product configurations, as follows:[17]

Total utility for the 2.6 GHz, 120 GB, $649 personal computer
$$= 0.6 + 0.7 \text{ 1 } 0.4 = 1.7$$

Total utility for the 2.8 GHz, 160 GB, $999 personal computer
$$= 0.9 + 0.8 + 0.3 = 2.0$$

Thus the latter combination of attributes is likely to be more attractive to the customer than the former.

Like the results in multidimensional scaling, the results in conjoint analysis are specific to individuals; that is, a set of utility values is generated for *each* respondent. We must therefore pool utility values across respondents if we are to make generalizable inferences. Some approaches can yield pooled utilities and also aid in estimating market shares for products with different combinations of attribute levels. For example, researchers Terry Vavra, Paul Green, and Abba Krieger used conjoint analysis in conjunction with a computer simulator to examine consumer reactions to and acceptance of E-ZPass, an electronic toll collection system.[18] Conjoint analysis has had several hundred commercial applications within the past few years.[19] Ready access to high-speed computers and the practical appeal of conjoint analysis results are likely to further increase the use of the technique in the future. Even some of the data collection problems associated with conjoint analysis, such as the difficulty of systematically formulating descriptive profiles when the number of attributes is large and of presenting the profiles without overwhelming respondents, are being overcome by using computers to construct the stimuli, present them to respondents, record their preferences, and transfer the data immediately to a central computer's memory.[20]

The advent of high-speed computers at relatively low cost paved the way for a new way of marketing with the use of databases. Many analytical tools were developed to analyze large databases. The collection of these tools is popularly referred to as *data mining*. We shall look at some of these tools.

Data Mining Tools for Gaining Customer and Market Insights*

Various companies—such as banks, airlines, health care firms, dot.coms, and retailers—also have data mining tools at their disposal, which enables them to gain valuable insights about their markets and customers.[21] A case in point is Amazon.com, a major online player that relies heavily on data mining to gain customer insights.

CASE IN POINT ▶ **Amazon** Amazon.com is a data mining giant, collecting and storing reams of data from its 40 million customers. Although it started simply as a bookseller, Amazon now sells a dizzying array of products on its website and has become a recognized leader in the world of personalization. It routinely conducts market basket analysis to uncover which items are bought together, as well as the sequence in which those items are purchased. This information helps the company make accurate recommendations that match individual customer needs. Using your past purchases, and even your "clicks" on items that you don't buy, Amazon personalizes its website so that everyone who signs in has his or her own personalized "gateway" page and Amazon store. Every Web page you browse is customized so that the products or product categories that are likely to be of the greatest interest to you appear at the top of the page. Furthermore, Amazon recommends books, CDs, DVDs, and other products on the basis of the buying and browsing patterns of other customers who bought the same titles you did. Finally, it lets you know about new releases that appear to match your preferences.

When you buy a book, Amazon will even try to pair it with another book—specifically, the title purchased most often at the same time as the book you bought. Amazon also offers U.S. customers individualized bargains according to their preferences.

All this personalization through data mining adds up to more than $5 billion in sales for the Seattle-based company. Data mining allows Amazon.com to practice personalized "one-to-one" marketing,[22] though in no way is it the only company to use data mining. Increasingly, organizations such as Ford, Wal-Mart, Kmart-Sears, and many others have become active users of data mining.[23] ◀

Data mining comprises various forms of analysis, such as market basket, classification, scoring models, and forecasting or prediction. In addition, offshoots of data mining, such as text, audio, and video mining, have begun to provide some interesting new business applications.

*This section on data mining was written by Professor M. J. Xavier, Institute for Financial Management and Research (IFMR), Chennai, India.

Data Mining

Data mining is an analytic
process for exploring data
to find consistent patterns
or systematic relationships
between variables and then
to validate those findings by
applying the detected
patterns to new subsets of
data.

Data mining is an analytic process designed to explore data (usually large amounts of business or market-related data) to find consistent patterns or systematic relationships between variables. Once those relationships have been discovered, the data mining process attempts to validate the findings by applying the detected patterns to new subsets of data. Because the key focus of any data mining exercise is to uncover interesting and useful patterns from the databases, it is also sometimes known as *knowledge discovery in databases (KDD)* or *predictive analytics.*

The data requirements for a typical data mining project can be quite significant. Even data storage (data warehousing) requires sophisticated technologies. As was described in Chapter 4, a data warehouse is a centralized database that consolidates companywide data from a variety of operational systems. In emphasizing the capture of data from diverse sources for later access and analysis, data warehousing selectively extracts and organizes data from various online transaction-processing or Web-browsing applications and other sources. Data mining accesses the data from the data warehouse and uses well-established statistical techniques, automated machine-learning techniques (techniques that use artificial intelligence algorithms), neural networks, genetic algorithms, and sophisticated mathematical models to generate insights about customer behavior. For example, working with Sun Microsystems and Accenture, Visa EU has created one of Europe's largest data warehouses to store details about the 3 billion credit and debit card transactions it processes every year across 26 different countries.[24] The power of this vast pool of financial data enables Visa EU to help member banks understand their customers' behavior better than ever before.

Data mining also can uncover details about such important issues as emerging usage patterns in a newly defined market segment, high-margin customers with increasing buying velocity, undetected trends in customer account losses, and customer lifetime values. For instance, Harrah's Entertainment uses a sophisticated mathematical forecasting model to assess a customer's lifetime value on the basis of his or her first visit to a casino.[25] The following example shows an interesting application of social networks to understanding telecommunications consumers' behavior.

CASE IN POINT ▶ **Social Networking—Are You an Alpha or an Omega User?** Until recently, telecommunications companies relied on analyses of aggregated data about individual users to develop customer profiles. But now they have discovered that it is not how many calls a customer makes but rather the communication patterns between customers—the traffic patterns among social networks—that are relevant for developing profitable segments. For example, two customers with the same number of minutes of calls per month might exhibit very different social networks. Whereas one could be using a mobile phone mostly to reach his or her parents, the other could be using it to stay in touch with friends. Similarly, some consumers might use voice calls to communicate with their professional contacts, but use SMS (short message service) to communicate with their social friends. Social network analysis even enables companies to explore who makes more calls and who receives more calls. People who love to communicate and to keep social groups connected and informed are labeled "Alpha users." Alpha users generally adopt communication technologies earlier than their peers in the same social network, which makes it easier to penetrate this segment with a new service or product. Alpha users also are within a phone call's reach of 52 to 86 percent of all customers in that segment. Penetrating the Alpha-user segment then leads to the second class of subscribers, namely, Omega users. These customers receive many calls but don't place many outbound calls.[26] ◄

To handle complex data mining tasks, several new software packages are available. Some of the better-known packages, such as STATISTICA Data Miner, SPSS Clementine, Affinium Model, Insightful Miner, SAS Analytics, and KXEN, incorporate analytical tools for data mining.[27]

Data Mining Procedures

Data mining procedures include the following:

- *Association.* Looking for patterns that connect one event or characteristic to another
- *Sequence,* or *path, analysis.* Looking for patterns in which one event leads to a later event
- *Classification.* Looking for new patterns by segmenting the data into groups
- *Clustering.* Finding and visually documenting groups of facts or groups of customers not previously known to be similar
- *Scoring models.* Developing propensity scores for individual customers
- *Forecasting/prediction.* Discovering patterns in data that can lead to reasonable predictions about the future

Association and sequence or path analyses are commonly used in market basket analysis; classification and clustering are used for segmentation analysis; scoring models work in conjunction with RFM analysis; and forecasting or prediction is employed to predict campaign response rates. We now describe and discuss some of these models, methods, and analyses.

Association and Market Basket Analysis

Market basket analysis examines customers' shopping carts to determine items that are most frequently purchased together.

A **market basket analysis** involves an algorithm that examines a long list of transactions to determine which items are most frequently purchased together. It takes its name from the image of a person in a supermarket throwing all of his or her items into a shopping cart (a "market basket"). In addition, it acknowledges that, in retailing, most purchases are bought on impulse. Studies conducted by the Point-of-Purchase Advertising Institute (POPAI) suggest that grocery shoppers make two-thirds of all their purchase decisions after they enter the store, a ratio that has more or less held constant since 1965, when POPAI first conducted its studies. Market basket analysis gives clues as to how a customer builds his or her basket, as the following example illustrates.

CASE IN POINT ► **Beauty Care, Greeting Cards, and Seasonal Candies Go Together**[28] Mind Meld, Inc., a data mining company, analyzed 32 weeks' worth of point-of-sale data containing 8 million market baskets. Market basket analysis revealed that "beauty-conscious" customers bought greeting cards 25 percent of the time and seasonal candies 16 percent of the time. Based on insights from this market basket analysis, the supermarket chain moved greeting cards and seasonal candies adjacent to the beauty care area, resulting in increased sales of both. ◄

Knowing which products sell together can be beneficial to any business. An obvious benefit is the increase in sales that a retail store might achieve by reorganizing its products so that things that sell together are placed in close proximity. This placement facilitates impulse buying and helps ensure that customers who would have bought a product in the past do not forget to buy it because they fail to see it. In addition, effective product placement has the side benefit of improving customer satisfaction; once they have found one of the items they want, customers do not have to look all over the store for other things that they normally buy with that one item. Online stores and catalog merchants obtain the same benefit by being able to determine the most effective way to group and display items on websites and in catalogs. As the earlier Case in Point showed, Amazon.com puts market basket analysis to excellent use by suggesting products that go together.

But the recommendations from a market basket analysis are not always quite so straightforward. Suppose a store finds that a popular toy is being bought along with candies 65 percent of the time. Potential marketing implications of such a finding could be

1. Keep the toy and candies close to each other in the store.
2. Bundle candy bars with the toy.
3. Bundle the toy with candy and another slow-moving item (to promote the slow-moving item).
4. Raise the price on one and lower it on the other.
5. Keep the toy and candies at opposite ends of the store to ensure that customers pass as many items as possible to gather the toy and the candy.

Input to a market basket analysis normally consists of a list of sales transactions organized in the form of a table; each column in the table represents a product, and each row represents either a sale (if the goal of the analysis is to determine which items sell together at the same time) or a customer (if the goal is to determine which items the same person buys together). The table cells generally contain only binary values: 1 (bought product) or 0 (did not buy product). The following example explains how a company might use a market basket analysis.

Suppose we monitor the shopping carts of eight customers, as shown in Exhibit 15.11, who might purchase any of eight products (A–H). The transactions of the eight customers appear in their shopping carts. For example, customer 1

**Exhibit 15.11
Shopping Carts of Eight
Customers**

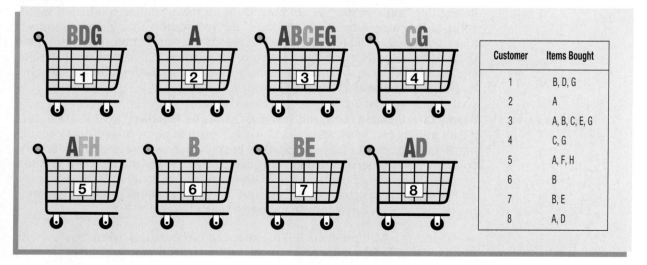

Customer	Items Bought
1	B, D, G
2	A
3	A, B, C, E, G
4	C, G
5	A, F, H
6	B
7	B, E
8	A, D

bought products B, D, and G; customer 2 bought A only; customer 3 bought A, B, C, E, and G; and so on. These data then can be summarized as in Table 15.6.

Furthermore, the products can be cross-tabulated, as shown in Table 15.7. The numbers on the diagonal indicate the number of times the individual products were purchased, and the other numbers indicate the number of times they were purchased in pairs. The first row in Table 15.7 indicates that product A has been bought once with every other product. From the second row, we can see that product B has been bought once with A, C, and D, and twice with E and G. Note that B was never bought with F or H. These data can be visualized in many different forms. Market basket analysis can produce any number of association rules, but only the best rules should be used for developing a marketing campaign. There are two measures of the quality of an association rule: support and confidence.[29]

■ **Support**   To determine the *support* that a combination or association receives from the data, we can form rules, such as the following: "The support for a person's buying products C and G is 25 percent; namely, two out of the eight

TABLE 15.6
Transaction Data for Market Basket Analysis

Customer	A	B	C	D	E	F	G	H
1	0	1	0	1	0	0	1	0
2	1	0	0	0	0	0	0	0
3	1	1	1	0	1	0	1	0
4	0	0	1	0	0	0	1	0
5	1	0	0	0	0	1	0	1
6	0	1	0	0	0	0	0	0
7	0	1	0	0	1	0	0	0
8	1	0	0	1	0	0	0	0

TABLE 15.7
Cross-Tabulation for Market Basket Analysis

	A	B	C	D	E	F	G	H
A	4	1	1	1	1	1	1	1
B	1	4	1	1	2	0	2	0
C	1	1	2	0	1	0	2	0
D	1	1	0	2	0	0	1	0
E	1	1	1	0	2	0	1	0
F	1	0	0	0	0	1	0	1
G	1	2	2	1	1	0	3	0
H	1	0	0	0	0	1	0	1

total transactions include both C and G."[30] Support can also be used to measure a single item; for instance, the support for product C is 25 percent, because it occurs in two of the eight transactions. Similarly, support for product G (occurring in three out of eight transactions) is 37.5 percent. Measuring the support of a single item is where the central diagonal of the table can be useful.

■ **Confidence** Support, however, is an incomplete measure of the quality of an association rule. Is 25 percent support for the combination of C and G a good rule? A customer's purchase of C can't really tell us whether or not he or she will also buy G. What is needed is a measure of how confident we can be, given that a customer has purchased one product, that he or she will also purchase another product.

The *confidence* of an association rule represents the support for the combination divided by the support for the condition.[31] Using our previous example, the support for the combination (G + C) is 25 percent because it occurs in two of the eight transactions. However, the support for condition G is 37.5 percent; therefore, we obtain a confidence rating of 25% ÷ 37.5% = 67%. Note also that confidence is directional. The confidence of the rule "If a customer purchases G, then he or she will buy C" is 25% ÷ 37.5% = 67%.

The same logic can also be extended to multiple items. Thus far, we have looked at only association rules involving two items, but more accurate rules sometimes emerge when more than two items are considered. Performing a market basket analysis that considers higher numbers of items in groups must occur iteratively; first pairs are found, then sets of three, then four, and so on. The number of calculations required to perform the analysis varies exponentially with the number of products to be considered. In other words, the number of calculations for n items is proportional to the number of items to be considered at one time raised to the nth power. Market basket analyses that include more than two items therefore result in multidimensional tables that can be difficult to visualize. However, despite the difficulties of visual representation, the use of data mining software allows meaningful rules to emerge.

■ **Sequencing and Market Basket Analysis** A sequencing tool is very similar to an association tool, but it adds time to the analysis and produces rules such as the following: "People who have purchased a digital camera are three times more likely to purchase a camcorder in the time period two to four months after the camera was purchased."

Sequencing requires a primary identification (ID), such as a customer ID, which connects transactions occurring at different times. By taking pairwise combinations of all transactions that have the same primary ID (say, were purchased by the same customer) and computing the time difference between each pair, the algorithm identifies all before-and-after item pairs.

An example of the application of sequencing rules might be website design. A Web company can collect data about the Web pages visited by consumers and the sequences in which those pages were accessed. Analyzing the data using appropriate data mining techniques might reveal patterns and sequencing rules that suggest the most effective website design to maximize ease of navigation.

■ **Advanced Market Basket Analysis** The discussion thus far has focused primarily on using data mining to uncover aggregate-level patterns in a given database. However, more sophisticated market basket analyses are possible when a customer's ID can be linked to each transaction through some mechanism, such as scanning customers' loyalty cards when they make purchases in a retail store.

The scope of market basket analysis thereby expands because customers' transaction data may be enhanced by the background information the retailer collected from them when they enrolled in the loyalty program.

For example, a deeper understanding of a buyer's purchasing behavior can be gained by examining questions like the following:

- How often does the buyer shop?
- How much does the buyer spend?
- How often does the buyer purchase a specific item?
- How many units of a specific item does the buyer purchase during a shopping trip?
- What competitive or complementary items does the buyer purchase?
- In which departments of the store does the buyer shop?
- How do frequent buyers' demographics and purchasing patterns compare with those of occasional buyers?
- How do nonbuyers of a specific item compare with buyers in terms of demographics and purchasing patterns?

Advanced market basket analyses can answer questions like these and provide managers with valuable insights for devising effective marketing strategies to enhance the in-store product mix, as well as to cross-sell products.

Classification Models

One of the most popular classification algorithms currently being used in data mining is the *decision tree*, otherwise known as automatic interaction detection, regression tree, answer tree, classification tree, or classification and regression tree (CART). This technique quickly analyzes a large data set that may contain many potential explanatory variables and identifies those with the greatest influence on a particular dependent variable.

The basic idea underlying the decision tree technique is to hierarchically segment individuals included in a database, on the basis of a designated categorical dependent variable, such as bought or did not buy a product. The explanatory variables are also categorical and might include, for instance,

- Demographics (age group, gender, occupation)
- Attitudes (agree or disagree with various statements)
- Previous behavior (bought or did not buy another product)

The technique creates a decision tree, a logical model represented as a binary (two-way-split) tree that shows how well the value of a target variable (dependent variable) can be predicted by using the values of a set of predictor variables (explanatory variables). An example of a decision tree is shown in Exhibit 15.12.

The rectangular boxes in the tree are called *nodes*, and each represents a set of records (rows) from the original data set. In this case, the original data included 150 customers, of whom 50 used a particular product. Nodes with *child nodes* (nodes 1 and 3) are called *interior nodes*, whereas those without child nodes (nodes 2, 4, and 5) are called *terminal* or *leaf nodes*. The topmost node (node 1) is called the *root node*. (Note that, unlike a real tree, the roots of decision trees are at the top.) In the construction of a decision tree, a binary split must divide the rows in a particular node into two groups (child nodes), then split the child groups in the same way.[32] This process is called *recursive partitioning*. The

Exhibit 15.12
A Sample Decision Tree

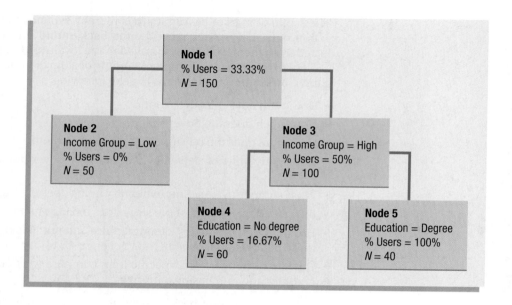

most appropriate split is selected to construct a tree that can be used to predict the value of the target variable.

In this case, the first split is based on the income variable, and we find that all users of the product are high-income customers. The second split is based on the education variable and shows that 100 percent of customers with a college degree from the high-income group ($N = 40$) use the product, whereas only 16.67 percent (10 out of 60) of those with no degree use the product. According to this decision tree, the company should therefore target high-income customers with a college degree.

In addition to the decision tree analysis, clustering (a brief description of which appears in this chapter as part of multivariate techniques) is used extensively to classify customers (or other units) into managerially useful groups. Both hierarchical and k-means clustering methods find application in data mining problems that involve classification or segmentation.

Scoring Models and RFM Analysis

Recall that data mining builds models by using inputs from a database to predict customer behavior. Further examples of such behavior might include attrition when a magazine subscription ends, cross-product purchasing, willingness to use an ATM card in place of a more expensive teller transaction, and so on. The prediction provided by a model is often called a *score*; a score (typically a numerical value) is assigned to each record in the database and indicates the likelihood that the specific customer will exhibit a particular behavior. For example, if a model is designed to predict customer attrition, a high score would indicate that the customer is likely to leave, whereas a low score would indicate the opposite. After scoring a set of customers, these numerical values suggest the most appropriate prospects for a targeted marketing campaign.

One of the most commonly used scoring methods—recency, frequency, and monetary value analysis, or RFM—has been helpful in improving response rates to marketing campaigns for more than 25 years. The analysis is based on three simple concepts:

1. Customers who purchased *recently* are more likely to buy again than customers who have not purchased in a while.

2. Customers who purchase *frequently* are more likely to buy again than customers who have made just one or two purchases.

3. Customers who *spent the most money* in total are more likely to buy again. The most valuable customers tend to continue to become even more valuable.

Thus RFM analysis is a means to segment the customer database to find those who are more likely to respond to, say, a catalog. This information will help the company lower its costs and increase its profits because it will mail catalogs to the more likely customers far more frequently than it will to customers who are unlikely to purchase from the catalog. For an RFM analysis, researchers need a database that contains information about the date of the most recent visit by each customer, the number of visits to date, and the value of the customer's total purchases thus far.

To assign a recency score, the database is sorted by the date of the customer's most recent visit, and the top 20 percent of customers are given a score of 5. The next 20 percent in terms of recent purchases is coded as 4, and so forth. Thus everyone in the database receives a recency score of 5, 4, 3, 2, or 1. A test promotion directed at a representative sample drawn from the database might elicit a response like that shown in Exhibit 15.13.[33] Purchase/visit frequency can be sorted in the same way, with the top 20 percent assigned a score of 5 and so on. The higher the number of visits, the greater the likelihood is that the customer will respond to new offers. Finally, the value of the customer's total purchases can be similarly assigned scores of 5, 4, 3, 2, or 1.

Now the entire customer base can be segmented into 125 segments according to the different combinations of the RFM scores, from 111 to 555. The highest score on all three dimensions is 555, whereas 111 represents the lowest score on all the dimensions. In between, there exist a variety of combinations, such as 543, 245, 234, 412, and so on.

Typically, the top segments tend to have higher response rates for promotional campaigns, and therefore the most responsive segments are targeted for promotional offers and new product introductions.

However, a possible danger of this approach is that a firm may end up neglecting potentially lucrative customers who currently reside in the lower-RFM categories. It is therefore advisable for a firm to select some random customers from low-score RFM segments and include them in its marketing campaigns or surveys, just in case.

Exhibit 15.13
Recency Scores and Response Rates

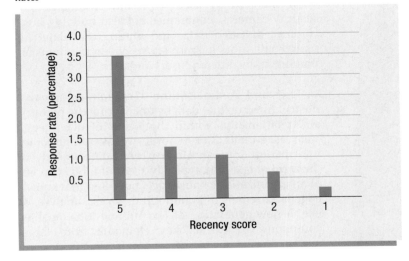

Forecasting, or Prediction, Models

The most commonly used forecasting, or prediction, models are logistic regression and neural networks. **Logistic regression** is a variation of ordinary regression that is used when the dependent (response) variable is dichotomous, coded as either 1 or 0 to represent the occurrence or nonoccurrence of some outcome event. For instance, in a new-product study, the customer buys or does not buy the

Logistic regression is a type of regression analysis in which the dependent variable is dichotomous, coded as either 1 or 0, to represent the occurence or nonoccurence of some outcome event.

product; in a bank loan study, a borrower might make timely repayments or turn into a defaulter. The independent (input) variables in logistic regression are continuous, categorical, or both. Unlike ordinary linear regression, logistic regression does not assume that the relationship between the independent variables and the dependent variable is linear, nor does it assume that the dependent variable or error terms are distributed normally. The form of the model is as follows:

$$\log\left(\frac{p}{1-p}\right) = \beta_0 + \beta_1 X_1 + \beta_2 X_2 + \ldots + \beta_n X_n$$

where p is the probability that $Y = 1$ (the event occurrence), and $X_1, X_2, \ldots, X_n$ are the independent variables (predictors). $\beta_0, \beta_1, \beta_2, \ldots, \beta_n$ are known as the regression coefficients, which are estimated from the data.

Other sophisticated models are also being developed for prediction, such as the neural network model. *Neural network models* mimic the functioning of the human brain and basically work on the principle of biological neurons (see Exhibit 15.14). In the brain, the dendrites in the neurons receive inputs, the soma processes the inputs, and the axon turns the processed inputs into outputs. Neural networks similarly take inputs and process them using various kinds of models and transformations to produce the output that most closely matches the actual data. Although neural network models may use either single- or multiple-layer processing, Exhibit 15.15 shows a diagram of a two-layer neural network.

A neural network acquires knowledge through learning, and this knowledge is stored in the interneuron connections. Compared with discriminant analysis and logistic regression, neural network models have been found to have greater prediction accuracy, but their problem stems from their diagnostics. Because the layers of the neural network are "black boxes," it is difficult to assess the relative importance of the input variables. With large problems, the modeling may consume a huge amount of computer time; normally, neural network programs require many hours of computation before final predictions emerge.[34]

New Trends in Data Mining

To cope with the vast accumulation of data by organizations, data mining methods have rapidly increased in sophistication. For instance, to mine insights from the text data included in millions of e-mails or from the large volumes of voice data that call centers generate, techniques such as text and audio mining are being increasingly used. With the proliferation of security cameras, companies are also building huge volumes of video data, and mining that data. Although still in its nascent stages, video mining is attracting many different users and uses.[35]

Exhibit 15.14
Biological Neuron

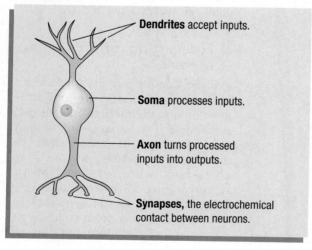

Dendrites accept inputs.

Soma processes inputs.

Axon turns processed inputs into outputs.

Synapses, the electrochemical contact between neurons.

■ **Text and Audio Mining** Text mining analyzes unstructured textual data by uncovering the patterns and relationships within thousands of documents, such as e-mails, call reports, websites, and other information sources. Unstructured data, mostly in the form of text files, typically account for 85 percent of an organization's knowledge, but often that knowledge is extremely difficult to find, access, analyze, or use. A new generation of text mining tools enables companies to extract key elements from large, unstructured data sets; discover relationships among

Exhibit 15.15
A Two-Layer Neural Network

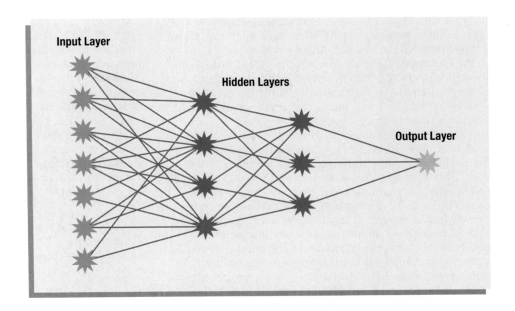

documents; and summarize the information. Many organizations have deployed or are considering such software to deal with the mountains of text they generate, even though specialized skills are needed to make such implementations work.[36]

Audio mining employs these same text mining tools after voice data are converted into text data. Several software packages exist to convert audio files to text files.

■ **Video Mining** The latest trend is to mine video data to discern patterns and extract valuable nuggets of information. For example, retail stores have started using computer software that sorts through video footage to determine, for example, how many and what types of people walk through a certain area of the store or stop to look at a certain product.[37]

Video mining enables stores to sell products more efficiently. Fewer resources are wasted on products that do not sell, so the products offered can be of higher value, and consumers can find better-quality products for the money they spend. For example, valuable answers to questions such as how long a customer spent looking at a particular display or product label, or how many customers passed a given area at a given time, can be gleaned from generated video data. The software can even be programmed to perform special tasks, such as watching the number of people at each checkout line in a store and alerting the manager when another cash register needs to be opened.[38]

SUMMARY

A variety of multivariate techniques, broadly classified into dependence and inter-dependence techniques, were discussed in this chapter. We focused on providing a conceptual understanding of these techniques, along with their potential applications and limitations. The dependence techniques covered in this chapter included analysis of variance (ANOVA) and discriminant analysis;

the interdependence techniques covered included factor analysis, cluster analysis, multidimensional scaling, conjoint analysis, and data mining.

The seeming statistical sophistication of multivariate techniques, coupled with the ready access to computer programs incorporating them, may tempt researchers to rush into using them without adequately considering their appropriateness for a given situation. Yielding to the temptation may lead to meaningless results, however.

In addition, applications of multivariate techniques, despite their apparent quantitative rigor, may not be totally free of researcher subjectivity. For instance, it is up to the researcher to decide which independent variables to include in any application involving the use of dependence techniques. Yet the choice of a particular set of independent variables can greatly influence quantitative results and the inferences they imply.

With the availability of high-speed computers and analytical tools, marketers are now better equipped to handle large volumes of transaction data and customer data. Data mining helps marketers to mine nuggets of information by examining patterns and trends in the data. The primary applications of data mining include market basket analysis, classification, scoring models, and forecasting or prediction. Association in market basket analysis helps marketers to understand patterns of buying by looking at items bought together. Classification typically employs decision tree analysis, or traditional *k*-means or hierarchical clustering methods. Scoring models—recency, frequency, and monetary value analysis, or RFM—examine customer decisions to help marketers predict customers' responses to marketing decisions. Forecasting or prediction models help marketers predict consumer behavior for new offerings. Logistic regression is the most used prediction tool, as it can handle both categorical as well as continuous predictor variables. Companies also use neural network models for prediction. The new trend is to use text, audio, and video mining methods.

REVIEW AND DISCUSSION QUESTIONS

ACE
self-test

1. What is the key distinction between dependence and independence techniques? Give an example of each technique.

2. When is interaction effect said to occur? Illustrate this effect with a suitable example.

3. State and illustrate the two key purposes of discriminant analysis.

4. Describe in your own words what factor analysis is and indicate its potential benefits.

5. Explain how cluster analysis and discriminant analysis differ.

6. Define *conjoint analysis* and state its potential applications.

7. "Multivariate techniques, although mathematically sophisticated, are not free of researcher or decision maker subjectivity." Defend this statement by pointing out some subjective aspect of each technique discussed in the chapter.

APPLICATION EXERCISES

1. A marketer of a refrigerated fruit drink has developed three new package designs for the product, which will enable the drink to be stored at room temperature. The marketer wants to know if any or all of these package designs may result in significantly higher sales than the current package design, which requires refrigerated storage. Suggest a suitable research approach for realistically evaluating the alternative package designs. What techniques would you use to analyze the research data to fulfill the marketer's information needs? Explain your answer.

2. A random sample of 600 respondents consists of 300 users (group 1) and 300 nonusers (group 2) of a certain product. The means and standard deviations of the age (variable *A*) and income (variable *B*) of the respondents in the two groups are as follows:

Group 1: $\bar{A}_1 = 30$ $\bar{B}_1 = \$15,000$
$S_{1A} = 3$ $S_{1B} = \$100$

Group 2: $\bar{A}_2 = 40$ $\bar{B}_2 = \$20,000$
$S_{2A} = 4$ $S_{2B} = \$90$

A discriminant analysis of the age and income data for the two groups produced the following discriminant function:

$$Y = v_A A + v_B B$$

where $v_A = .10$ and $v_B = .01$

a. From the discriminant analysis, would you classify a person age 25 with an income of $18,000 as a user or a nonuser? Why or why not?

b. Is one of the two independent variables more important than the other in discriminating between users and nonusers? If so, what exactly is the relative importance of one variable with respect to the other? If not, why not?

3. Consider the following factor-loading matrix:

	F_1	F_2	F_3
X_1	.90	.02	.05
X_2	.80	.02	.10
X_3	.05	.90	.02
X_4	.03	.03	.95
X_5	.75	.05	.10
X_6	.10	.80	.05
X_7	.60	.06	.08
X_8	.05	.85	.03

a. What proportion of the total variance in the original set of variables is explained by the three factors taken together?

b. What are the achieved communalities for X_4 and X_7? How would you interpret these values?

c. Are the three factors easy to interpret? Why or why not?

4. A bank conducted a survey of customers and obtained preference rankings for various hypothetical bank profiles, which were constructed using the following characteristics and levels within each characteristic.

Operating hours:

A. 8:00 A.M. to 3:00 P.M. weekdays

B. 9:00 A.M. to 5:00 P.M. weekdays

C. 9:00 A.M. to 5:00 P.M. weekdays plus 9:00 A.M. to noon Saturdays

Online transactions (to facilitate routine transactions 24 hours every day):

A. Yes   B. No

Monthly service charge:

A. None   B. $5   C. $15   D. $20

Conjoint analysis of the data yielded the following utility values for various levels of each of the three characteristics.

Operating hours:	A = 0.3
	B = 0.3
	C = 0.8
Online transactions:	A = 0.6
	B = 0.3
Monthly service charge:	A = 1.0
	B = 0.8
	C = 0.4
	D = 0.1

a. Which of the three bank characteristics is most crucial in influencing customer preference?

b. Will the bank benefit more by operating from 8:00 A.M. to 3:00 P.M. weekdays, providing no online transactions, and assessing no monthly service charge or by operating from 9:00 A.M. to 5:00 P.M. weekdays plus 9:00 A.M. to noon Saturdays, providing online transactions, and assessing a monthly service charge of $15? What if the service charge were changed to $20 in the latter alternative?

6. Compute the support for an individual's buying products B and G for the shopping cart purchases presented in Exhibit 15.11. What is the confidence rating of the purchase of B given the purchase of G? Also compute the confidence rating of the purchase of G given the purchase of B.

 SPSS EXERCISES

1. Constantine Karvonides, owner of Athenaeum Booksellers (see Cases 14.1 and 15.1), commissioned a research study to gauge the level of customer satisfaction with current operations and was looking over some of the results, trying to get a sense of how customers perceived the store. The survey was designed and administered by a local research firm. The research director of the firm had conducted some preliminary analysis of the data using SPSS software. Karvonides was interested specifically in reviewing the output of a one-way ANOVA to determine whether or not customers' overall satisfaction varied with level of education. Satisfaction was measured on a 5-point scale, with 1 being "very dissatisfied" and 5 being "very satisfied." Educational qualifications were measured by a categorical scale, with 1 being "some college or less," 2 being "college graduate," and 3 being "postgraduate." Help Karvonides interpret the ANOVA results provided below.

ANOVA

OSAT (Overall Satisfaction with Athenaeum Booksellers)

	Sum of Squares	d.f.	Mean Square	F	Sig.
Between groups	26.700	2	13.350	94.353	.000
Within groups	19.667	139	.141		
Total	46.366	141			

Descriptives

OSAT (Overall Satisfaction with Athenaeum Booksellers)

	N	Mean	Std. Deviation	Std. Error	95% Confidence Interval for Mean		Minimum	Maximum
					Lower Bound	Upper Bound		
1.00 Some college or less	48	3.08	.65	9.34E-02	2.90	3.27	2	4
2.00 College graduate	65	4.00	.00	.00	4.00	4.00	4	4
3.00 Postgraduate	29	4.00	.00	.00	4.00	4.00	4	4
Total	142	3.69	.57	4.81E-02	3.60	3.79	2	4

2. Constantine Karvonides also wanted to review the output of a randomized factorial design to determine whether or not respondents' overall satisfaction differed based on level of education and gender. (Measurement scales for satisfaction and education were the same as in the preceding exercise.) Help Karvonides interpret the factorial ANOVA results provided here and on the next page. Specifically, interpret the main effects in light of interaction effects. Remember, care must be exercised when significant interaction effects are present.

Between-Subjects Factors

		Value Label	N
GENDER	1	Female	68
	2	Male	74
NEWED: New educational levels	1.00	Some college or less	48
	2.00	College graduate	65
	3.00	Postgraduate	29

Tests of Between-Subjects Effects

Dependent Variable: OSAT (Overall Satisfaction with Athenaeum Booksellers)

Source	Type III Sum of Squares	d.f.	Mean Square	F	Sig.
Corrected model	35.373[a]	5	7.075	87.524	.000
Intercept	1687.072	1	1687.072	20871.617	.000
GENDER	2.483	1	2.483	30.720	.000
NEWED	24.292	2	12.146	150.263	.000
GENDER * NEWED	5.693	2	2.847	35.218	.000
Error	10.993	136	8.083E-02		
Total	1980.000	142			
Corrected total	46.366	141			

[a]R squared = .763 (Adjusted R squared = .754)

1. Grand Mean

Dependent Variable: OSAT (Overall Satisfaction with Athenaeum Booksellers)

Mean	Std. Error	95% Confidence Interval	
		Lower Bound	Upper Bound
3.706	.026	3.656	3.757

2. Gender

Dependent Variable: OSAT (Overall Satisfaction with Athenaeum Booksellers)

Gender	Mean	Std. Error	95% Confidence Interval	
			Lower Bound	Upper Bound
1 Female	3.848	.035	3.779	3.918
2 Male	3.564	.037	3.490	3.638

3. New Educational Levels

Dependent Variable: OSAT (Overall Satisfaction with Athenaeum Booksellers)

New educational levels	Mean	Std. Error	95% Confidence Interval	
			Lower Bound	Upper Bound
1.00 Some college or less	3.119	.041	3.037	3.200
2.00 College graduate	4.000	.036	3.930	4.070
3.00 Postgraduate	4.000	.054	3.892	4.108

4. Gender * New Educational Levels

Dependent Variable: OSAT (Overall Satisfaction with Athenaeum Booksellers)

Gender	New Educational Levels	Mean	Std. Error	95% Confidence Interval	
				Lower Bound	Upper Bound
1 Female	1.00 Some college or less	3.545	.061	3.426	3.665
	2.00 College graduate	4.000	.054	3.894	4.106
	3.00 Postgraduate	4.000	.067	3.867	4.133
2 Male	1.00 Some college or less	2.692	.056	2.582	2.803
	2.00 College graduate	4.000	.047	3.908	4.092
	3.00 Postgraduate	4.000	.086	3.830	4.170

CASE 15.1 ATHENAEUM BOOKSELLERS (PART B)

When he first took over operations at Athenaeum Booksellers, Constantine Karvonides knew that, to compete with large national bookstore chains, he would need to develop a strong product offering with high levels of service.[1] He had just commissioned a research study to gauge the level of customer satisfaction with current operations and was looking over some of the results, trying to get a sense of how customers perceived the store.

Background

Athenaeum Booksellers has been a local fixture in downtown San Francisco for the past 35 years. Athenaeum's merchandising strategy is to be the authoritative community bookstore that carries a dominant selection of titles in all subjects, including an extensive selection from small, independent publishers and university presses. The comprehensive title selection is diverse and reflects the interests of both the local community and visitors to the area. Athenaeum Booksellers also offers a café, a children's section, a music department, a magazine section, and a calendar of ongoing events, including author appearances and children's activities, which make it an active part of the community. Athenaeum creates a comfortable atmosphere with ample public reading space. The café offers coffee, tea, sandwiches, and bakery items, listening stations for customers to preview selected compact discs, and public restrooms.

Analyzing the Results of the Survey

Designed by a local research firm, the survey was administered to assess consumer satisfaction on a number of different aspects of Athenaeum Booksellers.[2] The survey was administered to individuals who visited the store over a one-week period. It was administered each day that week at different times, to obtain a good cross-section of customers. A total of 142 usable surveys were completed, and the research director of the firm had conducted some preliminary analysis of the data using SPSS software. (Output from the analyses appears in Table 1.) Constantine Karvonides wanted specifically to review the output of a preliminary factor analysis on a number of items, to determine whether or not they were capturing all the different facets of customer satisfaction. His review of the findings would also help him assess whether any additional underlying facets were driving satisfaction.

CASE QUESTION

1. Interpret the factor analysis results provided in Table 1 and discuss their implications for Karvonides.

TABLE 1
Bookstore Factor Analysis

Variables considered: visually appealing importance (VAIMP); wide selection importance (WSIMP); knowledgeable staff importance (KSIMP); availability of books on discount importance (ABDIMP); friendly service importance (FSIMP); convenient hours importance (CSHIMP); low price importance (LOPRIMP)

Total Variance Explained

Factor	Initial Eigenvalues Total	% of Variance	Cumulative %	Extraction Sums of Squared Loadings Total	% of Variance	Cumulative %	Rotation Sums of Squared Loadings Total	% of Variance	Cumulative %
1	3.110	44.435	44.435	2.780	39.708	39.708	2.686	38.372	38.372
2	1.829	26.127	70.562	1.359	19.408	59.116	1.452	20.744	59.116
3	.607	8.671	79.233						
4	.498	7.118	86.351						
5	.483	6.893	93.243						
6	.295	4.212	97.456						
7	.178	2.545	100.000						

Extraction method: principal axis factoring.

Rotated Factor Matrix[a]

	Factor	
	1	*2*
KSIMP	.953	
FSIMP	.796	
WSIMP	.722	
VAIMP	.692	
LOPRIIMP		.694
ABDIMP		.687
CSHIMP		.642

Extraction method: principal axis factoring.
Rotation method: varimax with Kaiser normalization.
[a]Rotation converged in three iterations.

CASE NOTES

1. For a more complete discussion of Athenaeum Booksellers, see Case 14.1, "Athenaeum Booksellers (Part A)."
2. A copy of the questionnaire can be found at the end of Case 14.1.

This case was written by Jeanne L. Munger (University of Southern Maine) in collaboration with the textbook authors, as a basis for class discussion rather than to illustrate either effective or ineffective marketing practice.

CASE 15.2 THE PANKEY INSTITUTE (PART C)
(www.pankey.org)

Christian B. Sager, executive director of the Pankey Institute, commissioned a research study to assess various aspects of the continuous education services the organization provides to dentists. Several factors relating to the educational experience were identified in the initial analysis,[1] which Mr. Sager was interested in confirming through further analysis of the data.

The initial data reduction of the 15 questions (Q1–Q5, Q6a–c, Q7–Q10, and Q12–Q14) resulted in five factors:

- *Enjoyment.* Four items loaded on the enjoyment factor: "I enjoyed the course"; "I liked the visiting instructors"; "I liked the in-house instructors"; and "Overall, I enjoyed the week at Pankey."
- *Value for the money.* Three items loaded on the "value for the money" factor: "The price for the course was very reasonable"; "Compared to other continuing education courses that I have taken, the Pankey course was a good value for the money"; and "The total course

expense (including the cost of travel and lost work days) was worth the money."
- *Newness of material.* Two items loaded on the "newness of material" factor: "A lot of the course material was new to me" and "Some of the material was difficult to comprehend."
- *Environment/staff.* Three items loaded on the environment/staff factor: "All of the instructors were experts"; "The support staff were all very helpful"; and "The dental equipment was state-of-the-art."
- *Applicability of material.* Three items loaded on the "applicability of material" factor: "More of the course should have been devoted to (a) dental procedures, (b) managing the dental practice, and (c) hands-on learning of clinical procedures."

Background

Founded in 1972, the Pankey Institute promotes excellence in dentistry and helps dentists educate their patients about the availability and benefits of comprehensive oral care. The Pankey Institute is acknowledged as one of the world's most prestigious centers of advanced dental education. The institute provides a series of courses laid out as building blocks of the concepts and principles that make up optimal dentistry.

Further Analysis of the Results

The goal of this phase of the analysis was to verify the factors identified by the consultants and then to analyze the effects of participants' age on the various factors identified through the data reduction phase. Mr. Sager was eager to learn the results of this phase of the analysis. A lot of work had already been completed, and he looked forward to the insights that would emerge from the final analysis.

CASE QUESTIONS

1. Using data reduction (factor analysis), verify the factors identified by the consultants. (*Hint:* Focus on questionnaire items Q1–Q5, Q6a–c, Q7–Q10, and Q12–Q14, using the *principal components analysis* and *varimax rotation* options in SPSS; for further

details about principal components analysis and varimax rotation, contact your instructor or consult books like those cited in this chapter's notes 7 and 10.)

2. Examine the effects of age on the various factors identified through the data reduction stage. (*Hint:* Use ANOVA.)

3. What changes to the existing questionnaire, if any, would you recommend based on the factor analysis and ANOVA results? Justify your recommendations.

CASE NOTE

1. A more complete discussion of the Pankey Institute, along with a condensed version of the questionnaire, appears in Case 13.2, "The Pankey Institute (Part A)." Additional analyses appear in Case 14.2, "The Pankey Institute (Part B)."

This case was written by Jeanne L. Munger (University of Southern Maine) in collaboration with the textbook authors, as a basis for class discussion rather than to illustrate either effective or ineffective marketing practice.

Communicating with Research Users

Part Five

16 Presenting Research Results

Chapter Objectives

After reading and understanding the material in this chapter, you should be able to:

- Assess the nature of the audience for a written report or an oral presentation.

- Identify the components of a written report and indicate what each component should contain.

- Apply the principles of SIMPLE (short, interesting, methodical, precise, lucid, and error free) to a report or presentation.

- Define the following graphical illustrations and indicate when each is likely to be most appropriate: pie chart, line chart, stratum chart, and bar chart.

- Graphically represent information contained in one-way and two-way tabulations.

- Identify unique oral presentation characteristics that call for special attention and effort during preparation.

End of Textile Quota: Is China Going to Be the Big Bad Wolf?[1]

Presenting the results of research in an easy-to-understand fashion is critical to making an impact on decision makers. Using appropriate tables, charts, and figures adds to the clarity of any report. The following example, based on an article in the *New York Times* from December 14, 2004, illustrates this point. The article presented detailed information about textile exports from the top 25 exporting countries. We present the same information on the next page in two different ways. Which one is better? Decide for yourself.

First, here is the information in tabular form:

Country	Textile Exports as Percentage of Total Textile Exports
China	31.1
Italy	8.4
Germany	6.2
United States	5.3
Korea	4.7
France	3.9
Turkey	3.9
India	3.8
Taiwan	3.7
Belgium	3.4
Mexico	3.1
Britain	2.5
Pakistan	2.2
Indonesia	2.1
Others (11 countries)	15.6
Total	100.0

Now compare the table with the following graphical presentation of the same information.

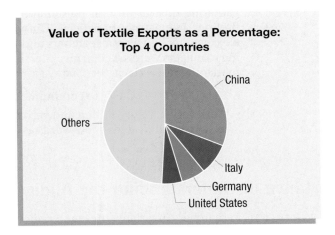

Alternatively, the information can be presented for the top 14 countries in terms of the same percentage of exports presented in the table.

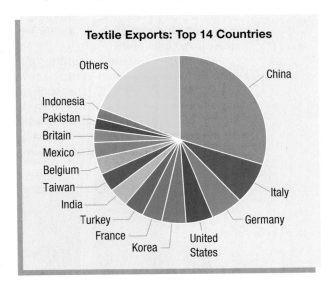

As you can see, the pie chart is better than the tabular format when the number of components is small and the relative sizes of those components are different. However, we lose information when we collapse the number of categories, as in the first chart. Pie charts are not useful when there are numerous components and when the relative sizes of components are not very different, as shown in the second pie chart. The tabular format is better when many categories exist. This chapter is about communicating research results in the most effective manner. ■

Although it is the last sequential step of the research process, communicating the results of a research project to decision makers is by no means last in importance.

Indeed, whether and to what extent research findings have an impact on decision making critically depends on how well they are communicated.

Effective presentation is the critical difference between a written report's gathering dust or an oral presentation's falling on deaf ears—and the research findings being truly beneficial. Unfortunately, communication is perhaps the weakest link between researchers and research users. When a sample of marketing managers were asked to give their best advice to college students interested in marketing research careers, many gave answers like the following:

- Develop a good ability to communicate well, both orally and in writing.
- Work very hard on written and verbal communication skills, especially on how to say a great deal in as few words as possible.[2]

Importance of Understanding the Audience

Researchers invariably present a project's description and findings in the form of a written report. Frequently they also supplement the written report with an oral presentation to highlight key findings and answer any questions decision makers may have. Whether results are written or oral, however, their potential impact depends on how well the information is tailored to fit the background and needs of its audience. Researchers sometimes attempt to impress rather than communicate with decision makers. Misunderstanding between research providers and users is the inevitable result.

Gaining a good understanding of audience characteristics and needs is therefore the foremost step in writing a research report or preparing an oral presentation. Ask yourself questions such as: From which organizational levels do audience members come? How busy are these individuals likely to be? How familiar are they with the project? In what aspects of the project are they most likely to be interested? Do they have the background and training to easily understand technical complexities and terminology related to the project?

Preparing an effective written report requires a good understanding of its audience, which might sometimes consist of individuals from different functional areas and organizational levels.

Researchers may not always be able to find accurate answers to questions like these. Nevertheless, being sensitive to such questions is a prerequisite for ensuring a good report or presentation. Moreover, when the audience consists of multiple groups with widely disparate backgrounds and interests, a researcher should prepare several separate reports or presentations, if feasible, and present the results to each group separately to maximize the overall impact of the research project. Thus it is important to be user oriented at this final and most critical stage of a research project.[3]

This chapter focuses primarily on written reports. However, most of the points covered apply to oral presentations as well. At the end of the chapter, we offer guidelines for making good oral presentations.

Components of the Written Report

The following sections discuss the various report components and their purpose.

Transmittal Letter

As its name implies, the *transmittal letter* introduces the report to its audience. It typically follows the style of a business letter and includes a brief description of the report's highlights. The contents of the executive summary section, which we will discuss shortly, can be incorporated into the transmittal letter if the entire report is brief. The transmittal letter is optional when the researcher personally delivers the report to its readers.

Title Page

The *title page* contains the title of the study, the name and affiliation of the report's author, the date of the study, and the name and affiliation of the person requesting the study. An attractively laid out title page is important for making a good first impression on the reader.

Table of Contents

When a report contains many sections, a *table of contents* helps the reader quickly locate any desired section. The contents page does not customarily include the title of the study; it is labeled "Table of Contents" or simply "Contents." When the body of the report contains numerous tables, figures, or other illustrations, a separate page, titled "List of Tables," "List of Figures," or the like, is desirable following the contents page.

Executive Summary

The *executive summary* is a carefully distilled synopsis of the entire report and typically should be no more than a few pages long. More appropriate in lengthy or technically complex reports, it should succinctly describe the primary purpose of the study, the general methodology used, the significant findings, and the key conclusions and recommendations. Because the summary is often the only section of a report that busy executives, who may well be the people with final authority to act on the study's findings, will have time to read thoroughly, writing it is an important task. A carelessly written executive summary is bound to create a poor image of the study and hurt its chances of having an impact.

A useful starting point for drafting an executive summary is to outline the main study objectives (issues about which information was sought through the study) and list all the findings that relate to each. This kind of outline will facilitate pulling together in one place findings from different sections of the study pertaining to the same objective.

To illustrate, suppose a firm marketing food products commissions a consumer survey in which a key objective is "To identify distinguishing features, if any, of users of our brand of cake mix vis-à-vis users of competing brands." Findings from several different sections of the survey questionnaire, sections focusing on brand preference, purchase frequency, usage behavior, and demographics, will be applicable to this objective. Organizing these findings under a common objective and examining them collectively will help identify key insights to be included in the executive summary. For instance, examining one-way and two-way tabulations of responses to questions about brand preference, purchase frequency, usage behavior, and demographics may suggest something like the following for inclusion in the executive summary:

> Users of our brand of cake mix, although similar to users of competing brands in several respects, also have a number of distinguishing characteristics. Specifically, users of the various brands do not differ significantly with respect to age, education, and household size. However, the median income of households using our brand is higher than that of households using competing brands ($45,000 versus $35,000). Moreover, the purchase frequency of our brand is lower than for competing brands (6 versus 10 boxes per household per year). Finally, users of our brand seem to be more brand loyal than users of competing brands (7 out of 10 users of our brand said they are likely to buy the same brand in the future, whereas only 5 out of 10 users of competing brands said so). Thus our brand enjoys an upscale, premium image, which has been the goal of our advertising campaign during the past two years. However, for our future campaigns we might consider themes that also promote more frequent purchases by households using our brand.

Main findings and implications pertaining to the various research issues or objectives addressed by a study can be transformed into brief sections like the one illustrated above. These sections, along with several introductory paragraphs briefly describing the study's purpose and methodology, form the building blocks of an effective executive summary. A concisely written executive summary that organizes the key findings by research objectives can also aid the researcher in drafting the full report: it can serve as a skeleton for structuring and fleshing out the body of the report. In fact, the sequencing of topics covered and results presented in the executive summary should be the same as in the body of the report. Readers who want more information about a particular section can then quickly turn to the corresponding section in the main body of the report.

Body of the Report

The *body* offers readers a comprehensive picture of the study by discussing all phases of it. Its five sections correspond to the various research project steps discussed earlier in the book, starting with a definition of the project's purpose and concluding with an interpretation of its findings. The sections can be divided into suitable subsections if they become lengthy or complex. Although their actual contents will vary from one study to another, they should focus on certain general issues, outlined next.

Purpose   This section provides a clear definition of the research problem and lists the study's objectives. A brief discussion of the rationale for the objectives and their relevance to the problem at hand is also appropriate for this section.

Method   This section describes and justifies the procedures used in generating and analyzing the data for the study. The types of issues to be addressed in this section include the following:

- What overall research approach or design (exploratory, conclusive, or exploratory followed by conclusive) was used in the study? Why was this design the most appropriate one?
- Did the study rely solely on secondary data, or was primary data collection also involved? What sources of secondary data were used?
- How were primary data, if any, gathered (through observation, questioning, or both)? What constituted the study population, and how was the sample selected from it? If the questioning approach was used, what method was used to administer the questionnaire (mail, telephone, online, or face-to-face interviews)? During which period were the data collected?
- What techniques were used to analyze the collected data? For instance, were the analyses limited to construction of one-way and two-way tables, and computation of summary statistics, or did they employ more advanced statistical procedures?

Findings   This section presents and discusses the results from all the analyses conducted. As recommended for the executive summary, an effective approach for this section is to group the findings by research objective. However, this section should offer much greater detail than the executive summary. For instance, whereas the executive summary might present only the key insights from a series of tables, the body of the report should present the tables in their entirety and discuss all the insights they reveal. Graphical illustrations (to be discussed later) are an effective way to present the findings in an economical yet interesting fashion.

Conclusions   This section briefly reviews the study, summarizes the inferences stemming from it, and highlights the evidence supporting each inference. It typically should be quite brief, because its purpose is to recapitulate the main points discussed in earlier sections. This section could also include a set of recommendations if requested by whomever commissioned the study. Some managers may want the researcher to make specific recommendations; others may prefer that the researcher simply report and interpret the findings, without recommending how the managers should act on them.

Limitations   This section includes any cautionary notes that qualify the results of the study. Any unforeseen or unavoidable methodological weakness or external events that might have a bearing on the study's conclusions should be covered here. For instance, if the demographic composition of the study sample is markedly different from that of the population of interest, this discrepancy must be explicitly acknowledged. Moreover, a brief discussion of why the discrepancy arose and how it might influence the generalizability of the study's findings should be included.

In summary, the body of the report, consisting of the sections described above, is essentially a report within a report.

Addenda

Addenda are relevant attachments referred to, but not included in, the body of a report. A typical addendum is a list of references. This list is necessary when numerous citations—data sources, websites, past studies, articles, books, and so on—are included in the main report. When there are only a few citations, you can reference them in footnotes on the pages where they appear instead of having a separate list of references.

Another addendum to research reports is an appendix (or set of appendixes). Questionnaires, raw data tables, formulas, complex calculations, and similar items usually appear at the end of a report as a set of appendixes. A questionnaire containing a summary of responses to each question is a particularly useful appendix because it simultaneously presents the actual questions asked and a bird's-eye view of the answers. Research in Use 16.1 describes illustrative excerpts from such a questionnaire. In general, any study-related material whose placement in the body of a report may be distracting rather than enlightening should be relegated to the appendix section.

Preparing Effective Written Reports

No one can acquire good writing skills overnight; they have to be cultivated through constant practice over a period of time. Preparing good written reports is also a skill that improves only with practice. This section offers a checklist of key features that an effective research report should contain and demonstrates their importance. Further details are available in the references cited in this chapter.

SIMPLE is a mnemonic representing the key features of effective written reports and oral presentations—short, interesting, methodical, precise, lucid, and error free.

We can summarize the desirable features of a research report in one word: **SIMPLE**—**s**hort, **i**nteresting, **m**ethodical, **p**recise, **l**ucid, and **e**rror free. Although these six features overlap to some degree, each is important enough to be discussed separately.

Make It Short

Decision makers usually have no more than a few hours to read a report summarizing a study that may have taken weeks or months to complete. Hence, the report must be as succinct as possible. It should cover in detail only those aspects of interest to research users and have a direct bearing on their decision making. This is not an easy task, however. Having labored long on a project, researchers may be tempted to explain everything they did, perhaps to obtain the audience's appreciation for their efforts. This temptation is likely to be strong among those unaccustomed to writing research reports.

How concise should a report be to be labeled *short?* There is no standard length for a report. The ideal length depends on the needs of the audience and hence will vary from one situation to another. A good rule to remember is that a report must not contain material irrelevant to its intended audience.

Make It Interesting

A report does not have to be humorous or entertaining, but it must be *interesting* enough to grab its readers' attention. There is just too much competition for the time managers have to devote to research reports. Therefore, an uninteresting report may not even be fully read, let alone have an impact on decision making.

You can prepare an interesting report if you understand the audience and write in a style appealing to them;[4] focus the report's content on issues that are relevant to the audience and important for them to know; and use suitable illustrations and other visual aids, a topic we will discuss later.

Make It Methodical

A written report must be *methodical,* so that readers will be able to follow it readily. The various sections within the report must be logically sequenced to ensure smooth transitions. The number of sections and the best way to arrange them depend to some degree on the nature of the project and the audience. However, the following general outline is helpful for structuring reports in most situations:[5]

1. Transmittal letter
2. Title page
3. Table of contents
4. Executive summary
5. Body of the report
    a. Purpose
    b. Method
    c. Findings
    d. Conclusions (and recommendations if requested)
    e. Limitations
6. Addenda
    a. List of references
    b. Appendix

Not all sections listed in this outline are necessary in every report.

Make It Precise

A *precise* report is a clear report, one composed of unambiguous statements. It is also comprehensive and contains all the information necessary for readers to get a complete and true picture of the study. Clarity is a function of writing style and report format, which we will discuss further in the following sections.

Comprehensiveness means providing enough details about the study—for example, nature of the sample, data collection procedures, analysis techniques—to help readers decide how valid and generalizable the study's findings are. To ensure objectivity and ethics, researchers have an obligation to inform research users about potential limitations of a study.

As we have seen throughout this book, to expect practical research projects to be perfect is unrealistic. Experienced research users are well aware of this shortcoming. Consequently they are bound to view with skepticism reports that sound too good to be true. Contrary to what some researchers may believe, a report that acknowledges a study's limitations is likely to create a better impression of the study than a report that fails to do so.

Report writers must be careful, though, not to overdo reporting of limitations by listing every little problem the study encountered. Doing so will not only lengthen the report unduly but also give the study a poor image. Furthermore, merely acknowledging all the limitations cannot salvage a study that is badly flawed because of researcher carelessness. In short, a report summarizing a

National Insurance Study Questionnaire with Summary of Study Findings

An economical way to present all the data collected through a survey is to include in the research report a copy of the questionnaire containing summary statistics for the various questions (for instance, frequency distributions for questions with categorical responses and means and standard deviations for questions with scaled responses). Shown here are two excerpts from a questionnaire that was included in a report on a survey of National's customers (as mentioned previously, National is a major insurance company whose name has been disguised). In both excerpts, N is the sample size, and the other numbers are percentages unless stated otherwise. The following excerpt illustrates the presentation of summary statistics for statements involving rating scales.

Directions: The following set of statements relates to your feelings about National Insurance Company. For each statement, please show the extent to which you believe National has the feature described by the statement. Circling a "1" means that you strongly disagree that National has that feature, and circling a "7" means that you strongly agree. You may circle any of the numbers in between that show how strong your feelings are. There are no right or wrong answers—all we are interested in is a number that best shows your perceptions about National.

[Mean scores underlined] **Reliability**	Sample Size (N)	Strongly Disagree					Strongly Agree		Std. Dev.
1. When National promises to do something, it does so.	277	1	2	3	4	5.33	6	7	1.67
2. When you have a problem, National shows a sincere interest in solving it.	278	1	2	3	4	5.59	6	7	1.65
3. National performs the service right the first time.	275	1	2	3	4	5.20	6	7	1.77
4. National provides its services at the time it promises to do so.	275	1	2	3	4	5.46	6	7	1.65
5. National maintains error-free records.	266	1	2	3	4	5.45	6	7	1.59

The next excerpt relates the presentation of the summary statistics for questions involving categorical or open-ended responses.

---

1. Would you recommend National to a friend interested in insurance services?

Yes	1	235	
No	2	32	N = 267

2. How long have you been using the services of National?

Less than 1 year	1	36	N = 271
1 to less than 2 years	2	16	
2 to less than 5 years	3	26	
5 years or more	**4**	**193**	**Median**

3. Have you recently had a problem with the service you received from National?

Yes	1	80	
No	2	180	N = 260

4. If you did have a problem, was it resolved to your satisfaction?

Yes	1	47	
No	2	30	N = 77

The following information is solely for statistical purposes and will be kept confidential. Please circle the number that corresponds to your answer.

1. Your gender is:

Male	1	144	
Female	2	132	N = 276

2. Your marital status is:

Single	1	20	
Married	2	219	
Widowed	3	12	
Divorced	4	24	N = 275

3. Your age is:

Under 25	1	20	
25–44	**2**	**219**	**Median**
1–64	3	12	
65 or over	4	24	N = 275

4. Your total annual family income is:

Under $10,000	1	12	
$10,000–$19,999	2	20	
$20,000–$29,999	3	59	
$30,000–$49,999	**4**	**106**	**Median**
$50,000–$64,999	5	38	
$65,000 or over	6	32	N = 267

5. The highest level of schooling you have completed is:

High school or less	1	102	
Some college	**2**	**86**	**Median**
College graduate	3	50	
Graduate school	4	35	N = 273

reasonably well-conducted study—one whose limitations were beyond the researcher's control—will be more credible when it mentions the key limitations than when it does not.

Make It Lucid

The *lucidity* of a report is critical to its effectiveness for several reasons. First, the clearer a report, the less time readers need to understand what it says and the more time they can spend digesting its contents. As mentioned earlier, most managers can devote only a limited amount of time to research reports. Hence, the more time they can devote to digesting rather than simply understanding a report's contents, the greater the potential impact of the report will be. Second, a report that lacks clarity risks confusing its readers and leading them to conclusions unwarranted by the study and unintended by the report writer. Third, an unclear report can annoy its readers and create a poor image of the quality of the entire research project.

How does a researcher prepare a clear report? A report that is short, interesting, methodical, precise, and error free is bound to be clearer than one that does not possess these characteristics. There are, however, a few other, more specific guidelines for enhancing report clarity.

One prerequisite for developing a clear report is to thoroughly understand the audience and to write in a style compatible with their background. A frequent complaint of managers is that research reports are too technical. The source of this complaint is invariably the report writer's failure to pay adequate attention to the audience. Technically complex material may be clear to the report writer and may even be viewed as a means for impressing the reader. However, more often than not, such material will neither enlighten nor impress the reader. On the contrary, it is more likely to result in dismissal of the report as being too theoretical to be of practical value.

Devoting a little extra time and effort to translating technical statements into plain language can greatly improve report clarity, as the following illustrations demonstrate:

- *Technical statement.* Owing to severe multicollinearity between the independent variables (personal selling expenditures and advertising expenditures), it is difficult to interpret their regression coefficients (estimated beta values) and hence their impact on the dependent variable (sales).

- *Plain-language translation.* Because personal selling and advertising expenditures for our product have moved together closely (changed in the same direction) in the past, it is difficult to say which of these two types of expenditures may be responsible for changes in our product's sales.

- *Technical statement.* According to our analysis of the survey data, the difference between mean sales per store in regions A and B is statistically significant beyond an alpha level of .05, based on a two-tailed *t*-test.

- *Plain-language translation.* According to our analysis of the survey data, the odds are less than 5 in 100 that the observed difference between mean sales per store in regions A and B could have occurred merely by chance.

The preceding examples are not meant to suggest that a report should be written in a style that talks down to its reader. Technical terminology (especially when it will help reduce a report's length) is appropriate if the audience is familiar with such terminology. Indeed, explanations of technical aspects in lay terms may run the risk of insulting a sophisticated audience. The bottom line is that the nature of the audience determines how technical a report can be without losing clarity.[6]

Appropriate tables, charts, or figures can add to the clarity of a report by conveying the contents of written material much more effectively and concisely. For instance, consider the following excerpt from an article published in a leading marketing journal (in this excerpt, ES1 and ES2 refer to samples selected in two different studies):

> A comparison of the demographic profiles between ES1 and ES2 revealed no major differences. . . . In ES1, the typical respondent was white (85.5 percent), married (72.7 percent), male (66.8 percent), and employed in a white-collar job (36.4 percent). Fifty-five percent of the respondents reported an income of less than $20,000, 48.2 percent had completed high school or less, and 44 percent were under 45 years of age. In ES2, 59.7 percent were male, 70.2 percent were married, 28.9 percent held white-collar jobs, and 81.8 percent were white. Approximately 43 percent of the sample were under 45, 53.2 percent reported having a high school education or less, and almost 50 percent stated that they had a family income of less than $20,000 a year.[7]

The information conveyed by this excerpt would have been much clearer had it been presented in tabular form, as presented below.

	Percentage of Respondents	
Respondent Characteristic	*ES1 Sample*	*ES2 Sample*
White	85.5	81.8
Married	72.7	70.2
Male	66.8	59.7
White-collar employee	36.4	28.9
Income less than $20,000	55.0	50.0
High school education or less	48.2	53.2
Under 45 years of age	44.0	43.0

We will discuss the use of tables and charts further in the section on graphical illustrations.

Make It Error Free

To make a good impression on readers, a report must be *error free*—free of arithmetical, grammatical, and typographical mistakes, however minor they may be. Checking a completed report thoroughly should take no more than a fraction of the time required to put the report together. Yet, perhaps because of a premature feeling of relief that the task is done, writers often look over their final drafts hastily or not at all.

The price of carelessness can be quite high. Incorrectly typed numbers, percentages that do not add up, misspelled words, and other minor errors are usually major distractions to readers. Moreover, a report with several such errors will make readers skeptical about the quality of the project itself. Checking a report more than once, preferably with the help of someone good at editing and proofreading, is a wise investment of the report writer's time.

Graphical Illustrations

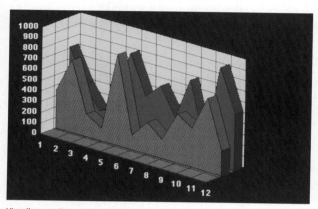

Visually appealing graphical illustrations can bring a report to life and provide the audience with refreshing breaks from the monotony of text and tables.

As the example concerning the ES1 and ES2 samples shows, presenting data in tabular form is usually more effective than describing them in the body of a report. Sometimes a report's clarity can be further improved by recasting the data in tables as graphical illustrations (charts, graphs, and so on), especially when the tables are complex or confusing. Visually appealing graphical illustrations can also add to a report's communication effectiveness by giving its audience refreshing breaks from the monotony of words and numbers.

A report writer's imagination is the only limit on the number of ways tabular data can be transformed into appropriate graphical illustrations. Nevertheless, only a handful of basic charts and graphs is available, variations of which are frequently used. To describe these basic formats, let's consider the hypothetical data in Table 16.1 pertaining to market shares of six brands of toothpaste in a certain region.

Suppose Table 16.1 is presented to the manager in charge of marketing brand X. Close examination of the table should offer the manager several key insights. For example, the two dominant competitors of brand X are brands A and B, and brand X's market position has been weakening over the years. These insights, and others not immediately apparent from the table, can be communicated more efficiently and effectively through graphical illustrations, such as those discussed next.

Pie Charts

A **pie chart** is a circle divided into several slices whose areas are proportionate to the quantities to be represented on the chart.

A **pie chart** is a circle divided into several slices whose areas are proportionate to the quantities to be represented on the chart. The relative sizes of the slices are shown as percentages. A pie chart is excellent for showing the decomposition of a

TABLE 16.1
Market Shares of Six Toothpaste Brands

Year	Brand X	Brand A	Brand B	Brand C	Brand D	Brand E
1996	30	29	25	5	5	6
1997	22	35	22	7	6	8
1998	25	25	30	10	5	5
1999	25	29	28	8	6	4
2000	28	30	25	6	6	5
2001	25	28	28	6	7	6
2002	22	30	29	6	6	7
2003	22	27	32	7	7	5
2004	20	29	33	5	7	6
2005	18	28	34	7	8	5

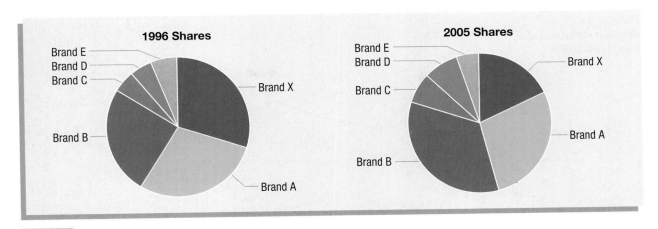

Exhibit 16.1
Pie Charts of Market
Shares in 1996 and 2005

total quantity into its components—for example, the contributions made by a firm's product lines to its sales or profits; the income distribution of households using a certain product; the allocation of a total budget to various expense categories; the market shares of firms within an industry or brands within a product category. Exhibit 16.1 illustrates two pie charts showing the market shares of the six toothpaste brands in 1996 and 2005.

The two charts in Exhibit 16.1 clearly show the loss of brand X's market share, apparently to brand B, between 1996 and 2005. Table 16.1 offers the same insight, but not as vividly as Exhibit 16.1. Although a single pie chart by itself can be quite revealing, a comparison of pie charts over time, as in Exhibit 16.1, or a comparison of related pie charts at the same point in time (such as pie charts showing the relative contributions of a firm's product lines to its sales and profits) can be even more insightful.

Using different shadings or colors for the various slices of a pie chart can improve its effectiveness. Also, limiting the number of slices to about six or seven is preferable. Too many slices will clutter the chart and diminish its visual impact. When a total quantity has numerous components, lump minor components (those making relatively small individual contributions to the total) into an "Other" category to avoid overcrowding the chart.

Constructing a pie chart may not be helpful when the total consists of numerous components, each contributing about equally to the total. For instance, when a firm's marketing budget is allocated to 20 different categories, each accounting for about 4 to 6 percent of the budget, a pie chart is likely to be no better than a table showing the allocations.

In short, pie charts are most effective when the number of components is relatively small and the relative sizes of those components are dissimilar. Constructing pie charts under other circumstances may merely add to the length of a report without improving its effectiveness.

Line Charts

A **line chart** is a two-dimensional graph typically used to show movements in one or more items over time. The horizontal axis is customarily the time axis, and the vertical axis represents values of the items. Exhibit 16.2 is a line chart showing changes in market shares of the toothpaste brands during the period 1996 to 2005.

Exhibit 16.2 summarizes the data in Table 16.1 in a very revealing fashion. A glance at the exhibit offers key insights (brand X's share has been steadily slipping in almost symmetric contrast to brand B's increasing share) that only a very careful scrutiny of Table 16.1 will reveal.

A **line chart** is a two-dimensional graph typically used to show movements in one or more items over time.

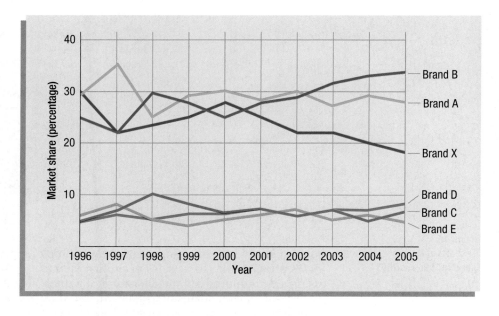

For a line chart to be most effective, the trends corresponding to different items must be shown by lines of different colors or of different form, as in Exhibit 16.2. Also, as in the case of pie charts, one should not include more than a few items on a line chart. Too many lines on one chart will give it a crowded appearance and cause confusion.

Stratum Charts

A **stratum chart** is a two-dimensional graph with time plotted along the horizontal axis and values of the items plotted along the vertical axis.

A **stratum chart** is also a two-dimensional graph with time along the horizontal axis and values of the items plotted along the vertical axis. The area of the graph is divided into several horizontal layers, or strata, one corresponding to each item. At any given time, the width of each stratum represents the relative magnitude of the corresponding item at that time. Exhibit 16.3 is a stratum chart summarizing the data in Table 16.1.

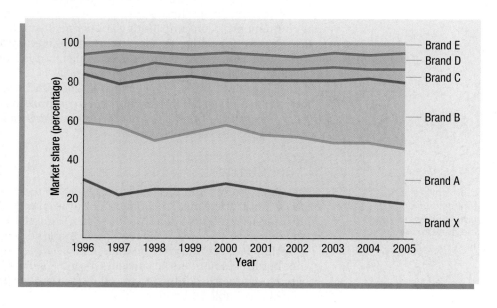

The lowest stratum in Exhibit 16.3 corresponds to brand X. The line defining the upper boundary of this stratum represents the same market share values as the brand X line in Exhibit 16.2. The second lowest stratum in Exhibit 16.3 corresponds to brand A. The line defining the upper boundary of this stratum represents the sum of the market shares of brands X and A. Similarly, the upper boundary of the third lowest stratum represents the combined share of brands X, A, and B.

Thus a stratum chart is a cumulative line chart. Also, its information content is similar to that of a series of pie charts constructed over a period of time; that is, it tracks the changes in relative magnitudes of the items over time. Just as with pie and line charts, having a fairly small number of items (strata) and making the strata distinct by using different colors or shadings are critical for a stratum chart's effectiveness.

Bar Charts

A **bar chart** consists of a series of bars (of equal thickness) whose heights (or lengths, if the bars are horizontal) represent values of the items.

A **bar chart,** as its name implies, consists of a series of bars (of equal thickness) whose heights (or lengths, if the bars are drawn horizontally) represent values of the items. Exhibit 16.4 contains two bar charts showing the market shares of toothpaste brands in 1996 and 2005.

The information conveyed in Exhibit 16.4 is the same as that conveyed in Exhibit 16.1. How, then, do we decide whether to use a pie chart or a bar chart? There is no cut-and-dried answer. A pie chart is preferable, however, when the values to be pictured are relative magnitudes (market shares, budget shares, and other types of percentages), because the concept of slicing up a pie seems intuitively appropriate for representing relative shares. Bar charts are appropriate for depicting actual or absolute magnitudes (sales of different product lines, expenditures on different marketing activities). The heights or lengths of the bars can be made to correspond to the absolute magnitudes of items, yet the areas occupied by the bars will provide a visual picture of relative magnitudes of the items.

Bar charts can also be used to show changes over time by, for example, plotting time along the horizontal axis, constructing one vertical bar at each point in time, and dividing each bar into segments so that their heights correspond to the values of the items at that point in time. The visual impact of such a time series bar chart is similar to that of a stratum chart. Exhibit 16.5 shows a bar chart that conveys the same information as the stratum chart in Exhibit 16.3.

Exhibit 16.4
Bar Charts of Market Shares in 1996 and 2005

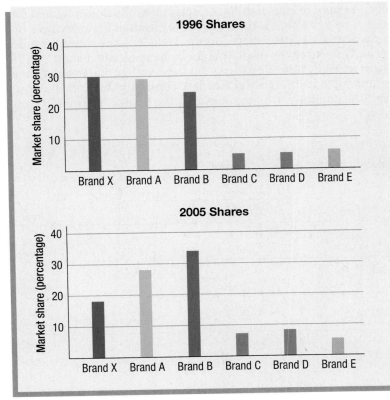

Graphical Representation of One-Way and Two-Way Tabulations

Potential applications of the various charts described above go beyond the representation of market shares and trend lines. Indeed, several of those charts can be used to pictorially summarize information contained in

Exhibit 16.5
Bar Chart of Market Shares from 1996 to 2005

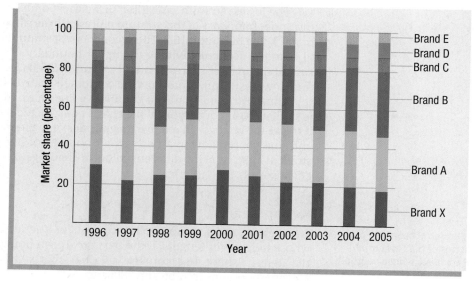

one-way and two-way tabulations, which are perhaps the most widely used procedures to analyze survey data in practical research projects. Research in Use 16.2 describes how one firm used a series of bar charts to visually represent one-way tabulation of responses for a number of questions with categorical responses.

Bar charts can also clearly and quickly communicate information contained in two-way tabulations. To illustrate, consider the two-way tabulation shown in Table 16.2. This table shows a cross-tabulation of responses (obtained from a survey of 1,000 consumers) pertaining to two variables: consumers' ages (coded <30, 30–50, and >50) and extent of consumption of a certain product (heavy, medium, and light). Although we can infer the nature of the association between these two variables from the pattern of percentages in the table, we can convey it much more efficiently and effectively by displaying the percentages in a chart such as Exhibit 16.6. There is clearly a strong association between age and extent of consumption. The under-30 group has the heaviest consumption, and the 30–50 group the lightest consumption, with the consumption level of the over-50 group falling in between.

TABLE 16.2
Two-Way Tabulation of Age Versus Extent of Consumption

| Age | Extent of Consumption | | | Total |
	Heavy	Medium	Light	
<30	125 (50%)	65 (26%)	60 (24%)	250 (100%)
30–50	60 (15%)	80 (20%)	260 (65%)	400 (100%)
>50	65 (18%)	205 (59%)	80 (23%)	350 (100%)
Total	250 (25%)	350 (35%)	400 (40%)	1,000 (100%)

Note: All percentages are based on row totals; some percentages have been adjusted slightly to make them add to 100.

The Roper Organization

The Roper Organization, a leading marketing research company, conducted a personal-interview survey of American youth. The study was commissioned by Warner-Lambert Company with the objective of ascertaining young people's perception of their family, their school, and the major social issues that confront them. A total of 1,000 youths between the ages of 8 and 17 participated in the study. The end of the report included the study questionnaire accompanied by a summary of the responses (similar to the illustrative excerpts presented in Research in Use 16.1). The following is a sample section from that questionnaire. (The numbers are percentages of respondents checking the answer categories.)

Here is list of things some young people told us they are concerned about today. (HAND RESPONDENT CARD.) Would you please read down that list and for each thing tell me if it is something you personally are very concerned about, sort of concerned about, or not really concerned about at all? First, (read them). (ASK ABOUT EACH.)

	Very Concerned	Sort of Concerned	Not Really Concerned	Don't Know/Refused
a. Pollution of our air and water	47	38	13	2
b. The use of drugs by professional athletes	52	25	20	3
c. The possibility of war	65	20	12	3
d. The spread of the disease called AIDS	65	20	10	3
e. The increasing number of divorces among parents	39	33	25	3
f. The possibility that you may someday have to fight in a war	47	26	25	2
g. The kidnapping of children and teenagers	76	16	8	1

Each row of numbers in this section is essentially a one-way tabulation of responses pertaining to the issue in question.

The discussion of these responses in the body of the report was accompanied by the following bar chart. This bar chart, in which each bar is a pictorial summary of one national concern, quickly and efficiently communicates the findings to the reader. Notice that the issues are ordered differently in the bar chart than in the questionnaire. The ordering of the issues on the bar chart (from those of most to least concern) enhances the chart's effectiveness.[a]

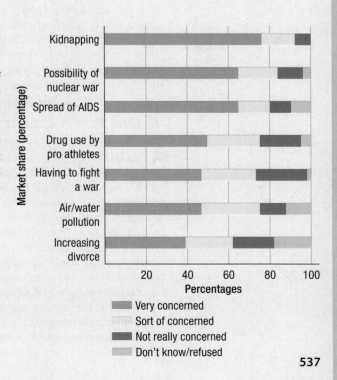

537

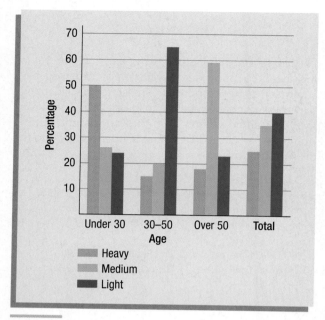

Exhibit 16.6
Bar Chart of Information in
Table 16.2

A bar chart similar to Exhibit 16.6 is not the only approach to graphically representing two-way tabulations. For instance, instead of the four clusters of three bars each shown in Exhibit 16.6, a researcher can construct four pie charts with each containing three slices.

Computer Graphics

The proliferation of personal computers and the availability of a variety of computer graphics software packages have greatly enhanced the options available for presenting research findings as graphical illustrations.[8] Many computer graphics programs have the capability to import pictures, movies, and animation, and to incorporate sound in presentations. The user can peruse visual displays of the resulting pictures and obtain hard copies of the most effective ones. These capabilities should simplify the task of determining the best way to graphically portray a study's findings. In fact, computer experts predict that, in the near future, "some graphics software will feature artificial intelligence that will be able to select automatically the most effective graph for a particular set of data."[9]

Many graphics software programs are becoming an integral part of today's desktops. For example, Microsoft PowerPoint is readily available on most desktops. Presentations can also be linked to the Web, allowing distant clients to view them. Researchers can easily coordinate their written reports with their oral presentations by creating colorful slides of key charts included in the report. The upshot is that written reports and oral presentations without graphical illustrations are more an exception than the rule today and are bound to become even more so in the future.

The ease of generating graphical illustrations of a study's results does not mean that a diagram or chart should be produced for every result. Although graphical illustrations can make a report interesting and add to its clarity, too many of them may clutter up the report and annoy the audience. The number of illustrations to use and the appropriate formats for them should therefore be carefully determined to avoid confusing, meaningless, or misleading illustrations.[10]

Oral Presentations

Oral presentations, like written reports, must also be SIMPLE: short, interesting, methodical, precise, lucid, and error free. However, making an effective oral presentation is in some ways more difficult than writing a good report because of the direct interaction with the audience. Any sign of faltering during an oral presentation will make an unfavorable impression on the audience and may lower the self-confidence of the presenter. An effective oral presentation requires meticulous preparation of what will be said and how it will be presented. It also requires planning for contingencies such as a breakdown of visual equipment or a series of unexpectedly tough questions from the audience. Therefore, even a 30-minute presentation may need many hours (or days) of preparation. Carefully planning and rehearsing an oral presentation is critical to its effectiveness.

Details for putting together and delivering a good oral report can be found in several excellent books.[11] However, the following three general tasks, covered while discussing written reports, are especially important for the success of oral presentations:

1. *Research the audience.* Know who your audience will be, learn about their backgrounds and information needs, and anticipate the questions they may ask.
2. *Choose the main points of the study to be covered during the presentation.* Be careful not to select too many main points.
3. *Make good use of visual aids*—flip charts, transparencies, slides, and so on—to improve presentation clarity and maintain audience interest.

Concerning the third point, given the proliferation of technology and equipment for creating visual aids, such aids are expected by audiences and used by presenters in virtually all oral presentations. Indiscriminate use of visual aids, however, is likely to be of little help. Visual aids must be chosen and sequenced with care, with each one containing a simple, relevant message. Table 16.3 provides a number of suggestions for the proper use of slides. Many of these suggestions can also enhance the effectiveness of other forms of visual aids.

TABLE 16.3
Guidelines for Effective Use of Slides

Word Slides
- Keep them brief; use key words only.
- Use bullets and color to highlight key points.
- Break up the information to make a series of progressive slides.

Box Charts
- Use for organization charts, flow charts.
- Simplify to keep them legible.
- Break up complex charts into a series. (Show flow chart divided by time periods; show organization chart with the overall chart and departmental "closeup.")

Bar Charts
- Use for data arranged in segments (by month, year, and so on).
- Choose vertical or horizontal bars (both within horizontal slide format).
- Add drop shadow for dimensional bars.
- Show complex facts clearly by using multiple or segmented bars.
- Divide the slice into a series if that improves effectiveness.

Pie Charts
- Use to emphasize the relationship of the parts to the whole.
- Select single pie or double.
- Consider options such as drop shadow for dimensional effect, pulled-out slices, and so on.
- Arrange the slices to make your point most effectively (see opening vignette).
- Divide the slice into a series if that improves effectiveness.

Line Charts and Stratum Charts
- Use to display trends or continuous data.
- Decide whether a line chart or a stratum chart is more effective.
- Select baseline and scale for maximum effectiveness.
- Use callouts to identify key points in chart.
- Divide extensive data into a series of charts.

Other Graphics
- Use logos and illustrations in subdued colors in the background, as "watermarks"—an effective way to add visual interest and continuity to a presentation.

SUMMARY

The foremost step in communicating the results of a research project is to gain a good understanding of the audience and its information needs. The most common vehicle for communicating research findings is the written report. To be effective, a written report must be SIMPLE: short, interesting, methodical, precise, lucid, and error free. Although these six features are interrelated, each has certain distinct requirements:

- *Short.* A report should discuss only those aspects of a study that are relevant and important from the reader's standpoint. Other aspects, such as methodological details, which may fascinate researchers but frustrate readers, must be omitted or only briefly stated.

- *Interesting.* The style, format, and contents of a report must attract and maintain the attention of readers.

- *Methodical.* The sections of a report and their contents must be chosen with the readers in mind and arranged in a logical sequence. Although there is no standard research report format, the outline suggested in this chapter should be helpful.

- *Precise.* A report must be clear and comprehensive. Clarity is a function of writing style and format. Comprehensiveness implies that the report must contain enough detail to provide an accurate, complete picture of the study; the report should acknowledge key limitations and how they may affect the interpretation of the results.

- *Lucid.* The report must be written in language that is familiar to its readers. It should use simple words and sentences, as well as appropriate tables and charts, to communicate its contents clearly and quickly.

- *Error free.* Even seemingly minor arithmetical, grammatical, or typographical errors in a report may annoy its readers and undermine the credibility of the report. Sufficient time and effort must be devoted to finding and correcting such errors before finalizing the report.

A variety of graphical illustrations—such as pie charts, line charts, stratum charts, and bar charts—can be employed to enhance the clarity and effectiveness of a report. The number and types of graphical illustrations to use must be determined with care. Haphazard use of illustrations will merely add to a report's length or, worse, may confuse or mislead readers.

In addition to submitting written reports, researchers often make oral presentations of their findings. Many of the guidelines for preparing good written reports apply to making effective oral presentations as well. Understanding the audience, distilling from the study the main messages to be conveyed, and making good use of appropriate visual aids are particularly important for oral presentations. A successful oral presentation requires spending adequate time and effort on planning and rehearsing.

REVIEW AND DISCUSSION QUESTIONS

1. The last step in the research process—communicating research results—may well be the most important step. What are the major reasons why?

2. Two desirable features of a written report are that it be short and precise. Is there likely to be any conflict between these two features? If so, how would you reconcile such a conflict? If not, why not?

3. "To have an impact on readers, a research report must be humorous and entertaining." Discuss this statement.

4. Why is the executive summary such a critical component of a research report?

APPLICATION EXERCISES

1. Recast the following statements in less technical language:
   a. "On the basis of our survey, the 95 percent confidence interval for the proportion of households with DVDs is .4 ± .05."
   b. "The regression of sales (dependent variable) on advertising expenditures (independent variable) produced an R^2-value of .9, which was statistically significant ($F = 55.8$, $p < .01$)."

2. Go through a business publication such as *Business Week* or *Fortune* and pick out any three graphical illustrations. State what type of chart each illustration is and identify and describe its positive and negative features.

3. Using the data in Table 16.1, compute the rate of change in market shares for brands X, A, and B from year to year (1996 to 1997, 1997 to 1998, and so on). Diagram these changes using a line chart and a bar chart. Which of these two charts is more effective? Why?

4. Can a pie chart or a stratum chart be used to depict the market share changes computed in question 3? Why or why not?

5. Ms. Smith, a researcher at XYZ Company, is delighted because management just informed her that she needs to make only a brief oral presentation of a study she recently completed; she does not have to develop a written report. "Thank goodness I don't have to go through the torture of writing up my findings!" she thinks. What advice would you give to Ms. Smith in developing her oral presentation?

INTERNET EXERCISES

1. Go to CNN (www.cnn.com) and evaluate the way the results of the QuickVote question of the day are presented. Could the results have been presented more effectively? If so, create the new chart.

2. Go to Forrester (www.forrester.com) and evaluate the way the results in one of the company's reports are presented. Could the results have been presented more effectively? If so, create the new chart or charts.

CASE 16.1 NATIONAL INSURANCE COMPANY

Jill Baxter, vice president of customer relationship management at National Insurance Company, had recently commissioned a survey of the company's customer base. The primary purpose of the survey was to ascertain how customers perceived National's quality of service and to identify areas for improvement. (To view a copy of the survey questionnaire, see Exhibit 12.2.) Jill requested Jeff Lord, a manager in National's marketing research department, to analyze the survey data and prepare a report for her. Drawing on his strong statistical background (he had double-majored in marketing and statistics in his undergraduate program), Jeff quickly conducted a variety of analyses of the data and prepared a "report" that basically consisted of a series of tables summarizing his analyses. (Several of these analyses are included as illustrations in Chapters 12, 13, and 14.) Jill was impressed by the report's technical sophistication and statistical detail, but she was also overwhelmed and frustrated by it. She therefore requested Jeff to prepare a more readable, three-to-four-page executive summary. After struggling a bit, Jeff drafted an executive summary, reproduced below. He was not entirely happy with this draft and was wondering how he could improve it.

Draft of Jeff's Executive Summary

We did a major mail survey of our customers and received replies from 285 of them. The survey questionnaire had four sections. The first section contained twenty-two 7-point ("Strongly disagree" to "Strongly agree") statements that had a Likert scale–type format. These statements were organized into five categories or dimensions related to National's service quality:

1. Reliability (Sample statement: "When National promises to do something, it does so.")
2. Empathy (Sample statement: "National treats you with care.")
3. Tangibles (Sample statement: "National has modern-looking equipment.")
4. Responsiveness (Sample statement: "Employees of National give you prompt service.")
5. Assurance (Sample statement: "The behavior of National employees instills confidence.")

For each statement, customers were asked to circle one number on the 7-point scale that best represented their assessment of National. National's overall ratings for each of the five service dimensions were obtained by averaging the ratings on the set of items pertaining to each dimension (all analyses were conducted using the SPSS software package). National's overall ratings were as follows: reliability, 5.4265; empathy, 5.5557; tangibles, 5.6233; responsiveness, 5.6097; and assurance, 5.7480. Clearly, National's weakest performance is on reliability, and its strongest performance is on assurance.

The second section of the survey questionnaire consisted of a constant-sum scale that asked respondents to allocate a total of 100 points among the five attributes based on how important they considered each attribute to be. Analysis of these responses produced some interesting results—namely, that reliability (on which National's performance is weakest) is the most important attribute; the average number of points allocated to reliability was 28.81 (the relative importance scores for the other dimensions were as follows: empathy, 17.55; tangibles, 11.09; responsiveness, 22.70; and assurance, 19.85. Recommendation: *National must take immediate action to improve the reliability of its service.*

Section 3 of the survey questionnaire asked respondents to indicate (1) their overall evaluation of National's service quality on a scale of 1 to 10; (2) whether they would recommend National to a friend; (3) how long they had been doing business with National; (4) whether they had experienced any recent problem with National's service; and (5) if they did experience a problem, whether it was resolved to their satisfaction. The final section of the survey questionnaire focused on demographics and included questions about the respondent's gender, marital status, age, family income, and education level.

Responses to questions from the last two sections of the survey, along with responses to appropriate questions from the first two sections, were analyzed using the following techniques: one-way tabulation, cross-tabulation, chi-square analysis, correlation analysis, and regression analysis. The broad objectives of these analyses were to (1) understand the nature of the composition of the sample (vis-à-vis National's entire customer base); (2) determine whether customers' assessment of National's service quality, as well as their willingness to recommend National, differed across different customer groups based on demographics and problem experience; and (3) determine the extent to which perceptions of service quality on the five dimensions influenced overall service quality perceptions. The key findings from these various analyses are summarized in the following sections.

Respondent Profile

About 52 percent of the respondents were male, and 48 percent were female. This sample distribution did not differ significantly (p-value = .546) from the population distribution based on a chi-square test. Almost 80 percent of the respondents were married. A similar percentage of respondents (79.6 percent) were in the 25–44 age group; this was a significantly higher percentage (based on a chi-square test) than in the population, which had only 70 percent in the 25–44 age group. The modal family income category for the sample was $39,000 to $49,999 (with 39.7 percent of the respondents); the remaining respondents were fairly evenly distributed below and above this income bracket. Fewer than one-third of the respondents (31.1 percent) had a college degree; the modal education category was "high school or less" (with 37.4 percent). The vast majority—71.2 percent—had been doing business with National for five years or more; based on a chi-square test, this percentage was significantly higher than the population percentage (65 percent).

Differences Across Customer Groups

Males and females did not differ significantly in terms of their willingness to recommend National to others (based on cross-tabulation and chi-square analysis). Similarly, willingness to recommend was not associated with either marital status or age. On the other hand, there was some evidence that willingness to recommend was associated negatively with income (chi-square = 10.639; p-value = .059) and education level (chi-square = 10.007; p-value = .019).

The analyses produced two other interesting insights. First, males and females did not differ significantly in terms of their overall evaluation of National's service quality (the mean ratings given by males and females were, respectively, 7.87 and 7.83 on the 10-point scale). Second, those who were and those who were not willing to recommend National differed substantially in terms of their overall evaluation of the company's service quality; mean ratings for the two groups, respectively, were 8.45 and 3.34. The second result has an important managerial implication: delivering superior service quality should be a top priority for National to stimulate positive word-of-mouth communications from current customers.

Association Between Dimensional and Overall Service Quality Ratings

The results of correlation analyses showed that ratings on each of the five quality dimensions were significantly associated with overall service quality ratings. The strongest correlation was for responsiveness (.863), and the weakest correlation was for tangibles (.504). Moreover, all five correlations were statistically significant at a p-value of .001 or less. Clearly, then, perceptions of National's service quality on the five individual dimensions critically influence National's overall service image from the customer's standpoint. Results from a multiple regression analysis (with overall service ratings as the dependent variable and ratings on the five dimensions as independent variables) further support the above conclusion: the R^2 value for this regression was .810, suggesting that more than 80 percent of the variance in overall perceptions was accounted for by the individual dimensional ratings.

Conclusions

On the whole, National's quality of service seems to be good, but it could be improved. Customers' ratings average between 5.4 and 5.7 (on a 7-point scale) for the five dimensions. Customers' overall rating is around 7.8 (on a 10-point scale). Although these are decent ratings, there seems to be some room for improvement. One area on which management needs to focus immediately is the reliability of National's service. Among the five service quality dimensions, reliability was rated as most important to customers; yet National's perceived performance on this attribute is the weakest. Another issue National needs to look into is why higher-income and highly educated customer groups are apparently less likely to recommend National than are lower-income and less educated customers.

CASE QUESTIONS

1. On a scale of 1 to 10, what is your overall rating of Jeff's executive summary? Support your rating by listing the key weaknesses and strengths of the executive summary.

2. Critically evaluate the content of the executive summary. Specifically:

   a. Does it contain all the components that an excellent executive summary should have? If not, what components are missing?

   b. Does it have any unnecessary information that could be minimized or eliminated to make it more effective?

3. Critically evaluate the organization of the executive summary. What suggestions would you make to Jeff to help him organize it more effectively?

4. Prepare a detailed outline for a revised executive summary that is likely to be much more useful to Jill Baxter.

CASE 16.2 THE PANKEY INSTITUTE (PART D)
(www.pankey.org)

Christian B. Sager, executive director of the Pankey Institute, commissioned a research study to assess overall satisfaction with the continuous education services that the organization provides to dentists. The overriding objective was to gain insight into the factors that affect participants' decisions to return to the Pankey Institute for coursework beyond the first training program.

Several analyses were conducted to better assess the value of different aspects of the instructional program. First, an initial data reduction had been completed and later confirmed. A set of five factors were identified and correlated with one another. The effects of demographic items on other demographic items were then studied. A further analysis examined the impact of gender and practice location on the five factors. The effects of the various factors on overall satisfaction were also investigated. Finally, the effects of age on the five factors were analyzed.

Now it was time to present the findings to the rest of the executives responsible for the program. It is your job to present the overall plan of analysis, an executive summary, and a report of the findings, and then prepare a PowerPoint presentation.

CASE QUESTIONS

1. Describe your overall plan of analysis.

2. Based on your analysis of the Pankey data set, prepare an executive summary and report outlining your managerial recommendations.

3. Based on the analysis and report, prepare a PowerPoint presentation.

This case was written by Jeanne L. Munger (University of Southern Maine) in collaboration with the textbook authors, as a basis for class discussion rather than to illustrate either effective or ineffective marketing practice.

Appendix 1

Areas Under the Standard Normal Curve (Areas to the Left)

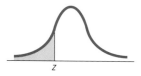

z	0	1	2	3	4	5	6	7	8	9
−3.0*	.0013	.0013	.0013	.0012	.0012	.0011	.0011	.0011	.0010	.0010
−2.9	.0019	.0018	.0017	.0017	.0016	.0016	.0015	.0015	.0014	.0014
−2.8	.0026	.0025	.0024	.0023	.0023	.0022	.0021	.0021	.0020	.0019
−2.7	.0035	.0034	.0033	.0032	.0031	.0030	.0029	.0028	.0027	.0026
−2.6	.0047	.0045	.0044	.0043	.0041	.0040	.0039	.0038	.0037	.0036
−2.5	.0062	.0060	.0059	.0057	.0055	.0054	.0052	.0051	.0049	.0048
−2.4	.0082	.0080	.0078	.0075	.0073	.0071	.0069	.0068	.0066	.0064
−2.3	.0107	.0104	.0102	.0099	.0096	.0094	.0091	.0089	.0087	.0084
−2.2	.0139	.0136	.0132	.0129	.0125	.0122	.0119	.0116	.0113	.0110
−2.1	.0179	.0174	.0170	.0166	.0162	.0158	.0154	.0150	.0146	.0143
−2.0	.0228	.0222	.0217	.0212	.0207	.0202	.0197	.0192	.0188	.0183
−1.9	.0287	.0281	.0274	.0268	.0262	.0256	.0250	.0244	.0239	.0233
−1.8	.0359	.0351	.0344	.0336	.0329	.0322	.0314	.0307	.0301	.0294
−1.7	.0446	.0436	.0427	.0418	.0409	.0401	.0392	.0384	.0375	.0367
−1.6	.0548	.0537	.0526	.0516	.0505	.0495	.0485	.0475	.0465	.0455
−1.5	.0668	.0655	.0643	.0630	.0618	.0606	.0594	.0582	.0571	.0559
−1.4	.0808	.0793	.0778	.0764	.0749	.0735	.0721	.0708	.0694	.0681
−1.3	.0968	.0951	.0934	.0918	.0901	.0885	.0869	.0853	.0838	.0823
−1.2	.1151	.1131	.1112	.1093	.1075	.1056	.1038	.1020	.1003	.0985
−1.1	.1357	.1335	.1314	.1292	.1271	.1251	.1230	.1210	.1190	.1170
−1.0	.1587	.1562	.1539	.1515	.1492	.1469	.1446	.1423	.1401	.1379
−.9	.1841	.1814	.1788	.1762	.1736	.1711	.1685	.1660	.1635	.1611
−.8	.2119	.2090	.2061	.2033	.2005	.1977	.1949	.1922	.1894	.1867
−.7	.2420	.2389	.2358	.2327	.2296	.2266	.2236	.2206	.2177	.2148
−.6	.2743	.2709	.2676	.2643	.2611	.2578	.2546	.2514	.2483	.2451
−.5	.3085	.3050	.3015	.2981	.2946	.2912	.2877	.2843	.2810	.2776
−.4	.3446	.3409	.3372	.3336	.3300	.3264	.3228	.3192	.3156	.3121
−.3	.3821	.3783	.3745	.3707	.3669	.3632	.3594	.3557	.3520	.3483
−.2	.4207	.4168	.4129	.4090	.4052	.4013	.3974	.3936	.3897	.3859
−.1	.4602	.4562	.4522	.4483	.4443	.4404	.4364	.4325	.4286	.4247
−.0	.5000	.4960	.4920	.4880	.4840	.4801	.4761	.4721	.4681	.4641

(continued)

Appendix 1 (concluded)

z	0	1	2	3	4	5	6	7	8	9
.0	.5000	.5040	.5080	.5120	.5160	.5199	.5239	.5279	.5319	.5359
.1	.5398	.5438	.5478	.5517	.5557	.5596	.5636	.5675	.5714	.5753
.2	.5793	.5832	.5871	.5910	.5948	.5987	.6026	.6064	.6103	.6141
.3	.6179	.6217	.6255	.6293	.6331	.6368	.6406	.6443	.6480	.6517
.4	.6554	.6591	.6628	.6664	.6700	.6736	.6772	.6808	.6844	.6879
.5	.6915	.6950	.6985	.7019	.7054	.7088	.7123	.7157	.7190	.7224
.6	.7257	.7291	.7324	.7357	.7389	.7422	.7454	.7486	.7517	.7549
.7	.7580	.7611	.7642	.7673	.7704	.7734	.7764	.7794	.7823	.7852
.8	.7881	.7910	.7939	.7967	.7995	.8023	.8051	.8078	.8106	.8133
.9	.8159	.8186	.8212	.8238	.8264	.8289	.8315	.8340	.8365	.8389
1.0	.8413	.8438	.8461	.8485	.8508	.8531	.8554	.8577	.8599	.9621
1.1	.8643	.8665	.8686	.8708	.8729	.8749	.8770	.8790	.8810	.8830
1.2	.8849	.8869	.8888	.9807	.8925	.8944	.8962	.8980	.8997	.9015
1.3	.9032	.9049	.9066	.9082	.9099	.9115	.9131	.9147	.9162	.9177
1.4	.9192	.9207	.9222	.9236	.9251	.9265	.9279	.9292	.9306	.9319
1.5	.9332	.9345	.9357	.9370	.9382	.9394	.9406	.9418	.9429	.9441
1.6	.9452	.9463	.9474	.9484	.9495	.9505	.9515	.9525	.9535	.9545
1.7	.9554	.9564	.9573	.9582	.9591	.9599	.9608	.9616	.9625	.9633
1.8	.9641	.9649	.9656	.9664	.9671	.9678	.9686	.9693	.9699	.9706
1.9	.9713	.9719	.9726	.9732	.9738	.9744	.9750	.9756	.9761	.9767
2.0	.9772	.9778	.9783	.9788	.9793	.9798	.9803	.9808	.9812	.9817
2.1	.9821	.9826	.9830	.9834	.9838	.9842	.9846	.9850	.9854	.9857
2.2	.9861	.9864	.9868	.9871	.9875	.9878	.9881	.9884	.9887	.9890
2.3	.9893	.9896	.9898	.9901	.9904	.9906	.9909	.9911	.9913	.9916
2.4	.9918	.9920	.9922	.9925	.9927	.9929	.9931	.9932	.9934	.9936
2.5	.9938	.9940	.9941	.9943	.9945	.9946	.9948	.9949	.9951	.9952
2.6	.9953	.9955	.9956	.9957	.9959	.9960	.9961	.9962	.9963	.9964
2.7	.9965	.9966	.9967	.9968	.9969	.9970	.9971	.9972	.9973	.9974
2.8	.9974	.9975	.9976	.9977	.9977	.9978	.9979	.9979	.9980	.9981
2.9	.9981	.9982	.9982	.9983	.9984	.9984	.9985	.9985	.9986	.9986
3.0[†]	.9987	.9987	.9987	.9988	.9988	.9989	.9989	.9989	.9990	.9990

*For $z \leq -4$, the areas are 0 to 4 decimal places.

[†]For $z \geq 4$, the areas are 1 to 4 decimal places.

Source: Weiss, *Introductory Statistics*, pp. 576–577. Reprinted by permission of Pearson Education, Inc.

Appendix 2

Chi-Square Distribution (Values of χ^2_α)

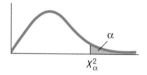

d.f. \ α	.995	.99	.975	.95	.90	.10	.05	.025	.01	.005
1	.00	.00	.00	.00	.02	2.71	3.84	5.02	6.63	7.88
2	.01	.02	.05	.10	.21	4.61	5.99	7.38	9.21	10.60
3	.07	.11	.22	.35	.58	6.25	7.81	9.35	11.34	12.84
4	.21	.30	.48	.71	1.06	7.78	9.49	11.14	13.28	14.86
5	.41	.55	.83	1.15	1.61	9.24	11.07	12.83	15.09	16.75
6	.68	.87	1.24	1.64	2.20	10.64	12.59	14.45	16.81	18.55
7	.99	1.24	1.69	2.17	2.83	12.02	14.07	16.01	18.48	20.28
8	1.34	1.65	2.18	2.73	3.49	13.36	15.51	17.54	20.09	21.96
9	1.73	2.09	2.70	3.33	4.17	14.68	16.92	19.02	21.67	23.59
10	2.16	2.56	3.25	3.94	4.87	15.99	18.31	20.48	23.21	25.19
11	2.60	3.05	3.82	4.57	5.58	17.28	19.68	21.92	24.72	26.76
12	3.07	3.57	4.40	5.23	6.30	18.55	21.03	23.34	26.22	28.30
13	3.57	4.11	5.01	5.89	7.04	19.81	22.36	24.74	27.69	29.82
14	4.07	4.66	5.63	6.57	7.79	21.06	23.68	26.12	29.14	31.32
15	4.60	5.23	6.26	7.26	8.55	22.31	25.00	27.49	30.58	32.80
16	5.14	5.81	6.91	7.96	9.31	23.54	26.30	28.85	32.00	34.27
17	5.70	6.41	7.56	8.67	10.09	24.77	27.59	30.19	33.41	35.72
18	6.26	7.01	8.23	9.39	10.86	25.99	28.87	31.53	34.81	37.16
19	6.84	7.63	8.91	10.12	11.65	27.20	30.14	32.85	36.19	38.58
20	7.43	8.26	9.59	10.85	12.44	28.41	31.41	34.17	35.57	40.00
21	8.03	8.90	10.28	11.59	13.24	29.62	32.67	35.48	38.93	41.40
22	8.64	9.54	10.98	12.34	14.04	30.81	33.92	36.78	40.29	42.80
23	9.26	10.20	11.69	13.09	14.85	32.01	35.17	38.08	41.64	44.18
24	9.89	10.86	12.40	13.85	15.66	33.20	36.42	39.36	42.98	45.56
25	10.52	11.52	13.12	14.61	16.47	34.38	37.65	40.65	44.31	46.93
26	11.16	12.20	13.84	15.38	17.29	35.56	38.89	41.92	45.64	48.29
27	11.81	12.88	14.57	16.15	18.11	36.74	40.11	43.19	46.96	49.65
28	12.46	13.56	15.31	16.93	18.94	37.92	41.34	44.46	48.28	50.99
29	13.12	14.26	16.05	17.71	19.77	39.09	42.56	45.72	49.59	52.34
30	13.79	14.95	16.79	18.49	20.60	40.26	43.77	46.98	50.89	53.67
50	27.99	29.71	32.36	34.76	37.69	63.17	67.50	71.42	76.15	79.49
100	67.33	70.06	74.22	77.93	82.36	118.5	124.3	129.6	135.8	140.2
500	422.3	429.4	439.9	449.1	459.9	540.9	553.1	563.9	576.5	585.2
1000	888.6	898.8	914.3	927.6	943.1	1058	1075	1090	1107	1119

Source: Weiss, *Introductory Statistics*, p. 579. Reprinted by permission of Pearson Education, Inc.

Appendix 3

Student's t-Distribution (Values of t_α)

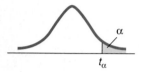

d.f.	$t_{.10}$	$t_{.05}$	$t_{.025}$	$t_{.01}$	$t_{.005}$
1	3.08	6.31	12.71	31.82	63.66
2	1.89	2.92	4.30	6.96	9.92
3	1.64	2.35	3.18	4.54	5.84
4	1.53	2.13	2.78	3.75	4.60
5	1.48	2.02	2.57	3.36	4.03
6	1.44	1.94	2.45	3.14	3.71
7	1.42	1.89	2.36	3.00	3.50
8	1.40	1.86	2.31	2.90	3.36
9	1.38	1.83	2.26	2.82	3.25
10	1.37	1.81	2.23	2.76	3.17
11	1.36	1.80	2.20	2.72	3.11
12	1.36	1.78	2.18	2.68	3.05
13	1.35	1.77	2.16	2.65	3.01
14	1.35	1.76	2.14	2.62	2.98
15	1.34	1.75	2.13	2.60	2.95
16	1.34	1.75	2.12	2.58	2.92
17	1.33	1.74	2.11	2.57	2.90
18	1.33	1.73	2.10	2.55	2.88
19	1.33	1.73	2.09	2.54	2.86
20	1.33	1.72	2.09	2.53	2.85
21	1.32	1.72	2.08	2.52	2.83
22	1.32	1.72	2.07	2.51	2.82
23	1.32	1.71	2.07	2.50	2.81
24	1.32	1.71	2.06	2.49	2.80
25	1.32	1.71	2.06	2.49	2.79
26	1.32	1.71	2.06	2.48	2.78
27	1.31	1.70	2.05	2.47	2.77
28	1.31	1.70	2.05	2.47	2.76
29	1.31	1.70	2.05	2.46	2.76
∞	1.28	1.64	1.96	2.33	2.58

Note: The last row of the table (d.f. = ∞) gives values for z_α. For example, the table shows that $z_{.10} = 1.28$ and $z_{.05} = 1.64$.

Source: Weiss, *Introductory Statistics*, p. 578. Reprinted by permission of Pearson Education, Inc.

Critical Values of the Sample Correlation Coefficient r

d.f. \ α	.10	.05	.02	.01
1	.988	.997	.9995	.9999
2	.900	.950	.980	.990
3	.805	.878	.934	.959
4	.729	.811	.882	.917
5	.669	.754	.833	.874
6	.622	.707	.789	.834
7	.582	.666	.750	.798
8	.549	.632	.716	.765
9	.521	.602	.685	.735
10	.497	.576	.658	.708
11	.476	.553	.634	.684
12	.458	.532	.612	.661
13	.441	.514	.592	.641
14	.426	.497	.574	.623
15	.412	.482	.558	.606
16	.400	.468	.543	.590
17	.389	.456	.528	.575
18	.378	.444	.516	.561
19	.369	.433	.503	.549
20	.360	.423	.492	.537
21	.352	.413	.482	.526
22	.344	.404	.472	.515
23	.337	.396	.462	.505
24	.330	.388	.453	.496
25	.323	.381	.445	.487
26	.317	.374	.437	.479
27	.311	.367	.430	.471
28	.306	.361	.423	.463
29	.301	.355	.416	.456
30	.296	.349	.409	.449
40	.257	.304	.358	.393
50	.231	.273	.322	.354
60	.211	.250	.295	.325
70	.195	.232	.274	.302
80	.183	.217	.257	.283
90	.173	.205	.242	.257
100	.164	.195	.230	.254

Note: A value given in the table is the *right-hand* critical value for a *two-tailed* test at the significance level indicated. The left-hand critical value is just the negative of the right-hand critical value.

Source: Weiss, *Introductory Statistics*, p. 586. Reprinted by permission of Pearson Education, Inc.

Appendix 5

Values of $F_{.05}$

d.f. for Denominator	d.f. for Numerator								
	1	2	3	4	5	6	7	8	9
1	161.4	199.5	215.7	224.6	230.2	234.0	236.8	238.9	240.5
2	18.51	19.00	19.16	19.25	19.30	19.33	19.35	19.37	19.38
3	10.13	9.55	9.28	9.12	9.01	8.94	8.89	8.85	8.81
4	7.71	6.94	6.59	6.39	6.26	6.16	6.09	6.04	6.00
5	6.61	5.79	5.41	5.19	5.05	4.95	4.88	4.82	4.77
6	5.99	5.14	4.76	4.53	4.39	4.28	4.21	4.15	4.10
7	5.59	4.74	4.35	4.12	3.97	3.87	3.79	3.73	3.68
8	5.32	4.46	4.07	3.84	3.69	3.58	3.50	3.44	3.39
9	5.12	4.26	3.86	3.63	3.48	3.37	3.29	3.23	3.18
10	4.96	4.10	3.71	3.48	3.33	3.22	3.14	3.07	3.02
11	4.84	3.98	3.59	3.36	3.20	3.09	3.01	2.95	2.90
12	4.75	3.89	3.49	3.26	3.11	3.00	2.91	2.85	2.80
13	4.67	3.81	3.41	3.18	3.03	2.92	2.83	2.77	2.71
14	4.60	3.74	3.34	3.11	2.96	2.85	2.76	2.70	2.65
15	4.54	3.68	3.29	3.06	2.90	2.79	2.71	2.64	2.59
16	4.49	3.63	3.24	3.01	2.85	2.74	2.66	2.59	2.54
17	4.45	3.59	3.20	2.96	2.81	2.70	2.61	2.55	2.49
18	4.41	3.55	3.16	2.93	2.77	2.66	2.58	2.51	2.46
19	4.38	3.52	3.13	2.90	2.74	2.63	2.54	2.48	2.42
20	4.35	3.49	3.10	2.87	2.71	2.60	2.51	2.45	2.39
21	4.32	3.47	3.07	2.84	2.68	2.57	2.49	2.42	2.37
22	4.30	3.44	3.05	2.82	2.66	2.55	2.46	2.40	2.34
23	4.28	3.42	3.03	2.80	2.64	2.53	2.44	2.37	2.32
24	4.26	3.40	3.01	2.78	2.62	2.51	2.42	2.36	2.30
25	4.24	3.39	2.99	2.76	2.60	2.49	2.40	2.34	2.28
26	4.23	3.37	2.98	2.74	2.59	2.47	2.39	2.32	2.27
27	4.21	3.35	2.96	2.73	2.57	2.46	2.37	2.31	2.25
28	4.20	3.34	2.95	2.71	2.56	2.45	2.36	2.29	2.24
29	4.18	3.33	2.93	2.70	2.55	2.43	2.35	2.28	2.22
30	4.17	3.32	2.92	2.69	2.53	2.42	2.33	2.27	2.21
40	4.08	3.23	2.84	2.61	2.45	2.34	2.25	2.18	2.12
60	4.00	3.15	2.76	2.53	2.37	2.25	2.17	2.10	2.04
120	3.92	3.07	2.68	2.45	2.29	2.17	2.09	2.02	1.96
∞	3.84	3.00	2.60	2.37	2.21	2.10	2.01	1.94	1.88

(continued)

Appendix 5 (concluded)

			d.f. for Numerator						
10	12	15	20	24	30	40	60	120	∞
241.9	243.9	245.9	248.0	249.1	250.1	251.1	252.2	253.3	254.3
19.40	19.41	19.43	19.45	19.45	19.46	19.47	19.48	19.49	19.50
8.79	8.74	8.70	8.66	8.64	8.62	8.59	8.57	8.55	8.53
5.96	5.91	5.86	5.80	5.77	5.75	5.72	5.69	5.66	5.63
4.74	4.68	4.62	4.56	4.53	4.50	4.46	4.43	4.40	4.36
4.06	4.00	3.94	3.87	3.84	3.81	3.77	3.74	3.70	3.67
3.64	3.57	3.51	3.41	3.41	3.38	3.34	3.30	3.27	3.23
3.35	3.28	3.22	3.15	3.12	3.08	3.04	3.01	2.97	2.93
3.14	3.07	3.01	2.94	2.90	2.86	2.83	2.79	2.75	2.71
2.98	2.91	2.85	2.77	2.74	2.70	2.66	2.62	2.58	2.54
2.85	2.79	2.72	2.65	2.61	2.57	2.53	2.49	2.45	2.40
2.75	2.69	2.62	2.54	2.51	2.47	2.43	2.38	2.34	2.30
2.67	2.60	2.53	2.46	2.42	2.38	2.34	2.30	2.25	2.21
2.60	2.53	2.46	2.39	2.35	2.31	2.27	2.22	2.18	2.13
2.54	2.48	2.40	2.33	2.29	2.25	2.20	2.16	2.11	2.07
2.49	2.42	2.35	2.28	2.24	2.19	2.15	2.11	2.06	2.01
2.45	2.38	2.31	2.23	2.19	2.15	2.10	2.06	2.01	1.96
2.41	2.34	2.27	2.19	2.15	2.11	2.06	2.02	1.97	1.92
2.38	2.31	2.23	2.16	2.11	2.07	2.03	1.98	1.93	1.88
2.35	2.28	2.20	2.12	2.08	2.04	1.99	1.95	1.90	1.84
2.32	2.25	2.18	2.10	2.05	2.01	1.96	1.92	1.87	1.81
2.30	2.23	2.15	2.07	2.03	1.98	1.94	1.89	1.84	1.78
2.27	2.20	2.13	2.05	2.01	1.96	1.91	1.86	1.81	1.76
2.25	2.18	2.11	2.03	1.98	1.94	1.89	1.84	1.79	1.73
2.24	2.16	2.09	2.01	1.96	1.92	1.87	1.82	1.77	1.71
2.22	2.15	2.07	1.99	1.95	1.90	1.85	1.80	1.75	1.69
2.20	2.13	2.06	1.97	1.93	1.88	1.84	1.79	1.73	1.67
2.19	2.12	2.04	1.96	1.91	1.87	1.82	1.77	1.71	1.65
2.18	2.10	2.03	1.94	1.90	1.85	1.81	1.75	1.70	1.64
2.16	2.09	2.01	1.93	1.89	1.84	1.79	1.74	1.68	1.62
2.08	2.00	1.92	1.84	1.79	1.74	1.69	1.64	1.58	1.51
1.99	1.92	1.84	1.75	1.70	1.65	1.59	1.53	1.47	1.39
1.91	1.83	1.75	1.66	1.61	1.55	1.50	1.43	1.35	1.25
1.83	1.75	1.67	1.57	1.52	1.46	1.39	1.32	1.22	1.00

Source: Weiss, *Introductory Statistics,* p. 584–585. Reprinted by permission of Pearson Education, Inc.

Appendix 6

National Insurance Company Data Analysis Using Microsoft Excel®

Using Excel's COUNTIF Function to construct a Frequency Distribution for the Variable USE

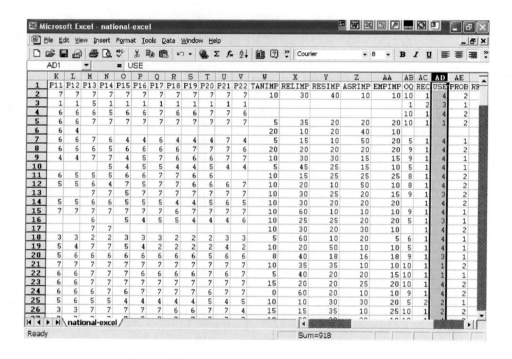

For a detailed description of the data, we refer you to Chapter 12.

All screen captures in this appendix reprinted by permission from Microsoft Corporation.

Frequency Distribution—Excel Output

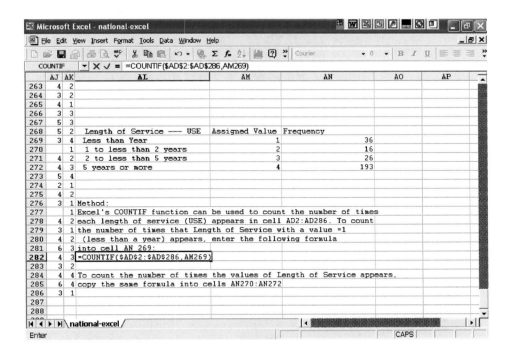

Using Excel's Chart Wizard to Construct Bar Charts

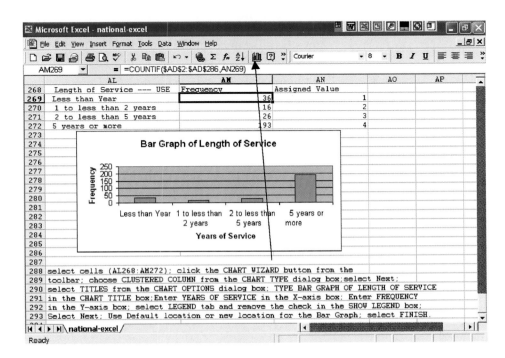

Computing Descriptive Statistics—Overall Quality of Services Provided by National

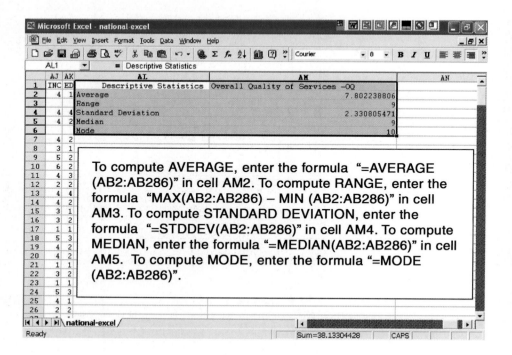

So far, we've used statistical functions to compute descriptive statistics for a data set. These functions can only be used to compute statistics one at a time: mean, range, standard deviation, median, and mode. Excel also provides a variety of data analysis tools. We will show how we can use those tools to compute descriptive statistics all at once for the variable OQ (Overall Service Quality). Follow the steps outlined here:

1. In the Excel worksheet (National Insurance datasheet), select *TOOLS* from the menu.
2. Choose the *DATA ANALYSIS* option.
3. Choose *descriptive statistics* from the list of statistical analysis tools.
4. When the *Descriptive Statistics* dialog box appears,
   a. Enter "AB1:AB286" (column containing the variable OQ) in the *Input Range* box.
   b. Select *Grouped by Columns*.
   c. Select *Labels in First Row*.
   d. Select *Output Range*.
      i. Enter "AL1" in the *Output Range* box (for the descriptive statistics to appear on the worksheet).
   e. Select *Summary Statistics*.
   f. Click *OK*.

Descriptive Statistics—Excel Dialog Boxes

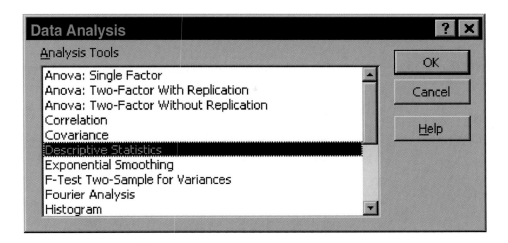

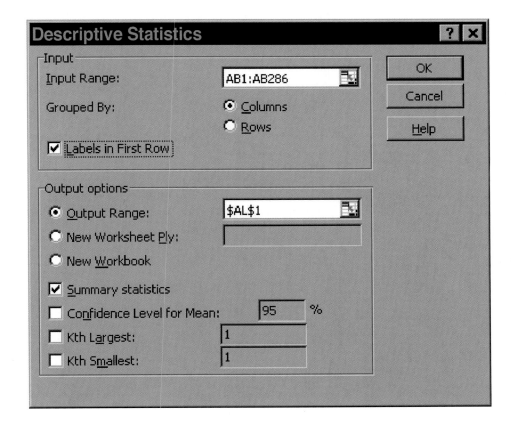

Descriptive Statistics of the Variable OQ—Overall Service Quality—Excel Output

Cells AL1:AM15 contain the Excel output.

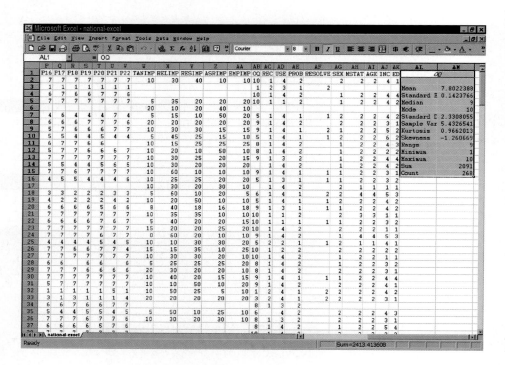

We used the data analysis tool to compute descriptive statistics for one variable, OQ. We can also compute for several variables. On the following page we show how to compute descriptive statistics for five variables (TANIMP, RELIMP, RESIMP, ASRIMP, EMPIMP).

Descriptive Statistics for Importance by Service Dimension

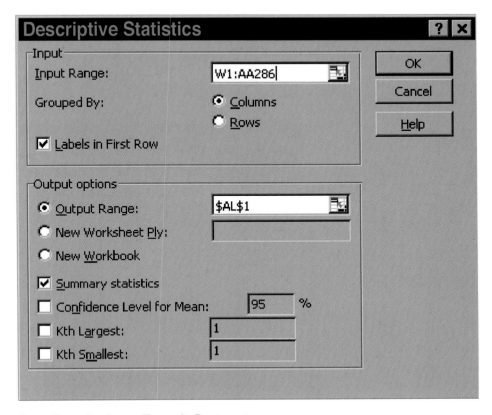

Descriptive Statistics—Excel Output

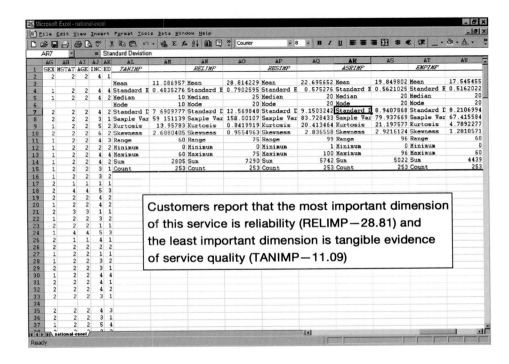

Customers report that the most important dimension of this service is reliability (RELIMP—28.81) and the least important dimension is tangible evidence of service quality (TANIMP—11.09)

Are there any significant differences between males and females in terms of how they perceive National's service quality?

This calls for a *t*-test. To conduct a *t*-test, we first created the two groups— Females and Males. The Female column contains Overall Service Quality data as reported by the female respondents. The Male column contains Overall Service Quality as reported by the male respondents.

Conducting a T-Test Using Excel

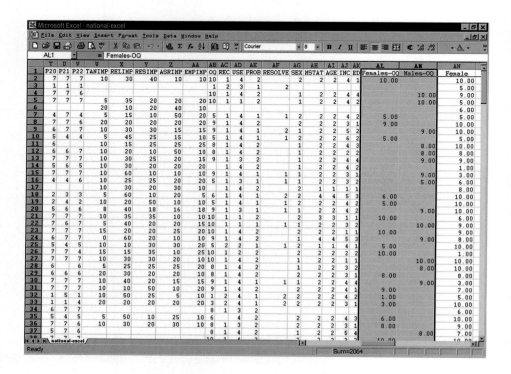

To conduct a *t*-test, follow the steps described below:

1. Select *Tools* from the menu.
2. Choose the *Data Analysis* option.
3. Choose *t-Test: Two-Sample Assuming Equal Variances*.
4. *t-Test: Two-Sample Assuming Equal Variances* dialog box appears.

   a. Enter "AL1:AL286" in the *Variable 1 Range* box.
   b. Enter "AM1:AM286" in the *Variable 2 Range* box.
   c. Enter "0" in the *Hypothesized Mean Difference* box.
   d. Select *Labels*.
   e. Enter ".05" in the *Alpha box*.
   f. Select *Output Range*.
   g. Enter "AN16" in the *Output Range* box (for placing the output).
   h. Click *OK*.

T–Test—Excel Dialog Boxes

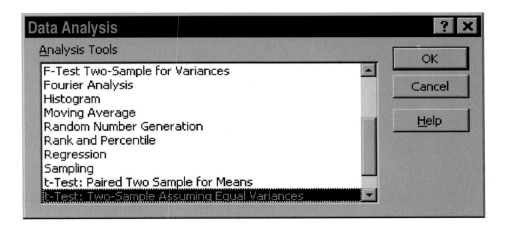

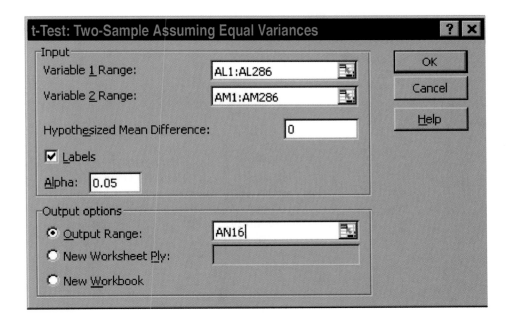

T-Test Results—Excel Output

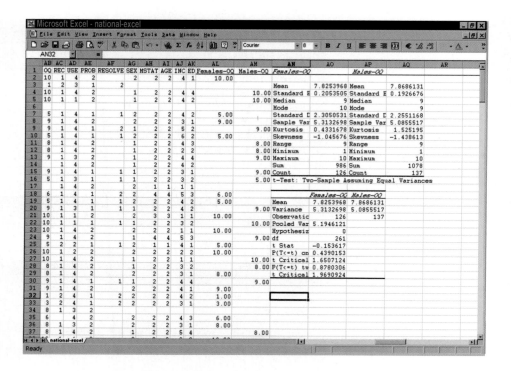

Descriptive statistics for the two groups are shown in cells AN1:AQ15. *t*-test results are shown in cells AN16:AP29. The findings show that the *p*-value $[P(T \leq t)] = .878$, as shown in cell AO28. Because the *p*-value (.878) is greater than the level of significance, $\alpha = 0.05$, we do not have sufficient evidence to reject the null hypothesis of no differences between men and women. This finding should be obvious simply by looking at the mean ratings of the two groups (cells AO3 and AQ3) and the relatively small standard errors (cells AO4 and AQ4). For the sake of clarity, we have reproduced the descriptive statistics and the *t*-test results in the next two tables.

Females-OQ		Males-OQ	
Mean	7.8253968	Mean	7.8686131
Standard error	0.2053505	Standard error	0.1926676
Median	9	Median	9
Mode	10	Mode	9
Standard deviation	2.3050531	Standard deviation	2.2551168
Sample variance	5.3132698	Sample variance	5.0855517
Kurtosis	0.4331678	Kurtosis	1.525195
Skewness	−1.045676	Skewness	−1.438613
Range	9	Range	9
Minimum	1	Minimum	1
Maximum	10	Maximum	10
Sum	986	Sum	1078
Count	126	Count	137

T-Test: Two-Sample Assuming Equal Variances

	Females-OQ	Males-OQ
Mean	7.8253968	7.8686131
Variance	5.3132698	5.0855517
Observations	126	137
Pooled variance	5.1946121	
Hypothesized mean difference	0	
d.f.	261	
t Stat	−0.153617	
$P(T \leq t)$ one-tail	0.4390153	
t Critical one-tail	1.6507124	
$P(T \leq t)$ two-tail	0.8780306	
t Critical two-tail	1.9690924	

Descriptive Statistics for the Five Service Dimensions

The five service dimensions are computed as follows:

Reliable = (p1 + p2 + p3 + p4 + p5)/5
Empathy = (p6 + p7 + p8 + p9 + p10)/5
Tangible = (p11 + p12 + p13 + p14)/4
Response = (p15 + p16 + p17 + p18)/4
Assure = (p19 + p20 + p21 + p22)/4

	Reliable	Empathy	Tangible	Response	Assure
Mean	5.4265152	5.5557252	5.6232877	5.6097328	5.7480469
Standard error	0.089809	0.0879349	0.071953	0.0953081	0.0894114
Median	5.8	5.8	5.75	6	6.25
Mode	7	7	7	7	7
Standard deviation	1.4592232	1.4233499	1.0648066	1.5426971	1.430582
Sample variance	2.1293323	2.025925	1.133813	2.3799145	2.0465648
Kurtosis	1.0560167	0.7869989	2.7464616	0.8169834	1.2573402
Skewness	−1.17647	−1.150716	−1.150555	−1.232299	−1.352646
Range	6	6	6	6	6
Minimum	1	1	1	1	1
Maximum	7	7	7	7	7
Sum	1432.6	1455.6	1231.5	1469.75	1471.5
Count	264	262	219	262	256

Correlations Among the Five Service Dimensions

Steps for using Excel:

1. Select *Tools* from the menu.
2. Choose the *Data Analysis* option.
3. Choose *Correlation* from the list of tools.
4. When the *Correlation* dialog box appears:
   a. Enter "AP1:AU286" in the *Input Range* box (please note: AP1:AU286 contains all the five service dimensions and the overall Service Quality).
   b. *Grouped by:* Columns.
   c. Check *Labels* in the first row.
   d. Select *Output Range.*
   e. Enter "AV1" in the *Output Range* box for posting the output.
   f. Click *OK.*

Data Analysis Dialog Box

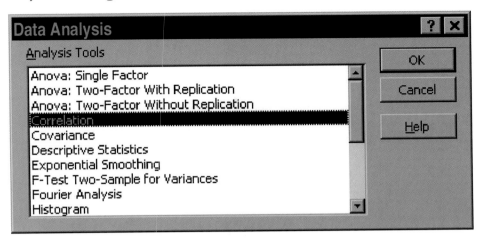

Correlation Dialog Box

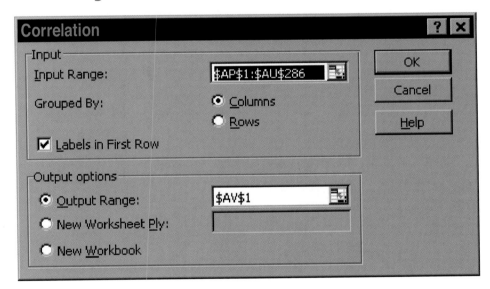

The Excel output is shown below.

	Reliable	Empathy	Tangible	Response	Assure	OQ
Reliable	1					
Empathy	0.8259666	1				
Tangible	0.5813179	0.6484511	1			
Response	0.8671382	0.8821064	0.6071428	1		
Assure	0.8419368	0.8731867	0.567311	0.9209463	1	
OQ	0.8464963	0.8215294	0.5038271	0.8625135	0.8594677	1

Note: OQ stands for Overall Service Quality.

Conduct a multiple regression analysis wherein overall service quality perception is the dependent variable and the average ratings along the five dimensions are the independent variables. What specific inferences can you make from the results of this analysis?

Excel doesn't work well when there are many missing values. Therefore, we created a new dataset from the original National dataset by deleting the data with missing values (similar to SPSS—*Listwise* procedure). After eliminating the data with missing values, we were left with only 206 data points. The partial dataset is shown below.

Conducting Multiple Regression Using Excel

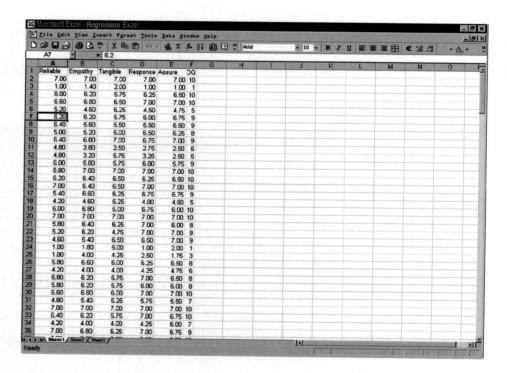

1. Select *Tools* from the menu.
2. Select the *Data Analysis* option.
3. Choose *Regression* from the list.
4. The *Regression* dialog box will appear.

   a. Enter "F1:F207" in the *Input Y Range* box (this column contains the dependent variable, overall service quality, OQ in our data set).

   b. "A1:E207" in the *Input X Range* box (these five columns contain the independent variables, reliable, empathy, tangible, response, and assure).

   c. Select *Labels* to indicate that the first cell contains variable labels.

   d. Select *Confidence Level*. Enter "95%" in the in the *confidence level* box.

   e. Select *Output Range*. Enter "F1" to post the regression output.

   f. Click *OK*.

Regression—Excel Dialog Boxes

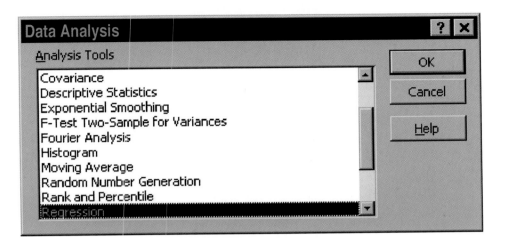

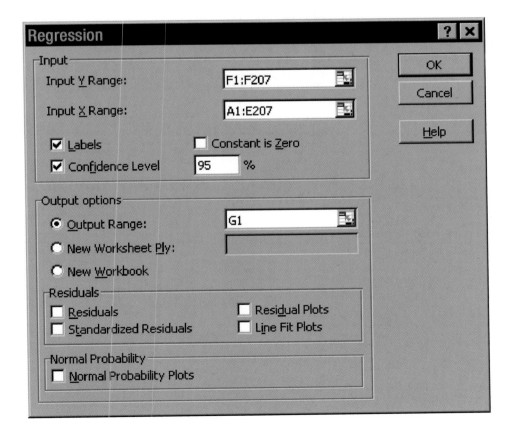

Regression—Excel Output

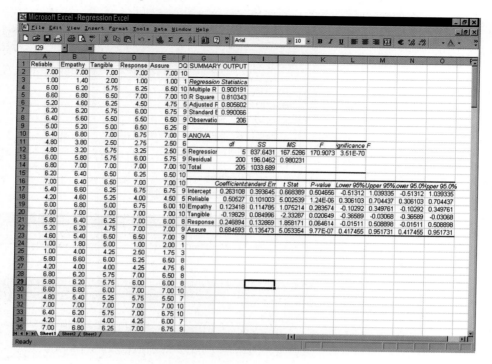

For the sake of clarity, we have reproduced the Excel regression output in the table on the next page.

SUMMARY OUTPUT

Regression Statistics	
Multiple R	0.900191
R-square	0.810343
Adjusted R-square	0.805602
Standard error	0.990066
Observations	206

ANOVA

	d.f.	SS	MS	F	Significance F
Regression	5	837.6431	167.5286	170.9073	3.51E–70
Residual	200	196.0462	0.980231		
Total	205	1033.689			

	Coefficients	Standard Error	t-Stat	P-Value	Lower 95%	Upper 95%	Lower 95.0%	Upper 95.0%
Intercept	0.263108	0.393645	0.668389	0.504656	−0.51312	1.039335	−0.51312	1.039335
Reliable	0.50527	0.101003	5.002539	1.24E206	0.306103	0.704437	0.306103	0.704437
Empathy	0.123418	0.114785	1.075214	0.283574	−0.10292	0.349761	−0.10292	0.349761
Tangible	−0.19829	0.084996	−2.33287	0.020649	−0.36589	−0.03068	−0.36589	−0.03068
Response	0.246894	0.132869	1.858171	0.064614	−0.01511	0.508898	−0.01511	0.508898
Assure	0.684593	0.135473	5.053354	9.77E–07	0.417455	0.951731	0.417455	0.951731

Note that all variables except empathy are significantly related to overall service quality (as indicated by the t-test of significance). The R-square of .81034 indicates a strong relationship between these variables and overall quality.

Glossary

Acquiescence bias (yea-saying) The bias resulting from a respondent's tendency to agree with whatever side is presented by one-sided questions.

Ad hoc research project A discrete, situation-specific project that is initiated and completed in response to a particular question, or set of related questions, raised by a decision maker.

Analysis of variance (ANOVA) A technique for detecting relationships between a metric-scaled dependent variable and one or more categorical (nominal or ordinal) independent variables.

Anchor label A label that defines one of the two extremes of a rating scale.

Applied research Research that is conducted to solve a specific problem.

Attitude A respondent's evaluative judgment.

Attribute A personal or demographic characteristic, such as education level, age, size of household, or number of children.

Balanced scale An equal number of positive/favorable and negative/unfavorable response choices.

Bar chart A graph that consists of a series of bars (of equal thickness) whose heights (or lengths, if the bars are horizontal) represent values of the items.

Basic research Research that is conducted to generate knowledge.

Behavioral variables Variables relating to such things as frequency of visits to a store or extent of magazine readership.

Belief What respondents consider (correctly or incorrectly) to be true.

Block Group A U.S. Census Bureau–defined geographic unit consisting of about a dozen city blocks or 340 households.

Buyer profile A description of the most promising (likely) buyers of a given product or service based on a number of key demographic variables, such as income, education, and age.

Cartoon test (balloon test) A pictorial technique like the TAT. The respondent is asked to examine the stimulus picture and fill in the empty "balloons" with words reflecting thoughts or verbal statements of the characters involved.

Case (observation) Each sample unit for which data are available within a data set.

Case study method An in-depth examination of a unit of interest.

Census study A study that involves drawing inferences from the entire body of units of interest.

Centralized organizational structure An organizational structure by which one corporate department caters to all of the firm's research needs.

Central limit theorem An assumption that, when the sample size is sufficiently large, the sampling distribution associated with a sampling procedure displays the properties of a normal probability distribution.

Central tendency A number depicting the "middle" position in a given range or distribution of numbers.

Chi-square contingency test A test widely used for determining whether there is a statistically significant relationship between two categorical (nominal or ordinal) variables.

Classification data Data that are useful in obtaining a profile of the respondent sample and in cross-classifying responses to other questions that pertain directly to the study objectives.

Cluster analysis An analysis technique that segments objects (such as customers, market areas, products) into groups so that objects within each group are similar to one another on a variety of characteristics.

Cluster sampling A sampling technique in which clusters of population units are selected at random and then all or some of the units in the chosen clusters are studied.

Coding A term broadly referring to the set of all tasks associated with transforming edited responses into a form that is ready for analysis.

Coefficient of determination A global measure of how much better predictions of the dependent variable made with the aid of the regression equation are than those made without.

Comparative rating scale A scale that provides all respondents with a common frame of reference.

Complex question A question that is not completely understood by, or sounds complicated to, the respondent.

Computerized interviewing An interviewing technique in which the questionnaire appears on a monitor and the responses are entered directly into computer memory.

Conclusive research Research that helps investigators verify insights and select the appropriate course of action.

Confidence level The complement of the significance level (1– significance level).

Conjoint analysis A technique for deriving the utility values that customers presumably attach to different levels of an object's attributes; requires respondents to compare hypothetical profiles of products, brands, and so on.

Constant-sum scale A scale that has a natural starting point (zero) and asks respondents to allocate a given set of points among several attitude objects.

Construct validity Assesses the nature of the underlying variable or construct measured by the scale by examining the scale's convergent and discriminant validity.

Content (face) validity The extent to which the content of a measurement scale seems to tap all relevant facets of an issue that can influence respondents' attitudes.

Contrived observation A technique in which observations are conducted in an environment artificially set up by the researcher.

Control group A unit or units participating in an experiment but not exposed to the experimental treatment.

Convenience sampling A sampling technique in which the researcher's convenience forms the basis for selecting a sample of units.

Cover letter A letter that informs potential respondents of what a study is about and, more critically, convinces them of the importance of participating in that study.

Cross-sectional study A one-time study involving data collection at a single period in time.

Crowded one-on-one interview An interview technique in which up to three client personnel are present in the room and observe a depth interview as it is conducted by a professional interviewer in a conventional fashion.

Data accuracy The extent to which collected data are error free and trustworthy.

Data file (data set) An organized collection of data records.

Data mining The process of digging deeply into vast amounts of data to extract valuable and statistically valid information that cannot be obtained through queries.

Data record A record containing all the coded data pertaining to a single sample unit.

Data warehouse A centralized database that consolidates companywide data from a variety of operational systems.

Decentralized organizational structure An organizational structure in which each constituency has its own marketing research arm.

Decision rule A guideline that specifies the sample evidence necessary to reject the null hypothesis.

Dependence technique An analysis technique in which one variable is designated as the dependent variable and the rest are treated as independent variables.

Dependent (criterion) variable In multivariate analysis, a variable that is presumed to be influenced by one or more independent variables and is conventionally plotted along the Y-axis in a scatter diagram.

Descriptive analysis An analysis that consists of computing measures of central tendency and dispersion, as well as constructing one-way tables. It helps the researcher summarize the general nature of the study variables.

Descriptive research Research that aims to describe something.

Dichotomous question A question that offers just two answer choices, typically in a yes/no format.

Direct observation Observation that captures the actual behavior or phenomenon of interest.

Discriminant analysis A technique for identifying the distinguishing features of prespecified subgroups of units that are formed on the basis of some categorical dependent variable.

Disguised observation Observation of which respondents are unaware.

Disguised question A question used to examine issues for which direct questions may not elicit truthful answers.

Disproportionate stratified random sampling A sampling technique in which the sample consists of units selected from each population stratum according to how varied the units within the stratum are.

Double-barreled question A question that raises several separate issues but provides only one set of responses.

Editing The process of examining completed data collection forms and taking whatever corrective action is needed to ensure that the data are of high quality.

Electronic group interviewing (EGI) An interviewing technique in which keypads or electronic devices are used to reduce unproductive discussion time. Each participant is provided with a keypad, and all participants are connected to a common video display screen visible to the entire group.

Experiment A procedure by which one (or sometimes more than one) independent (or cause) variable is systematically manipulated and data on the dependent (or effect) variable are gathered, while controlling for other variables that may influence the dependent variable.

Experimental group The unit or units exposed to experimental treatment.

Experimental research Research that allows one to make causal inferences about relationships among variables.

Expert system (ES) A computer-based, artificial intelligence system that performs tasks normally associated with human intelligence. It is programmed to reason and infer rather than merely to crunch numbers or store and retrieve information.

Exploratory research Research that seeks to develop initial hunches or insights and to provide direction for any further research needed.

External marketing research Marketing research conducted by agencies outside the firm.

External source A source outside the organization.

External validity The extent to which observed results are likely to hold beyond the experimental setting.

Factor analysis A data and variable reduction technique that attempts to partition a given set of variables into groups (called *factors*) of maximally correlated variables.

Factorial ANOVA A technique used to analyze data from a factorial design experiment; that is, one intended to investigate the impact of *more than one* categorical independent variable on a metric-scaled dependent variable.

Field (preliminary) edit A quick examination of completed data collection forms, usually on the same day they are filled out.

Field experiment A research study conducted in a natural setting in which one or more independent variables are manipulated by the experimenter under conditions controlled as carefully as the situation will permit.

Filter question A question that qualifies respondents for a subsequent question or ensures that the question is within their realm of experience.

Final (office) edit An edit that is conducted after all the field-edited data collection forms are received in a central location.

Focus group (focus group interview) A research technique that relies on an objective discussion leader or moderator who introduces a topic to a group of respondents and directs their discussion of that topic in a nonstructured and natural fashion.

Forced-choice scale An interview question response scale that does not give respondents the option to express a neutral or middle ground.

Funnel sequence A question sequence that begins with a very general question on a topic and gradually leads to a narrowly focused question on the same topic.

Geocoding (address geocoding) The process of appending latitudes and longitudes to addresses or other geographic locations to display them on a map or to access related locational information.

Geographic information system (GIS) Decision support computer software that stores, displays, and analyzes geographic data.

Graphic rating scale A scale that presents a continuum, in the form of a straight line, along which a theoretically infinite number of ratings are possible.

History effect Specific external event or occurrence during an experiment that is likely to affect the dependent variable.

Human observation An observation technique in which people observe and note their impressions of others' behavior.

Incidence rate The proportion of the general population possessing the characteristic of interest.

Independent (explanatory or predictor) variable In multivariate analysis, a variable that is presumed to influence a dependent variable and is conventionally plotted along the *X*-axis in a scatter diagram.

In-depth interview A one-on-one interview with customers that explores issues in depth.

Indirect observation Observation that involves examining the results or consequences of the behavior or phenomenon under study.

Inferential analysis Data analysis aimed at testing specific hypotheses.

Information Data that have been analyzed and interpreted to aid in decision making.

In-house marketing research Marketing research conducted by a firm itself.

Instrument variation effect A bias that relates to differences between pretest and posttest measurements owing to changes in the instruments (questionnaires) or procedures used to measure the dependent variable.

Interaction effect An effect that is present when the relative impact of treatment levels of one factor varies across treatment levels of another factor.

Interdependence technique An analysis technique in which there are no dependent or independent variable designations; all variables are treated equally in a search for underlying patterns of relationships.

Internal source Source within an organization.

Internal validity The extent to which observed results are due solely to experimental manipulation.

Internet (Web-based) survey A survey that involves no interviewers and is conducted over the Web.

Interval scale A scale that has all the properties of an ordinal scale, with meaningful interpretations of the differences between scale values being possible.

Inverted-funnel sequence A question sequence that begins with specific questions on a topic and gradually leads to a more general question on the same topic.

Itemized rating scale A rating scale that has a set of distinct response categories; any suggestion of an attitude continuum underlying the categories is implicit.

Judgment sampling A sampling technique in which the researcher exerts some effort in selecting a sample deemed to be most appropriate for the study.

Key-informant technique A research technique that involves interviewing knowledgeable individuals.

Laboratory experiment A research study conducted in a contrived setting in which the effect of all, or nearly all, influential but irrelevant independent variables is kept to a minimum.

Leading (loaded) question A question that steers respondents toward a certain answer, regardless of their true responses.

Likert scale A scale that consists of a series of evaluative statements (or items) concerning an attitude object. Respondents are asked to rate the object on each statement (or item) using a five-point agree/disagree scale.

Line chart A two-dimensional line graph typically used to show movements in one or more items over time.

Logistic regression A type of regression analysis in which the dependent variable is dichotomous, coded as either 1 or 0 to represent the occurrence or nonoccurrence of some outcome event.

Longitudinal study A repeated-measurement study that collects data over several periods in time.

Mail survey A survey that involves no interviewer and that is sent to the respondent through the mail.

Manipulation check A check consisting of formal measurements of the independent (or causal) variables to make sure the experimental manipulations worked as planned.

Market basket analysis A kind of analysis that examines customers' shopping carts to determine items that are most frequently purchased together.

Marketing concept An organizational philosophy that emphasizes determining customers' needs first and then coordinating all activities to satisfy those needs.

Marketing decision support system (MDSS) A marketing information system that allows decision makers direct access to data and answers the "what if" questions raised by them.

Marketing information system (MkIS) A continuing and interacting structure of people, equipment, and procedures designed to gather, sort, analyze, evaluate, and distribute pertinent, timely, and accurate information to marketing decision makers.

Marketing mix A combination of product, price, promotion, and place (the four Ps) designed for a target market.

Marketing plan A formal document that specifies an organization's resources, objectives, strategy, and implementation and control efforts in marketing a specific product.

Marketing research A set of techniques and principles for systematically collecting, recording, analyzing, and interpreting data to aid marketing decision makers.

Marketing research ethics Principles of conduct that govern the marketing research profession.

Marketing research process An interrelated sequence of steps that make up a marketing research project.

Marketing response function A mathematical model that represents the relationship between marketing input and output variables.

Marketing strategy A plan that enables an organization to make the best use of its resources to meet marketing objectives.

Matching Forming groups in such a way that the composition of units is similar across groups with respect to one or more specific characteristics.

Maturation effect The effect of physiological or physical changes in the units that occur with the passage of time on the dependent variable being measured.

Mean The simple average of various numbers.

Measurement The assignment of numbers to responses based on a set of guidelines.

Measurement level A measure that indicates how powerful the data are—whether they are nominal, ordinal, interval, or ratio.

Measure of dispersion A measure that describes how responses are clustered around the mean or a central value.

Mechanical observation An observation technique in which machines and devices record human activities.

Median The category into which the 50th percentile response falls when all responses are arranged from lowest to highest (or highest to lowest).

Metric data Data with interval or ratio properties.

Micro marketing The process of tailoring the marketing mix for a local neighborhood.

Micro merchandising The practice by which stores customize the products on their shelves to meet the needs of local customers.

Missing-value category A question category that codes questions for which answers should have been obtained but, for some reason, were not.

Mixed organizational structure An organizational structure in which the corporate research function coexists with and complements a decentralized research function.

Mode The most frequently occurring value for a variable.

Mortality effect An effect that occurs when certain participating units drop out of an experiment, and as a result, the set of units completing the experiment significantly differs from the original set of units.

Multicollinearity A condition that exists when independent variables in a multiple regression equation are highly correlated among themselves.

Multidimensional scaling Scaling intended to infer the underlying dimensions from a series of similarity or preference judgments provided by customers about objects (products, brands, and so on) within a given set.

Multiple-category question A question that has more than two answer choices.

Multiple-item scale A survey that contains a number of statements pertaining to the attitude object, each with a rating scale attached to it. The combined rating, usually obtained by summing the ratings on the individual items, is treated as a measure of attitude toward the object.

Multiple regression analysis A mathematical relationship (called the *regression equation*) between a designated dependent variable (Y) and two or more designated independent variables (Xs).

Multivariate analysis A form of analysis in which two or more variables are analyzed simultaneously.

Natural observation An observation technique in which customer reactions and behavior are observed as they occur naturally in a real-life situation.

Nominal scale A scale in which numbers are no more than labels and are used solely to identify different categories of responses.

Noncomparative rating scale A scale that implicitly permits respondents to use any frame of reference, or even none at all.

Nondisguised observation An observation technique in which respondents are aware they are being observed.

Nonforced-choice scale A scale that gives respondents the option to express a neutral attitude.

Nonmetric data Data with only nominal or ordinal properties.

Nonparametric procedure An analysis technique suitable for nonmetric data.

Nonprobability sampling A subjective procedure by which the probability of selection for each population unit is unknown beforehand.

Nonrepresentative-sample bias A bias that occurs when the units participating in an experiment are not representative of the larger body of units to which the experimental results are to be generalized.

Nonsampling error Any error in a research study other than sampling error.

Nonstructured observation Observation in which a study's data requirements cannot be broken into a set of discrete, clearly defined categories.

Nonstructured question A question that does not always use the same wording for every respondent and does not have fixed responses.

Null hypothesis A statement suggesting that no difference or effect is expected. The null hypothesis is said to be directional when it contains an inequality (i.e., $\leq$ or $\geq$). It is said to be nondirectional when it includes a strict equality (i.e., =).

Observational method A research method that involves human or mechanical observation of what people actually do or what events take place during a buying or consumption situation.

One-sided question A question that presents only one aspect of the issue on which respondents' reactions are being sought.

One-tailed hypothesis test A test in which values of the test statistic leading to rejection of the null hypothesis fall only in one tail of the sampling distribution curve.

One-way table A table that shows the distribution of data pertaining to categories of a single variable.

Online interviewing An interviewing technique in which respondents selected from a database are invited to visit a website to respond to an electronic survey.

Ordinal scale A more powerful scale than a nominal scale in that the numbers possess the property of rank order.

Original source A researcher who actually collects data.

Paired-comparison rating scale A survey consisting of a question seeking comparative evaluations of two objects at a time.

Parameter The actual, or true, population mean value or population proportion for any variable (income, product ownership, and so on).

Parametric procedure An analysis technique suitable for metric data.

Pearson correlation coefficient (product moment correlation) A measure of the degree of association between variables that are interval or ratio scaled.

Personal interview An interview in which there is face-to-face contact between interviewers and respondents.

Pie chart A circle diagram divided by radii into several sections whose areas are proportionate to the quantities to be represented on the chart.

Population (universe) The entire body of units of interest to decision makers in a situation.

Power In an hypothesis test, the probability of rejecting H_0 when H_0 is false.

Predictive validity A determination of how well the attitude measure provided by a scale predicts some other variable or characteristic it is supposed to influence.

Pre-experimental design A design that exerts little or no control over the influence of extraneous factors.

Pretesting Administering a questionnaire to a limited number of potential respondents and other individuals capable of pointing out design flaws.

Pretesting effect An effect that occurs when responses given during a later measurement are influenced by those given during a previous measurement.

Pretest-manipulation interaction bias A special form of reactive bias unique to experiments relying on premeasurement of consumers before they are exposed to the experimental manipulation. It arises when the premeasurement increases or decreases respondents' sensitivity to the experimental manipulation.

Primary data Data collected specifically for a research project.

PRIZM group One of the 62 buyer types in the PRIZM system (such as Greenbelt Families, New Beginnings).

PRIZM system Developed by Claritas Inc., this system segments or divides U.S. neighborhoods into 62 different buyer types based primarily on U.S. Census Bureau demographic data.

Probability sample A sample in which each element in the population has a known, nonzero chance of inclusion.

Probability sampling An objective procedure by which the probability of selection is known in advance for each population unit.

Projective technique A technique by which a fairly ambiguous stimulus is presented to respondents, who, by reacting to or describing the stimulus, indirectly reveal their own inner feelings.

Propensity to buy The percentage likelihood that a group of consumers (for instance, a PRIZM group) will purchase a certain product or service within a given time period.

Propensity to buy index An index that shows the likelihood that a group of consumers will purchase a certain product or service within a given time period, relative to a regional or national average. An index of 100 means average, 200 means twice the average, 50 means half the average, and so forth.

Proportionate stratified random sampling A sampling technique in which the sample consists of units selected from each population stratum in proportion to the total number of units in the stratum.

Qualitative research The collection, analysis, and interpretation of data that cannot be meaningfully quantified or summarized in the form of numbers.

Quantitative research The collection, analysis, and interpretation of data that involves larger, more representative respondent samples and the numerical calculation of results.

Query A word cue that enables users to search a database and obtain the desired information efficiently.

Questionnaire A set of questions designed to generate the data necessary to accomplish a research project's objectives.

Questionnaire format A function of the level of structure and disguise desired during data collection.

Question with implicit assumptions A question the responses for which can be greatly influenced by what respondents assume in answering it.

Quota sampling A sampling technique in which a prespecified quota of units is selected from each population segment or cell based on the judgment of the researchers or decision makers.

RAM (rapid analysis measurement) A wireless interactive dialing device that allows participants to register their reactions to the product or service they are shown by turning a dial.

Random assignment The distribution of the sample units chosen for a study to various groups on a strictly objective basis so that the group compositions can be considered equivalent.

Range A measure of dispersion of responses, calculated as the difference between the largest and smallest response values.

Ratio scale A scale that possesses all the properties of an interval scale, with the ratios of numbers on these scales having meaningful interpretations.

Raw variable A variable directly defined by the questionnaire data.

Reactive bias A form of bias in which participants exhibit abnormal or unusual behavior simply because they are participating in an experiment.

Reliability A measurement of how consistent or stable the ratings generated by the scale are likely to be.

Research process An interrelated sequence of steps that make up a research project.

Research proposal A document that briefly describes the purpose and scope, specific objectives, sample design, data collection procedures, data analysis plan, timetable, and estimated cost for the contemplated project.

Response latency The speed with which a respondent provides an answer.

Sampling The selection of a fraction of the total number of units of interest to decision makers.

Sampling distribution A representation of the statistical values obtained from every conceivable sample of a certain size chosen from a population by using a specified sampling procedure along with the relative frequency of occurrence of those statistical values.

Sampling error The difference between a statistic value generated through a sampling procedure and the parameter value, which can be determined only through a census study.

Sampling frame A listing of population units from which a sample is chosen.

Sampling study A study whereby inferences are drawn from a sample taken from the population.

Scatter diagram A two-dimensional graph in which data on two metric-scaled (interval or ratio) variables are plotted.

Secondary data Data that have already been collected by and are readily available from other sources.

Secondhand source A researcher who uses data collected by an original source to generate his or her own summaries and interpretations.

Selection effect An effect that occurs when multiple groups participating in an experiment differ on characteristics that have a bearing on the dependent variable.

Semantic-differential scale A scale similar to the Likert scale in that it consists of a series of items to be rated by respondents. However, the items are presented as bipolar adjectival phrases or words that are placed as anchor labels of a seven-category scale with no other numerical or verbal labels.

Sensitivity A measurement that focuses specifically on a scale's ability to detect subtle differences in the attitudes being measured; closely tied to reliability.

Sentence completion test A test in which respondents are asked to finish a set of incomplete sentences.

Shopping mall intercept interview An interview in which respondents are intercepted in shopping malls and interviewed.

significance level A measure that refers to the upper-bound probability of a Type I error.

SIMPLE A mnemonic representing the key features of effective written reports and oral presentations—short, interesting, methodical, precise, lucid, and error free.

Simple random sampling A sampling technique in which every possible sample of a certain size within a population has a known and equal probability of being chosen as the study sample.

Simple regression analysis A mathematical relationship (called the *regression equation*) between one variable designated as the dependent variable (Y) and another designated as the independent variable (X).

Single-item scale A scale that attempts to measure feelings through just one rating scale.

Single-source database A database that contains, in an integrated fashion, data for individual households on household characteristics, product purchases, and exposure to marketing stimuli.

Skip pattern A pattern that arises when questions that are not relevant to certain respondents are skipped.

Skewed response distribution A distribution in which a large proportion of responses are piled up toward one end of the range of data obtained.

Slope In a plotted diagram, a line that represents the change in the predicted value of the dependent variable per one-unit change in the independent variable, assuming all other variables likely to influence the dependent variable remain the same.

Spearman correlation coefficient A measure of association between two ordinal variables.

Split-ballot technique A technique that involves using two versions of the same questionnaire—one version including questions presenting only one side of the issue, and the second version including questions presenting only the other side.

Split-half reliability A measure of the degree of consistency across items within a scale; assessable for multiple-item scales only.

Standard deviation A measure of dispersion; the degree of deviation of the numbers from their mean, calculated as the square root of the variance.

Standard error The standard deviation of the different sample statistic values that are obtained through repeated selection of samples from the same population. It can be interpreted as an average amount of sampling error associated with the sampling procedure.

Stapel scale A variation of the semantic-differential scale in which respondents rate attitude objects using a ten-item scale with just numerical labels.

Statistic An estimate of a parameter from sample data.

Statistical efficiency A measure of the precision of the population estimate generated by a sampling procedure. For a given sample size, a sampling procedure that generates a more precise estimate than another is statistically more efficient.

Stratified random sampling A sampling technique in which the chosen sample is forced to contain units from each of the segments, or strata, of the population.

Stratum chart A two-dimensional graph with time plotted along the horizontal axis and values of the items plotted along the vertical axis.

Structured observation Observation in which a study's data requirements are well established and can be broken down into a set of discrete, clearly defined categories.

Structured question A question that is presented verbatim to every respondent and with fixed response categories.

Supervisory control The ability to minimize interviewer errors such as failure to follow instructions, mistakes in recording answers, and cheating.

Syndicated data Secondary data sold by research firms.

Systematic sampling A sampling technique in which a "cluster" of units is pulled from a population by selecting the first unit randomly and the remaining units systematically.

Systems-oriented marketing research Research that makes appropriate marketing information available on a regular, integrated basis.

Telephone survey A data collection method by which there is only voice contact between interviewers and respondents.

Test marketing A form of field experiment; used to assess the market's reactions to a new product and its associated marketing mix.

Test-retest reliability A measure of the stability of ratings over time. It relies on administering the scale to the same group of respondents at two different times.

Test statistic A standard variable the value of which is computed from sample data and compared with a critical value (obtained from an appropriate probability table) to determine whether to reject the null hypothesis.

Thematic apperception test (TAT) A nonstructured, disguised form of questioning in which respondents are shown a series of pictures, one at a time, and asked to write a story about each.

Trade area The geographic area surrounding a store that represents where the vast majority of the store's customers come from.

Transformed (recoded) variable A new variable constructed from data on raw variables.

Treatment Each specific level at which an independent variable is set in an ANOVA procedure.

True experimental designs Designs that have built-in safeguards for controlling all threats to internal and external validity.

Two-tailed hypothesis test A test in which values of the test statistic leading to rejection of the null hypothesis fall in both tails of the sampling distribution curve.

Type I error An error committed if the null hypothesis is rejected when it is true.

Type II error An error committed if the null hypothesis is *not* rejected when it is false.

Unbalanced scale A scale that has a larger number of response choices on the side of the scale where the overall attitude of the respondent sample is likely to fall.

Univariate analysis A form of analysis that focuses on one variable.

Validity The extent to which a rating scale truly reflects the underlying variable it is attempting to measure.

Variance A measure of dispersion of responses around their mean, calculated as the average of squared deviations about the mean.

Videoconference focus group A form of focus group that allows clients at multiple sites to view focus groups from remote locations.

Word association test A test in which words are read aloud to each respondent one at a time and the respondent is asked to say the first word that comes to mind as soon as each stimulus word is presented. The responses are then interpreted.

Y-intercept The predicted value of the dependent variable when all independent variables are set to zero.

Zaltman's Metaphor Elicitation Technique (ZMET) A technique that tries to bring to the surface the mental models that drive consumer thinking by analyzing metaphors that consumers use. A metaphor is a figure of speech that implies comparison between two unlike entities.

Chapter Notes

Chapter 1

1. Fredrik Dahlsten, "Managing Customer Knowledge—Towards Market Orientation and Innovation in an Automotive Organisation" (Ph.D. diss., Department of Project Management, Fenix Research Program, Chalmers University of Technology, Göteborg, Sweden, 2004).

2. A good discussion of marketing strategic planning can be found in many marketing textbooks. For example, see Philip Kotler, *Marketing Management* (Englewood Cliffs, NJ: Prentice Hall, 2000), 63–98; Charles W. Lamb, Jr., Joseph F. Hair, Jr., and Carl McDaniel, *Marketing* (Cincinnati: South-Western, 2002), 28–59.

3. Meredith Levinson, "Data Mining for Carbs," *CIO*, April 15, 2004. See also www.tgifridays.com and www.cxo.com.

4. Nichola Groom, "Low-Carb Food Sales Slow as American Craze Cools," *Yahoo! News*, November 2, 2004, news.yahoo.com.

5. Deborah Ball, "Unilever Cuts Outlook for 2004, May Change Five-Year Targets," *Wall Street Journal*, September 21, 2004; Ian Bickerton and Adam Jones, Comment & Analysis, *Financial Times*, August 23, 2004.

6. "Pizza Hut Introduces Buffalo Chicken Pizza," April 28, 2004, restaurantbiz.com.

7. "Q1 2004 Yum! Brands, Inc. Earnings Conference Call—Final," *Fair Disclosure Wire*, April 22, 2004. See also www.lexis-nexis.com.

8. C. Chitti Pantulu, "Pizza Hut Zooms on Indigenisation," *Economic Times*, April 7, 2004; Ken Hoffman, "Keeping Track of Carbs Never Tasted So Good," *Houston Chronicle, Thursday 2 Star Edition, Dining Guide*, August 19, 2004, 9.

9. "N-Gage QD Cheaper Than Expected," May 24, 2004, *megagames.com*; Chris Nuttall, "Nokia Admits N-Gage Errors," *Financial Times*, May 13, 2004; Victor Godinez, "New Version of N-Gage Has Fewer Problems but May Not Gain Fans," *Dallas Morning News*, June 30, 2004, www.dallasnews.com; www.nokia.com.

10. Bob Tedeschi, "Amazon Rumor Ruffles DVD Rivals," *New York Times*, October 25, 2004, www.nytimes.com; Peter Grant, "Renting at an Online Video Store," *Wall Street Journal*, September 7, 2004, online.wsj.com/article/0,,SB109665182349533938,00.html; Andrew Bary, "Fast Forward," Barron's Online, September 27, 2004, online.barrons.com; Nick Wingfield, "TiVo Strikes Deal with Netflix for Online Delivery of Movies," *Wall Street Journal*, October 1, 2004; Stefanie Olsen, "Akimbo Debuts Video on Demand on Amazon," *New York Times*, October 25, 2004, www.nytimes.com.

11. Don Fernandez, "What Women Want—Concept Car Designed by a Female Team Shows Volvo Is Listening to Its Audience," *Atlanta Journal-Constitution*, April 10, 2004, global.factiva.com.

12. www.business2000.ie.

13. Definition of marketing research is reprinted by permission of the American Marketing Association, Chicago, IL. © 2002 by the American Marketing Association. All rights reserved.

14. Kathleen Kerwin, with David Welch and Christoper Palmeri, "Steering away from Guzzlers," *BusinessWeek*, May 31, 2004, global.factiva.com.

15. "Enabled Products Slowly but Surely Making the Home 'Smarter' Reports In-Stat/MDR," *Business Wire*, July 7, 2004, global.factiva.com.

16. A good discussion of these products can be found in many business publications. Only a few are listed here. Danylo Hawaleshka, "A Mighty Mini," *Maclean's* (Toronto), March 18, 2002; Peter Newcomb, "Sound Judgment," *Forbes*, June 1, 1998; Mat Toor, "Sony's MiniDisc Goes Big on 'Small' Equity," *Marketing* (London), November 4, 1993; Christine Y. Chen, "Iridium: From Punch Line to Profit," *Fortune*, September 2002, 42; Fred George, "Satcom Revolution: Iridium Comes on Strong How About $1.49 per Minute for Any Call from Your Airplane?" *Business & Commercial Aviation*, September 2002, 116; Sydney Finkelstein, "Learning from Corporate Mistakes: The Rise and Fall of Iridium," *Organizational Dynamics* (Fall 2000): 138; David Leafe, "Business: Digital TV—Vision On," *Accountancy* (London; July 2002): 50; Rebecca Buckman, "Set-Top Setback: Microsoft Miscues Turned TV Foray into Costly Lesson—Software Giant Put $10 Billion on Cable, Came up Short; Partners Remained Wary—Nightmare of the 'Frankenbox,'" *Wall Street Journal, Eastern Edition*, June 14, 2002.

17. www.kelloggcompany.com.

18. Glenn Voss, A. Parasuraman, and Dhruv Grewal, "The Roles of Price, Performance, and Expectations in Determining Satisfaction in Service Exchanges," *Journal of Marketing* (October 1998): 46–61; Dhruv Grewal, Kent B. Monroe, and R. Krishnan, "The Effects of Price Comparison Advertising on Buyers' Perceptions of Acquisition Value, Transaction Value, and Behavioral Intentions," *Journal of Marketing* (April 1998): 46–59.

19. www.claritas.com.

20. www.clusterbigip1.claritas.com/claritas/Default.jsp?main=2&submenu=rrr&subcat=rrr5.

21. www.cnn.com/ELECTION/2004/special/polls/index.html.

22. Names obtained from a client list provided by Opinion Research Corporation, Princeton, NJ.

23. See "The Voice of the People Survey," surveyed exclusively for World Economic Forum by Gallup International at www.voice-of-the-people.net. The study covered 60 countries across all five continents. Gallup International conducted more than 65,000 interviews to gauge the global mood around 2004. For a full report, visit www.gallup-international.com.

24. Thomas C. Kinnear and Ann R. Root, *1994 Survey of Marketing Research* (Chicago: American Marketing Association, 1995).

25. Richard Kitaeff, "The Great Debate: Centralized vs. Decentralized Marketing Research Function," *Marketing Research* (Winter 1994): 59.

Chapter 2

1. John Tietjen and Kathy Thornhill, C-P New York, interview with author. Information reprinted courtesy of Colgate USA.

2. Yum! Brands, Inc., Event Brief, 2004 Q2 Earnings Conference Call—Final, June 14, 2004, Fair Disclosure Wire, www.apdigitalnews.com/emmw_fdwire.html; CCBN, Inc., www.ccbn.com/.

3. This is one source of friction between marketing managers and marketing researchers.

4. Greg Steinmetz and Carl Quintanilla, "Whirlpool Expected Easy Going in Europe, and It Got a Big Shock," *Wall Street Journal*, April 10, 1998.

5. Special Section on Whirlpool, April 3, 2003, www.appliancemagazine.com/. This article contains detailed comments on Whirlpool's management, strategies, and operations. See also Daily Briefings, "Why Whirlpool Is Cleaning Up," Business-Week Online, July 30, 2004, www.businessweek.com.

6. Lucas Allison, "When Every Penny Counts: How Creativity Allows Fisher-Price to Stretch Its Market Research Dollars," *Sales & Marketing Management* (February 1996): 74–75.

7. Lawrence D. Gibson, "Defining Marketing Problems," *Marketing Research* (Spring 1998): 5, 12.

8. Richard Lee, "Captain Morgan Jumps Malt Ship," *Stamford Advocate,* November 1, 2002, global.factiva.com.

9. Deborah Ball and Christopher Lawton, "Diageo Needs a Trendy, New Drink," *Wall Street Journal* (Brussels), September 18, 2002.

10. www.acnielsen.com/us/measure.

11. www.acnielsen.com/us/measure/scantrak.htm.

12. www.infores.com/public/prodserv/AB/bscan.htm.

13. It has been suggested that, to design a project properly, one should start by focusing on how the research results will be used (and therefore what the final report should contain) and then work one's way "backward." See Alan R. Andreasen, "Backward Market Research," *Harvard Business Review*, May–June 1985, 179–182.

14. Burger King Consumer Research Group Report.

15. www.vnu.com/vnu/page.jsp?id=84 (accessed February 2, 2005).

16. www.infores.com/ (accessed February 5, 2005).

17. http://www.imshealth.com/ims/portal/front/indexC/0,2773,6599_10525_0,00.html (accessed February 2, 2005).

18. http://www.gfk.com/index.php?lang=en&contentpath=http%3A//www.gfk.com/english/unternehmen/ueberblick.php%3Flang%3Den (accessed February 2, 2005).

19. "MTV, Nickelodeon, VH1 Turning TV Research into a Science," www.cnn.com/showbiz/tv/9905/07/know.audience.ap/.

20. Based on information from www.pazsaz.com/primegrd.html.

21. www.m-w.com.

22. www.ama.org.

23. Laura Rohde, "Privacy Issues Plague Google's Gmail," *IDG News Service*, April 15, 2004, www.pcworld.com/news/article/.

24. Laura Rohde, "Cry for Antispam Laws Grows Louder," *IDG News Service*, September 22, 2003, www.pcworld.com/news/articles/.

25. P. F. Bone and R. J. Corey, "Moral Reflections on Marketing," *Journal of Macromarketing* (Fall 1998): 104–114. See also O. C. Ferrell and Steven J. Skinner, "Ethical Behavior and Bureaucratic Structure in Marketing Research Organizations," *Journal of Marketing Research* (February 1988): 103–109.

26. J. R. Sparks and S. D. Hunt, "Marketing Researcher Ethical Sensitivity: Conceptualization, Measurement, and Exploratory Investigation," *Journal of Marketing* (April 1998): 92–109.

27. Claria Corporation website, www.claria.com/companyinfo/ (accessed October 17, 2004).

28. Perez, Jesus Alejandro, "U. Texas-Austin: Spyware Proves to Be an Annoyance at U. Texas-Austin Campus," U-WIRE, October 14, 2004, global.factiva.com.

29. Edward Diener and Rick Crandall, *Ethics in Social and Behavioral Research* (Chicago: University of Chicago Press, 1978), 3.

30. Sparks and Hunt.

31. Ibid., 92.

32. Quoted in "MTV, Nickelodeon, VH1 Turning TV Research into a Science," May 7, 1999, www.cnn.com.

33. "Pizza Hut Suing Papa John's over 'Better Ingredients' Claim," *Marketing News*, September 14, 1998, 38.

34. Adapted from "How Unethical Firms 'Prey' on Marketing Research Suppliers," *Marketing News*, Section 2, September 18, 1981, 16.

Chapter 3

1. See www.maytag.com for details on Maytag Corporation.

2. Nita Rollins, "Mixing It Up: Maytag and Fitch Innovate Kitchen Products and Best Practices," *Design Management Review* (Winter 2004): 20–25.

3. See www.fitchworldwide.com for more details.

4. Cheskin is a leading consulting and research firm. Fitch:Worldwide is a leading design firm. In 2003 Cheskin and Fitch collaborated on a study of the state of innovation in more than 27 industries. They identified six cultural characteristics that bode well for innovation. For more details on the innovation study entitled *Cheskin and Fitch:Worldwide: Fast, Focused and Fertile: The Innovation Evolution, 2003,* go to www.cheskin.com or www.fitchworldwide.com.

5. See *2004 Annual Report,* www.sgi.com.

6. Steven E. Prokesch, "Mastering Chaos at the High-Tech Frontier: An Interview with Silicon Graphics's Ed McCracken," *Harvard Business Review,* November–December 1993, 135–144.

7. Eric von Hippel, Stefan Thomke, and Mary Sonnack, "Creating Breakthroughs at 3M," *Harvard Business Review,* September–October 1999, 47–57.

8. "Bay Area McDonald's Restaurants Launch the Giving Meal," *Business Wire,* July 1, 2004, global.factiva.com.

9. Claritas Website, www.claritas.com (accessed October 26, 2004).

10. Johny K. Johansson and Ikujiro Nonaka, "Market Research the Japanese Way," *Harvard Business Review,* May–June 1987, 16–19.

11. Tim Stevens, "Lights, Camera, Innovation," *Industryweek,* July 19, 1999, 32–35.

12. Ibid.

13. Fleishman-Hillard Knowledge Solutions, *2004 Annual Meeting Survey: A Report to World Economic Forum, January 2004* (St. Louis, MO: Fleishman-Hillard, Inc.). See also www.weforum.org for more details about the 2004 annual meeting.

14. Hans Zeisel, *Say It with Figures* (New York: Harper & Row, 1968), 202. See also Yoram Wind and David Lerner, "On the Measurement of Purchase Data: Surveys Versus Purchase Diaries," *Journal of Marketing Research* (February 1979): 39–47, for a study that emphasizes the pitfalls of surveys relying on respondents' memories.

15. Vicki Morwitz, "Why Consumers Don't Always Accurately Predict Their Own Future Behavior," *Marketing Letters* 8 (1997): 57–70; Vicki Morwitz and David Schmittlein, "Using Segmentation to Improve Sales Forecasts Based on Purchase Intent: Which 'Intenders' Actually Buy?" *Journal of Marketing Research* (November 1992): 391–405; Vicki Morwitz, Joel H. Steckel, and Alok Gupta, *When Do Purchase Intentions Predict Sales?* Marketing Science Institute, Report No. 97-112, 1997.

16. "Honomichal Global Top 25," *Marketing News,* August 25, 2004, H27.

17. For an in-depth discussion on consumer panels, see Seymour Sudman and Brian Wansink, *Consumer Panels,* 2nd ed. (Chicago: American Marketing Association, 2002).

18. Gilbert A. Churchill, Jr., *Marketing Research: Methodological Foundations* (Fort Worth, TX: Dryden, 1999), 118–121, provides an excellent discussion of the additional capabilities of a true panel beyond those of an omnibus panel.

19. For a complete discussion of the advantages and limitations of panels, see Seymour Sudman and Robert Ferber, *Consumer Panels* (Chicago, IL: American Marketing Association, 1979). See also Steven E. Finkel, *Causal Analysis with Panel Data* (Thousand Oaks, CA: Sage, 1995); Zeisel, *Say It with Figures,* chap. 13.

20. Sudman and Ferber, *Consumer Panels,* p. 6.

Chapter 4

1. Ben Bold, "Unilever Reinforces Worldwide Commitment to CRM," *Brand Republic*, June 3, 2004; Bill Britt, "Unilever Starts CRM Activity," *Marketing Direct*, March 31, 2004; "Jigsaw Puts Database on the Open Market," *Precision Marketing*, January 30, 2004; "Home Shopping Giants Join Forces for Major Data Blitz," *Precision Marketing*, May 9, 2003; "DIRECT: Cadbury Creme Egg Aims Easter Work at Families," *Marketing*, April 3, 2003; "The Name Game," *Brand Republic*, January 24, 2003.

2. Karen E. Klein, "Small Talk: Advice from the Small-Business Experts: Researching Market Size, Competition," *Los Angeles Times*, October 14, 1998.

3. The Association of Pool & Spa Professionals(APSP) is located at 2111 Eisenhower Avenue, Alexandria, VA 22314; 703-838-0083; www.theapsp.org.

4. "China: Telecoms & Technology," Economist Intelligence Unit, Business, China, August 30, 2004,www.economist.com/countries/China/?.

5. Pragati Verma, "Now, A Net-connected PC for Rs 12K," *Economic Times*, October 26, 2004.

6. "A Case for Common Definitions: National Assn. of Drug Stores Tells Information Resources Inc. and AC Nielsen Co. to Find Ways of Developing Common Product and Category Definitions," *Chain Drug Review* 19: 2.

7. "Pharma Company Acquires Purell from GOJO Industries," *Hospital Business Week*, November 7, 2004; Phil Mulkins, "Do Hand Sanitizers Beat Soap and Water?" *Tulsa World*, November 2, 2004; Jack Neff, "Purell, Clorox, Kleenex Benefit: Flu Fear Equals Marketer Bonanza," *Advertising Age*, October 25, 2004, 8.

8. For more information on these 318 economic areas, see www.bea.gov/bea/regional/docs/msalist.htm. See also the Census Bureau at www.census.gov/population/www/estimates/aboutmetro.html and the White House at www.whitehouse.gov/omb/inforeg/msa99.pdf for the current definition of MSAs.

9. Rachel Swarns, "Hispanics Debate Census Plan to Change Racial Grouping," *New York Times*, October 24, 2004.

10. Gemma Charles, "Burger King in Global Star Wars Promotion," *Primedia Insight-Promo Online Exclusive*, Section: People Moves, May 5, 2005, p. 6; Amy Johannes, "Star War Premiums, Sweeps Invade Burger King," *Promotion Xtra*, March 30, 2005; "Critics Take Aim at Star Wars' Meals," *CNNMoney.com*, May 24, 2005.

11. For detailed information on key capabilities and limitations of microdata files, check www.census.gov or contact the U.S. Department of Commerce, Bureau of the Census, Data User Services Division, U.S. Government Printing Office, Washington, DC.

12. http://www.nopworld.com/.

13. www.findsvp.com/services/scrgstudies/indproducts.cfm.

14. Milton Liebman, "Competitive Edge," *Medical Marketing & Media*, February 1, 2003.

15. Christopher Westphal and Teresa Blaxton, *Data Mining Solutions* (New York: Wiley, 1998).

16. Thomas Davenport, "Putting the Enterprise into the Enterprise System," *Harvard Business Review*, July–August 1998, 121–131.

17. David Orenstein, "Sales Data Helps 7-Eleven Maximize Space, Selection," July 5, 1999, www.computerworld.com.

18. Adapted from Philip Kotler, *Marketing Management* (Englewood Cliffs, NJ: Prentice Hall, 2000), 100.

19. Design and implementation aspects of marketing information systems are discussed in several books on the subject, such as Kimball P. Marshall, *Marketing Information Systems* (Danvers, MA: Boyd & Fraser, 1996).

20. Amy Borrus, "How Marriott Never Forgets a Guest," *BusinessWeek*, February 21, 2000, 74.

21. Phaedra Hise, "Why Didn't I Think of That? Delivering the Kids," *Inc.*, July 1, 1995, www.inc.com.

22. For a detailed discussion of these data warehouse and data mining tools, see Peter Jacobs, *Data Mining: What General Managers Need to Know*, Harvard Management Update No. U9910D, October 1999. See also Kurtis M. Ruf, "Drowning in Data," www.ruf.com.

23. Jacobs, *Data Mining*.

24. For more detailed discussion of decision support systems, see Robert C. Blattberg, Rashi Glazer, and John D. C. Little, *The Marketing Information Revolution* (Cambridge, MA: Harvard Business School Press, 1994). See also Trish Baumann, "How Quaker Oats Transforms Information into Leadership," *Sales & Marketing Management*, June 1989, 79–80.

25. Peter R. Peacock, "Data Mining in Marketing: Part I," *Marketing Management*, Winter 1998, 9–18. See also Peter R. Peacock, "Data Mining in Marketing: Part II," *Marketing Management*, Spring 1998, 15–25; Claudia Imhoff, "If the Star Fits . . . Part 1," *DM Review*, April 2000, 28; Wayne Eckerson, "BI Free Agency," *DM Review*, April 2000, 36–37.

26. For guidelines on how to obtain estimates from managers, see, for example, Max H. Bazerman, *Judgment in Managerial Decision Making*, 4th ed. (New York: Wiley, 1998).

27. www.acnielsen.com.

28. Dana Canedy, "Advertising—New Ad Campaign for Hershey's Coming on Strong," *New York Times*, February 25, 1999.

29. David Orenstein, "Sales Data Helps 7-Eleven."

30. Kathleen Melymuka, "Coca Cola: Marketing Partner," *Computerworld*, December 14, 1999, www.computerworld.com.

Chapter 5

1. Amy Merrick, "New Population Data Will Help Marketers Pitch Their Products," *Wall Street Journal*, February 14, 2001; *Beverage World*, December 15, 2004; Brad Carlson,"Boise Entrepreneur Combines Geography, and Statistics, to Increase Customer Base," *The Idaho Review*, October 25, 2004 (Monday); "The African-American Shopper," *Convenience Store News*, July 12, 2004; Kathy Chu, "Visa Aggressively Courts High Spenders," *Associated Press*, July 12, 2004; "The Real Deal," *Progressive Grocer*, October 15, 2004; Lisa van der Rool, "Digital Lifestyles Targets Teens," *Adweek.com*, July 12, 2004; Julie Jargon, "Kraft Tailors Items to Hispanic Tastes; Wants Bigger Slice of Growing Market," *Crain's Chicago Business*, August 30, 2004 (Monday), 6; Jane Conti, "Selling to Asian-American," *National Underwriter*, November 8, 2004, 14.

2. Ibid.

3. Ibid.

4. Christian Harder, *ArcView GIS Means Business*, Environmental Systems Research Institute, Inc., 1997, 4.

5. Ibid.

6. Ibid. See also David J. Curry, *The New Marketing Research Systems* (New York: Wiley, 1993); Michael J. Weiss, *The Clustered World* (Boston: Little, Brown, 2000).

7. Based on "Managing Your Data of the MapXtreme," chap. 10 in *User Manual*, published by MapInfo, www.mapinfo.com.

8. Harder, *ArcView GIS Means Business*, 9.

9. Philip Kotler, *Marketing Management*, 10th ed. (Englewood Cliffs, NJ: Prentice Hall, 2000), 145.

10. Louise Morrison, "Targeting Markets," April 25, 1999, www.insideboulder.com/business/25dsrc.html. Due to privacy restrictions, personal buying habit data are not available on an individual household basis. In this example, Dean Stoecker is looking only at an estimate of the household buying data derived from the GIS system, not the actual household data.

11. This section is adapted from Harder, *ArcView GIS Means Business,* chap. 2.

12. *Ace 2004 Annual Report,* www.acehardware.com/corp/annrep2004/index.jsp (accessed June 10, 2005). Ace Hardware material courtesy of Ace Hardware Corporation.

13. Harder, *ArcView GIS Means Business,* 18. See also www.esri.com/data/online/tiger/document/area/topics/aaaad.html.

14. Researchers should also note that zip codes and Block Groups change over time. Block Groups are redrawn every 10 years with each new U.S. Census. Many postal zip codes are redrawn much more frequently. As a result, if a marketer wants to assess changes in a zip code's or Block Group's population over time, the marketer should first check to ensure that the boundary has remained constant during the focal time period. For further information on zip codes, see www.oseda.missouri.edu/jgb/zip.resources.html; see also www.census.gov/geo/ZCTA/zcta.html.

15. According to Tom Spencer, vice president/senior practice leader at Claritas Inc., the radius of a trade area is related to, but not the same as, the drive time to a business. Today's GIS have the ability to use drive time or drive distance to define a trade area. Also, not all trade areas are circular. Firms that have access to customer addresses are using these data to help identify irregularly shaped trade areas.

16. Harder, *ArcView GIS Means Business.*

17. Most firms do not want to disclose the specific tactics they use to find new store sites; they consider this information to be highly confidential. Thus the Connie's Café case will describe the general tactics used in the restaurant and retail industries. The data presented are fictitious.

18. Based on personal interviews with Bob Rycroft, vice president, Carlson Restaurants Worldwide, and Tom Spencer, vice president, Claritas Inc. The case does not reflect the techniques used by Carlson Restaurants.

19. www.ftc.gov/privacy/glbact/glb-faq.htm#G.

20. David R. Anderson, Dennis J. Sweeney, and Thomas A. Williams, *Statistics for Business and Economics,* (Mason, OH: South-Western, 1999), 604.

21. Tim Curry, Jack Coolbroth, and Steven Bogue, *A Regional Insert Program for 2001/2002 Mercury Grand Marquis: Grand Marquis Profile and Competitive Analysis,* Mathews Marketing, June 2001; Mercury Grand Marquis insert advertisement, Summer 2001.

22. Mercury Vehicles website, www.mercuryvehicles.com/news_events/nw_main.asp (accessed November 3, 2001).

23. Jay Garza, Young & Rubicam, Irvine, California, interview with author, January 15, 2002. Courtesy of Young & Rubicam Point of Contact Advertising, Irvine, CA.

24. Mercury Vehicles website, www.mercuryvehicles.com/news_events/nw_main.asp (accessed November 3, 2001).

25. Curry, Coolbroth, and Bogue, *A Regional Insert Program.*

26. Ibid.

27. www.claritas.com. According to Tom Spencer, vice president/senior practice leader at Claritas Inc., when PRIZM was introduced nearly 30 years ago, it stood for Potential Rating Index for Zip Markets. However, as data for smaller geographies were released by the Census Bureau, PRIZM was reconstructed to apply to these smaller geographies. Today PRIZM can still be applied at the zip code level but is more commonly applied at the Block Group or zip + 4 level.

28. Curry, *The New Marketing Research Systems.*

29. Claritas Inc., "Summary Lifestyle Descriptions: PRIZM Cluster Narratives," 1996, 1999.

30. Ibid.

31. R. L. Polk & Company website, www.polk.com/news/features/Co_overview.asp (accessed November 3, 2001).

32. Driver's Privacy Protection Act, 18 USC 2721–2725, prohibits the release of drivers' names and addresses but allows the release of their five-digit zip codes. See www.nydmv.state.ny.us/forms/mv15dppa.pdf.

33. The standard method of computing an average, which was just described, essentially weights each zip code estimate by the population size. Some firms use an alternative approach and weight the estimates from each zip code equally by taking an average of the averages.

34. Curry, Coolbroth, and Bogue, *A Regional Insert Program.*

35. Steve Bogue, Mathews Marketing Group, interview with author, October 23, 2001.

36. www.srds.com.

37. Courtesy of Young & Rubicam Point of Contact Advertising, Irvine, CA.

38. Web-based resources for learning more about GIS include www.esri.com, www.freedemographics.com, www.gis.com, and www.directionsmag.com. See www.zdnet.com/eweek/stories/general/0,11011, 382 745,00.html.

Chapter 6

1. Sharon McDonnel, "Showers, Golf, Skating Available at Airports," *New York Times*, December 8, 2003; Chris Jones, "An Issue of Flyways and Buyways," *Las Vegas Review-Journal*, November 11, 2004; Ted Jackovics, "Tampa, Fla., Airport Aims to Peg Travel Trends," *Tampa Tribune*, October 22, 2004.

2. See, for example, Gilbert A. Churchill, Jr., *Marketing Research: Methodological Foundations*, 7th ed. (New York: Dryden, 2000), 224.

3. Joshua D. Macht, "The New Market Research," *Inc.*, July 1, 1998, 86–94. See www.inc.com (search on "marketing research").

4. Justin Martin, "Ignore Your Customer," *Fortune*, May 1, 1995, 121–126.

5. Martin, ibid.; Macht, "The New Market Research." See also www.inc.com (search on "marketing research").

6. Stanley Marcus, "My Biggest Mistake," *Inc.*, July 1, 1999, 95.

7. In recent times, however, observational techniques have become popular in developing new products and customer satisfaction studies. For discussion, see Edward F. McQuarrie, *Customer Visits* (Thousand Oaks, CA: Sage, 1998). See also Edward F. McQuarrie, *The Market Research Tool Box* (Thousand Oaks, CA: Sage, 1996), chap. 4.

8. For further elaboration of the importance and benefits of using multiple data collection methods, see Barbara L. Watts, "Mixed Methods Make Research Better," *Marketing News*, February 28, 2000, 6; Bob Qureshi and Jenny Baker, "Category Management and Effective Consumer Response: The Role of Market Research," *Marketing and Research Today* (February 1998): 23–31.

9. Jan Callebaut, Madeleine Janssens, Dirk Lorre, and Hendrik Hendrickx, *The Naked Consumer* (Antwerp, Belgium: Censydiam Institute, 1994).

10. Rene Ross, "In-Home CAPI: A New Era in Data Collection?" *Quirk's Marketing Research Review* (November 1999): article no. 0526. See also www.quirks.com/articles.

11. Anne Marie Borrego, "Will They Bite?" *Inc.*, November 16, 1999. See also www.inc.com/articles.

12. Joseph Rydholm, "On the Front-line of On-line," *Quirk's Marketing Research Review* (July 1998): article no. 0348. Access www.quirks.com/articles.

13. Robert Hays, "Internet-based Surveys Provide Fast Results," *Marketing News,* April 13, 1998, 13. See also Dana James, "Precision Decision," *Marketing News,* September 27, 1999, 23–24.

14. J. D. Mosley-Matchett, "Leverage the Web's Research Capabilities," *Marketing News,* April 13, 1998, 6.

15. John R. Dickinson, A. J. Faria, and Dan Friesen, "Live vs. Automated Telephone Interviewing," *Marketing Research* (Winter 1994): 28–34. See also Leif Gjestland, "Net? Not Yet," *Marketing Research* (Spring 1996): 26–29.

16. "China: Telecoms & Technology," *Economist Intelligence Unit—Business China,* August 30, 2004; Pragati Verma, "Now, a Net-connected PC for Rs 12K," *Economic Times,* October 26, 2004; Borrego, ibid.

17. There are numerous online companies offering quick turnaround service; go to google.com and search on "online surveys" or "online survey companies."

18. Kim Cross, "Stats to Go," *Business2.com,* October 10, 2000, 284.

19. Humphrey Taylor, John Bremer, Cary Overmeyer, Jonathan W. Siegel, and George Terhanian, "Using Internet Polling to Forecast the 2000 Elections," *Marketing Research* (Spring 2001): 26–30.

20. Gary S. Vazzana and Duane Bachmann, "Fax Attracts," *Marketing Research* (Spring 1994): 19–25. See also Joseph Rydholm, "Fax-based Surveys Give PC World Magazine Flexibility and Quick Turnaround at Low Cost," *Quirk's Marketing Research Review* (February 1994): article no. 0076; David Liu and Nanda Ganesan, "Fax Versus Mail in Gathering Data: An Analytical Study," *Quirk's Marketing Research Review* (May 1996): article no. 0045. Access www.quirks.com/articles.

21. Patricia E. Moberg, "Biases in Unlisted Phone Numbers," *Journal of Advertising Research* (August–September 1982): 54–55; Gerald J. Glasser and Gale D. Metzger, "National Estimates of Nonlisted Telephone Households and Their Characteristics," *Journal of Marketing Research* (August 1975): 359–361; Timothy R. Graeff, "Uninformed Response Bias in Telephone Surveys," *Journal of Business Research* (March 2002): 251–259; David Whitlark and Michael Geurts, "Telephone Surveys," *Marketing Research* (Fall 1998): 13.

22. Moberg, ibid. See also Peter S. Tuckel and Harry W. O'Neill, "Call Waiting," *Marketing Research* (Spring 1995): 7–13.

23. Sony's survey: One out of every four households has caller ID; eight out of ten adults say they get three unwanted phone calls at home every day; the favorite features, in order of importance, are caller ID display, built-in answering machine, speed dialing. For more details, see "Who's Tying Up That Phone Line?" *New York Times,* January 28, 1999. See also Peter Tuckel and Trish Shukers, "The Answering Machine Dilemma," *Marketing Research* (Fall 1997): 5–9; Peter S. Tuckel and Harry W. O'Neill, "Call Waiting," *Marketing Research* (Spring 1995): 7–13; David Whitlar and Michael Geurts, "Phone Surveys," *Marketing Research* (Fall 1998): 13–17.

24. Cihan Cobanoglu, Bill Warde, and Patrick J. Moreo, "A Comparison of Mail, Fax and Web-based Survey Methods," *International Journal of Market Research* 43 (2001): 441–452; Robert Klassen and Jennifer Jacobs, "Experimental Comparison of Web, Electronic and Mail Survey Technologies in Operations," *Journal of Operations Management* (November 2001): 713–728; Cindy Claycomb and Stephen S. Porter, "Riding the Wave: Response Rates and the Effects of Time Intervals Between Successive Mail Survey," *Journal of Business Research* (May 2000): 157–162.

25. Arthur Saltzman, "Improving Response Rates in Disk-By-Mail Surveys," *Marketing Research* (Summer 1993): 32–39.

26. One study involving a mail survey of respondents in a sample of firms found that, in terms of improving response rates, the size of the incentive really may not matter as much as the fact that some incentive is included; see Milton M. Pressley and William L. Tullar, "A Factor Interactive Investigation of Mail Survey Response Rates from a Commercial Population," *Journal of Marketing Research* (February 1977): 108–111; Gail Gaboda, "Phone Cards Help Researchers Reward Respondents," *Marketing News,* September 15, 1997, 14; Kathleen V. Schmidt, "Prepaid Phone Cards Present More Info at Much Less Cost," *Marketing News,* February 14, 2000, 4.

27. Reid Kanaley, "AOL Internet-Access Membership Continues to Climb," *Knight Ridder/Tribune Business News,* December 6, 2001; Dana James, "Precision Decision," *Marketing News,* September 27, 1999, 23.

28. Ibid., 23–24.

29. See www.websiteoptimization.com for U.S. connectivity.

30. Humphrey Taylor, "The Global Internet Research Revolution: A Status Report," *Quirk's Marketing Research Review* (November 1999Carticle no. 0534. See www.quirks.com/article.

31. James, "Precision Decision," 23. See also Joseph Rydholm, "On the Front Line of On-line."

32. James, "Precision Decision," 23.

33. A good discussion of interviewer-induced errors in survey research is available in Charles F. Cannell, Kent H. Marquis, and Andre Laurent, *A Summary of Studies of Interviewing Methodology,* U.S. Department of Health, Education, and Welfare, Publication No. (HRA) 77-1343 (Washington, DC: U.S. Government Printing Office, 1977).

34. Jeff Rosenblum and Chris Grecco, "The Future of On-Line Research," *Quirk's Marketing Research Review* (July 1998): article no. 0357; see www.quirks.com/articles.

35. Brad Frevert, "Is Global Research Different?," *American Marketing Association Marketing Research* 12 (Spring 2000): 49-51; Jacqueline Arsivaud, "Conducting Research Outside the United States: A Primer," *Quirk's Marketing Research Review* (November 1996): article no. 0049; Ravi Iyer, "A Look at the Indian Market Research Industry," *Quirk's Marketing Research Review* (November 1997): article no. 0294; "Who's Tying up That Phone Line?" *New York Times,* January 28, 1999; QMMR Staff, "Q&A: Research in Europe," *Quirk's Marketing Research Review* (November 1997): article no. 0296; Michael Halberstam, "Surveying International Markets Demands Special Attention," *Quirk's Marketing Research Review* (February 1998): article no. 0306; Tom Pearson, "Keys to Conducting International Research: Quality Control Will Help Lead to Success," *Quirk's Marketing Research Review* (November 1998): article no. 0378; Chris Van Derveer, "Demystifying International Industrial Research," *Quirk's Marketing Research Review* (April 1996): article no. 0001; Barton Lee, Tony Zhao, and David Tatterson, "Emerging Trends in China's Marketing Research Industry," *Quirk's Marketing Research Review* (November 1998): article no. 0373; Stephen Phillips, "An Insider's Guide to Conducting Effective Research in Developing Countries," *Quirk's Marketing Research Review* (November 1998): article no. 0374; Barton Lee and Alexander Wong, "An Introduction to Marketing Research in China," *Quirk's Marketing Research Review* (November 1998): article no. 0050; Jerry Stafford, Mark Stapylton-Smith, and Geoff Hutton, "Omnibus Research in Asia has Unique Demands," *Quirk's Marketing Research Review* (June 1996): article no. 0027; Steven Lewis, "The Language of International Research," *Quirk's Marketing Research Review* (November 1997): article no. 0295; Loretta Adams, "Market Research and Measurement in Mexico: Key Guide Posts," *Quirk's Marketing Research Review* (January 1995): article no. 0121; Jennifer Mitchell, "Yes, You Can! Tips on Conducting Telephone Research in Latin America," *Quirk's Marketing Research Review* (November 1998): article no. 0380;

Bjorn Huysman, "Telephone Research in Asia," *Quirk's Marketing Research Review* (November 1998): article no. 0379; Kent Hamilton, "An International Marketing Research Checklist," *Quirk's Marketing Research Review* (November 1998): article no. 0376; Humphrey Taylor, "The Global Internet Research Revolution: A Status Report," *Quirk's Marketing Research Review* (November 1999): article no. 0534; Eduardo Smithson, "Conducting Marketing Research in Chile," *Quirk's Marketing Research Review* (November 1999): article no. 0533; Wander Meijer, "Marketing Research in Asia: It's the Economy, Stupid!" *Quirk's Marketing Research Review* (November 1999): article no. 0530; QMRR Staff, "Q&A: Conducting Research in Egypt and Israel," *Quirk's Marketing Research Review* (November 1999): article no. 0529; James Velayas, "How Important Is Your International Market Research Project?" *Quirk's Marketing Research Review* (January 2000): article no. 0554; Bill MacElroy, "International Growth of Web Survey Activity," *Quirk's Marketing Research Review* (November 2000): article no. 0629; Raeleen D'Augostino Mautner, "Five Tips to Doing Research in Italy," *Quirk's Marketing Research Review* (November 2000): article no. 0626; Eileen Moran, "Managing the Minefields of Global Product Development: Tips on International Market Research for Global Products," *Quirk's Marketing Research Review* (November 2000): article no. 0625.

36. Will Wade, "Turning Video Data into Better Branch Service." *American Banker*, July 7, 2004.

37. Gerry Khermouch, "Consumers in the Mist," *BusinessWeek*, February 26, 2001, 93–94.

38. Debbie Gage, "What People Buy, and How They Buy It," *Baseline*, December 1, 2002.

39. Robert V. Kozinets, "The Field Behind the Screen: Using Netnography for Marketing Research in Online Communities," *Journal of Marketing Research* (February 2002): 61–72.

40. Bob Becker, "Take a Direct Route When Data-gathering," *Marketing News*, September 27, 1999, 29.

41. For additional details about the STM, go to www.msistrategic.com. See also Research in Use 8.1 in Chapter 8.

42. Please see www.decisioninsight.com for more details.

43. Paula Kephart, "Virtual Testing," *Marketing Tools* (June 1998); www.american demographics/mt.

44. Claudia Montague, "Quick Reliable Test Marketing Is a Virtual Reality," *Marketing Tools* (April–May 1994); www. demographics.com.

45. Ely Dahan and John R. Hauser, "The Virtual Customer" (working paper, Sloan School of Management, Massachusetts Institute of Technology, December 2000). See also Ely Dahan and John R. Hauser, "Product Development: Managing a Dispersed Process," in *Handbook of Marketing*, ed. Barton Weitz and Robin Wensley (London: SAGE Publications Limited, 2002). See www.mit.edu/vc for copies.

46. Beth Kurcina, "Use Videos to Obtain Crucial POP Info," *Marketing News*, November 20, 2000, 16.

47. Michael L. Ray, *Unobtrusive Marketing Research Methods* (Columbus, OH: Franklin University Library, 1993), p. 15.

48. James Guyette, "Drawing from Big Boxes," *Aftermarket Business*, July 1, 2003.

49. Based on Steve Lewis, manager of store programs, Office Depot, Delray Beach, FL, interview with author.

50. Leigh Dyer, "Shopping Spies Help Retail Businesses Keep Eye on Service," *Charlotte Observer*, October 10, 2004.

51. Julie Schlosser, "Scanning for Dollars," *Fortune*, January 10, 2005, 60.

52. Howard Wolinsky, "Firm Studies Product Use to Help Clients," *Chicago Sun-Times*, May 12, 2004.

53. Alison Stein Wellner, "The New Science of Focus Groups," *American Demographics*, March 1, 2003.

54. Several articles discuss response latency measures and their use in marketing research; see James MacLachlan and John G. Myers, "Using Response Latency to Identify Commercials That Motivate," *Journal of Advertising Research* (October–November 1983): 51–57; David A. Aaker, Richard P. Bagozzi, James M. Carman, and James M. MacLachlan, "On Using Response Latency to Measure Preference," *Journal of Marketing Research* (May 1980): 237–244.

55. Katherine Bowers, "Subliminal Messages," *Women's Wear Daily*, March 19, 2003.

56. For further discussions of VOPAN and its use, see, for example, Ronald Nelson and David Schwartz, "Voice Pitch Gives Marketer Access to Consumer's Unaware Body Responses," *Marketing News*, January 28, 1977, 21; Nancy J. Nighswonger and Claude R. Martin, Jr., "On Using Voice Analysis in Marketing Research," *Journal of Marketing Research* (August 1981): 350–355.

57. Steve McClellan, "Nielsen Picks 'People Meter' Panel," *Broadcasting & Cable*, June 8, 2004.

58. For more information on the controversy surrounding people meters, see Peter Barnes and Joanne Lipman, "Networks and Ad Agencies Battle over Estimates of TV Viewership," *Wall Street Journal*, January 7, 1987; David Lieberman, "The Networks' Big Headache—Nielsen's New 'People Meter' Could Batter Their Ad Revenues," *BusinessWeek*, July 6, 1987, 26–28; David F. Poltrack, "Living with People Meters," *Journal of Advertising Research* (June–July 1988): RC-8–RC-10.

59. Hiawatha Bray, "DoubleClick Backs off on Net Data/Bows to Protests on Use of Personal Information," *Boston Globe, Business Section*, March 3, 2000, C1.

60. John Labate, "Privacy Suit over Online Ad Company's Database," *Financial Times, Saturday USA Edition*, January 29, 2000, 3. See also Amy Harmon, "Software Monitors E-Mail with Ease," *San Jose Mercury News, Business Section*, November 26, 2000, 1G, 8G, 12G.

61. Nick Wingfield, "The Tricky Task of Tracking Web Users," *Wall Street Journal*, November 22, 1999.

62. Peter Benesh, "Corporate Espionage Taking over Where Cold War Spying Left Off," *Investor's Daily, Section A*, October 10, 2000, 10; Paul Davidson, "Oracle-Style Investigations Common, Experts Say," *USA Today, Money Section*, June 29, 2000, 3B.

63. For a detailed discussion of observational methods, see Bill Abrams, *Observational Research Handbook* (Chicago: NTC Business Books, 2000).

Chapter 7

1. Cate Corcoran, "How Star Retailers Turn Fast," *Women's Wear Daily*, November 10, 2004.

2. Ellen Day, "Researchers Must Enter Consumer's World," *Marketing News*, August 17, 1998, 17.

3. John W. Mullins, Sarah H. Sittig, and Carol A. Brown, "Pioneering Practices for New Product Development at US West," *Marketing Management* (Winter 2000): 39.

4. Judith Langer, "15 Myths of Qualitative Research: It's Conventional, but Is It Wisdom?" *Marketing News*, March 1, 1999, 13–14.

5. Dana James, "Qualitative—Outlook2000," *Marketing News*, January 17, 2000, 14.

6. Kate Maddox, "The ROI of Research," *BtoB*, April 5, 2004.

7. Jack Honomichl, "Research Revenues on the Rise in '99," *Marketing News*, June 5, 2000, H2, H6. See also Patricia Sabena, "10 Trends in Qualitative Research," *Quirk's Marketing Research Review* (December 1999): article no. 0547.

8. *Group Interviewing, An Internal Manual* (*update*) (Cincinnati, OH: Burke, Inc.), p. 7.

9. Ellen Day, "Know Consumers Through Qualitative Research," *Marketing News,* January 5, 1998, 14.

10. Bobby J. Calder, "Focus Groups and the Nature of Qualitative Marketing Research," *Journal of Marketing Research* (August 1977): 360.

11. Naomi R. Henderson, "The Magic of Eight," *Quirk's Marketing Research Review* (December 1997): article no. 0283. See also Norton Paley, "Getting in Focus: Market Research," *Sales & Marketing Management* (March 1995): 92–96.

12. Thomas L. Greenbaum, *Focus Group Research,* 2nd ed. (Thousand Oaks, CA: Sage, 1998). See also Richard A. Krueger, *Focus Groups,* 2nd ed. (Thousand Oaks, CA: Sage, 1994). That rules of thumb are just that, and not universal laws, is emphasized in at least one controlled study (as opposed to studies involving focus groups conducted in practice), which found that two four-member groups are better than one eight-member group; see Edward F. Fern, "The Use of Focus Groups for Idea Generation: The Effects of Group Size, Acquaintanceship, and Moderator on Response Quantity and Quality," *Journal of Marketing Research* (February 1982): 1–13.

13. Judith Langer, "Focus on Women: 3 Decades of Qualitative Research," *Marketing News,* September 14, 1998, 21–22. See also Greenbaum, *Focus Group Research,* pp. 46–47.

14. "Claiborne Returns to Realities," *Cosmetics International,* April 23, 2004.

15. Peter DePaulo, "The Risk of Missing Something Important," *Quirk's Marketing Research Review* (December 2000): article no. 0636.

16. Barry E. Jacobs, "Take Action Against Dumbing Down of Qualitative Research," *Marketing News,* March 1, 1999, 20. See also Martin M. Buncher, "Focus Groups Seem Easy to Do and Use, but They're Easier to Misuse and Abuse," *Marketing News, Section 2,* September 17, 1982, 14.

17. Greenbaum, Focus Group Research.

18. Langer, "15 Myths of Qualitative Research," 13–14. See also Fern, "The Use of Focus Groups for Idea Generation."

19. Burke, Inc., is one such group. See www.burke.com.

20. For an interesting and insightful discussion of problems stemming from professional respondents, see Hazel Kahan, "'Professional' Respondents Say They're Better for Research Than 'Virgins,' but They're Not," *Marketing News, Section 1,* May 14, 1982, 22.

21. James Cowley, "Anyone Can Run Research Focus Groups, Right," *Marketing News,* March 1, 1999, 15. See also Naomi R. Henderson, "Secrets of Our Success— Insights from a Panel of Moderators," *Quirk's Marketing Research Review* (December 2000): article no. 0645; "Focus Group Moderators Should Be Well Versed in Interpretative Skills," *Marketing News,* February 18, 1981, 23.

22. Dona Vitale, "Getting More out of Groups by Putting More In," *Marketing News,* March 1, 1999, 18.

23. Dean Bates, "Moderator's Gender Can Influence a Focus Group," *Marketing News,* March 1, 1999, 17.

24. Richard A. Krueger, *Moderating Skills in Focus Groups,* 2nd ed. (Thousand Oaks, CA: Sage, 1994), 100–121.

25. Andrew Wright and L. F. Fitkin, "Focus Group Videos: A Survival Guide," *Quirk's Marketing Research Review* (December 1997): article no. 0279.

26. Michael L. Garee and Thomas R. Schori, "'Position' Focus Group Observers for the Best View," *Marketing News,* September 14, 1998, 29; Thomas Greenbaum, "Making It Work For You Behind the One-Way Mirror," *Quirk's Marketing Research Review* (December 1995): article no. 0149.

27. Michelle Wirth Fellman, "Qualitative Research Must Anticipate Technology Changes," *Marketing News,* December 7, 1998, 4. See also Michelle Wirth Fellman, "Videoconference Focus Groups Gaining Airtime," *Marketing News,* November 9, 1998, 2, 16.

28. Thomas Greenbaum, "The Focus Group Bill of Rights," *Quirk's Marketing Research Review* (October 1996): article no. 0055.

29. Jonathan Hall, "Moderators Must Motivate Focus Group," *Marketing News,* September 11, 2000, 26–27.

30. Greenbaum, *Focus Group Research.* See also Krueger, *Focus Groups;* Ellen Day, "Know Consumers Through Qualitative Research," *Marketing News,* January 5, 1998, 14.

31. Although a majority of researchers hold this view, it is not unanimously believed; for some differing viewpoints, see, for example, Fern, "The Use of Focus Groups for Idea Generation"; Naomi R. Henderson, "The Art and Science of Effective Qualitative Interviews," *Quirk's Marketing Review* (December 1998): article no. 0390.

32. Bill Dalbec, "Stage an Intervention for the Focus Group," *Marketing News,* February 26, 2001, 46–47; Winslow "Bud" Johnson, "The Collage," *Quirk's Marketing Research Review* (December 1999): article no. 0544; Mike Anastas, "Visuals Stimulate Richer Response in Focus Groups and Individual Interviews," *Quirk's Marketing Research Review* (December 1994): article no. 0068.

33. Jonathan Hall, "Moderators Must Motivate Focus Group," 27.

34. Michelle Wirth Fellman, "Mesmerizing Method Gets Real Results," *Marketing News,* July 20, 1998, 1, 38.

35. Ibid.

36. Art Shulman, "Enhancing Market Research with Kids," *Quirk's Marketing Research Review* (November 1994): article no. 0099; Lynn Kaladjian, "Children's Qualitative Research Past and Present," *Quirk's Marketing Research Review* (December 1996): article no. 0009; Eve Zuckergood, "Releasing the Child Within," *Quirk's Marketing Research Review* (December 1998): article no. 0384.

37. Thomas Greenbaum, "Focus Groups with Physicians Have Different Requirements Than Those with Consumers," *Quirk's Marketing Research Review* (January 1992): article no. 0396.

38. John Simons, "Taking on Viagra," *Fortune,* June 9, 2003.

39. Michele Holleran, "Understanding Minority Health Needs Through Focus Groups and Cluster Sampling Techniques," *Quirk's Marketing Research Review* (April 1998): article no. 0331.

40. Tom Lowry and Roberts Dexter, "Wow! Yao! For U.S. Brands Selling in China, NBA Sensation Yao Ming Is One Hot Ticket," *BusinessWeek,* October 25, 2004.

41. Sharon Waxman, "Onscreen, It's the Season of Cynicism," *New York Times,* December 14, 2004. For other applications of focus groups in the area of advertising, see Sara Eckel, "Cheese Whiz—A Fresh Ad Strategy Transforms Easy Mac into an Appetizing Product for Moms and Teens," in David J. Lipke, "Ready for a Close-up: Market Research Moves into the Spotlight," *American Demographics,* March 2001, www.americandemographics.com. See also Lisa Gubernick, "Are Market Research Groups out of Focus?" *Adweek,* September 5, 1983, 22; "Behind the Scenes at an American Express Commercial," *BusinessWeek,* May 20, 1985, 84–88.

42. Stuart Elliott, "A City Seeks to Sell Itself, Complete with a Brand-Identity Campaign," *New York Times,* December 10, 2004.

43. George Parker, "Interviewing Interactively," *Marketing News,* January 19, 1998, 7.

44. Ibid.

45. Janet Aschkenasy, "Dialing up Research: A Handheld Device Can Mean the Difference Between Participating in a 401(k) Plan or Not," *Financial Planning,* April 1, 2004.

46. Michelle Wirth Fellman, "Qualitative Research Must Anticipate Technology Changes," *Marketing News,* December 7, 1998, 4; Michelle Wirth Fellman, "Videoconference Focus Groups Gaining Airtime," *Marketing News,* November 9, 1998, 2, 16. See also Jospeh Rydholm, "The Next Best Thing to Being There," *Quirk's Marketing Research Review* (December 1995): article no. 0159.

47. Joseph Rydholm, "More, Better, Fast," *Quirk's Marketing Research Review* (March 1996): article no. 0040.

48. Dana James, "Outlook 2001—Qualitative Research," *Marketing News,* January 1, 2001, 13. See also Dana James, "Outlook 2000—Qualitative Research," *Marketing News,* January 17, 2000, 14.

49. Casey Sweet, "Anatomy of an On-line Focus Group," *Quirk's Marketing Research Review* (December 1999): article no. 0548.

50. James Heckman, "Turning the Focus Online," *Marketing News,* February 28, 2000, 15. See also Trenton Haack, "Focus Groups Without Walls—or Borders," *Quirk's Marketing Research Review,* article no. 0628. See also Charles E. Ramirez, "Execs Use Internet to Watch Consumers Focus PC Trades Mirror for Web to Hear About Products," *Detroit News, Business Section,* July 20, 2000, 2.

51. Sweet, "Anatomy of an On-line Focus Group."

52. Casey Sweet and Jeff Walkowski, "Online Qualitative Research Task Force: Report of Findings," *Quirk's Marketing Research Review* (December 2000): article no. 0643. See also Thomas Greenbaum, "Internet Focus Groups Are Not Focus Groups—So Don't Call Them That," *Quirk's Marketing Research Review* (July 1998): article no. 0355.

53. See www.websiteoptimization.com for recent Internet statistics. See also Winslow "Bud" Johnson, "Using Online Focus Groups for E-Commerce Research," *Quirk's Marketing Research Review* (June 2000): article no. 0598.

54. Dana James, "Outlook 2001—Qualitative Research," *Marketing News,* January 1, 2001, 13.

55. Ibid.

56. Mark B. Palmerino, "Take a Quality Approach to Qualitative Research," *Marketing News,* June 7, 1999, H35–H36.

57. Constance Gustke, "Built to Last," *Sales & Marketing Management* (August 1997): 78–82.

58. Cesar Miguel Escano, "MARKETING Children Power," *Business World,* March 26, 2004. See also Joseph Rydholm, "The World Is Not Enough," *Quirk's Marketing Research Review* (April 2000): article no. 0576.

59. Gerald Zaltman, "Metaphorically Speaking," *Marketing Research* (Summer 1996): 13; Gwendolyn Catchings-Castello, "The ZMET Alternative," *Marketing Research* (Summer 2000): 6–12.

60. Detailed discussion of the analysis and interpretation of responses to word association tests, as well as to other projective techniques, is beyond the scope of this textbook. However, several books on motivation research that treat this topic in detail are available; see, for example, George Horsley Smith, *Motivation Research in Advertising and Marketing* (Westport, CT: Greenwood Press Reprint, 1971).

61. Henry A. Murray, *Explorations in Personality* (New York: Oxford University Press, 1938).

62. Smith, *Motivation Research in Advertising and Marketing,* 142–143.

63. Gerald Zaltman and Robin Higie, *Seeing the Voice of the Customer: The Zaltman Metaphor Elicitation Technique,* Marketing Science Institute, Report No. 93–114. See also Gerald Zaltman and Robin Higie, "Seeing the Value of the Customer: Metaphor-based Advertising Research," *Journal of Advertising Research* (July–August 1995): 35–51.

64. www.britannica.com.

65. Donald E. L. Johnson, "Metaphors Help Architects Get into the Minds of Hospitals' Patients," *Health Care Strategic Management*, November 1, 2004.

66. Tracy Teweles, "Beyond Human Oddities: How to Mine Consumer Brains to Build Powerful Brands," *Quirk's Marketing Research Review* (May 1988): article no. 0335.

67. Lynn Kaladjian, "Children's Qualitative Research Past and Present," *Quirk's Marketing Research Review* (December 1996): article no. 0009. See also www.quirks.com/articles.

68. Many practitioners are suggesting the use of projective techniques to uncover consumer motivations in a focus group or in-depth interview setting. See Glenn Livingston and Sharon Livingston, "Making Projectives Projectable," *Quirk's Marketing Research Review* (February 1995): article no. 0116; Winslow "Bud" Johnson, "The Collage," *Quirk's Marketing Research Review* (December 1999): article no. 0544.

Chapter 8

1. Calmetta Y. Coleman, "Eddie Bauer's Windows Add Electronics," *Wall Street Journal*, November 28, 2000.

2. Irwin P. Levin, *Relating Statistics and Experimental Design—An Introduction* (Thousand Oaks, CA: Sage, 1999).

3. For a compelling argument, see Fred N. Kerlinger and Howard B. Lee, *Foundations of Behavioral Research*, 4th ed. (New York: Harcourt, 1999).

4. See, for example, Claire Selltiz, Marie Jahoda, Morton Deutsch, and Stuart W. Cook, *Research Methods in Social Relations* (New York: Holt, Rinehart and Winston, 1959), 83–88.

5. The two definitions are adapted from Kerlinger and Lee, *Foundations of Behavioral Research*, 398, 401.

6. Although these forms are the two most commonly used forms of validity in experimental research, they are by no means the only ones. For definitions and a comparative discussion of other forms of validity, see Thomas D. Cook and Donald T. Campbell, *Quasi-Experimentation: Design and Analysis Issues for Field Settings* (Chicago: Rand McNally, 1979), 80–91.

7. Indeed, several research studies have shown that laboratory experiments have a tendency to overestimate the effect of experimental manipulations. For an example of such a study involving price manipulations in a laboratory setting, see John Lynch, Jr., "On the External Validity of Experiments in Consumer Research," *Journal of Consumer Research* (December 1982): 25–44. See also J. E. McGrath and D. Brinberg, "External Validity and the Research Process," *Journal of Consumer Research* (June 1983): 109–124; John R. Nevin, "Laboratory Experiments for Estimating Consumer Demand: A Validation Study," *Journal of Marketing Research* (August 1974): 261–268; John G. Lynch, Jr., "Theory and External Validity," *Journal of the Academy of Marketing Science* (Summer 1999): 367–376; Bobby J. Calder and Alice M. Tybout, "A Vision of Theory, Research, and the Future of Business Schools," *Journal of the Academy of Marketing Science* (Summer 1999): 359–366.

8. For a succinct discussion of test-marketing, see Philip Kotler, *Marketing Management, The Millennium Edition* (Upper Saddle River, NJ: Prentice Hall, 2000), 346–354. Another classic reference concerning test-marketing is N. D. Cadbury, "When, Where, and How to Test Market," *Harvard Business Review* (May–June 1975): 96–105.

9. Joshua D. Macht, "The New Market Research," *Inc.*, July 1, 1998, 86–94; Justin Martin, "Ignore Your Customer," *Fortune*, May 1, 1995, 121–126. A thought-provoking article that makes this point forcefully, with several excellent examples, is "Marketing Researchers: Investigate Why New Products Succeed, Not Why They Fail," *Marketing News, Section 1*, September 18, 1981, 13. See also Edward M. Tauber, "Forecasting Sales Prior to Test Market," *Journal of Marketing* (January 1977): 82.

10. Chris Ayers, "McCafe Stirs It with Starbucks in America," *The Times* (London), *Business Section,* May 1, 2001, 27; Doral Chenweth, "McDonald's Tests Have to Pass in Columbus," *Columbus Dispatch, Business Section,* July 25, 2000; Kate MacArthur, "McD's Aims to Get Happy with Pizza: Testing New Kid's Meal in Ill., Wis.," *Crain's Chicago Business,* March 6, 2000, 32; Gary Strauss, "Fast Food: New Meals, Menus," *USA Today, Money Section,* June 16, 1992, 10B; "Marketing: McDonald's Lobs Pizza in Burger Wars," *The Independent* (London), March 18, 1990, 27; Eben Shapiro, "McDonald's Hopes Pizza Will Be the Next McHit," *New York Times, Section D,* September 20, 1989, 1; "McPizza," *The Economist,* September 23, 1989, 83; "McPizza? McDonald's Tests Three-Minute Pizza on Dinner Crowds," *Toronto Star,* August 28, 1989, B1; Stuart Elliott, "McDonald's Hopes McPizza Will Deliver," *USA Today,* August 25, 1989, 1B.

11. See, for example, Glen L. Urban and Gerald M. Katz, "Pre-Test-Market Models: Validation and Managerial Implications," *Journal of Marketing Research* (August 1983): 221–234; J. Hauser, G. Urban, and J. Roberts, "Prelaunch Forecasting of Automobiles," *Management Science* (April 1990): 401–420; Andre Gabor, C. W. J. Granger, and Anthony P. Sowter, "Real and Hypothetical Shop Situations in Market Research," *Journal of Marketing Research* (August 1970): 355–359.

12. Joshua D. Macht, "The New Market Research," *Inc.,* July 1, 1998, www.inc.com. See also Lucianne Englert, "Virtual Shopping Adventures," *Research and Creative Activity,* Indiana University Research Publication, September 1999, www .indiana.edu/~reapub.

13. "Household Based Retail Food Purchase Scanner Data for 2002 and 2003." *FedBizOpps,* July 14, 2004; Michael Garry, "The Privacy Hurdle," *Supermarket News,* November 15, 2004; Ellen Pedersen, "Top of Mind Optimization: It's All About the Data," *Brandweek,* October 25, 2004; "Branded Deli Meat and Cheese Sales Data Available to Retailers: FreshLook Marketing Creates First Syndicated Database for Deli," *PR Newswire,* October 5, 2004; for more information, go to www.iri.com and www.acnielsen.com.

14. Gordon A. Wyner, "Learn and Earn Through Testing on the Internet," *Marketing Research* (Fall 2000): 37–38.

15. Karen Becker-Olsen, "And Now, a Word from Our Sponsor," *Journal of Advertising,* July 1, 2003.

16. Ely Dahan and John R. Hauser, "The Virtual Customer," *Journal of Product Innovation Management,* September 2, 2002, 332–353; Ely Dahan and V. Seenu Srinivasan, "The Predictive Power of Internet-Based Product Concept Testing Using Visual Depiction and Animation" *Journal of Product Innovation Management,* March 2000. See also Joseph Wilkie, Christine Adams, and Azra Girnius, "First Systematic Comparison Between Mall-Intercept and Internet Interviewing" (European Society for Opinion and Marketing Research, Worldwide Internet Conference, London, February 21, 1999).

17. This is not an exhaustive list of threats to internal validity. Rather, it represents threats that are most likely to be present in experimental designs used in marketing, particularly those designs to be discussed in the next chapter. Donald T. Campbell and Julian C. Stanley, *Experimental and Quasi-Experimental Designs for Research* (Chicago: Rand McNally, 1979), and Cook and Campbell, *Quasi-Experimentation,* provide more comprehensive coverage of threats to internal validity.

18. As we will see in Chapters 9 and 10, even slight changes in a questionnaire can lead to big differences in responses. For a discussion of the extent to which responses can be influenced by the characteristics of the interviewer, see M. Venkatesan, "Laboratory Experiments in Marketing: The Experimenter Effect," *Journal of Marketing Research* (May 1967): 142–146.

19. As in the case of internal validity threats discussed in this chapter, these three biases are not the only external validity threats, although virtually all other external

validity threats are related to these biases. For further details, consult Campbell and Stanley, *Experimental and Quasi-Experimental Designs;* Cook and Campbell, *Quasi-Experimentation.* One point worthy of note concerning the names given to the validity threats: external validity threats are labeled *biases* rather than *effects* merely to distinguish them from internal validity threats.

20. Kerlinger and Lee, *Foundations of Behavioral Research,* 345.

21. Urban and Katz, "Pre-Test-Market Models," and Gabor, Granger, and Sowter, "Real and Hypothetical Shop Situations," offer several examples illustrating non-representative-sample bias and reactive bias associated with consumer panels.

22. For a clear and concise review of validity issues and limitations of marketing experiments, see John G. Lynch, Jr. , "Theory and External Validity," *Journal of the Academy of Marketing Science* (Summer 1999), 367–376.

23. For a comprehensive treatment of experimental designs, see Campbell and Stanley, *Experimental and Quasi-Experimental Designs for Research*; Seymour Banks, *Experimentation in Marketing* (New York: McGraw-Hill, 1965).

24. For further discussion of manipulation checks, see the classic article by Barbara C. Perdue and John O. Summers, "Checking the Success of Manipulations in Marketing Experiments," *Journal of Marketing Research* (November 1986): 317–327

25. Louise H. Kidder, Selltiz Wrightsman, and Stuart W. Cook, *Research Methods in Social Relations* (New York: Holt, Rinehart and Winston, 1981), 18.

26. Levin, *Relating Statistics and Experimental Design,* 13–14.

Chapter 9

1. Ronald Alsop, "Delivery & Image: UPS vs. FedEx," *Wall Street* Journal, February 19, 2004; Ronald Alsop, "In Business Ranking, Some Icons Lose Luster," *Wall Street Journal*, November 15, 2004. See also www.reputationinstitute.com and www .harrisinteractive.com/expertise/reputation.asp.

2. V. Kumar and Anish Nagpal, "Segmenting Global Markets: Look Before You Leap," *Marketing Research* (Spring 2001): 8–13.

3. Gordon C. Bruner II, Karen E. James, and Paul J. Hensel devote an entire volume to the scales reported in articles published from 1994 to 1997 in *Marketing Scales Handbook* (Chicago: American Marketing Association, 2001).

4. Don A. Dillman, *Mail and Telephone Surveys: The Total Design Method* (New York: Wiley, 1978); Don A. Dillman, *Mail and Internet Surveys: The Tailored Design Method* (New York: Wiley, 1999).

5. See, for example, Jagdish N. Sheth, Banwari Mittal, and Bruce I. Newman, *Customer Behavior* (Fort Worth, TX: Harcourt, 1999), 389–391. Some researchers believe attitudinal data and techniques must give way to study of actual customer behavior. For example, Don E. Schultz maintains that the traditional attitudinal research attempting to identify how customers feel, think, and intend to act about a product is outdated and inefficient. He argues instead for examining actual purchasing and usage patterns. See Don E. Schultz, "Losing Attitude," *Marketing Research* (Fall–Winter 1995): 9–15.

6. Steve E. Ballou, "Effective Research Requires a Good (Measurement of) Attitude," *Marketing News,* September 15, 1997, 15.

7. Stuart W. Cook and Claire Selltiz, "A Multiple-Indicator Approach to Attitude Measurement," *Psychological Bulletin* 62 (1964): 38.

8. Steven P. Brown and Douglas M. Stayman, "Antecedents and Consequences of Attitudes Towards the Ad: A Meta-Analysis," *Journal of Consumer Research* (June 1992): 34–53; Dhruv Grewal et al., "Comparative Advertising: A Meta-Analysis of the Empirical Evidence," *Journal of Marketing* (October 1997): 1–15.

9. Perception Research Services International, *Multidimensional Communications Research* (brochure), 1, www.prsresearch.com.

10. For a discussion of characteristics of good performance rating scales, see James H. Myers, *Measuring Customer Satisfaction: Hot Buttons and Other Measurement Issues* (Chicago: American Marketing Association, 1999).

11. Joseph Duket, "Comment Cards and Rating Scales: Who Are We Fooling?" *Quirk's Marketing Research Review* (May 1997): article no. 0257, www.quirks.com/articles.

12. E. B. Feltser, "The Numbers Game: Refining Multi-Point Scales," *Quirk's Marketing Research Review* (March 1997): article no. 0252, www.quirks.com/articles.

13. James H. Myers and W. Gregory Warner, "Semantic Properties of Selected Evaluation Adjectives," *Journal of Marketing Research* (November 1968): 409–412. See also Scott MacStravic, "Scale Scoring in Health Care Customer Surveys," *Quirk's Marketing Research Review* (February 1994): article no. 0077, www.quirks.com/articles.

14. Steven Lewis, "The Language of International Research," *Quirk's Marketing Research Review* (November 1997): article no. 0295, www.quirks.com/articles.

15. Eileen Moran, "Managing the Minefields of Global Product Development: Tips on International Market Research for Global Products," *Quirk's Marketing Research Review* (November 2000): article no. 0625, www.quirks.com/articles.

16. Tony Siciliano, "Magnitude Estimations: A Realistic Scaling Technique for International Research," *Quirk's Marketing Research Review* (November 1999): article no. 0532, www. quirks.com/articles.

17. Vikas Mittal and Wagner A. Kamakura, "Satisfaction, Repurchase Intent, and Repurchase Behavior: Investigating the Moderating Effect of Customer Characteristics," *Journal of Marketing Research* (February 2001): 131–142.

18. Jum C. Nunnally and Ira H. Bernstein, *Psychometric Theory* (New York: McGraw-Hill, 1994).

19. Paired-comparison ratings are also used as input for an analysis technique called *multidimensional scaling*.

20. Pamela L. Alreck and Robert B. Settle, *The Survey Research Handbook* (Homewood, IL: Irwin, 1994). Several researchers address the complexities of measuring customer satisfaction in *Marketing Research*: Terry Grapentine, "Problematic Scales," *Marketing Research* (Fall 1994): 8–12; Dick R. Wittink and Leonard R. Bayer, "The Measurement Imperative," *Marketing Research* (Fall 1994): 14–22; Diane H. Schmalensee, "Finding the 'Perfect' Scale," *Marketing Research* (Fall 1994): 24–27; Terry C. Gleason, Susan J. Devlin, and Marbue Brown, "In Search of the Optimum Scale," *Marketing Research* (Fall 1994): 28–33. See also Randy Brandt, "Satisfaction Studies Must Measure What the Customer Wants and Expects," *Marketing News,* October 27, 1997, 17; Brad Gale, "Satisfaction Is Not Enough," *Marketing News,* October 27, 1997, 18; Irwin Press, "Guidelines Needed for Healthcare Performance Measures," *Marketing News,* October 27, 1997, 19; Susan J. Devlin, H. K. Dong, and Marbue Brown, "Selecting a Scale for Measuring Quality," *Marketing Research* (Summer 1993): 12–17.

21. Rensis Likert, "A Technique for the Measurement of Attitudes," in *Attitude Management,* ed. Gene F. Summers (Chicago: Rand McNally, 1970), 149–158.

22. General procedures for generating an initial item pool and then narrowing it are discussed by Gilbert A. Churchill, Jr., "A Paradigm for Developing Better Measures of Marketing Constructs," *Journal of Marketing Research* (February 1979): 64–73. See also David W. Gerbing and James C. Anderson, "An Updated Paradigm for Scale Development Incorporating Unidimensionality and Its Assessment," *Journal of Marketing Research* (May 1988): 186–192. For a specific illustration of how a Likert scale is developed, see William J. Lundstrom and Lawrence M. Lamont, "The Development of a Scale to Measure Consumer Discontent," *Journal of Marketing Research* (November 1976): 373–381.

23. Details about this work are given in Charles E. Osgood, George J. Suci, and Percy H. Tannenbaum, *The Measurement of Meaning* (Urbana: University of Illinois Press, 1957).

24. Kumar and Nagpal, "Segmenting Global Markets: Look before You Leap," 12.

25. Nunnally and Bernstein's *Psychometric Theory* provides an excellent detailed discussion of reliability assessment.

26. A more rigorous measure of internal consistency among scale items is *Cronbach's alpha,* or *coefficient alpha.* For details about the procedure involved in computing this measure of reliability, see L. J. Cronbach, "Coefficient Alpha and the Internal Structure of Tests," *Psychometrica* 16 (1951): 297–334. See also the review article on various aspects of reliability by J. Paul Peter: "Reliability: A Review of Psychometric Basics and Recent Marketing Practices," *Journal of Marketing Research* (February 1979): 6–17.

27. Churchill, "A Paradigm for Developing Better Measures." See also Mildred L. Patten, "Conducting Item Try-Outs and an Item Analysis," in *Questionnaire Research* (Los Angeles: Pyrczak Publishing, 1998), chap. 6.

28. Patten, *Questionnaire Research.*

29. Sara Eckel, "Cheese Whiz—A Fresh Ad Strategy Transforms Easy Mac into an Appetizing Product for Moms and Teens," in David J. Lipke, "Ready for a Close-up—Market Research Moves into the Spotlight," *American Demographics* (March 2001), www.americandemographics.com. See also Lisa Gubernick, "Are Market Research Groups out of Focus?" *Adweek,* September 5, 1983, 22. See "Behind the Scenes at an American Express Commercial," *BusinessWeek,* May 20, 1985, 84–88, for other applications of focus groups in the area of advertising.

Chapter 10

1. "Circuit City Puts the Consumer First by Commissioning BizRate.com to Measure Its In-Store Customer Satisfaction Performance," *Business Wire,* July 16, 2001; Lauren Gibbons Paul, "Browser Beware," *Inc., Special Report,* June 30, 2001, 77.

2. One of the classic books on questionnaire design is Stanley L. Payne, *The Art of Asking Questions* (Princeton, NJ: Princeton University Press, 1951). More recent books on this subject are Seymour Sudman and Norman M. Bradburn, *Asking Questions* (San Francisco: Jossey-Bass, 1982), and Mildred L. Patten, *Questionnaire Research* (Los Angeles: Pyrczak Publishing, 1998).

3. Jonathan E. Brill, "The Exploratory Open-Ended Survey Question: A Potential Bonanza That's Typically a Waste," *Quirk's Marketing Research Review* (March 1995): article no. 131, www.quirks.com/articles.

4. Terra Friedrichs, "Asking the Right Questions in Telephone Interviews," *Quirk's Marketing Research Review* (May 1977): article no. 0263, www.quirks.com/articles.

5. A good discussion of multiple-category questions is provided by Pamela L. Alreck and Robert B. Settle, *The Survey Research Handbook* (Homewood, IL: Irwin, 1994).

6. Payne, *The Art of Asking Questions,* 134.

7. Del I. Hawkins and Kenneth A. Coney, "Uninformed Response Error in Survey Research," *Journal of Marketing Research* (August 1981): 373.

8. This drawback is mitigated by the fact that several statistical software packages offer coding instructions and analysis options for handling questions with multiple responses. For instance, the well-known SPSS 10.0 version has a "Multiple Response" routine for analyzing data generated by multiple-response questions. Researchers can and do use such a routine to code and tabulate data obtained from multiple-category questions that permit more than one response to be checked.

9. An alternative way to handle a lengthy questionnaire is suggested by Marco Vriens, Michael Wedel, and Zsolt Sandor, "Split-Questionnaire Designs: A New Tool in Survey Design and Panel Management," *Marketing Research* (Summer 2001): 14–19. The authors suggest that splitting a long questionnaire into several subcomponents, asking respondents to respond to only a fraction of the original

questionnaire, and using multiple imputation techniques to solve the problem of missing data will yield high-quality data.

10. V. Kumar and Anish Nagpal, "Segmenting Global Markets: Look Before You Leap," *Marketing Research* (Spring 2001): 8–13.

11. Steven Lewis, "The Language of International Research," *Quirk's Marketing Research Review* (November 1997): article no. 0295, www.quirks.com/articles.

12. See, for example, Alfred M. Falthzik and Marvin A. Jolson, "Statement Polarity in Attitude Scales," *Journal of Marketing Research* (February 1974): 102–105.

13. Payne, *The Art of Asking Questions,* 90–92, contains a more detailed discussion and additional examples of questions with unbalanced alternatives. See also Joseph Duket, "Comment Cards and Rating Scales: Who Are We Fooling," *Quirk's Marketing Research Review* (May 1997): article no. 0257, www.quirks.com/articles.

14. Eileen Moran, "Managing the Minefields of Global Product Development: Tips on International Market Research for Global Products," *Quirk's Marketing Research Review* (November 2000): article no. 0625, www.quirks.com/articles. See also Paula Lyon Andruss, "Going It Alone: U.S. Research Firms Must Put Time, Thought into European Studies," *Marketing News,* September 11, 2000, 19.

15. Terra Friedrichs, "Asking the Right Questions in Telephone Interviews," *Quirk's Marketing Research Review* (May 1997): article no. 0263, www.quirks.com/articles. The article recommends that it is better to ask warmup questions first, leading up to tough questions, in the Asia-Pacific region and Latin America.

16. Paula Lyon Andruss, "Slow Boat to China: Worth Eyeing More Than Ever—Carefully," *Marketing News,* September 10, 2001, 1, 11.

17. Sudman and Bradburn, *Asking Questions,* 219–221, contains a good discussion of the funnel sequence and its pros and cons.

18. Ibid.

19. Thomas W. Miller, "Make the Call: Online Results Are Mixed Bag," *Marketing News,* September 24, 2001, 30–35.

20. Don A. Dillman, *Mail and Internet Surveys: The Tailored Design Method* (New York: Wiley, 1999).

21. See, for example, ibid.

22. Shelby D. Hunt, Richard D. Sparkman, Jr., and James B. Wilcox, "The Pretest in Survey Research: Issues and Preliminary Findings," *Journal of Marketing Research* (May 1982): 269–273; quotation on 272.

23. Ironically, however, the study by Hunt, Sparkman, and Wilcox, ibid., found that, under certain circumstances, telephone pretests were able to detect more errors than face-to-face pretests could.

24. Dillman, *Mail and Internet Surveys.*

25. Rick Weible and John Wallace, "Cyber Research," *Marketing Research* (Fall 1998): 19–24, 31. See also Phil Levin and Bill Ahlhauser, taking the "pro" position, and Dale Kulp and Rick Hunter, taking the "con" position, in "Internet Interviewing," *Marketing Research* (Summer 1999): 33–36; Joshua Grossnickle and Oliver Raskin, "What's Ahead on the Internet," *Marketing Research* (Summer 2001): 9–13.

26. Marcie Levine, "How to Become a Survey Expert: Eight Tips to Help You Build Successful Customer Surveys," *Quirk's Marketing Research Review* (February 1999): article no. 0465, www.quirks.com/articles.

27. Scott M. Smith and David B. Whitlark, "Men and Women Online: What Makes Them Click?" *Marketing Research* (Summer 2001): 20–25.

28. This SurveyTime.com survey was prepared by Scott M. Smith, Ph.D., president of SurveyTime.com and professor of marketing, Brigham Young University, and Ryan Smith, director of sales, SurveyTime.com

29. Several online research companies offer survey templates for a variety of applications. For example, www.surveypro.com and www.surveytime.com contain several questionnaire examples.

30. Thomas W. Miller, "Can We Trust the Data of Online Research?" *Marketing Research* (Summer 2001): 26–32.

31. See, for example, Alreck and Settle, *The Survey Research Handbook.*

32. For a detailed treatment of cover letter design, see Paul Erdos, *Professional Mail Surveys*, rev. ed. (Melbourne, FL: Krieger Publishing, 1983), chap. 12.

33. The survey on office supply stores was developed by Smiti Sinha, Martin Jackson, Gina Rosano, Carlos Missagia, Ahmad Saadat, Raj Srinivasan, and Rajesh Jaiswal.

Chapter 11

1. www.gallup.com.

2. See www.harrisinteractive.com.

3. See www.acnielsen.com/products/reports/scantrack for more details.

4. Jodi Wilgoren, "Judges Rule Against Use of Sampling for Census," *Los Angeles Times*, August 25, 1998, www.latimes.com.

5. www.census.gov.

6. Victor Cook and David Frigstad, "Take It to the Top," *Marketing Research* (Fall 1997): 23–29. In this article, the authors argue that B2B research should be based on Delphi samples, panels of decision makers who constitute a universe of knowledge—a small-scale census study.

7. "Circuit City Puts the Customer First by Commissioning BizRate.com to Measure Its In-Store Customer Satisfaction Performance," *Business Wire*, July 16, 2001, www.businesswire.com. See also Humphrey Taylor, Cary Overmeyer, Jonathan W. Siegel, and George Terhanian, "Using Internet Polling to Forecast the 2000 Elections," *Marketing Research* (Spring 2001): 26–30. In this article, the authors argue that the capital costs of setting up everything needed to do good online research are significant. However, the marginal cost of data collection is relatively small. Even this study used an online panel (obviously a sample, not a census) to predict the presidential election.

8. Gallup Organization, *The Gallup Omnibus*, brochure.

9. Gonzalo R. Soruco and Timothy P. Meyer, "The Mobile Hispanic Market: New Challenges in the '90s," *Marketing Research* (Winter 1993): 6–11. The article argues that Hispanics have varied demographic characteristics and exhibit different degrees of mobility and assimilation. For example, suburban Hispanics differ from urban Hispanics, and therefore differences have to be taken into consideration while drawing stratified sampling.

10. Diane H. Schmalensee, "Rules of Thumb for B2B Research," *Marketing Research* (Fall 2001): 28–33. In this article, the author provides 10 rules of thumb for conducting research in the B2B environment. The article talks about usefulness of judgment sampling in a B2B environment and the need to talk to multiple respondents (using a snowballing technique) within a business organization.

11. For a discussion of the properties of a normal distribution, see any introductory statistics textbook, such as D. R. Anderson, D. J. Sweeney, and T. A. Williams, *Modern Business Statistics with Microsoft Excel* (Cincinnati: South-Western, 2003).

12. A few remarks about the expressions for the standard deviation are in order. First, $n-1$ in the denominator (rather than n) ensures that the sample standard deviation is an *unbiased* estimate of the population standard deviation. Second, a "finite population correction factor" is applied to this expression when the sample size is relatively large compared with the population size. Specifically, when the sample size (n) is more than about 10 percent of the population size (N), the expression for s is multiplied by the factor—$(N-n)/(N-1)$—resulting in a lower

value for *s*. Third, more convenient computation formulas are available if one wants to calculate the sample standard deviation by hand. Further information on these issues can be found in most basic statistic textbooks; see, for instance, Anderson, Sweeney, and Williams, *Modern Business Statistics with Microsoft Excel*.

Chapter 12

1. Reversing the wording of some items is but one way to attempt to uncover less-than-truthful respondents. Other approaches include deliberately planting certain questions (sometimes referred to as "sleeper" questions) intended to reveal whether a respondent is too consistent or not consistent enough.

2. For a discussion of computer-assisted coding of open-ended responses, see Serge Luyens, "Coding Verbatims by Computers," *Marketing Research* (Spring 1995): 21–25. See also Joseph Rydholm, "Dealing with Those Pesky Open-Ended Responses," *Quirk's Marketing Research Review* (February 1994): 70–79, www.quirks.com/articles.

3. A number of statistical software packages offer special coding instructions and analysis options for handling questions that permit multiple responses. For instance, the well-known SPSS 10.0 Windows package has a "MULTIPLE RESPONSES" routine for analyzing data generated by multiple-response questions.

4. The skewness of a response distribution can be regarded as the extent to which it departs from the structure of a typical bell-shaped distribution. Several ways to quantify the extent of skewness are available. A good discussion of skewness is in Ken Black and David L. Eldredge, *Business & Economic Statistics Using Microsoft Excel* (Cincinnati: South-Western, 2002), 76–78, 80–82.

5. "How to Keep Well-Intentioned Research from Misleading New-Products Planners," *Marketing News, Section 2*, January 6, 1984, 8. See also Thomas T. Semon, "Don't Be Mean: Simple Average Is Not Enough," *Marketing News*, July 20, 1998, 16.

Chapter 13

1. Further discussion of the assumptions that must be met for use of parametric and nonparametric methods, as well as the pros and cons of the two methods, is available in several excellent books. See, for example, Sidney Siegel and N. J. Castellan, *Nonparametric Statistics for the Behavioral Sciences*, 2nd ed. (New York: McGraw-Hill, 1988); W. J. Conover, *Practical Nonparametric Statistics*, 3rd ed. (New York: Wiley, 1998).

2. Selecting an appropriate analysis technique in a situation can be more complex than our discussion here might suggest. However, a comprehensive presentation of all the intricacies entailed in choosing a proper analysis procedure is very involved. An excellent discussion with a step-by-step flow diagram for selecting a technique after taking into account a variety of considerations is given in Frank M. Andrews, Laura Klem, Patrick M. O'Malley, Willard L. Rodgers, Kathleen B. Welch, and Terrence N. Davidson, *Selection of Statistical Techniques for Social Science Data: A Guide for SAS* (Raleigh, NC: SAS Institute, 1998).

3. The hypothesis tests listed in Table 13.2 are not meant to be exhaustive. Discussions of a greater variety of tests are given in many standard statistics books, such as Conover, *Practical Nonparametric Statistics*, and Bruce L. Bowerman, Richard T. O'Connell, and Michael L. Hand, *Business Statistics in Practice* (New York: McGraw-Hill/Irwin, 2001), 728–777.

4. For a comprehensive discussion of this issue, see Hans Zeisel, *Say It with Figures* (New York: Harper & Row, 1968), ch. 3; Darrell Huff, *How to Lie with Statistics* (New York: Norton, 1954), highlights several pitfalls related to percentages in general.

5. Procedures for verifying the assumption from sample data can be found in basic statistics textbooks, such as Charles H. Brase and Corrinne P. Brase, *Understanding Basic Statistics* (Boston: Houghton Mifflin, 2001).

Chapter 14

1. Susan E. Woodward, "The Consumer Confusion in the Mortgage Market," Sand Hill Econometrics, June 14, 2003, www.sandhillecon.com. See also Kenneth Harney, "Nation's Housing; Many Factors Decide Mortgage Broker Fees," *Patriot Ledger* (Quincy, MA), *Housing Section*, August 22, 2003, 15.

2. Andrew Reeves, "Courting Votes in Disasters," *Cincinnati Post,* May 18, 2004, A6.

3. Gerald Carlino and N. Edward Coulson, "Compensating Differentials and the Social Benefits of the NFL," *Journal of Urban Economics* (July 2004): 2–50. See also Daniel Gross, "A Team Makes a City a High-Rent District," *New York Times*, May 2, 2004, 36.

4. G. Stacy Sirmans and David A. Macpherson, *The Value of Housing Characteristics,* National Association of Realtors, December 2003; for full report, see www .realtor.org/Research.nsf/files/fullrptsirmansmacpherson2.pdf/$FILE/ fullrptsirmansmacpherson2.pdf. See also Kenneth R. Harney, "Sum of Its Parts? What's It Worth," *Washington Post*, February 7, 2004, F1.

5. For a discussion of the derivation and interpretation of the formula for r_s, see Sidney Siegel and N. J. Castellan, *Nonparametric Statistics for the Behavioral Sciences,* 2nd ed. (New York: McGraw-Hill, 1988).

6. Further discussion of these assumptions can be found in many statistics textbooks. See, for example, Ken Black and David L. Eldredge, *Business and Economic Statistics Using Microsoft Excel* (Cincinnati: South-Western, 2002), 488–492. See also Norman R. Draper and Harry Smith, *Applied Regression Analysis* (New York: Wiley, 1998).

7. See, for example, Black and Eldredge, *Business and Economic Statistics*, 488. See also Draper and Smith, *Applied Regression Analysis.*

8. For further discussion of the rationale for this requirement and the extent to which one can deviate from it without reducing the meaningfulness of the resulting regression equation, consult an advanced multivariate book, such as J. Johnston and J. Dinardo, *Econometric Methods* (New York: McGraw-Hill/Irwin, 1997).

9. See, for example, Douglas C. Montgomery, Elizabeth A. Peck, and G. Geoffrey Vining, *Introduction to Linear Regression Analysis*, 3rd ed. (New York: Wiley, 2001).

10. For example, see Eleonora Malpa and Patrick McPhillips, "Regression Analysis Is a Key to Actionable Results in CSM," *Quirk's Marketing Research Review* (October 1995), article no. 0142, www.quirks.com/articles.

11. Many practitioners have expressed similar viewpoints. For example, see George Butler, "What Mother Never Told You About Linear Regression," *Quirk's Marketing Research Review* (October 2000) article no. 0622; William McLauchlan, "Regression-based Satisfaction Analyses: Proceed with Caution," *Quirk's Marketing Research Review* (October 1992), article no. 0429; Doug Grisaffe, "Appropriate Use of Regression in Customer Satisfaction Analyses: A Response to William McLauchlan," *Quirk's Marketing Research Review* (February 1993), article no. 0189; www.quirks.com/articles.

12. Modifications of the basic technique are available for dealing with situations involving nonlinearity. For details, see Draper and Smith, *Applied Regression Analysis.*

13. For these formulas and the rationale underlying them, see, for instance, Black and Eldredge, *Business and Economic Statistics*, 480–482. See also Montgomery, Peck, and Vining, *Introduction to Linear Regression.*

14. An excellent treatment of this issue is given in Draper and Smith, *Applied Regression Analysis.*

15. A technique called *partial correlation analysis* is available for examining the association between a dependent and an independent variable after statistically factoring out the effect of other independent variables. For details, see the classic book on regression, Fred N. Kerlinger and Elazar J. Pedhazur, *Multiple Regression in Behavioral Research* (New York: Holt, Rinehart and Winston, 1973), ch. 3.

16. For example, see Draper and Smith, *Applied Regression Analysis*, and Johnston and Dinardo, *Econometric Methods*.

Chapter 15

1. http://conjoint.mit.edu/demos/crossover/Pages/car-intro1.html.

2. http://conjoint.mit.edu/demos/ski/Pages/intro1.html.

3. http://conjoint.mit.edu/demos/camera/Pages/logon-demo.html. More details pertaining to the Polaroid example can be found in Case 8.1.

4. http://conjoint.mit.edu/demos/bags/Pages/atr-price.html.

5. For a good discussion of contrasts, see Roger E. Kirk, *Experimental Design: Procedures for Behavioral Sciences* (Pacific Grove, CA: Brooks/Cole, 1995), ch. 4.

6. Paul E. Green, Abba M. Krieger, and Terry G. Vavra, "Evaluating New Products," *Marketing Research* (Winter 1997): 12–21.

7. Joseph F. Hair, Rolph E. Anderson, Ronald L. Tatham, and William C. Black, *Multivariate Data Analysis*, 5th ed. (New York: Prentice-Hall, 1998), ch. 5. This book contains detailed discussion of all multivariate techniques discussed in this chapter. See also William Neal, "Using Discriminant Analysis in Marketing Research: Part 1," *Marketing Research* (September 1989): 79–81; William Neal, "Using Discriminant Analysis in Marketing Research: Part 2," *Marketing Research* (December 1989): 55–60.

8. Jum C. Nunnally and Ira Bernstein, *Psychometric Theory* (New York: McGraw-Hill/Irwin, 1994).

9. A factor analysis that attempts to capture all the variance in the original variables is sometimes called *principal components analysis*. A variation of this procedure, called *common factor analysis*, attempts to capture only the part of the total variance shared by all the original variables. For further discussion of the distinction between the two procedures, see Hair, Anderson, Tatham, and Black, *Multivariate Data Analysis*, 100–103.

10. When the initial factor-loading matrix is difficult to interpret, one can sometimes make the pattern of loadings clearer through a process called *factor rotation*. Details of factor rotation are complex and can be found in advanced texts, such as Nunnally and Bernstein, *Psychometric Theory*, and Harry H. Harman, *Modern Factor Analysis* (University of Chicago Press, 1976).

11. A number of applications of factor analysis in scale development have been reported in the marketing literature; see, for example, William O. Bearden, David M. Hardesty, and Randall L. Rose, "Consumer Self-Confidence: Refinements in Conceptualization and Measurement," *Journal of Consumer Research* (June 2001): 121–134.

12. Several marketing research firms specialize in performing cluster analysis to identify useful customer segments for their clients. For a discussion of several such firms and the services they offer, see G. Ray Funkhouser, Anindya Chatterjee, and Richard Parker, "Segmenting Samples," *Marketing Research* (Winter 1994): 40–46.

13. For additional details, see Hair, Anderson, Tatham, and Black, *Multivariate Data Analysis*, 90, 95.

14. For extensive references on multidimensional scaling, check www.ncl.ac.uk/mds; Henry Assael and D. F. Poltrack, "Relating Products to TV Program Clusters," *Journal of Advertising Research* 39 (1999): 41–52; R. L. Andrews and A. K. Manrai, "MDS Maps for Product Attribute and Market Response: An Application of Scanner Panel Data," *Marketing Science* 18 (1999): 584–604.

15. Further discussion of the two approaches is given in P. E. Green and V. Srinivasan, "Conjoint Analysis in Consumer Research: Issues and Outlook," *Journal of Consumer Research* (September 1978): 103–123.

16. Brian Orme and W. Christopher King, "Conducting Full-Profile Conjoint Analysis over the Internet," *Quirk's Marketing Research Review* (July 1998): article no. 0359, www.quirks.com/articles.

17. This computation assumes that a simple, linear, additive conjoint model underlies the customer preference rankings.

18. Terry G. Vavra, Paul E. Green, and Abba M. Krieger, "Evaluating EZPass," *Marketing Research* (Summer 1999): 5–16. See also Paul E. Green, Abba M. Krieger, and Terry G. Vavra, "Evaluating New Products," *Marketing Research* (Winter 1997): 12–21. The marketing field abounds with examples of conjoint analysis. For example, see Jonathan Weiner, "Consumer Electronics Marketer Uses a Conjoint Approach to Configure Its New Product and Set the Right Price," *Marketing Research* (Summer 1994): 7–11; Mary P. Tonneberger, "In Search of Perfect Plastic," *Quirk's Marketing Research Review* (May 1992): article no. 0414, www.quirks.com/articles.

19. Joel Huber, "What We Have Learned from 20 Years of Conjoint Research: When to Use Self-Explicated, Graded Pairs, Full Profiles, or Choice Experiments," *Sawtooth Software Research Paper Series,* http://www.sawtoothsoftware.com/download/techpap/whatlrnd.pdf (accessed August 6, 2006). (Also part of Sawtooth Software Proceedings, 1997.) The Spring 1997 issue of *Marketing Research* also contains several articles on conjoint analysis and its applications.

20. For an illustration involving Internet-based data collection, see Ely Dahan and John R. Hauser, "The Virtual Customer" (working paper, Sloan School of Management, Massachusetts Institute of Technology, December 2000), mitsloan.mit.edu/vc/; Ely Dahan and John R. Hauser, "Managing a Dispersed Product Development Process," in *The Handbook of Marketing,* ed. Barton Weitz and Robin Wensley (New York: Sage, 2002); Brian Orme and W. Christopher King, "Conducting Full-Profile Conjoint Analysis over the Internet," *Quirk's Marketing Research Review* (July 1998): article no. 0359, *www.quirks.com/*articles.

21. Visa EU, "Visa Harnesses Power of Card Data," press release, October 21, 2002, www.visaeurope.com/pressandmedia/press113_pressreleases.html (accessed February 26, 2005); "Kmart Expands NCR Data Warehouse to 70 Terabytes," www.tgc.com/dsstar/00/1003/102254.html (accessed February 26, 2005).

22. Ron Deruyter, "Amazon.com Uses 'Personalization' to Lure Customers," *The Record* (Kitchener-Waterloo, Ontario), June 16, 2004, Wednesday Final Edition, Business.

23. Simon Lloyd, "The Direct Approach," *Business Review Weekly,* February 24, 2005; Evan Schuman, "At Wal-Mart, World's Largest Retail Data Warehouse Gets Even Larger," *eWEEK,* October 13, 2004, www.evanschuman.com/clips/largest.html (accessed February 26, 2005).

24. Visa EU, "Visa Harnesses Power of Card Data."

25. Gary Loveman, "Diamonds in the Data Mine," *Harvard Business Review* 81 (2003): 109–113.

26. Tomi T. Ahonen, "Customer Segmentation: Are You an Alpha or Omega User?" *Total Telecom,* www.totaltele.com (accessed February 1, 2005).

27. Robert A. Nisbet, "How to Choose a Data Mining Suite, DM Direct Special Report," *DM Review,* March 23, 2004, www.dmreview.com/article-sub.cfm?articleID=1000465 (accessed February 26, 2005).

28. Thomas J. Blischok, *Every Transaction Tells a Story: Creating Customer Knowledge Through Market Basket Analysis,* White Paper, Mind Meld, Inc., 1999.

29. R. Agrawal, T. Imielinski, and A. Swami, "Mining Association Rules Between Sets of Items in Very Large Databases," *Proceedings of the ACM SIGMOD Conference on Management of Data* (Washington, D.C., 1993, 207–216).

30. In probability terms, support is merely the intersection of C and G, and reflects the event containing the sample points that belong to both C and G. It is normally denoted as $P(C \cap G)$. For more details on probabilities, see David R. Anderson,

Dennis J. Sweeney, and Thomas A. Williams, *Essentials of Statistics for Business and Economics*, 4th ed. (Mason, OH: South-Western, 2006).

31. In probability terms, confidence relies on Bayes' theorem, according to which $P(C|G) = P(C \cap G) \div P(G)$.

32. Recent C5.0 algorithm will split into any number of categories that are necessary; CART uses binary splits based on logistic models.

33. Arthur Middleton Hughes, *The Customer Loyalty Solution: What Works (and What Doesn't) in Customer Loyalty Programs* (New York: McGraw-Hill, 2003).

34. D. Agrawal and C. Schorling, "Market Share Forecasting: An Empirical Comparison of Artificial Neural Networks and Multinomial Logit Model," *Journal of Retailing* 72 (1996): 383–407; Björn Vroomen, Philip Hans Franses, and Erjen Van Nierop, "Modeling Consideration Sets and Brand Choice Using Artificial Neural Networks," *European Journal of Operational Research* 154 (2004): 206–217.

35. Joseph Pereira, "Marketing Researchers' Cameras Tracking Shoppers in Stores; Video Miners' Tell Merchants Who's Buying, Browsing," *Hartford Courant, Business Section, Thursday Statewide Edition*, December 23, 2004.

36. Drew Robb, "Taming Text; Companies Are Increasingly Using Text Mining Tools to Harness the Information in Their Unstructured Data," *Computerworld*, June 21, 2004, 40; Ralph Kisie, "Early Warning: The Auto Industry Has a Tool to Fight a Multibillion Dollar Warranty Problem. It's Called Text-Mining Software," *Automotive News*, October 18, 2004, 1; Colin Shearer, "Anticipating Consumer Behavior with Analytics," *CRM Today*, www.crm2day.com/library/EEplpkZllyASiURqyN.php.

37. Joseph Pereira, "Video Miners Use Hidden Cameras in Stores," *Wall Street Journal*, December 21, 2004.

38. Kelly Sitch, "Mining Software Studies Shoppers," *The Collegian*, January 11, 2005.

Chapter 16

1. "Competition Means Learning to Offer More Than Just Low Wages," *New York Times*, December 14, 2004; "Textile Quotas to End Soon, Punishing Carolina Mill Towns," *New York Times*, November 2, 2004.

2. A. Parasuraman and Deborah G. Wright, "A Study of Marketing Research Jobs for College Graduates: Implications for Educators," in *1983 AMA Educators' Proceedings*, ed. Patrick E. Murphy, Gene R. Laczniak, Paul F. Anderson, Russell W. Belk, O. C. Ferrell, Robert F. Lusch, Terence A. Shimp, and Charles B. Weinberg (Chicago: American Marketing Association, 1983), 184. This material is very relevant even today.

3. The importance of understanding the audience and how to do so effectively are discussed succinctly in Mary Munter and Lynn Russell, *Guide to Presentations* (Englewood Cliffs, NJ: Prentice-Hall, 2002), chs. 1 and 2. See also Gary Blake and Robert W. Bly, *The Elements of Technical Writing* (New York: Macmillan, 1993); Ron Blicq and Lisa Moretto, *Technically-Write*, 5th ed. (Upper Saddle River, NJ: Prentice-Hall, 1999); Robert A. Day, *How to Write and Publish a Scientific Paper*, 3rd ed. (Phoenix: Oryx, 1988); David A. McMurrey, *Online Technical Writing— Online Textbook*, www.io.com/,hcexres/tcm1603/acchtml/acctoc.html; David Porush, *A Short Guide to Writing About Science* (New York: HarperCollins, 1995).

4. Gustav W. Friedrich, and Lynda Dee Dixon, *Strategic Communication in Business and the Professions*, 4th ed. (Boston: Houghton Mifflin, 2002); Scot Ober, *Contemporary Business Communication*, 4th ed. (Boston: Houghton Mifflin, 2001); Michael Netzely and Craig Snow, *Guide to Report Writing* (Englewood Cliffs, NJ: Prentice-Hall, 2002).

5. See the online writing lab at owl.english.purdue.edu.

6. One formula frequently used to assess the clarity of written material is called the Fog Index, developed by Robert Gunning. Details on this formula are given in Robert Gunning, *The Technique of Clear Writing* (New York: McGraw-Hill, 1952).

7. Richard M. Durand, Hugh J. Guffey, Jr., and John M. Planchon, "An Examination of the Random Versus Nonrandom Nature of Item Omissions," *Journal of Marketing Research* (August 1983): 307.

8. For a listing of available computer graphics software packages, see Kristen DeTienne, *Guide to Electronic Communication* (Englewood Cliffs, NJ: Prentice-Hall, 2002); Dennis O. Gehris and Linda Szul, *Communication Technologies* (Englewood Cliffs, NJ: Prentice-Hall, 2002). Also visit www.marketingpower.com, an American Marketing Association website.

9. See Munter and Russell, *Guide to Presentations,* ch. 5; Ober, *Contemporary Business Communication,* chs. 13 and 14.

10. For a discussion of situations in which certain graphical illustrations are more appropriate than others, as well as the pros and cons of each, see Ober, *Contemporary Business Communication,* ch. 11.

11. A succinct discussion is given in Ober, *Contemporary Business Communication.* Also consult online writing lab owl.english.purdue.edu.

Research in Use Sources

Chapter 1

a. Meera Louis, "Modern Marketing Helps Sell Life as a Nun," *Wall Street Journal*, May 11, 1999, p. B1.

b. Burger King Corporation research information used with permission from Burger King Corporation and Douglas Riggan, Manager, Consumer Research, Burger King.

c. Allison S. Wellner, "Research on a Shoe String," *American Demographics*, April 2001.

Chapter 2

a. Allison Lucas, "When Every Penny Counts: How Creativity Allows Fisher-Price to Stretch Its Market Research Dollars," *Sales & Marketing Management* (February 1996): 74–75. © 1996 VNU Business Media, Inc. Used with permission.

Chapter 3

a. Judith Weintraub, "Low-Carb Trend Squeezing Orange Juice Industry," *The Star-Ledger*, September 22, 2004; Dow Jones & Reuters; Factiva (http://global.factiva.com).

b. Reprinted by permission of *Harvard Business Review*. From "Creating Break-throughs at 3M," by Eric Von Hippel, Stefan Thomke and Mary Sonnack, Sept.–Oct. 1999. Copyright © 1999 by the Harvard Business School Publishing Corporation. All rights reserved.

Chapter 4

a. Carl Bialik, "Reports on Spam Levels Paint Differing Views of the Problem," Wall Street Journal Online, September 21, 2004, www.wsj.com.

b. Burger King Corporation research information used with permission from Burger King Corporation and Douglas Riggan, Manager, Consumer Research, Burger King.

Chapter 5

a. Extracts from Mark Hammond, "GIS Lands on the Map Cover Story: Business Mapping Helps Companies Make Right Moves," *eWEEK*, January 29, 1999. Additional material from "Chips with Your Pizza is Guaranteed to Be Hot Stuff!" *Leicester Mercury*, September 3, 2003. Dow Jones & Reuters.

b. Based on Neil Weinberg, "Damn the Torpedoes," January 26, 1998, www.forbes.com. Additional material from Michael Rogers, "When Maps Go Live: The ancient art of mapping is in the midst of a revolution that will change the way we view the earth," Newsweek Web Exclusive, August 12, 2003. Dow Jones & Reuters.

Chapter 6

a. Andy Cohen, "In Control," *Sales & Marketing Management*, June 1999, pp. 32–38; www.johnsoncontrols.com.

b. "Who's Afraid of the Big Dad Wolf?", Market Wire, October 26, 2004; Arif Mohamed, "RFIC Poised to Move Beyond Supply Chain," *Computer Weekly*, November 2, 2004; Brian Trent, "Technology and Tomorrow: A Challenge to Liberty," *Humanist*, November 1, 2004. See also Wikipedia website (http://en.wikipedia.org/wiki/RFID).

c. Written by Raghavan Srinivasan, Deputy Managing Director, TNS India.

d. "Vauhini Vara, "Companies Mine Blogs for Market Research," *Wall Street Journal Online*, December 3, 2004. See http://online.wsj.com/article/0,,SB110071998028976955,00.html.

e. "Spies Like Us—An Interview with Tom Stemberg, CEO of Staples," *Inc.*, August 1998, 45–48; James Heckman, "Souped Up: CEO Morrison Sets the Table for Innovation, Growth," *Marketing News*, March 29, 1999, E2, E4.

Chapter 7

a. "Pennzoil-Quaker State Company Uses Internet Focus Groups to Evaluate Products; Total Shine from Blue Coral/Slick 50 Gets High Marks," *PR Newswire, Financial News Section*, September 20, 2000; Alison Stein Wellner, "I've Asked You Here Because …," *BusinessWeek, Frontier, What Works Section*, August 14, 2000; Sarah Schafer, "Getting a Line on Customers," *Inc.*, December 15, 1996, www.inc.com.

b. Jennifer Carroll, "Connecting What Is Learned with What Is Done: At Gannett, Different Strategies Aim at the Same Goal of Attracting Younger Readers," *Neiman Reports*, December 22, 2003.

c. See also Cesar Miguel Escano, "MARKETING Children Power," *Business World*, March 26, 2004.

d. Steve Hamm, "Tech's Future," *BusinessWeek*, September 27, 2004, 82–89; Brian Bremmer and Hiroko Tashiro, "Shimano—The Tour De France's Other Winner," *BusinessWeek Online, Asian News*, www.businessweek.com (accessed August 9, 2004).

Chapter 8

a. "KaBloom Ltd.," *Hoover's Company Basic Records*, December 15, 2004; Jonathan Sidener, "Power Play," *San Diego Union-Tribune*, December 13, 2004; S. Muralidhar, "Kellogg's Cheez-It Is Here with Indian Touch," *Business Line, A Financial Daily from The Hindu Group of Publications*, April 30, 2002, www.blonnet.com; Steve Persall, "McQueen's Reign of Cool," *St. Petersburg Times*, December 10, 2004; Bruce Horovitz, "Fast Food Could Soon Mean Fast Fruit as Chains Test Dishes," *USA Today*, November 8, 2004, B3; "Hardee's Unveils New 'Monster,'" November 15, 2004, http://money.cnn.com; Bruce Horovitz, "Burger King to Offer Whopper of a Breakfast Sandwich," *USA Today*, March 29, 2005, www.usatoday.com. See also CEO's North American presentation at www.allieddomecq.com; Chris Reidy, "Dunkin' Donuts Parent Tests 'Combo' Restaurant Format: Allied Domecq's Recipe for Growth: Doughnuts, Sandwiches, Ice Cream," *Boston Globe*, August 3, 2000, C1.

b. For more details, see the Litmus Simulated Test Market System (STM) offered by Harris Interactive Inc., a Rochester, New York–based global research company (www.harrisinteractive.com/advantages/marketingsciences.asp).

c. Cris Prystay, "Global Firms Target Rural India: Companies Like Hyundai Motor Use Road Shows to Gain Favor with the New Middle Class," *Wall Street Journal Europe*, July 2, 2003.

d. Rex Briggs, R. Krishnan, and Norm Borin, "Integrated Multi-Channel Communication Strategies: Evaluating the Return on Marketing Objectives—The Case of the 2004 Ford F-150 Launch," *Journal of Interactive Marketing* (Summer 2005): 81–90.

Chapter 9

a. "Reynolds Wrap Aluminum Foil Ranks #1 in Overall Brand Equity," www.harrisinteractive.com/equitrend. See also www.brandkeys.com/awards for information on the customer loyalty index; see www.interbrand.com/best_brands_2004 for details on Interbrand methodology. See "The 100 Top Brands—The Global Brand Scoreboard," *BusinessWeek*, August 2, 2004, 68, bwnt.businessweek.com/brand/2003/index.asp, for details on 2002 and 2003 brand scoreboards. See www.burke.com/bmr/brand_equity.htm for details on Burke's methodology. For a detailed discussion on brand equity, see Kevin Lane Keller, *Strategic Brand Management* (Englewood Cliffs, NJ: Prentice Hall, 2002).

b. Measures presented here are based on several articles—for example, Darrel K. Rigby and Dianne Ledingham, "CRM Done Right," *Harvard Business Review,* November 1, 2004; Stephen H. Haeckel, Lewis P. Carbone, and Leonard L. Berry, "How to Lead the Customer Experience," *Marketing Management* (January– February 2003): 18, 19–23; Leonard L. Berry and Neeli Bendapudi, "Clueing in Customers," *Harvard Business Review,* February 1, 2003; Werner Reinartz and V. Kumar, "The Mismanagement of Customer Loyalty," *Harvard Business Review,* July 1, 2002; Eric Almquist, Carla Heaton, and Nick Hall, "Making CRM Make Money," *Marketing Management* (May–June 2002): 17–21; Bruce A. Corner, "Measuring Customer Relationships," *Marketing Management* (May–June 2002): 10–11; Lawrence A. Crosby, Sheree L. Johnson, and Richard T. Quinn, "Is Survey Research Dead?" *Marketing Management* (May–June 2002): 25–29; James D. Lenskold, "Marketing ROI: Playing to Win," *Marketing Management* (May–June 2002): 31–35.

Chapter 11

a. © The Gallup Organization. All rights reserved. Reprinted with permission.

b. "Our Survey Standards," *American Demographics,* August 2001, p. 1.

Chapter 12

a. From *The Nielsen Researcher,* (Spring 1987), pp. 6–8, published by Nielsen Marketing Research, Nielsen Plaza, Northbrook, IL 60062. Used by permission.

b. For complete details on the study, refer to www.pewresearch.org.

Chapter 16

a. The American Chicle Youth Poll," a report published by the Warner-Lambert Company, 201 Tabor Road, Morris Plains, NJ 07950.

Name Index

Organization Index

Subject Index

Photo and Cartoon Credits